The Nano Age of Digital Immunity Infrastructure Fundamentals and Applications

The Intelligent Cyber Shield for Smart Cities

The Nano Age of Digital Immunity Infrastructure Fundamentals and Applications

The Intelligent Cyber Shield for Smart Cities

By

Dr. Rocky Termanini

CRC Press
Taylor & Francis Group
Boca Raton London New York

CRC Press is an imprint of the
Taylor & Francis Group, an **informa** business

CRC Press
Taylor & Francis Group
6000 Broken Sound Parkway NW, Suite 300
Boca Raton, FL 33487-2742

International Standard Book Number-13: 978-1-138-05295-6 (Hardback)

Visit the Taylor & Francis Web site at
http://www.taylorandfrancis.com

and the CRC Press Web site at
http://www.crcpress.com

Contents

Preface

April 29, 2015: The US military said this week that it has made great progress in its efforts to develop a self-guided bullet; it steers itself via tiny fins to the target. As mentioned by my friend Dr. Kristina Nyzell, "Researchers at the University of Washington have been able to successfully infect a computer with malware coded into a strand of DNA."

Einstein once said: "We cannot solve problems with the same mindset that created them." He was right. Today, cyber defense and malware attacks use the same mindset and technologies. The world today is riding a see-saw with endless swing. Neither side is claiming victory. The present antivirus weapons that we're using are not smart enough to immobilize or deflect the massive preemptive attacks that are mutilating our societal fabric. Disaster recovery will not heal the post-traumatic stress disorder of people. No one is interested in post-mortems or digging graves.

We're going to talk about immunity, the brain, Smart Cities, artificial intelligence, and nanotechnology. The most fascinating component is the brain, which is our inner cosmos—the infinitely dense tangle of billions of brain cells and their trillions of connections.

In his book *Do No Harm: Stories of Life, Death, and Brain Surgery*, the British neurosurgeon Dr. Henry Marsh wrote, "If I got pain in my hand the pain is not actually in the hand, the pain is in my brain. My brain creates a three-dimensional model of the world and associates the nerve impulses coming from the pain receptors in my hand with pain in the hand and it creates this illusion that the pain is actually in the hand itself, and it isn't."

The concept of *bridging* is the cornerstone of information delivery and transfer. We cannot move from Point A to Point B unless we have a connection. This concept is fundamental in blueprinting a network of smart objects.

An interesting revelation: On February 14, 2014, the *Smithsonian* magazine published an article titled "Ancient Cities Developed in a Surprisingly Similar Way to Modern Ones!" The same mathematical equations that describe patterns of modern urban sprawl are equally suited to explaining the development of ancient cities. Take, for example, the Teotihuacan ruins in Mexico. Memphis was the capital of Ancient Egypt for over eight consecutive dynasties and reached the peak of prestige as a center for the worship of the god of creation and artworks. The sphinx served as the city guard and became an eternal memorial of power and prestige. When security deteriorated, the city could not sustain its prosperity and became victim to invaders.

There was a continuity of thinking between the past and the present to build the utopian city.

This book is the Rosetta Stone of cybersecurity of the future. We're talking about a decade or two from now, when fiction concepts will become reality. The concept of digital immunity has never been mentioned in any security seminar or even considered before. In fact, no technology company has ever thought about how to replicate the human immune system and create a digital replica for the business world. Since our immune system is made up of nano objects at the molecular and atomic levels, a digital immunity system will also be built with nanotechnology driven by the hyper-intelligence module of artificial intelligence. It is an idea further than Mars. There are no books on the topic. Digital immunity is the Holy Grail of Smart Cities. It is a technological revolution that everybody should know about.

There are 595 cybersecurity conferences per year around the world, according to www.concise-courses.com, which keeps a daily track and manages a *directory* on cybersecurity continuing education. These conferences are purposely held in glamorous cities such as Dubai, to attract more attendees and to cover all areas of the cybersecurity continuum, from cryptography to artificial intelligence innovation in machine learning. These conferences have a single purpose: to connect with prospects, to exhibit prototypes, and to give away pens and bags in exchange for business cards. These conferences tend to be grandiose and pompous, and invite special speakers to discuss the same theme of "how to win the war against cybercrime." It is the same hash and rehash discussed from different corners. Conferences are social hubs to take selfies with admired attendees or even with competitors. I reviewed the conference directory and, to my amazement, none of these big rallies mentioned the term *digital immunity*. These assemblages gathered over 350,000 security and information and communication technology consultants and chiefs, and no one knew about the benefits of immunity. No, I don't think Steve Jobs, Bill Gates, Jeff Bezos, Larry Page, Sergey Brin, or Mark Zuckerberg will ever reach the pedestal of Einstein, Marie Curie, Steven Hawking, Thomas Edison, Louis Pasteur, or Alexander Fleming. The difference is quite immense. The lords of present technologies have become ruthless billionaires who own islands and lots on the moon, while the first group saved humanity but died poor.

The world has not yet realized that human immunity can be replicated to protect the digital world. The real paradox is how technology stumbles on itself due to lack of vision. The World Health Organization (WHO) stated: "The two public health interventions that have had the greatest impact on the world's health are clean water and vaccines." Immunizations save an estimated 2.5 million lives each year from tuberculosis, diphtheria, tetanus, pertussis (whooping cough), polio, measles, hepatitis B, and Hib infections. When digital immunity becomes the *de facto* of cyber defense, most of the massive cyberattacks will be eradicated. Digital immunity will use artificial intelligence molecular-scale technologies to shield systems at the atomic level, where conventional attacks will never reach. Digital immunity will also go nano!

If we're seriously planning to build Smart Cities, then we need to seriously think about building a smart security *grid* that is cyberattack-proof and can withstand massive attacks. Smart City designers should have the inspiration of skyscraper engineers.

Let's learn a few things from the engineering tricks behind the world's super tall and super slender skyscrapers. Let's take as a good example Dubai's Burj Khalifa, currently the world's highest skyscraper. But it's numbers, not words, that make these structures so inspiring, specifically complicated engineering calculations. While it's dizzying to think of what's required to construct these massive buildings, the math has gotten even more complicated. According to Bill Baker, the structural engineer for Skidmore, Owings & Merrill, the company responsible for the Burj Khalifa, the trend toward taller, thinner buildings has presented new spins on old engineering challenges. There are two crucial factors that need to be carefully computed and simulated: the height-to-width of the structure and the wind, which is the "dominant force," says Baker. Skyscraper designers want to "confuse the wind," says Baker. Air pushing against the surface of a tall tower creates vortices, concentrated pockets of force that can shake and vibrate buildings (the technical term is vortex shedding). The aim of any skyscraper design is to break up these vortices. Facades often have rounded, chamfered, or notched corners to help break up the wind, and sometimes, open slots or grooves will be added to let the wind pass through and vent, in effect disrupting the air flow.

"It's interesting that the aerodynamics of the building are almost counterintuitive," says DeSimone Consulting and Engineering company in New York. "We don't want smooth shapes, we want shapes that break up the air flow."

By the same analogy, we can say that there are two critical factors in designing a secure Smart City. The first one is to build a smart digital immunity infrastructure that will be the foundation to protect the information fabric of the city. The second factor is the cognitive intelligence to capture all incoming preemptive cyberattacks before intrusion and build vector knowledge for future invasions. The antivirus legacy technologies have contributed a great defense, but they now have a great opportunity to embrace digital immunity and develop new smart tools that will beat any malware dogfight.

We wrote this book to assist cybersecurity experts in understanding the fundamentals and applications of digital immunity to protect Smart Cities. We realized the urgent need to write the book because everyone is talking about cybersecurity in general "generic" terms and not in terms of securing Smart Cities. Here's what the Department of Homeland Security's Fiscal Years 2014–2018 Strategic Plan said about infrastructure security: "Enhance security for the Nation's critical infrastructure from terrorism and criminal activity by (1) identifying critical infrastructure and related vulnerabilities; (2) developing and deploying a scalable assessment methodology depending on the level of threat and the nature of the target; (3) inserting and/or developing appropriate technologies; (4) tracking protective measures of our partners across the homeland security enterprise; and (5) conducting investigations that maximize disruption of criminal enterprises that pose the greatest risk to the United States." This is an academic hocus-pocus document that leads nowhere. It doesn't have any scientific substance and lacks the vibrant engineering pulse.

We consider this book to be the Rosetta stone of cybersecurity of the future. The concept of digital immunity has never been tackled or used before, and astonishing like the first landing on the moon. In fact, no technology company has ever thought about how to replicate the human immune system or create a digital replica for the business world. There are no books on the topic. Digital immunity will be the backbone of Smart Cities. It is a technological revolution that everybody should know about.

Dr. Chris Shar, from Pennsylvania State University, eloquently said

> We can be sure that the global battlefield of the 21st century will be over information—the dissemination or withholding of facts, the interpretation of events, the presentation or distortion of ideas and ideologies, and the communication of messages and symbols carefully prepared to provoke a particular reaction, either conscious or unconscious, from a target audience.

Digital immunity is a superintelligent, protective, *shrink-wrapped* shield that tightly envelopes a Smart City. We cannot build a Smart City without digital immunity.

This book provides a systematic course starting from the human immune system all the way to the digital immune system for Smart Cities, which uses a communication "grid" for the protection of its critical infrastructures and key assets. The Smart City is a multiplexed metropolis where ubiquitous data services will make cities more livable, more efficient, more sustainable, and perhaps more democratic. But more importantly, Smart Cities have a Smart Grid to protect all vital information hubs and home area networks from malicious exploits and "zero-day" black holes. Smart Cities need two things: a digital nervous system and a digital immune system. The former will facilitate the dynamics of data; and the latter will protect the city's data. As the American author Jane Jacobs wrote in her influential 1961 book, *The Death and Life of Great American Cities*: "Cities have the capability of providing something for everybody, only because, and only when, they are created by everybody." To achieve this wonderful utopia, Smart Cities will be blessed with smart security that will protect all the information arteries like our body's immune system. The Smart Vaccine™ is the Holy Grail of digital immunity.

A couple of notes worth mentioning: First, some of the charts are duplicates but with different captions to add to the dimensionality of the concept. Second, and more importantly, we're thinking about establishing the Digital Immunity Foundation as an independent agency to pursue and promote digital immunity for our digital world. We will approach the federal government for research funding under the label "Immunize America," and at the same time capture all innovative ideas from antivirus technology providers, invite academia to participate in launching an aggressive research campaign, and, of course, last but not least, the leading technology companies of Silicon Valley.

Finally, I would like to thank all my readers for their interest in digital immunity and hope that this book will inspire and encourage them to share their innovative ideas and be an active member of the foundation.

I hope my points have been well taken. I humbly express my gratitude and gratitude to all the people who worked with me to make it happen. I also thank my publisher, Richard O'Hanley from CRC Press, and Michelle van Kampen from Deanta Global, for their gracious support and coaching knowledge to release this book.

Dr. Rocky Termanini
Walnut Creek, California

Acknowledgments

It is difficult to quantify the gratitude I have for the many people who pushed me uphill to finish this book. It is recognition of their encouragement and inspiration. It is also recognition of those people who were amazed by the concept of digital immunity as a replica of our human immune system.

Lina Termanini, senior manager, Ernst Young, San Francisco, California

Nadia Hinedi, attorney at law

Dr. Zafer Termanini, orthopedic surgeon

Dr. Sami Termanini, general medicine, Adelaide, Australia

Ms. Mia Termanini Williams, business consultant, Blackhawk, California

Dr. Eesa Bastaki, president, University of Dubai, Dubai, UAE

Dr. Bushra Al Blooshi, manager of Research & Innovation, Dubai Electronic Security Center, Dubai, UAE

Ms. Irene Corpuz, security head, Abu Dhabi, UAE

Dr. Yigal Arens, director, USC/Information Science Institute, Los Angeles, California

Dr. Adel Al Alawi, professor, University of Bahrain, Bahrain

Dr. Kristina Nyzell, founder Disruptive Play, Sweden

Mr. Firas Abras, founder of Septimus Tech and cofounder of SMSbiotech, Los Angeles and Riyadh

Dr. Siripong Malasri, dean of engineering, Christian Brothers University, Memphis, Tennessee

Meshal Bin Hussain, vice president, Dubai Holding, Dubai, UAE

John and Danielle Cosgrove, Cosgrove Computer Systems, Elsegundo, California

Ahmad Hassan, director, Risk Management and Compliance, DU Telecom Co., Dubai, UAE

Ms. Amna Almadhoob, senior security and researcher, AMX Middle East, Bahrain

Ms. Kelly MacDonald, owner Taillight Music and Video Production, Portland, Oregon

I would also like to thank the rest of my visionary and creative friends for their gracious assistance.

Dr. Rocky Termanini

Chapter 1

The Rise of the Smart City

Overpopulation Misery

Today, 54% of the world's population lives in urban areas, a proportion that is expected to increase to 66% by 2050. Projections show that urbanization combined with the overall growth of the world's population could add another 2.5 billion people to urban populations by 2050, with close to 90% of the increase concentrated in Asia and Africa, according to a new United Nations report published on July 10, 2014, in New York. The report lists 28 mega-cities worldwide, with 453 million residents about 12% of the world's urban dwellers. Of today's 28 mega-cities, 16 are located in Asia, 4 in Latin America, 3 each in Africa and Europe, and 2 in North America. By 2030, the world is projected to have 41 mega-cities with 10 million inhabitants or more.

Tokyo remains the world's largest city, with 38 million inhabitants, followed by Delhi with 25 million; Shanghai, with 23 million; and Mexico City, Mumbai, and São Paulo, each with around 21 million inhabitants. Osaka has just over 20 million, followed by Beijing with slightly less than 20 million. The New York–Newark area and Cairo complete the top 10 most populous urban areas with around 18.5 million inhabitants each.

We do not consider that these statistics are very comforting or static, while the population of the world is ballooning by 80 million per year. Overpopulation is an undesirable condition where the existing human population exceeds the carrying capacity of Earth. Overpopulation is caused by a number of factors: reduced mortality rate, better medical facilities, preventive medicine, more support to overcome poverty, lack of family planning, and the depletion of precious resources. Conflicts over water are becoming a source of tension between countries, which could result in wars. Such conflicts cause more diseases to spread and make them harder to control. Starvation is a huge issue facing the world and the mortality rate for children is being fueled by it. Poverty is the biggest hallmark when we talk about overpopulation. Let's not forget global warming and Arctic melting and how these directly impact the habitat of human beings. The Arctic sea ice could potentially harm human beings by reducing certain animal habitats that are used for subsistence.

The land area of the world is fixed and it doesn't expand or grow; the same goes for our atmosphere. We're limited to 29% of the world's total area. The United Nations in its "2016 World Population Data Sheet" estimated that the world's population is 7.4 billion. We're in fact living in a virtual bubble. We do not have underwater or lunar cities to live in. According to a report published in February 2015 by the Brilliantmaps.com website, there are 4037 cities in the world with over 100,000 people. By 2030, the world is projected to have 41 mega-cities with more than 10 million inhabitants. All the good spots of the world have been populated with metropolitan cities, fertile farmlands, jungles, and rivers. Our natural resources are also being consumed at an alarming rate. Desolate and barren areas like the African Sahara, Death Valley, the Empty Quarter of Saudi Arabia, and the Amazon swamp are extremely hostile and inhospitable. We can also add the North and South poles to the list of inhospitable areas.

Historic Smart Cities

Old castles were once likened to a protected city with their moats and high walls. Take for example, the Krak des Chevaliers, a massive hilltop structure located in Syria. It is the largest crusader castle in the world, and one of the most important preserved medieval castles in the world. The Krak des Chevaliers was impossible to invade or penetrate without help from inside. These historical fortresses held great strategic importance and had accommodation and supplies to last a long time. Castles had a central alert system and a network of escape tunnels, and a communication protocol (smoke and mirrors) to communicate with nearby friendly castles.

Figure 1.1 shows how the city of Ur looked some 5800 years ago. The two concentric walls are called curtain walls, which surrounded the city to create multiple lines of defense. The walls were 30 feet high on a solid foundation of 20 feet deep and 20 feet thick. The city had a life span of 4600 years, and was a model for other cities and medieval castles. It was the state of the art of engineering and defense (Figure 1.1).

The citadel of Aleppo (the industrial capital of Syria) is considered one of the oldest and largest castles in the world, dating back to the middle of the third millennium BC. This circular citadel is located at the top of a 3000-foot hill and overlooks 100 miles of farmland. The prophet Abraham is said to have milked his sheep on the citadel hill. It is surrounded by a 500-foot wide moat and 50 feet of fortified limestone walls. Aleppo is an outstanding example of a 12th-century city with its military fortifications constructed as its focal point following the success of Salah El-Din against the Crusaders (Figure 1.2).

Figure 1.1 The Sumerian city of Ur on the Euphrates River in Mesopotamia is a model of a Smart City, founded in 3800 BC. Ur was the most important port on the Persian Gulf, and it extended much further inland than it does today. All the wealth that came to Mesopotamia by sea had to pass through Ur.

The encircling ditch and defensive wall above a massive, sloping, stone-faced glacis, and the great gateway with its machicolations comprise a major ensemble of military architecture at the height of Arab dominance. See Figure 1.3 to get an idea of how secure the city was. When there's danger, an early warning smoke signal alerts the residents to get inside the gates, which will be locked. Invading the city would take months after breaking down the gates.

During the medieval ages, there were over 30,000 castles with remarkable construction engineering that surpasses any of the high-rise buildings of today. Medieval castles were more than just large fortresses with massive stone walls, they were ingeniously designed fortifications that used many brilliant and creative ways to protect their inhabitants from attacking enemies. Although old cities did not have the cutting-edge technologies of today, citizens lived a peaceful life in harmony with the city leaders. Bureaucracy was only one layer and it was transparent. Crimes were limited to family disputes. The judicial system was simple and punishment was swift without the complicated proceedings of Watergate or Simpson.

A biblical story worth mentioning, since we're talking about building a Smart City, is the legendary city of Babel and its famous tower. It was eloquently described in http://www.ancient-origins.net/:

> One of the many fantastic stories in the Book of Genesis is the Tower of Babel. The gist of the story is thus: All human beings used to speak the same language. As they came to settle in Mesopotamia, they decided to

Figure 1.2 The citadel of Aleppo is the most prominent historic architectural site in Aleppo. It was recognized as a World Heritage Site by UNESCO in 1986. Its majestic stature forms the center of the city; in fact, the city wraps around it, extending a spider-like infrastructural web of streets forming the city's organic urban form. The entire mound was covered with large blocks of gleaming limestone that unified the built structure with the hill, thus increasing its visual scale. It was also surrounded by a moat filled with water to protect against intruders. (© 2014 Copyright MERIT CyberSecurity Group. All rights reserved.)

build a city with a tower to reach the heavens. Through this endeavor, mankind intended to create a name for himself. God, however, had other plans. Mankind's language was confused, and they were scattered over the earth. As a result, the city and the tower were never completed. Regardless of whether one believes that this story actually took place, there are several interesting ways of looking at it ... Although language was confused, and mankind scattered across the world, I can't help but think that we've come full circle, almost at least. Take this article as an example. It will probably be read by people from different parts of the world. In that sense, we are connected, rather than scattered. Also, through translations, we are able to overcome language barriers. Moreover, at times we may even communicate through empathy, without the need for speech. Yet, there's one part of the story we have not achieved. The people in the story of the Tower of Babel were working together to build a monument. Sadly, human beings aren't quite doing that today. Wars, the exploitation of the poor, and human trafficking

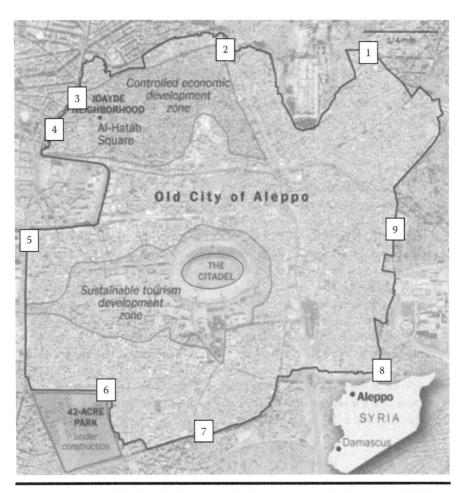

Figure 1.3 The Old City of Aleppo was in fact a Smart City in terms of defense sophistication, nine massive steel gates, citizen prosperity, and great leadership. The citadel was built as a replica of the city with formidable protection and intricate escape tunnels. (© 2014 Copyright MERIT CyberSecurity Group. All rights reserved.)

are just some examples of the ways in which we are destroying our fellow man/woman, instead of cooperating with him/her. Perhaps it's time we finish building the Tower of Babel.

The lesson learned from the legend of Babel is that human behavior is independent of time, place, religion, and even technology. We live in such complex mind-boggling Babel cities. We may be able to connect all our belonging and appliances to a common *smart* net, but we will end up with a *smart* gridlock and a self-inflicted massive denial of service.

The Democracy of Technology

Technology crime has reached epidemic levels, and the reasons are simple: first, you can commit a crime on the Internet as a human or as a dog. Second, launching a cyberattack from anywhere in the world is almost untraceable. The Internet can be used as a crime tool, or as a scaffold for a terrorist act. Technology by design is a moving target driven by human knowledge for good and evil. Information and communications technology (ICT) has emerged as the most powerful driver to achieve superiority in all domains of life. ICT has shifted techno-power from the Western world to Eastern Europe and Asia. The Internet belongs to everyone. It doesn't have boundaries and is totally democratic in nature. The Internet has created unprecedented new opportunities for cybercrime, which has been creeping into our societal order and has been creating major havoc and irreparable sinkholes. The Internet has opened a new Pandora's box of cybercrime, driven by evil creativity and wicked innovation. In fact, cybercrime has become a prosperous career in deep underground organizations. *Crime-as-a-service* has become more effective and lethal than an AK47. The malware continuum has also presented serious challenges for law and criminal justice, as it struggles to adapt to crimes that no longer take place in the terrestrial world, but in the virtual environment of cyberspace.

We all remember the classic engineering quote "if you can measure it, you can control it." The cybercrime phenomenon cannot be measured like speed, weight, density, or volume. The two prominent metrics that we could use to evaluate the malevolence of cybercrime are risk and vulnerability. Risk is *the probability that a threat will exploit a vulnerability that causes harm to an asset.* It can be quantitatively represented by the following formula:

$$\text{Risk} = \frac{\text{Threat} \times \text{Vulnerability}}{\text{Countermeasures}} \times \text{Impact}$$

Now, let's look at risk from a different angle: risk is the "damage" caused by an act multiplied by probability weighed against the cost of the damage:

$$\text{Risk} = \frac{\text{Impact} \times \text{Probability of an event to occur}}{\text{Cost}}$$

Impact is the effect on the organization should a risk event occur. Probability is the likelihood (threat) that the event could occur within a given timeframe. Cost (countermeasures) is the amount it takes to mitigate or reduce the risk to an acceptable level.

General Michael Hayden, former head of the US National Security Agency and later the Central Intelligence Agency, presented the formula of risk as

$$\text{Risk} = \text{Threat} \times \text{Vulnerability} \times \text{Consequence}$$

while vulnerability is defined as the *conditional probability* of success knowing an attack will occur in the future:

$$\text{Vulnerability} = \text{Probability (Success} \mid \text{Attack)} = P_V(S \mid A)$$

CSO magazine published a survey on the 2015 US Cybercrime Survey and painfully stated: Cybersecurity incidents are not only increasing in number, they are also becoming progressively destructive and target a broadening array of information and attack vectors. It's clear that adversaries continue to advance their threats, techniques, and targets. They are investing in technologies, sharing intelligence, and training their crews to attack with purpose and competence.

Technology continues to expand in every direction and permeates into our businesses and homes. Technology is responsible for the emergence of a new breed of kids who call themselves geeks (not nerds). They have cultivated their own freakish culture, terminology, and habits. They want to differentiate themselves from mainstream society. If you go to Google or Facebook, you will see miniature eggheaded Einsteins. They are massively ahead of their time. These are the people you pick on in high school and wind up working for as an adult. They feed on "digital Twinkies" and have the tenacity of a marathoner and the ambition of a Himalayan. In the cybercrime camp, we also have an army of hardcore hell-raisers (on the payroll of the Devil), just as smart as the white hatters, receiving crime orders from the dark web lords. Whizz kids with an IQ of over 200 roam around cyberspace (slide the highways) cracking bank servers, medical records, and government registries, and spying for clients. Many of them join adversary electronic armies (major league of cyber terrorism) to develop strategic attacks against critical infrastructures.

It is evident that malware engineering, which is not taught in academia, has become the most enticing and challenging field for the young generation. Distributed denial-of-service (DDoS) attacks have become the darling of hackers and cyber terrorists. Each attack is designed to humiliate chief technology officers (CTOs) and chief security officers (CSOs), and to cripple the backbone of a business. DDoS is an *invasion* of guided botnet missiles aimed like a tsunami to clog central business servers and cause a major loss of business and money.

Here's an interesting revelation: the second amendment to the constitution states: "A well-regulated Militia, being necessary to the security of a free State, the right of the people to keep and bear Arms, shall not be infringed." Americans are divided over the interpretation of this amendment. Could citizens own cyber arms to protect their private lives? Obviously, no debate has been organized to discuss this very slippery issue. Time will tell.

Disruptive Technology

Since the dawn of life, man has been suffering from disruptive technology. Clayton Christensen, who crafted the term "disrupted innovation," brought up an interesting phenomenon on how successful, outstanding companies can do everything "right" and yet still lose their market leadership, when new and unexpected competitors rise and take over the market. Almost every day, we witness how David beats Goliath in the technology domain. It is well-served justice. We can modestly claim that the biggest disruptive technology that humanity has ever encountered is the Internet. Stephen Hawking once said, "It is said that fact is sometimes stranger than fiction, and nowhere is this more true than in the case of black holes." Well, we can say the same thing about the Internet. It is a colossal gravitational force that has been expanding like the universe in every direction, and we are all captive inside it. It started with a "big bang" of four computers in 1969, and today, according to www.internetworldstats.com, we have 3,675,824,813 users as of June 2016. With fast geometric progression, we will hit the 5 billion mark in 2025. Disruptive technology casualties outnumber the beneficiaries. It is a fact of life. It displaces an established technology and shakes up the industry or a ground-breaking product that creates a completely new industry.

It is fair to say that the Internet is the *digital universe* of the world. There is a remarkable parallelism between our stellar universe, the human brain, and the Internet. They are abysmally deep and complex, immeasurable in size, but phenomenally scalable with unlimited processing power.

It is not fair to say that the Internet has been responsible for the demise of thousands of companies. The longevity of a company is the future visibility of its management. It's like blaming a large piece of ice for sinking the Titanic to the bottom of the Atlantic. Techno-evolution is a one-directional temporal process known to be disruptive and often fatal for the unprepared. Take, for example, Radio Shack, Borders, Blockbuster, Alpha Graphics, and PIP. Blockbuster was flying high before they crashed due to pilot error. The Internet stole the thunder from some of the most glamorous companies such as IBM, Microsoft, Kodak, Xerox, and Nokia, and thousands more lie at rest in the tech-graveyard. How about floppies, Zip drives, flash cards, and CDs? We thought that they would last forever. Charles Darwin was right when he said, "It is not the strongest of the species that survives, nor the most intelligent that survives. It is the one that is most adaptable to change."

So, how do technology companies adapt to change? Adaptation to change is equal to survival. Evolution, however, is a gradual genetic change from one generation to another. A principle mechanism of evolution is natural selection, in which individuals, superior in survival or reproductive ability, contribute selective genes to future generations, thereby gradually increasing the frequency of the favorable alleles (mutated genes) in the whole population.

One mammal transformed the world once its speed and power were harnessed. It is the first thing that allowed man to travel faster than his two legs could carry him on land. It is the creature that a few of us, as equestrians, know and appreciate in our current-day lives. The unsung hero is the horse. We've had 6000 years of history of the horse since its domestication. The horse served its time honorably. Then, along came the combustion engine in 1866, but it took the automobile nearly 50 years to dislodge the horse from farms, public transport, and wagon delivery systems throughout the world. The Big Shift brought us into another disruptive innovation: from horse dung to car smog. The energy crises of the 1970s and 1980s created a renaissance in electric vehicle manufacturing with the mass marketing stage launched in the 21st century. Then, the real big disruptive idea showed up on the horizon. Driverless robotic cars dazzled the public and Detroit auto companies panicked and scrambled to reinvent themselves as firms that provide all sorts of transportation options, from ride-hailing services to cars that drive themselves.

The old canonical axiom resonates in our ears: "time is what keeps everything from happening at once." In 1886, Karl Benz, the German mechanical engineer, designed and built the first practical car powered by an internal combustion engine. Although the automobile certainly eliminated piles of manure in city streets in the 19th century, it introduced a whole new set of global pollution complications.

A city is a large and permanent human settlement run by a local government. Cities do not have growth restrictions. They grow organically where each city has its own demography and unique geography, and of course, the vision of its leader. There are three kinds of cities: *Aleppo* (northern Syria), which is arguably the oldest city in the world; *Shanghai*, the most populous metropolis with 24 million people; and *Dubai* in the UAE, an example of a fast-growing city.

The Rise of Nanotechnology and Artificial Intelligence

These two innovative technologies will be covered in more detail in the upcoming chapters. We wanted to mention these two giant technologies and their contribution to sustained "nano" cybersecurity. Our focus here is digital immunity (DI) as the best protection for a Smart City. We will talk about how cybersecurity got immersed into these two technologies and brought a totally different perspective to the whole security continuum.

Artificial intelligence (AI) will be merged with the nano world and create super intelligent computing machines that will be the best protection for a Smart City. But let's make sure we understand how these two technologies will work hand in hand for the welfare of a Smart City.

Nanotechnology is science, engineering, and technology conducted at the nanoscale, which is about 1–100 nanometers. Nanoscience and nanotechnology involve the ability to see and to control individual atoms and molecules. Everything on Earth is made up of atoms—the food we eat, the clothes we wear, the buildings and houses we live in, and our own bodies. With new tools for scientists to use, such as the scanning tunneling microscope (STM) and the atomic force microscope

(AFM), the age of nanotechnology was born. Nanotechnology hasn't entered the new domain of DI, but it will.

AI creates thinking machines that can perform a million times better than our biological brain. DI replicates the human immune system (IS) for the digital world, which is molecular even down to the atom level. Cybersecurity—still in first gear—has been able to put the malware genie back in the bottle. AI will create highly intelligent molecular software (nanobots) that will live and roam among the molecules of nanogrids, nano rubber tubes, and motherboard circuits. It is not science fiction. It is the reality of the future.

Back to the Smart City

Here's another revelation: the human body is actually a smart system. In fact, the body resembles the most miraculous Internet of Things (IoT) system. There are over 40 billion cells in the body and each and every cell is equipped with a smart receptor (sensor) that reliably sends and receives intelligent signals from the brain. There are two types of neural signals: (1) the *sensory signal* (neuron) such as sight, sound, feeling, taste, and sense of touch, which is sent to a central unit in the brain for translation and response; and (2) the *motor signal*, which is sent back to the receptor for action. The brain registers the transaction as a knowledge record. The IS goes on alert to eradicate the unwanted guest. Figure 1.4 shows how the human grid is interconnected to form the human IoT replica.

Here's our definition of a Smart City: a city that resides at the top of a very intelligent grid like the human nervous system (NS). A Smart City needs a central coordination center to capture, analyze, and respond to all the messages in the city. A Smart City needs a very conductive *real-time* grid to safely transport the intelligent messages without collision or conflict. And finally, a Smart City needs sensors that are connected to all devices to collect and receive intelligent messages. This is the basic layout of the city. No Smart City is complete without a predictive defense mechanism that predicts and detects all incoming surprise attacks. City enemies can quickly design a distributed attack that tarnishes the glamour of the city. Just think about the human body without an IS. Adaptive DI is the Holy Grail of a Smart City. Hacking guerillas have a team of savvy cyberspies who could fire an army of Trojans and profile all the defense technologies in the city, and return to their ateliers and craft a nasty invasion of the same city technologies.

Figures 1.5 and 1.6 give an idea of the challenges to setting up a Smart City, and how to combat residual chaos that has grown in the city for hundreds of years, respectively.

Let's go back to the NS and see how marvelously it works. We know that the NS is pathologically connected to all the cells in the body; however, that's not as impressive as its autonomic (driverless) feature that drives the NS. We define autonomic processing as self-managing, self-optimizing, self-configuring, and even self-healing functionalities. The NS operates fully in two astonishing autonomic

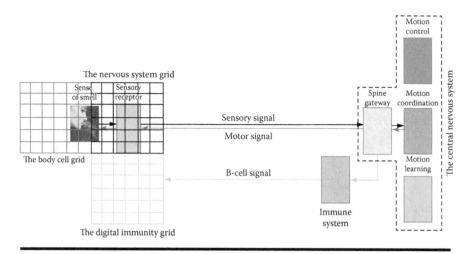

Figure 1.4   The human body is an overwhelmingly "smart" IoT network where every cell is an active device. Inside the body there are three interconnecting grids: (1) the cell location grid; (2) the nervous grid; and (3) the immune B-cell grid. A Smart City should follow the same pattern with two superimposed pathologically connected grids: the city smart grid (CSG) and the smart vaccine grid (SVG). (© 2014 Copyright MERIT CyberSecurity Group. All rights reserved.)

modes. The *fighting mode* where all resources are mobilized to surround and eradicate any surprise attack. The IS is then called upon to intercept the attack and learn about how it smuggled itself into the body for similar future attacks. The *normal mode* is to reset the orderly functions of the body and replenish all resources. The IS and the NS have tightly coupled grids that exchange sensory and mobile signals, and alert and emergency messages.

One lateral thought to learn about building a secure Smart City is to visit some of the most memorable castles and cities from the Old World. The first

Figure 1.5   Air conditioners in high-rise apartments. Residents wither under oppressive heat and humidity. Installing IoT apps would be a most grueling project.

Figure 1.6 The design of synchronized traffic lights in a Smart City is a major challenge but it will reduce accidents and eliminate road rage among drivers and pedestrians.

impression would be the brilliant defense engineering that was blueprinted to protect the city. Technology may have been rudimentary by our standards, but the engineering mind was as creative and innovative as ours. The major fear was bushwhacked attacks and repeated invasions. A city defense system should have three vital expert components: how *to predict* an attack, how to *detect* an incoming attack, and how *to eliminate* a sneaky attack. These three critical features are still alive today and they are an integral part of a Smart City's defense structure.

Smart Cities should be designed with a fully autonomic security system that predicts, fights, and eliminates mischievous aggression on the city. Without this level of security sophistication, the city and its residents will be vulnerable and defenseless. Let's forget the old saying: *the chain is as strong as its weakest link.*

The Need for Operations Research and Urban Informatics

One of the most remarkable disciplines of modern science is operations research (OR). In fact, with OR we can reach any feasible solution no matter how complex or complicated the problem. OR specialists work in the most prestigious public and private institutions in the world. During WWII, close to 1000 men and women in Britain were engaged in operational research. About 200 operational research scientists worked for the British Army. It is a full spectrum of engineering and math knowledge. Take, for example, queuing theory, which is used to solve traffic gridlock and waiting lines at banks. Airports use queuing models to simulate airplane movements and parking spaces. Emergency departments use queuing systems to determine the number of treatment rooms and physicians needed to minimize the triage of patients. One of the most popular applications of queueing theory is to help optimize the synchronization of traffic lights to maximize car movement in congested city streets. Let's not forget the phone companies that use queuing systems to analyze line bandwidth and phone call delays. Thus, queuing theory, known also as mathematical modeling, describes the performance of a random phenomenon in terms of arrival, wait time, service time, and turnaround time.

Simulation is another technique, like mathematical modeling, to build a replica *model* of a real-world system in a laboratory and analyze the behavior of the model to determine the breakdown areas under increasing workloads. Take, for example, crash testing a new car model to determine the safety threshold from the front, side, and rollover. Data will be collected and sent back to engineering. How about the Apollo 11 project?

> NASA estimated that it had taken more than 400,000 engineers, scientists and technicians to accomplish the moon landings—reflecting the vast number of systems and subsystems needed to send men there. Rick Robinson, director of technology for Amey, bluntly confessed: Many examples of "Smarter City" projects have demonstrated that in principle technologies such as social media, information marketplaces and the "internet of things" can support city-level objectives such as wellbeing, social mobility, economic growth and infrastructure resilience. But these individual results do not yet constitute a normalized evidence base to indicate which approaches apply in which situations, and to predict in quantitative terms what the outcomes will be. (https://www.theguardian.com/science/2009/jul/02/apollo-11-back-up-team)

The Bumpy Road to the Smart City

The first step to wisdom is to get a feel of the future. The Smart City is a fuzzy moving topic that cannot be thoroughly defined. The Smart City is a deep ocean with unknown depths and many unforeseeable surprises. Everyone is talking about Smart Cities as an expert, but the truth is that we know enough to be dangerous. It's like moving the Empire State Building one inch to the north. Pushing or pulling it will not work. You have to tear it down and build it one block at a time from the bottom up. The National Institute of Standards and Technologies (NIST) has been trying to develop an IoT-enabled Smart City framework, but it admits that there are lots of slippery slopes ahead. Here is how NIST described a Smart City sticky situation:

> Two barriers currently exist to effective and powerful Smart City solutions. First, many current Smart City ICT deployments are based on custom systems that are not interoperable, portable across cities, extensible, or cost-effective. Second, a number of architectural design efforts are currently underway (e.g., ISO/IEC JTC1, IEC, IEEE, ITU and consortia) but have not yet converged, creating uncertainty among stakeholders. To reduce these barriers, NIST and its partners are convening an international public working group to compare and distill from these architectural efforts and city stakeholders a consensus framework of common architectural features to enable Smart City solutions that meet the needs of modern communities.

The June 2016 issue of *Government Technology Magazine* discussed the difficulties of building a Smart City: In addition to varied pressures, city managers slowly came to discover that the new technologies, while promising, were not always ready for prime time. Tools that worked on the lab bench didn't always deliver when deployed in real-life situations. "Everyone bought into this big-bang vision, but when they started to deploy they discovered the solutions were not fully developed and ruggedized. People couldn't have known that: These things cannot be tested in the lab. They have to be tested in a living context," Cisco's Anil Menon said.

Mike Zeto, AT&T's Smart Cities general manager, also concerned about too many unknowns, said: "If we can prove it can be done over a narrowly defined area, that gives the city the ammunition to go to their key stakeholders and show that three to five solutions do add more value than siloed point solutions deployed departmentally." "You show that a holistic strategy can be deployed and proven. Then you can raise the funds you need to take the key learnings from that framework and deploy them across the city."

Anil Menon, global president of Smart-Connected Communities at Cisco, expressing his concern about the lack of a holistic blueprint of a Smart City, said: "Even as the scope of the smart city ambition has been scaled back, IT managers have more finely honed their ultimate ambition: to make life better. Today it's not just about servers and routers. Now the city managers and deputy mayors are talking about outcomes. How can I decrease congestion? How can I create a better tourist experience? This is a very different conversation than we've seen in the past."

At the Sixth Annual Smart City Expo World Congress in June 2016 in Dubai, Kathryn Willson, director, Microsoft CityNext, said: "Most cities so far have been trying to figure out how to squeeze efficiencies out of the systems they have." For more mature IT organizations, the implementation of smart tools will have to come hand in hand with a smartening up of IT's underlying bone structure. "Now they are trying to figure out: What is the platform position they need to take to move forward? They are trying to understand the Internet of Things, to understand big data, in order to understand how all of these things are going to fit together."

In June 2016, *Government Technology Magazine* had an eye-popping article titled "A New Smart City Model Is Emerging," highlighted the following: "Technology is not the only component to a Smart City. It is also about having smart public–private partnerships, smart planning, the integration of physical infrastructure into digital infrastructure."

All this fancy talk leads to one conclusion, while everyone is excited about Smart Cities, there's an underlying concern about how and where to start. In a near-zero visibility situation, the best alternative is to build a model of a Smart City by using simulation and predictive analytical tools to evaluate the integration process of the Smart City. We formulated a complex polynomial that represents all the influencing variables that make up Smart City solutions:

$$V_{\text{scity}} = V_{\text{mgmt}} + V_{\text{plan}} + V_{\text{egov}} + V_{\text{budget}} + V_{\text{safety}} + V_{\text{performance}}$$

$$V_{\text{security}} + V_{\text{energy}} + V_{\text{health}} + V_{\text{demographics}}$$

$$V_{\text{infras}} + V_{\text{traffic}} + V_{\text{waste}} + V_{\text{IoT}} + V_{\text{water}}$$

As we can see, building a Smart City is a complex endeavor, as risky as going to Mars. Each one of these variables represents a cluster of sub-variables pertaining to a smart solution. It will require a top-notch domain specialist to build such a highly intricate organism. Furthermore, we should determine the impact of one variable on the others. Take, for example, $V_{\text{performance}}$, which discusses the issue of the hardware and software capacity and scalability. Performance management requires a good understanding of the city's workload, the user habits, and which applications are used the most. City connectivity may require 50,000 devices to be connected as part of the IoT. This is in itself a monumental and tedious undertaking. The collection of user data is like walking around the globe on foot.

One way to crack this big hard nut with a wedge and hammer, is to resort to quantitative modeling. With the help of big data and analytics, urban planners can now use simulation to anticipate the impact of each variable of the big city polynomial. Laura Adler, a doctoral student from Harvard University, drew on her real-world experience when she said:

> The most fundamental benefit of simulation is the ability to mitigate the problem of "unintended consequences" by using realistic models to predict effects on land valuation, employment patterns, and transportation mode choice. In urban planning, optimizing one system often comes at the expense of functionality in other areas: the construction of much-needed housing can lead to overburdening the local

transportation infrastructure; campaigns for water conservation can, ironically, damage a city's water infrastructure.

Simulation allows planners to anticipate cascading effects across urban systems from water management to energy and waste management to parking. Simulations are an important bridge between theory and experiment: without affecting real-world situations, designers can predict the outcome of interventions across a range of scenario specifications. Simulations have thus become an indispensable tool for urban planners.

Today, online data collection and sensor systems are generating unprecedented quantities of data, enhancing the predictive power of statistical models. Spatial information systems are becoming more advanced, allowing for better geographical analysis and compelling visualizations that can communicate potential outcomes to citizens. And the growth—by leaps and bounds—of computing power allows planners to easily calculate the interrelationships of multiple urban systems. AI and human intelligence will merge to generate expert systems and reasoning engines that will improve the way we live.

Shopping for a Smart City Simulator

The marriage of experimental science with simulating and modeling natural phenomena using high-performance computing (HPC) has been a fruitful one. Experimentation provides raw data for simulating a natural process, and supports or disproves a working hypothesis. Simulation helps urban planners and scientists know how well or poorly they understand what they are studying by comparing the simulation against observations of the real thing. The connection between HPC-based simulation and experimentation moves science forward faster than experimentation alone, eliminating unlikely hypotheses and pointing in more rewarding directions. Researchers are now exploring a new twist in simulation-based discovery. Two currents in computation, machine learning and data analytics, popularly called "big data" are poised to transform this way of doing science.

Academia provides simulation systems for research, which are excellent tools for urban planning. The University of California in Berkeley has *UrbanSim*, which allows users to run simulations, draw from a library of open data, and produce visualizations. It is a free and open source. UrbanSim aims to help urban planners better understand the impact of interventions. Simulated scenarios with different input parameters can be shared with citizens for discussion and feedback.

The Massachusetts Institute of Technology (MIT) has developed *CityScope*, an urban simulator (http://cp.media.mit.edu/) that integrates physical representation with projections and visualization tools. Using sophisticated analytics, users can see the different results by setting different rules for infrastructure and mobility

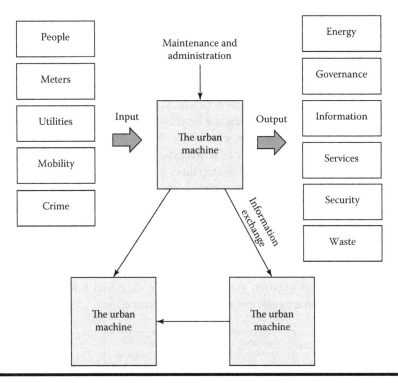

Figure 1.7 **The real-time city is now real! In recent years, the increasing deployment of sensors and hand-held electronics has allowed a new approach to the study of the built environment. The way we describe and understand cities is being radically transformed alongside the tools we use to design them and the impact on their physical structure. (From MIT Senseable City Lab 3-2015. http://senseable.mit.edu/cityways/.)**

systems. A visualization tool helps planners predict, quantify, and visualize the results of urban transformation (Figure 1.7).

Emerson College in Boston has a simulator program called *Participatory Chinatown* that specializes in community engagement through digital simulation. The program uses a multiplayer game format to engage citizens in a number of simulated neighborhood activities inside a digital re-creation of Boston's Chinatown.

On the public side, governments are aware of the power of simulation and have started to develop their own tools to help public officials access, analyze, and interpret urban data. Australia's "urban intelligence network," or *AURIN* (https://aurin.org.au/), is a state-run resource for the nation's cities and towns that provides datasets and online tools for analysis, modeling, and visualization. The program aims to support "evidence-based policy and decision-making" in cities and towns across the country. By centralizing data and analytics tools, AURIN ensures that individual cities can limit redundant efforts and better learn from one another's experiences.

A similar program from the École Polytechnique Fédérale de Lausanne, called *CitySim*, allows designers to estimate energy demand and plan for the integration of renewable energy sources. In 2015, MIT sponsored a conference called "Computers in Urban Planning and Urban Management" (http://cp.media.mit. edu/). Researchers around the globe are hard at work modeling diverse urban systems to meet different city challenges.

Arizona State University created the *WaterSim* model to estimate the water supply and demand for the Phoenix metropolitan area. Users can explore how water sustainability is influenced by the various scenarios of regional growth, drought, climate change impacts, and water management policies. WaterSim allows users to change variables one by one, and then see how each change affects the water sustainability of the region and its various communities.

As technology evolves and moves forward, legacy tools are being replaced with new ones. The Internet has been a blessing for urban city developers. And with the rise of geographic information systems (GIS), big data, and knowledge engines, simulation has become interactive and more subject specific.

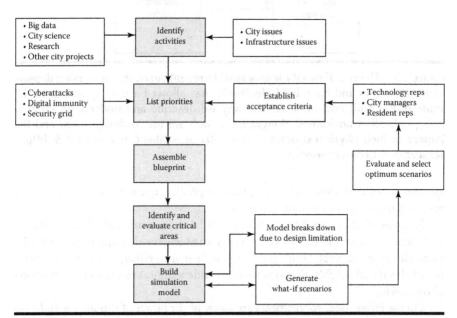

Figure 1.8   Building a Smart City is a new discipline of engineering. The project needs business strategists, experienced urban engineers, hands-on computer scientists, and cybersecurity gurus. This is the holistic blueprint to navigate safely to a well-designed Smart model City. (© 2014 Copyright MERIT CyberSecurity Group. All rights reserved.)

Figure 1.8 represents the basic methodology blueprint showing the systematic approach to develop a model Smart City.

The New Science of Cities: Urban Informatics

Since 2005, more than a dozen new laboratories, departments, and schools have been launched with a common purpose—to pursue deeply quantitative and computational approaches to understanding the city. If present trends continue, by 2030, new urban science institutions could connect thousands of researchers and students, and represent more than $2.5 billion in current and future investment. As urban planning moves from a centralized, top-down approach to a decentralized, bottom-up perspective, our conception of urban systems is changing. We're not going to be able to build Smart Cities unless we resort to a new scientific approach, as we explain next.

In the book *The New Science of Cities*, Michael Batty suggests that to understand cities (or building a new Smart City for that matter), we must view them not simply as places in space but as systems of networks and flows. To understand space, he argues, we must understand flows, and to understand flows, we must understand networks—the relations between objects that comprise the system of the city. Drawing on the complexity sciences, social physics, urban economics, transportation theory, regional science, and urban geography, and building on his own previous work, Batty introduces theories and methods that reveal the deep structure of how cities function.

The book presents the foundations of a new science of cities, defining flows and their networks and introducing tools that can be applied to understanding different aspects of a city's structure. It examines the size of cities, their internal order, the transport routes that define them, and the locations that fix these networks. The book also introduces methods of simulation that range from simple stochastic models to bottom-up evolutionary models to aggregate land-use transportation models. Then, using largely the same tools, the book presents design and decision-making models that predict interactions and flows in future cities. These networks emphasize a notion with relevance for future research and planning: that design of cities is a collective action (see Figure 1.9a,b).

Scientists and governments are finding ways to unite two extraordinarily profound developments in human history: the digital revolution and global urbanization. The result is the nascent field of urban informatics, the use of data to better understand how cities work. Using urban informatics, large-scale data and analytics can be interpreted to address problems and create solutions for operations, planning, and development.

This intersection of cities and computing has spawned an area of urban science widely described as urban informatics. Literally, merging the Oxford English

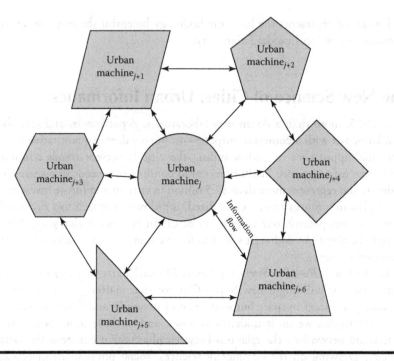

Figure 1.9 **(a) To build new Smart Cities, we must view them not simply as places in space but as systems of networks and flows. We must understand flows, and to understand flows, we must understand networks—the relations between objects that comprise the system of the city.**

definitions for these two terms yields a working meaning: "the collection, classification, storage, retrieval, and dissemination of recorded knowledge of, relating to, characteristic of, or constituting a city." But is this too limiting? As Foth explains, urban informatics is

> An emerging field populated by researchers and practitioners at the intersection of people, place and technology with a focus on cities, locative media and mobile technology. It is interdisciplinary in that it combines members of three broad academic communities: the social (media studies, communication studies, cultural studies, etc.), the urban (urban studies, urban planning, architecture, etc.), and the technical (computer science, software design, human–computer interaction, etc.), as well as the three linking cross sections of urban sociology, urban computing, and social computing.

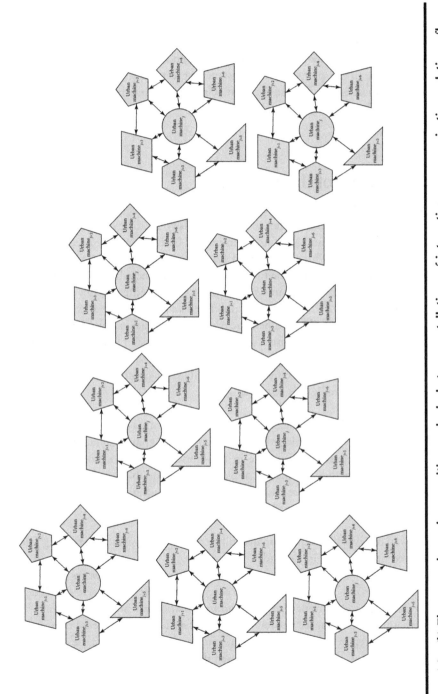

Figure 1.9 (b) **The new urban science—cities are looked at as constellations of interactions, communication, relations, flows, and networks.**

A brilliant synthesis of how concepts from complexity science change our understanding of cities. Scaling, fractals, and simulation models are clearly explained and used to demonstrate how flows and networks shape cities and how they can be better predicted and managed for improving urban planning and design. A great book for an emerging urban science. (Denise Pumain, Université Panthéon-Sorbonne, Institut Universitaire de France)

Reality Drivers of the Smart City

Why do we need Smart Cities? What are the major benefits and incentives? As a matter of fact, we do not have a choice. Everything is going to be smart. Technology is our gravitational force and all of us are immersed in it. If someone needs to know where we're heading, let him or her read Ray Kurzweil's book *The Singularity Is Near*, and how he has crystal balled the future. He is an incredible mega-thinking machine. Wall Street described him as the "restless genius." Interestingly enough, he doesn't believe in death. *Wired* magazine published an article titled "Ray Kurzweil's Plan: Never Die." Kurzweil has joined the Alcor Life Extension Foundation, a cryonics company. In the event of his declared death, Kurzweil plans to be perfused with cryoprotectants, vitrified in liquid nitrogen, and stored at an Alcor facility in the hope that future medical technology will be able to repair his tissues and revive him. His futuristic paradigm is fascinating:

> Within a few decades, machine intelligence will surpass human intelligence, leading to The Singularity—technological change so rapid and profound it represents a rupture in the fabric of human history. The implications include the merger of biological and nonbiological intelligence, immortal software-based humans, and ultra-high levels of intelligence that expand outward in the universe at the speed of light.

Kurzweil believes that superhumans will be able to agglomerate everything into a connected universe within a decade.

Alvin Toffler is another futurist and the author of the book *Future Shock*, in which he synthesized disparate facts from every corner of the globe. He concluded that the convergence of science, capital, and informatics was producing such swift change that it was creating an entirely new kind of society. He predicted the consequences to culture, the family, government, communication, the city, the economy, and the invention of the Internet. He insisted that

The illiterate of the 21st century will not be those who cannot read and write, but those who cannot learn, unlearn, and relearn. One of his predictive revelations that hits the nail on the head is:

Industrial vomit … fills our skies and seas. Pesticides and herbicides filter into our foods. Twisted automobile carcasses, aluminum cans, non-returnable glass bottles and synthetic plastics form immense middens in our midst as more and more of our detritus resists decay. We do not even begin to know what to do with our radioactive wastes—whether to pump them into the earth, shoot them into outer space, or pour them into the oceans. Our technological powers increase, but the side effects and potential hazards also escalate.

Building a new Smart City or upgrading a metropolitan city to the Smart City level is an excruciating push-up exercise. The project might encounter the same fiasco as the biblical city of Babel (1894 BC). Human rivalry and horn locking set the stage for collision entropy. The jumble of languages and plans was described in *Greek Apocalypse of Baruch, 3:5–8*, "When God saw this He did not permit them, but smote them with blindness and confusion of speech, and rendered them as thou seest." Building a Smart City dwarfs the mission to the moon and back, simply because it doesn't have a definite start and finish. "Those who cannot remember the past are condemned to repeat it" (George Santayana).

The Smart City is a major *disruptive phenomenon* characterized by two driving waves: the first one is *the unstable human chemistry* that creates massive social turbulence, which includes leadership clashes, polarized politics, territorial wrangles, vision myopia, and financial drought. The second driving wave is *technological hysteria*, which has been raging for the last 20 years, promoted by technology providers, engineers, and academic researchers. They set up endless conferences in glamorous cities like Dubai and Singapore about Smart Cities, but very few of them have tackled the issues of financing, investment, and policy—they are more likely to describe the technology and engineering solutions behind schemes that appear to create new efficiencies and improvements in transport and energy systems, but that, in reality, are unsustainable because they rely on one-off research and innovation grants. Rick Robinson, director of technology at Amey, brutally admitted "And because Smart Cities are usually discussed as projects between technology providers, engineers, local authorities and universities, the ordinary people who vote for politicians, pay taxes, buy products, use public services and make businesses work are not even aware of the idea, let alone supportive of it... The vast majority of Smart City initiatives to date are pilot projects funded by research and innovation grants. There are very, very few sustainable, repeatable solutions yet."

The world is divided on how real the Smart City is. Today, we do not have a model Smart City that can be copied or replicated. If we had a Smart City, then some interesting questions would be raised: How did it start? How long did it take, how much money was spent, who was involved in building it? How is it going to be run and managed? If we ask 10 urban domain experts, we will get 10 different answers. The consequence of the lack of cohesion and focus among the scientific community is that very little real money is being invested in Smart Cities to create the outcomes that cities, towns, regions, and whole countries have set out for themselves in thousands of Smart City visions and strategies. When we systematically analyze the present situation, we discover three hideous faults (sleeping giants) that need to be addressed before we suffer from serious and embarrassing economic and social consequences. First, many grants are not focused on the "bottom-up" construction of a Smart City's infra-structures, connectivity, and residents' safety. Research and innovative projects do not seem to be part of the holistic blueprint of a Smart City. Second, many of the investments have focused on smart technology and transforming our world into a commercial environment on a scale that is primarily commercial to develop new products and services that consumers want to buy. It is conve-nient for consumers and profitable for companies; but it is far from guaranteed to create resilient, socially mobile, vibrant, and healthy cities. These products will reduce our life expectancy and social engagement by promoting high-fat, high-sugar takeaway food on our smartphones to be delivered to our couches by drones while we immerse ourselves in multiplayer virtual reality games. Thirdly, investors in property development are not genuinely interested in Smart City development. They turn around and get a hefty "short-term" return by selling the properties that they build. At the same time, they invite the telecom compa-nies to install connectivity in those buildings. Investors deliberately select areas where there is no mobile coverage.

It goes without saying that the vast majority of private investments are simply made in the interests of profitable returns. Political leaders are not shaping the mar-kets in which those investments are made or influencing public sector procurement practices to create broader social, economic, and environmental outcomes. We need to persuade political leaders to act—the leaders of cities and local authorities and, more generally, national politicians. We need to approach "Smart Cities" not as a technology initiative but as a political and economic issue made urgent by impera-tive challenges to society.

Introducing Smart City Value Chain

Smart City Value Chain = Vision + Funding + People + Ecology + Technology

The polynomial shows that in order to sustainably add value to the lives of Smart City citizens, we need to develop a *value chain* that describes the transformation cycle of data into value and the components that need to be taken into account while proceeding with this approach. Moreover, some transversal layers come across this value chain to make it effective and resilient. Figure 1.10 is Michael Porter's supply chain, as applied to the Smart City.

The Smart City value chain (SCVC) will be discussed in detail in Chapter 2.

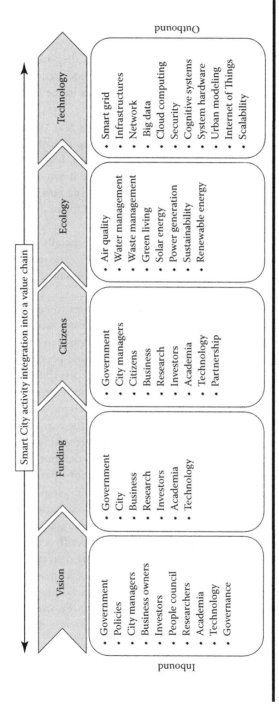

Inbound

Vision
- Government
- Policies
- City managers
- Business owners
- Investors
- People council
- Researchers
- Academia
- Technology
- Governance

Funding
- Government
- City
- Business
- Research
- Investors
- Academia
- Technology

Citizens
- Government
- City managers
- Citizens
- Business
- Research
- Investors
- Academia
- Technology
- Partnership

Ecology
- Air quality
- Water management
- Waste management
- Green living
- Solar energy
- Power generation
- Sustainability
- Renewable energy

Technology
- Smart grid
- Infrastructures
- Network
- Big data
- Cloud computing
- Security
- Cognitive systems
- System hardware
- Urban modeling
- Internet of Things
- Scalability

Outbound

Smart City activity integration into a value chain

Figure 1.10 The implementation of a Smart City is an adventure (a Smart City is a journey). Each step consists of "smart" initiatives or projects that allow movement forward, to test and to experiment, to capitalize on what does and what does not work, and so to form part of the city's transformation process. (© 2014 Copyright MERIT CyberSecurity Group. All rights reserved.)

Glossary

ACORN: A commercial product that splits people and families into different groups who share common characteristics based on where they live. Each of these groups has a profile that describes what they are like in terms of a wide range of behaviors and circumstances. Produced by CACI with a European-wide version and one for each country in the North Sea region based on local data.

Business process re-engineering: Basically changing the way you do things and deliver services. This generally involves looking in detail at the internal processes you use—who collects information, where is it sent, who makes decisions, how are they actioned—to see if some of them can be speeded up or removed. It often involves comparing how similar processes are delivered and looking at e-government tools to see if they can deliver improvements such as electronic forms.

Channel shift: Persuading customers to use cheaper—generally online—ways of getting services or information instead of more expensive ones. This is particularly the case where services can be accessed on a self-service basis via things like electronic forms or directories.

Channel strategy: Describing the best way for customers to contact their local authority in terms of customer satisfaction and cost-effectiveness and then producing an action plan to deliver that. The action plan can include making sure that the services are available in a way that people can easily use, and marketing the new ways we want them to access those services.

Co-design: Working together with customers to decide how services will be delivered. This generally means more than simply carrying out a consultation process asking for views and involves talking to the customer face to face. In the best cases, it will include in-depth customer testing and even asking them to say how services work before starting to design them.

Community profile: A pen picture of what we know about a particular area. This should include statistical information about the people and businesses based in the area and issues like crime, health, education, and so on. It can also look at the physical environment, for example, open spaces and roads; hard and soft resources such as schools, health services, clubs, and societies; and the range and level of services being delivered in that area.

Control: In testing new resources or approaches, a control is an area that has similar characteristics to the place where the test is taking place but where nothing new is done. This means that you can be reasonably sure that any changes in the test area are the result of what you are doing rather than general outside changes.

CRM (customer relationship management): A computer database on which you record information about what services people have requested and been given.

Customer journey: The process that people go through to access a service from their point of view rather than that of the organization. Who do they have to talk to (and how many)? How long do they have to wait? What information do they have to provide? How are they treated and feel at each stage? The output looks like a standard process map, but includes an assessment of their level of satisfaction at each stage.

Customer profile: A pen portrait of a group of people or families who share similar circumstances. These circumstances include the sort of homes they live in, income and employment, skills, the size and age of the family, and their habits in areas such as health, entertainment, shopping, and so on. It will also include which services they regularly use. These are produced by matching statistical information (80% of people in this sort of job live in this sort of house) and building on this by attaching survey and other information where you look at the views or behavior of each profile.

Data matching: Taking two or more datasets with a common element such as an address and adding them together so that you can see where there are statistical matches—60% of people who borrow library books also go to museums.

Data protection: Making sure that personal information gathered by public or private organizations in the delivery of a service is not used for other purposes or shared without the permission of the individual involved.

e-Government: Using ICTs—especially the Internet—to deliver services that in the past have been delivered by talking to a person face to face or on the phone or on paper. These services can be internal processes as well as customer services and will include using the Internet or computer-based information to support a person-to-person service delivery.

Focus groups: A representative group of customers who are brought together to talk through issues based on their knowledge and experience. They can be representative either because their characteristics match those of the general public or because they have particular needs or interests or belong to a particular group. Generally, focus groups will have specific questions you want them to give answers to, but the discussion is more open ended than you would get with a questionnaire.

Geospatial data: Any data that has an address attached to it. This can be a postal address, an area such as a local government electoral division, or a map reference.

GIS (geographic information systems): Computer systems that present information in map form rather than words, figures, or other sorts of pictures.

ICT (information and communications technology): Not just computers but also telephones or any technology that stores, manipulates, communicates, or displays information electronically.

Indicators: Data that helps us understand what is happening in the real world. This can relate to a process (what we do, such as the number of forms we process), outputs (what we produce, such as the value of the welfare benefits we pay), or outcomes (what difference we make, such as a cut in the number of people below the poverty line). They can be indicators of actual change (numbers of qualifications that children get) or a proxy indicator (the number of potholes we fill in as an indication of how good the roads are). In some countries such as England, central government sets out national indicators that other public sector organizations have to report on regularly and are used to assess how well they are serving their local citizens and businesses.

Intermediaries: People we do not directly employ, who help customers get access to our services. They can be friends and family of the customer, voluntary organizations helping particular groups, or other public sector organizations that offer one-stop services or can signpost what is available from other agencies.

Knowledge management: A structured approach to making sure that people in the organization know about how services are delivered and the customers being served is available to everyone in the organization who needs it, when they need it. This is commonly done using networked computers including intranets or the Internet.

Marketing: The process of making sure your products or services achieve their full potential in terms of sales or take-up. The full marketing process includes understanding customers and rivals in the marketplace, product design, and pricing as well as marketing communications (Marcomms), such as advertising, branding, and publicity.

MOSAIC: A commercial product that splits people and families into different groups who share common characteristics based on where they live. Each of these groups has a profile that describes what they are like in terms of a wide range of behaviors and circumstances. This product is produced by Experian with a European-wide version and one for each country in the North Sea region based on local data.

National indicators: The central government in England sets out National Indicators that other public sector organizations have to report on regularly and are used to assess how well they are serving their local citizens and businesses.

OAC: An open source product that splits people and families into different groups who share common characteristics based on where they live. Each of these groups has a profile that describes what they are like in terms of a range of behaviors and circumstances. Produced by the Office of National Statistics in the United Kingdom.

Outcomes: The difference we make, such as a cut in the number of people below the poverty line or a reduction in CO_2 gases.

Outputs: What we produce such as the value of the welfare benefits we pay or the number of people we train.

Personas: A description of a typical member of a group such as a customer profile or priority group as if they were a real, named, individual.

PRINCE: A UK-based, very structured project management methodology that is widely used by the public sector. The full PRINCE methodology is thorough and can be over-complex for small projects so many councils in England use "cut-down" versions that are more appropriate.

Process mapping: A visual way of representing the process of delivering services to internal and external customers. This will typically look at each stage to understand which agencies and officers are involved, what the information flows are, where decisions are made, and any points where eligibility criteria are used. It is particularly useful where there are several ways in which the process can be started. Having mapped out the process, it is then easier to compare with similar processes to see if there is room for improvement. For example, is the process for applying for a concessionary bus pass the same for a student as a pensioner or someone on state benefits?

Qualitative analysis: Looking at information that has been gathered as a result of open-ended questions. There is often a quantitative element to this through either comparing the number of people who gave similar answers or raised similar issues or through taking the answers from a small representative group and multiplying them by the number of people in that group across your area. Although the questions are open ended, it is still important to use the same set of questions with everyone so that comparing answers is easier.

Quantitative analysis: Looking at information that has been gathered as a result of questions that have predetermined answers from which people choose. Sample sizes are generally bigger than for qualitative work although they are generally still representative of the population as a whole rather than the whole population and answers are then multiplied to estimate the view of the whole population. There is still a subjective element to take account of as the answers given depend on the way the question is asked.

Note that it is generally advisable to use both qualitative and quantitative techniques—you can use qualitative work to test the questions and answers with a bigger sample group or you can take the answers to quantitative work to get more detail with an in-depth discussion with a smaller group.

Social marketing: Using marketing techniques to change people's behavior rather than simply increasing the take-up of a product or service. Examples would be encouraging people to take more exercise or eat more healthily, or to recycle more of their rubbish. Encouraging a channel shift is a social marketing exercise.

Super output area: The geographical area in which information from the national census is published in Britain. Generally speaking, this is the smallest area in which statistics are published and super output areas (SOAs) are used to build up to larger areas like local government electoral boundaries or areas such as post codes.

Systems integration: Using software and data standards to link together or share information held on different computer systems. It is more and more common to do this using Internet-based standards such as XML schemas.

Unit costs: The average cost of delivering a particular transaction or service. For example, customers may have to fill in a form to request a service. The unit cost of this will vary between face-to-face, telephone, and online methods because the cost of staff supporting that transaction and the building costs of face-to-face services will differ for each channel. The costs that are included, and then divided by the volume of transactions, can vary, but direct customer access staff, buildings, and ICT costs should always be included.

User needs: Understanding what customers need, not just in terms of the services they get, but the way they access those services. This should always be assessed by actually asking customers, although there are a range of ways in which this can be done.

Source: http://www.smartcities.info/glossary. Intercommunale Leiedal, client of MERIT CyberSecurity.

Bibliography

www.internetworldstats.com

http://www.wsj.com/articles/path-strains-under-housing-boom-1465173966

http://www.latimes.com/local/california/la-me-drought-consequences-20150901-story.html

http://web.mit.edu/cron/project/CUPUM2015/proceedings/Content/_html/cupum2015_modeling_sessions.htm

https://www.theguardian.com/science/2009/jul/02/apollo-11-back-up-team

https://sustainability.asu.edu/dcdc/watersim/

http://cp.media.mit.edu/

http://harborresearch.com/smart-cities-not-smart/

https://www.mindtools.com/pages/article/newSTR_66.htm

https://elab.emerson.edu/projects/participation-and-engagement/participatory-chinatown

https://aurin.org.au/

https://www.wired.com/2002/11/ray-kurzweils-plan-never-die/

https://theurbantechnologist.com/2016/02/01/why-smart-cities-still-arent-working-for-us-after-20-years-and-how-we-can-fix-them/

https://www.thenatureofcities.com/2015/07/26/ecologically-smart-cities-keeping-urban-ecosystems-centre-stage-in-indias-smart-cities-programme/

https://www.eurescom.eu/news-and-events/eurescommessage/eurescom-message-winter-2015/the-value-grid-of-smart-cities.html

Smart Grid: http://www.whatissmartgrid.org/smart-grid-101/smart-grid-glossary

Chapter 2

Challenges of the Smart City

Anatomy of the Challenge

The Cambridge Dictionary describes the term "challenge" as "Something needing great mental or physical effort in order to be done successfully." This definition is too generic and lead to nowhere. We will extend the definition and make it compatible with Smart Cities.

City urbanization projects are complex endeavors that cannot be totally quantified or blueprinted with accurate parameters. There are risks involved when activities interact, cross over, and interlink. Then, projects will suffer from technical as well as technological conflicts, plus the fact that project participants will have divergent opinions that make the challenge more difficult. A challenge ends either in success, which leads to victory, or failure, which ends in defeat.

Life challenges enable us to see ourselves at our best and our worst. In meeting a challenge, we become witnesses to our ability to go where we haven't gone before, do what we've never done before, and arrive at a new place in our lives. Indeed, once witnessed, the courage, fortitude, self-trust, and even the humility that helped carry us through can never be "unwitnessed."

We all remember the classic engineering quote "if you can measure it, you can control it." The cybercrime phenomenon cannot be measured like speed, weight, density, or volume. The two prominent metrics that we could use to evaluate the malevolence of cybercrime are risk and vulnerability. Risk is *the probability that a threat will exploit a vulnerability that causes harm to an asset*. It can be quantitatively represented by the following formula:

$$\text{Risk} = \frac{\text{Threat} \times \text{Vulnerability}}{\text{Countermeasure}} \times \text{Impact}$$

Now, let's look at risk from a different angle: risk is the "damage" caused by an act multiplied by probability weighed against the cost of the damage:

$$\text{Risk} = \text{Impact} \times \text{Probability of an event to occur}/\text{Cost}$$

Impact is the effect on the organization should a risk event occur. Probability is the likelihood (threat) the event could occur within a given time frame. Cost (countermeasures) is the amount it takes to mitigate or reduce the risk to an acceptable level.

General Michael Hayden, former head of the US National Security Agency and later the Central Intelligence Agency, presented the formula of risk as

$$\text{Risk} = \text{Threat} \times \text{Vulnerability} \times \text{Consequence}$$

In simple terms, we can define vulnerability as the likelihood of the success of a particular threat category against a particular organization. Mathematically, vulnerability is defined as the *conditional probability* of success knowing an attack will occur in the future:

$$\text{Vulnerability} = \text{Probability}(\text{Success}|\text{Attack}) = P_V(S|A)$$

The challenge is to test one's ability to accept risk without knowing the outcome (Figure 2.1). City administrators and government need a big dose of challenge in order to attain their objectives.

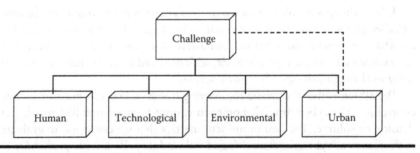

Figure 2.1 City administrators and government need to accept and overcome the challenge before they launch their commitment to build a Smart City. It is within their ability to accept risk without knowing the outcome. Urban commons is a controversial model that has a unique framework based on city and culture.

The Four Challenges of Smart Cities

First: The Human Challenge

The first component is the *human challenge*. While the latest smart gizmo tends to grab the headlines, industry experts are urging urban leaders to focus more on Smart City challenges with their citizens, rather than the technology; engaging residents in the city's administration through dialogue and collective decision-making using websites and mobile apps. There are two types of concerns that we must address.

1. *Behavioral concern* is about the level of synergism challenge of the leaders who are in command of the project. We can brutally promulgate that the failure of Smart City projects falls on the shoulders of the leaders who started with joy but could not come up with a cohesive plan. Project failure is the result of myopic planning, reluctance to accept change, and, above all, over expectation and excitement. Kimberly Lewis, senior vice president of the US Green Building Council, stated a very stern fact: "key challenges are being exacerbated by assumptions that any Smart City technological advancement automatically creates mass impact on the entire city population. However, it's becoming clear that Smart City technology is not a magic wand that can be waved to eliminate persistent challenges faced by poorer citizens."

   Governance is another critical challenge that needs to be carefully orchestrated with qualified city experience and lots of egoless team playing. Government leaders are being urged to develop technology strategies around the needs of citizens first, rather than prioritizing the technology and figuring out whether the public benefits later.

2. *Human rights concern* is about the citizens who are left in the dark. In the underdeveloped countries of Africa and Southeast Asia, citizens are under a totalitarian regime, which has full control over the mass media, the educational system, and the economy, and is responsible for political repression, capital punishment, restriction of speech, mass surveillance, and the establishment of forced labor camps, in addition to having no respect for human rights.

Smart Cities and Eradication of Poverty

The idea behind building Smart Cities is to rejuvenate the ailing urban system, improve the urban infrastructure and quality of life (QoL), and achieve a sustainable QoL for urban citizens (Figure 2.2).

The question now is: If Smart Cities offer QoL to its urban citizens, could Smart Cities eradicate extreme poverty?

Poverty is defined as a *socio-economically marginalized population*. It creates a Himalayan challenge for Smart City planners and developers. Ironically, cities are

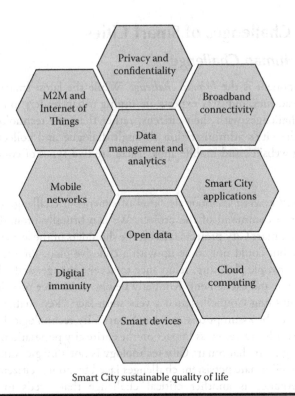

Smart City sustainable quality of life

Figure 2.2   The elements that will contribute to sustainable quality of life in a Smart City.

considered the growth engines of an economy, but they also attract a large proportion of poverty. Consequently, posh urban sprawls exist amid impoverished habitats called *slums* where the poor inhabitants are condemned to live in sub-human conditions. In 1995, the United Nations defined extreme poverty as "a condition characterized by severe deprivation of basic human needs, including food, safe drinking water, sanitation facilities, health, shelter, education and information. It depends not only on income but also on access to services." The World Bank published its Global Monitoring Report for 2015/2016 in which it defines "extreme poverty" as living on less than $1.90 per day.

Global poverty is estimated to have declined in 2012 to 902 million people, or 12.8% of the global population, according to the most recent data from the World Bank's Global Monitoring Report. The poverty headcount is forecast to fall in 2015 to 702.1 million, a poverty rate of 9.6%, the first time that the share of people living in extreme poverty would be in single digits. The number of people living in extreme poverty has decreased from 1.9 billion to 1.2 billion over the span of the last 20–25 years. Despite solid development gains, progress has been uneven and significant work remains. With an estimated 900 million people in 2012 living on less than $1.90 a day—the updated international poverty line—and a projected 700 million in 2015, extreme poverty remains unacceptably high, as documented in the World Bank's Global Monitoring Report. If we remain on our current trajectory, many economists predict we could reach global poverty "zero" by 2030–2035. Although most regions continue to reduce poverty, meeting the global poverty target by 2030 remains aspirational in all but the most optimistic of scenarios.

The incidence of extreme poverty has gone down from almost 100% in the 19th century, to 9.6% in 2015. While this is a great achievement, there is absolutely no reason to be complacent: a headcount ratio of 9.6% means that 655 million people are still living in extreme poverty. Where do they live?

John Wilmoth, director of the Population Division in the UN's Department of Economic and Social Affairs, came up with an interesting revelation: "The concentration of population growth in the poorest countries presents its own set of challenges, making it more difficult to eradicate poverty and inequality, to combat hunger and malnutrition, and to expand educational enrolment and health systems, all of which are crucial to the success of the new sustainable development agenda. India expected to become the largest country in population size, surpassing China around 2022, while Nigeria could surpass the United States by 2050."

The global human population growth amounts to around 75 million annually, or 1.1% per year. Figure 2.3 shows that while the world's population is growing, poverty is systematically being eradicated. Governments are racing to build Smart Cities from old cities, which is a great endeavor worth pursuing. The reason is obvious. Big cities are contaminated with big crimes, which is the causality of extreme poverty. So, cities are fighting the crippling effects of poverty with effective remedies such as affordable centrally located housing; youth and family service support including food, clothing, and mental health; strong schools and education services especially for struggling and nontraditional learners; job training focused on employability; access to quality early care and learning; access to quality health care; and encouraging family wage jobs.

Second: The Technological Challenge

The second component is the *technological challenge*. The National Academy of Engineering (NAE) published a report identifying several critical technological problems in the 21st century that, if solved, would change the world. The report focused on four areas: *sustainability, health, vulnerability,* and *joy of living*. "As the population grows and its needs and desires expand, the problem of sustaining civilization's continuing advancement, while still improving the QoL, looms more immediate," they wrote in their report. "Old and new threats to personal and public health demand more effective and more readily available treatments. Vulnerabilities to pandemic diseases, terrorist violence, and natural disasters require serious searches for new methods of protection and prevention." The NAE, however, cautiously stated that without the economic and political will, none of the

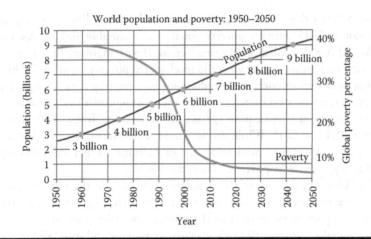

Figure 2.3   A graph clearly showing how poverty is going to dwindle despite the significant growth in population. Combatting hunger and malnutrition, increasing education and employment, and migrating to Smart Cities are the main drives for quality of life. (From US Census Bureau, International Data Base, August 2016 Update.)

challenges would be met. "Despite environmental regulations, cheaper polluting technologies often remain preferred over more expensive, clean technologies."

Smart Cities and Eradication of Cybercrime

Here's an interesting revelation: The first canonical rule is that "Malware runs on Steroid, Security runs on Diesel." Cybercrime is an extension of human creativity. The criminal mind is designed with synthetic intelligence and creativity. In fact, cybercrime is the most influential incentive in the creation of smart security. The brutal truth is that the whole continuum of crime will not be totally eradicated because it is part of the human psycho-infrastructure. There is a strong biological basis for criminality. The CBS hit television show Criminal Minds talks about criminals. "Those who kill in the spur of the moment tend to have a poorly functioning prefrontal cortex, the area that regulates emotion and impulsive behavior. In contrast, serial killers and others who carefully plan their crimes exhibit good prefrontal functioning! Criminals carry criminal gene in their DNA!" Cybercrime is a very real threat in our Internet-connected society. With 1.5 million cyber-attacks annually, this translates into over 4000 cyberattacks every day or 170 attacks every hour. It boils down to three attacks every minute!

So, cybercrime is an astronomical space with no boundaries (Figure 2.4). Cybercrime is the most challenging war against the human race. Ironically, cybercrime accompanies populations everywhere and settles in congested cities (as we can see in Figure 2.4). Crime and poverty are cousins and belong to the

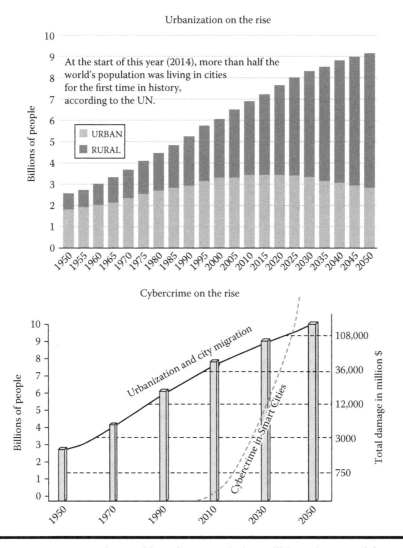

Figure 2.4 By 2050, the world's urban population will have increased from 3.9 billion to 6.4 billion, resulting in 67% of the world's population inhabiting urban areas. As the urban pilgrimage continues to increase, cybercrime will continually accelerate at an exponential rate, using AI technology to penetrate Smart Cities and bring every system to a screeching halt.

same family. In a few years, Smart Cities could eradicate poverty and reduce crime, but it would be logarithmically more challenging to eradicate cybercrime. The reason is obvious: cybercrime requires systematic planning, and it is location independent, transparent, and targets establishments for money or information, and of course critical infrastructures. In fact, Smart Cities will be the most fertile grounds to launch the next generation of cybercrime

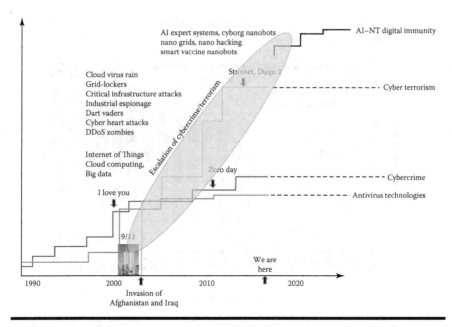

Figure 2.5 Cyber terrorism (shaded area), although it started late, has surpassed antivirus technology in sophistication. True cybercrime eradication will be done by digital immunity technology. (From National Institute of Standards and Technology, 2014.)

(Chapter 6). If we look at Figure 2.5, we notice that cyber terrorism has accelerated and surpassed cyber crime, as indicated by a steeper line. Cyber-terrorism requires a new generation of defense. Antivirus technologies (AVTs) are not smart enough to defend Smart Cities. We will discuss the new paradigm of digital immunity (DI) as a futuristic adaptive defense with a different approach to shield Smart Cities from all evil.

Urbanization may offer prosperity and QoL to urban citizens, but it will also be a haven for hackers, crackers, and spies to drill holes into the urban fabric. We can imagine these buccaneers using a Smart City like a technology laboratory to optimize their cyber arsenal. They will have access to city clouds, city sensors, machine-to-machine (M2M), the smart grid, and infrastructure critical systems. Thus, urbanization will yield diminishing returns. We will discuss the topic of cybercrime in more detail in Chapters 4 and 5.

A Smart City is a space where citizens live and breathe, and are strapped to the Internet. We may deprive someone of his or her freedom and incarcerate him or her—that's misery number one. Or we may punish someone by depriving him or her from accessing the Internet—that's misery number two. Particularly the young generation who have been nurtured on milk and the Internet. Internet deprivation is another virtual prison.

Internet's Compatibility Iceberg

Tim Berners-Lee, inventor of the World Wide Web, is both worried and optimistic about the future of his creation. Vint Cerf, the "father of the Internet," says that he is worried that all the images and documents we have been saving on computers will eventually be lost. "I worry a great deal about that, … Old formats of documents that we've created or presentations may not be readable by the latest version of the software because backwards compatibility is not always guaranteed, and so what can happen over time is that even if we accumulate vast archives of digital content, we may not actually know what it is," said Dr. Cerf. He was right. If we take a document that was written in IBM's report program generator (RPG) on System/3, it will be excruciatingly arduous to convert it to XML. We will discuss later the difficulties for Smart Cities to integrate disparate and incompatible software systems.

It is true that there are five ultra-disruptive technologies that are impacting the human race: autonomous vehicles, genetic engineering, cryptocurrencies, immersive technologies, and cognitive computing and neuromorphics. These technologies created such powerful seismic shocks in our societal fabric and rapidly made entire well-established industries obsolete overnight. The real prophetic wonder, referred to as the Internet (Inter+Net), came like a colossal sand storm and turned our social order upside down and inside out. Disruptive technologies have a cycle of survivability that follows the recognized Gartner Hype Curve—which shows the trend of emerging technologies—from maturity to adoption while the Internet grew like a big bang and proliferated at an exponential rate, beyond any imagination or predictability. The Internet is an incredible *epidemic* that must have been described somewhere in the Bible—who knows? It is as contagious as the Plague of London. It is a physical phenomenon with as incredible a gravitational pull as the black hole. We all pay homage to the Internet.

The Internet created a deep digital divide in the security domain. On one side of the divide, the Internet created a fertile ground for the full continuum of crime. On the other side, the defense technologies seem antiquated and lack scalability and integration.

The Aging Antivirus Technologies

AVT providers suffer from innovation anemia and lack of vision. They have been kickboxing one another for dominance of the market. After evaluating 20 AVT products, James Sanders from TechRepublic said that "The status quo for paid security products, however, is absolutely lacking. With this in mind, it is well overdue to roll up your sleeves, cross your arms, and get serious about desktop security." Even Symantec confessed about the problem: "Symantec is aware of buffer overflow and memory corruption findings in the Antivirus Decomposer engine used in various configurations by multiple Symantec products, … Symantec would like to thank Travis Ormandy with Google's Project Zero, for reporting these to us and working closely with us as we addressed the issues." What kind of sanity is this? Symantec could not discover the defects on its own? The big challenge here is that sending tens of thousands of advisory notes to Internet of Things (IoT) users to patch the holes is a major endless chore.

AVT providers have done a great job during the data center and client–server generation (up to the nineties). Neil Rubenking of *PC Magazine* wrote the report "The Best Antivirus Protection of 2017" in which the 10 leading systems were selected. It was no surprise that the same 10 got selected every year. They all took the same test and all got an A. The user community is still agonizing from two miseries. The first one is new attacks that AVT providers did not have well-tested solutions for, and the second is new defects on existing systems that are made public and need to be patched. Take, for example, Symantec Antivirus, which is supposed to be one of the best. The critical security vulnerabilities that have been found within Symantec and Norton products are "as bad as they get," according to security researchers. Charlie Osborne from ZDNet waved a red flag when she said "Google's bug-hunting Project Zero team disclosed multiple critical flaws found within Symantec's core engine, used as the backbone of both consumer and enterprise security products."

A curse also fell on Trend Micro, a leading AVT provider, where serious password vulnerability created remote command execution holes and dumped private data to any remote user. Thanks to the work of Google's Project Zero security team. Project Zero is a team of security experts at Google assigned to find zero-day vulnerabilities. They have successfully been intercepting serious malware traps since July 15, 2014.

Smart Cities are already immersed in the generation of Internet of Everything (IoE), smart mobile, smart meters, smart sensors, smart traffic control, M2M, wearable devices, big data, the cloud, and critical infrastructure systems. This is the brand-new landscape of computing that will make urbanization attractive with higher sustainable QoL.

AVT providers have to jump on the artificial intelligence (AI) and nanotechnology (NT) bandwagon and develop cognitive and predictive expert systems in order to protect an "airtight" Smart City. Cybercrime and its big brother cyber terrorism are in the driving seat and in control. Cybercriminals have established a global reputation of regularly and promptly following orders from governments and corporations around the world. They have a massive amount of *smart software bombs* (SSB), and their latest product, called *the virus rain*, is designed specifically to knock down the infrastructures of Smart Cities. *Wired* magazine published an interesting report on "How a Remote Town in Romania Has Become Cybercrime Central." The article, which was published in January 2011, described how the city of Râmnicu Vâlcea adopted the name *Hackerville*.

> It's something of a misnomer; the town is indeed full of online crooks, but only a small percentage of them are actual hackers. Most specialize in ecommerce scams and malware attacks on businesses. According to authorities, these schemes have brought tens of millions of dollars into

the area over the past decade, fueling the development of new apart-
ment buildings, nightclubs, and shopping centers. Râmnicu Vâlcea is a
town whose business is cybercrime, and business is booming.

When we compare the sophistication of the technological defense of the security camp to the effective execution and planning of the malware camp, we realize
how wide the divide is. It is like comparing the rifle used in the civil war, while
the evil camp uses Star Wars lightsabers and ray blasters. Pathetic! AVTs will be
covered in detail in Chapter 4.

Forbes magazine published an interesting report titled "Cyber Crime Costs
Projected to Reach $2 Trillion by 2019," in which it describes the reason for the stun-
ning jump from billions to trillions. Juniper Research estimates that the increase in
IoT-connected devices will reach over 46 billion units by 2021. Thus, there's a strong
correlation between the crime cost (damage) and the ballooning of the IoT. The crime
cost will hit Smart Cities hard and the figures will triple again. We can state the
following corollary: "Security in Smart Cities should be the most crucial challenge
on the implementation menu, it will be the straw that will break the back of the
camel." While Smart Cities are being built, professional cyber malware strategists are
building symmetrical smart systems to reduce the risk of defeat. Amazing *star wars*
are looming on the horizon. Here's what Albert Einstein said about creativity: "The
world we have made as a result of the level of thinking we have done thus far creates
problems we cannot solve at the same level of thinking at which we created them."

Cybersecurity, the Technological Divide

One of the biggest challenges—even headaches—that faces Smart Cities is *cybercrime.* One of the marvels of the human immune system (HIS) is that no backdoor
virus or Trojan could sneak into the body, from anywhere, without its knowledge.
This is because the white blood cells are incredibly cognitive and smart machines
that will rush to the infectious spot and eliminate the foreign invaders. These cells
are the defending army and are running in the streams of blood like a nebulous
grid watching over every cell in the body. This is impressive, isn't it? We need to
build a cognitive early warning predictive system to protect a city and its critical
infrastructures.

This computer security flaw doesn't work in the human immune environment
because once a cell becomes inactive (dead), it is kicked out of the body permanently and loses all its living privileges. It cannot masquerade as a living cell.

Another major hole in computer security is that computers are not capable of
remembering any previous attacks, like the M-cells of the human body. This is a
fundamental feature of the HIS acquired by vaccination. As governments around
the globe barrel headlong into the Smart City wave, cybersecurity experts are raising the alarm about the proliferation of unsecured technology. Survey after survey shows how cyber hackers have taken control of cyberspace and are fabricating

the full spectrum of malware, and marketing it from underground smart portals as a "crime-as-a-service" with hefty national and international contracts against governments and technology companies. All adversary countries have their own electronic army sending a barrage of smart missiles that outsmart firewalls, demilitarized zones (DMZS; zones of an untrusted network to protect a trusted network), and honeynets, and steal intellectual properties. Networked cyber terrorist groups have started using second-generation AI cognitive systems to shut down power and uranium enrichment plants. They even use slave cyborgs to commandeer commercial airplanes and to inject self-mutating viruses into a city's smart grid to paralyze IoT systems. The Russian hack crusade that disrupted the US presidential elections, like an act of God, is a vivid example of how vulnerable our infrastructures are. Marketing "master keys" to open remote data vaults and steal private records is another creative malware act that hangs like the sword of Damocles over the heads of city managers. We'll discuss these cyberattacks in detail in Chapters 5 and 6.

Digital Immunity: The New Miraculous Paradigm

Here is an interesting revelation: During the plague of Athens in 430 BC, the Greeks realized that people who had previously survived smallpox did not contract the disease a second time. In fact, these survivors were often called upon to attend to those afflicted with smallpox, according to a 1998 article in the *International Journal of Infectious Diseases*. A disease causes a disorder in the HIS. It is a declaration of an immunological war between attacking pathogens and antigenic mobilization of defending cells. Adaptive immunity is the holy grail of human healing. Like any science, the mechanics of adaptive immunity can be blueprinted and applied to the digital world. It is the only way to put the malware genie back in the bottle.

On December 17, 1903, the Wright brothers successfully replicated a bird flying with their three-axis control invention. Human immunity was added to the annals of human wonders as super physicians and chemists raced to learn more about its mystery. It took 300 years of sweat and frustration before immunology produced a mature immune system based on molecular recognition of the attack. Fortunately, for most of us, our immune systems keep steadfastly vigilant in monitoring themselves to ensure that each cellular component behaves and interacts symbiotically to generate protective immune responses. Amazingly, the concept of human immunity can also be replicated and applied to the digital world. It is a revolutionary leap forward in the future of cybersecurity.

Recipe for Digital Immunity

Here's a short synopsis of an innovative concept called "digital immunity." It mirrors the functionality of the HIS. Without this wonderful autonomic defense system, the Earth will turn into a massive graveyard. The intelligence of this HIS surpasses the intelligence of any system in existence.

The success and efficacy of DI comes from smart components that work together:

Digital Immunity = Early Warning + Nano Smart Grid + Episode Memory

+ AI Reasoning Engine + The Smart Nano Vaccine

+ Human Knowledge + Cybercrime Knowledge

The first one is the early warning component, the smart component of DI, often referred to as the early warning predictor (EWP). The EWP is an inference reasoning engine that relies on the Bayesian network model (BNM) to generate a probabilistic attack forecast. The smart grid is the nervous system that connects all the critical systems together. The episode memory is the knowledge base that stores all the attacks and how they were eradicated. The AI reasoning engine works with the early warning to determine the probability of an attack using the Bayesian model. The Smart Vaccine is the smart vaccinator of all the critical systems. It is the commander of the vaccinator army. An army of smart vaccines replicates the responsibilities of the human B-cells and M-cells, to vaccinate the critical system with an adaptive vaccine code. Human knowledge is the knowledge engine that stores the experience of the security experts that adds to the predictive reasoning. Cybercrime knowledge is the other knowledge engine that contains cybercrime episodes from big data and global law enforcement agencies. Chapter 9 describes the DI architecture in molecular detail.

We Call It Digital Immunity

Smart City computers can also be immunized with the help of an artificially intelligent agent called the "Smart Vaccine™." It is the holy grail of DI. DI is a pioneering concept that was never thought of before. After thoroughly studying immunology and the way it works, it was possible to replicate the human model and blueprint an architecture for the digital world. We called it "digital immunity." It is the most advanced technology that will defend Smart Cities. We will explain why DI is the most suitable security layer for Smart Cities.

It is ironic that the United States has the largest "think tank" in the world, with a massive brain power that could conquer anything except cybercrime. There's so much hub-bub on the subject of cybersecurity that the focus has become more political than technological. InfoSec Conferences (https://infosec-conferences. com/#jan18) lists 47 conferences on cybersecurity and crime for the month of January 2018. This is concrete proof that the subject of combatting cybercrime is a very crucial "challenge" and it dominates the minds of chief information officers (CIOs) and chief security officers (CSOs) (Figure 2.6).

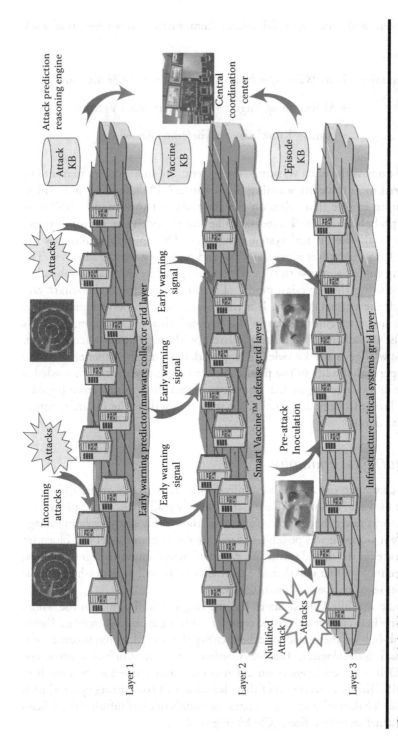

Figure 2.6 Digital immunity is a live composite environment that operates on several smart grids that support the vaccination process of the critical systems. The nano grids are highways that transport software vaccine, nano agents, state–stateless messages, alerts, and status messages. (© 2014 Copyright MERIT CyberSecurity Group. All rights reserved.)

Oh, another crucial item that joins the list of challenges is Smart City cybersecurity. Smart Cities will not offer its citizens a sustained QoL if AVTs suffer from a design defect and lack of quality control. In fact, AVTs need to deploy autonomic computing, grid computing, and AI to support the urbanization establishment.

Cybercrime lords and terrorists have got away with zero-day attacks and the business world has suffered from global viral epidemics. Now, cyber terrorists have found Smart City clouds, which is the best place to market their latest product "Attack-as-a-service." Meanwhile, a silent worm called *Stuxnet* with its ingenious camouflage was able to penetrate Natanz nuclear enrichment plant, in November 2007, and create havoc. Cyber-terrorism has become a real strategic weapon against Smart Cities, launched from anywhere in the world. There are 455 terror schools and institutes that graduate professional terrorists with formal degrees in modern terrorism. Viral attacks have become self-mutating, self-healing, and self-navigating, outsmarting the best firewalls, moats, and the Great Wall of China. Curiosity is in fact the mother of invention.

A nano digital virus—given the name nano cyborg (cybernetic organism)—is the most diabolical invention of the 21st century. It is the mastery of a new breed of creative nerds of the third kind, who can hatch an ingenious piece of code to create a technological holocaust for millions of people. These goons do it for money and for political or religious reasons. They surpass the intelligence of a rocket scientist and challenge the perseverance of a rock climber. Hackers and the hacking syndrome will be discussed throughout the book.

In the genesis of the Smart City, connectivity is the nervous system that connects all the devices together. In other words, Smart Cities live by their smart grids. Without a smart grid, there won't be a Smart City! The city connect function. Here are all the smart activities performed by a city's smart grid:

- The early warning predictive defense will detect the attack
- An alert is sent to the city's coordination center and the Smart Vaccine command
- An alert is dispatched to all devices and critical systems
- An army of smart vaccines (vaccinators) is mobilized
- All devices and systems are innoculated
- The attack is captured and the payload is reverse engineered

We will discuss the DI system in detail in Chapter 9.

Third: The Environmental Challenge

The third component is the environmental challenge, which is most important. Here's why: According to the United Nations Population Fund, 2007 was considered the turning point when city dwellers formed the majority of the global population for the first time in history. Today, the trend toward urbanization continues. In

2014, 54% of the world's population lived in cities—and it's expected to reach 66% by 2050. Migration forms a significant challenge as it is the driver of this urban population growth.

The challenge here is that a systematic focus on urban ecosystems, via the protection of urban commons, is essential to provide a robust, adaptive, and resilient pathway toward greater urban sustainability. The rapid growth of cities is starkly apparent. Urban expansion—with half-cooked plans—will certainly degrade and destroy natural habitats across large cities and small towns. It will transform urban forests, lakes, and wetlands into polluted travesties of their former ecological vigor, and convert them into vast expanses of concrete construction. Building an ecologically Smart City is quite a challenging endeavor.

The International Federation of the Red Cross and Red Crescent Societies (IFRC; www.ifrc.org), the world's largest humanitarian organization, gracefully illuminated us with this poignant definition of human vulnerability: Vulnerability in this context can be defined as the diminished capacity of an individual or group to anticipate, cope with, resist, and recover from the impact of a natural or manmade hazard. The concept is relative and dynamic. Vulnerability is most often associated with poverty, but it can also arise when people are isolated, insecure, and defenseless in the face of risk, shock, or stress.

We all agonize when it comes to the oldest disease of humanity, which is poverty and extreme child poverty. Aristotle once said "Poverty is the parent of revolution and crime." Gandhi reminded us that "Poverty is the worst form of violence." We see it in our cities and it will remain one of the worst challenges for humanity. Poverty is the brother of crime. And if history is written by the rich, the poor get blamed for everything. Do we think Smart Cities could eradicate poverty? Do we think Smart Cities are immune from poverty? These are very opaque questions.

Smart and resilient cities don't just look for innovative technologies—they seek to empower its citizens, especially those from marginalized or poverty-stricken communities. In November 2016, the *Indian Express* published an article titled "The Overrated Urban Spinoff: Agriculture's Contribution to Poverty Reduction Is Five Times More than That of Metropolitan Centers" (Figure 2.7).

Humans around the world are moving en masse into the urban and peri-urban worlds. At the same time, information and communication technologies (ICTs) are exposing a wide array of utopian and militant ideologies to the rising masses of city dwellers. Displaced from rural homes, traditions, and lifestyles, they are eager to find a quality of life (QoL) amid all the alienating turmoil they experience around them.

Pressing men and women so close together in howling, marching formations obliterates individuality. But even with all our electronic diversions, is loneliness any less prevalent now than it was when Arendt published her magnum opus in 1951? People are currently more isolated than ever, more prone to the symptoms of the lonely, totalitarian mind, or what psychiatrists call "racing thoughts."

Figure 2.7 After all, building a city is not just about building residential blocks and roads. It is about combining an array of strict rules and technological marvels to make urban life simpler and more rewarding in the 21st century.

Fourth: The Urban Commons Challenge

The term "urban commons" is a bizarre term that surfaced in the middle of the urbanism movement. It is one of the most innovative steps toward a Smart City, although it is very controversial. The document "The Regulation on Collaboration between Citizens and the City for the Care and Regeneration of Urban Commons" defines urban commons as

> the goods, tangible, intangible and digital, that citizens and the Administration, also through participative and deliberative procedures, recognize to be functional to the individual and collective wellbeing, activating consequently towards them, ..., to share the responsibility with the Administration of their care or regeneration in order to improve the collective enjoyment.

We can provide our own explanation of the term: Cities are complex socioeconomic systems and the idea of a "city as a commons" is an interesting one. Those living in an urban area all share the same space, and all benefit from (or suffer under) the same system of city management. It makes sense that those sharing these experiences should have some say in how their lives in the city are governed—and alternative forms of collaborative management and/or governance arrangements are one way forward.

"What makes the city a commons?" At this point, we would say it is not entirely clear—but it is a fascinating area for exploration—and one that has the potential to increase the "value" we get from our urban spaces through changing the way we perceive and govern the space around us. Professor Sheila R. Foster, associate dean, Fordham University School of Law, published the paper "Collective Action and Urban Commons." She eloquently describes the difficulties and challenges in setting up a proper urban commons (Figure 2.8).

Urban residents share the local resources in which they have a common stake. These resources range from local streets and parks to public spaces to a variety

Figure 2.8 The contrast between the two cities is mind-boggling. Dubai's Jumeirah Palm city (a) was built from scratch in 2001. The slum in Mexico City (b) was built by the Aztecs in 1325, and creating an urban commons would be a gargantuan endeavor. (a) Smart City model using Urban Commons in Dubai, UAE. (b) Neza Chalco Itza, Mexico City, Mexico. It contains an epic 4 million inhabitants, is the world's largest slum, and has the highest crime rate in Mexico.

of shared neighborhood amenities. These shared resources suffer from the same rivalry and free-riding problems and end up failing the mission. There's no well-established strategy to keep the mission on track while the existing government regulations are counterproductive and impede progress. Professor Foster calls the failure of successful collective actions and control "regulatory slippage," when local government oversight and management of the resources significantly decline, creating chaos, competition among users, rivalry, and resource degradation. The city ends up with streets, parks, and vacant land that were once thriving urban spaces but have become overrun, dirty, prone to criminal activity, and virtually abandoned by most users. The proposed solutions to the rivalry, congestion, and degradation that afflict common urban resources are to have a more assertive central government role or privatization of the resource. So far nothing happened, I argue, because of the potential costs to the local government during times of fiscal strain, costs to communities where the majority of residents are non-property owners, and costs to internal community governance. What happened instead, however, are various forms of cooperative groups of users. Scholars have largely ignored collective action in the urban context, and have assumed that collective action is unlikely in urban communities where social disorder exists. The paper highlights the ways in which common urban resources are being managed by groups of users in the absence of government coercion or management and without transferring ownership into private hands. This collective action occurs in the shadow of continued state and local government ownership and oversight of the resources. Formally, although the state continues to hold the regulatory reigns, in practice we see the public role shifting away from a centralized governmental role to what I call an "enabling" one in which state and local government provide incentives and lend support to private actors who are able to overcome free-riding and coordination problems to manage collective resources. This paper develops this enabling role, marks its contours and limits, and raises three normative concerns that have gone unattended by policymakers.

All Cities Are Smart, Not Dumb Cities

Urban technology expert Francis Pisani also has some interesting radical ideas about Smart Cities that are worth mentioning. He embarked on a world tour in 2012 and 2014 to look for examples of urban innovation. He then gave a clued-up account of this in an e-book published by UNESCO (available in English and French). A couple of points in his e-book are worth mentioning.

He criticized the term "Smart Cities," and said "because humanity has not done anything more intelligent than cities. All cities are smart. So, I think the question becomes: what is the process to make a city smarter?"

On the issue of how well the government is doing to help urban citizens, he said "I would like to see politicians who are technology-savvy and to put the question high on their agenda, but it's not happening. City officials often have a poor understanding of technology. Many just want their cities to be 'smart', and give the keys to IT companies that say: we are going to make it happen! That's not the best way to proceed."

He was asked about the vulnerability of Smart Cities, and his answer was "As the number of connected objects increases, cyber criminals have bigger targets and we become more dependent on electricity. In this regard, connected cities are more vulnerable. However, disconnecting is not the solution. We are moving from an internet of people to an internet of everything, with billions of connected objects, of which only a few are seriously protected from intrusion. The problem is the lack of awareness about how fragile the system is. Many cities want to use IT massively, but they don't have a budget to protect their systems, and this is a source of weakness." In his reply to the question "Are you aware of any cases where IT is used to prevent crimes effectively?" Francis Pisani stated "I don't know of many technologies today that are useful in crime prevention. CCTV cameras have indeed been a key tool to identifying and capturing many terrorists responsible for attacks, including the recent ones in Brussels, but only after the facts. And studies in the UK show that these cameras, which today are part of IT networks, have only a modest effect in preventing crime. The point is nothing will ever guarantee that a city is a hundred percent safe. Therefore, we should focus on *resilience* rather than security. The difference is that you can still do your best to protect yourself, but accepting the notion of failure." Finally, he was asked his opinion about people finding Smart Cities more attractive. His answer was "I don't know of anybody who moved to a city because it is supposed to be smarter. When I was in Korea, I visited Songdo, a place designed to be 'smart' and found out that they have problems to get people to live there. I certainly did not move to Barcelona because it's smart—as I said, I think all cities are—but rather because it's trying to go forward: it's a creative ecosystem. You will never get me to say that one place is better than another. I only see good and bad examples, and Barcelona is certainly a good one."

Vendors Interoperability Challenge

Hewlett Packard used to market its products with the slogan "one vendor one solution." This expression not only became short-sighted and unethical, it also became dangerous. There's no one technology provider that could offer the whole spectrum of ICTs. Technology companies such as IBM, Microsoft, HP, Nokia, Texas Instruments, and SAP, who used to brag *what is good for us is good for the country*, lost their glitter and were dethroned. The answer is very simple: they got too big and greedy, product quality decreased, and the market was inundated with half-cooked products. These companies ran out of creativity and innovation. Management resisted change and ignored the wave of disruptive technologies that were displacing established market-leading firms, products, and alliances. Customers switched to more effective and newer products.

One of the key issues facing modern cities today is to avoid municipalities being locked in to technology from a single provider, and to ensure that they are free to transition to the most convenient products and services for citizens offered by competitors. As more and more cities launch projects to become smart, a substantial need is emerging: the ability to share the various models across the world so that they can be replicated anywhere. The basic concern is to avoid cities or districts becoming self-contained, "locked-in" islands, captive of a single company that holds all the enabling technology. New initiatives have started to focus on interoperability and open software.

Two challenges currently exist to produce effective and powerful Smart City solutions. First, many current Smart City ICT projects are based on custom systems that are not interoperable, portable across cities, extensible, or cost-effective. Second, several standards organizations such as the International Organization for Standardization (ISO) and the Institute of Electrical and Electronics Engineers (IEEE) have been struggling to formulate an interoperability framework. To overcome these challenges, the National Institute of Standards and Technologies (NIST) formed a working group to finalize a consensus framework of common architectural models to facilitate the development of solutions that meet the needs of Smart Cities.

The Kurzweil Future Vision

When we talk about walking on the thin ice of a challenge, Dr. Ray Kurzweil, head of engineering at Google, is the technologist who can do it. Ray Kurzweil not only possesses the power of futuristic vision, he lives ahead of his time. He lamented once about "crashed" inventions when he said "I realize that most inventions fail not because the R&D department can't get them to work, but because the timing is wrong—not all of the enabling factors are at play where they are needed. Inventing is a lot like surfing: you have to anticipate and catch the wave at just the right moment." Kurzweil went further on AI. "Once non-biological intelligence matches the range and subtlety of human intelligence, it will necessarily soar past it because of the continuing acceleration of information-based technologies, as well as the ability of machines to instantly share their knowledge." He added: "Intelligent Nano robots will be deeply integrated in the environment, our bodies and our brains, providing vastly extended longevity, full-immersion virtual reality incorporating all of the senses … and enhanced human intelligence."

The UN Appeal for the Smart City

On September 19, 2006, Secretary General Kofi Annan addressed the General Assembly of the UN with a farewell statement. The following is the text of the address at the opening of the general debate of the sixty-first session:

> When I first spoke to you from this podium, in 1997, it seemed to me that humanity faced three great challenges. One was to ensure that globalization would benefit the human race as a whole, not only its more fortunate members. Another was to heal the disorder of the post-cold war world, replacing it with a genuinely new world order of peace and freedom, as envisaged in our Charter. And the third was to protect the rights and dignity of individuals, particularly women, which were so widely trampled underfoot.

> Prior to the Smart City Event, we have interviewed several important stakeholders and partners about their vision on Smart Cities. This week, we were curious to find out everything about the biggest challenges for the development of a successful Smart City Project.

> The number of extreme events associated with climate change is increasing and so cities must learn to develop resilience to them, especially those more vulnerable due to their location e.g. in coastal regions. City planners and developers need to consider how best to site and build infrastructure to limit the risks, and all cities will require rapid action plans that set out how to cope and limit long-term damage in the face of any disruption of major infrastructure.

> "Increased urbanization will give increased problems for cities in terms of infrastructure, their ability to meet existing environmental targets and also on their ability to attract new residents and companies, which bring wealth and prosperity to a city" (James Huntley, vice president at Energy Schneider Electric).

> Therefore, a growing number of cities have set their own targets to reduce greenhouse gas emissions, often with more ambitious figures than their own country. This makes sense as cities account for 70% of all greenhouse gas emissions globally while they currently occupy just 2% of the planet's surface. While cities function much more efficiently than suburban environments because of their density, for the same reason, they also offer the fastest route to greenhouse gas reduction, for example, through sustainable city regeneration projects and broad energy-efficiency and clean transport initiatives.

The Himalayas K2 Challenge

Talking about sheer challenge, here's one that will open your eyes and imagination: K2, also known as *Godwin Austin*, is considered the world's toughest mountain to climb, it is also the world's second-highest peak. It is familiarly called *The Savage Mountain* and is arguably the hardest climb in the world. The first ascent was in 1954. Its routes are steeper and more difficult than those to the top of Everest, and the surrounding weather is significantly colder and less predictable than on Everest. Reaching the top of K2 is the equivalent of an Olympic gold in mountaineering! It was first summited in 1954 by two Italian climbers, Lino Lacedelli and Achille Compagnoni. Forty-nine climbers have died on K2, 22 while descending from the summit. In terms of accidents that happen on the descent, it is the most deadly mountain in the world. The statistics for female climbers are particularly dramatic. Some even say that *K2 is cursed for women*. Five women have reached the top, but out of those five, three died on the descent and, just as a matter of interest, the other two have since died on other 8000 m peaks. In spite of these dangers, the mountain continues to lure climbers from around the world. It is the ultimate extreme challenge (Figure 2.9). In scaling Everest you are a great climber—but in scaling K2 you are a *true climber to other climbers*.

MerriamWebster gives us a skewed definition of challenge: "an action, statement, etc., that is against something: a refusal to accept something as true, correct, or legal. A difficult task or problem: something that is hard to do." This definitely applies to building a Smart City from scratch, or even upgrading to Smart City level.

Many governments attempt to discourage migration from rural areas to cities, but these measures are, by and large, unsuccessful. Since large cities enjoy preferential treatment in terms of infrastructure and industrial development, they serve as magnets for the "have-nots." Regardless of a big city's allure, many observers now feel that conditions for the ever-growing numbers of urban poor are most likely worse than for their rural counterparts (Figure 2.10).

While it is true that the more obvious ill effects of urban life—emotional stress, loss of family structure, congested traffic, noise, environmental pollution—affect people from all income levels, many city dwellers may also take for granted their access to basic public services, such as drinking water supply, housing, solid waste disposal, transportation, and health care.

Quality of Life

"Quality of life" has quickly become a catch-all term, but confusion over what it actually means could have serious negative consequences according to some recent research. QoL is subjective and multidimensional, encompassing positive and

Figure 2.9 The Himalayan K2—located on the border between Pakistan and Xinjiang, China. It is 8,611 m (28,251 ft) high.

negative features of life. It's a dynamic condition that responds to life events: a job loss, illness, or other upheaval can change one's definition of "quality of life" rather quickly and dramatically.

The *World Happiness Report*, published by the United Nations, offers metrics that are used in measuring each country's happiness. Each annual report is available to the public on the World Happiness Report website (www.worldhappiness.report).

Have you been to Australia? It's a unique world, known as the "Land Down Under." Australia's racial and cultural diversity, as well as its different flora and fauna, draw people to it. The outback and wide vistas contrast sharply with the cosmopolitan cities to offer visitors and residents unique experiences. The reason Australia draws immigrants is because of the QoL, world-class educational opportunities, climate, international sports, and the natural wonders of sea and landscape. So what does QoL mean? It simply means:

There is no thermometer today that can help measure the temperature of your QoL. There are few things that we cannot assign a *numerical value* to or a key

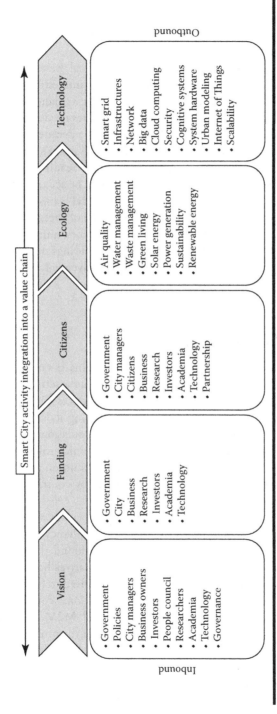

Figure 2.10 The implementation of a Smart City is an adventure (a Smart City is a journey). Each step consists of "smart" initiatives or projects that allow movement forward, to test and to experiment, to capitalize on what does and what does not work, and so to form part of the city's transformation process.

performance indicator (KPI), such as religious faith, happiness, or anger. The big open question remaining is how to correlate the numerical results of indices with the real perception of QoL. How is the transition from the objective measures of smartness to an intangible entity of well-being possible?

Miimu Airaksinen, professor at the Finnish Technical Research Centre and actively involved in the CITY keys project, highlights an interesting point: "Today we are talking quite a lot about the Internet of Things, but we should focus more on the Internet of meaningful things (...) the indicators values needed to be flexible."

Nanotechnology will pave the way for higher QoL in a decade or less, when we will have a smart nano-implant that will measure our physical and mental "stress" and translate it into numerical values—pretty much like reading blood pressure. Let's call it a "stressometer," where its sensor readings will be accumulated monthly at a city's health center, and will be interpreted by a medical team—part of the city management—indicating with high granularity the cause of stress. These stressometer readings will be correlated with the city's QoL indicators, numerically showing the QoL profile of a citizen. A report card will show readings on health, wealth, family, children, employment, city politics, social involvement, city traffic, and food.

Urbanization Is a Blessing or Curse

Proponents of population growth argue that it maintains essential genetic biodiversity and enables economic growth, while opponents assert that population growth strains already scarce natural resources and reduces QoL. While some argue that the world is already overpopulated, or reaching its carrying capacity, others disagree. Analysts and economists argue that population growth is not a bad thing, as it essentially encourages and enables economic growth and prosperity. Urbanization causes environmental and economic strain on land and people. Additionally, urbanization can indirectly affect society by contributing to health problems as a result of pollution and food shortages.

Despite the increasing investment in Smart City initiatives across the United Kingdom, new research conducted by Smart City consultancy Arqiva, together with YouGov (http://www.rudi.net/node/256690), has found that 96% of Brits surveyed online are not aware of any "Smart City" initiatives being run by their local city council in the last year. "Councils desperately need to find a way to harness the enthusiasm of the tech-savvy younger generation," concluded Arqiva's business development director of Smart Metering and M2M, Sean Weir. He added "There seems to be a dire lack of understanding of the progress and impact being made by the UK's cities—resulting in almost half of our citizens (48%) feeling that Smart Cities across the UK are still more than five years away. Without the proper support these initiatives will die on their feet, so far greater communication is needed on what exactly is happening and why people should care. If done correctly, they create powerful advocates to spread awareness—if done wrong, and they risk their city's economic future." Cities are not aware of the latest urban technologies.

It seems that there is so much malaise about a clear definition of "Smart City" that businesses are not aware of city urban planning. Professor Alessandro Aurigi from Plymouth University (https://www.plymouth.ac.uk/staff/alessandro-aurigi) eloquently said it right in his book *Making the Digital City*: "In sum, all the theories and predictions about our digital futures are affected basically by the same problem: on the one hand they try to describe as inevitable certain aspects of future technologies that are still to be shaped. On the other hand what has been shaped, and the Internet for instance is more and more becoming part of the fabric of everyday life, is getting so ubiquitous that it ends up being take for granted and not investigated and analyzed."

City administrators do not know how to participate in technology innovation and implementation processes, but sadly they are not invited to participate in the planning process. There is little cooperation and sharing among the neighboring cities on best urban practices.

As of 2014, nearly half of the world's population lives in an urban setting. Many people relocate to cities from rural areas in search of better job opportunities and access to services, such as health care and education. However, a higher concentration of people within a region can cause shortages of important resources, such as food and water. Stores of petroleum and natural gas, as well as ecosystems destroyed by massive deforestation to accommodate growing populations, cannot be immediately replaced. Increased industrial activity also raises pollution levels that contribute to respiratory health problems. A lack of appropriate sanitation and waste disposal systems increases the spread of infectious disease.

Urban communities must devise plans to contain health care costs while investing in hospitals and clinics at the same time. Preventative measures, such as environmentally friendly public transportation, can also be costly.

Urban areas may also undergo gentrification, a process in which wealthy young professionals relocate to once economically depressed areas. As the economic demographics in the area shift, the cost of living in the area rises and displaces the original inhabitants, often minorities whose culture significantly contributed to the character of the area.

Glossary

Advanced metering infrastructure (AMI): Advanced metering infrastructure is another term for smart meters—electricity meters that automatically measure and record usage data at regular intervals and provide the data to consumers and energy companies at least once daily. The opposite is automated meter reading (AMR)—meters that collect data for billing purposes only and transmit this data one way, usually from the customer to the distribution utility.

Automated meter reading (AMR): Automated meter reading is a technology that is used in utility meters for collecting the data that is needed for billing purposes. AMR, which works by translating the movement of the mechanical dials on a meter into a digital signal, does not require physical access or visual inspection. The data can be transmitted from the meter to the utility company by telephone, power line, satellite, cable, or radio frequency.

Demand response: Demand response refers to the capability of smart grid technologies to allow for reductions in electricity use targeted at times when demand is highest. These peak reductions can reduce the strain placed on the electrical grid and decrease the need for high-cost generation resources. Consumers participating in demand response activities are compensated for the service. When a utility issues a call for demand response, consumers do not have to take any action; the utility can simply send a signal to smart-capable appliances that take action based on pre-programmed consumer preferences.

Demand-side management: The term for all activities or programs undertaken by a *load-serving entity* or its customers to influence the amount or timing of electricity they use.

Distributed generation: Distributed generation (DG) refers to power generation at the point of consumption. Generating power on-site, rather than centrally, eliminates the cost, complexity, interdependencies, and inefficiencies associated with transmission and distribution. Like distributed computing (i.e., the PC) and distributed telephony (i.e., the mobile phone), distributed generation shifts control to the consumer.

Distribution automation: Distribution automation (DA) is a family of technologies including sensors, processors, communication networks, and switches that can perform a number of distribution *system* functions depending on how they are implemented. Over the last 20 years, utilities have been applying DA to improve reliability, service quality, and operational efficiency. More recently, DA is being applied to perform automatic switching, *reactive power* compensation coordination, and other feeder operations/control.

Dynamic pricing: Dynamic pricing refers to the family of rates that offer customers time-varying electricity prices on a day-ahead or real-time basis.

Electric grid: A network of synchronized power providers and consumers that is connected by transmission and distribution lines and operated by one or more control centers. When most people talk about the power "grid," they're referring to the transmission system for electricity.

Home area network (HAN): A communication network within the home of a residential electricity customer that allows the transfer of information between electronic devices, including but not limited to in-home displays, computers, energy management devices, direct *load* control devices, distributed energy resources, and smart meters. Home area networks can be wired or wireless.

Kilowatt hour (kWh): A kilowatt hour is the amount of energy you get from one kilowatt for one hour. Electricity use over time is measured in kilowatt hours. Your electric company measures how much electricity you use in kilowatt hours, abbreviated as kWh. A kilowatt is a unit of power equal to 1000 watts.

Load: The amount of electric power delivered or required at any specific point or points on a system. The requirement originates at the energy-consuming equipment of the consumers.

Off-peak hours: Those hours or other periods defined by the North American Energy Standards Board (NAESB) business practices, contracts, agreements, or guides as periods of lower electrical *demand.*

On-peak hours: Those hours or other periods defined by the NAESB business practices, contracts, agreements, or guides as periods of higher electrical *demand.*

Outage: The period during which a generating unit, transmission line, or other facility is out of service.

Peak load: The maximum load during a specified period of time.

Peak plant/peak load plant: A plant usually housing old, low-efficiency steam units, gas turbines, diesels, or pumped-storage hydroelectric equipment normally used during the peak-load periods.

Smart Cities: A city that harnesses digital technology and intelligent design to create a sustainable city where services are seamless and efficient and provide for a high QoL for citizens.

Smart devices: Typically an electronic device generally connected to other devices or networks via different protocols such as Bluetooth, NFC, Wi-Fi, 3G, and so on, that can operate to some extent interactively and autonomously.

Smart grid: The "grid" refers to our nation's electric power infrastructure. *Smart grid* is the application of information technology, tools, and techniques like smart meters, sensors, real-time communications, software, and remote-controlled equipment to improve grid reliability and efficiency.

Smart home: The integration of a smart meter along with Wi-Fi-enabled appliances, lighting, and other devices that conveniently change the way that a family interacts with its home and optimizes home energy consumption.

Smart meter: Smart meters, a common form of smart grid technology, are digital meters that replace the old analog meters used in homes to record electrical usage. Digital meters can transmit energy consumption information back to a utility on a much more frequent schedule than analog meters, which require a meter reader to transmit information.

Time-of-use pricing: Time-of-use pricing (TOU) typically applies to usage over broad blocks of hours (e.g., *on-peak* = 6 hours for summer weekday afternoon; *off-peak* = all other hours in the summer months) where the price for each period is predetermined and constant.

Variable peak pricing: Variable peak pricing (VPP) is a hybrid of time-of-use and *real-time pricing*, where the different periods for pricing are defined in advance (e.g., *on-peak* = 6 hours for summer weekday afternoon; *off-peak* = all other hours in the summer months), but the price established for the *on-peak* period varies by utility and market conditions.

Resources used to develop these definitions: NERC, DOE, ITRON, Wikipedia, IEEE, EEI, and EPRI. New terms were added by MERIT CyberSecurity.

Bibliography

United Nations Population Fund: https://www.unfpa.org

Designing the Urban Commons: http://designingtheurbancommons.org/

National Academy of Engineering: https://www.nae.edu/

Smart Cities vs. locked-in cities: http://www.youris.com/Energy/Ecocities/Smart-Cities-Vs-Locked-In-Cities.kl

Collective Action and Urban Commons: http://scholarship.law.nd.edu/ndlr/vol87/iss1/2/

Sheila Forster: https://papers.ssrn.com/sol3/papers.cfm?abstract_id=1791767

Urban Commons LLC: http://www.urban-commons.com/

Interview with Francis Pisani: http://www.youris.com/Energy/Ecocities/Cyber-Attacks--Are-Smart-Cities-Safer-Or-More-Vulnerable.kl

United Nations Populations Fund: www.unfpa.org

Global Monitoring Report 2015/2016: http://pubdocs.worldbank.org/en/503001444058224597/Global-Monitoring-Report-2015.pdf

http://pubdocs.worldbank.org/en/503001444058224597/Global-Monitoring-Report-2015.pdf#page=27

http://www.engineeringchallenges.org/14373/GrandChallengesBlog/8275.aspx

Gartner's Hype Curve: http://www.gartner.com/technology/research/methodologies/hype-cycle.jsp

Romania has become cybercrime central: https://www.wired.com/2011/01/ff_hackerville_romania/

http://theconversation.com/three-big-challenges-for-smart-cities-and-how-to-solve-them-59191

https://www.plymouth.ac.uk/staff/alessandro-aurigi

ZDNet report on Symantec: http://www.zdnet.com/article/symantec-antivirus-product-bugs-as-bad-as-they-get/

ZDNet on Trend Micro Password defect: http://www.zdnet.com/article/trend-micro-password-manager-had-remote-command-execution-holes-and-dumped-data-to-anyone-project/

http://readwrite.com/2016/09/25/human-factors-limit-smart-cities-technology-cl4/

https://www.theguardian.com/science/2008/feb/15/technological.challenges

Urban World Utopia or Global Dysgenic Idiocracy?: https://alfinnextlevel.wordpress.com/2015/10/23/urban-world-utopia-or-global-dysgenic-idiocracy/

Ernst Young Security Report: http://www.ey.com/Publication/vwLUAssets/ey-cyber-security-a-necessary-pillar-of-smart-cities/$FILE/ey-cyber-security-a-necessary-pillar-of-smart-cities.pdf

Securing Smart Cities: https://securingsmartcities.org/wp-content/uploads/2015/05/CitiesWideOpenToCyberAttacks.pdf

http://www.wikihow.com/Hack-a-Computer

Bologna Regulation for the Care and Regeneration of Urban Commons: http://wiki.p2pfoundation.net/Bologna_Regulation_for_the_Care_and_Regeneration_of_Urban_Commons

Elinor Ostrom: http://www.onthecommons.org/magazine/elinor-ostroms-8-principles-managing-commmons

http://www.ccri.ac.uk/what-makes-a-commons-cities-and-the-concept-of-urban-commons/

UN comprehensive study on cybercrime: http://www.unodc.org/documents/organized-crime/UNODC_CCPCJ_EG.4_2013/CYBERCRIME_STUDY_210213.pdf

Bologna Regulations. http://www.comune.bologna.it/media/files/bolognaregulation.pdf

Book References

Alessandro Aurigi, 2005, *Making the Digital City*, Ashgate Publishing, Brookfield, VT.

Jeffrey Carr, 2009, *Cyber Warfare*, O'Reilly Media, Sebastopol, CA.

Chapter 3

Critical Success Factors of Smart Cities

The Atlantis Story

The mystery of the lost city of Atlantis still captures the imagination of millions. Was it real or just a myth? In any case, Atlantis was a great Smart City, but later it ignored its critical success and slipped into oblivion. This is its story.

Over 11,000 years ago there existed an island nation located in the middle of the Atlantic Ocean populated by a noble and powerful race. The people of this "smart" island possessed great wealth thanks to the natural resources found throughout their island. The island was a center for trade and commerce. The rulers of this land held sway over the people and the land of their own island and well into Europe and Africa. This was the island of Atlantis.

For generations, the Atlanteans lived simple, virtuous lives. But slowly they began to change. Greed and power began to corrupt them. When Zeus saw the immorality of the Atlanteans, he gathered the other gods to determine a suitable punishment.

Soon, in one violent surge it was gone. The island of Atlantis, its people, and its memory were swallowed by the sea.

Plato said that Atlantis existed about 9000 years before his own time, and that its story had been passed down by poets, priests, and others. But Plato's writings about Atlantis are the only known records of its existence.

Anatomy of the Smart City

Smart City is a very complex term! A Smart City is basically a *modernized* city or an urban area that focuses on high-quality life and comfort with the contribution of visionary planners and enabling information and communication technologies (ICT). The grandiosity of a Smart City comes primarily in the design balance of multiple key components like government, the living standards of the public, economy, mobility, and environment with the help of strong funds and an ICT infrastructure. A Smart City can also be referred as a *digital city*. This term signifies a city that is digitally advanced and well developed. Any city can earn the title of smart when investments in human, social and traditional (transport), and modern ICT communication infrastructure fuel sustainable economic development and a high quality of life, with wise management of natural resources, through participatory action and engagement. Figure 3.1 shows a model of a Smart City that combines intelligent management, integrated ICTs, and active citizen participation. Most importantly, this Smart City's backbone is the smart grid, which carries the digital immunity system (DIS)—we also refer to it as the Digital Immunity Ecosystem. It is the cognitive shield that protects the city's smart grid. Grid computing offers secure connectivity, which is essential for the city to operate and offer quality of life to its citizens.

Microsoft's Zero-Day Cavity

The software giant Microsoft lost a lot of its glow and glamour due to zero-day holes in its cosmic software flagships Windows and Internet Explorer (IE). Since innovation is driven by technology, Microsoft has taken the lead and set the pace to establish its kingdom. System security was not an issue until Microsoft penetrated the Internet with its "half-cooked" IE, which was an annoying speed bump to progress. Its obituary reads "Here lies Microsoft's Internet Explorer due to continued severe sickness, Born August 1995 and buried January 2016, May it rest in peace." The antivirus companies have been marching to Microsoft's drum beat and are cautiously trying not to step on the turf of the software giant. Hardware vendors also pay homage to Microsoft. Software companies that challenge Microsoft are either doomed or acquired.

Here's the story of Microsoft's lengthy struggle to save IE. Released versions continued to have deep defects throughout its longevity of 20 years. The user community lost faith and jumped ship to Google's Chrome.

On November 2, 2016, the online magazine *Bleeping*, published a compelling reportage: "There's a tiny scandal brewing among two of Silicon Valley's elites after Google engineers have publicly disclosed a zero-day vulnerability affecting several Windows operating system versions before Microsoft could issue a patch to address the issue. On October 21, 2016 Google's engineers say they've detected

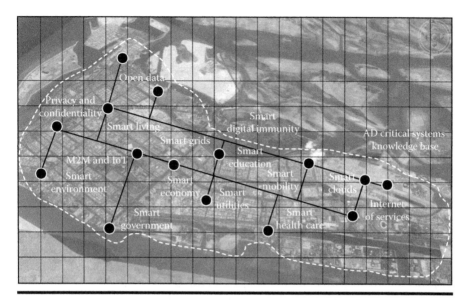

Figure 3.1 A model of a digital city, where all vital systems are connected together through the smart grid, which acts as the nervous system of the city. All the smart entities collaborate together and include smart grids, smart meters, smart homes, building automation, physical securities, life securities, facilities management, energy management, and other ICT infrastructure. (© 2014 Copyright MERIT CyberSecurity Group. All rights reserved.)

a sophisticated attack routine that combined two zero-days, one in Adobe Flash Player and the other affecting all Windows versions between Vista and Windows 10. Google notified both Adobe and Microsoft, asking them to provide patches. Five days later, Adobe released Flash Player patch that fixed the vulnerability that allowed an attacker to execute malicious code on the user's computer. At the time of this article, Microsoft has yet to release a security patch." Microsoft says that the zero-day flaw in Windows—revealed by Google—was exploited by Russian hackers via spear-phishing attacks. One lesson to be learned is *never trust complex systems. They will always bite the hand of the ones that created them*. Yeah, the little zero-day bug knocked Microsoft off its podium. It is no longer number one. The same applies to IBM, which used to fly high with its multiple virtual storage (MVS) and used to say "what's good for IBM, is good for the country." According to the Microsoft website, there are 400 million users of Windows 10, but 64% of these users are very active on Google's Chrome. But an article on the website Mashable (http://mashable.com/2015/07/29/microsoft-edge-vs-google-chrome/#p250NBaGHsq2) showed quantitatively that Chrome smokes Edge in speed and overall performance. We can say that in the computing industry, we're finding that a critical success factor (CSF) is very ephemeral and irreversible, but it deserves lots of respect. This is why we dedicated a full chapter to it.

Why Do We Need Critical Success Factors?

Believe it or not, CSFs apply to humans. All projects rely on human resources (HR) staff to handle key functions associated with project team hiring, compensation, and relations. To add value and support to the success of a project, HR planners must understand the nature and objective of the project, the project performance success criteria, and legal compliance. They must also define the optimum functional competencies for team members, manage compensations, and project cost red lines.

CSFs, also known as key results areas (KRAs), must be performed well if the project is to achieve its mission, objectives, or goals. By identifying your CSFs, you can create a common point of reference to help you direct and measure the success of your business or project.

CSFs are the *key* variables or conditions that have a tremendous impact on how successfully and effectively the Smart City design team meets its mission or the strategic goals or objectives of a project. The design team must perform the activities associated with CSFs to the highest possible standard in order to achieve their intended objectives and a successful project. Identifying CSFs can provide the Smart City teams with insight into which tasks are truly important, providing points of reference from which to direct the successful creation of a Smart City. A simple analogy would be a house of cards that is held together by some critical elements. If any of these elements failed, the whole structure would collapse. Let's not forget that human judgment is the most powerful driving factor in getting a project completed on time and within budget.

Criticality and Infrastructure Relationship

Before we delve into CSFs, let's first understand what criticality is. Criticality is a relative measure of the consequences of a failure mode and its frequency of occurrences. Criticality is very closely related to threats, risks, and attacks. We're going to use CSF as related to a Smart City, which is a complex system with many interrelated and interconnected components. Because the power grid is highly *critical*, this means that a blackout will have a very grave impact. The power grid is very complex and has many interconnections and components. Failure can either be human, mechanical, electrical, or in the design of the system. The resultant failure therefore can be catastrophic, critical, or marginal. Failure mode is defined as the way in which a failure is observed. It describes the way the failure occurs and its impact on equipment operation. A failure mode deals with the present, whereas a failure may have happened in the past and a failure effect may occur again in the future. Let's analyze the situation numerically. The formula for criticality due to a failure is

$$C_m = \beta\alpha\lambda_p t$$

$$\text{Modal criticality number} = \left(\text{Probability of next higher failure}\right)$$

$$\times \left(\text{Failure mode ratio}\right) \times \left(\text{Part failure rate}\right)$$

$$\times \left(\text{Duration of applicable mission phase}\right)$$

Total item criticality (C_r) is the joint probability of the item under all the failure modes:

$$C_r = \sum_{n=1}^{j} (\beta \alpha \lambda pt)^n$$

where:

β is the conditional probability that the failure will result in the identified severity classification, given that the failure mode occurs

C_r is the criticality probability

n is the initial failure mode of the item being analyzed where $n = 1, 2, 3, 4,\ldots, j$

j is the number of failure modes for the item being analyzed

Severity is an attribute associated with the damage caused by a cyberattack. There are four levels of severity: negligible, marginal, critical, and catastrophic (Figure 3.2).

Criticality of Reinforced Column

Now let's consider the inverse of CSF and call it critical failure factors (CFFs). In this case, they represent the threshold of failure that is more critical than success. To illustrate a CFF, we take a high-rise building that sits on a dozen reinforced concrete columns. The weight of the building is equally distributed over the 12 columns as shown in (Figure 3.3).

The reinforced columns were designed according to the standards of the American Concrete Institute (ACI) and passed all the safety codes. The columns transfer the weight of the building to the ground. The design of the columns included a safety factor and a critical limit of weight. Any column suffering from structural weakness due to earthquake, buckling, wind, shear moments, or a major explosion could impact the structure of the building and cause its collapse. The structural engineer must ensure that column design variables such as input, load, size, check, reinforcement, and footing have been calculated to the highest optimum level, and that the columns can handle several times the load factor.

Just for comparison, the Great Pyramid of Giza, Egypt, was built in 2580 BC. It took 9000 men working for 20 years to erect it. It has withstood all the coarse elements of nature. But what is more fascinating is that any stone block could be removed without affecting the structure of the pyramid.

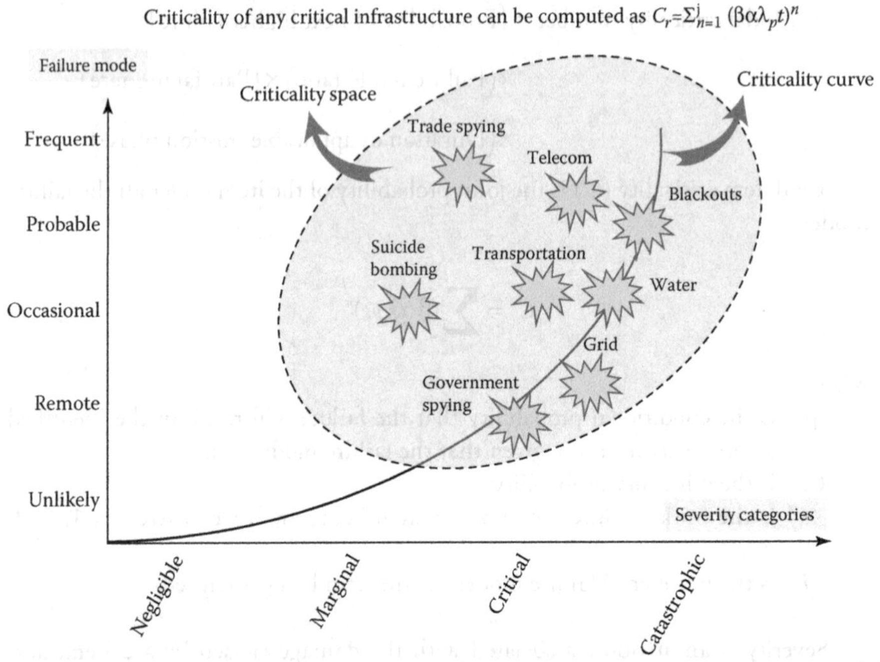

Criticality of any critical infrastructure can be computed as $C_r = \Sigma_{n=1}^{j} (\beta \alpha \lambda_p t)^n$

Figure 3.2 Most of the attacks on infrastructures are considered "critical" and associated with high failure probability. Smart Cities cannot afford to have infrastructures with high levels of vulnerability. Predictive analytics comes in handy to offer predictable future scenarios. (© 2014 Copyright MERIT CyberSecurity Group. All rights reserved.)

Safe design is achieved when the structural strength obtained by multiplying the nominal strength by the reduction factor Ø, exceeds or equals the strength needed to withstand the factored loads.

Ultimate design strength (U) = 1.2 D (dead load) + 1.6 L (live load)

Nominal strength × Ø = Ultimate design strength

where:
Dead load is the constant weight of the column
Active load is the dynamic weight of the column

WTC's Achilles Heel

Failure of Imagination

Right after the attack on the World Trade Center (WTC) in New York on 9/11, the investigative congressional commission on the attack put out a 567-page

The American Concrete Institute (ACI) Building
Code Requirements for Reinforced Concrete

Load compression

Buckling and steel load

Capacity of the column
Critical factor to be
carefully monitored

Strength of foundation

Figure 3.3 **The weakness of the column is a major criticality for the whole structure. Structural designers have to follow the American Concrete Institute standards, and make sure that the column will be able to carry the whole structure. It
is a key success factor. (© 2014 Copyright MERIT CyberSecurity Group. All rights
reserved.)**

report placing the blame on the national security apparatus. The panel's chairman,
Thomas Kean, put it this way: "We were unprepared. We did not grasp the mag-
nitude of a threat that had been gathering over a considerable period. As we detail
in our report, this was a failure of policy, management, capability, and, above all, a
failure of imagination." The attack on the WTC brought humiliation and indignity
to the whole nation. With all the massive engineering knowledge that had erected
one of the wonders of the world, no one realized that *heat* could bring this colossal
structure down. It was the straw that broke the back of the camel!

The WTC in New York City was built in August 1968 and opened in April 1973.
It was one of the marvels of the structural engineering world. With twin towers each
with 110 stories, it accommodated 50,000 workers and 200,000 daily visitors.

The final investigative analysis that was conducted by the National Institute
of Standards and Technologies (NIST) revealed an interesting theory as follows:
"based on its comprehensive investigation, NIST concluded that the WTC towers collapsed because: (1) the impact of the planes severed and damaged support

columns, dislodged fireproofing insulation coating the steel floor trusses and steel columns, and widely dispersed jet fuel over multiple floors; and (2) the subsequent unusually large number of jet-fuel-ignited multi-floor fires (which reached temperatures as high as 1,000 degrees Celsius, or 1,800 degrees Fahrenheit) significantly weakened the floors and columns with dislodged fireproofing to the point where floors sagged and pulled inward on the perimeter columns. This led to the inward bowing of the perimeter columns and failure of the south face of WTC 1 and the east face of WTC 2, initiating the collapse of each of the towers. Both photographic and video evidence—as well as accounts from the New York City Police Department aviation unit during a half-hour period prior to collapse—support this sequence for each tower.it was decided that heat was the main factor that made the structure weak and caused the collapse of the tower."

"The impact of the planes was not the primary cause of the collapse. The airplanes probably contained 60 tons of fuel each, maybe more. Airplane fuel contains 10× the energy, gram per gram, as TNT. Thus, the energy was equivalent to about 600 tons of TNT, more than half a kiloton. However, fuel doesn't explode unless it is well mixed with air. The building is a huge sail that could resist a 225 km/h hurricane." So, the NIST concluded that the CFF was heat. The building could withstand earthquakes and hurricanes, but not heat. It was a major vulnerability.

Even after the bombing of the WTC in 1993—eight years before 9/11—John Skilling, the chief structural engineer at WTC, commented: "To the best of our knowledge, little was known about the effects of a fire from such an aircraft, and no designs were prepared for that circumstance."

Heat Won, Steel Lost

In December 2001, Stanford University published a very revealing report about the vulnerabilities of the twin towers. Ronald O. Hamburger, a structural engineer investigating the September 11 disaster, presented his view and expertise: "The fuel in both jetliners burned off rapidly, despite media reports that the aircraft continued burning long after the crash .... The impact probably caused a failure of the fireproofing in the affected areas," he said. "We think that the fuel ignited several floors in the building, which had a devastating effect on the steel support beams. Steel is born of fire," Hamburger explained. "As it reheated, it expands and loses its rigidity. Above 1,000 degrees Fahrenheit, it loses a significant amount of its strength" (as shown in Figure 3.4). Hamburger went on to say that "the extreme heat from the fires might have caused the steel floors to expand and bow, which may have caused the support columns to bend inward and buckle. Heat also may have caused the steel flooring to separate from the columns, or the columns themselves may have heated up and buckled outward."

Aviation fuel (unleaded kerosene) burns at 800°F–1500°F, which is not hot enough to melt steel (2750°F). However, experts agree that for the towers to

Figure 3.4 The heat of the fire from the airplane fuel did not melt the support beams, but softened them, and the beams lost their strength and bent under the heavy load from above. The chain reaction accelerated until the beams hit the ground at a speed of 230 miles per hour. (© 2014 Copyright MERIT CyberSecurity Group. All rights reserved.)

collapse, their steel frames didn't need to melt, they just had to lose some of their structural strength—and that required exposure to much less heat. "I have never seen melted steel in a building fire," says retired New York deputy fire chief Vincent Dunn, author of *Collapse of Burning Buildings: A Guide To Fireground Safety*. "But I've seen a lot of twisted, warped, bent and sagging steel. What happens is that the steel tries to expand at both ends, but when it can no longer expand, it sags and the surrounding concrete cracks."

What Is Systems Science?

Systems science is an interdisciplinary field of science (combining several engineering and math disciplines) that studies the nature of complex systems, such as Smart Cities. It is conducted by Smart Cities system scientists to develop and monitor sustainable urban infrastructure and buildings, improve the power supply through smart grid technology, detect and counteract problems with aging urban infrastructure, calculate and communicate optimal transportation routes under congested traffic conditions, and deploy ubiquitous sensing devices to facilitate everyday activities in a crowded urban environment. Systems science includes the application of scaling laws and observations of urban systems at a macro-level. The Smart City provides a smart *dashboard* that enables observation of urban systems at a micro-level. We will cover the smart dashboard later.

In this chapter, we describe the steps toward a model that can unify the perspectives of the professions in the Urban Systems Collaborative. It begins with examples of Smart Cities and why this movement is so active. It describes how information technology (IT) plays roles in shaping new norms of behavior intended to facilitate the continuing growth of dense populations. It then explains a key hypothesis of the Urban Systems Collaborative that the increasing accessibility of information will enable us to develop urban systems models that are capable of helping citizens, entrepreneurs, civic organizations, and governments to see more deeply into how their city works, how people use the city, how they feel about it, where the city faces problems, and what kinds of remediation can be applied.

The idea is very simple: *In any organization, there are several factors such as profitability, employee's productivity, market share, and competition that are considered critical for the success of the organization. If any of the objectives associated with these factors are not achieved, the organization will fail—perhaps catastrophically so.*

Basic Definition of CSF

The concept of "critical success factors" was originally developed by D. Ronald Daniel of McKinsey & Company in 1961. It was then refined by John F. Rockart of the Massachusetts Institute of Technology's (MIT) Sloan School of Management in 1981.

Rockart defined CSFs as: "The limited number of areas in which results, if they are satisfactory, will ensure successful competitive performance for the organization. They are the few key areas where things must go right for the business to flourish. If results in these areas are not adequate, the organization's efforts for the period will be less than desired."

In this chapter, we discuss the importance of CSFs vis-à-vis the mission and strategic goals of Smart Cities. CSFs are part of the design of any project, much less for urban design. CSFs pertain to most "soft failure prone" areas during the design of Smart Cities. Even after the design, CSFs look at the very heart of the city's operations and how they perform relative to the CSF red lines.

CSFs are the measuring sticks for the activities, procedures, or areas that a business depends on for its continued survival. CSFs are unique to each environment, they even vary from one city to another, but regardless of the nature of the beast, they are the most reliable "visibility" gauges to manage the enterprise. We refer to CSFs as the *rivets* that hold all the components together.

Figure 3.5 shows a panoramic view of a typical Smart City. It includes all the active modernized components of the societal fabric. They are managed and controlled by scalable CSFs for the safety, security, and quality of life of all the residents.

In Figure 3.5, the two dotted lines represent the two smart grids. The *outer dotted line* is the Smart Vaccine Nanogrid (SVG), and the *inner dotted line* represents the Smart City Nanogrid (SCG), which is the grid that supports digital immunity. Cybercrime will be managed better and systematically eradicated through adaptive and predictive vaccination services, pretty much like human immunity.

The success of Smart Cities is in their *grid technology*, which builds a real-time environment in which citizens are interconnected and easily share information

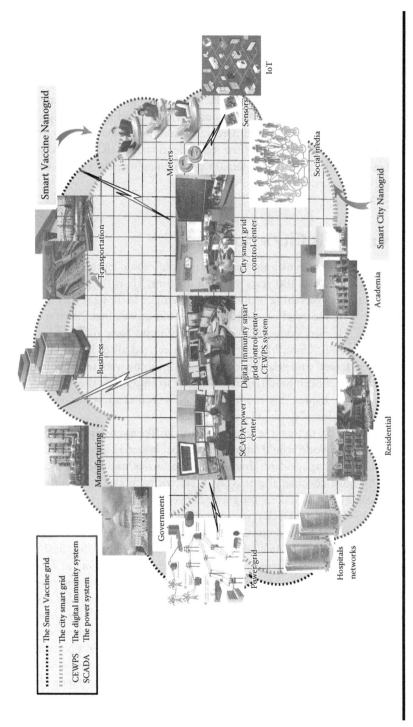

Figure 3.5   This is the world of Smart City. It includes all the active and modernized components of the societal fabric. They are managed and controlled by scalable critical success factors for the safety, security, and quality of life of all residents. We will discuss in more detail about the power grid in Figure 3.6. (© 2014 Copyright MERIT CyberSecurity Group. All rights reserved.)

anywhere in the city. A city without grid technology will never be a Smart City. Smart Cities live by their smart grids, which are their nervous system. They allow cities to breathe, to facilitate exchange of information, and to respond promptly to danger. Grid technologies elevate a Smart City to ubiquity city level, where citizens can use any available devices to interconnect them, to get any services anywhere and anytime through any kind of device. ICT has made a dream become reality. New advanced Internet technologies promote cloud-based services, big data, the Internet of Things (IoT), real-world user interfaces; use of smartphones, smart meters, networks of sensors, and radio-frequency identification (RFID); and more accurate communication based on the semantic web, opening new ways to collective action and collaborative problem solving.

The Power Grid Is City's Holy Grail

Nikola Tesla had a titanic multi-processing mind that could outrun the fastest computing machine. He was 100 years ahead of his time. He is the grand papa of the electricity that runs everything including the Internet. He thought that memories and thoughts were recorded on the brain and could be watched, like a movie, through the retina. He died alone and in massive debt in his New York hotel room in 1943 at the age of 86. Upon his death, the FBI declared all of his papers and research to be "top secret" and seized them. Eventually, some were returned to his family. Some have never been found, thus giving rise to conspiracy theories.

Visitors frequently request his room at The New Yorker Hotel, room 3327. Supposedly, they hope for a "spark" of inspiration.

It is incomprehensible to imagine what we would be like today without electricity or the Internet. The world would launch into global hysteria with higher crime, higher fatalities, higher car accidents, higher home robberies, and higher suicides.

A Smart City must consider the delivery of electricity to everyone in the city as a survival necessity. We all take it for granted. Everyone remembers New York's blackout of July 13–14, 1977, which resulted in citywide big-time looting and other disorder, including arson. How about the northeastern blackout (a 3500-megawatt power surge) that affected an estimated 55 million people in eight US states? This blackout resembled a massive implosion in many respects. Let me explain:

A software bug triggered out of sequence instructions in the main general electric energy's Unix energy management system. The bug propagated to other energy systems and stalled the alarm system. The failure deprived operators of both audio and visual alerts for important changes in system state. Systems thrashed backlog instructions and the backup system followed. The lack of alarms led operators to ignore phone alerts called from other stations. Then, the main control room lost power. The whole power grid went out of balance, which started to trigger a blackout cascade which reached New York City, and all hell broke loose. The bottom line is human error compounded with faulty systems.

Nuclear power plants and hydroelectric plants tried hard to save the power grid, Water supply pressure reduced and caused potential contamination of the water supply. The Amtrak grid was affected by the blackout and trains were severely disrupted. Transportation was severely impacted. Gas stations could not be used. Toll bridges stalled. Cellular communication devices were disrupted. Cable television systems were disabled. Commuters had to walk over 20 miles to get home. Subway commuters stayed in the dark for many hours. Some 55 million people were affected. The economic losses from the blackout exceeded $1 billion in New York City alone, according to figures released on August 20, 2003 by city comptroller William Thompson. The estimates included $800 million in unsold goods and services, as well as $250 million in spoiled food.

In ranking the CSF for a Smart City, power distribution is the number one priority, and number two, and number three. There will be future blackouts because as the power generation and distribution implement new technologies, there will be a steep learning curve and the body of knowledge will be accumulated over time.

In Figure 3.6, we focus primarily on the subject of power generation and delivery.

A Smart City Needs a Digital Cockpit

A Smart City's central coordination center (CCC) requires a smart *digital cockpit*, which comes with several dynamic and smart dashboards for each administrator in the CCC. A smart dashboard is a crystal ball that gives the administrator everything he or she needs to manage the duties of a Smart City. However, the administrator will need much more than a dashboard to display the key activities throughout a Smart City. Smart Cities need a smart, interactive, real-time steering mechanism to remotely monitor and acquire visibility over all the resources of the city. Like an airplane, Smart Cities need a cognitive dashboard with lots of artificial intelligence to keep the performance of the city within the range of critical factors. Figure 3.7 shows an example of a dashboard and the type of key performance indicator (KPI) with the critical success areas.

The dashboard is the smart *occipital lobe* that keeps the city in a safe and secure mode. We have listed some of the necessary control actions when the dashboard signals danger.

Quick reaction to incoming danger: The dashboard is equipped with a look-ahead logic, like a radar, if one of the KPIs is erratically accelerating toward the red line. Alert signals could also be sent from satellites.

Incoming problems and alternative rules: Once the dashboard shows that the system is crossing the red line, due to an abnormal workload runaway, the system will switch to a mirror system and continue without noticeable performance degradation.

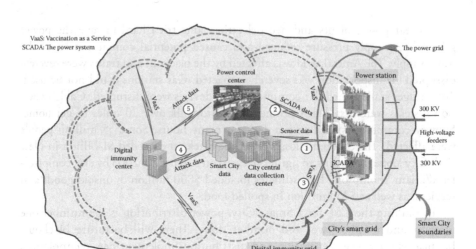

Figure 3.6 One of the most vital technologies that supports the Smart City is the smart grid. Without the smart grid, there wouldn't be a real Smart City. The dotted lines indicate two concentric grids. The outside dotted line is the CSG, and the inside dotted line is called the digital immunity grid (DIG). The diagram represents a power network to minimize congestion. The connections are numbered to simplify illustration: (1) sensor data; (2) SCADA control data collection; (3) vaccination service; (4) attack data sent to the database; (5) attack data sent to the digital immunity knowledge base. (© 2014 Copyright MERIT CyberSecurity Group. All rights reserved.)

Dispatch alerts: The dashboard is a smart communication steering wheel that receives and dispatches directives and relays alert instructions to all users.

Advanced analytics: The dashboard is connected to a smart performance analytics component that makes extensive use of statistical analysis, including explanatory and predictive modeling.

Collection of sensor data: Online sensor data from IoT devices will be cleaned and sent to the proper central system. The dashboard will graphically display the data collection workflow.

Real-time data collection: Real-time collection of a city's nano grid performance data is a vital process to guarantee that the key indicators are within the safety range of CSF.

Real-time data display: This functionality is extremely vital for a fast response in case there's an attack on the city grid. The dashboard will quickly locate the danger area and take the proper action. Three successive performance screens are shown in Figure 3.8a–c.

Digital vaccination: The digital immunity grid is the holy grail of a Smart City. It is the most intelligent, most smart, most cognitive security layer that is able to offer just-in-time vaccination to all the devices in the city. It is a new generation of defense

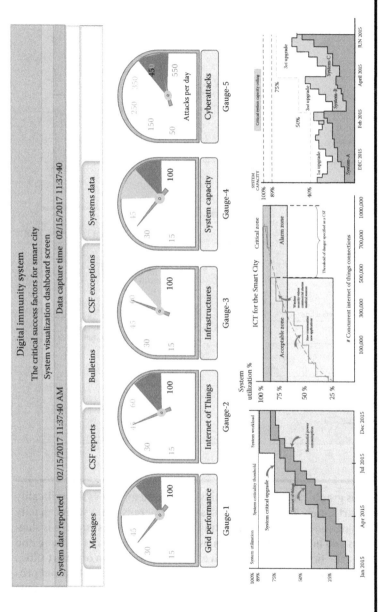

Figure 3.7 A dashboard that is the main visualization barometer of "the digital cockpit"—part of the analytics of the system. It provides real-time performance data from remote sensing devices. The collected data is compared to the "red zones" defined by the CSF rules. The Smart City control center (CCC) could have similar dashboards to keep track of the different activities and how far they are from the failure threshold. The cluster meters of the dashboard help the analyst in making the proper choices. (© 2014 Copyright MERIT CyberSecurity Group. All rights reserved.)

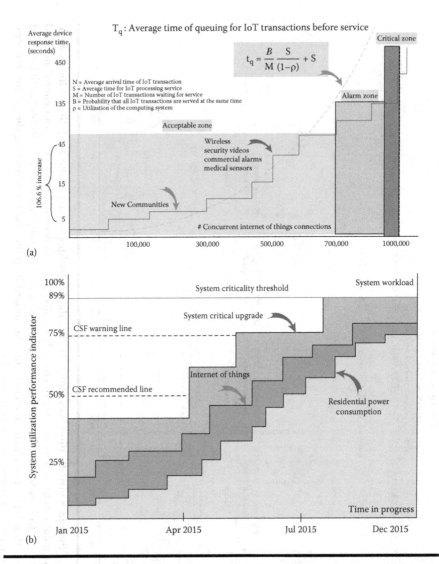

Figure 3.8 (a) This graph, part of the analytics of the system, shows the criticality of ICT for new Smart Cities. The critical success factor here is the system capacity to handle the present and future workload. If the computing infrastructure is sluggish, then residents will be discouraged from using important devices at home and at work. Upgrades take time and are expensive. The modernization of Smart Cities is driven by well-planned computing infrastructures (cloud, big data, Internet providers, security providers, and above all, reliable connectivity. (b) This screen, part of the analytics of the system, shows how IoT and residential power meters are growing, which translates into system workload. The quarterly growth is around 34%, which will put the city data collection in jeopardy. City capacity planners have to consider an upgrade, and determine the proper sizing of the upgrade.

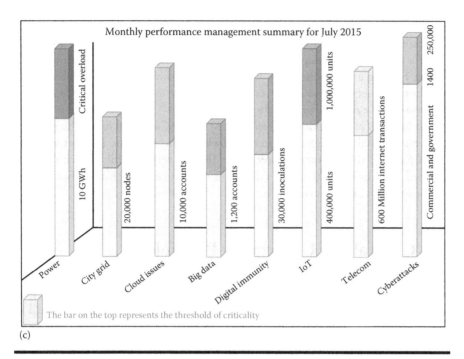

Monthly performance management summary for July 2015

Critical overload

10 GWh | Power
20,000 nodes | City grid
10,000 accounts | Cloud issues
1,200 accounts | Big data
30,000 inoculations | Digital immunity
400,000 units | IoT
600 Million internet transactions | Telecom
Commercial and government | 1400 | 250,000 | Cyberattacks
1,000,000 units

The bar on the top represents the threshold of criticality

(c)

Figure 3.8 (c) This screen, part of the analytics of the system, speaks for itself. If any of these Smart City activities reaches the critical threshold, the dashboard, three dimensionally, will highlight the activity and all its performance data. The system will automatically adjust itself, document the degradation "dip," and issue it to the system engineer who will interpret the data and report the results to the city administrator who will trace back to the IoT source device how the real attack problem occurred. (© 2014 Copyright MERIT CyberSecurity Group. All rights reserved.)

by offence. Digital immunity is a replication of the human immune system. It is the new security paradigm shift. We will discuss digital immunity in Chapters 9 and 10.

Crime data and forecast: The cognitive early warning predictive system (CEWPS) is the computing environment of digital immunity. It gathers all the attack episodes into a knowledge engine, and classifies them ontologically as a *knowledge model*. During the prediction process, which involves reasoning, the episodes will be part of the rules used by the reasoning engine that computes the best probabilistic forecast for future attacks.

Statistics on IoT: The IoT extends Internet connectivity beyond traditional devices like desktop and laptop computers, smartphones, and tablets to a diverse range of devices and everyday things that utilize embedded technology to communicate and interact with the external environment, all via the Internet. As objects become embedded with sensors and gain the ability to communicate, the new information networks promise to create new business models, improve business processes, and reduce costs and risks. The IoT doesn't function without cloud-based applications to interpret and transmit the data coming from all these sensors. The cloud is what enables the apps to go to work for you anytime, anywhere. IoT is an iceberg floating and no one really knows where it is heading. One problem is as stated by Gartner: *Where is all the data provided by those processors going to be stored and what are the problems around them?*

Linkage and communicate with other cities: Smart Cities will form a huge Smart Universe that will keep growing like a snowball downhill. The Internet will play *second fiddle* to the Internet of Everything (IoE). Everyone will live with sensors attached to his or her vital organs. All man-2-machine and machine-2-man devices will be sold at local pharmacies. That will be the day!

The Generalized Uncertainty Principle

The book *The System Bible*, realistically crafted by Dr. George Gall, highlights an interesting phenomenon in the world, called the *Uncertainty Principle*. It is appropriate to describe briefly what this principle means and how closely it is related to the reality of a Smart City's quality of life.

> At all times, there have been people who felt that things weren't working out very well. This observation has gradually come to be recognized as an ongoing fact of life, an inseparable component of the Human Condition …. In fact the biggest challenge that we face is that reality is more complex than it seems.
>
> Incredibly enough, the first breakthrough in recognition of the Generalized Uncertainty Principle did not come until the 1950's, when a daring—if anonymous—group of biologists toppled Watsonian determination with a short, pithy aphorism, now known as the Harvard Law of Animal Behavior: Under precisely controlled experimental conditions, a test animal will behave as it damn well pleases. We can say in summary that complex systems exhibit unexpected behavior.

Building or setting up a Smart City comes with a cloud of complex entities that deviate from the original plan, and start to develop goals of their own the instant they come into being. In the following, we list five *troublesome* areas that apply the Generalized Uncertainty Principle, but they are considered viable contributors to the success of Smart Cities.

Lack of vision and cooperation: A Smart City is supposed to perform well in a forward-looking way as regards the economy, people, governance, mobility, environment, and living, built on the smart combination of the endowments and activities of self-decisive, independent, and aware citizens.

Lack of integration and resource management: A Smart City monitors and integrates the conditions of all its critical infrastructures including roads, bridges, tunnels, rails, subways, airports, seaports, communications, water, power, even major buildings, and can better optimize its resources, plan its preventive maintenance activities, and monitor security aspects while maximizing services to its citizens.

Lack of infrastructure connectivity: A Smart City connects the physical infrastructure, the IT infrastructure, the social infrastructure, and the business infrastructure to leverage the collective intelligence of the city.

Lack of smartness initiative: A city that is striving to make itself "smarter" (more efficient, sustainable, equitable, and livable).

Lack of smart computing: A Smart City combines ICT and Web 2.0 technology with other organizational, design, and planning efforts to dematerialize and speed up bureaucratic processes and help to identify new, innovative solutions to city management complexity in order to improve sustainability and livability. The use of Smart Computing technologies to make the critical infrastructure components and services of a city—which include city administration, education, healthcare, public safety, real estate, transportation, and utilities—more intelligent, interconnected, and efficient.

Here's a canonical axiom that will augment your strategic thinking: If any structure, independent of its size, fails or deviates from its original design, this is due to human error and lack of associative CSF, or it was not integrated in the original design. The result is that *systems develop goals of their own the instant they come into being.*

The CSF and KPI, the Twin Brothers

KPIs are just as important as CSFs. In fact, there is a tight relationship between the two criteria as shown in Figure 3.9.

Let's take a small example to show how CSFs and KPIs work together:

System reliability is the ability of an item to perform a required function under given environmental and operational conditions and for a stated period of time

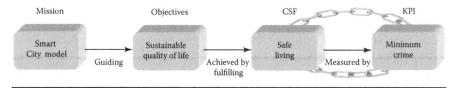

Figure 3.9 KPI is the only metric that can determine how well the planning of the Smart City initiatives is. It is a critical measure that needs to be used. As the old saying goes "if you can measure it, you can control it." It applies to the marvelous engineering work of the Smart City. (© 2014 Copyright MERIT CyberSecurity Group. All rights reserved.)

(ISO8402). A system is reliable if it doesn't breakdown very often. System reliability is a pivotal CSF and is monitored with the help of the available KPI.

System uptime (UT) is the time the system is working in full operation without problems.

System availability is the most important metric KPI. Numerically, it is the ratio of the uptime of the system over the total time (uptime + downtime). System availability means it is operational and available to users. System availability has decisive and crucial importance in the success of Smart Cities. Computing systems are the heart engines that pump computing energy to every citizen, business, and company under the umbrella of the city. If a massive cyberattack causes a massive blackout in the city, we can pull the plug from the wall and the city will come to a grinding halt.

Mean time between failure (MTBF) is the time the system is up and fully operational.

$$\text{MTBF (Uptime)} = \text{Total Time} - \text{Repair Time (MTTR)}$$

Mean time to repair (MTTR) is the time the system is being repaired, in other words, the system is down and not operational. Thus, we can consider system reliability. If MTTR is large or it happens very often, then the reliability of the system goes down (see Figure 3.10).

Smart Cities Are Made of Interdependent Structures

A structure is an arrangement and organization of interrelated elements that make up a system. Buildings are an example of load-bearing structures. Smart Cities are also made of several *load-bearing* structures. We define Smart Cities as a collection

$$\text{System availability} = \frac{\text{System uptime}}{\text{System uptime} + \text{Down time}} \times 100$$

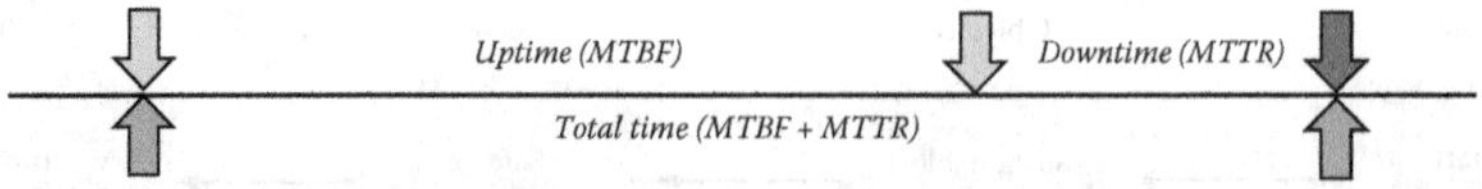

Uptime (MTBF)   Downtime (MTTR)

Total time (MTBF + MTTR)

Figure 3.10 **A Smart City's computing environment is crucial to all the operations that support the quality of life in the city. The most important metric is system availability, which means that the system is up and available to users to conduct their normal operations. Numerically, it is the ratio of uptime over the total time (uptime and downtime). The metric (MTTR) is notorious and it impacts system availability as well as system reliability. (© 2014 Copyright MERIT CyberSecurity Group. All rights reserved.)**

of organizational structures called "infrastructures." All structures carry their respective loads, which should not exceed their safety limit. The CSFs define these safety limits and their danger zones.

We selected eight of the most viable CSFs to measure the *quality* and *performance* of the Smart City design framework. Then, we tied these factors together and made them dependent on one another. Figure 3.11 shows a symbolic representation of how the CSF components are pathologically connected and lean on one another. If one factor breaks down, the whole structure will be in serious jeopardy. Figure 3.11 illustrates how the design and management of a Smart City are great challenges. That's why CSFs should be designed with great precision and transparency.

CSF-1—Management and organization: This factor is most important because it has to do with the synergistic behavior of team players. One bad person will spoil the whole project. The following are some of the bumps and hiccups that should be skillfully addressed by the head of the project: size of the project, social skills of the manager and his or her team, user team diversity, lack of alignment of organizational goals and projects, multiple or conflicting goals, resistance to change, turf, and conflicts.

CSF-2—Technology: This is a two-edged sword that requires great expertise to know which side of the sword you are on. A Smart City relies, among others, on a collection of smart computing technologies applied to critical infrastructure

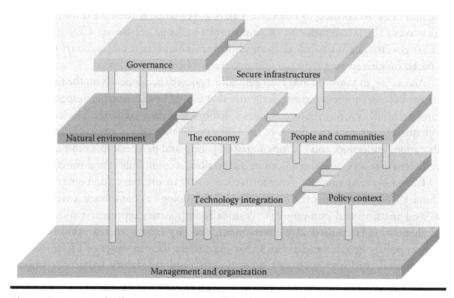

Figure 3.11 Symbolic representation of the house of CSF, we may call it the "CSF house of cards." Failure is a superior and opportunistic force that will overpower any weak object with defective design. Smart Cities CSFs were designed to protect the city from terminal implosion. (© 2014 Copyright MERIT CyberSecurity Group. All rights reserved.)

components and services. Smart computing refers to a new generation of integrated hardware, software, and network technologies that provide IT systems with real-time awareness of the real world and advanced analytics to help people make more intelligent decisions about alternatives and actions that will optimize business processes and business balance sheet results.

ICTs are key drivers of Smart City initiatives. The integration of ICT with development projects can change the urban landscape of a city and offer several potential opportunities, and it can enhance the management and functioning of a city. Despite proclaimed advantages and benefits of ICTs use in cities, their impact is still risky. Indeed, they can improve the quality of life for citizens, but they can also increase inequality and promote a digital divide.

Another potential area that needs to be clarified is the selection of the right ICT provider. A project like a Smart City needs several technology providers that need to collaborate and commit themselves to the success of the project. A Smart City project needs open systems that can interface with one another without any technical issues. The city management should insist on obtaining systems that comply with an approved system. It is an uphill battle with ICT providers.

CSF-3—Governance: Several cities have benefited from the emergence of ICTs that improve their governance. This ICT-based governance is known as "smart governance." It widely represents a collection of technologies, people, policies, practices, resources, social norms, and information that interact to support city governing activities. According to Forrester, smart governance is the core of Smart Cities initiatives. Thus, it represents an important challenge for Smart City initiatives. Smart governance is described as an important characteristic of a Smart City that is based on citizen participation and private/public partnerships.

According to Johnston and Hanssen, smart governance depends on the implementation of a smart governance infrastructure that should be accountable, responsive, and transparent. This infrastructure enables collaboration, data exchange, service integration, and communication. Some of the CSFs under the governance initiative are collaboration, leadership, and champion; participation and partnership; communication; data exchange; service and application integration; accountability; and transparency.

CSF-4—Policy context: Transformation from an ordinary (non-smart) city to a Smart City also entails the interaction of technological components with political and institutional components. Political components represent various political elements (city council, city government, and city major) and external pressures such as policy agendas and politics that may affect the outcomes of IT initiatives. Institutional readiness such as removing legal and regulatory barriers is important for the smooth implementation of Smart City initiatives. The policy context is critical to the understanding of the use of information systems in appropriate ways. Hence, an innovative government stresses the change in policies, because a government cannot innovate without a normative drive addressed in policy. Whereas innovation in technology for a Smart City can be relatively easily observed and broadly agreed upon, subsequent changes in the policy context are more ambiguous.

The policy context characterizes institutional and non-technical urban issues and creates conditions enabling urban development.

CSF-5—People and communities: Addressing the topic of people and communities as part of Smart Cities is critical, and traditionally has been neglected at the expense of more technological and policy issues of Smart Cities. Smart City projects are aimed at the quality of life of citizens and aim to foster more informed, educated, and participatory citizens. It is highly important to allow members of a city to participate in the governance and management of the city and become active users. Key players are needed to support the people initiative. The following are selected critical factors that should be studied and included in a Smart City project: digital divide, information and community administration, participation and partnership, communication, education, quality of life, and accessibility.

CSF-6—The economy: The economy CSF is the major driver of Smart City initiatives, and a city with economic competitiveness is one of the properties of a Smart City. Additionally, one of the key indicators to measure the level of a city's competitiveness is the capacity of the city as an economic engine. A Smart City framework consists of six main components: smart economy, smart people, smart governance, smart mobility, smart environment, and smart living. These components comprise the city's smart economy, which includes economic competitiveness as well as innovation, entrepreneurship, trademarks, productivity and flexibility of the labor market, and integration into the national and global market. Creating an environment for industrial development is pivotal to a Smart City. The economic outcomes of Smart City initiatives are business creation, job creation, workforce development, and improvement in productivity.

CSF-7—Built infrastructure: The reliability of an ICT infrastructure is pivotal for Smart Cities. The ICT infrastructure includes wireless infrastructure (fiber-optic channels, Wi-Fi networks, wireless hotspots, kiosks), service-oriented information systems, the IoT, the SVG, and the CSG. The performance of the ICT items is what will make the Smart City run its business. Any downtime of these devices will impact on the quality of life in the city. The implementation of an ICT infrastructure is fundamental to a Smart City's development and depends on factors related to its availability and performance. Here are some of the specific items that are tagged with high criticality: (1) real-time data monitoring and collection, (2) real-time Smart (AI) security and autonomic defense, (3) backup and recovery, (4) mobilize Smart Vaccine army for attack, (5) immunize all systems before attack, and (6) document all attacks.

CSF-8—The natural environment: Smart City initiatives are forward-looking on the environmental front. Core to the concept of a Smart City is the use of technology to increase sustainability and to better manage natural resources. Of particular interest is the protection of natural resources and the related infrastructure such as waterways and sewers, and green spaces such as parks. Together, these factors have an impact on the sustainability and livability of a city, so these should be taken into consideration when examining Smart City initiatives.

Four main modalities of natural resources conservation and management in influential areas of cities have proved effective: (1) urban and periphery oxygen-generating surfaces, (2) green-yellow belts, (3) regional activities parks, and (4) natural protected areas.

In summary, we would like to highlight the importance of three critical factors:

- To assess the *importance of natural resources* encountered in the influential areas of towns, and the factors affecting their balance.
- To identify the *main instruments used in the sustainable management of natural resources* in the areas of oxygen-generating surfaces, yellow-green belts, natural protected areas, and regional activities parks.
- To present solutions for an *integrated management of natural recourses* in influential areas of Smart Cities.

Critical Success Factors Value Chain

We all respect the proverb: *A chain is only as strong as its weakest link.* Let's introduce the rule of total probability, which states: Total probability allows us to calculate the likelihood of an event occurring that has been influenced by the occurrence of several other disjoint events (see Figure 3.12). It involves the idea of conditional probability, which is one of the axioms of probability. Total probability is just the addition rule for mutually exclusive events, where the mutually exclusive events are factored as a probability times a conditional probability. If any of the eight factors that we have listed in Figure 3.12 did not succeed (did not meet its objective), it would bring failure to the whole chain. Figure 3.12 shows how these factors are tied together, like the beams of a building.

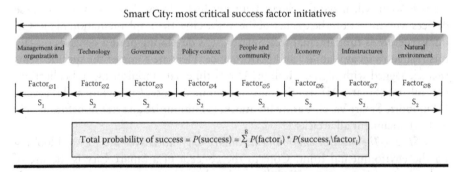

$$\text{Total probability of success} = P(\text{success}) = \sum_{1}^{8} P(\text{factor}_i) * P(\text{success}_i \backslash \text{factor}_i)$$

Figure 3.12 Smart Cities have eight success initiatives that have to succeed collectively. If any of these initiatives fails, then it will impede the success of the Smart City. The success of these initiatives follows a conditional probability as shown in the figure. (© 2014 Copyright MERIT CyberSecurity Group. All rights reserved.)

Matching Smart City Critical Issues with Best Solutions

When we build a subdivision, we draw complete blueprints for each substructure such as a concrete foundation, walls, and the electrical layout, and we hire contractors to build their assigned section within the projected time. All large building contractors know how to deal with other contractors without conflict. Once the building is completed and has the approval of the city, interested renters or buyers occupy it and the project cycle is done. Building a Smart City is totally different. Smart Cities are built while citizens are living in the city; the citizens are not relocated outside the city. Building new infrastructures while the city is populated is a major endeavor. In fact, the success of converting a city into a Smart City is doubly exhausting with major conflicts in pricing, people, the city, and safety codes.

We have listed some of the potential issues that need to be completed with the best techno-economic solutions. Figure 3.13 lists some of the challenging projects that will guarantee the completion of a Smart City.

As information systems have become pervasive in urban environments, they have created opportunities to capture information that was never previously accessible. This is highly valuable in enabling the detection of patterns of behavior or anomalies in such patterns whether at an aggregate or an individual level. This pervasiveness also enables the city agencies or individual citizens to capture, even unintentionally, photographs of incidents on the street—such as two apparently unrelated people engaged in a brief conversation—that historically were so transient

Infrastructure issue	Action recommended by the critical success factors
Critical city smart grid	Grid protection through digital immunity
Critical smart vaccine grid	The digital immunity protection shield of the Smart City Grid
Vaccination of critical systems	Grid alert should be followed by the vaccination of all city systems
City smart cloud	Connectivity to city grid, data privacy, and access control
Hardware connectivity	All systems and networks should be plug to plug compatible
Internet of Things	Sensor connectivity and metering
Application integration	Regardless of design, all systems should be connectable at the data level
Prediction of cyberattacks	Get leading time for citizens to prepare for alert
Technical management	Competency and experience in complex projects
ICT vendors	No one vendor solution
Operational cost management	Run away costs will drastically impede the progress of smart cities

Figure 3.13 Building a Smart City has many critical success factors. The figure shows selected ones for illustration purposes to demonstrate the gravity if one of these initiatives fails or lags behind. (© 2014 Copyright MERIT CyberSecurity Group. All rights reserved.)

that they would never have been noticed. And these photographs may now in a matter of minutes be visible, permanently, throughout the planet. So, this ability to make the invisible visible has many benefits, but it also needs to address serious issues of privacy and the protection of personal information.

Glossary

Action: A specific step to achieve a goal or objective. An action typically has assigned staff and schedule constraints.

Barrier: An external condition or organizational (internal) weakness that hinders an organization's ability to accomplish a goal or objective.

Critical success factors (CSFs): A handful of key areas where an organization must perform well on a consistent basis to achieve its mission.

Enabler: An external condition or organizational strength that facilitates an organization's ability to accomplish its goals or objectives.

Future scenarios: Multiple plausible futures that may develop due to external forces. Where a vision articulates a "preferred future," future scenarios taken together describe how, given different circumstances or environments, an organization might achieve its mission.

Goals: Broad, high-level aims that support the accomplishment of a mission.

Guiding principles: Directive statements that articulate the constraints an organization chooses to place upon the way it achieves its goals. Guiding principles embrace core values and are used to shape an organization's strategy. Guiding principles reflect long-term intentions, but are not necessarily permanent.

Information systems (IS): The means by which people and organizations gather, process, store, use, and disseminate information.

Information technology (IT): The hardware, software, and telecommunications that facilitate the acquisition, processing, storage, delivery, and sharing of information and other digital content in an organization. Also, the use of computing, electronics, and telecommunications technology in managing and processing information, especially in large organizations.

Initiative: A specific set of actions that implement a strategy.

IT strategy: A description of how information technology will support an organization's overall business strategy.

Mission: The primary business or purpose of an organization.

Objectives: Specific, quantifiable, lower-level targets that indicate the accomplishment of a goal.

Operational planning: The process of making decisions about the allocation of organizational resources (capital and staff) to pursue a strategy.

Performance measure: Performance targets relevant to each objective.

Strategic goal: A primary goal of an organization or enterprise that implies a particular strategy or set of strategies.

Strategic plan: A document that results from a strategic planning activity. It elaborates the organizational strategy and documents the elements that influence it.

Strategic planning: A process for defining an organization's strategy, or direction, and making decisions about how to allocate its resources to pursue this strategy, including its capital and people.

Strategy: A derived approach to achieving the mission, goals, and objectives of an organization. It supports the organizational vision, takes into account organizational enablers and barriers, and upholds guiding principles.

Sub-goal: A logical decomposition of a broader goal.

Vision: An ideal that an organization intends to pursue. It links the organization to the future by articulating instantiations of the successful execution of the mission.

Source: Previous document from Knowledge Base of MERIT CyberSecurity.

Bibliography

Zero-day computer: www.Bleepingcomputer.com

http://journals.isss.org/index.php/proceedings55th/article/view/1703

Understanding Smart Cities: http://dev5.ctg.albany.edu/publications/journals/hicss_2012_smartcities/hicss_2012_smartcities.pdf

CSF for humans: http://citeseerx.ist.psu.edu/viewdoc/download?doi=10.1.1.456.6914&rep=rep1&type=pdf

NIST: https://www.nist.gov/el/faqs-nist-wtc-towers-investigation

Stanford: http://news.stanford.edu/news/2001/december5/wtc-125.html

Application of big data to Smart Cities: https://jisajournal.springeropen.com/articles/10.1186/s13174-015-0041-5

NIST Security Report: http://nvlpubs.nist.gov/nistpubs/SpecialPublications/NIST.SP.800-182.pdf 114-5131862-1434662

CSF for Smart Cities: http://referaat.cs.utwente.nl/conference/25/paper/7590/critical-success-factors-for-a-smart-city-strategy.pdf

The critical success factor method: Establishing a foundation for enterprise security management: http://oai.dtic.mil/oai/oai?verb=getRecord&metadataPrefix=html&identifier=ADA443742

Smart City management: https://www.ctg.albany.edu/publications/journals/icegov_2011_smartcity/icegov_2011_smartcity.pdf

Smart City ICT framework: http://www.niua.org/sites/all/files/consultation-workshop/Nasscom_TechnologyArchitectureFramework.pdf

Electricity consumption: http://www.mpoweruk.com/electricity_demand.htm

Microsoft zero-day: http://www.bankinfosecurity.com/microsoft-says-russian-dnc-hackers-targeted-zero-day-flaws-a-9495

John Gall, 2003, *The Systems Bible: The Beginner's Guide to Systems Large and Small*, General Systemantics Press, Walker, MN.

Design of concrete columns: http://www.aboutcivil.org/reinforced-cement-concrete-design.html

Chapter 4

The Flat Tire of Antivirus Technologies

The Sun Goes Down

The computer industry carries diabolical genes. It is the nature of the beast.

The Internet started as an illegitimate baby in the village. Everyone raised their eyebrows and did not want to talk about it. Today, everyone in the world is worshiping the Internet. An incurable disease that is encroaching like the Big Bang.

A forecast by Gartner, published in November 2015, predicted that 6.4 billion Internet-connected things or devices would be in use in 2016. This number will be a staggering 20.8 billion by 2020. These things or devices will be used across a variety of industries covering both the consumer and business categories. It is an impressive forecast that focuses on connected "things" to the information highway. But what about a forecast about the astronomical and "uncontrollable" expansion of cyber malware? What kind of metrics should we use to forecast the strength of this tidal wave? Malware is a phenomenal type of energy that circulates around the world, but no one can control it, or harness it, or even recycle it into useful energy, since energy can be converted from one form into another. We're not there yet. We will be talking about this special topic in Chapters 7 and 10.

Quoting the Greek philosopher Heraclitus's famous statement "The only thing that is constant in this world is change," computer technology is constantly evolving into disruptive mode, which creates a new market and network but hurts established customers and products. Interestingly enough, disruptive products were presented by innovative companies such as Apple, Google, Amazon, and the Silicon Valley elite, and raised the innovation bar to the highest level. Disruptive products include the smartphone, Smart City, mobile Internet, online banking, online retail, Wikipedia, Internet of Things (IoT), Facebook, Twitter, the cloud, and goods delivery drones, and although these technologies brought true modernization to businesses and homes, at the same time, they also introduced smart malware and hacking.

Many of the antivirus technology (AVT) software companies have not brought out any *revolutionary* products equivalent to the iPhone. Steve Jobs sure did "put a ding in the universe."

Let's face it, the AVT companies suffer from several chronic problems:

Technology acceleration: Technology is galloping with gigantic strides, and will continue to accelerate depending on the dynamic changes in technology. A processor's yearly acceleration will be 85%!

$$\text{Processor acceleration} = \frac{(\text{Final speed}) - (\text{Initial speed})}{\text{Time}} = \frac{\text{Change in speed}}{\text{Time}}$$

$$= \frac{\text{IPhone 6 CPU speed} - \text{IPhone 3 CPU speed}}{7\text{-}2014 - 9\text{-}2007}$$

$$= \frac{1.4\,\text{GHz} - 800\,\text{MHz}}{7} = \frac{600}{7} = 85\%$$

Computing technology has moved from the desktop to the laptop to the iPad to the iPhone to the iWatch and to iGlasses. This is just the beginning. Technology has started to embrace the IoT, the Internet of Everything, man-to-machine, machine-to-machine, and body implants, and the parade goes on.

The Hardware Acceleration

The Legacy Era

IBM, nicknamed "Big Blue," was the General Motors (GM) of the computer industry. It was an unbeatable fortress with high-quality hardware and software products. IBM had 410,000 scientists, engineers, consultants, and sales professionals in over 175 countries. It was the largest of the eight major computer companies, the others being referred to as "the BUNCH" (Burroughs, UNIVAC, NCR, CDC, and Honeywell, plus GE and RCA).

On April 7, 1964, IBM introduced the revolutionary System/360, the first large "family" of computers to use interchangeable software and peripheral equipment. Riding the crest of the S/360 compatibility wave, IBM cemented its leadership position in the computer industry throughout the 1960s. IBM's gravitational force was dominant and monopolistically leveraged by the superb IBM/360. IBM became the de facto of the computing era from 1960 to 1968. It cannibalized the other seven computer companies, and all companies migrated to the 360 and paid homage to Big Blue. In June 1970, IBM announced the IBM S/370 and IBM grandiosity reached the highest level. It was better designed than the IBM/360 system.

In 1969, IBM's unbundling of software had a long-term impact. It gave rise to a multibillion-dollar software and services industry. The 360/MVS and its clone the 370/MVS operating systems opened the door for the software companies to launch and market their own MVS-compatible applications.

During the mainframe era, no one heard of cyberattacks. In fact, the word "cyber" has interesting roots. It derives from an old Greek word meaning (roughly) one who guides a boat, such as a pilot or rudder operator. Fast forward to the 20th century; Norbert Wiener was an American mathematician and a professor of mathematics at the Massachusetts Institute of Technology (MIT). He foresaw the rise of sophisticated robots, and realized that a robot would need something like a brain to control its mechanisms, as your brain controls your body. Wiener predicted correctly that this kind of controller would be difficult to design and build, so he sought a word to describe the study of these "intelligent" controllers. Not finding a suitable word in English, he reached back to the old Greek word, which he transliterated into English as "cybernetics." We quickly had a small rash of cyber words, such as *cybernetician*, *cyberspace*, *cybernation*, *cyborg*, and *cybercrime*.

Mainframes have hundreds of thousands of users interacting with them each day, through a local area network (LAN) or a private telephone line (systems network architecture [SNA]). This would suggest many more potential entry points for viruses. However, despite their difference, individual personal computers (PCs) are still more vulnerable to viruses and malicious code. On mainframes, only experienced administrators generally install new software and update code. In the PC world, both experienced and novice users download and install applications, some of which then infect the computers with malicious code. The AVT wasn't born yet. The Stone Age computer was bulky, heavy, and slow and it had to live in a refrigerated fishbowl of −12°C.

Then, the PC era kicked off from a garage. The first generation of PCs was relatively bulky and slow (Figure 4.1). It was a hobby before it became one of the largest industries in the world. Initially, Steve Jobs resented calling it a "home computer," preferring the term "personal computer." I love his quote: "I want to put a ding in the universe." He sure did.

In the beginning, there was water, then Bob Thomas, a computer engineer from Raytheon BBN, created the first computer virus in 1971, a non-malicious program called *Creeper*. A rudimentary replica to the modern antivirus software, called *Reaper*, was built and was able to neutralize Creeper on DEC PDP-10 machines. Then, the virus *Brain* was created in January 1986 to prevent copyright infringement, but the virus moved sectors of Microsoft MS-DOS computers and marked them as bad in the system, rendering those sectors unusable. It displayed a sarcastic and cryptic message "Welcome to the Dungeon."

Microsoft has unique visibility into an evolving threat landscape due to its hyper-scaled cloud footprint of more than 200 cloud services, over 100 data centers,

Apple II 1982   IBM PC 1981

Figure 4.1   Picture taken during the days of the Wild Wild West. In the next hundred years, these two boxes will be as famous as Leonardo da Vinci's Mona Lisa. These two magic boxes ushered in the beginning of a new computing paradigm. Personal computers opened their arms to welcome a very disruptive program called "the Virus."

millions of devices, and over a billion customers around the globe, and its investment in security professionals focuses on secure development as well as protection, detection, and responding functions. In summary, a systematic effort to mitigate attacks.

Symantec, the very popular AVT cybersecurity company, has also a global network of data centers. More than 32,000 organizations ranging from small businesses to the Fortune 500 across 100 countries use Symantec. Services are delivered on a highly scalable, reliable, and energy-efficient global infrastructure from 15 data centers around the globe.

Kaspersky Lab is a global cybersecurity company founded in 1997. Kaspersky Lab's deep threat intelligence and security expertise are constantly creating security solutions and services to protect businesses, critical infrastructure, governments, and consumers around the globe. The company's comprehensive security portfolio includes leading endpoint protection and a number of specialized security solutions and services to fight sophisticated and evolving digital threats. The company now has offices in 30 countries with 3000 employees. Over 400 million users are protected by Kaspersky Lab technologies and it helps 270,000 corporate clients protect what matters most to them. The company is well known for its discovery and dissection of the world's most sophisticated threats, including cyber-espionage and cyber sabotage threats such as Flame and miniFlame, Gauss, RedOctober, NetTraceler, Icefog, Careto/The Mask, Darkhotel, Regin, Cloud Atlas, Epic Turla, Equation, Stuxnet, and Duqu 2.0. Every day, the company automatically processes 310,000 new malicious advanced persistent threats (APT) files.

Sergey Ulasen, head of Infrastructure Development, Anti-Malware Research, is the guy who first discovered the notorious Stuxnet worm in 2010. In an interview, he said:

> My very first impression was that the anomalies found were due to some Windows misconfiguration or were the result of a conflict between installed applications. It's well-known of course that systems commonly get all in a tangle due to software conflicts .... Ultimately this incident confirmed to me that a security company needs strong threat analysis expertise. Dedicated teams need to concentrate on this analysis to ensure a company stays a step ahead of cybercriminals and at least keeps up with any cyber warfare going on – to be prepared to cope appropriately with either as and when it appears.

To add insult to injury, Sergey Ulasen traveled to Iran and helped the Iranians fish out the malware directly from the centrifuges.

Catch Me if You Can

The growth of both the Internet and the IoT is creating more connected devices, many of which are unsecure, to carry out larger distributed denial-of-service (DDoS) attacks. Due to the unsecure implementation of Internet-connected embedded devices, they are routinely being hacked and used in cyberattacks. Smart TVs and even refrigerators have been used to send out millions of malicious spam emails. Printers and set-top boxes have been used to mine Bitcoins and cybercriminals have targeted CCTV cameras (common IoT devices) to launch DDoS attacks. In Chapter 6, we will discuss the three generations of malware engineering. For example, there are remotely controlled software "robots" that can hack human genes and DNA, and commandeer airplanes; robot cyborgs to create havoc on command; and Kamikaze drones. The final battle of Armageddon is looming on the horizon.

There has been a phenomenal duality between virus flourishing and security software plateauing. Virus designers are superb system engineers who have wild imaginations and persistence, and have the upper hand in this deadly kickboxing dual.

For the last 27 years (1990–2017), the AVTs had not been able to catch up with malware. Hackers are great spies and opportunists. They know when, where, and how to attack. They are sharp shooters and excellent snipers. Hackers develop their own chat networks to exchange information and secrets. Hackers use a totally foreign language that no dictionary can decipher. We will discuss this in Chapter 7: Software Cyborgs of Tomorrow.

The world has a deep residual security concern of biblical proportions. Malware "engineering" has become the most prosperous and affluent business in the world.

You cannot smell or see malware, but business will suffer a massive convulsion from it. Malware designers are successful because they have the resources (especially the time) to test version after version, and to incrementally enhance their tactics up to the point where malware can infect a system and go undetected for months.

Antivirus companies have already lost their credibility due to fermenting marketing practices, drugging their loyal customers with lots of technical puff. Customers are not happy about the yearly renewal process.

Quality of Life in the Smart City

Now that the new technology tidal wave has arrived to shore, the Smart City with the more glamorous title "digital city" has become the new urban vision. Smart Cities have already stepped into the *second generation* of digital urbanism. Listing the goals of a Smart City is easy, implementing these goals is like climbing a one-mile high wall. There is no "one size fits all" set of goals for all cities. Each city comes with its own tailored schema design. But all Smart Cities have one common destination, which is "quality of life" (QoL) for all citizens. But how do we know that we have reached the summit of QoL? How can we measure quantitatively the QoL in cities? We must first think more clearly about what we mean by QoL. Many needs, values, and outcomes contribute to QoL and its perception. The polynomial of QoL has many influencing variables, but after evaluating all aspects of QoL, we decided to select the most "willingness" needs:

- To move to a new environment for a better life.
- To adapt to the new environment, including the neighborhood and new job.
- To be an achiever despite a sharp learning curve.
- To accept the challenge to help family to adjust to a new life.
- To accept the new technologies of a Smart City; in other words, IoT and connectivity to everywhere.
- To develop a positive attitude about planning the future.
- To learn more about safety and security in the city; safety needs such as protection from the elements, security, order, law, stability, and so on.
- To define biological and physiological needs such as air, food, drink, shelter, warmth, sex, sleep, and so on.
- To be active in the community.
- To learn about health care and educating one's children.
- To accept the challenge to manage stress and learn all about the disruptive technologies surrounding one's self and one's family.
- To realize personal potential and self-fulfillment, and seek personal growth and peak experiences.

AVT Meets the City's Smart Grid

Here's an important question to ask: could the present AVTs defend Smart Cities? The answer is a conditional "yes." To start with, none of the present AVT providers is ready to offer a smart and holistic security layer for the city. In fact, it would be more appropriate to change the term "antivirus" to "anti-malware."

The Smart Grid has evolved to take on a new meaning. It is a large network of connecting nodes that attaches computing devices, ranging from enterprise servers used for management systems to small specialized devices such as smart meters and control systems. Like the Internet, the Smart Grid consists of controls, computers, telecom adapters, automation, and new technologies and equipment working together; however, in this case, these technologies will work with the electrical grid to respond digitally to our quickly changing electric demand. Many of the devices are located in the field, exposing them to cyberattacks without the defenses provided by a corporate firewall. These remote devices not only play a critical role in the Smart Grid, but they also provide attractive and all too often easy targets for the motivated hacker.

The Smart Grid is an evolving network of new and legacy devices. Many legacy devices were designed years ago without security measures, but are now being connected to the Internet. In most cases, these devices lack the ability to detect and report traffic abnormalities, probes, or attacks, or to manage and control security policies. While legacy devices are gradually being replaced by newer systems with improved security, many of the devices have remained deployed for 10 years or more, often in remote areas or with difficult access, resulting in a very slow turnover to newer, more secure devices.

The "Smart Grid" is an intelligent, live, and breathing network that encompasses energy management systems, distribution management systems, advanced metering infrastructure, power generation management, and other systems. It offers the unique advantages of device interconnectivity, collaboration, activity sensing, and information metering. More importantly, the Smart Grid offers an exclusive cognitive security layer for the Smart City. AVT software doesn't have the logic to work with Smart Grids. It is a crucial component of the Smart City.

Now the good news: a digital immunity (DI) system is being designed using nanotechnologies (NT) and artificial intelligence (AI) components at the molecular level. This is like inventing the wheel with different tools and architecture. We will discuss the design in the following chapters. Cybercrime and cyber terrorism systems must be redesigned with new blueprints. The same will apply to AVT software.

The Age of AI and Nano

In the following chapters, we introduce two new technologies that have pushed aside all the other technologies and modernized most applications: AI and NT. AI is one of the greatest innovations because the acceleration of computing has opened up new avenues particularly in medicine and manufacturing. Driverless is a great invention that has taken the Smart City by storm. NT is another phenomenal science that has brought magic to Smart Cities and the whole living continuum. NT medical procedures could be reduced to the molecular scale and fix DNA and other human organs in a jiffy. "You can change the fate of cells by incorporating into them some new genes," said Dr. Axel Behrens, an expert in stem cell research from the Francis Crick Institute in London, who was not involved in the Ohio research. "Basically you can take a skin cell and put some genes into them, and they become another cell, for example a neuron, or a vascular cell, or a stem cell."

We're applying AI and NT to cybersecurity. In the next decade, digital immunity (DI) will become molecular and shove AVT aside. We have dedicated three chapters to the nano DI version.

Endpoint Protection Evaluation I

The Oxford English Dictionary defines the term "endpoint" as: *Special words or expressions used by a profession or group that are difficult for others to understand.* Very true! In the technical world of information technology (IT), obscure but precise language sometimes gets in the way of conceptual understanding. The term *endpoint* fits the bill. Symantec, for example, offered its own fancy explanation: "Symantec Endpoint Protection 14 is Artificial intelligence-fused with critical endpoint technologies, to deliver the most complete endpoint security on the planet." It did not explain anything about what an endpoint is. That's lots of polished veneer to impress the client, tagged with opaque award after award. Users have to resort to Google to find out what endpoint means. Oh, the number 14 next to endpoint protection stands for the version. How could a piece of software be reliable after 14 revisions? Why all of a sudden have AVT companies started to sprinkle AI endpoints on their websites?

Jennifer Burnham of Duva Blog eloquently defined the term as follows: "According to Wikipedia, *endpoint* is a hard-core punk band from Louisville, Kentucky. In the computer language, is a mobile device such as a laptop, phone, or tablet. The endpoint is a device or node that is connected to the LAN or WAN and accepts communications back and forth across the network, and to mean any device outside the corporate firewall."

Endpoint security is becoming a more common IT security function and concern as more employees bring mobile devices to work and companies allow its mobile workforce to use these devices on the corporate network.

In network security, endpoint security refers to a methodology of protecting the corporate network when accessed via remote devices such as laptops or other wireless and mobile devices. Each device with a remote connection to the network creates a potential entry point for security threats. Endpoint security is designed to secure each endpoint on the network that has been created by these devices.

Usually, endpoint security is a security system that consists of security software located on a centrally managed and accessible server or gateway within the network, in addition to client software being installed on each of the endpoints (or devices). The server authenticates logins from the endpoints and also updates the device software when needed. While endpoint security software differs by vendor, you can expect most software offerings to provide antivirus, antispyware, firewall, and also a host intrusion prevention system (HIPS).

Based on the performance of the AVT software over the last 20 years, malware has become more sophisticated and pervasive. Malware has moved out of single machines and has taken up residence in large business and government networks. That's where the money is. Malware today is the most dynamic and prosperous business in the world. Malware has become political, causing havoc and creating animosity between nations, and could tarnish the credibility of elections or even topple political regimes and governments.

AVT software providers still have a long way to go to win the war against malware. The reason they are not progressing is that they cannot forecast malware attacks. Another serious problem is that AVTs have been practicing "transport layer security (TLS) interception," which puts the client servers at high risk. We would like to articulate this grave subject: Lately, a lot of attention has been paid to software like Superfish and Privdog that intercepts TLS connections to manipulate HTTPS traffic. These programs create severe vulnerabilities that allow attacks on HTTPS connections.

So, the AVT providers install a root certificate into the user's browser and then they perform a so-called "man-in-the-middle" (MitM) attack. They present the user with a certificate generated on the fly and manage the connection to HTTPS servers themselves. Superfish and Privdog did this in an obviously wrong way: Superfish by using the same root certificate on all installations and Privdog by just accepting every invalid certificate from webpages. What about other software that also does MitM interception of HTTPS traffic?

The following are some of the technical deficiencies or "cracks" that need to be re-engineered in order to make endpoint protection/security suitable to protect the doors of a Smart City:

- Many AVT software providers use similar techniques to intercept HTTPS traffic. Take, for example, Avast, Kaspersky, and ESET. Avast enables TLS interception by default. By default, Kaspersky intercepts connections to certain webpages (e.g., banking), *there is an option to enable interception by default.* In ESET, TLS interception has an enabled and disabled option.
- Failing to deploy them to all endpoints—for example, any smartphone or tablet that is attached to a corporate network is an endpoint, and must be secured. If people use a virtual private network (VPN) to connect to their organization from remote locations, their devices become endpoints as well.

- Believing that endpoint security software can keep endpoints secure with technology, and therefore skimping on actual security policies, procedures, and training. No technology can deliver security if people undermine it.
- Failing to properly incorporate endpoint security into an overall security program. Ad hoc security is no longer sufficient; failure to properly design an overall program is going to leave holes that can—and likely will—be exploited by nefarious parties.
- The traditional endpoint security/malicious software detection approach is far from being sufficient, especially in corporate environments. More and more, it is being found that antivirus products can take months before adding the algorithms to recognize the more complex threats, leaving endpoints unprotected.
- AVT providers have not paid much attention to the behavior psychology of hackers and the analysis of their motivation to commit cybercrime. We discuss this issue in a later section in this chapter.

More AVT Flat Tire Stories

A recent study from CORE Security Technologies, a security company offering solutions against advanced cyber threats, revealed that malware could spend as much as six months on a system before it is identified using signature-based detection. To demonstrate the limitations of a prevention-centered approach to malicious software, they analyzed a sample set of tens of thousands of files sent to them by their customers. The files detected as malicious by their own Failsafe system were also scanned by the four most commonly deployed antivirus products. Here's what they found:

Within the first hour, the antivirus products missed nearly 70% of the malware. After 24 hours, still only 66% of the files were identified as malicious. At the seven-day mark, the accumulated total was 72%. After one month, 93% of the files were identified as malicious. More than six months passed before 100% of the malicious files were identified malware-alerts-per-week. The myth: many companies think that just because they may have a corporate antivirus installed, it means their business is fully protected.

Scott Dujmovich from Golden Tech, an IT solutions provider for the health care and financial services industries, admits that antivirus protection is becoming more and more irrelevant in terms of protecting networks against a breach. Also, modeling with "what-if" breach scenarios is a great tool to learn more about smart attacks. More importantly, making users part of the security solution will fix the weakest link in security today.

There are too many zero-day smart holes and backdoor Trojans loaded with mutating payload that are smarter than the AVT defense.

AVT providers should focus primarily on large companies such as Target, Home Depot, eBay, and Walmart, which need distributed security and protection tools, because those are the kinds of companies that get the biggest splash in the news. In the Target hacking, the hackers wormed their way into gathering more than 40 million debit and credit card numbers from Target's point of sale (POS) system, which was supposed to be protected by endpoint security/protection.

Superfish advertisement software was designed to help users find products by visually analyzing images on the web to find the cheapest ones. But it compromised security by intercepting connections and issuing fake certificates—the IDs used to identify websites—to trick sites into handing over data. This a practice commonly known as an MitM attack. Endpoint security/protection couldn't stop the hacking.

Then came PrivDog, which was developed by the founder of Comodo, and some versions of it are packaged with Comodo's own software. Comodo is a secure sockets layer (SSL) email certificate that ensures email cannot be read by anyone but the intended recipients. It also ensures that the destined message is not modified during transmission and allows recipients to confirm the identity of the message sender. Email certificates can be applied for and collected using Internet Explorer, Firefox, Opera, Safari, and Flock browsers. For best results, however, we recommend using Internet Explorer. Comodo secure email certificates allow the user to digitally sign his or her email as well as encrypt the email messages so that they cannot be read or edited during transmission. Comodo had a defect in its security/protection mechanism and it really put many users in jeopardy. Endpoint software would not have cleaned the mess.

Brad Deflin, president and founder of Total Digital Security, a managed security as a service provider, stated his view on endpoint security/protection: "For the last decade or so, our experience with endpoint security has not been good. A few market dominating incumbent providers held tremendous influence over the sales channels in the IT security industry, and, as a result, we saw very little innovation in the area of endpoint security. The solutions were clunky to operate and less than effective, certainly in terms of the hostile online environment we live in today."

Paul Paget, chief executive officer (CEO) of Pwnie Express, a wireless and wired threat detection security company, voiced his concern about proactively combatting endpoint security threats around wireless productivity tools, Bring Your Own Device (BYOD), and IoT devices. It is too much for the AVT providers to manage hack-proof exchange of information from outside the enterprise castle.

Tim Singleton, founder of Strive Technology Consulting, described the state of malware: "It sounds cynical, but if you rely on a single tool to prevent an attack and the bad guys figure out how to defeat that single tool, you're vulnerable. In reality, most security tools out there work quite well, but it is an arms race between the hackers and the security companies. The good guys plug a hole, the bad guys find a new one, the good guys plug that one, ad infinitum. If you are relying on a single solution for a security problem, you are vulnerable."

Smart Grids Need Smart Solutions

The human body is an incredible knowledge-generating utility powerhouse. It is designed as a fully autonomic control center for the whole body infrastructure. We could learn a lot from the human body grids and how they collaborate to help each other exchange vital information. In fact, some human grids loan its resources to other grids in distress. All the human grids need to be fully operational or the human body will not function properly. Smart Cities require a replica of the human layered Smart Grids. Figure 4.2 shows a model of the layered grids for a Smart City.

New, smarter cyber threats emerge every day and advanced, evasive techniques are becoming standard hacker protocol. Most security solutions, whether legacy or newer systems, adapt to new threats reactively, limited by their knowledge and detection logic. They rely on detecting threat signatures or suspicious behaviors.

Endpoint Protection Evaluation II

The most prevalent anti-malware solution is the endpoint detection and response (EDR). All AVT providers joined the EDR club and started aggressively promoting it to their customers. However, EDR solutions are not a substitute for, but rather can act in tandem with, other security measures. EDR tools are complimentary to a variety of other security measures and solutions, including data loss prevention solutions. Security Symantec has its own Symantec Endpoint Protection with the ability to protect all types of endpoints, even employee-owned devices. Kaspersky also joined the EDR parade. Kaspersky Endpoint Security for Business includes additional security features beyond simple Internet security, including email scanning, spam blocking, application control, hardware audits, non-Kaspersky software audits, firewall control, Wi-Fi control, antiphishing, terminal and cluster server protection, remote PC security, and proxy server support. It protects all endpoints, including PCs, remote PCs, virtual technologies, file servers, gateways, smartphones, Macs, Linux-based devices, and storage devices. Sophos Complete Security Suite is another reputable EDR solution that now protects 100,000 businesses and 100 million users in more than 150 countries. Sophos endpoint package includes antivirus, website blocking, heuristic technology (B-HAVE), a two-way firewall, email scanning, spam protection, and antiphishing.

F-Secure also has a remarkable business suite, which includes full endpoint security licenses for clients, workstations, Linux clients, servers, Linux servers, email servers, and Linux gateways. F-Secure performs well in third-party antimalware tests. In fact, in numerous third-party tests, F-Secure proved to be able to detect 100% of the malware test samples. The client-side security version includes web-browsing protection, email scanning, anti-rootkit technology, device protection, antispyware, and virus scanning.

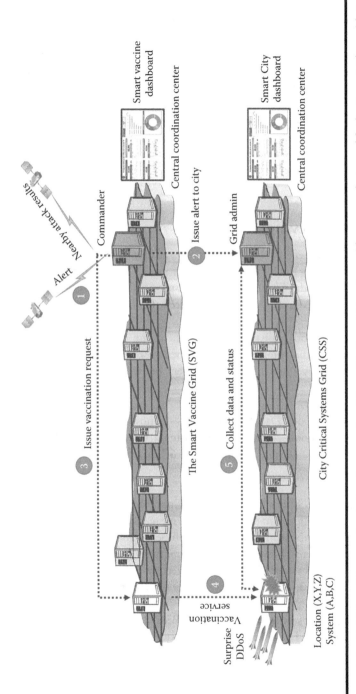

Figure 4.2 Grid to grid scenario. A simple scenario of how the Smart Vaccine grid communicates with the Smart City grid. In reality, the Smart Vaccine grid is a subset of the Smart City grid. By analogy, blood vessels and nerves run and work together.

Microsoft also has its System Center 2012 R2, where an endpoint protection manager deploys and configures endpoint protection, manages firewall settings, configures anti-malware policies, updates antivirus definitions, manages email alerts, and creates reports. It manages security protocols such as blocking incoming connections, suspicious downloads, and rootkit exploits; monitors spyware; and manages network profiles.

And finally, we have McAfee Endpoint Protection Suite. McAfee provides configurable endpoint protection for all types of endpoints and can manage strict compliance policies that medical, financial, and government agencies are required to enforce. The ePO can manage a large volume of endpoints, run complex queries, and streamline IT tasks.

Breaches Everywhere

But despite all the benefits bestowed upon the user community from endpoint protection/security technologies, the business world is still suffering from a rash of breaches all over the United States and Europe. The cybercrime statistics are mind-boggling. On March 3, 2015, CBS posted the following scary numbers:

> With 1.5 million annual cyber-attacks, online crime is a real threat to anyone on the Internet. That number means there are over 4,000 cyber-attacks every day, 170 attacks every hour, or nearly three attacks every minute.

Kelly Sheridan from DarkReading.com—a most trusted online community for security professionals—posted a hair-raising article on January 1, 2017: "Data Breaches Exposed 4.2 Billion Records in 2016," describing the state of the health of cyber breaches:

> There were 4,149 breaches reported during 2016 exposing over 4.2 billion records – approximately 3.2 billion more records than the previous all-time high exposed in 2013. In December 2016, Yahoo reported the single largest breach ever disclosed, impacting over 1 billion records. The number of reported breaches tracked by Risk Based Security has exceeded 23,700, exposing over 9.2 billion records.

This finding comes from the "2016 Data Breach Quick View Report," released on January 25 by Risk Based Security (RBS). Researchers discovered that the number of data breaches was consistent between 2015 and 2016, but their severity had skyrocketed.

The threat of data breaches will continue to grow as long as hackers' motivations remain the same. "As long as there is money to be made out of unauthorized access and data theft, malicious actors will continue to refine and improve their attack methods," she explains. "The wave of targeted phishing scams, seeking W2 details, that took place early in the first part of the year is a good example." While it's difficult to predict the future, data breaches will certainly continue. It's no longer enough for businesses to solely focus on prevention.

Morphisec, another pioneering security defense company, has brought a new armory of lethal weapons to antisepticize endpoint devices from onboard static and dynamic malware. Their applications are highly advanced and unique. "Moving Target Defense" is a polymorphic engine that takes the original customer's business applications and scrambles their process structures, which confuses all attack vectors.

There's a big misconception about the versatility of endpoint protection and security to defend inside and outside enterprises. Endpoints provide a vast attack surface for cybercriminals—80% of attacks penetrate via endpoints. Legacy security products do not protect adequately against advanced, evasive attacks, APTs, ransomware, and zero-days.

AVT providers are getting old and obese. It is time to inject new blood into the security industry. In all fairness, all AVT providers have done a great job serving their customers, but the "virus" has been designed with lots of autonomic features and the cognitive ability to fix itself and learn from its own mistakes. The virus family has become a huge community, which has expanded into a smart malware city. Let us give an example that simulates our reality: Let's say that we have 1000 AVT armies around the world, against 430 million new pieces of software drones, or over 1 million pieces of guided cyborgs each day. The overall total number of malware armies is now over 1.7 billion. What chance does ice have in hell?

Figure 4.3 is displayed for one purpose: to show the meteoric acceleration of AVT technology. Between 2010 and 2020, cybersecurity providers will be convinced that DI is the right solution for Smart Cities. The advantages of DI can be summarized as follows:

- DI will be a replica of the human immune system, inheriting most of the combat strategies of the (B and T) cells.
- DI will be designed with NT for the first time. Being molecular, the components of DI will have the advantage of their enhanced properties such as higher strength, lighter weight, increased control of the light spectrum, and greater chemical reactivity than their larger-scale counterparts.
- DI software will be empowered with super intelligence that exceeds the biological intelligence of hackers by one million fold.
- DI will be totally invisible and autonomic. It will regulate itself.
- DI, once in production mode, will be less costly and less labor intensive.
- DI will incarcerate malware with a life sentence.

Security technological sophistication

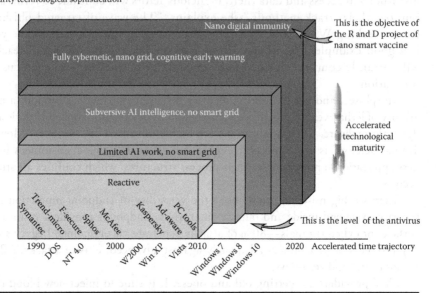

Figure 4.3 The digital immunity system CEWPS is two generations ahead of the present antivirus technology (AVT). The diagram shows the evolution of cybersecurity systems from the present to the ultimate one of digital immunity, which is the new paradigm of cybersecurity. It is the only practical way to remove the super glue of malware and protect Smart Cities. (© 2014 Copyright MERIT CyberSecurity Group. All rights reserved.)

Merger & Acquisition Technology

The merger/acquisition (M&A) statistics are mind-boggling. Technology companies merge or acquire other companies for several reasons. As the saying goes, *the big get bigger and the rich get richer.* Microsoft acquired 1500 companies to build a complete spectrum of applications for any business and industry. Microsoft has made nine acquisitions, each worth over US$1 billion: Skype (2011), Quantive (2007), Fast Search & Transfer (2008), Navision (2002), Visio Corporation (2000), Yammer (2012), Nokia (2013), Mojang (2014), and LinkedIn (2016) for a whopping US$26 billion. System security was not an issue until Microsoft penetrated the Internet with its "half-cooked" Internet Explorer, which was an annoying speed bump to progress. AVT companies had to march to Microsoft's drumbeat and cautiously not step on the turf of the software giant. Hardware vendors also paid homage to Microsoft. Software companies that locked horns with Microsoft were either doomed or acquired.

HP also went on a spree of high-priced acquisitions of 149 technology companies including Compaq for US$25 billion and Electronic Data System (EDS) for US$13.9 billion. The mergers were poorly planned, and as noted in a 2011 *Harvard*

Business Review article, study after study has shown that the failure rate of mergers and acquisitions is between 70% and 90%. That's even higher than the much-discussed divorce rate.

Symantec Corporation acquired 87 security companies, and the last acquisition was for Lifelock, a company that specializes in ID Theft protection for US$2.6 billion; Veritas Software for US$13.5 billion; and Verisign Certification Company for US$1.6 billion. Again, there's a risk in merging with a company for growth and market share. Mixing applications from both companies is a great challenge. Company cultures may clash and employee attrition may upset the users of the acquired company. Synergy may not happen as expected between the two AVT companies in the case of a hostile acquisition or take-over. Growth is another viable initiative for merging two competitive companies. M&A deals allow the AVT acquirer to eliminate future competition and gain a larger market share in its product's market. The downside of this is that a large premium is usually required to convince the target company's shareholders to accept the offer. It is not uncommon for the AVT acquiring company's shareholders to sell their shares and push the price lower in response to the company paying too much for the target company.

For financial and marketing stability and excessive management ambition, AVT companies resort to gobbling up software startups. According to Wikipedia, Microsoft acquired 200 companies between 1987 and 2017; Apple acquired 80 tech companies; Facebook purchased 61 companies; IBM added 187 companies to its technology arsenal; but Google topped everyone with 237 companies.

Merging with another company does not guarantee that cybersecurity will be better. Mergers inherit hidden system compatibility and employee cultural problems. Losing the focus on the desired objectives, failure to devise a concrete plan with suitable involvement and control, and lack of establishing necessary integration processes can lead to failure of any M&A deal. The *Financial Times Press* states that "Many research studies conducted over the decades clearly show that the rate of failures is at least 50 percent."

A merger is like acquiring an organ where multifaceted compatibility has to be satisfied. In mergers, acquisition will get the strength and the weakness of the acquired company. Software acquisition is a different breed of technology fusion. Merging two software systems could be done with a transparent bridging system or a hybrid adapter. The sole purpose of merging two software systems is to gain production and customers and reduce internal cost economies. Sometimes, merging two software systems can create more compatibility problems and less production.

Breaching Cases

Take, for example, the Yahoo and Verizon merger. Yahoo's stock plummeted Thursday as cybersecurity issues continued to rankle the company and reports surfaced that Verizon was looking to change the terms of—or possibly abort—its planned US$4.8 billion acquisition of the early Internet darling. Yahoo announced that a 2013 hack had compromised more than a billion user accounts. Names, email addresses, passwords, phone numbers, birthdays, and "in some cases, encrypted or unencrypted security questions and answers" were potentially accessed in the breach. It turned out that Yahoo uses what's known as a Message Digest (MD5) algorithm to protect and store passwords. MD5 was the most vulnerable and broken crypto algorithm. Yahoo was using Bitdefender antivirus.

Another antivirus blunder occurred at the US Department of Homeland Security (DHS) and the Federal Bureau of Investigation (FBI). A hacker with the Twitter handle @DotGovs released online the names and contact information of 29,000 DHS and FBI employees. How come EDR did not stop the hack?

How about the cyberattack on the Democratic National Committee (political organization)? The political organization's networks were illegally accessed by two separate cyber groups with possible affiliations to the Russian government's Main Intelligence Directorate (GRU) and Federal Security Service (FSB). The hacks zipped by the endpoint protection unhindered. The list of all unfortunate cyberattacks stretches for miles. It is paradoxically ironical when Gartner positions Symantec as a leader in Data Loss Prevention Magic Quadrant for the 10th consecutive time.

Recommendation

The world economy is smothered by the enthusiastic activities of virus writers, hackers, and spammers. The financial hemorrhage has already drained tens of billions of dollars every year and the mischief continues to breed more devastation and misery on small and large business. According to research carried out by Computer Economics, total losses in 2004 were close to US$18 billion, with a trend toward a 30%–40% annual growth rate.

From all the viral evidence on cybercrime, it seems that there's an atrocious asymmetrical war going on between security forces and malware black hat psychopaths who have been gaining significant advantage while designing superior cyber bombs and drilling underneath the sturdiest firewalls. This asymmetrical conflict looks like a cat and mouse chase!

In 2014, *Life Time Magazine* published a special magazine titled *Inside the Criminal Mind*. It describes in minute detail how to unlock the secrets behind the world's most notorious crimes. It is an outstanding documentary magazine that deciphers the psychology of people like Manson, the Zodiac killer, Al Capone, and Oswald. Unfortunately, it doesn't quite apply to cybercriminals who belong to a different breed of people.

If AI, cybernetics, and NT are the promising technologies that will bring us back to cyber victory, then these technologies should be taught in academia and practiced today, and not tomorrow, in the business world. Figure 4.4 is a simple engineering blueprint that we would like to recommend to the AVT world.

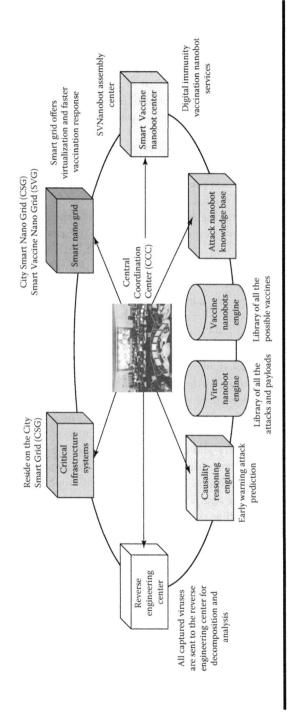

Figure 4.4 The digital immunity (DI) system with its nine remarkable autonomic and super intelligent components—the health recovery system for Smart Cities. (© 2014 Copyright MERIT CyberSecurity Group. All rights reserved.)

AVT Cannot Catch Hackers

A digital virus is the most important diabolical invention of the 21st century. It is the mastery of a new breed of creative *nerds of the third kind,* who can hatch an ingenious piece of code to create a technological holocaust for millions of people. He or she can do it for money or for political or religious reasons. He or she surpasses the intelligence of a rocket scientist and challenges the perseverance of a rock climber. The reality today is that *malware is running on steroid, security is running on diesel.*

It is appalling that all AVT software providers have been primarily focusing on malware detection and prevention, and not much on the psychological behavior of hackers. All AVT providers claim superiority and supremacy of their solutions over their competitors, and gauge their success by the number of "subscribed" customers and the blessings of consulting firms. In fact, most of the AVT portals come with lots of veneer wax and are adorned with big words and award banners. On its main page, Symantec has two reports from Gartner: "15 Years Running, a Leader in Gartner Magic Quadrant for Endpoint Protection Platforms" and "Gartner Positions Symantec as a Leader in Data Loss Prevention Magic Quadrant for the 10th Consecutive Time"; but, amazingly, none of them highlights the issue of the "psychology of hacking"!

Here's a revelation you should keep in mind: In medicine, all physicians honor the famous Hippocratic Oath that says, "I will use treatment to help the sick according to my ability and judgment, but never with a view to injury and wrongdoing." The physician has to know the history of the patient before prescribing the right medicine. Given a new understanding of the person/persons behind such a crime, the process will be a preliminary part of the crime handling process. Using the methods of *behavioral analysis,* it creates a new dimension of understanding the malicious activity and a network analysis of what occurred in the environment. AVT software providers regrettably do not mention much on the psychological motivation of hackers. Their marketing philosophy is based on three points: (1) creating awareness and fear in the user's mind about malware attacks and loss of data; (2) presenting their products as the only solution to protecting the user's information assets; and (3) claiming that they are the leader in the antivirus industry. All antivirus engines employ heuristic analysis in order to find previously unknown computer viruses or to detect new variants of known viruses. Heuristic analysis is often performed by antivirus software by running the suspect program in a virtual machine, allowing the antivirus program to see what the suspect program will do in a controlled environment before allowing the program to run on the user's actual computer. If the program performs any actions normally associated with malware, the antivirus will notify the user. This is also known as *file emulation.* Antivirus software can also decompile the suspected program and analyze the source code and see if it matches any known source code of known malware. Constantly changing computer viruses pose a challenge for heuristic analysis as its success depends on finding a balance between false positives and false negatives. Security professionals are improving heuristic analysis to limit the number of false positives, which can sometimes identify and quarantine non-threatening files.

Before we open the curtain on a new technology called "digital immunity," we want to highlight the importance of a systematic study of the root of hacking as it is the most influencing variable in the equation of cybercrime. Let's articulate:

In order to effectively and systematically combat computer crime and suppress hacking activities, lawmakers and computer professionals must understand the motivation behind this activity. The hacking community is a diverse and complicated universe, a mind-blowing nuclear reactor, keeping unsurmountable amounts of kinetic energy ready to control the world. By understanding the different types of hackers and what motivates their behavior, it is possible to understand the anatomy of computer crime, which will allow us to easily predict future activity. If the best offense is a good defense, then the best way to predict potential hacking attempts is to understand the mentality of hackers. One way of understanding the hacking mentality is by examining research based on *social psychology theory*. Though other fields use psychological profiling to help solve crimes like serial killings and terrorism, only a few studies have been done connecting psychological theory with computer crime. This research, while very in-depth, can be distilled down to a few basic principles: social learning via peer groups and justification of illegal activity. We're going to discuss the infrastructure of the hacking community, the different motivations of the various groups, and a simple explanation of the research involving the social learning theory and computer crime, in order to explain this behavior.

Hacking Psychological Profiling

Initially, the virus writing and hacking communities were very much two separate groups. Hacking required a totally different skillset and mindset from virus writing. Now, with the massive connectivity of the Internet, skillset and mindset are having some crossover. However, in general, hackers frown upon virus writers. After all, hacking requires system knowledge and skill and is somewhat "sexy" in today's counterculture, while virus writing is still looked down upon, mostly for its indiscriminate damage and lack of required skill.

The first step to wisdom is to admit that there is a security problem.

A hacker profile is a collection of inferences about the qualities of the person responsible for committing the crime of cyber hacking. An inference is a conclusion reached based on evidence and reasoning. There must be zillions of computer institutes that offer training mostly in the technical side of computer science. We would like to highlight an important point regarding training offered by AVT software providers. We examined the Symantec training courseware and were amazed that the courses were highly technical, but no classes are provided on the psychology of hacking and hackers. We feel that this is a serious black hole that needs to be plugged. We examined Kaspersky's training courses, but again nothing is provided on the psychological profiling and motivation of hackers. We believe that it is crucial for all AVT providers to organize a series of training courses on hackers.

The SANS Institute is one of the most reputable institutions of computer education. The *knowledge acquirers* assemblage is made up of auditors and network administrators, hardware and software engineers, and chief information security officers. They share the lessons they learn and jointly find solutions to the challenges they face. SANS also has a congregation of knowledge givers made up of security practitioners from global business organizations to academic institutions working together to help the entire information security community. SANS is the largest source for cybersecurity training and certification in the world. It also offers the largest collection of research documents on all aspects of information security. SANS is also empowered with Internet Storm Center (ISC), which monitors the level of malicious activity on the Internet, particularly with regard to large-scale infrastructure events. SANS has an extensive repertoire of courses that covers the whole spectrum of cybersecurity. Surprisingly, SANS does not have a dedicated seminar or class on the subject of hacker profiling.

ASIS International is the leading organization for security professionals, with more than 38,000 members worldwide. Founded in 1955, ASIS is dedicated to increasing the effectiveness and productivity of security professionals by developing educational programs and materials that address broad security interests, such as the ASIS Annual Seminar and Exhibits, as well as specific security topics. ASIS also advocates the role and value of the security management profession to business, the media, government entities, and the public. By providing members and the security community with access to a full range of programs and services, and by publishing the industry's No. 1 magazine *Security Management*, ASIS leads the way for advanced and improved security performance.

Global Information Assurance Certification (GIAC) is the leading provider and developer of cybersecurity certifications. GIAC tests and validates the ability of practitioners in information security, forensics, and software security. GIAC published a technical paper titled "Psychology and the Hacker – Psychological Incident Handling." It is great reading material on the psychology of hacking. Tables 4.1 and 4.2 give a cross-sectional stereotype view of hackers.

Steven M. Crimando, a member of the Association of Threat Assessment Professionals (ATAP), is an expert in threat assessment and threat management, and is frequently called upon by law enforcement agencies, the media, and the courts to provide insight into workplace, school, and community violence prevention and response, including acts of extreme violence such as active shooter incidents. He organizes a seminar titled Comprehensive Active Shooter Incident

Table 4.1 Behavior of the Hacker and Personal Attributes

Hacker Behavior	Profile 1	Profile 2	Profile 3
Number of respondents	350	10% reluctant to discuss	40% angry at corporates
Age range	15–60	Very excited to be called hackers	—
Mean age	26	—	Always looking for better opportunity
Yearly salary	$61,000–$100,000	Contact basis	40% did not divulge data
Education	60% community college	Attending conferences and black hat summits	Sharing hacking knowledge with peers
Mood and temper	10% high depression	20% pot smokers	30% hikers
Bipolar disorder	10%	—	—
Appearance	60% obese, grubby, long hair and beard	Junk food	Not too healthy
Male/female	10% female	Not too attractive	Very talkative
Internal characteristics	Handle stress and frustration	Spending long hours, not much sleep	Moderate drinking and party animal
Sports/hobbies	Baseball games on TV	Biking, mountain climbing	Very eager on green ecology
Social lifestyle	50% not married	Away from home, few friends	Harley club members

Table 4.2 Tableau with Finer Granularity Shedding More Light on Hackers' Lives and Motives, and How Well AVT Software Is Doing to Eliminate Attacks

Hacker Type	Hacker Behavior	Tools	Target	AVT Prevention	AVT Capture Ratio
Hobby hacker	Tinkerer, learner, moral disengagement, no malice	Basis DOS, Trojans, downloaded tools	Retail companies (Target, Kmart, etc.)	Honeypot, Firewall, AVT software	90%–100%
Malicious insider	Opportunist, disgruntled, no loyalty to company, lots of malice	Knows a lot about zero-days, and on the AVT; knows how to get the right hacking tools	Has own company, own bank, steals cash from company; compromises sensitive data	AVT cannot prevent these actions	45%–55%
Political hacktivist	Politically motivated, against regimes, wreaks havoc, works as a group, not interested in hacking systems	Defaces websites, political web graffiti, DOS attacks	Government websites, military websites, political websites and social media like Twitter and Facebook	Defacing is not a virus; AVT is not too effective against this type of attack	20%–50%
Religious activist	Loyal to a fanatical and radical religious group; fights for religious causes	Defaces websites, political web graffiti, DOS attacks	Government websites, military websites, political websites and social media like Twitter and Facebook	AVT are not too effective against this type of hacking	20%–40%

(Continued)

Table 4.2 (Continued) Tableau with Finer Granularity Shedding More Light on Hackers' Lives and Motives, and How Well AVT Software Is Doing to Eliminate Attacks

Hacker Type	Hacker Behavior	Tools	Target	AVT Prevention	AVT Capture Ratio
Spy	Secretive, vengeful, dislikes company of government; works for a foreign group, going after secret data	Trojans and backdoors, uses internal people to get to data; password cracker, contact with admins	Competitive companies, government, special secret project for military, computers	Hit and miss; not very effective in stopping spies	40%–60%
Document thief	Slick, professional spy, very knowledgeable in hacking, no ethics, no morals	Network tools, IRC, Trojans and backdoors, uses internal people to get to data; password cracker, contact with admins	Bank records, medical records, government records, engineering design blueprints	Hit and miss; not very effective against this type of hacking; it is happening daily	30%–50%
Cyber terrorist	Loyal, slick, professional with excellent knowledge, very motivated in hacking, no ethics, no morals	Network, IRC, Trojans and backdoors, uses internal people to get to data; password cracker, contact with admins	Military sites, government sites, airlines, critical infrastructures, government elections	Hit and miss; not very effective against this type of hacking; it is happening daily	20%–50%
Organized crime	Loyal to group, politically motivated, anti-establishment, full of hatred and malice, very knowledgeable in military and hacking	Network tools, IRC, Trojans and backdoors, uses internal people to get to data; password cracker, contact with admins	Military sites. government sites, banks, government elections	Hit and miss; not very effective against this type of hacking; it is happening daily	10%–30%

Management, in which he scientifically describes the behavior of criminals including cybercriminals (AVT providers should attend as well):

■ Identifies elements in the scope and prevalence of an active shooter threat.
■ Describes how the four-phase model of emergency management (mitigation, preparedness, response, recovery) can be applied as a comprehensive approach to managing the active shooter threat.
■ Describes critical differences in the warning signs of workplace violence versus warning behaviors associated with mass shootings.

Every organization and community is vulnerable to violence, regardless of its size or type. The active shooter threat is a dynamic, multifaceted problem that requires a multidimensional approach to prevention, response, and recovery. Case studies have indicated that shooters/hackers often begin planning and preparing for an attack weeks, months, and sometimes years ahead. The consequences for individuals, families, communities, and organizations can last for decades. This interesting seminar discusses the importance of mitigating the active shooter/hacker threat by understanding the *dynamics of the event*, planning for the full cycle of the event, and preparing those at risk with the necessary information and skills.

The Nano Cybercriminal

No one has ever described who is the nano cybercriminal and what are the qualifications to become one. Hackers once tinkered with AT&T digital phones—followers of Captain Crunch—making millions of free calls in the 1960s and 1970s; then, they started using modems and hacking into mainframes in the 1970s and 1980s; they subsequently exploited the LAN technology and the burgeoning Internet in the 1980s. Malware writers moved from boot-sector viruses on floppy disks to file-infector viruses and then to macro viruses in the 1990s and vigorously exploited worms and Trojans for attacks, and now NT is stepping into the manufacturing and business world. The cyber world has moved to greener pastures.

NT has made striking advances in medicine and biology, bioengineering, and electronics. And the turn is coming for cyber malware. We're going to have a new breed of criminals called *nano hackers*, who will be able to acquire the experience of NT, and turn it around to use it to do evil things. These criminals will learn about DI; they will study it and learn how it works.

Similarly, academia will teach NT as part of computer science. The field will be very inviting and many bright students will master nano software and hardware. Silicon valley giants will race to develop new tools and solutions.

In the next decade, the world will have the same dilemma as today. NT will get into the hands of cybercriminals.

Auditing the Hacker's Mind

One of the most precious materials on the behaviorism and the motivation chemistry of the hacker's mind is the book *Cyber Adversary Characterization: Auditing the Hacker Mind*. It gives a cross-sectional diagnosis of the mind of a miscreant motivated by a broad range of ulterior purposes. The book talks about vandals with limited impulse control, cyber terrorists who are on the payroll of the Devil, and ghouls with a lust for political espionage and malice. If AVT software providers read the book, they will definitely gain a broader knowledge on what triggers the mind of the hacker. All this pre-mortem work will pay off.

We said earlier that the AVT, with its present state of technology, is running on a flat tire and that it is time to complement it with another *asymmetrical* technology that would build a new defense barrier and enrich the AVT industry with a new "radical" dimension. It is called digital immunity! It is a totally new concept that will revolutionize cyber defense and elevate the technology bar to the highest level. We all agree with the classical proverb "Originality doesn't rely on creating something from nothing. It relies on putting together ideas and materials in a new way."

Digital Immunity: The Holy Grail

Here's a new revelation: During the plague of Athens in 430 BC, the historian Thucydides noted that people who had recovered from a previous bout of the disease could nurse the sick without contracting the illness a second time. No one knew at that time that human immunity could bring Athens back to life. Engineering, medicine, and the military became the most important elements for the survival of civilization. The first element is to build a healthy city, the second element is to maintain healthy citizens, and the third one is to defend the city.

One of the great contributions to humanity was the discovery of the vaccine. Without adaptive immunity, one-fourth of the human race would have been terminally ill. Dr. Edward Jenner and Louis Pasteur share this honorable credit. Smallpox was responsible for an estimated 300–500 million deaths during the 20th century alone. In the 1950s, an estimated 21 million deaths were reported. As recently as 1967, the World Health Organization (WHO) estimated that 15 million people contracted the disease and that 2 million died in that year. So, we studied the workings of the human immune system and we replicated its functionalities to protect the digital world.

George Stephenson invented the steam locomotive engine in 1820; Karl Benz invented the modern car in 1879; and the Wright brothers invented the airplane in 1903. These three inventions brought three new infrastructures to the modern world. Thomas Edison gave us electricity in 1879; Alexander Graham Bell gave us the telephone in 1876; and Thomas Johnson Watson gave us the IBM computer in 1953. Then, Leonard Kleinrock and Vinton Cerf gave us the Internet and that was the beginning of the electronic big bang that we are living in today. But we're still suffering from virus storms and rain. We thought that if immunity saved the human race, we could design a system that would save the digital world.

Then came the Internet as one of our greatest contributions to the world. We've developed great things on the web, but cybercriminals have outsmarted all the security systems and implanted mines and traps in almost every system. So far, our report card on fighting cybercrime is a D. Cyberattacks have become the next form of warfare. The news on the latest crop of criminal enterprises is that criminals are turning to cloud computing as a way to generate new "attacks-as-a-service," such as offering botnets for lease and sale, aid tools for cheating on games, and tools to facilitate credit card fraud, even spoiling the US presidential elections. It has been an uphill battle with successive calamities crippling our cyberspace, knocking down our critical infrastructures, and digging black holes in our social fabric.

The Cognitive Early Warning Predictive System (CEWPS™) (Figure 4.5), creator of the nano DI, is an incredible constellation of smart objects called "nanobots" that interact symbiotically with one another to deliver cognitive early warning alert messages, vaccination emergency responses, reverse-engineering lab work, attack prediction scenarios, attack episode storage, and knowledge base updates. CEWPS possesses an arsenal of the most advanced technologies including: AI, autonomic computing, grid computing, on-demand computing, virtualization, and semantics.

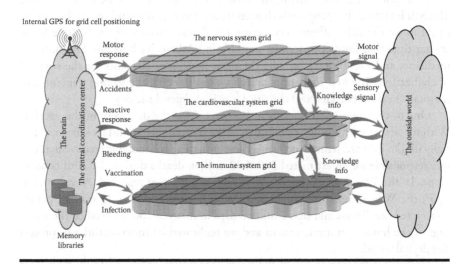

Figure 4.5 The human body is a universe of bits of energy and knowledge that energizes the human grids. Signals coming from outside are authenticated and routed to the proper grid for processing. The brain (the central coordination center) gives approval to respond and document the event in the library. Embedded security is a component of digital immunity, which provides defense by offence.

It can humbly be stated that CEWPS will be the most influential invention in the domain of digital computing (Figure 4.6).

Violet Blue, an award-winning author who writes for Ctnet, eloquently describes the psychological profile of hackers:

> The dark myth perpetuated in the media that most hackers attending hacker conventions are motivated by revenge, reputation enhancement, and personal financial gain at the expense of others was simply not supported by the data collected. Instead, apart from tending not to read others' body language cues very easily, most hackers attending conferences seem to feel that this personal liability can be compensated by their keen ability to focus on details in creative ways not commonly found in the general population. I think the practical conclusion here is that hackers have complicated gifts.

Theory of Reasoned Action

Developed by Martin Fischbein and Icek Ajzen in 1967, the Theory of Reasoned Action (TRA) aims to explain the relationship between attitudes and behaviors within human action.

$$\text{Criminal intent} = (\text{Benefit value} \times \text{Attained likelihood})$$

$$-(\text{Disadvantage value} \times \text{Realization likelihood})$$

Underlying the psychology of the criminal hacker may be a deep sense of inferiority. Consequently, the mastery of computer technology, or the shutdown of a major site, might bestow on him or her a sense of power. *It's a population that takes refuge in computers because of their problems sustaining real-world relationships ... Causing millions of dollars of damage is a real power trip.*

It seems evident that most AVT providers do not have any "formal" courses on the subject of *behavioral cyber criminology*. AVT software providers should focus on the *cause* and not the *effect*. Pre-mortem is more fact-finding than post-mortem, which is after the fact. In other words, AVT providers are in the business of *incident response* and shy away from *incident forecast modeling*. In other words, they deal with "what happened" rather than "Why did it happen." That explains why AVT software are reactive and not proactively predictive. Studying about criminal profiling can definitely contribute to learning more about cybercrime. Criminal profiling is a systematic knowledge structure referred to as "behavioral evidence analysis" (BEA).

We examined SANS's website (www.sans.org) and we were impressed by the variety of courses and training, but there was no mention of BEA.

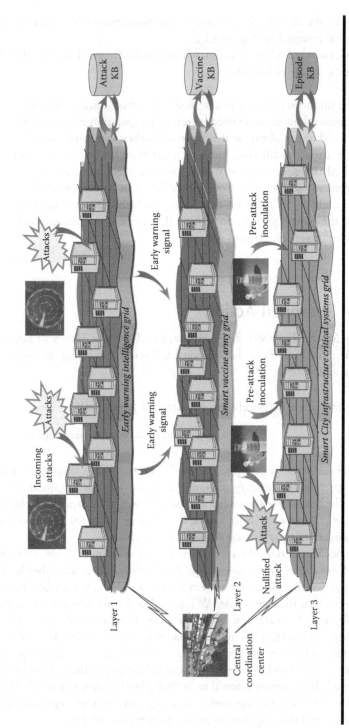

Figure 4.6 The top two grids are components of the digital immunity system, which is fully autonomic (driverless), guarding every device of the IoT and the critical infrastructures.

New, smarter cyber threats emerge every day and advanced, evasive techniques are becoming standard hacker protocol. Most security solutions, whether legacy or newer systems, adapt to new threats reactively, limited by their knowledge and detection logic.

In *The Art of War*, the most famous and most important military treatise in Asia for the last 2000 years, Sun Tzu said: "It is said that if you know your enemies and know yourself, you will not be imperiled in a hundred battles; if you do not know your enemies but do know yourself, you will win one and lose one; if you do not know your enemies nor yourself, you will be imperiled in every single battle."

AVT software producers have a social and ethical responsibility—before technical—to protect the business world and society from this growing evil. The focus of AVT software producers has been on selling inefficient products with glaring grandiosity, but the world is still suffering from the deep wounds of "hack ology." The psychological aspects of incidents will formulate more *direct* plans of action against the attackers—who are executing the evil act. The human element seems to have been lost in formal security education. We've made a complete circle, back to our previous statement: "the AVT business has been running a flat tire." We will articulate this weakness with more revealing facts.

When you visit a website whose URL starts with "https," a small padlock symbol appears in the browser window. This indicates that the website is secured using a digital certificate issued by one of a few trusted certification authorities (CAs). To ensure that the digital certificate is legitimate, the browser verifies its signature using standard cryptographic algorithms.

January 12: Operation Aurora Google publicly revealed that it has been on the receiving end of a "highly sophisticated and targeted attack on our corporate infrastructure originating from China that resulted in the theft of intellectual property from Google."

Wrong Crystal Ballers

Ken Olsen, founder of legendary minicomputer company Digital Equipment Corporation (DEC), stated: "There is no reason for any individual to have a computer at home." LOL. Ken Olsen is really eating his words. Forget the home, people have computers in their pockets. Even Bill Gates had myopic vision about the Internet. "I see little commercial potential for the internet for the next 10 years," Gates allegedly said at one Comdex trade event in 1994. Gates is a competitive guy. But in the end, Microsoft's reliance on proprietary technology ended up hamstringing the company in the long run. Current CEO Satya Nadella has gone a long way toward opening up the company's technology, to the delight of customers and developers.

Ballmer, the CEO of Microsoft, once said: "The Internet was designed for the PC. The Internet is not designed for the iPhone." And in a 2007 interview with

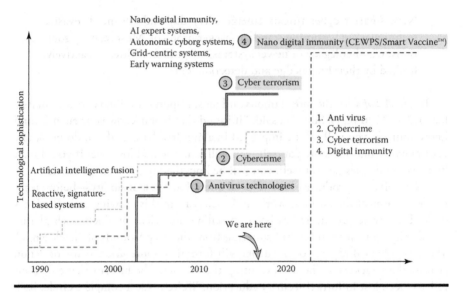

Figure 4.7   Cyber terrorism leads the way in the malware race, followed by cybercrime; AVT software trails behind. Since necessity is the mother of invention, digital immunity will prevail as the most intelligent, cognitive, and predictive shield to protect the Smart City from the Virus Rain™ and masquerading attacks. (© 2014 Copyright MERIT CyberSecurity Group. All rights reserved.)

USA Today, he said: "There's no chance that the iPhone is going to get any significant market share. No chance. It's a $500 subsidized item. They may make a lot of money."

Myopic vision led Ballmer, the Harvard drop out, to big surprises. The Internet became the juggernaut of the 20th century and the 21st century as well. Figure 4.7 shows that NT will cause the most phenomenal hysteria to plague the world. Everything that needs to be reliable, safe, and sturdy has to go nano.

Digital Immunity, the Holy Grail of Cybersecurity

If we go back to the basics and review how the human body fights disease, we conclude that immunity is defense by offense. There is *a striking similarity between cyberattack and body disease.* Both are pathogenic agents that sneak unexpectedly into infrastructure and internal systems, creating genetic/nutritional disorders and toxic agents, and spreading physical damage. We do know that the human body's immune system is the only robust defense mechanism that protects us from constant attack by potentially lethal invisible organisms.

Leveraging medical knowledge that leads us to immunity vaccines, we can take a similar approach to launch a new chapter in enterprise systems immunity. The

Smart Vaccine is the replication of the human immune system. The idea is fascinating and straightforward. Build a "defense by offense" mechanism to immunize any critical infrastructure or mission-critical enterprise system. This is the only way to outsmart cyber malware.

Since innovation is driven by technology, Microsoft has taken the lead and set the pace to establish its kingdom. System security was not an issue until Microsoft penetrated the Internet with its "half-cooked" Internet Explorer, which was an annoying speed bump to progress. Antivirus companies have been marching to Microsoft's drum beat and cautiously trying not to step on the turf of the software giant. Hardware vendors also paid homage to Microsoft. Software companies that challenged Microsoft were either doomed or acquired.

Microsoft has never been a security elite company and that's why AVT providers have had to remain under the radar of Microsoft, in order to survive. Most of them have survived because they did not advance beyond Microsoft's marching orders. Consumers were lured to buy an antivirus software with their new PCs and laptops as the ultimate "life jacket." The health of system security stagnated and did not offer any significant "radical" solution to address cyber terrorism. Zero-day attacks were big time and it was party time for the black hat community.

AVT Software Is the Hijacker!

Former Firefox developer Robert O'Callaghan, now a free agent and safe from the public relations (PR) tentacles of his corporate overlord, says that "antivirus software is terrible, AV vendors are terrible, and that you should uninstall your antivirus software immediately—unless you use Microsoft's Windows Defender, which is apparently okay."

Justin Schuh, Google Chrome's security chief and one of the world's top information security experts, believes that antivirus software is "my single biggest impediment to shipping a secure browser." He goes on to explain that meddling AV software delayed Win32 Flash sandboxing "for over a year" and that further sandboxing efforts are still on hold due to AVT software. "The man-in-the-middle (MitM) nature of antivirus also causes a stream of TLS errors," says Schuh, which in turn breaks some elements of HTTPS/HSTS.

These are two recent instances where browser developers have been increasingly upset with AVT software. Back in 2012, Nicholas Nethercote, another system engineer working on Firefox's MemShrink project, said "McAfee is killing us." In that case, Nethercote was trying to reduce the memory footprint of Firefox, and found that gnarly browser add-ons like McAfee were eating memory like pigs, among other things. If you venture off-piste into the browser mailing lists, anti-antivirus sentiment has bubbled away just below the surface for a very long time.

AVT software is incredibly invasive when it steps into the privileged areas of system memory. An antivirus, in an attempt to catch viruses before they can infect your system, forcibly hooks itself into other pieces of software on your computer, such as your browser, word processor, and even the operating system (OS) kernel. O'Callaghan gives one particularly shocking example: "Back when we first made sure ASLR was working for Firefox on Windows, many AV vendors broke it by injecting their own ASLR-disabled DLLs into our processes." ASLR, or address-space layout randomization, is one of the better protections against buffer overflow exploits.

In June 2016, Google's Tavis Ormandy, a Project Zero researcher, found 25 high-severity bugs in Symantec/Norton security products. "These vulnerabilities are as bad as it gets, they don't require any user interaction, they affect the default configuration, and the software runs at the highest privilege levels possible. In certain cases, on Windows, vulnerable code is even loaded into the kernel, resulting in remote kernel memory corruption." Over the past five years, Ormandy has found similar vulnerabilities in security software from Kaspersky, McAfee, Eset, Comodo, and Trend Micro; further details can be found at https://bugs.chromium. org. Studies in December 2007 showed that the effectiveness of antivirus software had decreased in the previous year, particularly against unknown or zero-day attacks.

Traditional AVT software relies heavily on signatures to identify malware. When a malware arrives into the hands of an antivirus firm, it is analyzed by malware researchers or by dynamic analysis systems. Then, once it is determined to be a malware, a proper signature of the file is extracted and added to the signatures database of the antivirus software. Many viruses start as a single infection and through either mutation or refinement by other attackers, can grow into dozens of slightly different strains, called "variants." Generic detection refers to the detection and removal of multiple threats using a single virus definition.

AVT programs have not been effective against new viruses, even programs that use non-signature-based methods that should detect new viruses. The reason is that the virus software developers "thoroughly" test their new viruses on major AVT software to make sure that they are not detected before releasing them into the wild. Pretty smart!

On December 2, 2016, as part of the IDG Contributor Network, *Computerworld* published an interesting report on AVT that although not very complimentary was very realistic. It said:

> Antivirus technology is probably older than most think, having been created in an early form in 1987 by developers who would curiously also go on to produce a virus authoring kit (perhaps renewing the old humorous urban legend about antivirus companies producing viruses to keep themselves in business).
>
> While the technology has improved over the years, its basic approach has always remained the same. It looks at incoming data from downloads, removable media and other sources for patterns of characters,

called signatures, which are known to indicate a malicious file. When identified, any such files are quarantined to prevent compromise of the system. The database of known signatures is updated frequently to account for new signatures.

The online consulting group GCN published an article prepared by (ISC)2 Government Advisory Council Executive Writers Bureau, Lou Magnotti, titled "Is Antivirus Software Still Relevant?":

> Federal agencies are big users of antivirus software, and regardless of their technical competence, government security professionals still find themselves victims of malware. Unfortunately, simply installing antivirus technology does not protect today's endpoints.

Final Analysis

In the final analysis, we present what we have learned about the harsh reality of the AVT industry:

- AVT software has not progressed at the same pace as malware software. It cannot and will not be able to exterminate, on their own turf, the massive attacks aimed at banks, governments, department stores, and computer companies.
- There is a very good reason why the malware industry gets high marks. Malware strategists plan their attack, rehearse it, and select the time and the place.
- There is no interest in cyber adversary characterization. AVT providers do not invest quality time and effort auditing the hacker mind, rating the attack with characterization metrics, or building and using cyberattack models.
- There is no methodology to build a knowledge engine for attacker profiling.
- AVT software is not suited to Smart City protection. A new design is required.
- AVT software is not suited to fighting global terrorism. A new design is required.
- AVT software is not equipped with a cognitive early warning predictive capability.
- AVT software doesn't have autonomic functionalities: self-configuring, self-healing, self-managing, and self-protecting.
- AVT software doesn't have Smart Grid functionalities to protect a Smart City.
- AVT software lacks radical innovation, not just endpoint protection. DI is the most viable security technology for a Smart City.

Glossary

Attribution: The process of establishing who is behind a hack. Often, attribution is the most difficult part of responding to a major breach since experienced hackers may hide behind layers of online services that mask their true location and identity. Many incidents, such as the Sony hack, may never produce any satisfactory attribution.

Backdoor: Entering a protected system using a password can be described as going through the front door. Companies may build "backdoors" into their systems, however, so that developers can bypass authentication and dive right into the program. Backdoors are usually secret, but may be exploited by hackers if they are revealed or discovered.

Black hat: A black hat hacker is someone who hacks for personal gain and/or who engages in illicit and unsanctioned activities. As opposed to white hat hackers (see White hat), who traditionally hack in order to alert companies and improve services, black hat hackers may instead sell the weaknesses they discover to other hackers or use them.

Botnet: Is your computer part of a botnet? It could be, and you might not know it. Botnets, or zombie armies, are networks of computers controlled by an attacker. Having control over hundreds or thousands of computers lets bad actors perform certain types of cyberattacks, such as a DDoS (see DDoS). Buying thousands of computers wouldn't be economical, however, so hackers deploy malware to infect random computers that are connected to the Internet. If your computer gets infected, your machine might be stealthily performing a hacker's bidding in the background without you ever noticing.

Brute force: A brute force attack is arguably the least sophisticated way of breaking into a password-protected system, short of simply obtaining the password itself. A brute force attack will usually consist of an automated process of trial-and-error to guess the correct password. Most modern encryption systems use different methods for slowing down brute force attacks, making it hard or impossible to try all combinations in a reasonable amount of time.

Bug: You've probably heard of this one. A bug is a flaw or error in a software program. Some are harmless or merely annoying, but some can be exploited by hackers. That's why many companies have started using bug bounty programs to pay anyone who spots a bug before the bad guys do.

Chip-off: A chip-off attack requires the hacker to physically remove memory storage chips in a device so that information can be scraped from them using specialized software. This attack has been used by law enforcement to break into PGP-protected Blackberry phones.

Cracking: A general term to describe breaking into a security system, usually for nefarious purposes. According to the *New Hacker's Dictionary* published by

MIT Press, the words "hacking" and "hacker" (see Hacker) in mainstream parlance have come to subsume the words "cracking" and "cracker," and that's misleading. Hackers are tinkerers; they're not necessarily bad guys. Crackers are malicious. At the same time, you'll see cracking used to refer to breaking, say, digital copyright protections—which many people feel is a just and worthy cause—and in other contexts, such as penetration testing (see Penetration testing or pen testing), without the negative connotation.

Crypto: Short for cryptography, the science of secret communication or the procedures and processes for hiding data and messages with encryption (see Encryption).

Dark web: The dark web is made up of sites that are not indexed by Google and are only accessible through specialty networks such as Tor (see Tor). Often, the dark web is used by website operators who want to remain anonymous. Everything on the dark web is on the Deep Web, but not everything on the Deep Web is on the dark web.

DDoS: This type of cyberattack has become popular in recent years because it's relatively easy to execute and its effects are immediately obvious. DDoS stands for distributed denial-of-service attack, which means an attacker is using a number of computers to flood the target with data or requests for data. This causes the target—usually a website—to slow down or become unavailable. Attackers may also use the simpler denial-of-service attack, which is launched from one computer.

Deep Web: This term and "dark web" or "dark net" are sometimes used interchangeably, though they shouldn't be. The Deep Web is the part of the Internet that is not indexed by search engines. It includes password-protected pages, paywalled sites, encrypted networks, and databases—lots of boring stuff.

DEF CON: One of the most famous hacking conferences in the world, which started in 1992 and takes place every summer in Las Vegas.

Digital certificate: A digital passport or stamp of approval that proves the identity of a person, website, or service on the Internet. In more technical terms, a digital certificate proves that someone is in possession of a certain cryptographic key that, traditionally, can't be forged. Some of the most common digital certificates are those of websites, which ensure your connection to them is properly encrypted. These get displayed on your browser as a green padlock.

Encryption: The process of scrambling data or a message making it unreadable and secret. The opposite is decryption, the decoding of the message. Both encryption and decryption are functions of cryptography. Encryption is used by individuals as well as corporations and in digital security for consumer products.

End-to-end encryption: A particular type of encryption where a message or data gets scrambled or encrypted on one end, for example, your computer or phone, and gets decrypted on the other end, such as someone else's computer. The data is scrambled in a way that, at least in theory, only the sender and receiver—and no one else—can read it.

Evil maid attack: As the name probably suggests, an evil maid attack is a hack that requires physical access to a computer—the kind of access an evil maid might have while tidying his or her employer's office, for example. By having physical access, a hacker can install software to track your use and gain a doorway even to encrypted information.

Exploit: An exploit is a way or process to take advantage of a bug or vulnerability in a computer or application. Not all bugs lead to exploits. Think of it this way: If your door was faulty, it could simply be that it makes a weird sound when you open it, or that its lock can be picked. Both are flaws but only one can help a burglar get in. The way the criminal picks the lock would be the exploit.

Forensics: On TV shows like *CSI*, forensic investigations involve a series of methodical steps in order to establish what happened during a crime. When it comes to a hack, however, investigators are looking for digital fingerprints instead of physical ones. This process usually involves trying to retrieve messages or other information from a device—perhaps a phone, a desktop computer, or a server—used, or abused, by a suspected criminal.

GCHQ: The UK's equivalent of the US National Security Agency. GCHQ, or Government Communications Headquarters, focuses on foreign intelligence, especially around terrorism threats and cybersecurity. It also investigates the digital child pornography trade. "As these adversaries work in secret, so too must GCHQ," the organization says on its website. "We cannot reveal publicly everything that we do, but we remain fully accountable."

Hacker: This term has become—wrongly—synonymous with someone who breaks into systems or hacks things illegally. Originally, hackers were simply tinkerers, or people who enjoyed "exploring the details of programmable systems and how to stretch their capabilities," as MIT Press's *New Hacker's Dictionary* puts it. Hackers can now be used to refer to both the good guys, also known as white hat hackers, who play and tinker with systems with no malicious intent (and actually often with the intent of finding flaws so they can be fixed), and cybercriminals, or "black hat" hackers, or "crackers."

Hacktivist: A "hacktivist" is someone who uses his or her hacking skills for political ends. A hacktivist's actions may be small, such as defacing the public website of a security agency or other government department, or large, such as stealing sensitive government information and distributing it to citizens. One often-cited example of a hacktivist group is Anonymous.

Hashing: Say you have a piece of text that should remain secret, like a password. You could store the text in a secret folder on your machine, but if anyone gained access to it you'd be in trouble. To keep the password a secret, you could also "hash" it with a program that executes a function resulting in garbled text representing the original information. This abstract representation is called a hash. Companies may store passwords or facial recognition data with hashes to improve their security.

HTTPS/SSL/TLS: This stands for hypertext transfer protocol, with the "S" for "Secure." The HTTP is the basic framework that controls how data is transferred across the web, while HTTPS adds a layer of encryption that protects your connection to the most important sites in your daily browsing—your bank, your email provider, and social network. HTTPS uses the protocols SSL and TLS to not only protect your connection, but also to prove the identity of the site, so that when you type https: //gmail.com, you can be confident that you're really connecting to Google and not an imposter site.

InfoSec: An abbreviation of "information security." It's the inside baseball term for what's more commonly known as cybersecurity, a term that irks most people who prefer InfoSec.

Jailbreak: Circumventing the security of a device, like an iPhone or a PlayStation, to remove a manufacturer's restrictions, generally with the goal to make it run software from non-official sources.

Keys: Modern cryptography uses digital "keys." In the case of PGP encryption, a public key is used to encrypt or "lock" messages and a secret key is used to decrypt or "unlock" them. In other systems, there may only be one secret key that is shared by all parties. In either case, if an attacker gains control of the key that does the unlocking, he or she may have a good chance at gaining access.

Lulz: An Internet-speak variation of "LOL" (short for "laughing out loud") that is regularly employed among the black hat hacker set, typically to justify a hack or leak done at the expense of another person or entity. For example: *y did i leak all contracts and employee info linked to Sketchy Company X? for teh lulz.*

Malware: This stands for "malicious software." It simply refers to any kind of malicious program or software that is designed to damage or hack its target. Viruses, worms, Trojan horses, ransomware, spyware, adware, and more are malware.

Man-in-the-middle: A man-in-the-middle or MitM is a common attack where someone surreptitiously puts himself or herself between two parties, impersonating them. This allows the malicious attacker to intercept and potentially alter their communication. With this type of attack, one can just passively listen in, relaying messages and data between the two parties, or even alter and manipulate the data flow.

Metadata: This is simply data about data. If you were to send an email, for example, the text you type to your friend will be the content of the message, but the address you used to send it, the address you sent it to, and the time you sent it would all be metadata. This may sound innocuous, but with enough sources of metadata—for example, geolocation information from a photo posted to social media—it can be trivial to piece together someone's identity or location.

NIST: The National Institute of Standards and Technology is an arm of the US Department of Commerce dedicated to science and metrics that support industrial innovation. The NIST is responsible for developing information security standards for use by the federal government, and therefore it's often cited as an authority on which encryption methods are rigorous enough to use given modern threats.

Nonce: A portmanteau of number and once, nonce literally means "a number only used once." It's a string of numbers generated by a system to identify a user for a one-time-use session or specific task. After that session, or a set period of time, the number isn't used again.

OpSec: Short for operational security, OpSec is all about keeping information secret, online and off. Originally a military term, OpSec is a practice and in some ways a philosophy that begins with identifying what information needs to be kept secret, and whom you're trying to keep it a secret from. "Good" OpSec will flow from there, and may include everything from passing messages on Post-Its instead of emails to using digital encryption. In other words: Loose tweets destroy fleets.

OTR: What do you do if you want to have an encrypted conversation, but it needs to happen fast? OTR, or off-the-record, is a protocol for encrypting instant messages end to end. Unlike PGP, which is generally used for email and so each conversant has one public and one private key in his or her possession, OTR uses a single temporary key for every conversation, which makes it more secure if an attacker hacks into your computer and gets a hold of the keys. OTR is also generally easier to use than PGP.

Password managers: Using the same crummy password for all of your logins—from your bank account, to Seamless, to your Tinder profile—is a bad idea. All a hacker needs to do is get access to one account to break into them all. But memorizing a unique string of characters for every platform is daunting. Enter the password manager: software that keeps track of your various passwords for you, and can even auto-generate super complicated and long passwords for you. All you need to remember is your master password to log into the manager and access all your many different logins.

Penetration testing or pen testing: If you set up a security system for your home, or your office, or your factory, you'd want to be sure it was safe from attackers, right? One way to test a system's security is to employ people—pen testers—to purposely hack it in order to identify weak points. Pen testing is related to red teaming, although it may be done in a more structured, less aggressive way.

PGP: "Pretty good privacy" is a method of encrypting data, generally emails, so that anyone intercepting them will only see garbled text. PGP uses asymmetric cryptography, which means that the person sending a message uses a "public" encryption key to scramble it, and the recipient uses a secret "private" key to decode it. Despite being more than two decades old, PGP is still a formidable method of encryption, although it can be notoriously difficult to use in practice, even for experienced users.

Phishing: This is really more of a form of social engineering than hacking or cracking. In a phishing scheme, an attacker typically reaches out to a victim in order to extract specific information that can be used in a later attack. That may mean posing as customer support from Google, Facebook, or the victim's cell phone carrier, for example, and asking the victim to click on a malicious link—or simply asking the victim to send back information, such as a password, in an email. Attackers usually blast out phishing attempts by the thousands, but sometimes employ more targeted attacks, known as spear phishing (see Spear phishing).

Plaintext: Exactly what it sounds like—text that has not been garbled with encryption. This definition would be considered plaintext. You may also hear plaintext being referred to as "cleartext," since it refers to text that is being kept out in the open, or "in the clear." Companies with very poor security may store user passwords in plaintext, even if the folder they're in is encrypted, just waiting for a hacker to steal it.

Pwned: This is computer nerd jargon (or "leetspeak") for the verb "own." In the video game world, a player that beats another player can say that he or she pwned him or her. Among hackers, the term has a similar meaning, only instead of beating someone in a game, a hacker that has gained access to another user's computer can say that he or she pwned him or her. For example, the website "Have I Been Pwned?" will tell you if your online accounts have been compromised in the past.

Rainbow table: A rainbow table is a complex technique that allows hackers to simplify the process of guessing what passwords hide behind a "hash" (see Hashing).

Ransomware: A type of malware that locks your computer and won't let you access your files. You'll see a message telling you how much the ransom is and where to send payment, usually requested in bitcoin, in order to get your files back. This is a good racket for hackers, which is why many now consider it an "epidemic," as people typically are willing to pay a few hundred bucks in order to recover their machine. It's not just individuals, either. In early 2016, the Hollywood Presbyterian Medical Center in Los Angeles paid around $17,000 after being hit by a ransomware attack.

RAT: Stands for remote access tool or remote access Trojan. RATs are really scary when used as malware. An attacker who successfully installs a RAT on your computer can gain full control of your machine. There is also a legitimate business in RATs for people who want to access their office computer from home, and so on. The worst part about RATs? Many malicious ones are available in the Internet's underground for sale or even for free, so attackers can be pretty unskilled and still use this sophisticated tool.

Red team: To ensure the security of their computer systems and to suss out any unknown vulnerabilities, companies may hire hackers who organize into a "red team" in order to run oppositional attacks against the system and attempt to completely take it over. In these cases, being hacked is a good thing because organizations may fix vulnerabilities before someone who's not on their payroll does. Red teaming is a general concept that is employed across many sectors, including as a military strategy.

Root: In most computers, "root" is the common name given to the most fundamental (and thus most powerful) level of access in the system, or it is the name of the account that has those privileges. That means the "root" can install applications and delete and create files. If hackers "gains root," they can do whatever they want on the computer or the system that they have compromised. This is the holy grail of hacking.

Rootkit: A rootkit is a particular type of malware that lives deep in your system and is activated each time you boot it up, even before your operating system starts. This makes rootkits hard to detect, persistent, and able to capture practically all data on the infected computer.

Salting: When protecting passwords or text, "hashing" (see Hashing) is a fundamental process that turns plaintext into garbled text. To make hashing even more effective, companies or individuals can add an extra series of random bytes, known as a "salt," to the password before the hashing process. This adds an extra layer of protection.

Script kiddies: This is a derisive term for someone who has a little bit of computer savvy and who's only able to use off-the-shelf software to do things like knock websites offline or sniff passwords over an unprotected Wi-Fi access point. This is basically a term to discredit someone who claims to be a skilled hacker.

Shodan: It's been called "hacker's Google" and a "terrifying" search engine. Think of it as a Google, but for connected devices rather than websites. Using Shodan, you can find unprotected webcams, baby monitors, printers, medical devices, gas pumps, and even wind turbines. While that sounds terrifying, Shodan's value is precisely that it helps researchers find these devices and alert their owners so that they can secure them.

Side-channel attack: Your computer's hardware is always emitting a steady stream of barely perceptible electrical signals. A side-channel attack seeks to identify patterns in these signals in order to find out what kind of computations the machine is doing. For example, a hacker "listening in" to your hard drive whirring away while generating a secret encryption key may be able to reconstruct that key, effectively stealing it, without your knowledge.

Sniffing: A way of intercepting data sent over a network without being detected, using special sniffer software. Once the data is collected, a hacker can sift through it to get useful information, like passwords. It's considered a particularly dangerous hack because it's hard to detect and can be performed from inside or outside a network.

Social engineering: Not all hacks are carried out by staring at a *Matrix*-like screen of green text. Sometimes, gaining entry to a secure system is as easy as placing a phone call or sending an email and pretending to be somebody else—namely, somebody who regularly has access to said system but forgot his or her password that day. Phishing (see Phishing) attacks include aspects of social engineering, because they involve convincing somebody of an email sender's legitimacy before anything else.

Spear phishing: And social engineering are often used interchangeably, but the latter is a more tailored, targeted form of phishing (see Social engineering), where hackers try to trick victims into clicking on malicious links or attachments pretending to be a close acquaintance, rather than a more generic sender, such as a social network or corporation. When done well, spear phishing can be extremely effective and powerful. As a noted security expert says, "give a man a 0day and he'll have access for a day, teach a man to phish and he'll have access for life."

Spoofing: Hackers can trick people into falling for a phishing attack (see Phishing) by forging their email address, for example, making it look like the address of someone the target knows. That's spoofing. It can also be used in telephone scams, or to create a fake website address.

Spyware: A specific type of malware or malicious software designed to spy, monitor, and potentially steal data from the target.

State actor: State actors are hackers or groups of hackers who are backed by a government, which may be the United States, Russia, or China. These hackers are often the most formidable, since they have virtually unlimited legal and financial resources of a nation state to back them. Think, for example, of the NSA. Sometimes, however, state actors can also be a group of hackers who receive tacit (or at least hidden from the public) support from their governments, such as the Syrian Electronic Army.

Tails: The Amnesic Incognito Live System. If you're really, really serious about digital security, this is the operating system endorsed by Edward Snowden. Tails is an amnesic system, which means your computer remembers nothing; it's like a fresh machine every time you boot up. The software is free and open source. While it's well-regarded, security flaws have been found.

Threat model: Imagine a game of chess. It's your turn and you're thinking about all the possible moves your opponent could make, as many turns ahead as you can. Have you left your queen unprotected? Is your king being worked into a corner checkmate? That kind of thinking is what security researchers do when designing a threat model. It's a catch-all term used to describe the capabilities of the enemy you want to guard against, and your own vulnerabilities. Are you an activist attempting to guard against a state-sponsored hacking team? Your threat model better be pretty robust. Just shoring up the network at your log cabin in the middle of nowhere? Maybe not as much cause to worry.

Token: A small physical device that allows its owner to log in or authenticate into a service. Tokens serve as an extra layer of security on top of a password, for example. The idea is that even if the password or key gets stolen, the hacker would need the actual physical token to abuse it.

Tor: Short for The Onion Router. Originally developed by the US Naval Research Laboratory, it's now used by bad guys (hackers, pedophiles) and good guys (activists, journalists) to anonymize their activities online. The basic idea is that there is a network of computers around the world—some operated by universities, some by individuals, some by governments—that will route your traffic in byzantine ways in order to disguise your true location. The Tor network is this collection of volunteer-run computers. The Tor Project is a nonprofit group that maintains the Tor software. The Tor browser is the free piece of software that lets you use Tor. Tor hidden services are websites that can only be accessed through Tor.

Verification (dump): The process by which reporters and security researchers go through hacked data and make sure that it's legitimate. This process is important to make sure that the data is authentic, and the claims of anonymous hackers are true, and not just an attempt to get some notoriety or make some money scamming people on the dark web.

Virus: A computer virus is a type of malware that typically is embedded and hidden in a program or file. Unlike a worm (see Worm), it needs human action to spread (such as a human forwarding a virus-infected attachment, or downloading a malicious program). Viruses can infect computers and steal data, delete data, encrypt it, or mess with it in just about any other way.

VPN: Stands for virtual private network. VPNs use encryption to create a private and secure channel to connect to the Internet when you're on a network that you don't trust (say a Starbucks or an Airbnb Wi-Fi). Think of a VPN as a tunnel from you to your destination, dug under the regular Internet. VPNs allow employees to connect to their employer's network remotely, and also help regular people protect their connection. VPNs also allow users to bounce off servers in other parts of the world, allowing them to look like they're connecting from there. This gives them the chance to circumvent censorship, such as China's Great Firewall, or view Netflix's US offerings while in Canada. There are endless VPNs, making it almost impossible to decide which ones are the best.

Vuln: An abbreviation for "vulnerability," it is another way to refer to bugs or software flaws that can be exploited by hackers.

Warez: Pronounced like the contraction for "where is" (where's), warez refers to pirated software that's typically distributed via technologies like BitTorrent and Usenet. Warez is sometimes laden with malware, taking advantage of people's desire for free software.

White hat: A white hat hacker is someone who hacks with the goal of fixing and protecting systems. As opposed to black hat hackers (see Black hat), instead of taking advantage of their hacks or the bugs they find to make money illegally, they alert the companies and even help them fix the problem.

Worm: A specific type of malware that propagates and replicates itself automatically, spreading from computer to computer. The Internet's history is littered with worms, from the Morris worm, the first of its kind, to the famous Samy worm, which infected more than a million people on Myspace.

Zero-day: A zero-day or "0day" is a bug that's unknown to the software vendor, or at least it's not patched yet. The name comes from the notion that there have been zero-days between the discovery of the bug or flaw and the first attack taking advantage of it. Zero-days are the most prized bugs and exploits for hackers because a fix has yet to be deployed for them, so they're almost guaranteed to work.

Source: Selected terms related to this chapter from www.if4it.com/it-glossary and from publications and educational seminars of MERIT CyberSecuritySource from Merit CyberSecurity Knowledge Base.

Bibliography

http://www.computerworld.com/article/3146996/malware-vulnerabilities/is-antivirus-software-dead-at-last.html

Is antivirus software still relevant?: https://gcn.com/articles/2015/01/08/antivirus-software-still-relevant.aspx

The best anti-virus companies: https://antivirus.thetoptens.com/

Evolution of software enterprise: http://www.zdnet.com/article/the-evolution-of-enterprise-software-an-overview/

The first anti-virus: http://www.thewindowsclub.com/which-was-the-first-windows-virus-which-was-the-first-antivirus

Evolution of anti-virus software: http://www.networkworld.com/article/2287721/tech-primers/the-evolution-of-antivirus-software.html

Symantec Data Sheet: https://www.symantec.com/content/dam/symantec/docs/data-sheets/data-loss-prevention-solution-en.pdf

Botnet of Things: https://www.technologyreview.com/s/603500/10-breakthrough-technologies-2017-botnets-of-things/

Internet of DNA: https://www.technologyreview.com/s/535016/internet-of-dna/

Microsoft blog on security: https://blogs.microsoft.com/microsoftsecure/2017/01/17/microsofts-cyber-defense-operations-center-shares-best-practices/

Symantec Data Security Center: https://www.symantec.com/content/dam/symantec/docs/data-sheets/data-center-security-server-ds-6.7-en.pdf

Stuxnet worm discovery: https://eugene.kaspersky.com/2011/11/02/the-man-who-found-stuxnet-sergey-ulasen-in-the-spotlight/

Brain dump: https://sviehb.wordpress.com/

Hacking lingo: http://www.dourish.com/goodies/jargon.html

Anti-virus era is over: https://www.technologyreview.com/s/428166/the-antivirus-era-is-over/

Psychology of the hacker: https://www.sans.org/reading-room/whitepapers/incident/psychology-hacker-psychological-incident-handling-36077

Living without anti-virus: http://exodusdev.com/blog/mike/living-dangerously-no-anti-virus-or-firewall

Heimdal Security. https://heimdalsecurity.com/blog/10-reasons-why-your-traditional-antivirus-cant-detect-second-generation-malware/

Protecting the Smart Grid: http://rtcmagazine.com/articles/view/103264Endpoint; security: http://www.webopedia.com/TERM/E/endpoint_security.html

Grid architecture: https://www.cs.fsu.edu/~engelen/courses/HPC-adv-2008/Grid.pdf

Grid architecture: http://www.csus.edu/indiv/c/chingr/mis270/architecture.pdf

Malware networks: https://techcrunch.com/2011/07/27/a-look-at-the-size-shape-and-growing-threat-of-malware-networks-infographic/

Weakness in Internet security: https://www.sciencedaily.com/releases/2008/12/081231005357.htm?utm_source=TrendMD&utm_medium=cpc&utm_campaign=ScienceDaily_TrendMD_0

AVT evaluation with 25 experts: https://digitalguardian.com/blog/data-security-experts-answer-what-biggest-misconception-companies-have-about-endpoint-security

Endpoint security and response: http://www.cybersecuritydocket.com/2015/05/08/edr-the-future-of-cybersecurity-and-incident-response/

Microsoft purchases: https://en.wikipedia.org/wiki/List_of_mergers_and_acquisitions_by_Microsoft

Cyber Breach 2017: https://www.identityforce.com/blog/2017-data-breaches

CBS: http://www.cbs.com/shows/csi-cyber/news/1003888/these-cybercrime-statistics-will-make-you-think-twice-about-your-password-where-s-the-csi-cyber-team-when-you-need-them-/

Morphisec: http://2zprirhczd51638uv19ng3rp.wpengine.netdna-cdn.com/wp-content/uploads/2016/12/ENDPOINT-SECURITY-AS-USUAL_Think-Again.pdf

The top reasons why M&A deals fail: http://www.investopedia.com/articles/investing/111014/top-reasons-why-ma-deals-fail.asp

AVT top 10: http://www.top10bestantivirus.com/

It might be time to stop using anti-virus: https://arstechnica.com/information-technology/2017/01/antivirus-is-bad/

Why do companies merge with or acquire other companies? | Investopedia: http://www.investopedia.com/ask/answers/06/mareasons.asp#ixzz4amYwtSEY

HTTPS intercept: https://blog.hboeck.de/archives/869-How-Kaspersky-makes-you-vulnerable-to-the-FREAK-attack-and-other-ways-Antivirus-software-lowers-your-HTTPS-security.html

High severity bugs in Symantec: https://arstechnica.co.uk/security/2016/06/severe-bugs-25-symantec-norton-products-details/

Security key: https://arstechnica.co.uk/security/2016/12/this-low-cost-device-may-be-the-worlds-best-hope-against-account-takeovers/

IMB report on global crime: https://www-01.ibm.com/common/ssi/cgi-bin/ssialias?htmlfid=SEL03094WWEN

SANA psychology and the hacker: https://www.sans.org/reading-room/whitepapers/incident/psychology-hacker-psychological-incident-handling-36077

Nation-state attacks: http://cdn2.hubspot.net/hubfs/150964/Ponemon_Report_Oct._2015_-_The_Rise_of_Nation_State_Attacks.pdf?t=1488835615078

Cognitive hacking: http://www.ists.dartmouth.edu/library/301.pdf

Chapter 5

DDoS Malware: The Curse of Virus Rain™

Introduction

A distributed denial-of-service (DDoS) attack is an Egyptian curse of biblical proportions! Heraclitus, the Greek philosopher, is quoted as saying "change is the only constant in life." We have translated his quote as "malware is the only constant hiccup in life."

On April 15, everyone in China is going to jump up and down simultaneously at noon, knocking the earth off its axis! And they are going to download whitehouse.gov simultaneously at noon, knocking the government's website off its axis!

In 2014, the denial-of-service (DoS) attack celebrated its 40th birthday. Born as the handiwork of a teenaged "computer geek," these attacks have since exploded in quantity—and sophistication.

A DoS attack is analogous to a large group of frantic people trying to get out of the main entrance of a building, causing a horrific stampede, trampling over one another, and blocking the rest of the crowd inside. A DoS is a famous queuing model where there's an infinity of arrivals and zero service.

The Virus Rain™

We refer to DDoS by a fancier term called the "Virus Rain™", which is made up of millions of distributed nano zombies unleashing clouds of stealth attack vectors to deliver millions of exploits. It is a replica of the classic attack on Pearl Harbor on December 7, 1941, a date that will live in infamy. Gary Sockrider at DDoS defense firm Arbor Networks said it right: "you ain't seen nothing yet." We created a nano-technology version of the attack (see Chapter 14), a unique scenario way ahead of its time—a nano attack on the city of San Francisco. Cyber terrorism is going to become so big—bigger than the Olympics or the Hajj— that it will eventually open the eyes of cybersecurity chiefs.

There are actually two versions of the Virus Rain: the classic version and the nano version. This book discusses both versions. The nano version is worse than the 1665 London bubonic plague because this attack is incurable, unstoppable, and invisible. It is at the molecular scale. Using antivirus technologies is like fighting with a bow and arrow. Only our version of Nano Digital Immunity will be able to stand against and defend systems.

The Virus Rain is an advanced version of the Japanese "Mirai" that hijacks "innocent" computer systems and surveillance cameras and turns them into zombies and remotely controlled "bots," which are used as part of a botnet in large-scale network attacks. These zombies will serve as remote launch pads for digital attacks primarily targeting online consumers of Internet of Things (IoT) devices. The attacked region turned shock and awe havoc from the heavy damage to most of the busy infrastructures web servers that controlled the region. The Virus Rain was written in C language, while the nano Virus Rain belongs to a different generation, built with artificial intelligence (AI) components. It is unfair to compare the two versions, as it is similar to comparing an F-22 and a buggy.

The Virus Rain is the harvest of a massive tactical brigade of programmable DDoS botnets—different from the nano botnet that fires "automatic rounds" with an unbelievable amount of payload at a speed of 620 Gbps. All the technologies of the attack are enabled and currently used today. The Russkill group focuses on flooding web servers with Hypertext Transfer Protocol (HTTP) requests, generating an immense amount of garbage traffic. Darkness DDoS bots create mammoth amounts of Internet Control Message Protocol (ICMP) and HTTP floods. Slowloris is another attack tool that causes a DoS to trick web servers about logging requests. Evil-minded zombie computers (slave) in addition create DDoS-for-hire services to cripple transportation. Erratic Demise's HTTP floods target servers with erroneous application programming interface (API) flags that read HTTP requests from a local server rather than reading them from a remote server.

The Mariposa botnet specializes in cyber scamming and DDoS. It was designed for the Virus Rain to carry 12 million unique IP addresses or up to 1 million individual zombie computers infected with the "Butterfly (*mariposa* in Spanish) bot", making it one of the largest botnets, capable of generating flawed attack as Transmission Control Protocol (TCP) SYN floods. Authors also advertised that the tool is capable of creating a full TCP connection instead. Mariposa also does not generate multiple threads and therefore does not create a significant amount of traffic.

The most recent attacks on financial institution have been launched via the BroBot *itsoknoproblembro* toolkit. This advanced toolkit supports multiple attack methods, including HTTP, HTTPS, and domain name system (DNS). The people behind this virus-like tool have been breaking into thousands of web servers with this malware and turning them into Brobots. After being compromised, the victim's server forms a new botnet, and is given commands to attempt to overwhelm targeted banks' servers with various attacks.

The was designed to send a tsunami of a million simultaneous attacks, launched from remote botnet clouds. It hit the heart of New England with payloads of DDoS firing mutating stealth-smart bombs, backdoor hemorrhoid Trojans, autonomic heart attack, and kamikaze agents. It was like the Four Horsemen of the Apocalypse, or the final battle of Armageddon. It is no longer just hacking, it is commandeering the Internet and reprogramming good devices into a Mongolian army of wicked zombies.

The National Cyber Emergency Response Team (CERT) estimates that the Virus Rain carries over 500,000 different types of "mutating" DDoS viruses that have been unleashed to paralyze the North East of the United States. It is uniquely referred to as "The Electronic Pearl Harbor 2" (Figure 5.1).

New, sophisticated DDoS attacks have increased throughout the world (Figure 5.2), and security experts predict that this trend will continue. The current defense tools are not capable defending businesses and homes. Akamai's most recent State of the Internet Security Report 2016 reveals that Internet and web attacks are increasing in number, severity, and duration. The latest statistic is a scary 125% over a year! The world is having serious problems with all the facets of malware. Protecting against DDoS attacks is only one aspect of securing a business, and, like every other aspect of security, it is changing constantly. DDoS attackers originally coordinated people, then there were botnets of PCs, then botnets of servers, and now botnets of IoT devices. At each point in the evolution of DDoS, the landscape has permanently changed. Today, there is a new baseline DDoS attack size, and organizations have to be ready to defend against it. We expect to see many more vulnerable and compromised devices before devices become more secure. The good news is that there are significant reasons for companies to invest in security in the future. Another piece of good news is that the resources used to fuel IoT botnets, while considerable, are not infinite. It is foreseeable that there will be contention for resources among botnets, meaning we may see the number of attacks increasing, but the size of many attacks will fall. The counter to this is that attackers will find new devices to compromise and once again increase their capabilities. This is not a system that will find equilibrium in the short term. Seven of 10 DDoS attacks greater than 300+ Gbps occurred in 2016, including three in the last quarter. Insecure IoT devices continue to be a big source of DDoS traffic. The largest DDoS attacks in Q4 came not from Mirai but from Spike botnets. Experts at Akamai spotted a new malware kit named Spike, which is used by bad actors to run DDoS attacks through desktops and IoT devices.

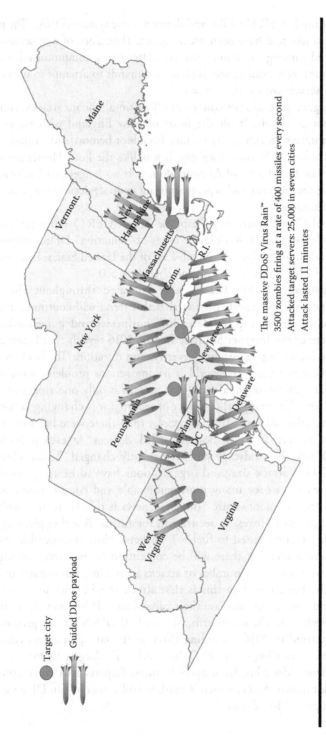

The massive DDoS Virus Rain™
3500 zombies firing at a rate of 400 missiles every second
Attacked target servers: 25,000 in seven cities
Attack lasted 11 minutes

● Target city

Guided DDos payload

Figure 5.1 Calamity is spelled DDoS, where raindrops are replaced by bomb drops. This is the Electronic Pearl Harbor 2. (©

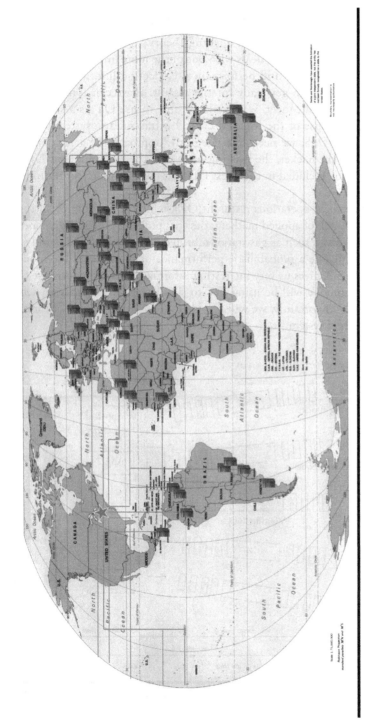

Figure 5.2 This is what a realistic Virus Rain DDoS looks like. All these slave servers from somewhere in the world are flooding the northeastern region of the United States with mutating attacks. (© 2014 Copyright MERIT CyberSecurity Group. All rights reserved.)

Queuing Theory Is Future Visioning

The timing is perfect to introduce queuing theory (QT) to learn more about forecasting DDoS attacks. QT deals with one of the more unpleasant experiences of life, predicting behavior and performance. Collecting information before an assault is the best way to get ready for the assault. If we can forecast weather, hurricanes, stocks, and cancer, we should be able to use QT as a smart model to measure our defense of the IoT and critical infrastructure systems (CIS). In order to combat DDoS, we need to strategically approach the attack and learn everything about the hacker, the hacking tools, and the hacked target. A knowledge engine will be included in the latest DDoS attack scenarios for training and better response.

QT is a branch of operations research (OR), which is the king of all the sciences. QT is a branch of applied mathematics that provides probabilistic modeling tools for *service systems* such as gas stations, bridge tolls, bank cashiers, and so on; the model will provide a probabilistic performance of the system. The model, as shown in Figure 5.3, gives us very interesting information that supports the operation of the system. We will be using QT to simulate DDoS attacks on selected targets, but more importantly, we will be able to forecast the arrival of the attack vectors to the target system.

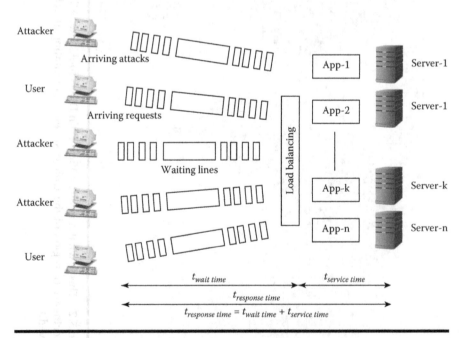

Figure 5.3 A simplistic model of a DDoS attacking a victim's multiple servers at the same time.

DDoS Attack Forecast and Mitigation Mathematical Performance Equations

Without QT science, it would not be possible to design defect-free anything, for example, highway traffic, bridge traffic, airplane movements, bank and grocery stores customer traffic; even in industrial engineering, system performance analysis, transportation planning, intersection traffic light design, and emergency department and paramedic arrival times. QT can be applied to any industry. The Internet uses QT tools to study big data access time to determine the arrival time of the attack to the target system, to calculate the number of attacks from different types, and the length of time for the service denial when the processor and memory are tied up. QT allows the analyst to conduct "what-if" scenarios to determine all the possible probabilities of the attack. Learning QT is beyond the scope of this book (wait until the next book). Every corporation would pay any amount to know when a cyberattack, or even its cloud, will hit its data center. The following is the most important information that we would like to get from the queuing model:

■ When will the attack occur?
■ How long is the queue of requests (attack and legitimate)?
■ What is the nature of the attack?
■ How long will the attack last?
■ How fast will the target system get saturated (the thrashing point)?
■ How many packets will hit the target system?

Basic Queuing Theory Formulas

λ = arrival rate of attacks to the server (User Datagram Protocol [UDP] and ICMP)
T_q = Average time for attack packet in the system (wait and process)
T_s = Average service time for a packet to be served in the system
N_w = Number of requests waiting in the queue
N_q = Number of requests waiting in the queue and being executed by the system
C = Number of servers used; $C = 1$ if there's one server
M = Random arrival/service rate stochastic following Poisson distribution
D = Deterministic service rate (constant rate)

M/D/1 Case (Random Arrival, Deterministic Service, and One Server)

Average mixed packets in waiting line $N_w = (2\rho - \rho 2) / 2(1 - \rho)$
Average total time per attack (wait and process) $E(v) = 2 - \rho / 2T_s(1 - \rho)$

Average waiting time per attack $T_w = \rho / 2T_s(1-\rho)$

M/M/1 Case (Random Arrival, Random Service, and One Server)

Utilization of the target server, mean service time/mean interarrival time $\rho = \lambda / T_s$

The probability of having zero requests in the systems $P_{zero} = 1-\rho$

The probability of having (n) attacks on the Smart Grid $P_n = \rho_n P_{zero}$

Average number of attack packets in queue and inside server $N_q = \rho / (1-\rho)$

Average time of attack packets in the server (wait + execution)

$T_q = T_s / (1-\rho) = \rho / \lambda(1-\rho)$

Average time for packet in waiting line $T_w = T_q - 1 / \rho$

Average number of packets in waiting line $N_w = \rho^2 / (1-\rho)$

Average number of packets in the queue including the one being served

$$N_q = \rho + \frac{\rho^2}{2(1-\rho)}\left[1+\left(\frac{\sigma_s}{T_s}\right)^2\right] \quad \text{(see Figure 5.4)}$$

Average time of packet entry in the queue including the one being served

$$T_q = T_s + \frac{\rho T_s}{2(1-\rho)}\left[1+\left(\frac{\sigma_s}{T_s}\right)^2\right] \quad \text{(see Figure 5.4b)}$$

M/M/C Case (Markovian, Random Service, and C Servers)

Expected average queue length

$$E(m) = P_0 \frac{\rho^{c+1}}{cc!} \frac{1}{(1-\rho/c)^2}$$

Expected average number of attacks/users in the system $E(n) = E(m) + \rho$

Expected average waiting time $T_w = T_q - 1/\rho$

Expected average total time (wait and process) $E(v) = E(n) / \lambda$

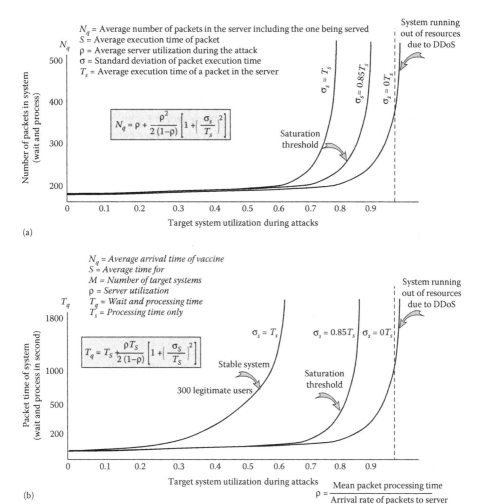

(a)

(b)

Figure 5.4 **(a) The depicted formula was developed by two Russian mathematicians, Khintchine and Polloeczek. The equation can be applied to DDoS attacks that use exponential interarrival times and any distribution of service times. Attack execution may vary and as the arrival of the packets increases, the utilization of the server escalates and eventually the system will asymptotically come to a screeching halt. (b) The waiting time and the time to process the request. (© 2014 Copyright MERIT CyberSecurity Group. All rights reserved.)**

The Famous Little Law

Dr. John Dutton Conant Little is an institute professor at the Massachusetts Institute of Technology (MIT), best known for his result in OR—Little's law.

Little's law provides a fundamental relationship between three key parameters in a queuing (or waiting line/service) system: *the average number of items in the system, the average waiting time (or flow time) in the system for an item*, and *the average arrival rate of items to the system*. The system can be very general. For example, it might include both the service facility and the waiting line, or it might be only the waiting line. An important feature of Little's law is that by knowing, perhaps via direct measurement, two of the three parameters, the third can be calculated. This is an extremely useful property since measurement of all three parameters may be difficult in certain applications. Little's law is applicable to many environments including manufacturing and service industries. We're going to apply Little's law to DDoS attacks on target systems. This is an unusual application but it works very well.

Little's law says that under steady-state conditions, the average number of items in a queuing system equals the average rate at which items arrive multiplied by the average time that an item spends in the system. If

N_q = average number of items in the queuing system

T_s = average waiting time in the system for an item

λ = average number of items arriving per unit time, the law is

$$N_q = \lambda T_s$$

Little's law tells us that the average number of packets in the attack server (N_q) is the effective arrival rate (λ) of DDoS packets times the average time that the server finishes work with the packet (T_s), or simply

> Number of attack packets that smuggled into the system
>
> = Arrival rate ackets fired from of the pbotnets
>
> × the time of the server to destroy the packet payload

Conquest against the DDoS Regime

The current security defense systems are only capable of detecting and mitigating simple and conventional attacks. The data center of a large corporation has a cybersecurity team working on detecting and mitigating attacks. This chapter briefly discusses the behavior of DDoS attacks and how they impact the systems of a victim. We're looking at a quantitative method to capture data on workload performance and system degradation during an attack.

Figure 5.5 depicts a strategic action plan to solidify the efforts of eradicating the *pre-attack* stage. That's the most ambitious endeavor, but it is the only way to stop DDoS attacks before they arrive into a city. The results of this synergistic endeavor will be collected and standardized into a central knowledge engine.

The technique of QT is very effective in providing significant system performance "capacity" during the time of the attack, but most importantly we will visually see the behavior of the server during the attack. With QT, we'll be able to have a handle on the issue of scalability, and what are the requirements to overcome the saturation of the system.

Despite a significant breadth of research into defenses, DoS attacks remain a significant problem in the Internet today. The DoS phenomenon has evolved rapidly over the last decade. DoS attacks were once caused by only a few attackers—often a single attacker—sending specially crafted packets designed to exploit flaws in a victim's particular TCP/IP TCP/IP implementation (e.g., the Teardrop or Land attack), and sometimes using Internet protocol (IP) spoofing (the forging of the source IP address field in the IP header to something other than the sending host's IP address) to hide their identity. DoS attacks have become an increasing risk, as the sophistication of the current malware technologies enables relatively inexperienced attackers to perform these attacks.

There are six concurrent activities that should be executed by professionals making up one team from academia, national agencies, ethical hackers, digital immunity specialists, and performance analysts.

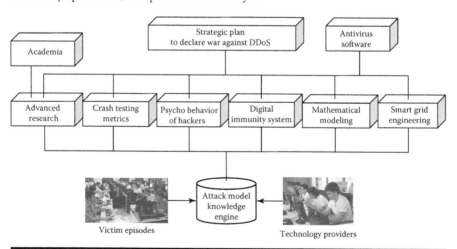

Figure 5.5 DDoS is the biggest nightmare to threaten Smart City security. Systematic decomposition is mandatory (divide and conquer) in order to win the Pork Chop Hill. (© 2014 Copyright MERIT CyberSecurity Group. All rights reserved.)

Advanced research: To think about the future, and what are the potential technologies that can be implemented to fight cybercrime. AI and nanotechnology will give cybersecurity the upper hand. In the following chapters, we will explain how they work.

Crash testing metrics: To examine system crashes second by second, like wind tunnel testing an airplane's metal durability. Collect data and convert it into standards and thresholds.

Psycho behavior of hackers: The human element is the most important factor in any crime. There are thousands of studies on the whole cybercrime continuum, but cybercrime is becoming exponentially more advanced and damaging. It is a major paradox that keeps dragging with time.

Digital immunity: This is the bright future of cybersecurity. It is the new paradigm that will help curb cybercrime and prove that AI and NT will put out the fire of malware.

Mathematical modeling: Everything in the world can be modeled including cybercrime. Cybercrime can be broken down into its components and replicated as a system help to explain the mechanics of the system, to study the effects breaking point of the different components, and to make conclusive predictions about its behavior.

Smart Grid engineering: Smart Cities are just as safe as their Smart Grids. A Smart Grid is not a network. It is the nervous and immune systems of a grid. Any attack alert on a city will be translated into a total response by an army of Smart Vaccine™ nanobots. Nanobots will be explained later.

DDoS Codification and Cataloguing

DDoS is systematic organized crime executed in cyberspace. Here's how it works (Figure 5.6).

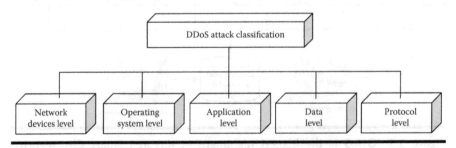

Figure 5.6 DoS attacks can be classified into five categories based on the attack protocol level, the architecture of the target, the sophistication of the operating system, and the security of the software and hardware.

Typically, a DDoS master program is installed on one computer using a stolen account. At a designated time, the master program communicates to any number of "agent" programs installed on computers anywhere on the Internet. When they receive the command, the agents initiate the attack. Using client/server technology, the master program can initiate hundreds or even thousands of agent programs within seconds. Website DDoS is executed by flooding one or more of a site's web servers with so many requests that it becomes unavailable for normal use. It is pretty much like the arrangement of the Roman army on the battlefield: the top general standing on a hill overlooking the battlefield and giving orders to use his tactics. The frontline is the most powerful soldiers who will do the brutal fighting. Behind them, the support line made up of intermediate officers who are the true commanders of the battle.

The Five Protocols of a DoS Attack

Network device level: Includes attacks that might be caused either by taking advantage of bugs or weaknesses in software, or by trying to exhaust the hardware resources of network devices.

OS-level DoS: Attacks that use the Ping of Death attack. In this attack, ICMP echo requests having total data sizes greater than the maximum IP standard size are sent to the targeted victim. This attack often has the effect of crashing the victim's machine.

Application-level attack: The *finger* bomb. A malicious user could cause the finger routine to be recursively executed on the hostname, potentially exhausting the resources of the host.

Data flooding attacks: An attacker attempts to use the bandwidth available to a network, host, or device to its greatest extent, by sending massive quantities of data and so causing it to process extremely large amounts of data. An attacker could attempt to use up the available bandwidth of a network by simply bombarding the targeted victim with normal, but meaningless packets with spoofed source addresses. An example is flood pinging. Simple flooding is commonly seen in the form of DDoS attacks.

DoS attacks based on protocol: Takes advantage of certain standard protocol features. For example, several attacks exploit the fact that IP source addresses can be spoofed. Several types of DoS attacks have focused on the DNS, and many of these involve attacking the DNS cache on name servers. An attacker who owns a name server may coerce a victim name server into caching false records by querying the victim about the attacker's own site. A vulnerable victim name server would then refer to the rogue server and cache the answer.

Figure 5.6 shows the five categories of DDoS attacks.

DDoS Needs Planning and Knowledge

DDoS is clearly exemplified in Revelation 12:9: "And the great dragon was thrown down, that ancient serpent, who is called the devil and Satan, the deceiver of the whole world." DDoS cybercrooks are the *dragon ninjas* of the Internet. We can also consider DDoS like an implosion of a structure that collapses inward. When a high-rise building implodes, it brings all the floors, one after another, to the ground. DDoS is a violent cyber implosion that brings any computing infrastructure down. It can steal data, corrupt private files, or silently snoop and prowl, and steal passwords and encryption code. DDoS has a domino effect!

DDoS has no universal standards because the software industry is rolling out much more sophisticated systems, and many of them are AI-centric and more resilient. In fact, we can say that "you can have any color as long as is malware." If heroin is a potent opiate substance, the Internet is more addictive than heroin for the young generation of today. Script kiddies, who have the lightning speed of learning, develop 78% of the malware. Kids prefer to write code and socialize on Internet relay chat (IRC) than go to a Saturday dance.

Grant Manser set up damaging software and sold it on the dark web at age 16. He created λ = arrival rate of attacks to the server (User Datagram Protocol [UDP] and ICMP), the software used by cyber hackers to crash 224,000 websites around the world from the bedroom of his family's home. The "stresser" program worked by bombarding websites, servers and email addresses with so much information that they crashed, with companies, schools, colleges, and government departments among the victims. He pleaded guilty to 10 charges but only received a suspended sentence.

Organized Crime in Cyberspace

It is hard to give a definitive answer on the number of crime service providers (CSP) in the United States or abroad. However, our research on dark web activities shows that between 2003 and 2008 there were over 300 CSP in the United States alone. In 2007, the Russian Business Network (RBN) rose to prominence as a high-profit, low-risk criminal enterprise selling "bulletproof" services to anyone willing to pay its fee. Its business model of earning high profits with almost zero risk of being caught made the RBN the darling of the Russian underworld. David Bizeul, a French security researcher who has written one of the best reports on the RBN to date, describes RBN as "a complete infrastructure to achieve malicious activities. It is a cybercrime service provider. Whatever the activity is—phishing, malware hosting, gambling, pornography … the RBN will offer the convenient solution to fulfill it."

Atrivo, another CSP company that was based in Concord, California, specialized in providing networks for spammers and other bad actors to use, many of whom were associated with the RBN. The RBN relied heavily on two networks hosted by Atrivo: *UkrTeleGroup*, which routed traffic through the Ukraine, and *HostFresh*, which routed traffic through Hong Kong and China. A report by Verisign's iDefense security laboratory named Atrivo as having the highest concentration of malicious activity of any hosting company in the world.

The Estonian company ESTDomains was based in Tartu, Estonia, but registered as a US corporation in Delaware. It was another active domain registrar that dealt almost exclusively with criminal elements engaged in setting up Internet scams. Estonia's Computer Emergency Response Team (CERT) reported the following: "To understand EstDomains, one needs to understand the role of organized crime and the investments coming from that, their relations to hosting providers in Western nations and the criminals who ply their trade through these services." In other words, ESTDomains was a cell for Russian organized crime's entree into the lucrative world of Internet crime. The Internet Corporation for Assigned Names and Numbers (ICANN) pulled the plug on ESTDomains' right to issue domain names, citing its CEO's criminal conviction as the cause.

Then came McColo, a San Jose–based web hosting service provider, which was responsible for hosting most botnet's command and control servers. McColo perfectly illustrates the key role that US-based businesses play in providing protected platforms for Russian organized crime enterprises that, in turn, are utilized as attack platforms by non-state actors in nationalistic and religious actions.

While the DDoS threat landscape continues to evolve (Figure 5.7), we discovered that four attack types continue to fall: volumetric, asymmetric, computational, and vulnerability based.

These attack categories have the following characteristics:

■ *Volumetric*: Flood-based attacks that can be at layers: the network layer 3, the transport layer 4, and the application layer 7 of the open system interconnection.
■ *Asymmetric*: Attacks designed to invoke timeouts or session-state changes.
■ *Computational*: Attacks designed to consume the central processing unit (CPU) and memory.
■ *Vulnerability based*: Attacks that exploit software vulnerabilities.

Defense mechanisms have also evolved to deal with these different categories (Figure 5.8). Today's high-profile organizations have learned to deploy sophisticated mitigation tools to maximize their security posture. F5Networks, headquartered in Seattle, is an American-based company that specializes in application delivery networking (ADN) technology, web security, cloud performance, availability of servers, and data storage devices, has recommended DDoS mitigation architecture that can accommodate specific data center size and industry requirements.

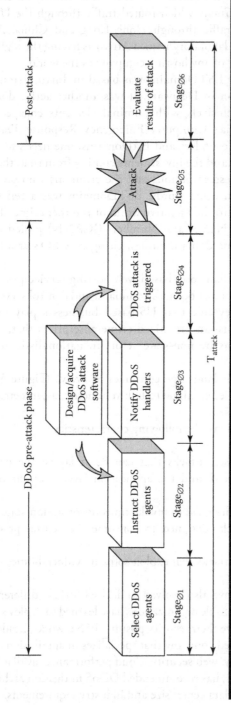

Figure 5.7 A DDoS attacker has to have a large reservoir of knowledge, a bulletproof plan, and wide angle vision. There are six stages to a DDoS attack. The attack is only as good as its plan. The success of one will trigger successive attacks from learning through accumulative previous experiences. Almost all DDoS attacks follow the same pattern. Skipping one stage makes the attack less successful. (© 2014 Copyright MERIT CyberSecurity Group. All rights reserved.)

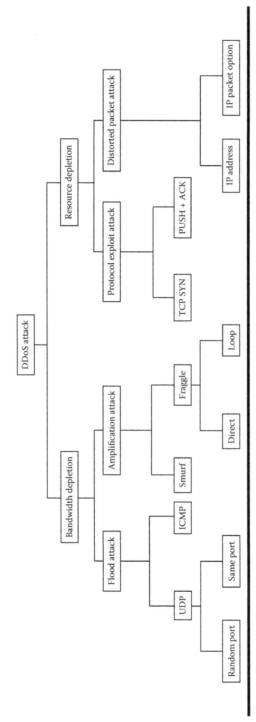

Figure 5.8 The dynamic proliferation of DDoS attack technologies has made it very challenging for corporate and law enforcement to control the attacks. Third-party zombies are very resource draining and DDoS is maliciously riding on their back.

You think massive outage is bad? Worse is expected. *Forbes* has learned that hackers (the masters) are selling access to a huge army of botnets made of *slave IoT zombies* designed to launch attacks capable of severely disrupting web connections. The Russian Business Network (RBN) is marketing crime-as-a-service (CaaS). This finding was revealed just days after compromised cameras and other IoT machines were used in an attack that took down Twitter, Amazon Web Services, Netflix, Spotify, and other major web companies.

The hackers claimed that they could generate 1 terabit per second of Virus Rain. That would almost equal the world record DDoS attack, which hit the French hosting provider OVH earlier in September 2016 at just over 1 terabit. For $4,600, anyone can buy 50,000 bots (hacked computers under the control of hackers), while 100,000 bots cost $7,500. Together, these bots can combine resources to overwhelm targets with data, in what's known as a DDoS attack.

Daniel Cohen, head of RSA's FraudAction business unit, said that he didn't know if the botnet for hire was related to Mirai, the epic network of weaponized IoT computers used to swamp Dyn—a DNS provider and the chief target of the Friday October 2016 attack—with traffic. But *Forbes* was able to find a forum post on Alpha Bay from the seller who goes by the name of *loldongs* and belongs to a gang of hooligans who created a Mirai-based botnet. The original post was on the 4 October, just a few days after the Mirai source code was made available to everyone. In a later post, in response to another user's request, loldongs claimed: "I can take down OVH easily." OVH is a French cloud computing company.

In the past, DDoS attacks were mostly volumetric, relying on the sheer volume of packets to disrupt targets. As DDoS defenses improved, and to get more bang for their buck, attackers began bringing other techniques to bear, such as reflection/amplification attacks. Reflection refers to spoofing a packet's source address, while amplification means the ability to send a small packet to a server and get a large response back, which will tie up the server to saturation point.

Arbor Network's Gary Sockrider described the next generation of DDoS: "We've already seen a the new model of Mirai with new features that actually can do spoofing of the source address, which now gives (attackers) the capacity to combine IoT botnets with reflection/amplification techniques. We haven't seen any of these in the wild yet, but we know the capability is already out there. So when you combine these two techniques, we're in the age of the multi-terabit DDoS attack now, and it's imminent."

DDoS Arsenal

DDoS is mushrooming every day and more potent artilleries are being used and sold. The aggressiveness of their vengeance *for the whole world* has made DDoS domain experts the most powerful cyborgs. They are risk takers who are persistent and dedicated, and this makes them feel great. Thus, it is very hard to give a definitive count of all the DDoS. Smart City planners have a major stumbling block because they want to "internize everything" in order to preserve energy, boost efficiency, and manage runaway costs. We have attempted to classify DDoS in Figure 5.8.

Hacker and Data Guardians

The most perplexing phenomenon in the age of the Internet is the following syndrome: How come malware marines always run faster than cyber defense wardens and outsmart them in every round? Well, it's easier to destroy than to build. It took 10,000 workers 5 years to build the World Trade Center, and 19 terrorists to bring the two towers down in 2 hours. Let's put physics aside and examine what makes the cortex of the hacker an anatomical marvel. The hacker is an invader, not a crusader. A hacker is a person capable of command and control of a system. He or she is an intelligent "lateral" thinker. Like a car mechanic, hackers have the appropriate tools for the appropriate task. They accumulate new tools from hacking friends. They are avid readers and excavators. Their cognitive skills provide them with a realistic plan before jumping into the fire. Strategic hackers go after vulnerable systems with holes and defects. Hackers are loyal to themselves and very few friends. Like engines, they measure more than twice before they cut. Hackers learn from their mistakes and keep their expertise to themselves. Obviously, they use the surprise element to break into firewalls. Hackers are a copy of navy seals, very adventurous and courageous in taking grave risks. Hackers have high definition vision, predictive analytics, and a phenomenal mental "what-if" simulation scenario of the assault. They thrive on success, not failure. Hackers have a great opportunity to become security gurus and draw excellent salaries and recognition.

Security specialists, on the other hand, police company policy followers and data guardians. The most dreadful position on the corporate pyramid is the chief information officer, briefly labeled the CIO. The fancy name started in 1981 at the Bank of Boston and was carved out at the MIT Sloan School of Management. CIOs are always caught between a rock and a hard place. CIOs are servants to the chief financial officer (CFO) and chief executive officer (CEO), and the sacrificial lamb when corporate information assets are bombed, stolen, or compromised.

The January 2015 issue of *CIO* magazine published an interesting article titled "2015 State of the CIO," which gave some eyebrow-raising statistics: only 24% of CIOs are doing a good job at protecting a company's information; 46% of CIOs are sidelined and have lost the trust of the CEO; and 34% of CIOs are involved in "turf wars" with peers in the C-suite.

Since information and communication technologies (ICT) are moving at an accelerated speed, CIOs are facing serious challenges keeping up with upgrades and cyberattacks. Newer technologies are bringing smarter attacks and more disorder. The two nightmares that a CIO legitimately fears are *surprise DDoS attack* and *getting fired*. The new system "The Cognitive Early Warning Predictive System, using the Smart Vaccine" provides the smartest layer of security for a Smart City, including assault detection, attack mitigation, incident response, and ongoing risk management.

Glossary

ACK or ACK-PUSH flood: In an ACK or ACK-PUSH flood, attackers send spoofed ACK (or ACK-PUSH) packets at very high packet rates that fail to belong to any current session within a firewall's state table and/or a server's connection list. The ACK (or ACK-PUSH) flood exhausts a victim's firewalls by forcing state table lookups and servers, thereby depleting their system resources that are used to match these incoming packets to an existing flow.

Amplified attacks (reflective): According to US CERT, certain UDP protocols, such as DNS, NTP, SNMPv2, NetBIOS, SSDP, CharGEN, QOTD, BitTorrent, Kad, Quake network protocol, and Steam protocol, have been identified as potential attack vectors using amplified (reflective) attacks. Most attacks using these protocols would be performed similarly to the DNS and NTP attacks.

Buffer overflow: Buffers can only hold specific amounts of data, and when capacity has been reached the data has to flow somewhere else, typically into another buffer, which can corrupt the data that is already contained in that buffer.

DNS amplified (reflective): Another possible way of taking advantage of a DNS flood is through attackers spoofing a victim's DNS infrastructure and through the use of Open Recursive DNS servers and extensions to the DNS protocol. Very small DNS requests can result in very large and high-volume DNS responses (i.e., amplification factor). Refer to DNS amplification attacks for more information.

DNS flood: In a DNS flood, attackers use the DNS as a variant of a UDP flood. Attackers send valid but spoofed DNS request packets at a very high packet rate and from a very large group of source IP addresses. Since these appear as valid requests, the victim's DNS server proceeds to respond to all requests. The DNS server can be overwhelmed by the vast number of requests. This attack consumes large amounts of network resources that exhaust the DNS infrastructure until it goes offline, taking the victim's Internet access (www) down with it.

Excessive verb—single session: In an excessive verb attack, attackers take advantage of a feature of HTTP 1.1 that allows multiple client requests within a single HTTP session. In this case, attackers can lower the session request rate of a HTTP attack in order to come under the radar of request rate–limiting features found on some attack defense systems deployed today.

This attack is viewed as a low-and-slow application-layer attack and normally consumes little bandwidth but eventually renders the victim's server unresponsive.

Excessive verb (HTTP GET flood): In a GET flood, attackers send large numbers of valid HTTP requests to a victim's web server. The HTTP request is most often a GET request and is directed to the most CPU-intensive process on the victim's web server. Each attacker can generate large numbers of valid GET requests so the attacker can use a relatively small number of attacking machines to take a system offline. HTTP GET floods are non-spoofed and the source IP address is the actual public IP of the attacker machine (or NAT firewall). The most common variant of this attack uses GET requests but an attacker can also use HEAD, POST, PUT, OPTIONS, or any other HTTP method to cause an outage. This attack is viewed as a low-and-slow application-layer attack and normally consumes little bandwidth but eventually renders the victim's server unresponsive.

Fake session attack: In a fake session DoS attack, an attacker sends forged SYN packets, multiple ACK packets, and then one or more FIN/RST packets. When these packets appear together, they look like a valid TCP session from one direction only. Since many modern networks utilize asymmetric routing techniques whereby incoming packets and outgoing packets traverse different Internet links to improve cost and performance, this attack is harder to detect. This attack simulates a complete TCP communication and is designed to confuse new attack defense tools that only monitor incoming traffic to the network and not bidirectional server responses. Two common variants of this DDoS attack are most often observed: the first variant sends multiple SYNs, then multiple ACKs, followed by one or more FIN/RST packets. The second variant skips the initial SYN and starts by sending multiple ACKs, followed by one or more FIN/RST packets. The slow TCP-SYN rate makes the attack harder to detect than a typical SYN flood.

Fraggle attack: In a Fraggle attack, attackers send spoofed UDP packets instead of ICMP echo reply (ping) packets to the broadcast address of a large network resulting in a DoS.

Fragmented ACK flood: In a fragmented ACK flood DDoS attack, large fragmented (1500+ byte) packets are sent to consume large amounts of bandwidth, while generating a relatively small packet rate. While the protocols allow for fragmentation, these packets usually pass through border routers, firewalls, and intrusion detection system/intrusion prevention system (IDS/IPS) devices uninspected or can consume excessive resources attempting to reassemble and inspect fragmented packets. The packet contents can be randomized, irrelevant data that can consume resources. However, this method can also be used as an advanced evasion technique designed to bypass deep packet inspection (DPI) devices altogether. The attacker's goal can be to consume all bandwidth of the victim's network or use fragmentation to hide insidious low-and-slow application-layer DDoS attacks, malware, overflows, brute force, and so on.

HTTP fragmentation: In a HTTP fragmentation attack, a non-spoofed attacker establishes a valid HTTP connection with a web server. The attacker proceeds to fragment legitimate HTTP packets into the smallest fragments possible and sends each fragment as slow as the server timeout will allow, which eventually holds the HTTP connection open for a long period of time without raising any alarms. By opening multiple extended sessions per attacker, the attacker can silently force a web application offline with just a handful of attacking machines.

ICMP flood: In an ICMP flood, attackers send highly spoofed ICMP packets in sufficiently large volumes to flood a network. The victim's network resources are overwhelmed by the large number of incoming ICMP packets. The attack consumes resources and available bandwidth, exhausting the network until it goes offline. ICMP floods can overwhelm a network with packets containing random or fixed source IP addresses. This attack is often viewed as a network-level volumetric attack and can be defeated by L3/L4 packet filtering.

ICMP fragmentation flood: In an ICMP fragmentation flood, attackers send highly spoofed, large fragmented ICMP packets (1500+ byte) at a very high packet rate and these packets cannot be reassembled. The large packet size can enlarge the bandwidth of an ICMP attack overall. In addition, it causes wasted CPU resources in an attempt to reassemble useless packets.

Intelligent DDoS mitigation systems (IDMS): Specifically designed to detect and mitigate DDoS attacks using more advanced techniques, IDMS equipment uses a combination of deep packet inspection (DPI), proxy inspection, and heuristic-based techniques to separate malicious traffic from good traffic. Services and solutions utilizing IDMS technologies can protect an organization from a DDoS threat.

IP NULL: In an IP NULL attack, attackers send packets whereby the IPv4 header field is used to specify which transport protocol is being used in its payload (e.g., TCP and/or UDP) and sets this field to a value of zero. Firewalls configured for just TCP, UDP, and ICMP may allow this type of packet through. If these packets arrive as a flood, a victim's server's CPU resources may be wasted in handling these packets.

Mirai botnet: The Mirai botnet code infects poorly protected Internet devices by using telnet to find those that are still using their factory default username and password. The effectiveness of Mirai is due to its ability to infect tens of thousands of these insecure devices and coordinate them to mount a DDoS attack against a chosen victim. Refer to RSA attack for more information about Mirai botnet.

Multiple verb—single request: In a multiple verb attack, attackers use a variation of the excessive verb attack vector. The attacking machines create multiple HTTP requests, not by creating them one after another, for example, during a single HTTP session attack, but instead by creating a single packet filled with multiple requests. It's a variant of the excessive verb attack whereby the attacker can maintain high CPU processing loads on the victim's server with very low attack packet rates. The low packet rates make the attacker nearly invisible to NetFlow attack detection techniques. Additionally, if the attacker selects the HTTP verb carefully, these attacks will bypass DPI technologies as well. This attack is viewed as a low-and-slow application-layer attack and normally consumes little bandwidth but eventually renders the victim's server unresponsive.

Non-spoofed UDP flood: In a non-spoofed UDP flood, attackers send non-spoofed UDP packets at a very high packet rate resulting in networks becoming overwhelmed by the large amount of incoming UDP packets. The attack consumes vast amounts of network resources and bandwidth, exhausting the network and forcing a DoS. The packets contain the valid public IP address of the attacker. This type of attack is harder to identify because it resembles good traffic.

NTP amplified (reflective): Attackers spoofing a victim's network time protocol (NTP) infrastructure use Open NTP servers, which send small requests resulting in a very high volume of NTP responses..

NTP flood: In an NTP flood, attackers use NTP as a variant of a UDP flood. Attackers send valid but spoofed NTP request packets at a very high packet rate and from a very large group of source IP addresses. Since these appear as valid requests, the victim's NTP server proceeds to respond to all requests. The NTP server can be overwhelmed by the vast number of requests. This attack consumes large amounts of network resources that exhaust the NTP infrastructure until it goes offline.

Ping flood: In a Ping flood, attackers use "ping," which is a variant of an ICMP and send highly spoofed ping (IMCP echo requests) packets at a very high rate and from random source IP ranges or as the IP address of the victim. Attackers can consume all available network resources and bandwidths, exhausting the network until it goes offline. Since the ping requests are most often well-formed and highly spoofed, a Ping flood cannot be easily detected by DPI or other detection techniques.

Ping of Death: A type of DoS attack in which the attacker sends a ping request that is larger than 65,536 bytes, which is the maximum size that an IP allows. While a ping larger than 65,536 bytes is too large to fit in one packet that can be transmitted, TCP/IP allows a packet to be fragmented, essentially splitting the packet into smaller segments that are eventually reassembled. Attacks take advantage of this flaw by fragmenting packets that when received would total more than the allowed number of bytes and would effectively cause a buffer overload on the operating system at the receiving end, crashing the system.

Random recursive GET: In a random recursive GET attack, attackers use a modified version of a recursive GET. This attack is designed primarily for forum sites or news sites whereby web pages are indexed numerically, usually in sequential order. The attacking GET statements will insert a random number within a valid range of page reference numbers, making each GET statement different from the previous one.

Recursive GET: A recursive GET attack is a variant of the excessive verb attack. In this case, an attacker identifies multiple pages and/or images and generates HTTP GET requests that appear to "scroll" through these pages or images trying to replicate a normal user. This attack can be combined with any of the verb attack methods to make this attack vector very difficult to detect because the requests appear to be legitimate.

RST/FIN flood: In an RST/FIN flood, attackers send highly spoofed RST or FIN packets at an extremely high rate that do not belong to any session within the firewall's state table and/or server's session tables. The RST or FIN flood DDoS attack exhausts a victim's firewalls and/or servers by depleting its system resources used to look up and match these incoming packets to an existing session.

Same source/Dest flood (LAND attack): In a LAND DDoS attack, a victim receives spoofed SYN packets at a very high rate that have the victim's IP range in both the source IP and the destination IP fields in the IP header. This attack exhausts a victim's firewalls and/or servers by exhausting its system resources used to compute this protocol violation. Although the packet's source and destination IPs are identically defined within a same source/Dest attack, the content of the packets are often irrelevant because the attacker is simply attempting to deplete system resources.

Slow read attack: In a slow read DDoS attack, attackers send valid TCP-SYN packets and perform TCP three-way handshakes with the victim to establish valid sessions between the attacker and the victim. The attacker first establishes a large number of valid sessions and begins to request to download a document or large object from each attacking machine. Once the download begins, the attacking machines begin to slow down the acknowledgment of received packets. The attacker will continue to slow down the receipt of packets, which consumes excess resources on the delivering server since all the associated processes appear to be in a very slow receiving network. Slow read attacks are always non-spoofed in order to hold sessions open for long periods of time.

Slow session attack: In a slow session attack, attackers send valid TCP-SYN packets and perform TCP three-way handshakes with the victim to establish valid sessions between the attacker and the victim. The attacker first establishes a large number of valid sessions then slowly responds with an ACK packet and incomplete requests to keep the sessions open for long periods of time. Normally, the attacker will set the attack to send an ACK packet with an incomplete request typically before the session timeout is triggered by the server. The "held-open" sessions can eventually exhaust the victim's server resources used to compute this irregularity. Low-and-slow tools have also been designed to consume all of the 65,536 available "sockets" (source ports), resulting in a server's inability to establish any new sessions. Slow session attacks are always non-spoofed in order to hold sessions open for long periods of time.

Slowloris attack: Slowloris sends partial requests to the target server, opening connections, then sending HTTP headers, augmenting but never completing the request. Slow HTTP POST sends headers to signal how much data is to be sent, but sends the data very slowly, using thousands of HTTP POST connections to DDoS the web server.

Smurf attack: A distributed DoS attack in which large numbers of ICMP packets with the intended victim's spoofed source IP are broadcast to a computer network using an IP broadcast address. Most devices on a network will, by default, respond to this by sending a reply to the source IP address. If the number of machines on the network that receive and respond to these packets is very large, the victim's computer will be flooded with traffic. This can slow down the victim's computer to the point where it becomes impossible to work on.

Specially crafted packet: In a specially crafted packet attack, attackers take advantage of websites with poor design, vulnerable web applications, and/or have improper integration with backend databases. For example, attackers can exploit vulnerabilities in HTTP, structured query language (SQL), service improvement plan (SIP), DNS, and so on, and generate specially crafted packets to take advantage of these protocol "stack" vulnerabilities to ultimately take the servers offline. They can also generate requests that will lock up database queries. These attacks are highly specific and effective because they consume huge amounts of server resources and are often launched from a single attacker. An example of a specially crafted DoS attack is MS13-039.

SSDP amplified (reflective): SSDP, otherwise known as the Simple Service Discovery Protocol, is a network-based protocol used for the advertisement and discovery of network services. SSPD allows universal plug-and-play devices to send and receive information using UDP on port 1900. SSDP is attractive to DDoS attackers because of its open state that allows spoofing and amplification.

Stacheldraht: (German for "barbed wire") Stacheldraht malware is written by Random for Linux and Solaris systems and acts as a DDoS agent. This tool detects and automatically enables source address forgery. It uses a number of different DoS attacks, including UDP flood, Internet Control Message Protocol (ICMP) flood, TCP-SYN flood, and Smurf attack.

SYN flood: In a SYN flood, the source network sockets become totally random and overwhelming and at the same time the destination network sockets become much more narrowed. In extreme cases, over 99% of the incoming packets are to one destination network socket. Read more about SYN floods.

SYN-ACK flood: In a SYN-ACK flood, attackers either flood a network with SYN-ACK packets from a sizeable botnet or they spoof a victim's IP address range. Typically, a smaller botnet sends spoofed SYN packets to large numbers of servers and proxies on the Internet that generate large numbers of SYN-ACK packets in response to incoming SYN requests from the spoofed attackers.

TCP NULL: In a TCP NULL attack, attackers send packets that have no TCP segment flags set (six possible), which is invalid. This type of segment may be used in reconnaissance, such as port scanning.

TOS flood: In a type of service (TOS) flood, attackers use the TOS field of an IP header. This field has evolved over time and is now used for explicit congestion notification (ECN) and differentiated services (DiffServ). While this type of flood isn't seen too often, two types of attacks may be launched based on this field. In the first, the attacker spoofs ECN packets to reduce the throughput of individual connections. This could cause the server to appear out of service or unresponsive to customers. In the second, the attacker utilizes the DiffServ class flags to potentially increase the priority of the attack traffic over that of the non-attack traffic. Utilizing DiffServ flags isn't a DDoS attack in itself; this function is aimed at increasing the effectiveness of the attack.

Tribe flood network: The TFN is a set of computer programs that conduct various DDoS attacks such as an ICMP flood, SYN flood, UDP flood, and a Smurf attack.

UDP flood: In a UDP flood, DDoS attackers send highly spoofed UDP packets at a very high packet rate using a large source IP range. The victim's network (routers, firewalls, IPS/IDS, SLB, WAF, and/or servers) is overwhelmed by the large number of incoming UDP packets. This attack normally consumes network resources and available bandwidth, exhausting the network until it goes offline.

UDP fragmentation: In a UDP fragmentation attack, attackers send large UDP packets (1500+ bytes) to consume more bandwidth with fewer packets. Since these fragmented packets are normally forged and have no ability to be reassembled, the victim's resources will receive these packets, which can possibly consume significant CPU resources to reassemble firewalls in order to remain up and running, and will begin to indiscriminately drop all good and bad traffic to the destination server being flooded. Some firewalls perform an early random drop process blocking both good and bad traffic. SYN floods are often used to consume all network bandwidth and negatively impact the performance of the target system.

Source: Selected terms related to this chapter from www.if4it.com/it-glossary and from publications and educational seminars of MERIT CyberSecurity.

Bibliography

DDOS: https://motherboard.vice.com/en_us/article/history-of-the-ddos-attack

DDoS attack on Twitter: http://spectrum.ieee.org/tech-talk/telecom/security/what-is-a-distributed-denialofservice-attack-and-how-did-it-break-twitter

DDoS amplification: https://arxiv.org/pdf/1505.07892.pdf

Bank info security: http://www.bankinfosecurity.com/search.php?keywords=DDoS#p-1

DDoS: http://ddos.inforisktoday.com/

Mirai code: https://techcrunch.com/2016/10/10/hackers-release-source-code-for-a-powerful-ddos-app-called-mirai/

Mariposa: https://en.wikipedia.org/wiki/Mariposa_botnet

DDoS malware: http://f6ce14d4647f05e937f4-4d6abce208e5e17c2085b466b98c2083.r3.cf1.rackcdn.com/ddos-malware-research-paper-pdf-w-777.pdf

Some of the largest and most disruptive distributed denial of service (DDoS) attacks: https://www.theguardian.com/technology/hacking

Verisign: http://f6ce14d4647f05e937f4-4d6abce208e5e17c2085b466b98c2083.r3.cf1.rackcdn.com/ddos-malware-research-paper-pdf-w-777.pdf

Must read: http://securityaffairs.co/wordpress/8259/security/ddos-attacks-so-simple-so-dangerous.html

Elsevier Queueing: http://www.fang.ece.ufl.edu/mypaper/comnet07wang.pdf

Botnet behavior: http://csjournals.com/IJCSC/PDF1-2/49.pdf

Queue management: http://www.professeurs.polymtl.ca/jose.fernandez/QueueManagementDoS.pdf

Taxonomy: https://pdfs.semanticscholar.org/0c0d/325c02f9d28b97e8cf5b0d87385f39d0be4d.pdf

Ultimate DDoS defender: https://www.researchgate.net/publication/261758696_AUGMENTED_SPLIT_-PROTOCOL_AN_ULTIMATE_AN_ULTIMATE_DDOS_DEFENDER

Empirical study: http://facweb.cs.depaul.edu/brewster/pubs/WiFi-DOS.pdf

Formulas: http://web.mst.edu/~gosavia/queuing_formulas.pdf

Formulas: http://irh.inf.unideb.hu/~jsztrik/education/16/SOR_Main_Angol.pdf

Glossary: https://www.corero.com/resources/glossary.html

Chapter 6

The Three Generations of DDoS

Kurzweil's Accelerating Intelligence

As a futurist, I find Dr. Ray Kurzweil's famous book, *The Singularity Is Near*, revolutionary and inspirational. In fact, you may need to buy an extra copy because you will wear the first one out. The book provides a superb definition of the term "evolution as a process of creating patterns in increasing order." Then, Kurzweil continues on to explain the pattern of evolution as applied to technology: "But a serious assessment of the history of technology reveals that technological change is exponential. Exponential growth is a feature of any evolutionary process, of which technology is a primary example. You can examine the data in different ways, on different timescales, and for a wide variety of technologies, ranging from electronic to biological, as well as for their implications, ranging from the amount of human knowledge to the size of the economy. The acceleration of progress and growth applies to each of them. Indeed, we often find not just simple exponential growth, but 'double' exponential growth, meaning that the rate of exponential growth (that is, the exponent) is itself growing exponentially."

In this chapter, we're going to explain how and why distributed denial of service (DDoS) follows Kurzweil's concept of acceleration evolution. In other words, DDoS is riding the forward motion of crime evolution. Just to give you a jolt of shock, DDoS will morph into an artificial intelligence (AI) computer with its own morals and ethics. It will have the formidable ability to store the mind of the hacker, and triggered by the hacker's implant, navigate autonomously on its own and self-destruct as a final act after the attack. So, if we start to comfortably ride driverless cars, there will soon be a time when DDoS will be hackerless. But this is just the beginning; cyber terrorism will raise the bar to another unsuspected level. It will be joining the uranium underground and stepping into the zone of dirty bombs. It looks like the Internet has opened the gates of hell. We will explain this paradigm in this chapter.

We have talked in detail about the present technologies of DDoS, but we have no interest in regurgitating the same content, because it looks like the present state of the art of antivirus technology (AVT) software is still behind Gartner's Hype Curve. DDoS is still at large and ferociously disturbing the quality of life of citizens of a Smart City. Let's not blame Russia, China, or any other hostile nation for slinging surprise cyber missiles into our cyberspace. We are the creators of the Internet. We gave it to the world on a silver platter, and now this good turn has reciprocated with malice and crime.

On his website, the journalist Brian Krebs describes the big cyber avalanche:

> A massive and sustained Internet attack on October 21, 2016, that has caused outages and network congestion today for a large number of Web sites was launched with the help of hacked "Internet of Things" (IoT) devices, such as CCTV video cameras and digital video recorders, new data suggests. Earlier today cyber criminals began training their attack cannons on Dyn, an Internet infrastructure company that provides critical technology services to some of the Internet's top destinations. The attack began creating problems for Internet users reaching an array of sites, including Twitter, Amazon, Tumblr, Reddit, Spotify and Netflix.

Mirai (Chinese name: "Linux.Gafgyt") is a Trojan horse that opens a backdoor on a compromised computer. Mirai's first public fiesta occurred on September 20, 2016, when it fired a huge DDoS attack against the website of journalist Brian Krebs, which reached 620 Gbps. Amazing! At the end September 2016, the hacker responsible for creating the Mirai malware released the *source code* for it, effectively letting anyone build his or her own attack army using Mirai.

At first, it was unclear who or what was behind the attack on Dyn. But one computer security firm said that the attack involved Mirai, the same malware strain that was used in the record 620 Gbps attack on my site on Friday October 21, 2016. Mirai is another version of Virus Rain™ that was described in Chapter 5.

According to researchers at security firm Flashpoint, the August 17, 2017 attack was launched at least in part by a Mirai-based botnet. Allison Nixon, director of research at Flashpoint, said the botnet used in today's ongoing attack is built on the backs of hacked IoT devices—mainly compromised digital video recorders (DVRs) and Internet Protocol (IP) cameras made by a Chinese hi-tech company called XiongMai Technologies. The components that XiongMai make are sold downstream to vendors who then use them in their own products.

The Three Generations of DDoS

Since technology is galloping at an exponential rate, DDoS serial cybercriminals continue to take advantage of zero-day and SQL injection vulnerabilities and build better malignant attacks. Cybersecurity and malware have become two sides of the same coin. This challenging duality has become the most arduous struggle in the age of the Internet. Based on our assessment of accelerating technology trends, we believe that DDoS technology in the next decade will be more devastating and will extend over three generations. DDoS will have a colossal impact on the life of Smart Cities. We can imagine that Smart Cities will connect with one another to form Smart Regions. Accordingly, DDoS will morph to become extended denial of service (EXoS).

Given that technological advances in cybersecurity are inherently heterogeneous and highly competitive, Smart Cities' lords of cybercrime will find fertile ground in multi-billion-dollar truly invisible high-tech smart systems beyond the imagination of any government or academic research (Figure 6.1).

Evolution and Generation of DDoS

The Law of Accelerating Returns

Kurzweil's big idea is that each new generation of technology stands on the shoulders of its predecessors—in this way, improvements in technology enable the next generation of even better technology. We can see this in the computer industry, where laptops run circles around legacy mainframes. So, when we say "accelerating returns," we mean that the acceleration can be measured in the "returns" of the technology—such as speed, efficiency, price performance, and overall "power"—which improve exponentially too.

First-Generation G1 DDoS: Internet Vandalism

The law of accelerating returns will certainly apply to DDoS progress and evolution. The first generation of DDoS is the state of the art of today. DDoS is a commodity that can be rented or engaged as a crime-as-a-service (CaaS) with the underground. DDoS criminals use foreign countries to launch their devastating multiple vector attacks. Another dimension of cyberattacks comes from mobile phones and tablets that are mobile and ready to setup a botnet made of a zombie army that is ready to attack a network, the public and private cloud, an e-commerce site, and prominent retail and financial websites.

The first-generation DDoS has been effective at winning malware battles, but is still short of crippling the critical infrastructures of a Smart City. AVT has been unable to conquer DDoS with lengthy stagnation and reactive tools. Crime lords

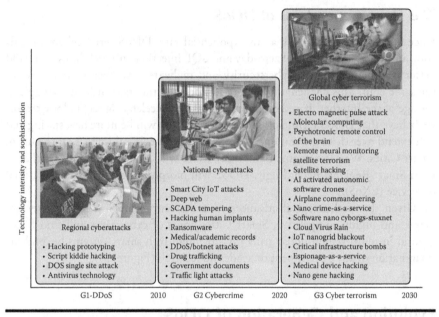

Regional cyberattacks
- Hacking prototyping
- Script kiddie hacking
- DOS single site attack
- Antivirus technology

National cyberattacks
- Smart City IoT attacks
- Deep web
- SCADA tempering
- Hacking human implants
- Ransomware
- Medical/academic records
- DDoS/botnet attacks
- Drug trafficking
- Government documents
- Traffic light attacks

Global cyber terrorism
- Electro magnetic pulse attack
- Molecular computing
- Psychotronic remote control of the brain
- Remote neural monitoring satellite terrorism
- Satellite hacking
- AI activated autonomic software drones
- Airplane commandeering
- Nano crime-as-a-service
- Software nano cyborgs-stuxnet
- Cloud Virus Rain
- IoT nanogrid blackout
- Critical infrastructure bombs
- Espionage-as-a-service
- Medical device hacking
- Nano gene hacking

Technology intensity and sophistication

G1-DDoS   2010   G2 Cybercrime   2020   G3 Cyber terrorism   2030

Figure 6.1   A panoramic view of how malware is growing exponentially from a DoS single site attack into molecular autonomic and remotely guided nanobots that burn Smart Cities like Nero decided to burn Rome for fun! Computing miniaturization will allow computers to be implanted in our organs, or psychotronically turn a whole Smart City into a terminal ward or an insane asylum.

and their ingenious hackers have started working on the second generation of this weapon of mass destruction. No longer are hackers basement-dwelling weirdos, as portrayed in Hollywood productions. They're business people.

Here's something that could be the tip of the hacking iceberg: We were impressed by five prisoners from Marion Ohio, who built two personal computers from parts, hid them behind a plywood board in the ceiling of a closet, and then connected those computers to the Ohio Department of Rehabilitation and Correction's (ODRC) network to engage in cybershenanigans. The computers were cobbled together from *spare parts* that prisoners had collected from Marion Correction Institution's RET3, a program that helped to rehabilitate prisoners by getting them to break down old PCs into component parts for recycling. In the future, prisoners will continue practicing cybercrime from their cells. They will contact their bot master and provide him or her with details on the security CCTV and gates. The next thing we're going to hear is that prison IoT security devices are compromised including security CCTV monitors and the electronic gate locks.

Nowadays, a simple how-to video on YouTube or a Bitcoin-prepaid stresser/booter is enough to successfully perform an attack against even large websites and applications, something unseen in previous years. DDoS attacks were using botnets to hack target devices. Brian Krebs is now probably the most in-demand cyber-security expert in the field: he was among the first to tell about the evolution of Mirai and cover some of the security breaches and vulnerabilities. For his many years of hard work as a security journalist, his investigations of computer hacks, and the paths that people take to become cybercriminals, he was chosen as a target. Akamai, which hosted Krebs's blog on a pro bono basis, could not withstand a record-setting 620 Gbps attack by Mirai botnet and shut him off. Krebs received extortion threats, with the threats clearly referencing DDoS attacks: "If you will not pay in time, DDoS attack will start, your web-services will go down perma-nently. After that, price to stop will be increased to 5 BTC (Bit Coin) with further increment of 5 BTC for every day of attack." As we all know, censorship doesn't work over the Internet. The first massive DDoS was an IoT-based botnet. Mirai took the credit for it.

Hundreds of thousands of routers, cameras, DVRs, and other connected devices, even Wi-Fi-enabled coffee makers, made one of the biggest media stories of 2017 in the professional security community, hunting down Dyn, one of the world's largest domain name system (DNS) providers.

A fast and merciless attack made the world's most visited websites unavailable for hours, causing extreme collateral damage in a thoughtful infrastructure attack. Before that, Mirai had raised the bar of a possible threat by performing a 1 Tbps attack on OVH, a French cloud hosting provider, one of the biggest in its class. A paradigm shift in the network security landscape was experienced in 2016. Qrator Labs and Wallarm made three predictions at the end of 2015 that were fully real-ized during 2016.

We've talked about evolution as an exponential process, and the seamless flow of progressive innovations. But generation is a different phenomenon and has a different perspective: we're interested in really trying to understand how digital media technologies and sociocultural practices co-evolve. Within that, we're inter-ested in whether it is possible to identify discrete historical moments marked by digital transformations with distinctive sociocultural characteristics of continuity and change. We noticed that the line between generations is fuzzy. But, no one is accepting that to have fixed values, everyone is open to new "disruptive" technolo-gies. Particularly, our young generation. We can say that Moor's law with slight modifications (Moor-2) can be applied to the processing speed of a youngster's mind. Moore's law is a computing term that originated around 1970; the simpli-fied version of this law states that "processor speeds, or overall processing power for computers will double every two years." The mind of today's youngster (boys and girls 13 years of age) has doubled in speed and agility of thinking, compared with the mind of the youngster in 2000. The primary driving force of Moor-2 law is the exponential immersion and the stereoscopic multidimensionality of the mental vision of a youngster's mind, which correlates with the accelerating speed of the Internet. Youngsters of the second generation are in fact cyber natives. The divergence between academic culture and the delights of relay chatting became irreconcilable. This social rebellion planted the seeds of the first generation of hacking!

It reminds us of Gary Larson's joke when the dinosaur leader gave a speech to his fellow countrymen: "The picture's pretty bleak, gentlemen … The world's climates are changing, the mammals are taking over, and we all have a brain about the size of a walnut."

The World Wide Web generation: It started after 1991 as a new paradigm shift (technical innovation), doubling every decade.

The mobile generation: On January 9, 2007, Steve Jobs unveiled the iPhone 3 to the public at the Macworld 2007 Convention at the Moscone Center in San Francisco. Apple made a profit of $266 million in three days and sold 1.4 million iPhones in 2007. It was reported by Steve Jobs on July 18, 2008 at the Moscone Center that sales would reach 1 billion by April 2017. Apple's App Store contains more than 2.2 million applications available for the iPhone. According to *2600: Hacker Quarterly*, there are over a million registered hack applications that can be bought, rented, or are free.

The Second-Generation G2 DDoS

Most dictionaries provide us with the same definition for the term "generation": "pertaining to any method or technology that is expected or intended to supersede present day techniques."

Technology is the most influential change agent that signals, with its disruptive turbulence, the start of the new generation. So how did the second generation start and when? Cybercrimes of the second generation will be syphoning the best of the latest technological developments of the next seven to eight years. The distinction between legitimate and illegal activity may also become increasingly blurred. Most of the laws of the land have holes and gaps or may not apply to cybercrime. The current proximity between criminal spamming and legitimate marketing techniques, such as behavioral advertising, already serves as an indicator for this. The challenge for legislators will be to delineate the circumstances under which these activities may legitimately be conducted, and to ensure that as far as possible these measures are harmonized internationally. Criminalization will naturally also require sufficient capacity to investigate, disrupt, and prosecute.

The second-generation G2 DDoS will be very innovation-intensive and prolific, and will breed and spread everywhere like ivy. Cybercrime will not only tag along the latest disruptive technologies, but, as in medicine, it will force its way into the healthy systems of most lucrative companies. But, before we talk about G2 DDoS, let's describe the rationale behind the genesis of a Smart City.

Faced with rapid urbanization, city planners are turning to technology to solve a wide range of problems associated with modern cities. Smart Cities are the result of deep technology immersion. They are set to enhance our quality of life, and offer us more tranquility and better security in our home and workplace. Although not all Smart Cities are alike, they share three fundamental disruptive technologies that have quickly integrated into Smart City's architecture:

1. *Second-Generation G2 DDoS*: AI-centric embedded with electronics, software, sensors, actuators, and network connectivity, which enable these objects to collect and exchange data. Homes will have smart devices and appliances connected to a home area network (HAN). The convenience, availability, and reliability of externally managed cloud-computing resources will continue to be an appealing choice for many home dwellers who have no interest or experience in IT. According to Gartner, nearly 20.8 billion devices will be on the IoT by 2020. We can imagine the cybercrime opportunities available to malware professionals.
2. *Wearable and Implant Devices*: The integrity and security of medical data will be one of the biggest advantages of the IoT. Hacking medical records is a profitable business. There are thousands of crime service providers (CSP) who specialize in identity theft of medical records. Even insurance companies resort to their services to collect evidence on insurance fraud from subscribers.
3. *Machine-to-Machine (M2M) Networks*: This is going to be the most influential paradigm shift that the IoT can offer. As a matter of fact, there is a little confusion about the similarity between M2M and the IoT. Simply put, M2M is where machines use a network or a city's grid to communicate with remote applications that monitor and control either the machine itself or the surrounding environment. On the other hand, in the IoT domain, all smart devices enable us to interact with our environment where the physical world merges with the digital world.

Health monitoring and wearable devices for patients are becoming extremely popular, as they are able to transmit a patient's real-time, vital sign data from his or her home to medical staff. Such Wi-Fi-powered devices include glucometers, scales, and heart rate and ultrasound monitors. Furthermore, wearable devices are gaining attention among the elderly and those with chronic illness. With the push of a button, a person is able to alert medical staff of an emergency situation.

The Dawn of G2 DDoS Attacks

The latest technological fantasy predicts that a highly digitized city will lead to urban utopia. But a Smart City is *idealistic hype*, although the term is very attractive. Every city is hopping on the Smart City bandwagon and stumping its own routine. It is the race of the century and the finish line is far away. Every city dreams of tying the Internet to everything. It is the same universal bogus myth of physical fitness delusion: any obese person can turn into Mr. Atlas in a couple of months. A huge canyon separates a digital city from being a Smart City. A Smart City should enhance livability, economic prosperity, IoT metering and analytics, energy efficiency management, and, above all, the security of the critical infrastructures of the Smart City. However, the biggest challenge for Smart Cities is the lack of a smart security grid to protect critical systems. This is a city's Achilles' heel.

Smart City Fight against G2 DDoS

G2 DDoS will mature in 2020, so how are we going to build a Smart City with the most advanced defense? Here are the most critical components required to reach the promised Smart City:

- *Smart Devices (IoT)*: Configured in the form of an IoT structure. A typical Smart City will have a grid that keeps track—according to Cisco flow—of 10,000,000,000,000,000,000,000 bytes of data over 18,200,000,000 connections. Comparing the human body, here's what we have: medical authorities estimate that the number of human cells is around 70 trillion, while estimates put the number of bacteria living in and on our bodies to be 100 trillion, meaning that we're well outnumbered by our prokaryotic friends!! The magic here is that all the cells are connected to several *grids* and real-time sensors are keeping us healthy. So, IoTs will be constantly surrounded by hostile self-propagating "worms" known to proliferate across multiple connected networks to acquire easily commoditized information such as health care information, social security numbers, and banking credentials, or even to take control of a significant number of systems, and finally, to tarnish the city's quality of life. DDoS payload vectors will be hovering over the Smart City like hyenas over a cadaver, trying to penetrate the city's Smart Grid. Many of the smart devices will morph into zombies that will join the attacking army.
- *City Smart Grid*: Without a Smart Grid there is no Smart City. The canonical rule is that the grid should be built as the city's ground zero that connects everything to everything (EtE), specifically, homes-to-business, homes-to-utilities, government-to-government, government-to-citizens, government-to-business, government-to-employees, and citizens-to-business (Figure 6.2).
- *Governance System*: To monitor citizens' accountability and sustain prosperity and economic growth.
- *Digital Immunity (The Smart Vaccine) Grid*: To protect all devices and infrastructure systems. The Cognitive Early Warning Predictive System (CDWPS) is the most advanced and smartest defense system, capable of stopping all DDoS attacks. The human body is grid-centric, with autonomic and self-regulating components that exchange intelligence data with one another. The blood grid alone is 100,000 miles, delivering oxygen and collecting waste. We'll be talking about it in detail in Chapter 9.

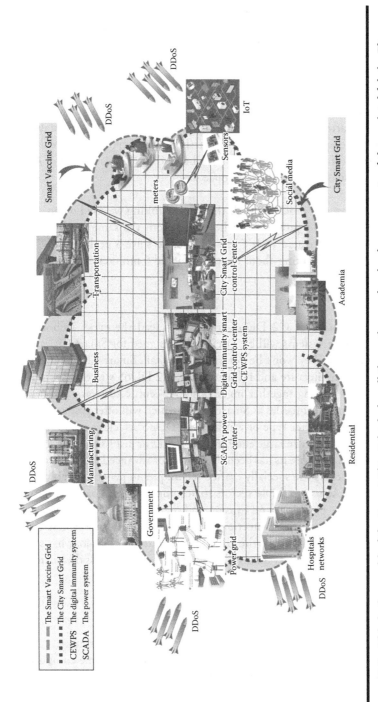

Figure 6.2 **This is the world of the Smart City. It includes all the active modernized components of the societal fabric. They are managed and controlled by scalable critical success factors for safety, security, and quality of life for all the residents. (© 2014 Copyright MERIT CyberSecurity Group. All rights reserved.)**

It is going to take a long time for Smart Cities to corral 21 million devices into one cohesive well-secured grid. Connecting IoT devices to the grid is only half the job. It will take at least 10 years before it becomes a reality. The management of the sensors and data from IoT devices is truly a mental agony leading to chaos and turmoil before Smart City achieves this monumental task.

The DDoS enterprise lords are also getting ready for the Smart City's IoT infrastructure, the Internet infrastructure, and the city's critical infrastructures.

Technology has artificially been augmenting not only our brains, but malware as well. AI will be the soul of G2 DDoS. The Darth Vaders of cybercrime are developing ultra-smart tools with great secrecy much beyond the sophistication of AVT security software systems. Albert Einstein once said:

> We cannot solve our problems with the same thinking we used when we created them. No problem can be solved from the same level of consciousness that created it. If I had an hour to solve a problem I'd spend 55 minutes thinking about the problem and 5 minutes thinking about solutions.

He was right.

The second generation of G2 DDoS attacks will lead the cyber technology industry. New malware systems will be specifically designed for Smart Cities and tested to make sure that they won't be detected if they fail. Smart City landscapes will have a different architecture and infrastructure. G2 DDoS strategists will not only be dexterous in putting together ingeniously AI-centric software "cyborgs," but they will also aim their missiles at Smart Cities, which will offer golden opportunities for a new and smarter type of warfare. G2 DDoS attackers are no longer solely interested in taking down large enterprise networks or just stealing data. One of the most dangerous new threats has been the growth of advanced targeted attacks (ATAs) in which attackers use specially crafted techniques to penetrate companies for specific goals. ATAs use multiple vectors to accomplish their goal, combining custom malware, spear phishing, and evasion and denial-of-service techniques to evade or disable existing security protections and steal customer- or business-critical information. In addition to ATA, the G2 DDoS assault menu-du-jour has some very ambitious attacks on the City Smart Grid (CSG). We will discuss the anatomy of the attacks first and then talk about defense solutions.

List of Intelligent Assaults

The following is a list of Smart City G2 DDoS futuristic potential assaults:

Cloud Computing: A Smart City will use the cloud to offload some computing overhead and switch to operating expenses from capital expenses, hardware performance elasticity, the business continuity benefits—they're all real. But so are the dangers of a DDoS disaster. There's a problem with moving your servers and data up to the cloud: it increases your attack surface. Suddenly, you're not the only one at risk from a DDoS attack. Other customers of the cloud service provider (CSP) are too, and that can have implications for you.

When a DDoS attack hits a CSP data center, the traffic may be targeted at a particular tenant, but because the attacker is using the CSP's Internet connection to reach that tenant, it will naturally choke off others' traffic too.

Andy Shoemaker, CEO of DDoS consulting at Nimbus DDoS, put it eloquently: "By the time the traffic gets to you or the customer, that's already being targeted: the damage is already done. It doesn't matter if you filter the traffic at the small end of the funnel. The big end of the funnel is already overflowing."

The CSP service-level criteria (SLC) centers on the system's capacity and a bandwidth Internet connectivity to and from its customers. This bandwidth is then limited or simply charged by usage, depending on the purchased service level. CSPs and similar utility companies provide a steady supply of power independent of the number of customers or workload. However, capacity and network bandwidth are service facilities and obey the laws of queuing metrics. In other words, they will reach a level of saturation and scalability creating a real bottleneck.

In Smart Cities, grid performance is a critical success factor (CSF) that cannot be ignored. A Smart City Grid workload is a composite of all IoT devices and all the city's infrastructures. Sizing hardware capacity requires knowledge and blackout experience. Malware service providers (MSP) know all the CSFs of the systems that run a city's grid, and that "the eggs are in one basket," takes place on the cloud. They will be carefully drumming up a series of DDoS at the right time. MSP criminals are cunning enough to ride on a defective *open source* such as Elasticsearch and then use Linux DDoS Trojan Mayday, and with that, they will have compromised several Amazon EC2 virtual machines (VMs). They were able to launch a user datagram protocol (UDP)-based DDoS attack from the compromised cloud instances. They utilized the outbound bandwidth of the CSP, Amazon in this case. This is a far from desirable situation for CSPs. If their public IP address range becomes linked to a DDoS attack, they could find it registered on blacklists or on individual organizations' firewall blacklists.

CSPs monitor their managed networks and will shut down the offending VM if needed. All cloud customers should have a well-configured, hardened, egress firewall on their perimeter, which will prevent the need for such a shutdown by the CSP in the first place. The egress filter would, for instance, block outgoing network time protocol (NTP) traffic or would block any requests to an external web server once a threshold of connections per second has been reached. This firewall should be monitored as well. It is one thing to block the traffic, but another to find the actual cause of it within the internal network.

The cause of DDoS traffic leaving the network is usually associated with the overflow of packets, installed on one or more systems, which link that infected system to a much larger, global botnet. Not only does this result in the DDoS-related issues mentioned before, but it usually gives the botnet owner full control of the infected systems, leading to risks of data theft, outages, and possibly even data ransom situations. Quality host-based malware detection and prevention tools are a must-have for any system.

Dedicated DDoS mitigation products could also be deployed for rapid response. The customer would direct all incoming and outgoing traffic through the mitigation "filter," which would purge the DDoS attack traffic from the stream. When using a third-party provider, the outgoing bandwidth of the CSP would still be consumed if the customer is (unknowingly) participating in a DDoS attack. The incoming bandwidth of the CSP would still be saturated when the customer is a target of a DDoS attack. This means that it is important to weigh up what solution works best for the environment.

A well-placed intrusion detection or prevention system could catch suspicious or malicious traffic as well. This might not only detect the DDoS traffic, but it could also detect and prevent the malware and botnet command and control traffic in the first place, which of course is a much better situation.

Autonomic Cyborg Attacks: This is another futuristic, horrifying, and creepy type of attack fabricated for Smart Cities. The attack combines two distinct technologies (autonomic computing and cybernetics), which have never been used in building a cyber invasion.

Cybernetics is the science that deals with "self-governance." A cybernetic machine controls itself by incorporating *feedback* signals—originally referred to as a "circular causal" relationship. So, if we build a machine with a specific goal, we can program it to steer itself until it reaches that goal.

We can say that any physical implants (tissues or artificial objects) inserted in a person's body makes that person a cyborg! In a typical example, a human with an artificial cardiac pacemaker or an implantable cardioverter defibrillator would be considered a cyborg (short for cybernetics and organism). These devices measure voltage potentials in the body, perform signal processing, and can deliver electrical stimuli, using this synthetic feedback mechanism to keep the person alive.

Cybernetics has created incredible futuristic systems that are used in medicine, the military, and space. Cybercriminals have been hiring cyberneticists for some pretty interesting demonic attack projects. Here is a modest list of some of the pioneering projects that will raise the bar of creativity to the highest level. The Defense Advanced Research Projects Agency (DARPA) is developing a neural implant to remotely control the movement of sharks. The shark's unique senses would then be exploited to provide data feedback in relation to enemy ship movement or underwater explosives.

The use of neural implants has recently been attempted, with success, on cockroaches. Surgically applied electrodes were put on the insect, which were remotely controlled by a human. The results, although sometimes different, basically showed that the cockroach could be controlled by the impulses it received through the electrodes. DARPA is now funding this research because of its obvious beneficial applications to the military and other areas.

Theorist Dr. Andy Clark, professor of philosophy and chair in logic and metaphysics at the University of Edinburgh, Scotland, suggests that interactions between humans and technology result in the creation of a cyborg system. In this model, "cyborg" is defined as a part biological part mechanical system, which results in the augmentation of the biological component and the creation of a more complex whole.

At the 2009 Institute of Electrical and Electronics Engineers (IEEE) Micro-Electronic Mechanical Systems (MEMS) Conference in Italy, researchers demonstrated the first "wireless" flying-beetle cyborg. Engineers at the University of California at Berkeley have pioneered the design of a "remote-controlled beetle," funded by DARPA. Filmed evidence of this can be viewed at http://appleseed.wikia.com/wiki/Cyborg. This was followed later that year by a demonstration of the wireless control of a "lift-assisted" moth-cyborg. Eventually, researchers plan to develop MEMS for dragonflies, bees, rats, and pigeons. For the MEMS cybernetic bug to be considered a success, it must fly 100 meters from a starting point, guided via computer into a controlled landing within 5 meters of a specific end. Once landed, the cybernetic bug must remain in place. Retinal implants are another form of cyberization in medicine.

Autonomic Computing: This is another technology that will, unfortunately, fall into the hands of malware traders. The term *autonomic* is derived from human biology. The autonomic nervous system monitors your heartbeat, checks your blood sugar level, and keeps your body temperature close to 98.6°F without any conscious effort on your part.

Malware planners and strategists will fabricate attack software systems with the unique characteristics of autonomic computing: self-configuring, self-healing, self-optimizing, and self-protecting. Here's an interesting scenario of how "lone wolf" cyber terrorists will surprise the world with a leading-edge quantum leap.

DDoS will become a software cyborg.

Ray Kurzweil also talked about "singularity," which is the merger of computer intelligence and human intelligence. He said that "By 2029, computers will have human-level intelligence ... the process towards this *singularity* has already begun... that leads to computers to have human intelligence, which will be stored inside our brains, and connected to the cloud, expanding who we are. Today, that's not just a future scenario," Kurzweil said. "It's here, in part, and it's going to accelerate."

In the next decade, our biological intelligence will merge with computer intelligence, and the technological change will be exponential and human progress will prevail. Smart Cities will contribute to the quality of citizens. AI, smart systems, cybernetics and autonomic computing, cloud computing, even nano-technologies, will bring a new wave of modernization to Smart Cities across all industries. Smart City Grids and clouds (public and private) will deploy a digital immunity (DI) paradigm as the smartest defense environment against raging information warfare.

Autonomic cyborg attack = Autonomic intelligence + Cybernetics intelligence

+ IRC network + Syndicated crime cloud

+ Cloud botnet + Selected cloud targets

Crime-as-a-Service for Smart City: The CaaS business model drives the digital underground economy by providing a wide range of commercial services that facilitate almost any type of cybercrime. Criminals are able to freely procure services such as the rental of botnets, denial-of-service attacks, malware development, data theft, and password cracking, to commit crimes themselves. This has facilitated the move by traditional organized crime groups (OCGs) into cybercrime areas. The financial gain that cybercrime experts receive from offering these services stimulates the commercialization of cybercrime as well as its innovation and further sophistication.

The anonymization techniques used in parts of the Internet, known as *darknets*, allow users to communicate freely without the risk of being traced. These are perfectly legitimate tools for citizens to protect their privacy. However, the features of these privacy networks are also of primary interest to criminals who abuse such anonymity on a massive scale for illicit online trade in drugs, weapons, stolen goods, forged IDs, and child sexual exploitation.

In the Smart City environment, current and future developments such as big and fast data, the Internet of Everything, wearable devices, augmented reality, cloud computing, artificial intelligence, and the transition to IPv6, will provide additional attack vectors and increased attack "surfaces" for criminals. This will be exacerbated by how emerging and new *disruptive* technologies will be used and how they will influence people's online behavior.

The new term will be *crime-as-a-business* (CaaB), or even crime-as-a-career (CaaC). This is an open invitation to graduates with knowledge in disruptive technologies to join the business of cybercrime. It starts with the lords of cybercrime, the chief malware officers, who are as ambitious as Amazon's Jeff Bezos or Alibaba's Jack Ma, with a market value of US$428 billion and US$231 billion, respectively.

In the next decade, the malware rockefellers will have created a deep-rooted CaaS conglomerate network with 50,000 satellite portals, supported by a global dark network of supply chains. We're going to call it "MalMart," which will undeniably be the world's biggest online cybercrime enterprise. It will grow exponentially with a market value of $550 billion and will offer first-class hacker-to-cracker, botmaster-to-botmaster, and mob-to-mob business and banking transactions via global web portals on private clouds. One of MalMart's unique services will be a complete portfolio of "prefab assembly required" cloud DDoS hacking tools. Then, MalMart will have a large network of cells for heavy-duty actors, who specialize in organized cybercrime and Mafia-like crime activities.

In 2017, Amazon has 341,000 employees serving 300 million loyal customers. Walmart employs 2.3 million associates around the world—1.5 million in the United States alone. By comparison, MalMart in 2025 will employ 500,000 hacktivists, insiders, spies, engineers, terrorists, information and communications technology (ICT) gurus, even politicians, to support 2,000,000,000 active members.

Games of the Drones: Unmanned aerial vehicles (UAVs), commonly referred to as drones, are reshaping the ways in which survey and mapping professionals operate. Industries that widely use UAVs for gathering data from the sky include utilities, construction, and agriculture because they can be quickly airborne and offer a more cost-effective solution than manned aircraft. But in the next decade, there will be ultra-smart software drones.

Serial hacker] Samy Kamkar is probably best known for creating and releasing the fastest spreading virus of all time, the MySpace worm Samy, and subsequently being raided for it by the US Secret Service, under the Patriot Act. In 2013, he chiseled an attack (and posted it online for others to exploit) that allowed him to fly his own serial drone that would seek out other flying robots in the sky, hack them, and turn them into a physical botnet army of UAVs under his control. The software, dubbed SkyJack, compromises smartphone wireless-phone wireless connections that remotely control drones, such as the wildly popular Parrot AR model, commonly sold at Costco, and allows hackers to commandeer a victim drone's flight control and camera systems.

The Samy Kamkar drone attack is a great tool for cybercriminals.

Over 500,000 Parrot AR models have been sold, and Kamkar's technique should prove useful to hijack other drones, such as those that will undoubtedly be delivering goods around cities in the coming years—misdirecting packages and pizzas in real time. The future of robotic crime looks promising indeed to Crime Inc., and it is beginning to dedicate significant resources to the effort.

The big revelation now is that drones can carry and guide DDoS missiles and bypass a Smart City's smart barricades. Drones can be fun; on the one hand, cyber predators have their ear to the ground and are evaluating every disruptive technology as it rolls off the production line. On the other hand, drone attacks show the importance of cybersecurity during the design of these platforms and their safety implications. Drone-DDoS is, in fact, a "de-authentication/dissociation" attack that aims to de-authenticate almost all of the city's mobile phones and make them insecure. Just imagine, 50,000 mobiles turn into a massive botnet under the control of a rancorous ghoul who wants to have fun on Friday afternoon.

In the next section, we will discuss more sophisticated and perilous attacks.

Imbedded chips: Biohacking, where computing devices are injected under the skin, provides a novel way to sneak through both physical and digital scans. That's why US Navy petty officer Seth Wahle, now an engineer at APA Wireless, implanted a chip between the thumb and forefinger—the purlicue apparently— of his left hand. It has a near field communications (NFC) antenna that pings Android phones, asking them to open a link. Once the user agrees to open that link and install a malicious file, their phone connects to a remote computer, the owner of which can carry out further exploits on that mobile device. Put simply, that Android device is compromised. In a demonstration for *Forbes*, Wahle used the Metasploit penetration testing software on his laptop to force an Android device to take a picture of his cheery visage.

Humans will become cyborgs in the "next step in human evolution."

At least that's according to Amal Graafstra, an amateur biohacker from Seattle. Amal is the cyborg who has implanted wireless chips under his skin to gain *superhuman* abilities. These chips allow him to enter his house, log on to his computer, start his motorcycle, and even activate his smart gun, all with just the wave of a hand. The 40-year-old father started a biohacking company, known as Dangerous Things, from his basement in 2013, where he makes implantable devices that can be shipped anywhere in the world. The chips, called radio-frequency identification (RFID) chips, use radio waves to wirelessly communicate with tags attached to objects.

Here's what James Cagney once said about crime: "you've reading a lot of stuff about 'crime don't pay.' Don't be a sucker! That's for yaps and small-timers on shoestrings. Not for people like us."

Car hacking is another attractive criminal technology that has car thieves drooling at the mouth. Hacking the internals of computing infrastructures is a true engineering skill that makes automobile manufacturers mentally bewildered and comatose. The more driving controls wired into a car's black box, the more astonishing hacking skills will prevail. Wireless, RFID, and Bluetooth technologies have been arming drones with funny names (New DJI Mavic, Yuneec Typhoon H, Air Dog, Parrot Disco) with techno-modern, remotely guided cyber missiles to attack autonomous cars.

Academic Malware Cells to Market Diplomas and Grades: By the next decade, malware will be so advanced and cultivated that governments will have to create a dedicated agency to fight malware, like a pandemic of infectious disease that will spread throughout the globe. Academia will also be severely infected with new offensives. Academic malware will spread globally and many reputable institutions that have earned a worldwide reputation will realize that they will be easy targets—like banks—for grade and diploma thefts.

Here's a chilling scenario of what will happen to the academic world. Several organized crime syndicates will specialize in academic terrorism. Most of their members will be gifted students who have been strangled by the medieval mentality of Don Quichotte's professors who preach asymmetrical education that has no mental protein leading to mind obesity, is not compatible with the modern world, is asymptotic thinking, and is insulting to the intelligence of the young mind.

Academia-as-a-service will open its membership to radicals who will intimidate institutions, ridicule their professors (knowledge givers) with their asymptotic thinking, and insult the intelligence of the young mind. The whole concept of classroom, attendance, exams, and grades will be so antiquated and defunct.

Academia focuses on grades and not on education. New graduates get a job based on their academic accomplishments exemplified by A or F.

Since DDoS is the AK-47 of the Internet, academic hackers will use DDoS to create shock and awe in Fortune 50 universities in a Smart City. The first attack will have an army of 3000 hijacked devices that are part of an invisible and covert botnet. Registration files will be abducted, divulging information on tuition payment transactions and credit card records between issuing and acquiring banks. The second attack will be on the academic database, robbing the grades, scrambling and encrypting them, and locking them in a cloud vault. The third attack will attack the diploma database, forge the names, use skeletal diplomas, and deliver fresh diplomas to clients overseas.

Deep Web: The Deep Web is the black hole of the Internet. It is estimated that 90% of all Internet data and websites are hidden from search engine indexing; this area of the Internet is known as the Deep Web. There is much confusion between the two, with some outlets and researchers freely interchanging between them. However, the dark web is not the Deep Web; it is only part of the Deep Web. The dark web relies on darknets, that is, networks where connections are made between trusted peers. Examples of dark web systems include The Onion Router (Tor) and the Invisible Internet Project (I2P). There is another smaller subset of the Deep Web that consists of darknet markets and sites about drugs, pornography, weapons, assassins, counterfeiting, forgeries, hacking, and the like. This section is called the *dark web*.

The next chapter of the Deep Web black market looks even bigger than ever before—and it'll play out on a global stage. Movies, books, television shows, and even a play are all in the works, bringing the narrative of the Deep Web to a mainstream audience like never before. What we've learned about the Deep Web in the past year is this: It's a hydra. Cutting off one head only means two more will grow in its place.

Tor, The Onion Router: We need to mention the value of anonymity and privacy that gave birth to "The Onion Router" with its famous acronym Tor. It is free software enabling anonymous communication. Tor directs Internet traffic through a free, worldwide, volunteer network consisting of more than 7000 relays to conceal a user's location and usage from anyone conducting network surveillance or traffic analysis.

Tor users can surf the Internet, chat, and send instant messages anonymously. It is used by a wide variety of people for both licit and illicit purposes. Tor has been used by criminal enterprises, hacktivism groups, and law enforcement agencies at cross-purposes, sometimes simultaneously; likewise, agencies within the US government variously fund Tor to track criminals. Tor is used for illegal activities, for example, to gain access to censored information, to organize political activities, or to circumvent laws against criticism of heads of state.

In the next decade, Tor developers will expand the software's capability and accessibility, no matter what level of tech literacy a person possesses. In short, everything Tor is doing is meant to give more people easy access to powerful anonymity, and the developers behind the project are almost all prominent liberation technology activists with their hands in projects all over the Internet and the world. Given Tor's proven ability to challenge authority and resist power, it's easy to see why governments around the world might be interested in keeping close tabs on those involved.

The future looks very bright for the Deep Web. Developers will integrate new technologies in cryptocurrency, encryption, and private networking. The Deep Web will be an active podium for whistleblowers to reveal government spying and track social networks. The Deep Web will be the right asylum for hacktivists who will reveal secret arms deals and the activities of drug cartels. The Deep Web will have hundreds of Edward Snowdens who will unearth the secrets of totalitarian governments and the political and religious persecution of citizens.

Drugs: When we talk about the future of drugs, there are three items that cannot be ignored:

1. From the beginning of time, and to the end of time, humans will love drugs. We have the greatest affinity to get high and suppress our distress. The Internet will be the train that will take people to euphoria land.
2. People who supply these intoxicants, particularly banned ones, will pocket a load of cash, and people will spend their last penny to get some.
3. Drugs will help people learn, think, relax, sleep, or simply to forget, for a bit. This prediction is not looking like a bad one; there is already a huge gray market in drugs that enhance athletic performance, image, and mood—and it's a market that is rapidly expanding.

The online drug trade, however, will be blazing a trail into the next decade and beyond, whether the world's police like it or not. The drug trading zone will remain highly resilient to any attempt to destroy it. In November 2013, the world's police— including the FBI, Europol, and Britain's National Crime Agency—closed the biggest online drug market, *Silk Road 2.0*, in a blaze of publicity during Operation Onymous. But just weeks later, the dark market was back doing a roaring trade.

The story of Silk Road is very stimulating! It was founded in February 2011 and the name "Silk Road" comes from a historical network of trade routes between Europe, India, China, and many other countries on the Afro-Eurasian landmass. Silk Road was an online black market and the first modern darknet market, best known as a platform for selling illegal drugs. As part of the Dark Web, it was operated as a Tor hidden service, such that online users were able to browse it anonymously and securely without potential traffic monitoring.

In March 2013, the site had 10,000 products for sale, 70% of which were drugs. In October 2014, there were 13,756 listings for drugs, grouped under the headings stimulants, psychedelics, prescription, precursors, other, opioids, ecstasy, dissociatives, and steroids/PED.

Mike Power, author of *Drugs 2.0: The Web Revolution That's Changing How the World Gets High*, described how the online drug trade might fare over the next decade or two. "At the moment, the online trade in drugs is a minority sport, a good way of buying high quality drugs," he told me. "Even now it's tipping over from early adopters into the mainstream. It will get bigger, easier to use, and more widespread. There will be more sites and more people using them because it is the perfect business model: anonymous, commission-based, peer-reviewed, postal drug dealing. Online dealing is not a replacement for trafficking cartels, it's never going to work on that level, but if you've got a kilo of MDMA it's the way to go."

Harvard Business Review published a very interesting report on drugs titled "Like It or Not, 'Smart Drugs' Are Coming to the Office." The unauthorized use of prescription drugs such as the ADHD medications Adderall and Ritalin and the narcolepsy drug Modafinil is now common among American university students. They use these drugs not to escape work and avoid responsibility but to be able to work more and better.

As we step into the third generation of the Internet, the landscape of drug crime will also be modernized accordingly. The rise of the criminal UAV is completely incompatible with our current security paradigm. The payment and delivery of drugs will be totally invisible and genuinely camouflaged through the Bitcoin crypto market on the dark cloud. DDoS drones (Category 1) will be programmed to create botnets with 1000 zombie slaves to keep law enforcement busy somewhere else. Category 2 messenger drones will create holding stations for the cryptocurrency payment information between brokers–buyers–sellers. Category 3 shipment delivery drones will carry the encrypted destination location of the parcel.

On the sports front, in the next decade, the issue of performance enhancing drugs (PED) will create a controversy hurricane of sport prejudice and political rivalry. In the 2028 Olympiad, contestants will be freely taking event-specific PED, such as anabolic androgenic steroids, ephedrine, blood doping, painkillers, and stimulants, and report doing so before their events. The Olympics will become the most veritable stage to assess the value of PED and their effects on athletes, by gender, race, and training. Athletes have been unfairly victimized and kicked out and banned from all future events. In the next decade, the International Olympic Committee (IOC), the International Amateur Athletics Federation (IAAF), the National Football League (NFL), and other reputable agencies will revise their policies and rules on PED.

Established in 2011, the Global Commission on Drug Policy (GCDP) is a key international reference regarding the impacts of the current drug control strategy, proposing innovative and effective policy recommendations that protect human rights, scale-up harm reduction, and promote development. It is composed of 23 political leaders and leading thinkers from across the political spectrum.

The GCDP surprised the world when, in 2014, it released a ground-breaking report that highlighted *five* pathways to drug policies, including (1) putting health and community safety first; (2) ensuring equitable access to controlled medicines;

(3) ending the criminalization of people who use or possess drugs; (4) promoting alternatives to incarceration for low-level actors in illicit drug markets, including cultivators; and (5) encouraging diverse experiments in legally regulated markets, beginning with, but not limited to, cannabis, coca leaf, and certain other psychoactive substances.

The GCDP yearly report published in 2016 examined in further detail the third proposed pathway concerning full decriminalization, understood as ending all criminal and civil penalties for drug consumption and possession for personal use, and why it is an essential step toward regulation in drug policy reform.

The commission chairman Kofi Annan, former UN Secretary General, said: "Punitive measures do not create a drug free society, we must learn to live with drugs so that they cause the least possible harm ... States must end all penalties both criminal and civil-for drug possession for personal use, and the cultivation of drugs for personal consumption or athletic performance enhancement, and implement alternatives to punishment for all low-level, non violent actors in the drug trade."

M2M Hacking: We don't have to wait 20 years before we automate our homes and cars, and connect them to a central hub in a Smart City. Technology is accelerating like a snowball down a hill. Pretty soon, our life will be full of over-automated items that get hacked every other day. Androids are the coming force. We are talking of the IoT—a world where sensors allow machines to talk to one another. And, as with our human-driven Internet, the IoT is a game-changing, hugely significant opportunity for the economy and business. Various research studies have pegged the value of the IoT at multiple trillions of dollars. Cisco1 and GE2 estimate that the size of the IoT pie is over $10 trillion. Research firm IDC estimates that, in 2020, over 40% of all data in the world will be data resulting from machines talking to one another. In the next decade, we're going to have more cyberattacks on our Smart Cities than all the global wars.

If the IoT estimates are over $10 trillion, then M2M crime will not be a small hiccup. There's no standard rule of thumb that will give us a definitive estimate on M2M crime. Cybercrime will continue its stratospheric growth over the next decade, according to a recent report published by Cybersecurity Ventures. While there are numerous contributors to the rise in cybercrime—which is expected to cost the world more than $6 trillion by 2021, up from $3 trillion in 2015—the most obvious predictor is a massive expansion of the global attack surface that hackers target. Putting things in perspective, here are some eye-popping stats related to an IoT turbulent boom.

- 300 billion connected devices by 2025
- $10 trillion cost of crime by 2020
- $79 billion smart-home industry
- 90% of cars will be connected by 2025
- 210 million wearable devices by 2025

A particularly vivid and realistic near-future fiction published last month in *New York Magazine*, described a cyberattack on New York that involved the hacking of cars, the water system, hospitals, elevators, and the power grid. In these stories, thousands of people die. Chaos ensues. While some of these scenarios overhype the mass destruction, the individual risks are all real. And traditional computer and network security isn't prepared to deal with them.

Cyber threats have evolved from targeting and harming computers, networks, and smartphones, to humans, cars, railways, planes, power grids, and anything with a heartbeat or an electronic pulse. As the planet morphs into a digital global society of interconnected people, places, and things, there's a whole lot of cyber that needs to be defended.

Social Security, Passport, and ID Theft: Passports and ID are uniquely powerful documents—and fake ones even more so. They act not only as a form of identification for crossing borders (including ones the buyer could normally not easily cross), but they can also be used for everything from opening bank accounts, applying for loans, purchasing property, and much more—so it is no surprise that they are a valuable commodity. There are several sites on the Deep Web claiming to sell passports and other forms of official ID, with prices varying from country to country, and seller to seller. As mentioned in the Introduction, the validity of such services is hard to verify without actually purchasing from them, and especially in cases of things like citizenship these services may well be simple scams preying on vulnerable people in different countries who are looking to obtain citizenship in order to remain in that country (Figure 6.3).

Medico-Ransomware: The most valuable commodity to citizens is not cash (that comes in at Number 2), medical records are the most precious strategic area for cyber thieves. If medical records get in the hands of crooks, they can easily get fast money from patients by kidnapping historical medical records from hospitals

Figure 6.3   US citizenship for sale for under 6000 USD. (From http://xfnwy-ig7olypdq5r.onion.to.)

and insurance institutions that convey more about the temporal health profile of patients.

In a ransomware attack, how do cybercriminals attack health care infrastructure, encrypt data, and then demand payment to recover access?

Although the standard vector is malicious email attachments—the most common being Word documents, Adobe files, archives, and JavaScript—other vectors include links to booby-trapped websites, compromised websites, malicious web ads, malware links in social networking posts, and unpatched versions of Microsoft Office and Adobe Reader or Flash.

So why is medico-ransomware on the rise in health care? A recent survey carried out by the University of Kent found that 41% of respondents hit by this type of malware paid the ransom. Each payment encourages future attackers to commit the same crime. Medico-ransomware takes less time and effort compared to stealing medical records, so the cost/benefit definitely favors the cybercriminals.

Here's how medico-ransomware predators go hunting. CryptoLocker is a ransomware Trojan that hit the Internet on September 5, 2013, targeting the Microsoft Windows platform. CryptoLocker uses social engineering techniques to trick the user into running it. More specifically, the victim receives an email with a password-protected ZIP file purporting to be from a logistics company. CryptoLocker propagates via infected email attachments and via an existing botnet. After the Trojan has downloaded the public key (PK), it saves it inside the following Windows registry key: HKCUSoftwareCryptoLockerPublic Key. Then, it starts encrypting files on the computer's hard disk and every network drive the infected user has access to, using RSA public-key cryptography, with the private key stored only on the malware's control servers. The single copy of the private key, which will allow you to decrypt the files, is located on a secret server on the Internet; the server will destroy the key after a time specified in this window. After that, nobody will ever be able to restore the files. To obtain the private key for this computer, which will automatically decrypt files, you need to pay.

Here's the big nut that ought to be cracked: Every citizen has medical (in or out patient) records at a hospital or ambulatory care unit (clinic), insurance claim records, and even legal medical records at a law firm during a dispute with hospitals. Hospitals get their revenues from patients, insurance, donations, and government grants. The Health Insurance Portability and Accountability Act (HIPAA) allows hospitals to transfer and exchange confidential patient records. When ransomware attacks, the damage can be devastating and in some cases, entire hospitals have been crippled for days. The thieves recognize both the value and the vulnerabilities of health care information and the security gaps that exist in the connected world.

Situation 1—User at Home: Let's say that the ransomware attacker uses CryptoLocker, which gets installed by a Zbot variant (Trojan used to carry out malicious tasks). After execution inside the user's computer, it adds itself to Startup under a random name and tries to communicate with a command and control server. A public key and a corresponding Bitcoin address will be sent to the user's computer. Using asymmetric encryption (a public key to encrypt and a private key for decrypting files), an email will be sent to the user asking him or her about the ransom. When the user refuses to comply with the attacker's demand, CryptoLocker begins encrypting databases, CAD files, financial data, and more than 70 types of files, and cripples the user's machine. Windows-savvy system users know how to circumvent the trap. Breaking the encryption is a very arduous task.

CryptoLocker doesn't freeze the user's computer, but it keeps everything running except personal files, such as documents, spreadsheets, and images, which are encrypted. The criminals retain the only copy of the decryption key on their server—it is not saved on the user's computer, so he or she cannot unlock the files without their assistance. Out of desperation, the user complies in the end, and will surrender and pay in Bitcoins. The attackers will mail him or her the instructions on how to create a bitcoin wallet and use the blockchain. Bitcoins will eventually get converted into dollars.

Situation 2—the Medical Records: This is the work of professional crooks who know what they're doing. They carefully craft an attack plan describing the details of the assault and their retreat without leaving a trace. They know where the servers are, and how to crack the database of the patient records. Crooks know the value of these records better than care providers. The attackers will initially perform a mass scan to find these unprotected MongoDB databases, then they will access the unprotected sites and hold the data for ransom using Harak1r1 0.2 Bitcoin ransomware. Medico-ransomware is viciously addictive and pervasive. It beats hijacking an airplane.

Situation 3—Insurance Records: This is another "cave of sesame" full of treasure that ransom attackers will go after to open. Every employed citizen, retired, below the poverty level, student, government employee, and even prisoner enjoys some sort of health insurance that includes members of the family. A health insurance claim record includes a wealth of personal information. Among a few other tidbits are eligibility and denial, social security numbers, dates of birth, physical addresses, and victims' full names, type of treatment, name of physician, psychiatric treatment, chronic ailment, prescribed medication, and laboratory results. But most importantly is the payment for each claim.

The Medical Bermuda Triangle: The National Health Care Anti-Fraud Association estimates that 3% of the health care industry's expenditure in the United States is due to fraudulent activities, amounting to a cost of about $51 billion. Other estimates attribute as much as 10% of the total health care spend in the United States to fraud—about $115 billion annually. Another study of all types of fraud committed in US insurance institutions (property-and-casualty, business liability, health care, social security, etc.) put the true cost at between 33% and 38% of the total cash flow through the system. The bottom line, fraud is one of the biggest money-making crimes in the United States. Currently, there's a limited cure for it, but a DI system will have nano anti-fraud smart functionalities to trap all the fraudulent transactions and tie them to the money matrix and crack wide open the exclusive club of the Lords.

Many hospitals and other industries use highly radioactive materials for medical imaging and other purposes. If these toxic substances are packed around conventional explosives, a device no bigger than a suitcase could contaminate several city blocks—and potentially much more if the wind helps the fallout to spread…

The lasting effects of a dirty bomb make this weapon especially attractive to terrorists. Fear of contamination would drive away tourists and customers, and the cleanup would be costly. Georgian police busted three separate groups of smugglers for attempting to traffic in nuclear materials. Georgian police caught a group of traffickers trying to sell a consignment of uranium for $200 million as the U.S.-led coalition advanced against ISIS in Syria and Iraq. The tactics of the terrorist group have been shifting. Rather than urging its followers to come and join the fight in Syria, ISIS recruiters now call for attacks against the West using whatever weapons are available. The continued erosion of the group's territory may not make it any less dangerous.

Obtaining ingredients for such a weapon is not, it turns out, the hard part. During the chaos that followed the Soviet collapse in the early 1990s, radioactive material was frequently stolen from poorly guarded reactors and nuclear facilities in Russia and its former satellite states.

The Bermuda Triangle occurs (Figure 6.4) when an insurance company becomes aware of a big fraud ring that is filing fraudulent claims under legitimate names. The insurance company sets up a deal with the medical hospitals to catch the fraudsters, who have already extorted ransom money from several hospitals after stealing millions of patient records. The insurance company has a dozen law firms that take care of all the legal proceedings and trials. The victim hospitals, the law firms, and the victim insurance companies hire the secret CaaS organization that specializes in tracking criminals. Law enforcement and other central government agencies hire them to do their dirty investigation work. CaaS knows the underground and many members of the Deep Web. They will track the fraudsters and bring their activities to the law firms as evidence of robbing and kidnapping citizen records for ransom purposes.

Third-Generation G3 DDoS

The third generation of DDoS is around the corner (Figure 6.5), but it will be fully functional in the next decade. As the saying goes "New technologies, new problems, new cybercrimes." Bruce Schneider eloquently said it: "If you think technology can solve your security problems, then you don't understand the problems and you don't understand the technology."

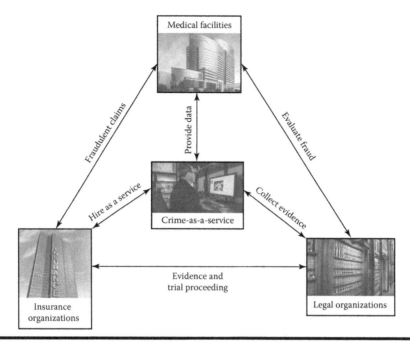

Figure 6.4 A fraud matrix showing how the fraud equation works: Patient with false sickness generates false treatment by provider, which creates a false a claim, which is paid by payor. Money ends up in the bank account of the syndicate. Legal hounds are hired by the insurance company to reveal the truth of the claim. The syndicate pays the lawyers and the legal process ends up in a cul-de-sac.

By the time we get to the 2040s, we'll be able to multiply human intelligence a billionfold. That will be a profound change that's singular in nature. Computers are going to keep getting smaller and smaller. Ultimately, they will go inside our bodies and brains and make us healthier, make us smarter. (Ray Kurzweil)

Mathematics is the study of the universe in numbers, structure, distance, and change. Cybersecurity is a polynomial (an equation) built with influencing variables that represent the inherent properties of an object (topic). So, to represent cybersecurity as an equation, we need to identify all the variables that influence the outcome of the equation.

The Internet will be the amphitheatre where evil and good will fight for supremacy. In the next 20 years, Smart Cities will be the outcome of the integration of technologies with new or existing urban landscapes. There is going to be a paradigm shift of what we experience and what we come to expect from the cities around us. These Smart Cities "will integrate cyber-physical technologies and

infrastructure to create environmental and economic efficiency while improving the overall quality of life."

The transformations of today's cities into Smart Cities will be an amalgamation of two major technologies—millions of analog/digital sensors connected to devices dispersed across a city, that is, the IoT and a Smart Grid that will connect all of these nodes together and enable real-time communication. By 2020, there will be more than 50 billion Internet-connected devices that will transform the way we live and work. This forecast is short-sighted and incomplete, as the human element will be the major success or failure factor in a Smart City. The use of innovative ICT applications, smartphones, and smart fixtures are all part of the process of making smart citizens. The harmony in a Smart City is the result of the aspiration and eagerness of citizens to practice governance rules as well as follow the technological rules. Also, in every stable ecosystem there's a corrective possess to keep the city in constant disciplinary mode. Smart Cities take time to mature and control.

Every city, including the smart ones, has three kinds of citizens: the first category is devoted to the prosperity of the city and comprises ardently patriotic and good citizens. The second category belongs to the herd of middle-class bourgeois who decide to migrate to a modernized metropolitan environment, seeking better employment opportunities. The third batch is made up of low-grade hooligans who are anti-everything and want to create opportunities to deploy their diabolic blueprints for sabotage and chaos. To be more devious, these outlaws farmed out all the engineering work to be done overseas and designed for smart cities showcase.

Getting Ready for the Big Malware Attacks

The planning department of malware will convene in the war room ready to set up a horrifying serial plan. But not before studying and assessing the impact and damage of the latest emerging and disruptive technologies:

1. Cybernetic robots are becoming co-workers
2. From wearables to implantable
3. AI machine learning as a service (MLaaS)
4. Genetically modified life forms
5. AI bot
6. Satellite terrorism
7. Driverless cars
8. Blockchain and Bitcoin
9. Immersive virtual reality
10. From augmented reality to mixed reality
11. Cyborg robots
12. Cybersecurity wars

Twelve emerging technologies—including the mobile Internet, autonomous vehicles, and advanced genomics—have the potential to truly reshape the world in which we live and work. Leaders in both government and business must not only know what's on the horizon but also start preparing for its impact.

One of the most perilous areas in the malware continuum is implantable medical devices (IMD), which will be under the IoT umbrella. Hacking human bodies is the most barbaric of all attacks. We have heart pacers, implantable defibrillators, diabetic pumps, cochlear pumps, infusion pumps, and neuro stimulators. Most of these life-threatening medical devices do not have a security mechanism in place.

Satellite Terrorism

In the next decade, satellite terrorism will be the latest technology invention to hurt many Americans.

Satellite terrorism is a lethal satellite technology, controlled by organized crime and a global "narco Nazi" system, and is being used to take hostile control of the United States. This technology will provide constant location, sight, sound, and thought surveillance, and can be used as an invisible weapon and torture instrument. Ruthless, sadistic criminals will be monitoring everyone and torturing, destroying, and killing those who get in their way or who don't fit their worldview. Satellite genocide, disguised as mental and physical illness, has occurred throughout the world over roughly the past half century.

Satellite energy will be used to attack the brain and body in numerous ways. The technology will transmit communication to and from the brain, causing people to "hear voices," and will be responsible for most "mental illness." It will cause physical pains and sensations literally from head to toe and physical illnesses, injuries, and diseases throughout the body. The technology will have the potential to cause major diseases such as cancer and AIDS.

Satellite technology will be used to maliciously torture people past their breaking point to suicide and violence. Most mass shootings and other inexplicable tragedies will be caused by this technology. Once this type of technology gets into the hands of cyber anarchists, they will use it to create weapons of mass control (WMC). US government satellite surveillance systems are a new way for cyber-criminals to gain possession not only of our financial lives, but our most precious resource: our minds. Organized remote satellite mental torture of citizens who live in a Smart City will be one of the most horrific and atrocious experiences that will create mass convulsions of biblical proportions.

The House of Cards

Every new technology and innovation brings new risks and vulnerabilities. These vulnerabilities will impact city administration, residents, businesses, and other organizations alike that conduct business there. Keeping in mind the new technologies and life in a Smarter City, just consider what could happen if one or more technology-reliant services didn't work. What would commuting look like with non-functioning traffic control systems, no street lights, and no public transportation? How would citizens respond to an inadequate supply of electricity or water, dark streets, and no cameras? What if garbage collection is interrupted in summertime and stinks up the streets? I guess it would be unpleasant and probably cause a lot of chaos in any city.

Simple bugs can cause big problems and have a big impact, Whether it's a water dam in Rye Brook or power grids, financial institutions, water systems, or online networks, all these infrastructures are going to be at risk and would be under assault like never before, and we need to do more about it. Recently, a police department in Massachusetts paid $750 to get its files back after being hit by ransomware. In February 2016, California's Hollywood Presbyterian Medical Center paid a ransom of about $17,000 in Bitcoins, one of at least six major health care systems victimized so far that year. In March 2016, the city of Plainfield, New Jersey, faced a demand for about $700 in Bitcoins to unfreeze their municipal servers. The technologies used by Smart Cities could pose a major cybersecurity threat and open the door for several possible cyberattacks. Each new and raw technology will create new opportunities for clever cyber city raiders. The Bible described it: For the love of money is a root of all kinds of evils. It is through this craving that some have wandered away from the faith and pierced themselves with many pangs—Timothy 6:10.

Technology is opening more gates for evil doers than good doers and city defenders. Anyone can join the big league malware club without passport or special privileges. The people who join the club should have a premeditated plan with a label "crime pays." There's no patriotism in practicing malware. Political and religious vengeance is the leading impulse. The primary aim is to drill holes into a Smart City's societal fabric and skillfully cripple several operations of selected critical systems.

In the next decade there will be great satellite defense systems equipped with cognitive and autonomic intelligence, specifically fabricated to beat satellite terrorism.

Electromagnetic Pulse Attack

By 2025, adversary countries will try to aggrandize their barbaric legacy by hiring highly paid technology freelancers to develop "customized" DDoS that will trigger an electromagnetic pulse (EMP) attack, targeting and destroying a Smart City's critical infrastructures. A major threat to America has been largely ignored by those who could prevent it. An EMP attack could wreak havoc on the nation's electronic systems—shutting down power grids, sources, and supply mechanisms. An EMP attack on the United States could irreparably cripple the country. It could simultaneously inflict large-scale damage and critically limit our recovery abilities.

Let's explain first what the EMP phenomenon is. An EMP is a high-intensity burst of electromagnetic energy caused by the rapid acceleration of charged particles. In simple terms, the explosion will create a highly turbulent electromagnetic wave (electron and gamma rays) that propagates in every direction, destroying any electromagnetic device. The higher the altitude, the further the deadlier electromagnetic waves will travel. That's the danger. In an attack, these particles interact and send electrical systems into chaos in three components: The first, the electromagnetic shock, disrupts electronics such as sensors, communications systems, protective systems, computers, and other similar devices. The second component has a slightly smaller range and is similar in effect to lightning. Although protective measures have long been established for lightning strikes, the potential for damage to critical infrastructure from this component exists because it rapidly follows and compounds the first component. The third component is slower than the previous two, but has a longer duration. It is a pulse that flows through electricity transmission lines, damaging distribution centers and fusing power lines. The combination of the three components can easily cause irreversible damage to many electronic systems. EMP is a burst of electromagnetic energy that creates an electromagnetic field around itself, which disrupts electronic devices, causing them to shut down within range. An EMP attack on the United States would leave the country with no electricity, no communications, no transportation, no fuel, no food, and no running water.

Americans remain gravely ill-prepared for an EMP attack. In fact, any US Smart City will have only three days' worth of food and health care provisions. Most Americans will not have enough batteries to keep flashlights working for any period of time, much less generator capabilities. And many of the country's most vulnerable citizens will rely on the electricity grid for medical equipment, such as dialysis machines and infusion pumps. Even standard medication will be difficult or impossible to come by if EMP disables pharmacies and transportation networks.

In the next decade, the damage from an EMP improvised attack will easily prove more severe. The EMP detonation will affect car and truck engines, aircraft ignition systems, hospital equipment, pacemakers, communications systems, and electrical appliances. Road and rail signaling, industrial control applications, and other electronic systems will all be susceptible to EMP. Electromagnetic energy on a radio frequency (RF) will travel through any conductive matter with which it comes into contact—from electrical wires to telephone wires, even water mains—which can spread the effects to areas far beyond ground zero.

A non-nuclear or improvised EMP is an RF (rather than gamma or X-ray frequency) weapon. While easier to conceal and not requiring a missile, an RF EMP must be detonated close to the target and does not produce as much damage as the nuclear version, affecting largely localized areas. But such a weapon could be harnessed as an "E-Bomb" (electromagnetic bomb), a stand-alone weapon that is easier to hide and maneuver. It is difficult to estimate the exact damage of an improvised attack, but in 1993 EMP testing by the US military shut down engine controls 300 meters away at a contractor site. Not large scale by any means, but damaging enough to cause concern.

So how could a Smart City protect itself from these colossal random electromagnetic raids? Before inaugurating a city as a Smart one, contingency planning will be an imperative prerequisite. The power grid as the backbone of the city should be sectionalized to circumvent total blackout. The power grid will be equipped with a grid of cognitive detection sensors (CDS) for early response. Primary substations will have "subterrain" backups for autonomic switchover. The city will go into cardiac arrest for a short period of time, before half of the city will be resuscitated with an auxiliary adjunct source of energy. The Internet will be down, and the IoT will suffer from the attack. The city will learn from this dreadful experience.

Extensive use of wireless RF networking for critical infrastructure and communications systems provides an alternative attack vector for the neutralization of an adversary's underlying industrial, civil, and communications infrastructure without the destruction of the hardware associated with those systems. Advances in munitions-based microelectronics and power technologies make possible the implementation of non-kinetic cyber and electromagnetic—or electronic warfare (EW)—attacks that could be delivered via artillery-launched munitions. The precision delivery of the non-kinetic effects (NKE) electronics payload close to the target allows low-power operation, which limits the geographical extent of impacted systems, and reduces the overall impact on the electromagnetic spectrum.

Backdoor Trojans will be replaced with a smart army of software drones and cyborgs that will attack a city's smart clouds and paralyze IoT networks. Evil technology will also remotely launch cyber heart attacks on critical installations, bridges, and driverless cars, and commandeer airplanes. The black hats, inspired by Star Wars, will develop a network of autonomic Darth Vaders guiding sith armies throughout Smart Cities. Star Wars will become cyberwars. AVT providers must reinvent themselves and develop new security solutions to be able to stand in front of their adversaries.

Washington Doesn't Understand the Internet

But Washington is waking up to the new reality: Politics as usual is not compatible with the Internet age, especially when it comes to laws and regulations governing the Web. And the Internet's key players—along with millions of passionate users who have tended to view Washington as disconnected from their lives—are realizing that they can't ignore what happens on Capitol Hill. Both sides must now face the long-simmering culture clash between Washington and the Internet, with implications that go far beyond a temporary Wikipedia blackout.

The Second-Generation Digital Native

If you are amazed to know the difference between a 1950 Mercedes and its newest version in 2017, then you are in for a big shock when we compare a 13-year-old from 1950 and the 2017 clone. We can also compare the telephone answering machine with a driverless and self-parking automobile, or the radial tire with a nanobot (nano robot) surgical object in the bloodstream to calibrate your DNA. Our digital natives were nurtured on Internet online magic while the 1950 youngster was nurtured on rock 'n' roll music. On the technology side, the Internet has created a new breed of people. Digital natives consider themselves citizens of the Internet.

Marc Prensky is an internationally acclaimed thought leader, speaker, writer, and designer in the field of education. He coined the term "digital native" to represent the new generation of internauts. He eloquently said: "It is amazing to me how in all the hoopla and debate these days about the decline of education in the US we ignore the most fundamental of its causes. Our students have changed radically. Today's students are no longer the people our educational system was designed to teach. Today's students are all 'native speakers' of the digital language of computers, video games and the Internet."

There are a number of labels to describe the young people currently studying at school, college, and university. They include the digital natives, the net generation, the Google generation, or the millennials. All of these terms are being used to highlight the significance and importance of new technologies within the lives of young people (Gibbons, 2007). People who were born before this new digital era, which began around 1980, are known as *digital immigrants*. According to Gibbons, digital immigrants may learn to use new technologies but they will still in some way be located in the past, unable to fully understand the natives. It is like the difference between learning a new language and being a native speaker. However, the war between natives and immigrants is ending. The natives have won. It was a bloodless conflict fought not with bullets and spears, but with iPhones and floppy disks. Now the battle between the haves and have-nots can begin. Simplistically speaking, the digital native–immigrant concept describes the generational switchover where people are defined by the technological culture with which they're familiar.

Michael Thomas, in his book *Deconstructing Digital Natives*, which is an unprecedented assemblage of critical scholarly perspectives on the digital native, talks about the technology of young people and new literacies. The current generation of young people will reinvent the workplace, and the society they live in. They will do it along the progressive lines that are built into the technology they use every day—of networks, collaboration, co-production, and participation. The change in behavior has already happened. We have to get used to it, accept that the flow of knowledge moves both ways, and do our best to make sure that no one gets left behind.

Being Internet savvy with free cyberspace available to smart digital natives, plus learning to be anti-establishment against the greedy corporate calcified culture and traditional brick-and-mortar academia, they turn to digital crime as a mental challenge to gain experience. Pretty soon, they slip into the digital crime domain as active members of the electronic army. The largest DDoS attacks ever are usually pulled off by bored digital natives.

There's no foolproof method to prevent kids from pulling the trigger on a DDoS attack at present. However, for mission-critical systems in newly built Smart Cities, you need to do something—and sitting on your hands waiting for an attack is not an option. DI is around the corner and will be the best cure for mushrooming malware. The reality is that cybercrime is much less cinematic.

Glossary

Altcoin: Altcoin is the term used to describe those digital currencies that do not have as big a market capitalization or do not have the recognition of the current incumbent cryptocurrencies, such as Bitcoin, litecoin, and dogecoin.

ASIC: Stands for application-specific integrated circuit, which is a specialized silicon chip that performs just one task. In the digital currency space, these chips process SHA-256 in order to mine Bitcoins and validate transactions.

ASIC miner: An ASIC miner is the hardware that houses the chip of the same name. You put it into your Internet connection via a modem or wireless as a separate circuit for bitcoin independent of your desktop computer.

Bitcoin: Bitcoin is a worldwide cryptocurrency and digital payment system called the first decentralized digital currency.

Bitcoin index: The live Bitcoin news Bitcoin index is a weighted average index that shows the value of one Bitcoin versus one single unit of currency of each of the majors in the Forex space—EUR, USD, JPY, GBP and AUD.

BitPay: BitPay is a payment processing company and software that allows merchants such as eBay, Amazon, and other online shopping channels to accept Bitcoin as payment for its goods and services.

Block chain: A block chain as dictated by the digital currency space is a term that refers to the total number of blocks for which miners have created hashes since the birth of the digital currency in question.

Block reward: This term refers to the "reward" that the miner receives for successfully hashing a transaction block.

BTC: This is the correct abbreviation used in the financed space for Bitcoin, similar to EUR for Euro.

Cryptocurrency: This is the generic term used to describe a currency that is purely based on mathematics such as Bitcoin litecoin.

Difficulty: In the Bitcoin world, this word is used to describe the difficulty a user encounters when trying to hash a new block in the Bitcoin block chain.

ECDSA: This abbreviation stands for political curve digital signature algorithm, which is the lightweight algorithm that the Bitcoin software uses to sign transactions in the protocol.

Exchange: An exchange is exactly how it sounds, somewhere where account holders can exchange one digital currency for another or a Fiat currency for a digital currency.

Faucet: When an individual or a team of individuals develops a digital currency, they may pre-mine a certain amount before release and give these pre-mined coins away. This is called a faucet.

Fiat: A Fiat currency is a traditional paperback currency that is regulated by an organization such as a central bank. Examples include the Euro, the US dollar, and the Australian dollar.

Genesis block: The Genesis block is the very first block in the block chain of any digital currency.

Hash: A hash is the mathematical term for an algorithm that takes a set of data of any length and composition and converts it into a fixed length and fixed composition piece of data.

Hash rate: This term refers to the amount of hashes that a particular Bitcoin miner can perform in a set period of time.

Mega hashes/sec: This term refers to the amount of hashing attempts possible by a given processor processing unit in a set period of time—normally one second.

Mining: Mining is the process used to create new Bitcoin and complete transactions in the block chain.

Output: When a Bitcoin transaction takes place, the output refers to the destination address used in the transaction.

Paper wallet: Some people prefer to store their Bitcoin in a paper wallet—a form of cold storage—in order to improve security. The term simply refers to a printed sheet of paper that holds a number of public Bitcoin addresses and corresponding private keys.

Proof of work: Proof of work simply refers to the output of any efforts to mine Bitcoins. In the Bitcoin block chain, the hashing of a block takes time and effort, meaning that the hash block can be considered proof of work.

Public key: The public key is a string of digits and letters (your Bitcoin address). When hashed with a corresponding string, known as a private key, it digitally signs online communication.

SHA-256: Every digital currency must have a cryptographic function that dictates how the hash is constructed. In Bitcoin, SHA-256 is this function, and is used as the basis for hash creation (i.e., Bitcoin's proof of work).

Transaction fee: Some transactions that occur in the Bitcoin block chain contain transaction fees. These transaction fees are paid to the miner that hashes the block in question.

Wallet: Bitcoin and other digital currency users use wallets to hold the private keys associated with particular public Bitcoin addresses, not bitcoins.

Source: Selected terms related to this chapter from www.if4it.com/it-glossary and from publications and educational seminars from MERIT CyberSecurity.

Bibliography

https://www.flashpoint-intel.com/
https://krebsonsecurity.com/2016/10/hacked-cameras-dvrs-powered-todays-massive-internet-outage/
https://krebsonsecurity.com/2012/10/the-scrap-value-of-a-hacked-pc-revisited/

Control risks in Smart Cities: https://www.controlrisks.com/en/our-thinking/analysis/smart-cities-and-cyber-threats

IDG Survey: https://www.a10networks.com/sites/default/files/A10-MS-23175-EN.pdf

http://www.bettycjung.net/Web1.htm

DDoS update: http://readwrite.com/2016/10/22/the-internet-of-things-was-used-in-fridays-ddos-attack-pl4/

http://readwrite.com/2017/04/12/fully-appreciating-the-amazing-things-ai-can-and-cant-yet-do-for-lawyers-cl1/

http://readwrite.com/2017/04/09/the-bots-invasion-is-on-powered-by-24b-in-funding-dl4/

The Register—the cloud: https://www.theregister.co.uk/2016/07/21/ddos_the_cloud_and_you/

AI and attacks: http://www.networkcomputing.com/wireless/artificial-intelligence-3-potential-attacks/237102029

From cyborg to cybercrime: http://www.huffingtonpost.co.uk/mark-hawtin/from-cyborg-to-cyber-mond_b_13510774.html

http://www-03.ibm.com/autonomic/pdfs/AC%20Blueprint%20White%20Paper%20V7.pdf

The Boeing 767: https://www.wired.com/2008/01/dreamliner-security/

Crime as a service: http://www.bankinfosecurity.com/interviews/crime-as-service-top-cyber-threat-for-2017-i-3406

Computerworld Anonymous: http://www.computerworld.com/article/2688411/report-crime-as-a-service-tools-and-anonymization-help-any-idiot-be-a-cyber-criminal.html

Disruptive technologies: https://disruptiveviews.com/cyber-criminals-crime-as-a-service/

Infosec: http://resources.infosecinstitute.com/cybercrime-as-a-service/#gref

Game of the drones: http://www.akuaroworld.com/the-game-of-drones-has-begun/

Ray Kurzweil: http://howtocreateamind.com/download/MA2013_Kurzweil.pdf

VeriChip: http://www.antichips.com/what-is-verichip.htm

FDA Approval of Verichip: http://www.nbcnews.com/id/6237364/ns/health-health_care/t/fda-approves-computer-chip-humans/#.WP578_nytPY

Chip hacking: https://www.forbes.com/sites/thomasbrewster/2015/04/27/implant-android-attack/#73b3cc6a1d23

Future of drugs: https://www.vice.com/en_us/article/the-future-of-drugs-max-daly-according-to-vice-531

BBC drugs: http://www.bbc.com/news/technology-22381046

https://www.blackhat.com/docs/eu-15/materials/eu-15-Balduzzi-Cybercrmine-In-The-Deep-Web-wp.pdf

http://kernelmag.dailydot.com/issue-sections/features-issue-sections/10386/tor-network-surveillance/

Drug Lord: https://www.vice.com/en_uk/article/the-scurvy-crew-silk-road-interview

Global Commission on Drug Policy: http://www.globalcommissionondrugs.org/

The report of GCDP 2016: http://www.globalcommissionondrugs.org/wp-content/uploads/2016/11/GCDP-Report-2016-ENGLISH.pdf

Smart Drugs: https://hbr.org/2016/05/like-it-or-not-smart-drugs-are-coming-to-the-office

Kofi Annan's speech on GCDP: http://www.spiegel.de/international/world/kofi-annan-on-why-drug-bans-are-ineffective-a-1078402.html

Deep Web market: https://deepwebmarket.wordpress.com/2015/10/11/become-a-citizen-of-the-usa-real-usa-passport/

How a DDoS is executed: https://securelist.com/blog/research/36309/black-ddos/

Hajime Botnet: https://securelist.com/blog/research/78160/hajime-the-mysterious-evolving-botnet/

Car jacking: https://securelist.com/analysis/publications/77576/mobile-apps-and-stealing-a-connected-car/

Bleak future for DDoS: http://gizmodo.com/todays-brutal-ddos-attack-is-the-beginning-of-a-bleak-f-1788071976

3D Gen: https://technologyevaneglist.wordpress.com/2016/05/29/threat-of-cyber-attacks-in-smart-cities/

The laser attack: https://motherboard.vice.com/en_us/article/watch-hackers-use-a-drone-mounted-laser-to-control-malware-through-a-scanner

Infrastructure attack: https://securityintelligence.com/news/smart-cities-big-problems-the-risk-of-malware-in-iot-enabled-infrastructure/

Why Smart Cities are smarter: http://www.thehindu.com/features/homes-and-gardens/why-smart-cities-need-smart-citizens/article8625075.ece

Satellite terrorism: http://www.gangstalkingmindcontrolcults.com/mike-patrick-satellite-genocide-letters-and-documents/

Dr. Hall: https://redice.tv/red-ice-radio/satellite-terrorism-surveillance-technology-implantable-microchips-biometric-id-cards-and-government-spying

Remote neural monitoring: http://www.stopthecrime.net/Remote%20Neural%20Monitoring.pdf

Neural satellite: http://www.stopthecrime.net/Remote%20Neural%20Monitoring.pdf

Smart City nightmare: https://hbr.org/2017/04/smart-cities-are-going-to-be-a-security-nightmare

America's next secret weapon: http://nationalinterest.org/blog/the-buzz/americas-next-secret-weapon-can-paralyze-city-19059

Medical ransomware: https://securityintelligence.com/ransomware-and-health-care-theres-more-at-risk-than-just-money/

https://www.tutorialspoint.com/mongodb/

Digital natives and immigrants: https://www.marcprensky.com/writing/Prensky%20-%20Digital%20Natives,%20Digital%20Immigrants%20-%20Part1.pdf

Children and the Internet: https://www.internetsociety.org

Chapter 7

Software Cyborgs of Tomorrow

Shaking Hands with Cybernetics

This chapter describes a new concept in computer science and in cybercrime. The term *cyborg* doesn't only apply to a human being with a body driven or controlled by technological devices, such as an oxygen tank, an artificial heart valve, or an insulin pump. Cyborgs could be designed from hardware components, software programs, or both.

In this book, we're specifically talking about nanotechnology (NT) components at the molecular and atomic scale, immersed with artificial intelligence (AI) algorithms, autonomic computing, and cybernetic purely software-centric components; thus, we refer to them as "Soft Cyborg" and "Cyborg Nanobot," which are synonymous. We're going to see these terms throughout the book. Although they share the same name, they are different kinds of cyborgs. They operate solely on the Internet and the cloud from satellites. The big lords of cybercrime and cyber terrorism, aware of the latest enabling technologies, decided to hire knowledgeable software engineers to build an arsenal of Soft Cyborgs that are equipped with formidable agility and intelligence in fighting, like the US Marines.

Everyone saw the movie The Terminator and worried about Kyle and Sarah being caught by the terminator. The *Los Angeles Times* called the film "a crackling thriller full of all sorts of gory treats.. loaded with fuel-injected chase scenes, clever special effects and a sly humor." The film also explores the potential dangers of AI dominance and rebellion. The robots will become self-aware in the future, reject human authority, and determine that the human race needs to be destroyed. The impact of this theme is so important that "the prevalent visual representation of

AI risk has become the terminator robot." This grim scenario will never happen, because our biological intelligence will always be in control.

AI will reach human levels by around 2030. If we follow AI to, say, 2045, we will have multiplied our human (biological) intelligence by a billion fold. The term "singularity," which is a captivating new term, will cause a cutting-edge paradigm shift in our lives. Singularity will usher the beginning of the AI age. Kurzweil invented the concept of the "law of accelerating returns," which states that the speed of technological change will increase exponentially. Thus, the exponential growth in computing technology might plausibly lead to superintelligence.

As computers increase in power, it becomes possible for people to build a machine that is more intelligent than humans; this superhuman intelligence possesses greater problem-solving and inventive skills than current humans are capable of. This superintelligent machine then designs an even more capable machine, or rewrites its own software to become even more intelligent; this (ever more capable) machine then goes on to design a machine of yet greater capability, and so on. These iterations of recursive self-improvement will accelerate, allowing enormous qualitative change before any upper limits imposed by the laws of physics or theoretical computation set in. But then, where will the Internet fit in the grand scheme of things? How will the Internet look in 2030? What will be the level of exponential evolution that we'll be living with?

What we have to think about is the fate of the Internet in 2030. This is a bewildering confession of what our reality is going to be. How would singularity impact a Smart City and cybercrime? If the superintelligent machine is the invention of man, then cybercrime will also be the work of man. Cybercrime will also follow the law of accelerating returns. Whenever technology approaches a barrier, new technologies will surmount it. Cybercrime in 2030 will be more imaginative and Machiavellian.

Digital technology avalanche dead ahead! More powerful converging core technologies, proliferating clouds and platforms, cognition available as a service, and an explosion on the new manufacturing frontier of "maker" tools, all increasingly accessible and affordable to anybody, anywhere, for any purpose. In a 2030 perspective, there are no technology barriers and no limits. We are just at the beginning of the real-world digital revolution. Virtually all digital futurologists continue to assume the future availability of effectively limitless computing power and memory. On the other hand, it is widely acknowledged that foreseeable physical and economic constraints could defeat Moore's law by the early 2020s. But this does not necessarily mean that raw computing power and memory capacity will not continue to explode. Why? First, because software is making the underlying computing hardware fully flexible. Second, radical new technologies not subject to the same constraints will be under development—notably optical or photonic computers that use visible light or infrared beams instead of electric currents to perform, and quantum computing, which harnesses the power of atoms to perform computational tasks. And there's the potential wonder material of graphene.

What Is a Soft Cyborg?

A cyborg (short for "cybernetic organism") is a nano robot of molecular size whose physiological functioning is aided by or dependent upon a mechanical or electronic device, and is controlled by a set of hardwired commands (software program), or controlled remotely by the masters of command & control (CC). We coined the term "Soft Cyborg" (SC) as an AI executable code imbedded in a software container. Soft Cyborgs are designed with autonomic and cybernetic software monolithic components that actuate self-regulating, self-navigating, self-monitoring functionalities once they are launched toward the target. They are AI programmed to work as a squadron. In the next two decades, Smart Cities will have intense storms of Cyborg Rain. A digital immunity system (DIS) will be designed with the same symmetrical technologies of Soft Cyborgs. Figure 7.1 shows the anatomy of the nano Soft Cyborg. Soft Cyborgs and Smart Vaccines are of similar nature. Soft Cyborg can be good or evil.

Description of the Anatomy of the Soft Cyborg: Nanobot

We assume that an attack will have a smart payload and sophisticated attack vector. Most destructive attacks seem to be politically motivated to spy on global corporations, governments, and large cloud centers.

The Soft Cyborg is a masterpiece of ingenuity engineering and malice. It is an invisible software booby trap to create havoc and most of the time some substantial destruction to vulnerable infrastructures. Soft Cyborgs and Smart Vaccines have a similar nanostructure. They look alike and operate in similar ways. They can be good Soft Cyborgs or bad Soft Cyborgs. To differentiate between them, we call the good Soft Cyborgs (Smart Vaccine Nanobots). We keep the name Soft Cyborgs for the evil ones.

The Soft Cyborg consists of seven interconnected components (see Figure 7.1) that work together without any conflict. All the components have the autonomic capability to fix themselves and repair any defect during a fight. The following is a brief description of each component:

1. *Actuator (Kernel)*: The commander in charge. Its main mission is to launch the planned attack without any glitches. The commander reports to the adversary master control center (MCC), which monitors the attack mission. Communication could be with the cloud or with a satellite.
2. *Deep Attack Algorithms*: "Algorithms" are mathematical equations and relations considered as logical rules to determine the probability of an attack succeeding. A deep attack algorithm uses historical data to help the Cyborg Nanobot take the safest course of action.
3. *Nano Missiles*: They are nano smart pieces of software that work as guided virus missile, fired by a kernel. The nano cyborg will guide itself toward the

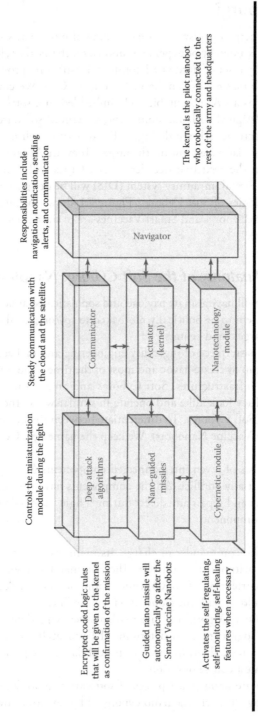

Figure 7.1 **The Soft Cyborg is an incredible nanobot software agent reduced to molecular scale with nanotechnologies magic tools. The nanobot is programmed with artificial intelligence technologies. Soft Cyborgs and Smart Vaccine Nanobots have a similar nanostructure, but one to create havoc and the other one to eliminate it. A digital immunity system (CEWPS) is made of Smart Vaccine Nanobots. The Smart Vaccine Nanobots incrementally learn from their own challenging missions. (© Copyright MERIT CyberSecurity Group. All rights reserved.)**

target. Depending on the nature of the attack, Nano Soft Cyborgs will form Cyborg Rain, which will be launched from a satellite of the cloud and penetrate the city grid. Sometimes, Nano Cyborgs will go into dormant mode and wait for the right moment to attack.

4. *Communicator*: The communication link with the rest of the cyborgs, or the cloud and the satellite. Responsibilities also include navigation, notifications, and sending alerts.

5. *The Cybernetics Module*: Acts as the reflex system and activates self-regulating, self-monitoring, and self-healing functionalities when necessary. In other words, it is the fully autonomic control system of the Cyborg Nanobot.

6. *The Navigator*: Controls the movement of the Soft Cyborg and keeps it on track. It is under a satellite navigation cognitive system.

7. *The Nanotechnology Module*: Responsible for the miniaturization of the cyborg to the right molecular scale before battle.

The Smart Vaccine™ is also a Soft Cyborg that installs the digital immunity (DI) defense layer in a Smart City. While a Soft Cyborg is the main saboteur of the DI, the Smart Vaccine is the only force that can outsmart Soft Cyborg attacks. Chapter 10 will discuss the internals of the Smart Vaccine.

The Soft Cyborg: Nanobot, Continued

Soft Cyborgs behave like social animals with their collective behaviors to solve difficult computational problems. They live in a hierarchical organization such as an army, taking orders from their commanders for specific attacks. Soft Cyborgs were created to do evil and commit crimes on the Internet, in Smart Cities, and on the cloud. Soft Cyborgs communicate with one another during attacks and collaborate through a special set of transactional messages (web services). In this respect, they are different from distributed denial-of-service (DDoS) attacks. They are in constant communication with their commanders. A Soft Cyborg army organization chart is shown in Figure 7.2. It is a menacing army that was designed by computer experts who were inspired by military formations and tactics, and have elevated the malware base to the highest level. In the next decade, information warfare will be highly intelligent and autonomous, at the same level of sophistication as driverless cars, or even flying cars.

Master Control Center (MCC): It is equivalent to the master control of a DDoS. A group of "master" hackers who give directives to commanders of the Soft Cyborg armies. The masters watch the battles remotely from start to finish.

Attack Planning Center: The center that provides the MCC and the Soft Cyborg commander with the necessary information on the potential target before the attack: location, size, architecture, infrastructure, risk, and expected outcome.

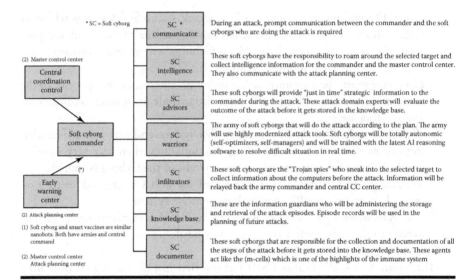

Figure 7.2 The hierarchy of the Soft Cyborg army and its responsibilities. The commander's messages, attack alerts, attack planning requests, attack in progress status, attack outcome, and documentation, all these transactions are working concurrently. It is a real war. (© Copyright MERIT CyberSecurity Group. All rights reserved.)

Soft Cyborg Army Commander: It gets directives from central command and control (CCC). The commander's responsibilities cover total management of the army and control of the attack from start to finish.

Soft Cyborg Communicator: This agent is to relay progress of the attack to the commander, as well as connect with central command.

Soft Cyborg Intelligence Officers: These Soft Cyborgs have the responsibility of roaming around the selected target and collecting intelligence information for the commander and the MCC.

Soft Cyborg Advisors: As the name implies, these Soft Cyborgs will provide "just in time" strategic information to the commander during the attack. These attack domain experts will evaluate the outcome of the attack before it gets stored in the knowledge base.

Soft Cyborg Warriors: The army of Soft Cyborgs that will carry out the attack according to the plan. The army will use highly modernized attack tools and will be educated on attack strategies and tactics. Soft Cyborgs will be totally autonomic (self-optimizers, self-managers) and will be trained with the latest AI reasoning software to resolve difficult situations in real time.

Soft Cyborg Infiltrators: These Soft Cyborgs are the "Trojan spies" who sneak into the selected target to collect information about the computers before the attack. Information will be relayed back to the army commander and MCC.

Soft Cyborg Knowledge Base Keeper: These are the information guardians who will be administering the storage and retrieval of the attack episodes. Episode records will be used in the planning of future attacks.

Soft Cyborg Documenters: These Soft Cyborgs are responsible for the collection and documentation of all the steps of an attack before they get stored in the knowledge base. These agents act like M-cells, which is one of the highlights of the immune system.

Soft Cyborg Knowledge Engines

Soft Cyborgs are modern warriors that will be designed and manufactured by "malware" expert systems. They are designed to sabotage operations under three categories: *Level 1*: Internet of Things (IoT) devices, city traffic lights, street security cameras, bridge tolls; *Level 2*: DDoS for the power grid, utility meters, medical records, and bank customer accounts; *Level 3*: electromagnetic pulse attacks to create massive disturbance in the city.

Soft Cyborgs (Smart Vaccine) rely heavily on machine learning techniques to acquire more experience. In AI, Soft Cyborgs autonomically train themselves and optimize their knowledge and connect to the AI knowledge bases to learn more about future battles. Figure 7.3 shows the five knowledge bases that contribute to the success of Soft Cyborg attacks.

We would like to supplement the reader with our definition of the term "knowledge" as it is heavily used throughout the book.

Experience: E_j is an event or an episode that we participate in or live through. We all learn from experience, regardless if it is an ugly, bad, or happy one. Experience

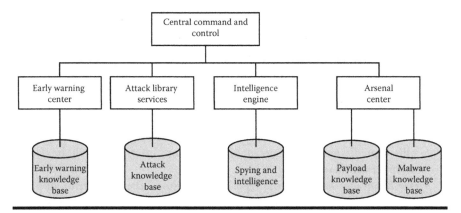

Figure 7.3 Soft Cyborg knowledge databases are considered "fulfillment centers" during attack cycles. When the army commander needs service, all the knowledge bases respond on time. (©Copyright MERIT CyberSecurity Group. All rights reserved.)

is cumulative and gets transformed into knowledge later. Experience is gained by repeated trials. We all experience it in life. Quantitatively speaking, experience is a function of time $f(t)$ with a start time E_{jt1} and a finish time E_{jt2}. Experience duration is expressed as $t_2 - t_1$. Experience can have many modes such as physical, emotional, mental, spiritual, vicarious, or virtual. The parameter j represents the experience mode.

So, E_j represents the experience for a particular mode m. When we add the time duration to a particular experience including its mode, we get the following:

$$E_j t_j . m$$

where m is the mode (1 = physical, 2 = mental, etc.). Once experience is stored in the brain, it gets magically converted into knowledge.

By definition, we consider a cyberattack as an independent discrete event that has a start and a finish. But knowing about past cyberattacks, $E_j - 1$ (*a priori*), can definitely help forecast incoming attacks. The cognitive early warning predictive system (CEWPS) is a smart machine that is built for one purpose in mind: to catch cyberattacks before they occur. That's the magic of CEWPS.

Knowledge on the other hand is different from experience. It is the derivative of experience.

$$K_t = d(Et) / d(t)$$

Knowledge can be defined as "the fact or condition of knowing something with familiarity gained through experience or association." The knowledge engine takes disparate experience episodes, $E_j t_j . m$, converts them into knowledge patterns, and catalogues them in the brain for subsequent neural response. Intelligence is another human characteristic but it refers to the fast ability to retrieve knowledge, connect pieces of knowledge together, or process knowledge quickly.

The database engine stores *a priori* knowledge extracted from previous cyberattacks on the Smart Grid. Attackers know that there's a Smart Grid and they design their attack vector to penetrate the grid from the weakest side and hide until the time comes to spread to the center of the grid.

The Early Warning Knowledge Base—The Attack Planning Center: It uses probabilistic prediction on the success of the mission. Information will be relayed to upper command.

Attack Knowledge Base: It is the repository that stores the software of all previous attacks and scenarios of future attacks. The knowledge base also contains "prefab" software components for different attacks. The Soft Cyborg browses through the catalogue and loads the necessary modules into his memory unit. The attack knowledge base contains thousands of attack modules and spare parts. One of the great features of the attack knowledge base is its attack optimizer, which will generate the best attack model from prompted queries. The attack knowledge base has a reverse-engineering engine that analyzes the attack and breaks it down to its atomic level to review the payload and how the attack is executed.

Spying and Intelligence Knowledge Base: To acquire more positional knowledge about the adversary. Satellites that carry special nanobots are transmitted behind enemy lines to relay encrypted information on the army and its arsenal.

Payload Knowledge Base: It is a registry of all known payloads anatomy and damage properties. Not all payload nanobots are alike. Each side keeps their armories secret. Information comes from internal sources.

Malware Knowledge Base: Malware comes in different forms and attacks. The commander of the Soft Cyborg Nanobot examines the different malware "blueprints" to gain more knowledge on adversaries. The Smart Vaccine has all these knowledge engines as well.

Soft Cyborg Satellite and Web Communication

Cloud computing will be big business. The market generated $100 billion a year in 2012, it is currently $127 billion (2017), and will reach $800 billion by 2030. The competition is getting extremely intense.

In the simplest terms, cloud computing means storing and accessing data and programs over the Internet instead of a computer's hard drive. The Soft Cyborg industry will be a deep-rooted business on the cloud. The industry will use *infrastructure-as-a-service* (IaaS) as its backbone, and offer its services to other Soft Cyborg groups. For example, Amazon rents out its infrastructure to its customer Netflix in the form of cloud services. The Soft Cyborg industry will have a collection of private inter-collaborated clouds connected to hijacked satellites to launch their cyborg attacks.

Like HTTP, Constrained Application Protocol (CoAP) can carry different types of payloads, and can identify which payload type is being used. CoAP integrates with XML, JSON, CBOR, or any data format of your choice. Like HTTP, CoAP is based on the wildly successful REST model: Servers make resources available under a URL, and clients access these resources using methods such as GET, PUT, POST, and DELETE.

Cloud service providers (CSP) are companies that offer network services, infrastructure, and business applications in the cloud. Cloud services are hosted in a data center that can be accessed by companies or individuals using network connectivity. Soft Cyborg leaders want to be invisible and will try to hide their existence on invisible clouds. They will definitely not be customers of Amazon, IBM, or Microsoft. They will develop their own cloud infrastructure. Cloud infrastructure is a collection of server hardware, networking gear, storage resources, and software that is needed to build applications that can be accessed by the cloud. In a cloud infrastructure, applications can be accessed remotely using networking services such as wide area networks (WANs), telecom services, and the Internet.

The components of cloud infrastructure are usually broken down into three categories: computing, networking, and storage. These resources need to work together to provide a cloud service. The categories break down as follows:

Computing: This part of the infrastructure provides the computing power for the cloud service and is usually provided by racks of servers powered by server chips. The servers can be tied together with virtualization software in order to split up the computing power for different clients or services.

Networking: Routers and switches are used to move data between the computing resources, the storage systems, and the outside world. These might be proprietary data center switches or white box switches running software-defined networking (SDN) software on commodity server hardware.

Storage: The cloud service usually requires large amounts of storage resources, which are often pooled and separated from the server hardware in separate racks that might use a combination of hard disks and flash storage. Storage systems have their own networking gear and storage software to manage high-performance connectivity with the service.

A cloud infrastructure likely contains very expensive combinations of server, networking, and storage hardware, but the key to making it work all together is software. This software is often referred to as "virtualization software" because it is capable of taking all of the hardware pieces and dynamically creating new networks that tie together the virtual resources so that they can be sold to different customers as services.

Components of the Satellite Infrastructures

The geosynchronous earth orbit (GEO) satellite communication network will become very competitive and increasingly more technologically advanced. The Soft Cyborg lords know that satellite/Internet communications are relatively inexpensive because there are no cable-laying costs and one satellite covers a very large area (Figure 7.4).

Whether traveling near Earth or deep in our solar system, every spacecraft is supported by a sophisticated "ground segment" comprising computer systems, nano software, nano telecommunication networks, and other resources that enable Soft Cyborg specialists to communicate with the CCC.

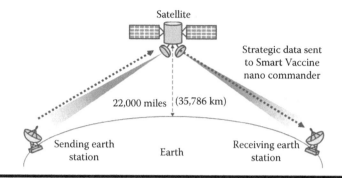

Satellite

Strategic data sent
to Smart Vaccine
nano commander

22,000 miles ⋮(35,786 km)

Sending earth
station

Earth

Receiving earth
station

Figure 7.4 Modern cyber nano warfare will rely heavily on satellite when transmitting strategic data against adversaries who in turn use their own satellite as well. (© Copyright The McGraw-Hill Companies, Inc., 2002. All rights reserved.)

The satellite and its ground stations are very strategic in Smart City Grid defense.

Summary of the Internet/Satellite Transactional Services and Messages

Soft Cyborg attacks from satellite are manifold operations equipped with multi-level, multi-tasked commands pointed at highly trained Smart Soft Cyborgs that are ready to go to holy war. Soft Cyborgs are confident to succeed and create chaos and havoc to quiet Smart Cities.

The messages are fully autonomic and self-monitoring.

Central Command General Messages: These are the general commands for administrative communication with the rest of the army.

Early Warning Messages to Central Command: The alert "classified" messages sent to central command, in case of any threatening situation.

Central Command Messages to Cloud 1 and Cloud 2: Communication of administrative messages to the associative clouds before and during an attack.

Central Command Messages to Soft Cyborg Barracks: Administrative and alert messages sent to the barracks for preparation for coming attacks.

Central Command Messages to Soft Cyborg Factory: Requests from central command to build Soft Cyborgs for provisioning and replenishment of the inventories.

Early Warning Alert Messages: In case of an emergency, alerts are sent directly to army commanders prior to attacks.

Communication with the Early Warning Knowledge Base: Queries on similar early warning attacks that can be studied before an attack.

Communication with the Attack Knowledge Base: Queries on similar historical attacks that can be studied to gain more knowledge before an attack.

Communication with the Spying and Intelligence Knowledge Base: Queries on similar historical attacks that can be studied to gain more intelligence knowledge before an attack.

Communication with the Payload Knowledge Base: Queries to find out the best type of payload to use for proper attacks.

Communication with the Malware Knowledge Base: Queries to find out the best type of attack strategy to use for proper attacks.

Attack Messages: Strictly confidential attack messages between the army commanders and Soft Cyborgs in the battlefield.

Attack Document: All attack episodes will be documented and stored in the attack episodes knowledge base for review and knowledge acquisition.

Future Cyber Warfare

As reality prevails, AI will reach human levels by around 2030. Follow that out further to, say, 2045, and we will have multiplied the human biological machine intelligence of our civilization a billion fold. Singularity will usher in the beginning of the AI age. It is an explosion into artificial superintelligence due to an exponential growth in computing technology. This technological acceleration confirms Kurzweil's concept of the law of accelerating returns in which the speed of technological change increases exponentially.

It isn't fair to compare the present to two decades from now. Digital Earth will become Smart Earth. Even logarithmic scaling would give us the wrong projection of 2017 to 2040. Advances will be seen in all industries across the board. Technology will be like an unstoppable runaway train. Cybersecurity and its counterpart cybercrime will be ardently competing for global dominance and sovereignty; and the Smart City will be the focal stage for both to demonstrate their superintelligence.

Nanobot Is the Rosetta Stone

Denying services, hacking files, or locking servers with ransomware will end up in the technology junkyard along with legacy systems. Medicine, in particular, will be the hotbed for both defense (that's the right term) and malware. It is the most important science in the existence of man. The reason is obvious: disease will create sickness, which will invade healthy people and will impede productivity. Sick people will end up getting terminally sick and eventually dying. The whole social fabric of Smart Cities will be full of holes and tears.

In the next 20 years, medical nanotechnology will be closer to God's miracles. The Russian millionaire Dimitry Itskov is pouring millions into a futuristic biomedicine project; he confidently claimed that "The ultimate goal of my plan is to transfer someone's personality into a completely new body."

At the conference of the US National Institutes of Health (NIH) Roadmap for Medical Research, there were the following provocative quotations: "What if doctors could search out and destroy the very first cancer cells that would otherwise have caused a tumor to develop in the body?" "What if a broken part of a cell could be removed and replaced with a minimum biological machine?" "What if pumps the size of molecules could be implanted to deliver life-saving medicines precisely when and where they are needed?" These scenarios may sound unbelievable, but they are the goals of the NIH's roadmap for nanomedicine initiative that will yield medical benefits as early as 10 years from now.

The futurist Ray Kurzweil seems to be correct on every prediction including the ones in biomedicine: "When nanotechnology is mature, it's going to solve the problems of biology by overcoming biological pathogens, removing toxins, correcting DNA errors, and reversing other sources of aging. We will then have to contend with new dangers that it introduces, just as the Internet introduced the danger of software viruses. These new pitfalls will include the potential for self-replicating nanotechnology getting out of control, as well as the integrity of the software controlling these powerful, distributed Nanobots."

Nanotechnology in Medicine

Nanobots will be able to travel through the bloodstream, go in and around our cells, and perform various services, such as removing toxins; sweeping out debris; correcting DNA errors; repairing and restoring cell membranes; reversing atherosclerosis; modifying the levels of hormones, neurotransmitters, and other metabolic chemicals; and a myriad of other tasks. For each aging process, we can describe a means for nanobots to reverse the process, down to the level of individual cells, cell components, and molecules.

Stopping and reversing aging is only the beginning. Using nanobots for health and longevity is just the early adoption phase of introducing nanotechnology and intelligent computation into our bodies and brains. The more profound implication is that we'll augment our thinking processes with nanobots that communicate with one another and with our biological neurons. Once non-biological intelligence gets a foothold, so to speak, in our brains, it will be subject to the law of accelerating returns and expand exponentially. Our biological thinking, on the other hand, is basically stuck.

This also offers golden opportunities to cybercriminals, because technology gives and technology takes. Nanomedicine, which is a branch of nanotechnology, will be the technology that will enable us to manipulate our DNA more easily than ever before. Soft Cyborgs are in fact Smart Nanobots programmed to circulate in the blood of a human, and get to his or her DNA and modify its structure.

In the next two decades, hackers will become biomedical engineers and specialize in DNA dredging terrorism (DDT). Feng Zhang, a biological engineer from Harvard, knows how to fix broken genes and track most intractable afflictions. DDT cybercriminals will know how serious and dangerous hijacking DNA records is. Once DNA forensic criminals have access to the centralized DNA database, after authorization and authentication, they will be able to manipulate a specific region of DNA and jumble up the crime investigation. Crime-as-a-service organizations could get a contract from a reputable law firm to break into the central DNA database and compromise the DNA sequence code of a defendant.

Cyber warfare in the next two decades (Figure 7.5) will use new arms from new technologies. There will be a new type of hackers—let's call them nano hackers. It is like jumping with one hop from disc operating system (DOS) to Windows 11. Hi-tech combat will be fought with AI smart weaponry at the molecular scale and at three levels (satellites, clouds, and grids). The wars between adversary Soft Cyborgs and security Smart Vaccine Nanobots will be atrocious, continual, and symmetrical in order to defeat the nano defense of a Smart City. The Smart Vaccine Grid is a nanogrid with cognitive and autonomic components. Cybercriminals will not be able to collect any intelligence on the internals of the Smart Vaccine and how nano DI will shield a Smart City from persistent Soft Cyborg attacks.

A Smart City is purposely designed with Smart Grid technology (Figure 7.6), which simply means smart connectivity. We're giving Smart Grid computing a new definition: It is like the human nervous system where the whole body is connected through pipelines to the brain. There will be two Smart Nano Grids to protect the city. The first grid is the Smart City Grid (SCG), which serves as the connectivity backbone of the IoT, the machine-to-machine (M2M), and the critical systems of the city's infrastructure. The second one is the Smart Vaccine Grid which provides the DI to the Smart City. The Smart Vaccine Grid will neutralize the Soft Cyborg attacks before the payloads hit the city.

Scenario of Soft Cyborg Attack on Beirut, Lebanon

The defense and critical infrastructure of many industrial nations (first and second worlds), including the United States, has become more reliant on satellite systems. This increased use and dependence comes with a downside. Because satellite systems are integrated into national security systems and emergency response systems and are critical components for the modern military, satellites have become an attractive target of cyberattacks. As the reliance grows, so do the threats of cyberattacks from criminals, terrorists, and nations.

This is a hypothetical scenario but it can be real. In the next two decade, Soft Cyborg Nano attack will be very highly advanced and focused on critical industrial systems such as supervisory control and data acquisitions (SCADAs) and city traffic lights. The city of Beirut in Lebanon is the jewel

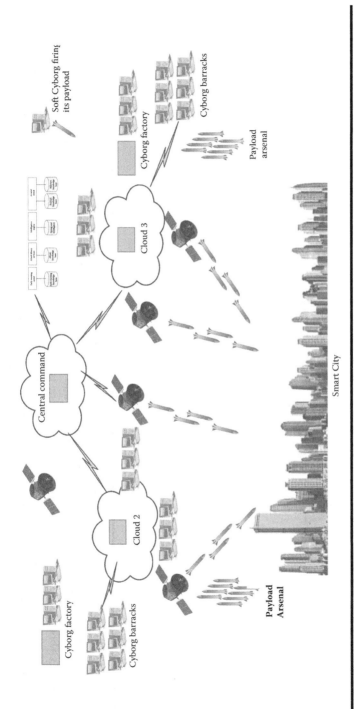

Figure 7.5 This is a typical scenario of how government and business satellites can be used for massive cyberattacks on a Smart City. Terrorists built a network of clouds and established their headquarters, and they were able to hack a few satellites from which they sent their Soft Cyborgs. They made their own soft cyborgs and had an immense knowledge base for their payloads. (© Copyright MERIT CyberSecurity Group. All rights reserved.)

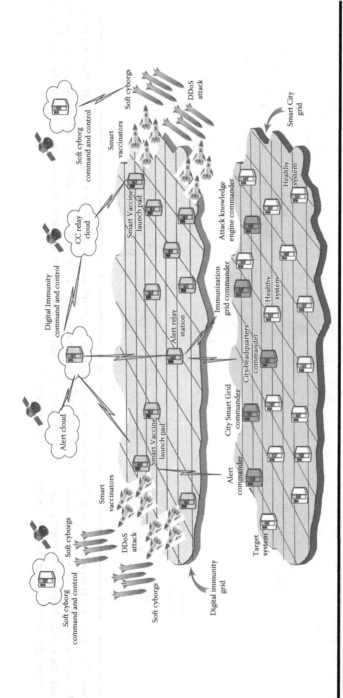

Figure 7.6 This is how cyber warfare will be in the next two decades. It is hi-tech combat fought at three levels (satellites, clouds, and grids). It is an atrocious perpetual war between two symmetrical forces that will try to outsmart the other. The main purpose of the Smart Vaccine Grid is to build a cognitive, robust, and scalable defense for the Smart City against the persistent attacks of Software Cyborgs. There are two Smart Grids. The first one is the Smart City Grid, which serves as the connectivity backbone of the IoT, the M2M, and the critical systems of the city infrastructures. The second one is the Smart Vaccine Grid, which provides digital immunity to the Smart City. The Smart Vaccine Grid will neutralize the Soft Cyborg attacks before the payloads hit the city. (© Copyright MERIT CyberSecurity Group. All rights reserved.)

of the Mediterranean Sea. Beirut has been ranked among the world's 50 most beautiful cities, according to the Condé Nast Traveler website. The Lebanese government received several grants from the UN and France to convert the city into the "Smart Beirut." Its natural beauty has placed the city as the fifth most charming capital in the world. Genesis 37:11 says "But while his brothers were jealous of Joseph, his father wondered .... When Joseph arrived, they tore off his beautiful coat and threw him into the dry well." The Middle East is a deep abyss infested with malware continuum coming from religious radicals, political agitators, and provocateurs. They organize a well-funded legitimate business front while they are on 3-D video connected to an underground virtual private network (VPN) of highly skilled and hands-on operatives. Most of them lived in the Western world, but over time, they became anti-establishment extremists. They formed intelligence cells and connected to several command and control (C&C) servers. They thoroughly examine every aspect of the target: location, time, team, tools. Often, they spend months examining the spot to minimize the risk of being caught.

The Great Brink's heist of 1950 wasn't a great success because the gang members were caught. Finally, the leader decided to confess, and most of the gang members received light sentences, but only $58k of the $2.7 million was recovered. After the tragedy of the World Trade 2001, terrorism became suicidal with many casualties, while cyber terrorism is going after money, confidential information, spying on citizens, or compromising the presidential elections of another country. But in the next two decades, cyber terrorism will migrate to a totally more advanced platform. The following is an excerpt from a nano attack.

On August 15, 2030, Smart Beirut (Figure 7.7) was hit by an unusual type of massive cyberattack, which caught the 1.9 million people living in the capital by surprise. Hundreds of incident response teams scrambled to catch up with the invisible attack. A citywide Smart Nano Grid was installed by a joint venture between Fujitsu and Siemens. The funding came from one of the oil-rich countries. The nanogrid connected over 1.5 million devices, plus minimized the blackouts in the city due to constant distributed attacks from anti-government groups. Conventional security methods were not effective. Antivirus vendors had incompatible software that could not coexist to defend the city. Consulting companies from the United States recommended Nano Smart Grid as the ultimate security approach. DI was a new concept for the Middle East, and Beirut wanted to be the first Smart City to implement DI.

No one knew the nature of the attack, which happened on a religious holiday. Systematically and with a progression of 5-minute intervals, the nano attack rapidly spread throughout the city's nanogrid and hit the whole city like a hurricane, bringing down the power grid, followed by the metro rail grid, automatic teller machines (ATMs), the traffic light grid, the hospital grid, the bridge toll, and the Telecom network.

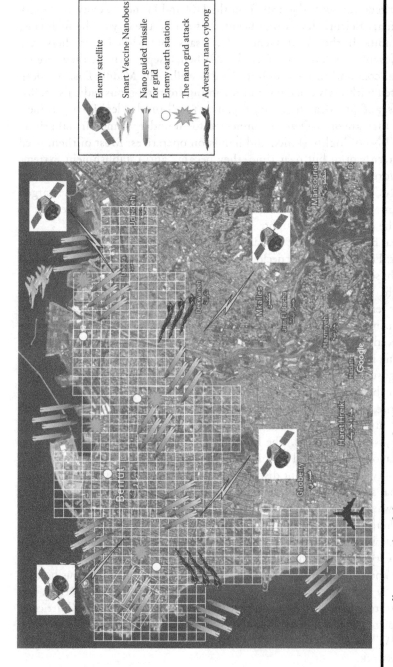

Figure 7.7 A live scenario of the nano attack (the nano cyborg attack) on Beirut, Lebanon. The Smart Vaccine Grid is not shown in the picture. The focus is on the attack on five critical infrastructures: the airport, the harbor, the medical district, the financial district, and the residential IoT.

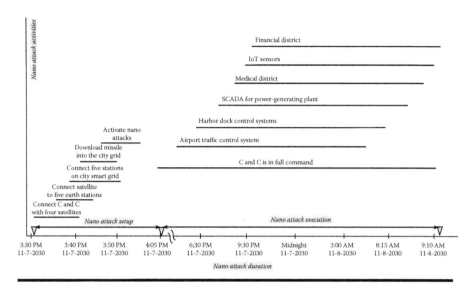

Figure 7.8 **The sequence of the nano attack activities, showing in the first part the nano attack setup, followed by the nano attack execution. (© Copyright MERIT CyberSecurity Group. All rights reserved.)**

The Computer Emergency Response Team (CERT) estimates that over 200,000 different types of viruses were unleashed to paralyze the city. Later, it was referred to as "The Cyborg Rain."

Cyborg Rain is the DDoS of the future. It is designed with much more advanced technologies and a more sophisticated attack strategy. Cyborg Rain will be deployed for Smart Cities. It will be hi-tech combat fought at three levels (satellites, clouds and grids). A time line showing the sequence of attack events of the Cyborg Rain is shown in Figure 7.8.

Glossary

Aaron: A computerized robot (and associated software), designed by Harold Cohen, that creates original drawings and paintings.

Alexander's solution: A term referring to Alexander the Great's slicing of the Gordian knot with his sword. A reference to solving an insoluble problem with decisive yet unexpected and indirect means.

Algorithm: A sequence of rules and instructions that describes a procedure to solve a problem. A computer program expresses one or more algorithms in a manner understood by a computer.

Alu: A meaningless sequence of 300 nucleotide letters that occurs 300,000 times in the human genome.

Analog: A quantity that is continuously varying, as opposed to varying in discrete steps. Most phenomena in the natural world are analog. When we measure and give them a numeric value, we digitize them. The human brain uses both digital and analog computation.

Analytical engine: The first programmable computer created in the 1840s by Charles Babbage and Ada Lovelace. The analytical engine had a random-access memory (RAM) consisting of 1000 words of 50 decimal digits each, a central processing unit, a special storage unit for software, and a printer. Although it foreshadowed modem computers, Babbage's invention never worked.

Angel capital: Refers to funds available for investment by networks of wealthy investors who invest in start-up companies. A key source of capital for high-tech start-up companies in the United States.

Artificial intelligence (AI): The field of research that attempts to emulate human intelligence in a machine. Fields within AI include knowledge-based systems, expert systems, pattern recognition, automatic learning, natural language understanding, robotics, and others.

Artificial life: Simulated organisms, each including a set of behavior and reproduction rules (a simulated "genetic code"), and a simulated environment. The simulated organisms simulate multiple generations of evolution. The term can refer to any self-replicating pattern.

ASR: *See* Automatic speech recognition.

Automatic speech recognition (ASR): Software that recognizes human speech. In general, ASR systems include the ability to extract high-level patterns in speech data.

BGM: See Brain-generated music.

Big bang theory: A prominent theory on the beginning of the Universe: the cosmic explosion, from a single point of infinite density, that marked the beginning of the Universe billions of years ago.

Big crunch: A theory that the Universe will eventually lose momentum in expanding and contract and collapse in an event that is the opposite of the big bang.

Bioengineering: The field of designing pharmaceutical drugs and strains of plant and animal life by directly modifying the genetic code. Bioengineered materials, drugs, and life forms are used in agriculture, medicine, and the treatment of disease.

Biology: The study of life forms. In evolutionary terms, the emergence of patterns of matter and energy that could survive and replicate to form future generations.

Bionic organ: In 2029, artificial organs that are built using nanoengineering.

Biowarfare agency (BWA): In the second decade of the 21st century, a government agency that monitors and polices bioengineering technology applied to weapons.

Bit: A contraction of the phrase "binary digit." In a binary code, one of two possible values, usually zero and one. In information theory, the fundamental unit of information.

Brain-generated music (BGM): A music technology pioneered by Neurosonics Inc., that creates music in response to a listener's brain waves. This brain wave biofeedback system appears to evoke the relaxation response by encouraging the generation of alpha waves in the brain.

BRUTUS.1: A computer program that creates fictional stories with a theme of betrayal; invented by Selmer Bringsjord, Dave Ferucci, and a team of software engineers at Rensselaer Polytechnic Institute in New York.

Buckyball: A soccer ball–shaped molecule formed from a large number of carbon atoms. Because of their hexagonal and pentagonal shape, the molecules were dubbed "buckyballs" in reference to R. Buckminster Fuller's building designs.

Busy beaver: One example of a class of noncomputational functions; an unsolvable problem in mathematics. Being a "Turing machine unsolvable problem," the busy beaver function cannot be computed by a Turing machine. To compute the busy beaver of n, one creates all the n-state Turing machines that do not write an infinite number of 1s on their tape. The largest number of 1s written by the Turing machine in this set that writes the largest number of 1s is the busy beaver of n.

BWA: See Biowarfare agency

Byte: A contraction for "by eight." A group of eight bits clustered together to store one unit of information on a computer. A byte may correspond, for example, to a letter of the English alphabet.

CD-ROM: *See* Compact disc read-only memory.

Chaos: The amount of disorder or unpredictable behavior in a system. In reference to the laws of time and chaos, chaos refers to the quantity of random and unpredictable events that are relevant to a process.

Chaos theory: The study of patterns and emergent behavior in complex systems comprised of many unpredictable elements (e.g., the weather).

Chemistry: The composition and properties of substances comprised of molecules.

Chip: A collection of related circuits that work together on a task or set of tasks, residing on a wafer of semiconductor material (typically silicon).

Closed system: Interacting entities and forces not subject to outside influence (e.g., the Universe). A corollary of the second law of thermodynamics is that in a closed system, entropy increases.

Cochlear implant: An implant that performs frequency analyses of sound waves, similar to that performed by the inner ear.

Colossus: The first electronic computer, built by the British from 1500 radio tubes during World War II. Colossus and nine similar machines running in parallel cracked increasingly complex German codes on military intelligence and contributed to the Allied forces' winning of World War II.

Combinatorial explosion: The rapid exponential growth in the number of possible ways of choosing distinct combinations of elements from a set as the number of elements in that set grows. In an algorithm, the rapid growth in the number of alternatives to be explored while performing a search for a solution to a problem.

Common sense: The ability to analyze a situation based on its context, using millions of integrated pieces of common knowledge. Currently, computers lack common sense. To quote Marvin Minsky: "Deep Blue might be able to win at chess, but it wouldn't know to come in from the rain."

Compact disc read-only memory (CD-ROM): A laser-read disc that contains up to a half billion bytes of information. "Read only" refers to the fact that information can be read, but not deleted or recorded, on the disc.

Complicated-minded school: The use of sophisticated procedures to evaluate the terminal leaves in a recursive algorithm.

Computation: The process of calculating a result using an algorithm (e.g., a computer program) and related data. The ability to remember and solve problems.

Computer: A machine that implements an algorithm. A computer transforms data according to the specifications of an algorithm. A programmable computer allows the algorithm to be changed.

Computer language: A set of rules and specifications for describing an algorithm or process on a computer.

Computing medium: Computing circuitry capable of implementing one or more algorithms. Examples include human neurons and silicon chips.

Connectionism: An approach to studying intelligence and to creating intelligent solutions to problems. Connectionism is based on storing problem-solving knowledge as a pattern of connections among a very large number of simple processing units operating in parallel.

Consciousness: The ability to have a subjective experience. The ability of a being, animal, or entity to have self-perception and self-awareness. The ability to feel. A key question in the 21st century is whether computers will achieve consciousness (which their human creators are considered to have).

Continuous speech recognition (CSR): A software program that recognizes and records natural language.

Crystalline computing: A system in which data is stored in a crystal as a hologram, conceived by Stanford professor Lambertus Hesselink. This three-dimensional storage method requires a million atoms for each bit and could achieve a trillion bits of storage for each cubic centimeter. Crystalline computing also refers to the possibility of growing computers as crystals.

CSR: See Continuous speech recognition.

Cybernetic artist: A computer program that is able to create original artwork in poetry, visual art, or music. Cybernetic artists will become increasingly commonplace starting in 2009.

Cybernetic chauffeur: Self-driving cars that use special sensors in the roads. Self-driving cars are being experimented with in the late 1990s, with implementation on major highways feasible during the first decade of the 21st century.

Cybernetic poet: A computer program that is able to create original poetry.

Cybernetics: A term coined by Norbert Wiener to describe the science of control and communication in animals and machines. Cybernetics is based on the theory that intelligent living beings adapt to their environments and accomplish objectives primarily by reacting to feedback from their surroundings.

Database: The structured collection of data that is designed in connection with an information retrieval system. A database management system (DBMS) allows monitoring, updating, and interacting with a database.

Debugging: The process of discovering and correcting errors in computer hardware and software. The issue of bugs or errors in a program will become increasingly important as computers are integrated into the human brain and physiology throughout the 21st century. The first "bug" was an actual moth, discovered by Grace Murray Hopper, the first programmer of the Mark I computer.

Deep Blue: The computer program, created by IBM, that defeated Gary Kasparov, World Chess Champion, in 1997.

Destroy-all-copies movement: In 2099, a movement to permit an individual to terminate his or her mind file and to destroy all backup copies of that file.

Destructive scan: The process of scanning one's brain and neural system while destroying it, with a view to replacing it with electronic circuits of far greater capacity, speed, and reliability.

Digital: Varying in discrete steps. The use of combinations of bits to represent data in computation. Contrasted with analog.

Digital video disc (DVD): A high-density compact disc system that uses a more focused laser than the conventional CD-ROM, with storage capacities of up to 9.4 gigabytes on a double-sided disc. A DVD has sufficient capacity to hold a full-length movie.

Direct neural pathway: Direct electronic communication to the brain. In 2029, direct neural pathways, combined with wireless communication technology, will connect humans directly to the worldwide computing network (the Web).

Diversity: Variety of choices in which evolution thrives. A key resource for an evolutionary process. The other resource for evolution is its own increasing order.

DNA: Deoxyribonucleic acid: the building blocks of all organic life forms. In the 21st century, intelligent life forms will be based on new computational technologies and nanoengineering.

DNA computing: A form of computing, pioneered by Leonard Adleman, in which DNA molecules are used to solve complex mathematical problems. DNA computers allow trillions of computations to be performed simultaneously.

DVD: See Digital video disc.

Einstein's theory of relativity: Refers to two of Einstein's theories. Einstein's special theory of relativity postulates that the speed of light is the fastest speed at which we can transmit information. Einstein's general theory of relativity deals with the effects of gravity on the geometry of space. It includes the formula $E = mc^2$ (energy equals mass times the speed of light squared), which is the basis of nuclear power.

EMI: See Experiments in musical intelligence.

Encryption: Encoding information so that only the intended recipient can understand the message by decoding it. PGP (pretty good privacy) is an example of encryption.

Entropy: In thermodynamics, a measure of the chaos (unpredictable movement) of particles and unavailable energy in the physical system of many components. In other contexts, a term used to describe the extent of randomness and disorder of a system.

Evolution: A process in which diverse entities (sometimes called organisms) compete for limited resources in an environment, with the more successful organisms able to survive and reproduce (to a greater extent) into subsequent generations. Over many such generations, the organisms become better adapted at survival. Over generations, the order (suitability of information for a purpose) of the design of the organisms increases, with the purpose of survival. In an "evolutionary algorithm" (See Evolutionary algorithm), the purpose may be defined as the discovery of a solution to a complex problem. Evolution also refers to a theory in which each life form on Earth has its origin in an earlier form.

Evolutionary algorithm: Computer-based problem-solving systems that use computational models of the mechanisms of evolution as key elements in their design.

Experiments in musical intelligence (EMI): A computer program that composes musical scores. Created by the composer David Cope.

Expert system: A computer program based on various artificial intelligence techniques that solves a problem using a database of expert knowledge on a topic. Also, a system that enables such a database to be made available to the nonexpert user. A branch of the artificial intelligence field.

Exponential growth: Characterized by growth in which size increases by a fixed multiple over time.

Exponential trend: Any trend that exhibits exponential growth (such as an exponential trend in population growth).

Femtoengineering: A proposed computing technology on the femtometer (one thousandth of a trillionth of a meter) scale. Femtoengineering requires harnessing mechanisms inside a quark. Molly discusses femtoengineering proposals with the author in 2099.

Florence Manifesto Brigade: A neo-Luddite group that is based on the "Florence Manifesto" written by Theodore Kaczynski from prison. Members of the brigade protest technology primarily through nonviolent means.

Fog swarm projection: In the mid- and late-21st century, a technology that will allow projections of physical objects and entities through the behavior of trillions of foglets.

Foglet: A hypothetical robot that consists of a human-cell-sized device with 12 arms pointing in all directions. At the end of the arms are grippers so that the foglets can grasp one another to form larger structures. These nano-bots are intelligent and can merge their computational capacities with one another to create a distributed intelligence. Foglets are the brainchild of J. Storrs Hall, a Rutgers University computer scientist.

Free will: Purposeful behavior and decision making. Since the time of Plato, philosophers have explored the paradox of free will, particularly as it applies to machines. During the next century, a key issue will be whether machines will evolve into beings with consciousness and free will. A primary philosophical issue is how free will is possible if events are the result of the predictable—or unpredictable—interaction of particles. Considering the interaction of particles to be unpredictable does not resolve the paradox of free will because there is nothing purposeful in random behavior.

General problem solver (GPS): A procedure and program developed by Allen Newell, J.C. Shaw, and Herbert Simon. GPS attains an objective by using recursive search and by applying rules to generate the alternatives at each branch in the recursive expansion of possible sequences. GPS uses a procedure to measure the "distance" from the goal.

Genetic algorithm: A model of machine learning that derives its behavior from a metaphor of the mechanisms of evolution in nature. Within a program, a population of simulated "individuals" is created and undergoes a process of evolution in a simulated competitive environment.

Genetic programming: The method of creating a computer program using genetic or evolutionary algorithms (See Evolutionary algorithm; Genetic algorithm).

God spot: A tiny locus of nerve cells in the frontal lobe of the brain that appears to be activated during religious experiences. Neuroscientists from the University of California discovered the God spot while studying epileptic patients who have intense mystical experiences during seizures.

Gödel's incompleteness theorem: A theorem postulated by Kurt Gödel, a Czech mathematician, that states that in a mathematical system powerful enough to generate natural numbers, there inevitably exist propositions that can be neither proved nor disproved.

Gordian knot: An intricate, practically unsolvable problem. A reference to the knot tied by Gordius, to be untied only by the future ruler of Asia. Alexander the Great circumvented the dilemma of untying the knot by slashing it with his sword.

GPS: See General problem solver.

Grandfather legislation: As of 2099, legislation that protects the rights of MOSHs (mostly original substrate humans) and acknowledges the roots of 21st-century beings (See MOSH).

Haptic interface: In virtual reality systems, the physical actuators that provide the user with a sense of touch (including the sensing of pressure and temperature).

Haptics: The development of systems that allow one to experience the sense of touch in virtual reality (See Haptic interface).

Hologram: An interference pattern, often using photographic media, that is encoded by laser beams and read by means of low-power laser beams. This interference pattern can reconstruct a three-dimensional image. An important property of a hologram is that the information is distributed throughout the hologram. Cut a hologram in half, and both halves will have the full picture, only at half the resolution. Scratching a hologram has no noticeable effect on the image. Human memory is regarded to be distributed in a similar way.

Holy Grail: Any objective of a long and difficult quest. In medieval tore, the Grail refers to the plate used by Christ at the Last Supper. The Holy Grail subsequently became the object of knights' quests.

Homo erectus: "Upright man." *Homo erectus* emerged in Africa about 1.6 million years ago and developed fire, clothing, language, and weapon use.

Homo habilis: "Handy human." A direct ancestor leading to *Homo erectus* and eventually to *Homo sapiens*. *Homo habilis* lived approximately 1.6–2 million years ago. *Homo habilis* hominids were different from previous hominids in their bigger brain size, diet of both meat and plants, and creation and use of rudimentary tools.

Homo sapiens: Human species that emerged perhaps 400,000 years ago. *Homo sapiens* are similar to advanced primates in terms of their genetic heritage and are distinguished by their creation of technology, including art and language.

Homo sapiens neanderthal (***neanderthalensis***): A subspecies of *Homo sapiens*. *Homo sapiens neanderthalensis* is thought to have evolved from *Homo erectus* about 100,000 years ago in Europe and the Middle East. This highly intelligent subspecies cultivated an involved culture that included elaborate funeral rituals, burying their dead with ornaments, caring for the sick, and making tools for domestic use and for protection. *Homo sapiens neanderthalensis* disappeared about 35,000–40,000 years ago, in all likelihood as a result of violent conflict with *Homo sapiens sapiens* (the subspecies of contemporary humans).

Homo sapiens sapiens: Another subspecies of *Homo sapiens* that emerged in Africa about 90,000 years ago. Contemporary humans are the direct descendants of this subspecies.

Human genome project: An international research program with the goal of gathering a resource of genomic maps and DNA sequence information that will provide detailed information about the structure, organization, and characteristics of the DNA of humans and other animals. The project began in the mid-1980s and is expected to be completed by around the year 2005.

Idiot savant: A system or person who is highly skilled in a narrow task area but who lacks context and is otherwise impaired in more general areas of intelligent functioning. The term is taken from psychiatry, where it refers to a person who exhibits brilliance in one very limited domain but is underdeveloped in common sense, knowledge, and competence. For example, some human idiot savants are capable of multiplying very large numbers in their heads, or memorizing a phone book. Deep Blue is an example of an idiot savant system.

Image processing: The manipulation of data representing images, or pictorial representations on a screen, composed of pixels. The use of a computer program to enhance or modify an image.

Improvisor: A computer program that creates original music, written by Paul Hodgson, a British jazz saxophone player. Improvisor can emulate styles ranging from Bach to jazz greats Louis Armstrong and Charlie Parker.

Industrial Revolution: The period in history in the late 18th and 19th centuries marked by accelerating developments in technology that enabled the mass production of goods and materials.

Information: A sequence of data that is meaningful in a process, such as the DNA code of an organism or the bits in a computer program. Information is contrasted with "noise," which is a random sequence. However, neither noise nor information is predictable. Noise is inherently unpredictable but carries no information. Information is also unpredictable; that is, we cannot predict future information from past information. If we can fully predict future data from past data, then that future data stops being information.

Information theory: A mathematical theory concerning the difference between information and noise, and the ability of a communications channel to carry information.

Intelligence: The ability to use optimally limited resources—including time—to achieve a set of goals (which may include survival, communication, solving problems, recognizing patterns, performing skills). The products of intelligence may be clever, ingenious, insightful, or elegant. R.W. Young defines intelligence as "that faculty of mind by which order is perceived in a situation previously considered disordered."

Intelligent agent: An autonomous software program that performs a function on its own, such as searching the Web for information of interest to a person based on certain criteria.

Intelligent function: A function that requires increasing intelligence to compute for increasing arguments. The busy beaver is an example of an intelligent function.

Internet computation harvesting proposal: A proposal to harvest the unused computational resources of personal computers on the Internet, thereby creating virtual parallel supercomputers. There were sufficient unused "computes" on the Internet in 1998 to create human brain capacity supercomputers, at least in terms of hardware capability.

Knee of the curve: The period in which the exponential nature of the curve of time begins to explode. Exponential growth lingers with no apparent growth for a long period of time and then appears to erupt suddenly. This is now occurring in the capability of computers.

Knowledge engineering: The art of designing and building expert systems. In particular, collecting knowledge and heuristic rules from human experts in their area of specialty and assembling them into a knowledge base or expert system.

Knowledge principle: A principle that emphasizes the important role played by knowledge in many forms of intelligent activity. It states that a system exhibits intelligence in part due to the specific knowledge relevant to the task that it contains.

Knowledge representation: A system for organizing human knowledge in a domain into a data structure flexible enough to allow the expression of facts, rules, and relationships.

Law of accelerating returns: As order exponentially increases, time exponentially speeds up (i.e., the time interval between salient events grows shorter as time passes).

Law of increasing chaos: As chaos exponentially increases, time exponentially slows down (i.e., the time interval between salient events grows longer as time passes).

Law of time and chaos: In a process, the time interval between salient events (i.e., events that change the nature of the process or significantly affect the future of the process) expands or contracts along with the amount of chaos.

Laws of thermodynamics: The laws of thermodynamics govern how and why energy is transferred.

The first law of thermodynamics (postulated by Hermann von Helmholtz in 1847), also called the law of conservation of energy, states that the total amount of energy in the Universe is constant. A process may modify the form of energy, but a closed system does not lose energy. We can use this knowledge to determine the amount of energy in a system, the amount lost as wasted heat, and the efficiency of the system.

The second law of thermodynamics (articulated by Rudolf Clausias in 1850), also known as the law of increasing entropy, states that the entropy (disorder of particles) in the Universe never decreases. As the disorder in the Universe increases, the energy is transformed into less usable forms. Thus, the efficiency of any process will always be less than 100%.

The third law of thermodynamics (described by Walter Hermann Nernst in 1906, based on the idea of a temperature of absolute zero first articulated by Baron Kelvin in 1848), also known as the law of absolute zero, tells us that all molecular movement stops at a temperature called absolute zero, or 0 Kelvin (–273°C). Since temperature is a measure of molecular movement, the temperature of absolute zero can be approached, but it can never be reached.

Life: The ability of entities (usually organisms) to reproduce into future genera-tions. Patterns of matter and energy that can perpetuate themselves and survive.

LISP (list processing): An interpretive computer language developed in the late 1950s at MIT by John McCarthy used to manipulate symbolic strings of instructions and data. The principal data structure is the list, a finite ordered sequence of symbols. Because a program written in LISP is itself expressed as a list of lists, LISP lends itself to sophisticated recursion, sym-bol manipulation, and self-modifying code. It has been widely used for AI programming, although it is less popular today than it was in the 1970s and 1980s.

Logical positivism: A 20th-century philosophical school of thought that was inspired by Ludwig Wittgenstein's *Tractatus Logico-Philosophicus*. According to logical positivism, all meaningful statements may be con-firmed by observation and experiment or are "analytic" (deducible from observations).

Luddite: One of a group of early-19th-century English workmen who destroyed labor-saving machinery in protest. The Luddites were the first orga-nized movement to oppose the mechanized technology of the Industrial Revolution. Today, the Luddites are a symbol of opposition to technology.

Magnetic resonance imaging (MRI): A non-invasive diagnostic technique that produces computerized images of body tissues and is based on nuclear magnetic resonance of atoms within the body produced by the application of radio waves. A person is placed in a magnetic field that is 30,000 times stronger than the normal magnetic field on Earth. The person's body is stimulated with radio waves, and the body responds with its own electro-magnetic transmissions. These are detected and processed by computer to generate a three-dimensional map of high-resolution internal features such as blood vessels.

Massively parallel neural nets: A neural net built from many parallel processing units. Generally, a separate, specialized computer implements each neuron model.

Microprocessor: An integrated circuit built on a single chip containing the entire central processing unit (CPU) of a computer.

Millions of instructions per second: A method of measuring the speed of a computer in terms of the number of millions of instructions performed by the computer in one second. An instruction is a single step in a computer program as represented in the computer's machine language.

Mind–body problem: The philosophical question: How does the nonphysical entity of the mind emerge from the physical entity of the brain? How do feelings and other subjective experiences result from the processing of the physical brain? By extension, will machines emulating the processes of the human brain have subjective experiences? Also, how does the nonphysical entity of the mind exert control over the physical reality of the body?

Mind trigger: The stimulation of an area of the brain that evokes a feeling usually (i.e., otherwise) gained from an actual physical or mental experience.

Minimax procedure or theorem: A basic technique used in game-playing programs. An expanding tree of possible moves and countermoves (moves from the opponent) is constructed. An evaluation of the final "leaves" of the tree that minimizes the opponent's ability to win and maximizes the program's ability to win is then passed back down the branches of the tree.

MIPS: See Millions of instructions per second.

Mission-critical system: A software program that controls a process on which people are heavily dependent. Examples of mission-critical software include life support systems in hospitals, automated surgical equipment, autopilot flying and landing systems, and other software-based systems that affect the well-being of a person or organization.

Molecular computer: A computer based on logic gates that is constructed on the principles of molecular mechanics (as opposed to the principles of electronics) by appropriate arrangements of molecules. Since the size of each logic gate (device that can perform a logical operation) is only one or a few molecules, the resultant computer can be microscopic in size. Limitations on molecular computers arise only from the physics of atoms. Molecular computers can be massively parallel by having parallel computations performed by trillions of molecules simultaneously. Molecular computers have been demonstrated using the DNA molecule.

Moore's law: First postulated by former Intel CEO Gordon Moore in the mid-1960s, Moore's law is the prediction that the size of each transistor on an integrated circuit chip will be reduced by 50% every 24 months. The result is the exponentially growing power of integrated circuit-based computation over time. Moore's law doubles the number of components on a chip as well as the speed of each component. Both of these aspects double the power of computing, for an effective quadrupling of the power of computation every 24 months.

MOSH: An acronym for mostly original substrate humans. In the last half of the 21st century, a human being still using native carbon-based neurons and unenhanced by neural implants is referred to as a MOSH. In 2099, Molly refers to the author as being a MOSH.

MOSH art: Art (usually created by enhanced humans) that a MOSH is theoretically capable of appreciating, although MOSH art is not always shared with a MOSH.

MOSH music: MOSH art in the form of music.

Moshism: An archaic term that is rooted in the MOSH way of life, before the advent of enhanced humans through neural implants and the porting of human brains to new computational substrates. An example of a Moshism is the word *papers* that refer to knowledge structures representing a body of intellectual work.

MRI: See Magnetic resonance imaging.

MYCIN: A successful expert system, developed at Stanford University in the mid-1970s, designed to aid medical practitioners in prescribing an appropriate antibiotic by determining the exact identity of a blood infection.

Nanobot: A nanorobot (robot built using nanotechnology). A self-replicating nanobot requires mobility, intelligence, and the ability to manipulate its environment. It also needs to know when to stop its own replication. In 2029, nanobots will circulate through the bloodstream of the human body to diagnose illnesses.

Nanobot swarm: In the second half of the 21st century, a swarm of trillions of nanobots can rapidly take on any form. A nanobot swarm can project the visual images, sounds, and pressure contours of any set of objects, including people. A swarm of nanobots can also combine their computational abilities to emulate the intelligence of people and other intelligent entities and processes. A nanobot swarm effectively brings the ability to create virtual environments into the real environment.

Nanoengineering: The design and manufacture of products and other objects based on the manipulation of atoms and molecules; building machines atom by atom. "Nano" refers to a billionth of a meter, which is the width of five carbon atoms (See Picoengineering; Femtoengineering).

Nanopathogen: A self-replicating nanobot that replicates excessively, possibly without limit, causing destruction to both organic and inorganic matter.

Nanopatrol: In 2029, a nanobot in the bloodstream that checks the body for biological pathogens and other disease processes.

Nanotechnology: A body of technology in which products and other objects are created through the manipulation of atoms and molecules.

Nanotubes: Elongated carbon molecules that resemble long tubes and are formed of the same pentagonal patterns of carbon atoms as buckyballs. Nanotubes can perform the electronic functions of silicon-based components. Nanotubes are extremely small, thereby providing very high densities of computation. Nanotubes are a likely technology to continue to provide the exponential growth of computing when Moore's law on integrated circuits dies by the year 2020. Nanotubes are also extremely strong and heat resistant, thereby permitting the creation of three-dimensional circuits.

Natural language: Language as ordinarily spoken or written by humans using a human language such as English (as contrasted with the rigid syntax of a computer language). Natural language is governed by rules and conventions sufficiently complex and subtle for there to be frequent ambiguity in syntax and meaning.

Neanderthal: See *Homo sapiens neanderthal* (*neanderthalensis*).

Neural computer: A computer with hardware optimized for using the neural network paradigm. A neural computer is designed to simulate a massive number of models of human neurons.

Neural connection calculation: In a neural network, a term that refers to the primary calculation of multiplying the "strength" of a neural connection by the input to that connection (which is either the output of another neuron or an initial input to the system) and then adding this product to the accumulated sum of such products from other connections to this neuron. This operation is highly repetitive, so neural computers are optimized for performing it.

Neural implant: A brain implant that enhances one's sensory ability, memory, or intelligence. Neural implants will become ubiquitous in the 21st century.

Neural network: A computer simulation of human neurons. A system (implemented in software or hardware) that is intended to emulate the computing structure of neurons in the human brain.

Neuron: Information-processing cell of the central nervous system. There are an estimated 100 billion neurons in the human brain.

Noise: A random sequence of data. Because the sequence is random and without meaning, noise carries no information. Contrasted with information.

Objective experience: The experience of an entity as observed by another entity, or measurement apparatus.

OCR: See Optical character recognition.

Operating system: A software program that manages and provides a variety of services to application programs, including user interface facilities and management of input–output and memory devices.

Optical character recognition (OCR): A process in which a machine scans, recognizes, and encodes printed (and possibly handwritten) characters into digital form.

Optical computer: A computer that processes information encoded in patterns of light beams; different from today's conventional computers, in which information is represented in electronic circuitry or encoded on magnetic surfaces. Each stream of photons can represent an independent sequence of data, thereby providing extremely massive parallel computation.

Optical imaging: A brain-imaging technique similar to MRI but potentially providing higher resolution imaging. Optical imaging is based on the interaction between electrical activity in the neurons and blood circulation in the capillaries feeding the neurons.

Order: Information that fits a purpose. The measure of order is the measure of how well the information fits the purpose. In the evolution of life forms, the purpose is to survive. In an evolutionary algorithm (a computer program that simulates evolution to solve a problem), the purpose is to solve the problem. Having more information, or more complexity, does not necessarily result in a better fit. A superior solution for a purpose—greater order—may require either more or less information, and either more or less complexity. Evolution has shown, however, that the general trend toward greater order does generally result in greater complexity.

Paradigm: A pattern, model, or general approach to solving a problem.

Parallel processing: Refers to computers that use multiple processors operating simultaneously as opposed to a single processing unit. (Compare with Serial computer.)

Pattern recognition: Recognition of patterns with the goal of identifying, classifying, or categorizing complex inputs. Examples of inputs include images such as printed characters and faces, and sounds such as spoken language.

Perceptron: In the late 1960s and 1970s, a machine constructed from mathematical models of human neurons. Early perceptrons were modestly successful in such pattern recognition tasks as identifying printed letters and speech sounds. The perceptron was a forerunner of contemporary neural nets.

Personal computer: A generic term for a single-user computer using a microprocessor, and including the computing hardware and software needed for an individual to work autonomously.

PGP: See Pretty good privacy.

Picoengineering: Technology on the picometer (one trillionth of a meter) scale. Picoengineering will involve engineering at the level of subatomic particles.

Picture portal: A visual display for viewing people and other real-time images. In later years, the portals project three-dimensional, real-time scenes. Molly's son, Jeremy, uses a picture portal to view the Stanford University campus.

Pixel: An abbreviation for picture element. The smallest element on a computer screen that holds information to represent a picture. Pixels contain data giving brightness and possibly color at particular points in a picture.

Pretty good privacy (PGP): A system of encryption (designed by Phil Zimmerman) distributed on the Internet and widely used. PGP uses a public key that can be freely disseminated and used by anyone to encode a message and a private key that is kept only by the intended recipient of the encoded messages. The private key is used by the recipient to decode messages encrypted using the public key. Converting the public key to a private key requires factoring large numbers. If the number of bits in the public key is large enough, then the factors cannot be computed in a reasonable amount of time using conventional computation (and thus the encoded information remains secure). Quantum computing (with a sufficient number of qu-bits) would destroy this type of encryption.

Price performance: A measure of the performance of a product per unit cost.

Program: A set of computer instructions that enables a computer to perform a specific task. Programs are usually written in a high-level language such as "C" or "FORTRAN" that can be understood by human programmers and then translated into machine language using a special program called a compiler. Machine language is a special set of codes that directly controls a computer.

Punch card: A rectangular card that typically records up to 80 characters of data in a binary coded format as a pattern of holes punched in it.

Quantum computing: A revolutionary method of computing, based on quantum physics, that uses the ability of particles such as electrons to exist in more than one state at the same time (See Qu-bit).

Quantum decoherence: A process in which the ambiguous quantum state of a particle (such as the nuclear spin of an electron representing a qu-bit in a quantum computer) is resolved into an unambiguous state as the result of direct or indirect observations by a conscious observer.

Quantum encryption: A possible form of encryption using streams of quantum-entangled particles such as photons (See Quantum entanglement).

Quantum entanglement: A relationship between two physically separated particles under special circumstances. Two photons may be "quantum entangled" if produced by the same particle interaction and emerging in opposite directions. The two photons remain quantum entangled with each other even when separated by very large distances (even when light-years apart). In such a circumstance, the two quantum-entangled photons, if each forced to make a decision to choose among two equally probable pathways, will make the identical decision and will do so at the same instant in time. Since there is no possible communication link between two quantum-entangled photons, classical physics would predict that their decisions would be independent. But two quantum-entangled photons make the same decision and do so at the same instant in time. Experiments have demonstrated that even if there were an unknown communication path between them, there is not enough time for a message to travel from one photon to the other at the speed of light.

Quantum mechanics: A theory that describes the interactions of subatomic particles, combining several basic discoveries. These include Max Planck's 1900
observation that energy is absorbed or radiated in discrete quantities, called
quanta. Also Werner Heisenberg's 1921 uncertainty principle stating that
we cannot know both the exact position and momentum of an electron or
other particle at the same time. Interpretations of quantum theory imply
that photons simultaneously take all possible paths (e.g., when bouncing
off a mirror). Some paths cancel each other out. Remaining ambiguity in
the path actually taken is resolved based on the conscious observation of
an observer.

Qu-bit: A "quantum bit" used in quantum computing that is both zero and one at
the same time, until quantum decoherence (direct or indirect observation
by a conscious observer) causes each quantum bit to disambiguate into a
state of zero or one. One qu-bit stores two possible numbers (zero and one)
at the same time. N qu-bits stores 2 to the Nth power possible numbers at
the same time. Thus, an N qu-bit quantum computer would try 2 to the
Nth power possible solutions to a problem simultaneously, which gives the
quantum computer its enormous potential power.

RAM: See Random-access memory.

Random-access memory (RAM): Memory that can be both read and written
with random access of memory locations. Random access means that locations can be accessed in any order and do not need to be accessed sequentially. RAM can be used as the working memory of a computer into which
applications and programs can be loaded and run.

Ray Kurzweil's cybernetic poet: A computer program designed by Ray Kurzweil
that uses a recursive approach to create poetry. The cybernetic poet analyzes word sequence patterns of poems it has "read" using Markov models
(a mathematical cousin of neural nets) and creates new poetry based on
these patterns.

Read-only memory (ROM): A form of computer storage that can be read from but
not written to or deleted (e.g., CD-ROM).

Reading machine: A machine that scans text and reads it aloud. Initially developed for those who are visually impaired, reading machines are currently
used by anyone who cannot read at their intellectual level, including reading disabled (e.g., dyslexic) persons and children first learning to read.

Recursion: The process of defining or expressing a function or procedure in terms
of itself. Typically, each iteration of a recursive-solution procedure produces a simpler (or possibly smaller) version of the problem than the previous iteration. This process continues until a subproblem whose answer
is already known (or that can be readily computed without recursion) is
obtained. A surprisingly large number of symbolic and numerical problems lend themselves to recursive formulations. Recursion is typically used
by game-playing programs, such as the chess-playing program Deep Blue.

Recursive formula: A computer-programming paradigm that uses a recursive search to find a solution to a problem. The recursive search is based on a precise definition of the problem (e.g., the rules of a game such as chess).

Relativity: A theory based on two postulates: (1) that the speed of light in a vacuum is constant and independent of the source or the observer, and (2) that the mathematical forms of the laws of physics are invariant in all inertial systems. Implications of the theory of relativity include the equivalence of mass and energy and of change in mass, dimension, and time with increased velocity (See also Einstein's theory of relativity).

Relaxation response: A neurological mechanism discovered by Dr. Herbert Benson and other researchers at the Harvard Medical School and Boston's Beth Israel Hospital. The opposite of the "fight or flight" or stress response, the relaxation response is associated with reduced levels of epinephrine (adrenaline) and norepinephrine (nor-adrenaline), blood pressure, blood sugar, breathing, and heart rates.

Remember York movement: In the second decade of the 21st century, a neo-Luddite web discussion group. The group is named to commemorate the 1813 trial in York, England, during which a number of the Luddites who destroyed industrial machinery were hanged, jailed, or exiled.

Reverse engineering: Examining a product, program, or process to understand it and to determine its methods and algorithms. Scanning and copying a human brain's salient computational methods into a neural computer of sufficient capacity is a future example of reverse engineering.

RKCP: See Ray Kurzweil's cybernetic poet.

Robinson: The world's first operational computer, constructed from telephone relays and named after a popular cartoonist who drew "Rube Goldberg" machines (very ornate machinery with many interacting mechanisms). During World War II, Robinson provided the British with a transcription of nearly all significant Nazi-coded messages, until he was replaced by Colossus (See Colossus).

Robot: A programmable device, linked to a computer, consisting of mechanical manipulators and sensors. A robot may perform a physical task normally done by human beings, possibly with greater speed, strength, and/or precision.

Robotics: The science and technology of designing and manufacturing robots. Robotics combines artificial intelligence and mechanical engineering.

ROM: See Read-only memory.

Russell's paradox: The ambiguity created by the following question: Does a set that is defined as "all sets that do not include themselves" include itself as a member? Russell's paradox motivated Bertrand Russell to create a new theory of sets.

Search: A recursive procedure in which an automatic problem solver seeks a solution by iteratively exploring sequences of possible alternatives.

Second Industrial Revolution: The automation of mental rather than physical tasks.

Second law of thermodynamics: Also known as the law of increasing entropy, this law states that the disorder (amount of random movement) of particles in the Universe may increase but never decreases. As the disorder in the Universe increases, the energy is transformed into less usable forms. Thus, the efficiency of any process will always be less than 100% (hence the impossibility of perpetual motion machines).

Self-replication: A process or device that is capable of creating an additional copy of itself. Nanobots are self-replicating if they can create copies of themselves. Self-replication is regarded as a necessary means of manufacturing nanobots due to the very large number (i.e., trillions) of such devices needed to perform useful functions.

Semiconductor: A material commonly based on silicon or germanium with a conductivity midway between that of a good conductor and an insulator. Semiconductors are used to manufacture transistors. Semiconductors rely on the phenomenon of tunneling (See Tunneling).

Sensorium: The product name for a total touch virtual reality environment, which provides an all-encompassing tactile environment.

Serial computer: A computer that performs a single computation at a time. Thus, two or more computations are performed one after the other, not simultaneously (even if the computations are independent). The opposite of a parallel processing computer.

Silicon Valley: The area in California, south of San Francisco, that is a key center of high-technology innovation, including the development of software, communication, integrated circuits, and related technologies.

Simple-minded school: The use of simple procedures to evaluate the terminal leaves in a recursive algorithm. For example, in the context of a chess program, adding up piece values.

Simulated person: A realistic, animated personality incorporating a convincing visual appearance and capable of communicating using natural language. By 2019, a simulated person will be able to interact with real persons using visual, auditory, and tactile means in a virtual reality environment.

Simulator: A program that models and represents an activity or environment on a computer system. Examples include the simulation of chemical interaction and fluid flow. Other examples include a flight simulator used to train pilots and a simulated patient to train physicians. Simulators are also often used for entertainment.

Society of mind: A theory of the mind proposed by Marvin Minsky in which intelligence is seen to be the result of the proper organization of a large number (a society) of other minds, which are in turn comprised of yet simpler minds. At the bottom of this hierarchy are simple mechanisms, each of which is by itself unintelligent.

Software: Information and knowledge used to perform useful functions by computers and computerized devices. Includes computer programs and their data, but more generally also includes such knowledge products as books, music, pictures, movies, and videos.

Software-based evolution: Software simulation of the evolutionary process. One example of software-based evolution is Network Tierra, designed by Thomas Ray. Ray's "creatures" are software simulations of organisms in which each "cell" has its own DNA-like genetic code. The organisms compete with one another for the limited simulated space and energy resources of their simulated environment.

Speaker independence: Refers to the ability of a speech recognition system to understand any speaker, regardless of whether or not the system has previously sampled that speaker's speech.

Stored-program computer: A computer in which the program is stored in memory along with the data to be operated on. A stored-program capacity is an important capability for systems of artificial intelligence in that recursion and self-modifying code are not possible without it.

Subjective experience: The experience of an entity as experienced by the entity, as opposed to observations of that entity (including its internal processes) by another entity, or by a measurement apparatus.

Substrate: Computing medium or circuitry (See Computing medium).

Supercomputer: The fastest and most powerful computer available at any given time. Supercomputers are used for computations demanding high speed and storage (e.g., analyzing weather data).

Superconductivity: The physical phenomenon whereby some materials exhibit zero electrical resistance at low temperatures. Superconductivity points to the possibility of great computational power with little or no heat dissipation (a limiting factor today). Heat dissipation is a major reason that three-dimensional circuits are difficult to create.

Synthesizer: A device that computes signals in real time. In the context of music, a (usually computer-based) device that creates and generates sounds and music electronically.

Tactile virtualism: By 2029, a technology that allows one to use a virtual body to enjoy virtual reality experiences without virtual reality equipment other than the use of neural implants (which include high-bandwidth wireless communication). The neural implants create the pattern of nerve signals that corresponds to a comparable "real" experience.

Technology: An evolving process of tool creation to shape and control the environment. Technology goes beyond the mere fashioning and use of tools. It involves a record of tool making and a progression in the sophistication of tools. It requires invention and is itself a continuation of evolution by other means. The "genetic code" of the evolutionary process of technology is the knowledge base maintained by the tool-making species.

Three-dimensional chip: A chip that is constructed in three dimensions, thus allowing for hundreds or thousands of layers of circuitry. Three-dimensional chips are currently being researched and engineered by a variety of companies.

Total touch environment: In 2019, a virtual reality environment that provides an all-encompassing tactile environment.

Transistor: A switching and/or amplifying device using semiconductors, first created in 1948 by John Bardeen, Walter Brattain, and William Shockley of Bell Labs.

Translating telephone: A telephone that provides real-time speech translation from one human language to another.

Tunneling: In quantum mechanics, the ability of electrons (negatively charged particles orbiting the nucleus of an atom) to exist in two places at once, in particular on both sides of a barrier. Tunneling allows some of the electrons to effectively move through the barrier and accounts for the "semi" conductor properties of a transistor.

Turing machine: A simple abstract model of a computing machine, designed by Alan Turing in his 1936 paper "On Computable Numbers." The Turing machine is a fundamental concept in the theory of computation.

Turing test: A procedure proposed by Alan Turing in 1950 for determining whether or not a system (generally a computer) has achieved human-level intelligence, based on whether it can deceive a human interrogator into believing that it is human. A human "judge" interviews the (computer) system and one or more human "foils" over terminal lines (by typing messages). Both the computer and the human foil(s) try to convince the human judge of their humanness. If the human judge is unable to distinguish the computer from the human foil(s), then the computer is considered to have demonstrated human-level intelligence. Turing did not specify many key details, such as the duration of the interrogation and the sophistication of the human judge and foils. By 2029, computers will be able to pass the test, although the validity of the test remains a point of controversy and philosophical debate.

Utility fog: A space filled with foglets. At the end of the 21st century, utility fog can be used to simulate any environment, essentially providing "real" reality with the environment-transforming capabilities of virtual reality (See Fog swarm projection; Foglet).

Vacuum tube: The earliest form of an electronic switch (or amplifier) based on vacuum-filled glass containers. Used in radios and other communication equipment and early computers; replaced by the transistor.

Venture capital: Refers to funds available for investment by organizations that have raised pools of capital specifically to invest in companies, primarily new ventures.

Virtual body: In virtual reality, one's own body potentially transformed to appear (and ultimately to feel) different than it does in "real" reality.

Virtual reality: A simulated environment in which you can immerse yourself. A virtual reality environment provides a convincing replacement for the visual and auditory senses, and (by 2019) the tactile sense. In later decades, the olfactory sense will be included as well. The key to a realistic visual experience in virtual reality is that when you move your head, the scene instantly repositions itself so that you are now looking at a different region of a three-dimensional scene. The intention is to simulate what happens when you turn your real head in the real world: The images captured by your retinas rapidly change. Your brain nonetheless understands that the world has remained stationary and that the image is sliding across your retinas only because your head is rotating. Initially, virtual reality (including crude contemporary systems) requires the use of special helmets to provide the visual and auditory environments. By 2019, virtual reality will be provided by ubiquitous contact lens–based systems and implanted retinal-imaging devices (as well as comparable devices for auditory "imaging"). Later in the 21st century, virtual reality (which will include all the senses) will be provided by direct stimulation of nerve pathways using neural implants.

Virtual reality auditory lenses: In 2019, sonic devices that project high-resolution sounds precisely placed in a three-dimensional virtual environment. These can be built into eyeglasses, worn as body jewelry, or implanted.

Virtual reality blocking display: In 2019, a display technology using virtual reality optical lenses (See Virtual reality optical lenses) and virtual reality auditory lenses (See Virtual reality auditory lenses) that creates highly realistic virtual visual environments. The display blocks out the real environment, so you see and hear only the projected virtual environment.

Virtual reality head-directed display: In 2019, a display technology using virtual reality optical lenses (See Virtual reality optical lenses) and virtual reality auditory lenses (see Virtual reality auditory lenses) that projects a virtual environment stationary with respect to the position and orientation of your head. When you move your head, the display moves relative to the real environment. This mode is often used to interact with virtual documents.

Virtual reality optical lenses: In 2009, three-dimensional displays built into glasses or contact lenses. These "direct eye" displays create highly realistic virtual visual environments overlaying the "real" environment. This display technology projects images directly onto the human retina, exceeds the resolution of human vision, and is widely used regardless of visual impairment. In 1998, the Microvision Virtual Retina Display provided a similar capability for military pilots, with consumer versions anticipated.

Virtual reality overlay display: In 2019, a display technology using virtual reality optical lenses (See Virtual reality optical lenses) and virtual reality auditory lenses (See virtual reality auditory lenses) that integrates real and virtual environments. The displayed images slide when you move or turn your head so that the virtual people, objects, and environment appear to remain stationary in relation to the real environment (which you can still see). Thus, if the direct eye display is displaying the image of a person (who could be a geographically remote real person engaging in a three-dimensional visual phone call with you, or a computer-generated simulated person), that projected person will appear to be in a particular place relative to the real environment that you also see. When you move your head, that projected person will appear to remain in the same place relative to the real environment.

Virtual sex: Sex in virtual reality incorporating a visual, auditory, and tactile environment. The sex partner can be a real or simulated person.

Virtual tactile environment: A virtual reality system that allows the user to experience a realistic and all-encompassing tactile environment.

Vision chip: A silicon emulation of the human retina that captures the algorithm of early mammalian visual processing, an algorithm called "center surround filtering."

World Wide Web (www): A highly distributed (not centralized) communications network allowing individuals and organizations around the world to communicate with one another. Communication includes the sharing of text, images, sounds, video, software, and other forms of information. The primary user interface paradigm of the "Web" is based on hypertext, which consists of documents (which can contain any type of data) connected by "links," which the user selects by a pointing device such as a mouse. The Web is a system of data-and-message servers linked by high-capacity communication links that can be accessed by any computer user with a "web browser" and Internet access. With the introduction of Windows98, access to the Web is built into the operating system. By the late 21st century, the Web will provide the distributed computing medium for software-based humans.

Y2K (year 2000 problem): Refers to anticipated difficulties caused by software (usually developed several decades prior to the year 2000) in which date fields used only two digits. Unless the software was adjusted to hand four-digit dates, this could have caused computer programs to behave erratically when the year became "00." It was thought that these programs would mistake the year 2000 for 1900.

Terms were selectively extracted for this chapter from the public domain of the International Foundation of Information Technology; www.if4it.com/it-glossary.

Bibliography

2030 forecast: http://www.businessinsider.com/21-technology-tipping-points-we-will-reach-by-2030-2015-11/#10-of-reading-glasses-will-be-connected-to-the-internet-by-2023-8

Ray Kurzweil: http://money.cnn.com/2015/06/03/technology/ray-kurzweil-predictions/

Neural Monitoring: https://www.linkedin.com/pulse/micro-chip-implant-whatever-implants-all-leads-remote-projjal-ghosh

Neural Monitoring: http://satelliteterrorism3.blogspot.com/2014/04/organized-gang-stalking-crime-victim.html

Cyber terrorism: https://www.nap.edu/read/11848/chapter/6#46

Satellite Network: http://www.irma-international.org/viewtitle/14070/

Satellite overview: https://www.isoc.org/inet97/proceedings/F5/F5_1.HTM

Satellite Standards: http://www.opengroup.org/cloud/cloud_iop/p6.htm

Satellite Intro: http://www.intelsat.com/wp-content/uploads/2013/01/5941-SatellitePrimer-2010.pdf

How do satellite communication: https://www.nasa.gov/directorates/heo/scan/communications/outreach/funfacts/txt_satellite_comm.html

Bitcoin Hacking: https://darkwebnews.com/help-advice/access-dark-web/

Knowledge Base: AI http://www.mkbergman.com/1816/knowledge-based-artificial-intelligence/

Conde Nast: www.cntraveler.com/

Chapter 8

The Amazing Architecture of the Human Immune System

Introduction

From DNA to the atoms inside us, the human body is a scientific marvel. Yes indeed, the human body is the most complex and elaborate constellation of heterogeneous pieces of mosaic assembled marvelously and exquisitely to perfection. We need to examine the anatomy of the human body before we penetrate the cosmos of human immune system (HIS).

The human body is an *autonomic* and *cybernetic* system with 12 interconnected components, each of which contributes to the whole. If one of them is not functioning properly, it will drastically impact the whole. It is overwhelming to realize that all the inventions in the world, from the beginning of time until today, were mentally configured in the brain. It is also hard to accept the reality that everyone dies of "brain death." Whether an old person suffers cardiac arrest resulting in a lack of oxygen and nutrients to the brain, or a younger person suffers a gunshot wound to the head resulting in brain death, it's the same diagnosis.

In this chapter, we're pushing the human body envelope into the future. Marvelous things are going to happen to our bodies. Technology is going to be our best companion in all aspects of life. We're going to highlight some of the greatest advances in science and engineering as applied to humans. As we learn the operating principles of the human body and brain, we will soon be able to design vastly superior systems that will last longer and perform better, without susceptibility to breakdown, disease, and aging. We could say "playing God" is the

245

highest expression of our human nature. The urges to improve ourselves, to master our environment, and to set our children on the best path possible have been the fundamental driving forces of all human history. Without these urges to "play God," the world as we know it wouldn't exist today! The combination of human-level intelligence with a computer's inherent superiority in speed, accuracy, and memory-sharing ability will be formidable.

The Anatomy of the Futuristic Human Body

In the next two decades, our bodies will be transform exponentially for the better. We will be healthier, smarter, more immune, and more active. In fact, we will ourselves be creating our own successors. We will become to the machine what the horse and the dog are to us; the conclusion being that machines are, or are becoming, animate.

The first half of the 21st century will be characterized by three overlapping revolutions: in genetics, nanotechnology, and robotics (GNR). These will usher in what we referred to earlier as the beginning of the singularity, where technology will merge with human intelligence.

In 2009, Canadian astronaut Robert Thirsk began a six-month stay on the International Space Station (ISS) orbiting around the Earth. The astronauts on the ISS place their lives in the hands of the space station's advanced life support system. For the astronauts to survive in space, the temperature and pressure within the ISS must be maintained. An adequate supply of oxygen must be provided, and waste gases, such as carbon dioxide, must be removed. Solid waste must also be removed, but urine is recycled to provide the crew with clean water. All of these functions are achieved with the help of advanced technology systems. All the systems on the ISS must work together to support life on board. The same is true inside your body. Like the life support system on the ISS, your organ systems must work together to keep you alive. For instance, your body needs systems that enable it to take in oxygen and remove carbon dioxide.

The human body is a masterpiece of complexity and beauty—a symphony of forty trillion cells working in concert. It is hard to grasp just how small the atoms that make up your body are until you look at the sheer number of them. An adult is made up of around 7,000,000,000,000,000,000,000,000,000,000 (7 octillion) atoms. When you see blood oozing from a cut in your finger, you might assume that it is red because of the iron in it, rather like rust has a reddish hue. But the presence of the iron is a coincidence. The red color arises because the iron is bound in a ring of atoms in hemoglobin called porphyrin and it's the shape of this structure that produces the color. Just how red your hemoglobin is depends on whether there is oxygen bound to it. When there is oxygen present, it changes the shape of the porphyrin, giving the red blood cells a more vivid shade.

Just like a chicken, our life started off with an egg. Not a chunky thing in a shell, but an egg nonetheless. However, there is a significant difference between a human egg and a chicken egg that has a surprising effect on your age. Human eggs are tiny. They are, after all, just a single cell and are typically around 0.2 mm across—about the size of a printed full stop. Your egg was formed in your mother—but the surprising thing is that it was formed when she was an embryo. The formation of your egg, and the half of your DNA that came from your mother, could be considered as the very first moment of your existence. And it happened before your mother was born. Say your mother was 30 when she had you, then on your 18th birthday, you are arguably over 48 years old.

Our senses set boundaries on what we can experience. Your body sets limits on what you can do. But what if the brain could understand new kinds of inputs and control new kinds of limbs—expanding the reality we inhabit? We're at a moment in human history when the marriage of our biology and our technology will transcend the brain's limitations. We can hack our own hardware to steer a course into the future. This is poised to fundamentally change what it will mean to be a human.

Inside the Human Machine

The body has a chemical plant far more intricate than any plant that man has ever built. This plant changes the food we eat into living tissue. It enables the growth of flesh, blood, bones, and teeth. It even repairs the body when parts are damaged by accident or disease. Power, for work and play, comes from the food we eat. The human body contains nearly 100 trillion cells. Other overwhelming facts about the brain (from http://www.human-memory.net/brain_neurons.html): The number of connections in the human brain is approximately 10^{15} (quadrillion = 1,000,000,000,000,000). Imagine an immense forest that stretches over half the United States, a single forest that covers one million square miles. Each square mile contains 10,000 trees and each tree contains 100,000 leaves. Imagine the vast number of trees in such a forest. The number of organized electrical connections in your brain is approximately equal to the number of leaves on those trees.

The picture of the world we "see" is artificial. Our brains don't produce an image the way a video camera does. Instead, the brain constructs a model of the world from the information provided by modules that measure light and shade, edges, curvature, and so on. This makes it simple for the brain to paint out the blind spot, the area of your retina where the optic nerve joins, which has no sensors. It also compensates for the rapid jerky movements of our eyes called saccades, giving a false picture of steady vision.

Our DNA is stored in 23 pairs of chromosomes within the nucleus of every cell in our body. Each cell has a full set of chromosomes which contain all the genetic material needed to determine the makeup of our entire bodies. That's why cloning of animals can be done with just one cell. All the genetic material that defines us is inside each and every cell of our body, from our hair follicles to toenails.

There are more non-human cells in our body than human ones. There are ten times more bacteria cells in our bodies than our own human cells. These bacteria are harmless or even help us perform key bodily functions, such as digestion. Even our DNA itself isn't all from human evolution. DNA includes the genes from at least eight retroviruses that were absorbed into our own genetic code at some point. The viral genes in our DNA now perform important functions, especially related to reproduction.

All body parts can repair themselves (except teeth). Innate human biology allows us to repair ourselves pretty easily for the most part. While any serious damage to the body can take a long time to heal, all our body parts have the ability to start healing and regenerating on their own—except teeth. Since the enamel of teeth is not a living tissue, it cannot regenerate, even if the injury goes deep enough to damage the living part of the tooth. That's why a chipped tooth always takes a visit to the dentist to be entirely fixed.

The 12 Biological Autonomic Systems

The infrastructure of the human body is a marvel of engineering second to none. Our bodies consist of 12 marvelous biological systems that carry out specific functions necessary for everyday living, as displayed in Figure 8.1. These systems collaborate and lean on one another when we confront danger or sickness. However, when one system requires some maintenance or develops some defect, medicine comes to our aid, but has limitations to what it can do. In the next two decades, medical nanotechnology will be a normal part of the practice of medicine. Nanomedicine will bail us out from chronic diseases, cancer, HIV, and all our biological pathogens, removing toxins, correcting DNA errors, and even reversing aging!

As nanotechnology is doing such a great job of contributing to the welfare of humanity, it will extend its contribution into the physical and cyber security. Digital immunity will be the Holy Grail that will bring quality of life to the present and future Smart Cities. Figure 8.1 is an isometric picture of the Human Motherboard, showing how holistically all the systems work together—listed randomly, not by importance.

1. The Circulatory System

The circulatory system moves blood, nutrients, oxygen, carbon dioxide, and hormones around the body. It consists of the heart, blood, blood vessels, arteries, and veins. In the average human, about 2000 gallons (7572 liters) of blood travel daily through about 60,000 miles (96,560 kilometers) of blood vessels, according to the Arkansas Heart Hospital (http://www.livescience.com/health). An average adult

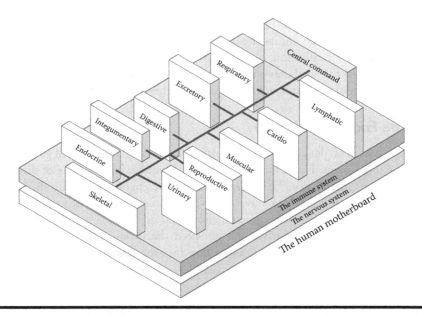

Figure 8.1 We decided to show the human anatomy as an engineering drawing to display the marvelous human autonomic systems. They all work together like the cylinders of car engine, and lean on one another when we confront danger or sickness. However, when one of the systems requires maintenance or repair, adaptive medicine comes to the rescue, but has limitations to what it could do. Nanomedicine comes to the true help. (© 2014 Copyright MERIT CyberSecurity Group. All rights reserved.)

has 5–6 quarts (4.7–5.6 liters) of blood, which is made up of plasma, red blood cells, white blood cells, and platelets. In addition to blood, the circulatory system moves lymph, which is a clear fluid that helps rid the body of unwanted material.

2. The Digestive System

The digestive system consists of a series of connected organs that, together, allow the body to break down and absorb food, and remove waste. It includes the mouth, esophagus, stomach, small intestine, large intestine, rectum, and anus. The liver and pancreas also play a role in the digestive system because they produce digestive juices. The entire system—from mouth to anus—is about 30 feet (9 meters) long.

The application of nanotechnology in cancer research has provided hope within the scientific community for the development of novel cancer therapeutic strategies. As gastrointestinal cancers contribute to more than 55% of deaths associated with cancer, tremendous efforts have been made toward the development of novel diagnostic and therapeutic methods for improving patient quality of life and lengthening survival. Advances in image-based detection, targeted drug delivery, and metastases ablation could go a long way to improve patient outcomes. Classical approaches generally do not meet patients' expectations due to a lack of specificity and poor patient stratification. More highly targeted and customized treatments are needed. Toward this goal, nanotechnologies and nano devices have been explored for their potential utilities in advancing targeted therapeutic approaches.

3. The Endocrine System

This is a system of glands that secrete hormones. The human body will go flip-flop without this system. Hormones are chemicals that affect the actions of different organ systems; there are eight major glands that secrete hormones into the blood. These hormones, like catalysts, travel to different tissues and regulate various bodily functions, such as metabolism, growth, and sexual function.

In the next two decades, we will not need the various organs that produce chemicals, hormones, and enzymes that flow into the blood and other metabolic pathways. We will be able to synthesize bio-identical versions of many of these substances, and we will be able to routinely create the vast majority of biochemically relevant substances. We are already creating artificial hormone organs. California-based Medtronic's MiniMed® 630G system, which includes a new user-friendly insulin pump, is available as an artificial pancreas, implanted under the skin, and will monitor blood glucose levels and release precise amounts of insulin, using a computer program to function like our biological pancreatic islet cells.

In the human body version 2.0, hormones and related substances (to the extent that we still need them) will be delivered via nanobots, controlled by intelligent bio-feedback systems to maintain and balance required levels. Since we will be eliminating most of our biological organs, many of these substances may no longer be needed and will be replaced by other resources required by the nanorobotic systems.

4. The Immune System

The immune system is the body's defense against bacteria, viruses, and other pathogens that may be harmful. It includes lymph nodes, the spleen, bone marrow, lymphocytes (including B-cells and T-cells), the thymus, and leukocytes, which are white blood cells. The drama of the immune system is that the more we learn about it, the more complex it gets. Thus, we're resorting to a new concept that will help us understand how deep the ocean of the immune system is.

In the next two decades, nanomedicine will be the emerging interdisciplinary fusion of nanotechnology, biology, and medicine. Pills the size of molecules will seek and destroy tumors. Miniscule robots, nanobots, will perform surgery inside patients with a precision never before achieved. Nanobots, a billionth of a meter across, will fix mutations in DNA, or repair neurons in the brain. Such are the possibilities as medicine enters the nano era. Nanomedicine will offer robotic replacements for human blood cells that perform hundreds or thousands of times more effectively than their biological counterparts. Dr. Freitas—a nanomedicine theorist and pioneer, who designed respirocytes (robotic red blood cells)—claims that a "runner could do an Olympic sprint for fifteen minutes without taking a breath." Dr. Freitas's robotic macrophages, called "microbivores," will be far more effective than our white blood cells at combatting pathogens. His DNA-repair robot would be able to mend DNA transcription errors and even implement necessary DNA changes. Other medical robots he has designed can serve as cleaners, removing unwanted debris and chemicals (such as prions, malformed proteins, and protofibrils) from individual human cells.

According to Feynman, Hibbs originally suggested to him (circa 1959) the idea of a medical use for Feynman's theoretical micromachines:

> A friend of mine (Albert R. Hibbs) suggests a very interesting possibility for relatively small machines. He says that … it would be interesting in surgery if you could swallow the surgeon. You put the mechanical surgeon inside the blood vessel and it goes into the heart and "looks" around …. It finds out which valve is the faulty one and takes a little knife and slices it out. Other small machines might be permanently incorporated in the body to assist some inadequately-functioning organ.

Richard Feynman, "There's Plenty of Room at the Bottom"

In the book Quantum Mechanics and Path Integrals, Nobel prize-winning physicist Richard P. Feynman and his student Hibbs considered the possibility of scaling down objects to molecular level. Today, 51 years later, is becoming a reality. Recently, Professor Ido Bachelet, Principal Investigator at the Nanotechnology Centre, Bar Ilan University in Israel, announced the treatment of cancer with nanomedicine. He indicates DNA nanobots can currently identify 12 different kinds of cancer tumors in humans and believes that within a very short time span, nanobots could cure cancer and repair spinal cord damage. Apart from detecting and identifying cancer cells, smart engineered nanobots have the ability to deliver medicaments in controlled-release form (Figure 8.2).

Here is a step-by-step explanation of how the new nano immune system works:

1. *Pathogen attack*: The smart nanobot (injected into the blood stream) rushes to the site of the attack.
2. *Send a sensory signal to the brain*: The brain receives the sensory signal and alerts the lymphatic network to the attack.
3. *The immune system receives the alert*: T-cells and B-cells are ready to respond.
4. *Immune system mobilized*: Ready to go to war.
5. *The B-cell army*: Prepared to go to war and heading toward the site of the attack.
6. *Generate antibody*: The vaccine that will capture the attacking pathogen.

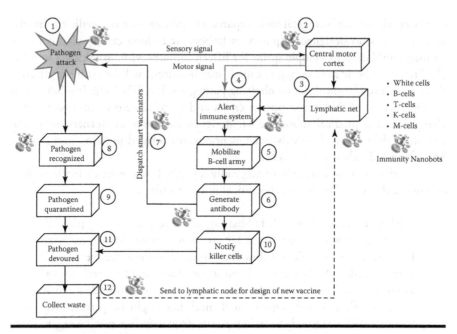

Figure 8.2 **This is how the biological immunity nanobots can help support the human immune system. In the next two decades, nanomedicine will be the emerging interdisciplinary fusion of nanotechnology, biology, and medicine. (© 2014 Copyright MERIT CyberSecurity Group. All rights reserved.)**

7. *Dispatch vaccination*: Vaccinators are at the site of the attack, ready to kill the pathogens.
8. *The pathogen is recognized*: The right vaccine was generated.
9. *Pathogen arrested*: Quarantined and taken into custody.
10. *Pathogens are killed*: and sent to forensics.
11. *Pathogen cut into pieces*: The parts are sent to the M-cells.
12. *Waste is collected*: All the waste material is collected and saved for the next battle.

Anatomy of the Biological Nanobots

Nanorobotics is an emerging technology field creating machines or robots whose components are at or near the scale of a nanometer (10^{-9} meters). More specifically, nanorobotics (as opposed to microrobotics) refers to the nanotechnology engineering discipline of designing and building nanorobots (popularly known as nanobots), with devices ranging in size from 0.1 to 10 micrometers and constructed from nanoscale or molecular components (Figure 8.3).

Nanobots are biological nanosystems designed to perform a specific task with precision at nanoscale dimensions. Nanomedicine's advantage over conventional

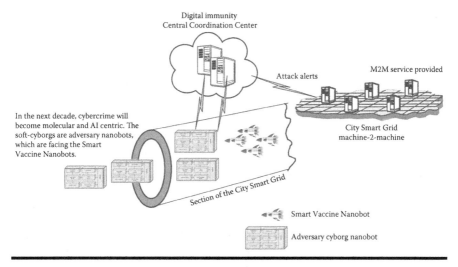

Figure 8.3 **Nanotechnology allows the viral battle to take place inside the nanogrid. The grid will be large enough to accommodate the traffic of the battle. Nanomedicine will offer robotics (nano carriers) to replace human blood cells; they will perform hundreds or thousands of times more effectively than their biological counterparts. (© 2014 Copyright MERIT CyberSecurity Group. All rights reserved.)**

medicine lies i its size. Nanobots could also be designed with software as a nano set of programmed instructions to do a specific task. We could refer to them as Soft Nanobots. In the cybersecurity domain, Soft Nanobots are similar to biological nanobots, but will be loaded onto the motherboard like "firmware." Soft Nanobots are also dynamic agents that roam throughout grids or network wires and transport information to its destination. For the sake of simplicity, we can say that Soft Nanobots are like web services.

5. The Lymphatic System

There are hundreds of lymph nodes, lymph ducts, and lymph vessels in the human body. They are located deep inside the body, such as around the lungs and heart, or closer to the surface, such as under the arm or groin. The lymphatic system's main job is to make and move lymph, a clear fluid that contains white blood cells, which help the body fight infection. The lymphatic system also removes excess lymph fluid from bodily tissues and returns it to the blood. It is also the waste management system of the body. Unlike blood, which flows throughout the body in a continuous loop, lymph flows in only one direction—upward toward the neck.

In the next two decades, we will be able to replace the spleen or the pancreas with smart and heavier-duty devices that will do better than the natural ones. Nanobots will interface with lymph nodes, control the amount of red blood cells and blood storage in the body, and help to fight infection. If the spleen detects potentially dangerous bacteria, viruses, or other microorganisms in the blood, it—along with the lymph nodes—creates white blood cells called lymphocytes, which act as defenders against invaders. Nanolymphocytes will be faster and more efficient at producing antibodies to kill foreign microorganisms and stopping infections from spreading. Humans who have lost a defective spleen will be able to get a computerized spleen and remain healthy. The body will accept these nanodevices, which will coexist with other natural organs.

6. *The Nervous System*

The nervous system controls both voluntary action (like conscious movement) and involuntary actions (like breathing), and sends signals to different parts of the body. The central nervous system includes the brain and spinal cord. The peripheral nervous system consists of nerves that connect every other part of the body to the central nervous system. Sensory neurons react to physical stimuli such as light, sound, and touch and send feedback to the central nervous system about the body's surrounding environment, according to the American Psychological Association, as described in the portal http://www.scribd.com/document/321127602/The-Nervous-System-is-a-Complex-Collection-of-Nerv. Motor neurons, located in the central nervous system or in peripheral ganglia, transmit signals to activate the muscles or glands.

Nanotechnology can be defined as the science and engineering involved in the design, synthesis, characterization, and application of materials and devices whose smallest functional organization in at least one dimension is on the nanometer scale or one billionth of a meter. In the next decade, applications to medicine and physiology imply materials and devices (nanobots) designed to interact with the body at subcellular (i.e., molecular) scales with a high degree of specificity. This can potentially translate into targeted cellular and tissue-specific clinical applications designed to achieve maximal therapeutic affects with minimal side effects, as shown in Figure 8.4. Bioelectronics medicine is an emerging discipline that uses nanotechnology to electrically stimulate the nervous system into producing the natural drugs the body needs to heal itself.

We would like to explain the incredible story of how surgical nanobots can do the work of the surgeon but from the veins of the injured (Figure 8.4). Biomedicine can mutate into a surgical team. This is how it works:

We start at the human grid, which is covered with billions of sensory receptors. An injury takes place at work and the employee starts to bleed and is in pain. The sensory signal (the pain signal) travels all the way to the brain's cortex motor region and continues its way to the motion coordinator. At the same time, the sensory signal goes to another part of the brain called the "movement forecaster," which receives some information from the motor learning center of the brain. The motor learning center relays the motor signal back to the motion coordinator and then to

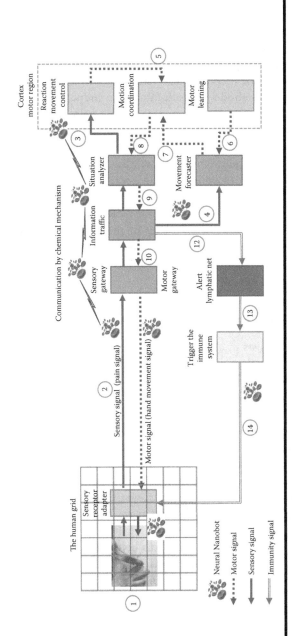

Figure 8.4 The critically injured person receives an immediate response for these nanosurgical systems to collaborate with the biological neurons under the command of the brain. The surgical nanobots will be injected in the nervous system and go into action immediately. This is going to happen in 2040. It will be reality, not virtual. (© 2014 Copyright MERIT CyberSecurity Group. All rights reserved.)

the situation analyzer, to determine the severity of the pain. An army of surgical nanobots gets motor instructions for the brain and rushes to the injury area. A signal from a sensory neuron travels to the lymphatic net, which in turn triggers the immune system (B-cells). An immune surgical nanobot accompanies the B-cells to the injury area, ensuring no microbes or pathogens sneak into the bloodstream. The accident triggers several sensory and motor signals at the same time.

New nanoparticles will be used to enable remote-controlled magnetic guiding for stem cell homing. The method will result in positive endpoints for treatment of many diseases, including stroke. Nanoparticles will also help increase the permeability of the blood–brain barrier with proper delivery of Lexiscan to the central nervous system.

In the next two decades, another practice will be common in neuromedicine: the use of iron nanoparticles for labeling human neural stem cells. This technique will help track the localization as well as the survival of stem cells. In patients with Parkinson's disease, magnetic resonance imaging (MRI) will detect these labeled stem cells, and it will be helpful for follow-up of the patient. Similarly, carbon nanowires and nanotubes are being tested for use in neural repair and regeneration. They have an influence on cellular signal transmission. They are showing promising results in neural regeneration and repair.

7. The Muscular System

The muscular system consists of about 650 muscles that aid in movement, blood flow, and other bodily functions. There are three types of muscle: skeletal muscle, which is connected to bone and helps with voluntary movement; smooth muscle, which is found inside organs and helps to move substances through organs; and cardiac muscle, which is found in the heart and helps pump blood.

University of Texas at Dallas researchers have made artificial muscles from carbon nanotube yarns that have been infiltrated with paraffin wax and twisted until coils form along their length. In the next two decades, people suffering from limb amputations will benefit greatly from nanomedicine. New artificial muscles made from nanotech yarns and infused with paraffin wax can lift more than 100,000 times their own weight and generate 85 times more mechanical power than the same size natural muscle.

The artificial muscles (Figure 8.5) are yarns constructed from carbon nanotubes, which are seamless, hollow cylinders made from the same type of graphite layers found in the core of ordinary pencils. Individual nanotubes can be 10,000 times smaller than the diameter of a human hair, yet pound-for-pound, can be 100 times stronger than steel.

Dr. Ray Baughman, team leader, and Robert A. Welch, professor of Chemistry, and director of the Alan G. MacDiarmid NanoTech Institute at UT Dallas, summarized this "playing God" work: "The artificial muscles that we've developed can provide large, ultrafast contractions to lift weights that are 200 times heavier than

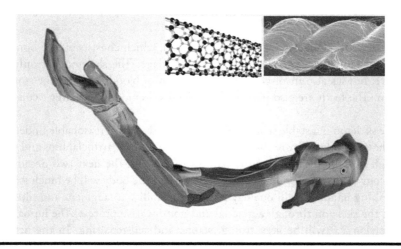

Figure 8.5 **In the next two decades, people suffering from limb amputations will benefit greatly from nanomedicine. New artificial muscles made from nanotech yarns and infused with paraffin wax can lift more than 100,000 times their own weight and generate 85 times more mechanical power than the same size natural muscle.**

possible for a natural muscle of the same size." But he believes that in the next two decades, artificial muscles will be part of fashionable nano-orthopedic medicine.

8. The Reproductive System

The reproductive system allows humans to reproduce. It is key to the production and survival of the human race. The male reproductive system includes the penis and the testes, which produce sperm. The female reproductive system consists of the vagina, the uterus, and the ovaries, which produce eggs. During conception, a sperm cell fuses with an egg cell, which creates a fertilized egg that implants and grows in the uterus.

Nanotechnology is an integrative discipline, which represents a unique combination of classical natural, mathematical, computer, and materials sciences, investigating and manipulating physical matter on the scale of nanometers. By the year 2000, nanotechnology was universally recognized as a landmark innovation, and named the sixth truly revolutionary technology introduced in the modern world.

In reproductive medicine, the use of investigational nanobiotechnological tools has already resulted in encouraging outcomes in the treatment of several high-impact conditions, creating significant opportunities for alternative non-invasive or minimally invasive treatments for several traditionally "surgical" pathologies. In the next two decades, nanomaterials will be tools for the detection and treatment of malignant and benign reproductive conditions. Nanomedicine will expand into reproductive biology, as well as highly delicate systems to combat reproductive diseases.

9. The Skeletal System

Our bodies are supported by the skeletal system, which consists of 206 bones that are connected by tendons, ligaments, and cartilage. The skeleton not only helps us move, but it's also involved in the production of blood cells and the storage of calcium. The teeth are also part of the skeletal system, but they aren't considered bones.

The skeleton is a stable structure, and we already have a reasonable understanding of how it works. We are able to replace parts of it (e.g., artificial hips and joints), although these procedures require painful surgery. In the next two decades, the technology in this area will be very successful, and the body will be much stronger. Interlinking nanobots will one day provide the ability to augment and ultimately replace the skeleton through a gradual and non-invasive process. The human skeleton version 2.0 will be very strong, stable, and self-repairing. In the next two decades, there will be bone banks, where most of the body's bones will be able to be replaced and safely installed and will properly interface with the other parts of the body.

In the next two decades, a new material that triggers stem cells to begin forming bone could enable a more effective treatment for hard-to-heal bone breaks and defects, says Dr. Akhilesh K. Gaharwar, a biomedical engineer at Texas A&M University, who is part of the team developing the biomaterial. It consists of nano-sized, two-dimensional particles embedded within a gel, which stimulates bone growth through a complex signaling mechanism without the use of proteins known as growth factor. Gaharwar is optimistic that "The dynamic and bioactive nano-composite gels we have developed will show strong promise in bone tissue engineering applications."

10. The Respiratory System

The respiratory system allows us to take in vital oxygen and exhale carbon dioxide in a process we call breathing. It is our oxygen generation and treatment plant. It consists mainly of the trachea, the diaphragm, and the lungs.

The application of nanotechnology has significantly increased in different spheres of life, including drug delivery systems, and will continue to be developed in the near future. The plausibility of the non-invasive administration of drugs via inhalation and avoidance of first-pass metabolism due to direct delivery at the affected site make the respiratory system an ideal target port for nanocarrier-mediated drug delivery systems. The development of several nanocarrier systems (liposomal, solid-lipid nanoparticles, polymeric nanoparticles) offers various potential advantages for respiratory drug delivery including fewer undesirable side effects.

In the next two decades, nanomedicine will be an emerging multidisciplinary field that will offer unprecedented access to living cells and promise the state of the art in cancer detection and treatment. Metastatic lung cancer is one of the most common cancers leading to mortality worldwide. Current treatment includes chemo- and pathway-dependent therapy aimed at blocking the spread and proliferation of these metastatic lesions. Development of nanomedicines as drug carriers (nanocarriers) that target cancer for therapy will draw upon principles in the fields of chemistry, medicine, physics, biology, and engineering. Given the zealous activity in the field, as demonstrated by more than 30 nanocarriers already approved for clinical use, and given the promise of recent clinical results in various studies, nanocarrier-based strategies are anticipated to soon have a profound impact on cancer medicine and human health.

11. The Urinary System

No system will operate properly or even survive unless it eliminates its own harmful waste. The urinary system eliminates a waste product called *urea* from the body, which is produced when certain foods are broken down. The whole system includes two kidneys, two ureters, the bladder, two sphincter muscles, and the urethra. Urine produced by the kidneys travels down the ureters to the bladder and exits the body through the urethra.

Although the urinary system is a closed system, over time it may have problems that need to be fixed. Using engineered nanodevices (nano carriers) and nanostructures as delivery systems for drug and gene therapy are particularly attractive goals in urological practice. It is inevitable that nano uroradiology will be clinically useful in the future in uro-oncology (bladder, prostate, and kidney) and in diseases other than cancer (e.g., urinary tract stones). Nanowires (sensing wires that can be coated with molecules that bind to proteins of interest and transmit their information through electrodes to computers) and nanotubes (cylinder-like assemblies of carbon atoms, with cross-sectional dimensions in the nanometer range, and lengths that can extend over a thousand times their diameter) allow several thousands of sensors to be placed on a single chip, offering even greater multiplexing advantage.

In the next two decades, further applications of nanotechnology in urology will be even more advanced, and will be potentially used to diagnose and treat prostate diseases. Surgical tools, such as "nano-tweezers," are already under development, and it is anticipated that their everyday use in microsurgical procedures such as vasectomy reversal and varicocele repair are only a few years away. In addition, nano probes aiding diagnostic procedures, e.g., "nano-urobots" that could be used for cystoscopy, ureteroscopy and fulguration of tumors, as well as searching the inferior vena cava and renal vein to detect venous involvement of renal cell cancer, may be imminent. Smart nanosensors with communication capability and synthetic therapeutic devices to provide minimally invasive therapies will undoubtedly be developed, with particular interest in urological tissue engineering for urinary tract reconstruction.

12. The Skin

The skin is the body's largest organ. It protects us from the outside world and is our first defense against bacteria, viruses, and other pathogens. Our skin also helps regulate body temperature and eliminate waste through perspiration. In addition to skin, the integumentary system includes hair and nails.

The skin is a phenomenal tool for investigation of nano carriers for drug delivery for topical and dermatological application. The physicochemical characteristics of the nanoparticles, such as rigidity, hydrophobicity, size, and charge are crucial to the skin permeation mechanism. Many nano carriers such as polymeric, inorganic, and lipid nanoparticles and nano emulsions have been developed and some, like carbon nanotubes and fullerenes, need further exploration for future use in skin care and dermatological treatments.

The skin has a total area of approximately 2 m^2. Nanotechnology promises to transform the diagnosis and treatment of dermatological conditions because of its interaction at the sub-atomic level with the skin tissue. The skin represents a marvelous vehicle through which these nanomaterials can be investigated for drug delivery, both with respect to active ingredient delivery and efficacy. Being the most exposed part to the external environment, it is more prone to the ill effects of radiation and ultraviolet rays.

The skin forms a barrier to the external environment and is impermeable to drugs due to epidermal cell cohesion and stratum corneum lipids. There is a requirement for efficient drug delivery systems past this barrier. Nanotechnology is the latest advance in cosmetics and skincare. Nanotechnology can be used to modify drug permeation/penetration by controlling the release of active substances and increasing the period of permanence on the skin, besides ensuring direct contact with the stratum corneum and skin appendages and protecting the drug against chemical or physical instability.

Nanostructured carriers are an upcoming option for drug delivery because of their advantages over conventional formulations. The physicochemical characteristics of nano carriers, such as rigidity, hydrophobicity, size, and charge, are crucial to the skin permeation mechanism. The use of nanoscale carriers in drug delivery is expected to increase drug specificity and thus reduce side effects by decreasing the dose of administered drugs. These colloidal particulate systems, with sizes ranging from 10 nm to 1000 nm, offer targeted drug delivery, sustained release, protection of labile groups from degradation, and low toxicity. Drug-release nano carriers, such as liposomes, micelles, and polymeric and solid-lipid nanoparticles as well as inorganic nanoparticles and sub-micrometric emulsions, are now available. For example, zinc oxide particles, normally opaque and greasy, vanish and have an elegant feel when broken down into nanoparticles.

Among the technologies used to develop elegant and effective cosmeceuticals, nanotechnology has a special place. In the cosmetic arena it is believed that the smaller particles are readily absorbed into the skin and repair damage easily and more efficiently.

Skin aging is the combined result of chemical products, pollution, stress, and irradiation from infrared and ultraviolet sources. Collagen plays an important role in skin rejuvenation and wrinkle reversal effect. The quantity of collagen in the skin decreases with age. The aging of the skin manifests itself in many ways: drying out, loss of elasticity and texture, thinning, damaged barrier function, appearance of spots, modification of surface line isotropy, and, finally, wrinkles. Most cosmeceuticals have been developed with claims of anti-wrinkle and firming, moisturizing and lifting, and skin toning and whitening activity. Antiaging products are the main cosmeceuticals in the market currently being made using nanotechnology.

The Vital Organs of Survival

One again, we want to list the *vital organs* because systems in general come with a criticality list that need to be carefully observed and maintained. Smart Cities also have a criticality list that needs to be watched and properly controlled. We're going to show the parallels between the vital organs of the human body and the Smart City vital organs, to acquire more knowledge and appreciation for the importance of the vital organs. For example, the digital immunity system is one of the vital systems; the CSG is another vital component.

The human body has five vital organs (Figure 8.6) that are essential for survival. The order is not important.

1. *The human brain* is the commander in chief, which controls the status of every cell in the body; no subordinate system can revolt against it. It is responsible for our thoughts, feelings, memory storage, and general perception of the world.
2. *The human heart* relentlessly pumps blood throughout the body. It is the energy generator of the body.
3. *The kidneys* control the body's waste and sewage. The kidneys take urea from the blood and combine it with excess body water and release it as urine.
4. *The liver* has over 500 functions. It filters toxins from the blood and creates bile, which breaks down fat and carries away waste; it produces cholesterol, regulates blood clotting, processes hemoglobin, controls detoxification of harmful chemicals, and breaks down drugs.
5. *The lungs* are the air filter of the body. They capture oxygen from the air we breathe, clean the carbon dioxide from it, and pass it to the heart for distribution.

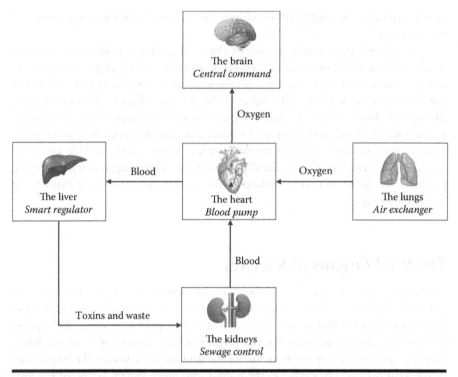

Figure 8.6 Although these organs are necessary for survival, people can live with one lung and one kidney and only part of their liver. The liver is the only organ that can completely regenerate. The heart is the organ that keeps blood and its cargo of oxygen and nutrients circulating throughout the body. The lungs allow the body to breathe. The liver and kidneys remove toxins. The brain controls all these functions and more. (© 2014 Copyright MERIT CyberSecurity Group. All rights reserved.)

The Miraculous Brain

The ancient Egyptians thought so little of brain matter that they made a practice of scooping it out through the nose of a dead leader before packing the skull with cloth before burial, while other organs—including the liver, intestines, and lungs—were carefully preserved in their own sacred Canopic jars. They believed consciousness resided in the heart, a view shared by Aristotle and a legacy of medieval thinkers. Even when consensus for the locus of thought moved northward into the head, it was not the brain that was believed to be the sine qua non, but the empty spaces within it, called ventricles, where ephemeral spirits swirled about.

During the 4th century BC, Aristotle thought that, while the heart was the seat of intelligence, the brain was a refrigerator as a cooling mechanism for the blood. Aristotle believed that the heart and not the brain was the center of sensation and movement:

And of course, the brain is not responsible for any of the sensations at all. The correct view, is that the seat and source of sensation is the region of the heart, the motions of pleasure and pain, and generally all sensation plainly have their source in the heart.

(Aristotle)

As late as 1662, philosopher Henry More scoffed that the brain showed "no more capacity for thought than a cake of suet, or a bowl of curds." In the 4th century BC, Hippocrates believed the brain to be the seat of intelligence (based on, among others before him, Archaeon's work).

With an estimated 100 billion neurons and 100 trillion synapses in the human brain, creating an all-encompassing map of even a small chunk is a daunting task. Using standard methods, it would take roughly 3 billion person years to generate the wiring diagram of a single cortical column, a narrow functional unit of neurons in the cortex, estimates Winfried Denk, a neuroscientist at the Max Planck Institute for Medical Research in Heidelberg, Germany.

A stunning revelation: *The brain's many regions are connected by some 100,000 miles of fibers called white matter—enough to circle the Earth four times.*

The brain controls all our bodily functions, but there are three things it cannot do:

- It cannot feel pain. The brain can feel pain from all over the body, but not within itself.
- The brain cannot store oxygen. A person can feel a lack of oxygen after only a few seconds. When someone stands up too quickly and becomes dizzy, this is an example of the loss of blood flow to the brain that can be sensed.
- The brain cannot store glucose (blood sugar). Diabetics who give themselves too much insulin can drop their blood sugar level and faint, and without immediate glucose infusion the brain can die.

When it comes to intelligence, it remains a big mystery how the brain's neurons can solve problems. The storage and manipulation of knowledge is a mystery, including why some people are smarter than others. Studying the anatomy of the brain is more challenging than scanning the deepest ocean.

Dr. Werner Gitt, in his book "Information: The Third Fundamental Quantity", described the processing power of the brain: Without a doubt, the most complex information-processing system in existence is the human body. If we take all human information processes together, i.e., conscious ones (language, information-controlled, deliberate voluntary movements) and unconscious ones (information-controlled functions of the organs, hormone system), this involves the processing of 1024 bits daily. This astronomically high figure is higher by a factor of 1,000,000 [i.e., is a million times greater] than the total human knowledge of 1018 bits stored in all the world's libraries.

The outer layer of the human brain, the cortex, is folded over on itself to allow more of it to be packed into the skull. If you flattened the average adult cortex out, it would cover 2500 square centimeters (a small tablecloth).

In the next two decades, the use of nanobots to support brain surgery, will be a significant improvement over surgically installed neural implants, which are beginning to be used today. Nanobots will be introduced without surgery, through the bloodstream, and if necessary can be directed to leave, so the process is easily reversible. They are programmable, in that they can provide virtual reality one minute and a variety of brain extensions the next. They can change their configuration and can alter their software. Perhaps most importantly, they are massively distributed and therefore can take up billions of positions throughout the brain, whereas a surgically introduced neural implant can be placed only in one or at most a few locations.

In the next two decades, nanotechnology will be fully mature, and will be ready to solve problems of biology by overcoming biological pathogens, removing toxins, correcting DNA errors, and reversing other resources of aging. Figure 8.7 shows the holistic architecture of the brain of 2040. However, we will then have to contend

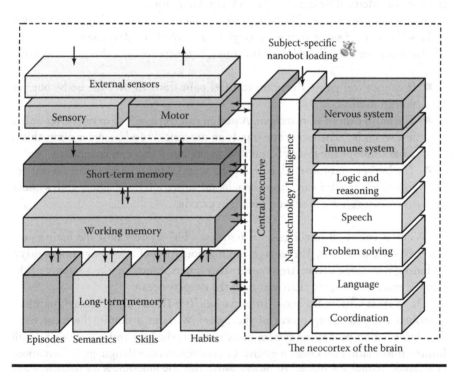

Figure 8.7 For the purposes of illustration and simplicity, we have translated the blob of the brain into an engineering drawing. An army of surgical (or treatment) nanobots will reside in the "Nanotechnology Intelligence" slate, working with the neocortex of the brain. This will be reality in 2040. (© 2014 Copyright MERIT CyberSecurity Group. All rights reserved.)

with new dangers that it introduces, just as the Internet introduced the danger of software viruses. These new pitfalls will include the potential for self-replicating nanotechnology to get out of control, as well as the integrity of the software controlling these powerful, distributed nanobots.

As the Nobelist Horst Störmer describes it, "Nanotechnology has given us the tools ... to play with the ultimate toy box of nature—atoms and molecules. Everything is made from it .... The possibilities to create new things appear limitless."

Types of Nanobots

Nanobots come in three different designs. The first type is the biological type, which is heavily used in nanomedicine, physics, and manufacturing. They can be propagated through the bloodstream, reach our cells, and perform various services, such as removing toxins, sweeping out debris, correcting DNA errors, repairing and restoring cell membranes, reversing atherosclerosis, modifying the levels of hormones, neurotransmitters, and other metabolic chemicals, and a myriad of other tasks. For each aging process, we can describe a means for nanobots to reverse the process, down to the level of individual cells, cell components, and molecules (Figure 8.8).

The second type is the hardware version and is made of nano electric circuits and electrometrical (low-voltage) components, which can be part of computer motherboards, sensor devices, alarms, and other useful control systems. The hardware type has a nano memory that can store hardwired programs to do specific tasks.

The third type is the software version, which will be the Rosetta stone of the cybersecurity world (Figure 8.9). It will bring a new dimension and a substantial paradigm shift. The software version is made of smart and autonomic nano programs that can be stored on the cloud or satellites, or roam around the grid looking for an object. There are two types of software nanobots: the *Cyborg Nanobot*

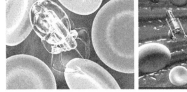  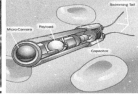

Figure 8.8 These fascinating new "biological" nanobots seek out and destroy cancerous tumors. Whether they're sneaking between cells or turning cockroaches into living 8-bit computers, nanobots are insanely fascinating. Now, they're about to become an army of impossibly small weaponized robots that can swarm into the human body, hunt down malignant tumors, and destroy them once and for all.

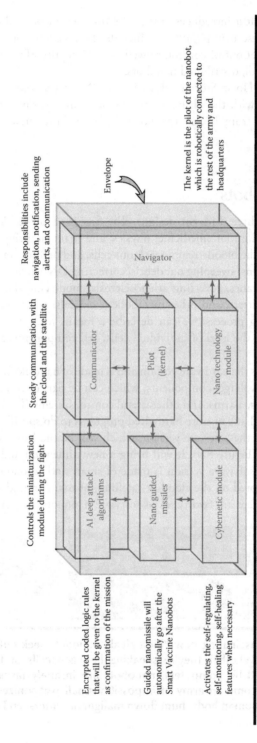

Figure 8.9   Architecture of a software cyborg nanobot.

(the cybernetic version), which is used by the adversaries; and the *Smart Vaccine Nanobot*, which is the digital immunity agent.

Uploading the Brain to a Computer

> People also started dreaming about how to come out from their BODIES...
>
> **According to Marshall Brain (founder of HowStuffWorks)**

The objective of this section is to give evidence that nanotechnology (NT) and artificial intelligence (AI) can enhance our intelligence and thus our intellectual performance. By the same token, NT and AI will bring more knowledge and intelligence to Smart Cities in all domains, and in particular offer digital immunity as a shield from malware attacks. Today, scientists are creating an artificial brain, by uploading a human brain into a machine that can think, respond, make decisions, and keep everything in its memory. Uploading the brain allows man to think faster and make better decisions without any effort. After the death of the body, the virtual brain will act as the man. The upload is possible using small robots known as nanobots. These robots are small enough to travel throughout our circulatory system. Traveling into the spine and brain, they will be able to monitor the activity and structure of our central nervous system. They will be able to provide an interface with a computer while we still reside in our biological form. Nanobots could also carefully scan the structure of our brain, providing a complete readout of the connection. This information, when entered into a computer, could then continue to function as us. Thus, the data stored in the entire brain will be uploaded into the computer. Imagine a day when you will be able to transfer your memories onto a computer. A day when you will have a "backup" of everything that is stored in your head. We call it mind transfer.

By 2045, humans will achieve digital immortality by uploading their minds to computers (Figure 8.10)—or at least that's what some futurists believe. This notion formed the basis for the Global Futures 2045 International Congress, a futuristic conference held on June 14–15, 2013.

Specifically, they believe that in a few decades, humans will be able to upload their minds to a computer, transcending the need for a biological body. The idea sounds like sci-fi, and it is—at least for now. The reality, however, is that neural engineering is making significant strides toward modeling the brain and developing technologies to restore or replace some of its biological functions.

Let's say you transfer your mind into a computer—not all at once but gradually, having electrodes inserted into your brain and then wirelessly outsourcing your faculties. Someone reroutes your vision through cameras. Someone stores your memories on a net of microprocessors. Step by step, your metamorphosis continues until at last the transfer is complete. As engineers get to work boosting the performance

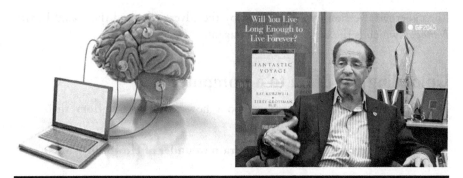

Figure 8.10 Bold predictions were made by Ray Kurzweil, director of engineering at Google, which have now been put under the microscope by Express.co.uk (http://www.express.co.uk/news/science/661470/EXPLAINED-How-we-will-soon-be-able-to-upload-our-MINDS-to-computers/amp). During a Global Future 2045 International Congress, he sensationally said, "We're going to become increasingly non-biological to the point where the non-biological part dominates and the biological part is not important anymore." The mind-boggling speech added that mankind will have machine bodies by 2100.

of your electronic mind so you can now think as a god, a nurse heaves your fleshy brain into a bag of medical waste. As you—for now let's just call it "you"—start a new chapter of existence exclusively within a machine, an existence that will last as long as there are server farms and hard-disk space and the solar power to run them. Are "you" still actually "you"?

Mind Upload = Mind Transfer = Reverse Engineering the Brain

These are popular terms for a process by which the mind, a collection of memories, personality, and attributes of a specific individual, is transferred from its original biological brain to an artificial computational substrate. Alternative terms for mind uploading have appeared in fiction and non-fiction, such as mind transfer, mind downloading, off-loading, side-loading, and several others. They all refer to the same general concept of "transferring" the mind to a different substrate.

Once it is possible to move a mind from one substrate to another, it is then called a *substrate-independent mind* (SIM). The concept of SIM is inspired by the idea of designing software that can run on multiple computers with different hardware without needing to be rewritten. For example, Java's design principle "write once, run everywhere" makes it a platform-independent system. In this context, substrate is a term referring to a generalized concept of any computational platform that is capable of universal computation.

We take the materialist position that the human mind is solely generated by the brain and is a function of neural states. Additionally, we assume that the neural states are computational processes and devices capable of universal computing that are sufficient to generate the same kind of computational processes found in a brain.

If the software of the brain is the critical element to a mind—and not the details of the hardware—then, in theory, we could shift ourselves off the substrate of our bodies. With powerful enough computers simulating the interactions in our brains, we could upload. We could exist digitally by running ourselves as a simulation, escaping the biological wetware from which we've arisen, becoming non-biological beings. That would be the single most significant leap in the history of our species, launching us into the era of transhumanism (Figure 8.11).

A technical hurdle to successful uploading is that the simulated brain must be able to modify itself. We would need not only the pieces and parts, but also the physics of their ongoing interactions—for example, the activity of transcription factors that travel to the nucleus and cause gene expression, the dynamic changes in location and strength of the synapses, and so on. Unless your simulated experiences changed the structure of your simulated brain, you would be unable to form new memories and would have no sense of the passage of time. Under those circumstances, would there be any point to immortality?

If uploading proves to be possible, it would open up the capacity to reach other solar systems. There are at least a hundred billion other galaxies in our cosmos, each of which contains a hundred billion stars. We've already spotted thousands of exoplanets orbiting those stars, some of which have conditions quite like our Earth. The difficulty lies in the impossibility that our current fleshy bodies will ever get to those exoplanets—there's simply no foreseeable way that we will be able to travel those kinds of distances in space and time. However, because you can pause

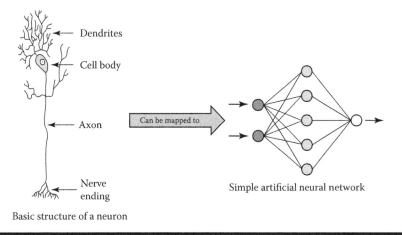

Basic structure of a neuron

Simple artificial neural network

Figure 8.11   Mapping the structure of a neuron into a simple artificial neural network. The single most significant leap in the history of our species, launching us into the era of transhumanism. (© 2014 Copyright MERIT CyberSecurity Group. All rights reserved.)

a simulation, shoot it out into space, and reboot it a thousand years later when it arrives at a planet, it would seem to your consciousness that you were on Earth, you had a launch, and then instantly you found yourself on a new planet. Uploading would be equivalent to achieving the physics dream of finding a wormhole, allowing us to get from one part of the universe to another in a subjective instant.

Imagine what it would be like to leave your body behind and enter a new existence in a simulated world. Your digital existence could look like any life you wanted. Programmers could make any virtual world for you—worlds in which you can fly, or live underwater, or feel the winds of a different planet. We could run our virtual brains as fast or slow as we wanted, so our minds could span immense swaths of time or turn seconds of computing time into billions of years of experience.

If biological algorithms are the important part of what makes us who we are, rather than the physical stuff, then it's a possibility that we will someday be able to copy our brains, upload them, and live forever in silica. But there's an important question here: is it really you? Not exactly. The uploaded copy has all your memories and believes it is you, just there, standing outside the computer, in your body. Here's the strange part: if you die and we turn on the simulation one second later, it would be a transfer. It would be no different to beaming up in Star Trek, when a person is disintegrated, and then a new version is reconstituted a moment later. Uploading may not be all that different from what happens to you each night when you go to sleep: you experience a little death of your consciousness, and the person who wakes up on your pillow the next morning inherits all your memories, and believes him or herself to be you.

The Superintelligent Human

The Concept of Singularity

The term "singularity" is polymorphic, with many faces, noticeably exponential; but above all, it ushers in the dawn of superintelligence, the new epoch of fusing technology and human intelligence. Ray Kurzweil describes our human capacity vis-à-vis technology: "Our intuition about the future is linear. But the reality of information technology is exponential, and that makes a profound difference. If I take 30 steps linearly, I get to 30. If I take 30 steps exponentially, I get to a billion."

The concept of singularity is simple, but mixing technology intelligence with human intelligence is tricky and an imbalance may occur, that is, technology intelligence could outpower human intelligence. Even after deactivation, we could end up with a runaway train. In 2040, we'll be able to multiply human intelligence a billionfold, by relying on technology intelligence. Computers are going to get smaller and smaller. Ultimately, they will go inside our bodies and brains and make us healthier and smarter.

How do we tie singularity to the Smart City? First, we need to be immersed with technology and experience biological cognitive enhancement. Singularity as defined by Kurzweil is "an expansion of human intelligence by a factor of trillions through merger with its nonbiological form [and] will occur within the next several decades."

In the next three decades, we're going to have three distinct spectra of technologies that will support Smart Cities. They will either complement each other or coexist together:

- Technologies to support Smart Cities and their infrastructure
- Technologies that will promote human superintelligence for Smart City citizens
- Technologies that support the quality of life of Smart City citizens

1. Technologies to Support Smart Cities and Their Infrastructure

A Smart City sounds very attractive, but no city is smart unless it has secured its critical infrastructure. The main components of a Smart City are smart infrastructure, smart governance, smart management, smart citizens, smart living, smart economy, smart environment, and smart connectivity. When all these components are weaved into one cohesive framework, then we have a very happy Smart City.

By definition, a critical infrastructure is a vital entity that supports the life of the city. Any damage or destruction to this entity will have a debilitating effect on the performance of the city.

The key success factor in developing a Smart City is connectivity where all its components are pathologically and holistically connected in real time to the city's centralized command center. Therefore, one of the most important prerequisites is to have a Smart Grid that ties all the pieces together. It is pretty much like the nervous system in the human body. A Smart City is only as smart as its sensors.

In 2040, the Smart City will be totally immersed in urban technologies. It will be more efficient and sustainable, with ultra-smart infrastructure systems. Digital immunity will be one of the most superintelligent defense systems to keep the Smart City immunized.

Infrastructure is not exactly the sexiest word in architecture. There are no "starchitects" proudly boasting their pipe designs or subsurface drainage systems. By its very definition—the underlying structures that support our systems—infrastructure is hidden from us and therefore often overlooked. But without it, our current cities couldn't possibly exist. Without finding ways to improve it, our future cities will struggle to survive.

Smart City infrastructure will undergo a major modernization phase. This will include two critical infrastructures necessary to the survival of the Smart City:

- *The City Smart Grid (CSG)* will connect all the critical infrastructure systems together with a smart and cognitive environment. The CSG will be managed with fully autonomic AI-centric systems that monitor and collect operations and status information without any human operators. All systems will be equipped with parallel redundancy.
- *The Smart Vaccine™ Grid (SVG)* will offer total digital immunity to the CSG prior to and during emergency situations.

2. Technologies That Will Promote Human Superintelligence for Smart City Citizens

Superintelligence is defined by Nick Bostrom in his captivating book, *Superintelligence Paths, Dangers, Strategies*, as "any intellect that greatly exceeds—in speed and quality—the cognitive performance of humans in virtually all domains of interest."

What can we expect when *smart* machines surpass humans in intelligence? Futurists predict that could become reality by 2040. The concept of *singularity* simply means that technology will eventually supersede human intelligence, creating an amazing world filled with "smart" machines. These machines will not only defeat us in chess and games like Jeopardy, but will also drive cars, write books, and replace humans in customer service, and, one day, emulate consciousness.

Singularity is one of the most disrupting paradigms of the 21st century. It is the most influential change agent in the history of mankind. Singularians defy mortality, disease, and aging, and transcend all biological limitations, while making a compelling case that a human civilization with superhuman capabilities is closer at hand than most people realize. As we move closer to the singularity, other breakthroughs will appear. Experts predict that over the next three decades, research in stem cells, genetic engineering, human-like robots, and nano-replicators that provide household essentials at little or no cost will make life more pleasurable for all of us. A positive post-singularity world could include affordable health care, providing most world citizens with indefinite lifespans, and a global economy strong enough to erase today's gap between the rich and poor.

On the negative side, superintelligence is going catapult cybercrime and cyber terrorism into an exponential trajectory with superintelligent weaponry, to cripple critical infrastructure systems in Smart Cities, contaminate the world of the Internet of things (IoT) with ransomware, and launch malicious massive Soft Cyborg attacks. Smart Cities will suffer from global smart paralysis.

3. Technologies That Support the Quality of Life of Citizens in Smart Cities

Quality of life (QOL) is the general well-being of individuals and societies, outlining negative and positive features of life. It observes life satisfaction, including everything from physical health, family, education, employment, wealth, religious beliefs, finance and the environment.

At the 2015 Fourth International SMART Conference, held in Brussels, Belgium, on July 2, 2015, experts presented 19 technical papers on various uses of smart technology, sensors, and other specialized technologies to optimize the use of energy, control pollution, and enhance health, well-being, and accessibility for the elderly and those with disabilities. Smart technology is not only about making life more convenient, it is also thought to be especially helpful toward *self-management of health care*, as well as giving the elderly, the chronically ill and persons with disabilities an enhanced quality of life. Smart Cities can take advantage of the IoT to make health care innovations a reality. As Jessica Mulholland eloquently said, "Through 2025, wearable health apps—like the Fitbit Flex … —will continue to improve and become more specialized to help people who want to be healthier."

One of the most crucial indicators of quality of life in Smart Cities in 2040 will be the amazing advances in medicine and how it will conquer cancer, coronary artery disease, stroke, diabetes, and Alzheimer's. Here's a fantastic voyage that will give us goose bumps, of how tumors will be defeated, as reported in the magazine *IEEE Spectrum*:

Researchers will be rolling up their sleeves and getting ready to tackle cancer. Today's cancer drugs work by circulating throughout the body, killing healthy cells along with cancerous ones. Even antibody-equipped drugs designed to target cancer cells don't always hit their marks. Injecting drugs into a tumor is out of the question because the pressure would cause cells to spew from it like a volcano, spreading the disease elsewhere. So why not deploy robots to deliver the medicine?

One of cancer therapy's holy grails is the delivery of drugs directly to tumors, thereby killing diseased cells while sparing healthy ones. A promising solution may be to deploy armies of carefully engineered microbot–bacteria hybrids in the body. The submarine-like bots are made by encasing magnetic nanoparticles and drug-carrying bacteria, which could power through fast currents in large blood vessels, transporting their cargo to the network of tiny vessels that lead inside a tumor. After a surgeon injects the bots into an artery, an MRI machine's magnetic forces, used for robotic navigation, pull and steer them toward the tumor. Fixing a magnetic "north" pole at the tumor entices the bacteria to swim toward it. The bacteria converge inside the tumor and die, releasing their drug payload.

This is just the beginning of a new era that will contribute to the sustained health of Smart City citizens. Nanomedicine and nanobiotechnology will also fuse into the human body and bring miracles. Across the globe, researchers are engineering a wide array of free-roaming robots to carry out precise and delicate tasks inside the human body.

One example is the magic *robot pill*, a capsule that contains a magnet, camera, wireless chip, and set of mechanical legs, powered by a DC motor and used to screen diseases.

Let's not forget the people who are on the payroll of the Devil. They will take any opportunity to use this technology for their evil plans. The Smart City is the selected Shangri-La. In two decades, all Smart Cities will be designed with the most sophisticated hiding cyber "quicksand" where the more they struggle in it, the faster they will sink.

Anyone can grasp Mr. Kurzweil's main idea: that mankind's technological knowledge has been snowballing, with dizzying prospects for the future. The basics are clearly expressed. But for those more knowledgeable and inquisitive, the author argues his case in fascinating detail in *The Singularity Is Near*, which is startling in scope and bravado.

Smart City Quality of Life (QOL) Indicators

Based on academic research and several initiatives, the following 10 indicators have been defined as an overarching framework for the measurement of well-being. Ideally, they should be considered simultaneously, because of potential trade-offs between them. We've tried to list them by importance:

1. *Life satisfaction*: Positive attitude about life and happiness.
2. *Health*: Healthy mind in a healthy body. Essential part of mental and psychological well-being.
3. *Material living conditions*: Happy family brings stability and optimism in life.
4. *Security and safety*: The most important factor in QoL.
5. *Work happiness*: Work can be a real trap and one of the causes of crime and divorces. Changing job is one solution. Getting psychological treatment is another option.
6. *Academia*: Particularly for the young generation. Parents should play a positive role in the education of the children. Online education is also very effective.
7. *Leisure and social interactions*: Sports participation is a factor for good living. Soccer games for kids are an excellent way to keep them from getting into trouble.
8. *Citizen participation activities*: Participation in community activities is a great way to learn more about how well a Smart City is doing.
9. *Ecology and environment*: Clean air, noise control, and waste management help tremendously to reduce stress and bad tempers.
10. *Data metering and analytics*: The best way to control energy costs.

The Magic of Superintelligent Digital Immunity

In the next two decades, Smart Cities will deploy superintelligent digital immunity (SDI) as the smartest and most advanced defense ecosystem for the critical systems of infrastructures and for the Internet of Things. SDI is ultra-intelligent—it is not only a system, but an environment that will surpass all the intellectual activities of any man, however clever. SDI follows the rules of singularity but in reverse. We take all the cyber hacking knowledge and security experts from big data and merge it with the intelligence of SDI.

Chapter 9 will discuss how SDI is designed and how it will defend Smart Cities beyond the expertise of cyber hackers.

Glossary of Human Anatomy

Action potential: A brief (one millisecond) event in which the voltage across a neuron reaches a threshold, causing a propagating chain reaction of ion exchange across the cell membrane. Eventually this causes neurotransmitter release at the terminals of the axon. Also known as a spike.

Alien hand syndrome: A disorder resulting from a treatment for epilepsy known as a corpus colostomy, in which the corpus callosum is cut, disconnecting the two cerebral hemispheres of the brain, also known as split-brain surgery. This disorder causes unilateral and sometimes intricate hand movements without the patient feeling they have volitional control of the movements.

Axon: The anatomical output projection of a neuron capable of conducting electrical signals from the cell body.

Cerebellum: A smaller anatomical structure that sits below the cerebral cortex at the rear of the head. This area of the brain is essential for fluid motor control, balance, posture, and possibly some cognitive functions.

Cerebrum: Human brain areas including the large, undulate exterior cerebral cortex, hippocampus, basal ganglia, and olfactory bulb. Development of this area in higher-order mammals contributes to more advanced cognition and behavior.

Computational hypothesis of brain function: A methodology for testing computational hypotheses about neural functionality articulated in models at the systems level.

Connectome: A three-dimensional map of all neuronal connections in the brain.

Corpus callosum: A strip of nerve fibers located in the longitudinal fissure between the two cerebral hemispheres that enables communication between them.

Dendrites: The anatomical input projections of a neuron that carry electrical signals initiated by neurotransmitter release from other neurons to the cell body.

Dopamine: A neurotransmitter in the brain linked to motor control, addiction, and reward.

Electroencephalography (EEG): A technique used to measure electrical activity at millisecond resolution in the brain by connecting conductive electrodes to the scalp. Each electrode captures the summation of millions of neurons underlying the electrode. This method is used to capture fast changes in brain activity in the cortex.

Functional magnetic resonance imaging (fMRI): A neuroimaging technique that detects brain activity with second resolution by measuring blood flow in the brain with millimeter resolution.

Galvanic skin response: A technique that measures changes in the autonomic nervous system that occur when someone experiences something new, stressful, or intense even if below conscious awareness. In practice, a machine is hooked up to the fingertip and the electrical properties of the skin are monitored, which change along with activity in the skin sweat glands.

Glial cell: Specialized cells in the brain that protect neurons by providing nutrients and oxygen to them, removing waste, and generally supporting them.

Neural: Of or relating to the nervous system or neurons.

Neuron: A specialized cell found in both the central and peripheral nervous systems, including brain, spinal cord, and sensory cells, that communicates to other cells using electrochemical signals.

Neurotransmitter: Chemicals that are released from one neuron to another recipient neuron, usually across a synapse. These are found in the central and peripheral nervous systems including the brain, spinal cord, and sensory neurons throughout the body. Neurons may release more than one neurotransmitter.

Parkinson's disease: A progressive disorder characterized by movement difficulties and tremors that is caused by the deterioration of dopamine-producing cells in a midbrain structure called the substantia nigra.

Plasticity: The brain's ability to adapt by creating new or modifying existing neural connections. The capability of the brain to exhibit plasticity is important after an injury in order to compensate for any acquired deficits.

Sensory substitution: An approach to compensate for an impaired sense in which sensory information is fed into the brain through unusual sensory channels. For example, visual information is converted into vibrations on the tongue or auditory information is converted into patterns of vibrations on the torso, allowing an individual to see or hear respectively.

Sensory transduction: Signals from the environment, such as photons (sight), air compression waves (hearing), or scent molecules (smell) are converted (transduced) into action potentials by specialized cells. It is the first step by which information from outside the body is received by the brain.

Split-brain surgery: Also known as a corpus callosotomy, the corpus callosum is severed as a measure to control epilepsy not cured by other means. This surgery removes the communication between the two cerebral hemispheres.

Synapse: The space typically between an axon of one neuron and a dendrite of another neuron where communication between neurons occurs by release of neurotransmitters. Axon–axon and dendrite–dendrite synapses also exist.

Transcranial magnetic stimulation (TMS): A non-invasive technique used to stimulate or inhibit brain activity using a magnetic pulse to induce small electric currents in underlying neural tissue. This technique is typically used to understand the influence of brain areas in neural circuits.

Ulysses contract: An unbreakable contract used to bind oneself to a potential future goal made when one understands one may not have the ability to make a rational choice at that time.

Ventral tegmental area: A structure comprising mostly dopaminergic neurons located in the midbrain. This area plays a critical role in the reward system.

Source: From previous document: Knowledge Base of MERIT CyberSecurity.

Bibliography

http://neurosciencenews.com/neurons-synapses-neuroscience-5119/

Smart Innovation: http://www.govtech.com/health/Smart-Innovations-to-Enhance-Citizens-Health-Care-Quality-of-Life.html

Quality of life equation: https://hqlo.biomedcentral.com/articles/10.1186/1477-7525-2-14

Ray Kurzweil, *The Singularity Is Near*, 2003, Penguin.

Facts about the human body: https://www.theguardian.com/science/2013/jan/27/20-human-body-facts-science

Muscular nanotechnology: http://www.zmescience.com/research/technology/artificial-muscles-nanotech-yarn-0432/

Engineering the immune system: http://www.hopkinsmedicine.org/research/advancements-in-research/fundamentals/in-depth/engineering-the-immune-system

Journal of Nanomedicine: https://www.omicsonline.org/open-access/smart-nanobots-the-future-in-nanomedicine-and-biotherapeutics-2155-983X-1000e140.pdf

The immortalist: http://www.bbc.com/news/magazine-35786771

Relation between Smart Grid and Smart City: http://www.mayorsinnovation.org/images/uploads/pdf/1-ieee.pdf

Chapter 9

The Miraculous Anatomy of the Digital Immune System

Introduction

We all remember the famous business metric "If you can measure it, you can control it." Well, the Internet has become a mega gravitational force ushering a new era of prosperity and cybercrime. We're riding the Internet whether we like it or not. Cybercrime and terrorism has been making drastic black holes in our societal fabric, and thriving on profound immorality and political poisoning. The World Trade Center disaster was above all, *a failure of imagination* as lamented by Senator Thomas Kean during the 9/11 commission report.

This chapter focus on two pivotal topics. First, describe the anatomical structure of the Cognitive Early Warning Predictive System (CEWPS), which creates the Intelligent Digital Immunity System (DIS), with smart components designed using Artificial Intelligence (AI) and Nanotechnology. Second, discuss the rational justification of using AI and Nanotechnology to build a distinctive and unique defense for Smart Cities. In summary, we will show how AI will interface with CEWPS and upload Human Intelligence (HI), which will augment its defense capabilities one million fold.

Forbes magazine, on November 11, 2014 made the point, with a bold title, that "America's Critical Infrastructure Is Vulnerable to Cyber Attacks". The article is a wakeup call, because the whole country is on thin ice with no real defense system to protect our critical systems. There is a lot of static noise and no kinetic movement forward. According to the Association of American Publishers, between 2001 and

2016, there are over 1500 published books on cybersecurity that talk about the re-hashing the same technology as the antivirus industry.

In Chapter 7, I highlighted the amazing Soft Cyborg technology—a kind of ugly and mean nanobot, and how they may go berserk and spew unlimited quantities of "gray goo" which will blanket the Earth smothering all life, in other words, our final battle—Armageddon.

On May 11, 2017, President Trump issued an executive order on strengthening the cybersecurity of federal networks and critical infrastructure. In the Executive order he highlighted:

> Within 90 days of the date of this order, the Secretary of State, the Secretary of the Treasury, the Secretary of Defense, the Attorney General, the Secretary of Commerce, the Secretary of Homeland Security, and the United States Trade Representative, in coordination with the Director of National Intelligence, shall jointly submit a report to the President, through the Assistant to the President for National Security Affairs and the Assistant to the President for Homeland Security and Counterterrorism, on the Nation's strategic options for deterring adversaries and better protecting the American people from cyber threats.

On January 13, 2015, President Obama gave a speech at National Cybersecurity Communications Integration Center in Arlington, Virginia. He ended his speech by saying: "And as long as I'm President, protecting America's digital infrastructure is going to remain a top national security priority." Both presidents use the same political rhetoric, which made our adversaries more active and aggressive in attacking the United States. Poking a hornet's nest is not constructive.

Since necessity is the mother of invention and to control global malware, which is like cancer, we need a radical change of direction, mindset, and tools to revolutionize cyber defense. Nanomedicine is catching up with cancer. Other medical nanobots can serve as cleaners, removing unwanted debris and chemicals (such as prions, malformed proteins, and protofibrils) from individual human cells.

In the domain of engineering, nanomaterials could be used to create highly sensitive sensors capable of detecting hazardous materials in the air. For example, carbon-based nanotubes are relatively inexpensive and consume minimal power. Other areas of nanotechnology pertinent to homeland security are emergency responder devices. Lightweight communications systems that require almost no power and have a large contact radius would give rescuers more flexibility. Nanotech robots could be used to disarm bombs or save trapped victims, reducing the risks to rescue workers. But the most exciting application of nanotechnology has been in the field of cybersecurity, with the design of Digital Immunity (DI) and the Smart Vaccine™ (SV) with the creation of nanobots.

Nanobot engineering is defined as the engineering of "smart" functional systems at the molecular scale. Nanotechnology is defined as "the design, characterization, production and application of structures, devices and systems by controlled manipulation of size and shape at the nanometer scale (atomic, molecular and macromolecular scale) that produces structures, devices and systems with at least one novel/superior characteristic or property".

The SV is actually an intelligent nanobot, programmable to do a specific function in DI. Since it is scaled at the molecular level, it can be a component of a chip, roam through computer cables, reside on a storage device, and communicate with other SVs. That's why it was called the Smart Vaccine™. It is the counterpart of B-cells, or T-cells in human immunity. We can also compare it to a neuron that transfers sensory and motor signals to and from the brain. The scaling down of CEWPS/SV to the nanomolecular level is the advantage that places the system ahead of its time. In this chapter and Chapter 10, we'll be describing in more detail the anatomy of the SV nanobot.

Smart Cities Are Like the Human Body

The closest analogy to the Smart City ecosystem is the human body which is holistically administered by the brain and 12 federated systems that act autonomically with perfect orchestration. No waterway on earth is so complete, so commodious, or so populous as the wonderful river of life, the "*Stream of Blood*". The violin, the trumpet, the harp, the grand organ, and all the other musical instruments, are mere counterfeits of the human voice.

Another marvel of the human body is the self-regulating process (so-called autonomic) by which nature keeps the body temperature consistently at 98 degrees. Whether in India, with the temperature at 130 degrees, or in the arctic regions, where the records show 120 degrees below freezing point, the body temperature remains the same, practically steady at 98 degrees despite the extreme to which is subjected. It was said that "All roads lead to Rome!". Modern science has discovered that all roads of real knowledge lead to the human body.

And you think cities are crowded now? For the first time in history, more than 50% of the world's population lives in cities. By 2030, more than 5 billion people will live in urban settings. But before we get to that kind of population density, we have to optimize our cities. We need to make them smarter, safer, and above all, more secure. Yes, technology can help. Modern cities compete with one another to attract businesses, talent, skills, and taxpayers. As a result, city administrations are becoming entrepreneurial, valuing innovation, technology, marketing, and communication. The Smart City ecosystem is a broad partnership between the public and private sector. City planners and developers, nongovernmental organizations, IT system integrators, software vendors, energy and utility providers, the automotive industry, and facility control providers, as well as technology providers for mobile technology, cloud computing, networking, system-to-system (S2S), and radio-frequency identification (RFID), all have a role to play.

Again, like the human body, component connectivity is one of the principal prerequisites for Smart City design. Smart Cities live by their smart grids which are the *nervous system* that allows cities to live and breathe, to facilitate exchange of information, and to respond promptly to danger. In case of a massive cyberattack on the city, which is highly probable. The DI smart grid will be the best savior. Chapter 11 describes the innovation of the DI grid and how all the avant-garde technologies converge (AI, Nanotechnology, Cybernetics, and HI) to bring a new paradigm shift in cybersecurity. With all the serial assaults of cybercrime, technology alone has not been able to win the battle, or the war. The integration of HI with technology will create an ultra-intelligent DI environment that will surpass all the intellectual activities of city attackers.

CEWPS provides all the intelligent nano components that make up DI for the Smart City. CEWPS is a *thinking machine* that reasons with its deep store of human *biological* knowledge written into its DNA. and its rapid response to threats is. CEWPS is designed with HI combined with technology intelligence. Dr. Eric Drexler, MIT, described the intelligence fusion concept: "As I discuss in *Engines of Creation*, if you can build genuine AI, there are reasons to believe that you can build things like neurons that are a million times faster. That leads to the conclusion that you can make systems that think a million times faster than a person." CEWPS is like a bullet train compared to a steam locomotive representing the Antivirus Technology (AVT) of today.

Like the brain which is the central nervous system including the spinal cord, CEWPS is the central intelligent system that controls the activities of DIS on a smart grid that spreads across the City Smart Nanogrid (CSNG) protecting all the critical systems of infrastructures and the sensor devices of the Internet of Things (Figure 9.1). The Digital Immunity Smart Nanogrid (DISG) is the combination of the nervous and immune systems together, and has the following autonomic responsibilities:

- Real-time alerts
- Send status information to central command
- Receive action information from central command
- Initiate defense by way of offense
- Regular vaccination of all Smart City systems
- Collect and document attack information

Keeping the city thriving on quality living is critical. Transportation strategies have an impact on public safety, the environment, energy, rapid response services, the ability to do business, and critical deliveries have to be

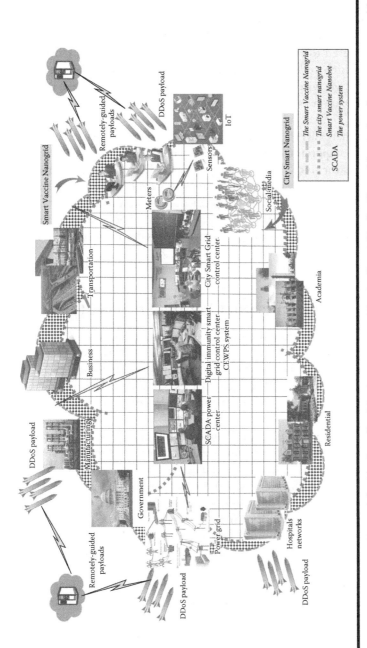

Figure 9.1 This is the top view of the battle. All critical systems are physically and logically reside on the city smart nanogrid and connected with adapters to the SV nanogrid (outer grid). When the attack profile is recognized and located on the grid, a convoy of SV fighters rush to the battle field and vaccination process is instantiated. The attacking virus is captured, its attack vector is analyzed, then it will be destroyed before it mutates and multiplies. SV has two types: one to capture the virus and quarantine it. The second type is to digest it and keep the remains for the next battle. Once the battle is documented, it will be to the added to the ViKB. (© 2014 MERIT CyberSecurity Group. All rights reserved.)

fit precisely in this gigantic jigsaw puzzle; while keeping the general quality of life at a high. Real-time traffic flow information, coupled with Telco, Global Positioning Systems (GPS), Machine 2 Machine (M2M) communication, Wi-Fi, and RFID technologies, as well as data analytics and prediction techniques, can all be used to enhance private and public travel. Smart Cities live by their sensors, which collect information about traffic conditions at critical city spots and send, via wireless or GPS communication, to centralized control systems. This data can, for example, influence the optimization of traffic light synchronization.

By definition, Smart City implies smart government, smart citizens, smart technologies, and more importantly, smart future. Predicting the future has always been a human endeavor since the beginning of time. History tells us interesting stories about how the future was predicted. Romans, Egyptians, and Greeks had high priests who influenced the rules with predictions about calamities, sickness, and wars. Temples were holy places where mysterious rituals performed by priests including sorcery, exorcism, and astrology. Today, we consider all these rituals nonsense without true scientific basis.

CEWPS Is the Electronic Shield of the Smart City

We would like to introduce definitions of some important terms:

CEWPS is the system, both hardware and software (DI is the product of CEWPS). SV (comparable to human B-cell) is the nanobot that eliminates adversary nano cyborgs, and installs DI in Smart Cities. CEWPS is the convergence of three futuristic technologies that will establish its leadership for the next two decades (Figure 9.2):

The first technology is HI where the combination of human-level intelligence with a computer's inherent superiority in speed, accuracy, and memory-sharing ability will be formidable. The second technology is AI, which allows CEWPS to become a *digital mind* with greatly superior serial power could run on a faster timescale than we do, and can reason and make decisions on its own imitating human knowledge and experience. The third technology is Nanotechnology, which is the most successful technology until now in the world of scientific industry. Nanotechnology empowered CEWPS with incredible features, which are not present in any security system today. Nanotechnology introduced the concept on miniaturization, which allowed CEWPS to build software robots (nanobots) at a molecular scale. By the 2020s nanobot technology will be viable in autonomic computing and SV applications. Nanobots are robots that will be the size of human blood cells (seven to eight microns) or even smaller. Billions of them could travel through smart grids, carrying vaccination services, and using high-speed wireless communication to communicate with other nanobots and Smart City central command computers.

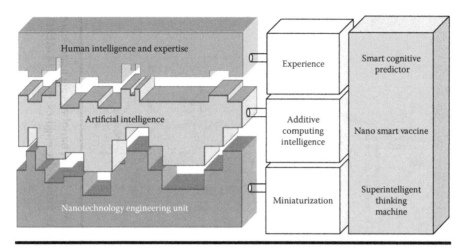

Figure 9.2   The architectural representation of CEWPS, the thinking machine of DI which immunizes all the Smart City devices. CEWPS is the composite of three enabling technologies. First, HI provided experience and cognitive power. Second, AI which expanded the intelligence of CEWPS and provided microscopic SVs nanobots. Third, nanotechnology which brought miniaturization and higher performance in spreading DI a million times faster than any software program, and any cyberattack before reaching the Smart City. (© 2014 MERIT CyberSecurity Group. All rights reserved.)

The 3D Nano Attack Scenario

Figure 9.3 represents a 3D futuristic scenario of nano defense of the Smart City. CEWPS which is nano intelligent system that generates DI through the Smart Vaccine Nanogrid (SVG). CEWPS is the nerve center of DI which integrates cloud computing, encryption technology, wireless computing, and nanobot logistics. CEWPS runs everything real time from its Command and Control Center (CCC) with the city headquarters center of the City Smart Grid (CSG). CEWPS has a whole menu of crucial responsibilities, not only to destroy the DDoS attacks, but to preserve a copy of the payload and keep its structure of the Virus Knowledge Base (ViKB) for future attacks. More importantly, CEWPS will keep all the Smart City systems routinely immunized. We will discuss how the SV nanobot will command the army of vaccinators (nanobots) to outsmart all attacks.

One of the most advanced components of DI (CEWPS) is its *Intelligent Early Warning Predictive* (IEWP) system. It will revolutionize preempted asymmetric and stealth attacks. The system is equipped with smart sensors on micro chips that will communicate with other friendly clouds and satellites and pass this information to the central component of the predictive system for analysis and accurate prediction. Telecoms will be more reliable, faster, and have wider bandwidth. The 5th generation of wireless will evolve and nanotechnology will create newer generations. We will discuss the internals of IEWP in the next section.

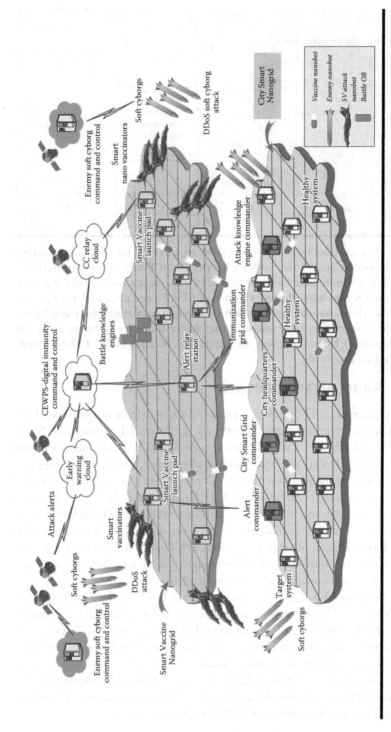

Figure 9.3 The 3D defense by offense scenario of CEWPS system. Nanobot army going after the DDoS, nanobot vaccinators are immunizing the city's smart grid. The battle episodes are documented and stored in the battle knowledge engines. (© 2014 MERIT CyberSecurity Group. All rights reserved.)

Anatomy of CEWPS and Its Intelligent Components

CEWPS comes with an arsenal of offensive and defensive systems. It is designed specifically to defend, by offense (Figure 9.4), Smart Cities and large metropolitan areas. CEWPS is in fact an incredible "brain" that controls a multitude of autonomic subsystems which are connected through CEWPS sensory and motor smart grid. This book often describes CEWPS with different configurations, depending on the subject and the content. CEWPS has nine subsystems headed by the Central Coordination Center (CCC), which acts as the nervous center and control hub. Figure 9.4 shows the nine interlinked operating subsystems.

Anatomical Composition of Digital Immunity (DI)

CEWPS Component 1: The Central Coordination Center (CCC)

The CCC is the nerve center of CEWPS; it is the brain of CEWPS. The center has several technical responsibilities that have to be met in order for the center to guarantee adequate protection and safety of the critical system. It is aware of all the security activities in the yard. It receives status data from all the subordinate systems and dispatches instructions and performatives based on the situation.

CEWPS comes with a multi-screen information dashboard (Figure 9.5) showing how the subsystem operate under normal conditions. The main objective of the Main Dashboard (MD) is to maintain optimum levels of operation for all the subscribed Infrastructure Critical Systems (ICS), catch all exceptions and abnormalities ahead of time, and most importantly, dispatch rapid response to alerts. The MD is the eyes, or the controls of the cockpit of a jumbo jet, for CEWPS.

Figure 9.5 shows how the MD screen looks, however, there are 60 dynamic sub screens to give the status of CEWPS-SV activities. The administrator can add, dynamically, additional screens, or run an ad-hoc SQL query on demand.

CEWPS draws its predictive clout from its accumulative knowledge reservoir. CEWPS collaborates with a group of prominent AVT providers who provide data on the latest cyberattacks in the world. Building a synergistic alliance with AVT providers gives CEWPS higher credibility, and more importantly, feeds CEWPS with a steady flow of fresh malware data ready to be converted into vaccine knowledge.

CEWPS Component 2: The Knowledge Acquisition Component

Where wisdom, experience, and knowledge are distilled. By analogy, we can compare the acquisition process to our sensory nervous system, which is made of cells that collect external sensory signals for distillation, filtration, and conversion into stimuli stored in the brain, before motor signals are instantiated and sent to the attack area. Here are some of the basic terms that we use thought the book:

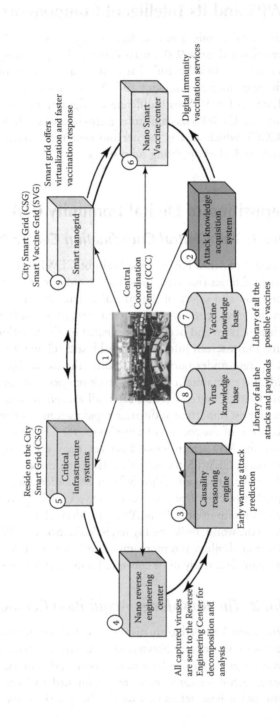

Figure 9.4 The pathological integration of nine operating components are equally critical. They receive commands from the CCC. During an attack, all the nano armies of SVs (B-Cells) are mobilized and fight together. The main focus is to protect the critical systems from the attack by vaccination and, at the same time, capture the virus and determine its identity and save it for the next attack. (© 2014 MERIT CyberSecurity Group. All rights reserved.)

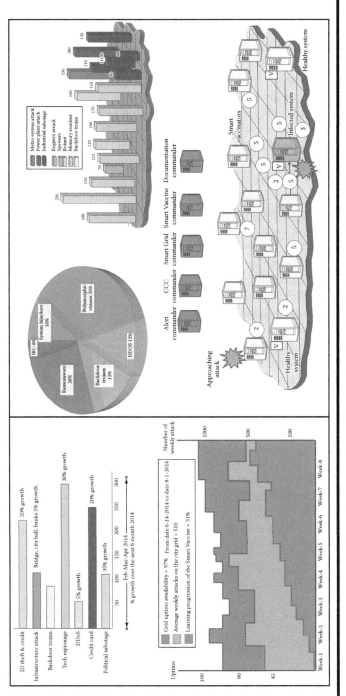

Figure 9.5 There are 20 dashboard screens, depending on the situation in the Smart City and the attack, screens flash out automatically depending on the defense status of the SV grid. (© 2014 MERIT CyberSecurity Group. All rights reserved.)

What Is Experience?

Experience is in fact a conscious event that creates a brain process that gets stored internally in the sensory cortex of the brain as *neural code*. Once an experienced episode gets into the brain, a memory record is created and is ready to be stored. There are three types of memory records: First, in the sensory stage which is the front-end. The registration of information during perception occurs in the brief sensory stage that usually lasts only a fraction of a second. It's your sensory memory that allows a perception such as a visual pattern, a sound, or a touch to linger for a brief moment after the stimulation is over. Second, after that first flicker, the sensation is stored in short-term memory which has fairly limited capacity; it can hold about seven items for no more than 20 or 30 seconds at a time. Third, long-term memory can store unlimited amounts of information indefinitely. People tend to more easily store material on subjects that they already know something about, since the information has more meaning to them and can be mentally connected to related information that is already stored in their long-term memory. That's why someone who has an average memory may be able to remember a greater depth of information about one particular subject. Most people think of long-term memory when they think of "memory" itself. Biologically, information must first pass through sensory and short-term memory before it can be stored as a long-term memory.

So, experience E_j is an event—or an episode that we participate in or live through. We all learn from experience, regardless if they are ugly, bad, or happy ones. Experience is cumulative and gets transformed in to knowledge later. Experience is gained by repeated trials. We all experience it in life. Quantitatively speaking, experience is a function of time $f(t)$ with a start time $E_j t_1$ and a finish time $E_j t_2$. Experience duration is expressed as $t_2 - t_1$.

Once experience is stored in the brain, it gets magically assembled with similar neural codes and become an episodic record of knowledge.

CEWPS considers a cyberattack as an independent discrete event that have a start and finish. But knowing about the past cyberattacks E_{j-1} (*a priori*) can definitely help forecasting incoming attacks. CEWPS is a smart machine and it is built for one purpose in mind: to catch cyberattacks before they occur. That's the magic of CEWPS.

What Is Knowledge?

Knowledge on the other hand is different from experience. It is the derivative of experience, as shown here.

$$K_t = \frac{d}{dt}(E_t)$$

Knowledge can be defined as "the fact or condition of knowing something with familiarity gained through experience or association." A knowledge engine takes disparate experience episodes $E_j t_j$ and converts them into knowledge patterns, and catalogues them in the brain for subsequent neural response. Intelligence is another human characteristic, but it refers to the fast ability of retrieving knowledge, connecting pieces of knowledge together, or processing knowledge quickly. CEWPS stores *a priori* knowledge extracted from previous cyberattacks on the smart grid. Attackers previously know that there's a smart grid and they design their attack vector to penetrate the grid from the weakest side and hide until the time comes for spreading to the center of the grid.

The Six Stages of a Cybercrime Episode

No one has ever analyzed a cyberattack on a smart grid in a Smart City. Let's not forget that the smart grid is not only a power grid. It is a resilient and secure network that connects all the critical infrastructures together. Smart grids are the new paradigm and technology and security vendors are jockeying to learn about it and introduce new products. Smart grid cyberattacks will usher the beginning of the new cyberwar and we had better be ready for it. CEWPS is designed to defend smart grids which are the backbones of future Smart Cities.

As we described earlier, a cyberattack is an unknown event that can be represented as a Bayesian Network (BN) model describing the conditional dependencies in probability distributions. We can deduce, from experience, that all cyberattacks have a similar pattern, and follow the same six stages as shown in (Figure 9.6).

So, the attack on the CSG has to be well studied, engineered, and executed. We're implementing nanotechnology as an innovative approach to design the CSG as well as Smart Vaccine Grid (SVG). In the following chapters we're discussing on detail the advantages of the new model of smart grids. The only way to penetrate the nanogrid is to use similar technologies. Cyber terrorists will eventually implement nanotechnology hacking tools in order to penetrate Smart Cities. Most of the cyberattacks on large installations or critical infrastructures are done with internal help. Nowadays, cyberattacks are driven mostly by political and religious motifs. Cyber terrorism is planned and executed by domain experts who know where the most vulnerable spots are in major cosmopolitan cities in the world. Each country has its own electronic army which is equipped with the latest symmetrical technologies. Cyber terrorists learn from their successes and failures and will try to launch several attacks at different locations on the grid. Most likely organized electronic armies have similar knowledge engines to CEWPS, where they model attacks and develop new payloads. In other words, Smart Cities are attacked by smart attacks.

The FBI, the Dutch KLPD (Korps Landelijke Politie Diensten), the International Criminal Police Organization (Interpol), the French Sûreté, and the German BKA (Bundeskriminalamt), all have automated fingerprint

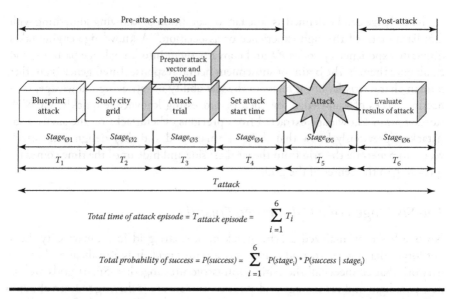

$$\text{Total time of attack episode} = T_{attack\ episode} = \sum_{i=1}^{6} T_i$$

$$\text{Total probability of success} = P(success) = \sum_{i=1}^{6} P(stage_i) * P(success \mid stage_i)$$

Figure 9.6 DDoS attackers must have a large reservoir of knowledge, bullet proof plan, and a wide-angle vision. There are six stages to a nano cyberattack. The attack is just as good as its plan. The success of one will trigger successive attacks with learning from previous ones. Almost all attacks follow the same pattern. Skipping one stage will make the success less successful.

identification systems (AFIS) that they share among each other in order to catch serial cyber terrorists. However, cybercriminals were one time security analysts with great knowledge of the state of the art, present AVTs. CEWPS will be a great help for the law enforcement agencies who are starting to use advanced technologies to track their malware enemies. CEWPS collects crime data from many global sources, which will be a be used in predictive reasoning in the inference engine. But the focus in CEWPS is primarily on pre-attack, rather than on post-attack.

Cybercrime Raw Data Distillation Process

The purpose of the data distillation process is to collect all cybercrime cases and normalize them into the Attacks Knowledge Base (AKB), before CEWPS can perform predictions. The Causality Reasoning Engine (CRE) will be discussed in CEWPS Component 3. The distillation process requires 5 basic steps as shown in (Figure 9.7).

Step 1: The raw data feeders: US global intelligence agencies and local law enforcement agencies have to feed fresh data and all historic data. The millions of criminal cases recordeded will enrich the knowledge base and enhance the performance of the inference engine.

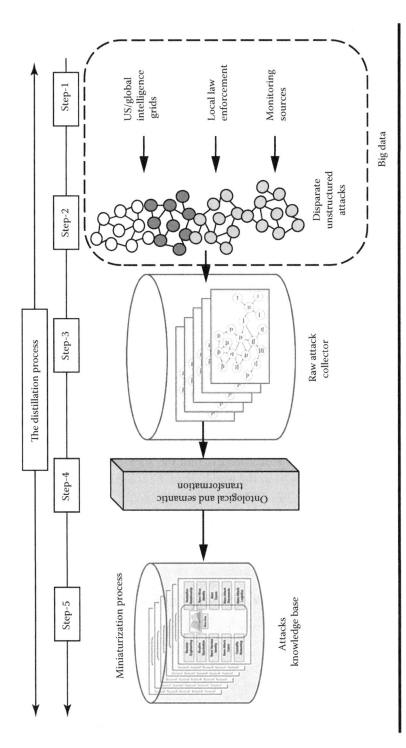

Figure 9.7 Unstructured attack cases are collected from different sources, filtered and transformed into uniform patterns, and then nanotechnology will be through a miniaturization process. The new CEWPS the system of DI will be scaled down to the molecular level. (© 2014 MERIT CyberSecurity Group. All rights reserved.)

Step 2: Raw input data: The crime case data is coming from many different law enforcement agencies, research organizations, and other crime repositories. As a result, data can be disparate, redundant, structured in different formats, or even processed by different software systems. Each country, for example, has its own proprietary finger or face identification system. The data collector will take care of homogenizing the data.

Step 3: Raw data collection: All unedited cybercrime episodes will be routed to an intermediate repository for cleaning and filtering. This process is pretty much like an iron mill where iron will be smelted and cast, or even like an oil refinery.

Step 4: Ontological and Semantic Transformation: In this step, we combine the attributes of each criminal case into an ontology record. Then combine all similar criminal cases together. We use ontology and semantics technologies (Figure 9.8) to standardize all the criminal records, before passing them to the causality prediction engine (discussed later in this chapter).

CEWPS comes with two knowledge bases. The first one is the AKB (Virus Library) and the second is the Vaccine Knowledge Base (VaKB) (Vaccine Library). The two knowledge bases will be discussed in components 8 and 9.

Step 5: The Attack Knowledge Base: CEWPS AKB is actually a very smart engine with high-level cognition and intelligence. It is an "expert library" that contains significant archival criminal episodes from around the world. CEWPS AKB uses special cybercrime taxonomy codes. CEWPS uses nanotechnology's miniaturization process to provide the SVG which is a nanogrid, with faster response and accurate information.

Cyber terrorism is the biggest global supply chain in the world with a monitory flow of 50 billion dollars per year. Cybercrime and its older brother cyber terrorism are the most affluent professions in the world. Forty-nine law enforcement agencies are regular crime data feeders into CEWPS AKB. CEWPS will have the biggest crime *repository*] in the world. The CEWPS AKB engine will be running 24/7 trying to clean up the data. Like crude oil, raw crime episodes go into an extensive distillation process that converts the raw data into a uniform structure. The formatted crime episode will then be routed into the AKB and will be transformed into a *knowledge model* before it goes into the inference engine for predictive induction.

CEWPS Component 3: The Reasoning Engine

Here, we would like to introduce two important terms used by the reasoning engine.

What Is Causality?

Causality is the relationship between an event (the cause) and a second event (the effect), where the second event is understood to be the consequence of the

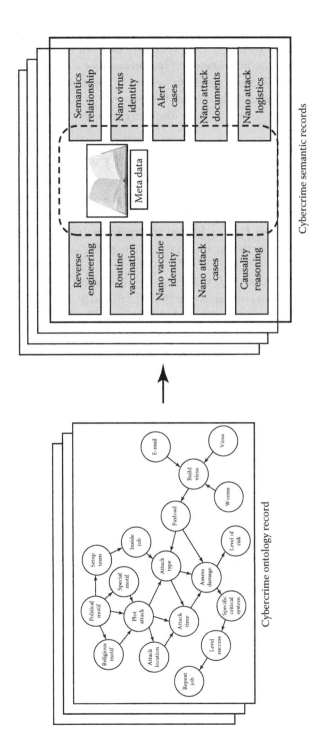

Figure 9.8 Shows the relationship between ontology and semantics. A crime ontology record is a collection of related attributes tied together. Converting all crime ontology records into a standardized format called the knowledge model.

first. It governs the relationship between events. There are, however, two cases of causality. First, necessary causes: If *x* is a necessary cause of *y*, then the presence of y necessarily implies the presence of *x*. The presence of *x*, however, does not imply that *y* will occur. Second, sufficient causes: If *x* is a sufficient cause of *y*, then the presence of *x* necessarily implies the presence of *y*. However, another cause *z* may alternatively cause *y*. Thus, the presence of *y* does not imply the presence of *x*.

What Is Prediction?

A prediction of this kind might be inductively valid if the predictor is a knowledgeable person in the field and is employing sound reasoning and accurate data. But as rule, predicting an event $E(tf)$ to happen in the future (tf), is perfectly valid, if previously, one or several similar events did occur at the same place and time $E(tf-1)$, $E(tf-2)$, $E(tf-3)$.

The probability that event $E(tf)$ will occur provided event $E(tf-1)$ did occur. Using probability formalism, we can write: $P(E(tf) \mid E(tf-1))$

In summary, we can deduce causal mechanisms from past data. Causality is an ingredient of CEWPS reasoning engine.

The *reasoning engine* is the *smart* guy component of CEWPS, often referred to as knowledge-based system. CEWPS refers to it as the Early Warning Predictor (EWP) which is an inference (reasoning) engine that relies on Bayesian Network Model (BNM) to generate probabilistic attack forecast. Some of the benefits of using BNMs are

- They are graphical models, capable of displaying relationships clearly and intuitively.
- They are directional, thus being capable of representing cause-effect relationships.
- They can handle uncertainty.
- They handle uncertainty though the established theory of probability.
- They can be used to represent both indirect and direct causation. BN is a set of local conditional probability distributions. Together with the graph structure, they are sufficient to represent the joint probability distribution of the domain

$$\Pr(X_1,\ldots,X_n) = \prod_{t=1}^{n} \Pr(X_i \mid Pa_i)$$

where Pa_i is the set containing the parents of X_i in the BN

We Can Forecast Weather—Why Can't We Predict Crime?

Let's take a look at other forecast systems such as weather and stock forecasting approaches. Weather forecasting is the application of science and technology to predict the state of the atmosphere for a given location. Weather forecasts are made by collecting (first step) quantitative weather data from weather satellites about the current state of the atmosphere on a given place and using scientific understanding of atmospheric processes to project how the atmosphere will change. The second step is to enter this data into a mathematical weather model to generate credible prediction results.

Anatomy of the Causality Reasoning Engine

The CRE is an AI-based system. It is commonly known as a reasoning inference engine (RIE). This type of engine is the holy grail of AI science. It is highly educated and a fast learner machine. Let's take a look at its anatomy in Figure 9.9.

An inference engine cycles through three sequential steps: *match rules*, *select rules*, and *execute rules*. The execution of the rules will often result in new facts or goals being added to the knowledge base which will trigger the cycle to repeat. This cycle continues until no new rules can be matched.

In the first step, matching the rules, the inference engine finds all of the rules that are triggered by the current contents of the knowledge base. In forward chaining the engine looks for rules where the antecedent (left hand side) matches some fact in the knowledge base. In backward chaining the engine looks for antecedents that can satisfy one of the current goals.

In the second step, selecting the rules, the inference engine prioritizes the various rules that were matched to determine the order to execute them.

In the third step, executing the rules, where the engine executes each matched rule in the order determined in step two and then iterates back to step one again. The cycle continues until no new rules are matched.

The AKB represents facts regarding cyberattacks, cybercriminal profiles, victims, and the impact of the attack. The world was represented as classes, subclasses, and instances and assertions were replaced by values of object instances. The rules worked by querying and asserting values of the objects. In addition to the input source of the AKB, there are two significant knowledge bases that participle into the reasoning process. The ViKB and the VaKB. They will be discussed later in this chapter.

CEWPS Component 4: Reverse Engineering Center

The center is responsible for decomposing all unknown attacking viruses and learning everything about their code and technologies. The pathology reports on captured and quarantined viruses will be catalogues and stored in the ViKB.

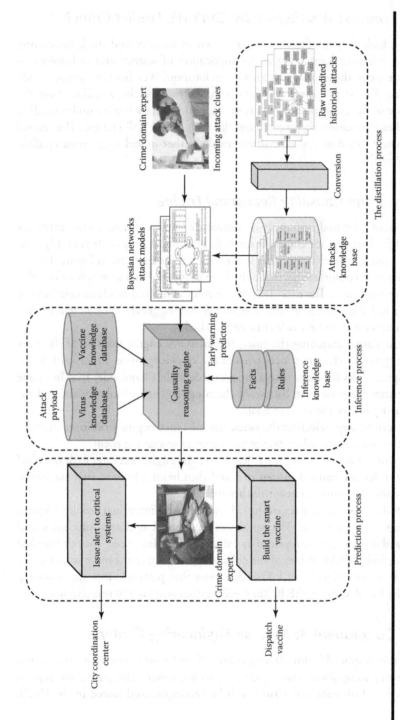

Figure 9.9 The CRE is the GPS of CEWPS. It is the EWP which extracts information about previous attacks, the strategy of defeat, and what kind of vaccine was used and the strategy of attack. The reasoning engine also gets information from the facts and rules. (© 2014 MERIT CyberSecurity Group. All rights reserved.)

Information coming from other forensics centers will also be stores in ViKB. Meanwhile, the corresponding antivirus vaccine will be stored in the VaKB. The Central Coordination Center (CCC) will receive daily bulletins from the Reverse Engineering Center (REC). The Smart Vaccine Nano Center (SVNC) is responsible for generating the SV nanobots and sending them to the city's nanogrid as a response to cyberattacks.

The tools of reverse engineering are categorized into debuggers or disassemblers, hex editors, monitoring, and decompile tools:

1. *Disassemblers*: A disassembler is used to convert binary code into assembly code and also used to extract strings, imported and exported functions, libraries, and so on. The disassemblers convert the machine language into a user-friendly format. There are different dissemblers that specialize in certain things.
2. *Debuggers*: This tool expands the functionality of a disassembler by supporting the CPU registers, the hex duping of the program, view of stacks, and so on. Using debuggers, the programmers can set breakpoints and edit the assembly code during run time. Debuggers analyze the binary in a similar way as the disassemblers and allow the reverser to step through the code by running one line at a time to investigate the results.
3. *Hex editors*: These editors allow the binary to be viewed in the editor and change it as per the requirements of the software. There are different types of hex editors available that are used for different functions.
4. *Portable executive and resource viewer*: The binary code is designed to run on a Windows-based machine and has a very specific data which tells how to set up and initialize a program. All the programs that run on Windows should have a portable executable that supports the DLLs the program needs to borrow from.

CEWPS Component 5: Smart City Critical Infrastructure (SCCI)

The Smart City Critical Infrastructure (SCCI) is a vital component of CEWPS which shields all critical systems of the city and keeps them in normal operating mode. The SVG is connected in real time to these devices and monitored at all times.

In the domain of terrorism, the term *critical infrastructure* became of paramount importance. In fact, certain national infrastructures are so vital that their incapacity or destruction would have a debilitating impact on the defense or economic security of the country. This is the reason we included the critical infrastructures as a part of the CEWPS environment. (Figure 9.10) shows graphically the 11 critical infrastructures with their respective criticality scale.

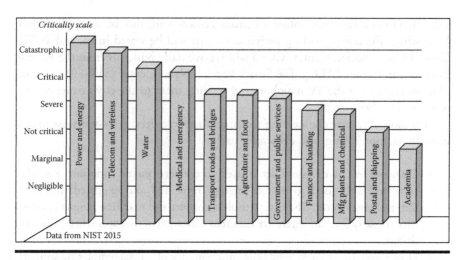

Figure 9.10   The 11 critical systems that manage the infrastructure in the Smart City ranked by criticality. There are six criticality levels and power and energy got the award for being the most catastrophic in case of a city or regional blackout. (NIST article, July 2017, Framework for Protecting Our Critical Infrastructure.)

What Is Criticality?

It is also appropriate to clarify the subject of criticality, because it is very closely related to threat, risk, and attacks. Criticality is a relative measure of the consequences of a failure mode and its frequency of occurrences. To say that the power grid is highly critical, means that a black out will create a very grave impact. The power grid is very complex and has many interconnections and components. Failure can be either human, mechanical, electrical, or in the design of the system. The resultant failure therefore can be either catastrophic, critical, or marginal. Failure mode is defined as "the way in which a failure is observed. It describes the way the failure occurs, and its impact on equipment operation. A failure mode deals with the present, whereas a failure cause happened in the past and a failure effect deals with the future." Let's analyze the situation numerically:

The formula of criticality due to a failure is

$$C_m = \beta \alpha \lambda_p t$$

$\text{Criticality}_{\text{mode}} = (\text{Probability of next higher failure}) \times (\text{Failure mode ratio}) \times (\text{Part failure rate}) \times (\text{Duration of applicable mission phase})$

Total item criticality (C_r) is joint probability of the item under all the failure modes:

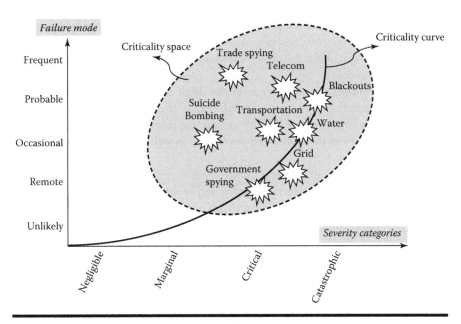

Figure 9.11 Most of the attacks on infrastructures are considered "critical" and associated with high failure probability. Smart Cities cannot afford to have infrastructures with high levels of vulnerability. Predictive analytics comes handy to offer predictable future scenarios. (© 2014 MERIT CyberSecurity Group. All rights reserved.)

$$C_r = \sum_{n=1}^{j} (\beta\alpha\lambda pt)_n$$

C_r = criticality probability
n = the initial failure mode of the item being analyzed where $n = 1,2,3,4\ldots j$
j = the number of failure modes for the item being analyzed

Severity is an attribute associated with the damage caused by the cyberattack. There are four levels of severity: negligible, marginal, critical, and catastrophic as shown in Figure 9.11.

What Is a Critical Infrastructure?

We keep using the term *critical infrastructure* everywhere. But what does it mean in terms of Smart Cities?

In a Smart City, energy, water, transportation, public health and safety, and other key services are managed in concert in order to support the smooth operation of critical infrastructure while providing for a clean, economic, and safe environment in which to live, work, and play. Timely logistics information will be gathered and supplied to the public by either the cloud, secure information highways, or social media networks.

The energy infrastructure is arguably the single most important feature in any city. If unavailable for a significant enough period of time, all other functions will eventually cease. This is why CEWPS utilizes the smart grid to offer on-demand vaccination services to immunize the power grid as well as the other critical infrastructure systems.

Critical infrastructure is a term coined by governments to represent the backbone of the Smart City's economy, security, and health. People are aware of it as the power they use at home, the water they drink, the transportation that moves them, and the communication systems they rely on to stay in touch with friends and family. The corollary of this can be stated as a Smart City cannot exist without a smart grid protecting its critical infrastructures.

How did a particular infrastructure become critical? This is an interesting question. Infrastructures were born with cities. The oldest infrastructures were aqueducts and roads. The Egyptians built canals and irrigations systems. They didn't make so many roads. Roads were not so important because they relied on the Nile for transportation. The Romans built aqueducts, roads, and bridges. As cities became more and more populated, the infrastructures became more important and additional sections were added to the old ones.

Engineering, medicine, and the military became the most important elements of a civilization's survival. The first is to build a healthy city, the second is to maintain healthy citizens and the third is to defend the city. George Stephenson invented the steam locomotive engine in 1820. Karl Benz invented the modern car in 1879. The Wright brothers invented the airplane in 1903. All these three inventions brought to the modern world three new infrastructures. Thomas Edison gave us the grace of electricity in 1879, Alexander Graham Bell gave us the telephone in 1876, and Thomas Johnson Watson gave us the IBM computer in 1953. Then Leonard Kleinrock and Vinton Cerf gave us the Internet and that was the beginning of the electronic "Big Bang" that we are living in today.

The reality of living defies predictions and forecasts. Today, 54% of the world's population lives in urban areas, a proportion that is expected to increase to 66% by 2050. Just 10 years ago, the number of Internet users was 910 million with a world population of 6.4 billion. This number has jumped to a whopping 3.1 billion with a world population of 7.2 billion. Cities are becoming more crowded, noisier, with more crime and poverty. But governments are fighting all these miseries by seriously considering jumping on the Smart City bandwagon. The strategy is to utilize innovation and ability to solve social problems and use information and communication technologies (ICTs) to improve this capacity. The intelligence here lies in the ability to solve a communities problem and use technology to transfer the solution. In this sense, intelligence is an inner quality of any territory, a place, city, or region where innovation processes are facilitated by information and communication technologies. What varies is the degree of intelligence, depending on the person, the system of cooperation, and the digital infrastructure and tools that a community offers its residents. Take for example Tokyo, it tops the population list and remains the world's largest city with 38 million dwellers. Amazingly, Tokyo is rated as the third most impressive Smart City on Earth. This is the secret:

Due to months of rolling blackouts due to lack of nuclear power, the need for the Japanese to innovate has never been greater. Japan's biggest companies are behind the Smart City revolution taking place around the globe and are using Tokyo as their proving ground. Panasonic, Sharp, Mitsubishi, and many other big names are working very hard to infuse smart technology into this massive city.

CEWPS Component 6: The Smart Vaccine Center (SVC)

One of the great contributions to humanity was the discovery of the vaccine. Without adaptive immunity, one-fourth of the human race would have been terminally ill. Because with the exponential acceleration of technology, it is like a runaway train with no control. The whole world needs quality of life not only Smart Cities. DI will offer similar contribution to the digital world. The SV is one of the most fascinating services that technology could offer to win the battle against cybercrime and terrorism. The SV is built with two avant-garde and cutting-edge technologies: AI and nanotechnology.

The SV was conceived with futuristic features that will be ready in a decade. SV has seven well programmed components, as shown in Figure 9.12, that work autonomically in any difficult battle situation against adversary nanobots, pretty much like human B-cells. Nanotechnology also offers incredible advantages in the design of nano SV, which is the new generation of smart weaponry against cyber malware.

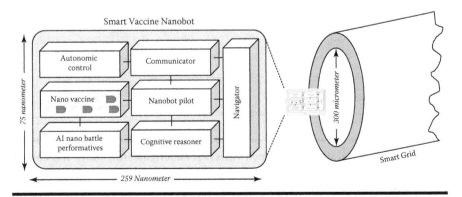

Figure 9.12 The ingenious structure of the nano SV, the SV nanobot can easily roam inside the blood and nerve vessels, and surprisingly inside the CSG. (© 2014 MERIT CyberSecurity Group. All rights reserved.)

CEWPS Component 7: The VaKB

The VaKB is the intelligent "pharmacy" that has all prescriptions of all possible vaccines that were manufactured for previous attacks. It works very closely with the causal reasoning engine. Further explanation will be provided in the next section.

CEWPS Component 8: The ViKB

The ViKB is the repository that contains all the attack payloads, attack descriptions, the source, and the expected target. It works very closely with the causal reasoning engine. Further explanation will be provided in the next section.

The VaKB and ViKB are critically important to the overall security of the smart grid as shown in (Figure 9.13). There will be situations where the virus is not available in the knowledge base and its matching vaccine is not ready, then the infected system will provide samples of the virus and a vaccine will promptly be fabricated for the rest of the systems on the grid.

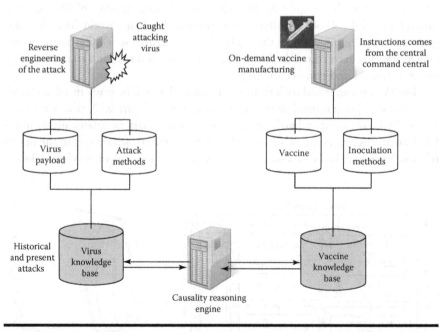

Figure 9.13 The parallelism between virus reverse-engineering (once it is caught for forensics) and vaccine processing is uncanny and fascinating. Using Bayesian visualization reasoning, CEWPS comes up with the amazing predictions to vaccinate the critical systems before the attack spreads to the other critical systems. (© 2014 MERIT CyberSecurity Group. All rights reserved.)

CEWPS Component 9: CEWPS Smart Nanogrid

We are now leaving the fourth generation of nanotechnology and entering the fifth one. We're going to achieve marvelous things including nanosystems that will outperform our present computing hardware and software. Nano could replace current technologies that send data through metal lines with metallic carbon nanotubes, which conduct electricity better than metal. When information is sent from one core to another, the outgoing electrical signal would be converted to light and travel through a waveguide to another core, where a detector would change the data back to electrical signals. Nanowires (NW) thus represent the best-defined class of nanoscale building blocks, and this precise control over key variables has correspondingly enabled a wide range of devices and integration strategies to be pursued. CEWPS is giving us the new generation of cybersecurity which is exemplified in a robust and intelligent environment called DI. One of the most advanced components of CEWPS is its smart nanogrid. Because without the grid, we wouldn't have DI, and without DI we will not have a securely intelligent Smart City. The city's Central Communication Center (CCC) is connected real time to the smart nanogrid through intelligent nano adapters as shown in Figure 9.14.

The CEWPS screen shows how the state of New Jersey counties and sub counties have been mapped into a grid-centric screen with all the critical systems that control the major infrastructures in the state. The grid has two-dimensional coordinates to facilitate the location of any particular system. Each critical system is

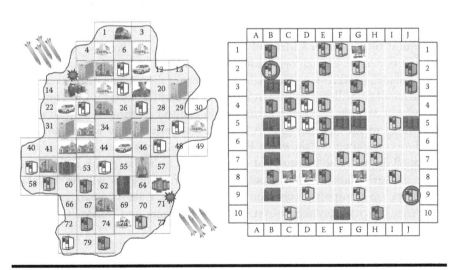

Figure 9.14   CEWPS has a great feature that no other system has, which is a graphical real-time representation of the city smart nanogrid during an attack and how the SV nanobots are neutralizing the attackers. (© 2014 MERIT CyberSecurity Group. All rights reserved.)

recognized by a location code and type of infrastructure. CEWPS was using infrastructure data from the state of New Jersey during its development.

The Smart Grid Model

During the design of CEWPS, we looked at the risk issue and how it can be managed best, we realized that the only way to be ahead of the malware curve, is to stay away from conventional technologies and jump into the two leading domains of AI and Nanotechnology. CEWPS and all its pioneering components can harness these two technologies to fabricate and assemble the "DI" of the future. We wanted to create a replica of the city with a smart grid over it with a huge variety of connections, different types of devices, sensors and meters, and selected critical infrastructures. The city would then be connected to a computerized screen as shown in Figure 9.14. All the coordinates of the devices on the city would be reflected in "real time" on the computerized screen. If a simulated attack hits the city, at specific square of the nanogrid, the computer screen will also indicate the location of the attack and its type. Then the model will dispatch an alert to all the subscribed citizens on the grid and at the same time, the SV nanobots will be rushing to the site of the attack.

Connectivity of Critical Systems to City's Smart Nanogrid

In the near future, Smart Cities will be equipped with two layers of special grids. The first one is the city nanogrid, and the second one is the DI grid. Both grids will be made of special nanomaterials such as nanotubes, nanowire or nanomesh. Nanotechnology will give us a smart nanogrid that will be used for DI. This futuristic wire of 300 nanometers in diameter will connect all the devices with meters and sensors to the city nanogrid. A special autonomic adapter will establish the real-time connectivity as shown in Figure 9.15. The city's Critical Infrastructure Systems (CIS) will also be equipped with adapters to interface with both the city smart nanogrid and the SV nanogrid. The nmart nanogrids will be the main "highways" to transport vaccination services, dispatch alerts, report attack outcome status, exchange system-to-system (S-2-S) messages, and broadcast important administrative instructions.

Anatomy of the Autonomic Adapter

The Autonomic Adapter (AA) engine is the smart interface between the CIS and the smart grid. It carries on its back the following important mechanisms:

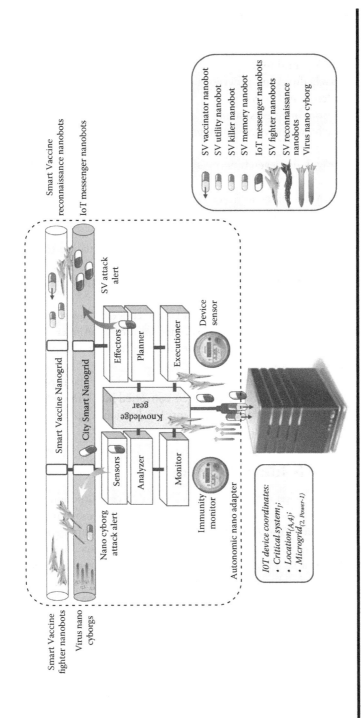

Figure 9.15 All city critical infrastructure systems, IoT devices will be connected to the AA. AI and Nanotechnology will make this a reality to spread DI in all Smart Cities. (© 2014 MERIT CyberSecurity Group. All rights reserved.)

- Delivery of the vaccination services to the CIS which is also called the client system.
- Sending out an attack outcome status to the City CCC for alert.
- Authentication of grid users.
- Vaccination schedules and provisions
- Security bulletins and alerts
- Attack data from infected systems
- Connectivity between system-to-system (S-2-S)

The AA engine includes seven functional components as shown in (Figure 9.15):

1. *The Effectors*: As the name indicates, it describes what is being done due to an attack. Effectors receive response services from the CCC and pass them to the planner for planning the counter attack.
2. *The Analyzer*: Provides the mechanism to evaluate the situation (normal versus attack) based on performance and security metrics and rules.
3. *The Monitor*: Monitors the sensors that provides real-time signals from the CIS, according to the rules of the analyzer.
4. *The Planner*: Prepares a list of nano vaccination services following the instructions coming from the CCC and passes them to the executioner.
5. *The Executioner*: Receives the vaccination services from the planner, and passes them to the CIS.
6. *The Knowledge Gear*: Gathers activity sensor and effector data from all four functional components of the AA and gets converted into knowledge and can be retrieved by any of the four components for decision support.

The Smart City Is Idealistic Hype

Let's start on a realistic note: the Smart City is idealistic hype; although the term is very attractive, it will not happen soon. It is a moving target with so many uneasy to control variables. For one thing, Smart Cities need inexhaustible approved budgets. but above all, a stable government led by a credentialed visionary leader. Building a Smart City takes at least 20 years to set up a "base city". No one has started a Smart City from scratch which is a futile endeavor, if not impossible. According to the United Nations, there are 196 capital cities on earth. None of them is a true Smart City. So, a Smart City is nothing but a cross-pollinated booming urbanite with some inherent beauty. It can be on the be ocean, in the ocean, or in the middle of the desert. The term Smart Cities is a bit ambiguous. Some people choose a narrow definition—i.e. cities that use information and communication technologies to deliver services to their citizens.

My favorite definition of a Smart City is: A booming metropolis with resilient and future-ready infrastructures, bundled with intelligent ICTs to secure the use of its key resources, and managed by a team of smart citizens and smart government. But the most influencing variable in the Smart City polynomial is its ability to secure itself from physical human-provoked attacks and catastrophes. A Smart City should have a mechanism to defend itself and mitigate and eliminate danger.

Protecting the Critical Infrastructures and Key Resources (CIKP) in the Smart City requires a brand-new approach to cybersecurity and a new set of technologies. CEWPS was specifically designed to meet the crucial security requirements in Smart Cities. CEWPS is two generations ahead of the present AVTs. What are the CIKP that Smart Cities have to worry about?

The National Strategy for Homeland Security has identified 13 critical sectors.

As we learn more about threats, means of attack, and the various criteria that make targets lucrative for terrorists, this list will evolve. The critical infrastructure sectors consist of: "First, agriculture and food, water, public health, emergency services, government. Second, the defense industrial base, information and telecommunications. Third, energy, transportation, banking and finance, chemicals and hazardous materials, and postal and shipping."

Smart cities should be characterized by optimum urban performance reflected in 13 critical sectors. But Smart Cities are more than the sum of those

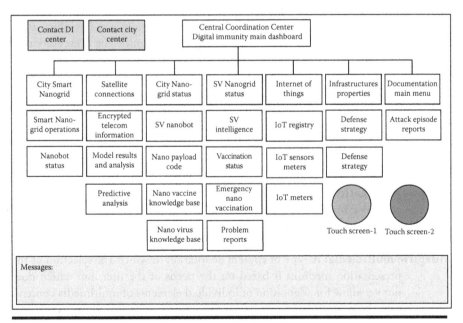

Figure 9.16   The CEWPS MD is the brain of the system. On the front it is a menu of options, but behind the screen, there are a nebulous traffic of communication nano signals that interact with one another. The administrator will monitor all the 25 screens, and let the system take charge autonomously of the battle. He will be in contact with the CCC of DI and the CCC of the Smart City. (© 2014 MERIT CyberSecurity Group. All rights reserved.)

sectors. We can say that a Smart City is a digitally intelligent city. In other words, it is the balanced hybrid mixture networked infrastructures and human capital. CEWPS (call it the Holy Grail) would only qualify to protect the 13 critical sectors of the city.

CEWPS MD

The CEWPS/SV system will have around 150 dynamic screens and 100 online reports categorized by component. The main screens for the DI system has 25 main screens as displayed in Figure 9.16.

Glossary

Accommodation: A process to which Piaget referred in his theory of cognitive development, whereby an individual's existing understanding is modified from a new experience.

Adaptable hypermedia systems: Systems in which users can explicitly set preferences or establish profiles through filling out forms to provide information for the user model, which is then used to determine the presentation of information.

Adaptable systems: Systems in which users have the ability to diagnose their own progress and modify student/user models as needed.

Adaptation model: The component of an adaptive hypermedia system that allows the system to modify information presentation so that reading and navigation style conform to user preferences and knowledge level and that specifies the way in which the user's knowledge modifies the presentation of information.

Adaptive navigation: Adaptive hypermedia techniques that modify the links accessible to a user at a particular time; link adaptation.

Adaptive presentation: Techniques that modify the contents of a page based on the user model; content adaptation.

Adaptive multimedia: A type of content adaptation in which the selection of the presentation medium is based on the needs of the user, but which does not yet allow for adaptation of individual elements of multimedia content.

Adaptive text presentation: A type of content adaptation in which the user model determines a page's textual content. While there are various techniques for adaptive text presentation, they look similar from the perspective of "what can be adapted," that is, those with varying user models see different textual content as the content for the same page.

Adaptive systems: Systems that modify the student/user model to adjust to progress and characteristics of users.

Adaptive tutoring systems: (ATS) what many refer to as intelligent tutoring systems, though Streitz is reluctant to ascribe intelligence to technical systems.

Aesthetic entry point: A way to introduce a topic that engages the senses through works of art that relate to the subject matter being studied. Also, concepts and examples have their own aesthetic properties, which can be examined and discussed in conjunction with the topic at hand.

Assimilation: A process of adaptation to interactions with the environment through which individuals add new experiences to their base of knowledge according to Piaget's theory of cognitive development.

Asynchronous learning: Directed study or "self-study" that does not occur in real-time or in a live instructor-led setting.

Asynchronous web technology: A type of computer-mediated communication that involves the use of the World Wide Web to provide information in non-real time.

Behaviorism: A major school of thought on the nature of learning and the properties of knowledge that was dominant in the 1950s and 1960s and focused on the observation of behavior and the adaptation of organisms to the environment. Behaviorist learning theories view knowledge as objective, given, and absolute.

Bodily-kinesthetic intelligence: A biopsychological potential which involves using one's body for processing information in order to solve problems or build products.

Bug catalog: A set of errors compiled and analyzed by an intelligent tutoring system to indicate where a particular learner is having difficulty.

Categorization: The basis of a cognitive learning theory developed by Jerome Bruner, a cognitive psychologist and educator. According to Bruner's theory, people interpret the world in terms of similarities and differences among various events and objects. While engaged in categorizing, people employ a coding system based on a hierarchical arrangement of categories that are related to each other, with successively more specific levels.

Common Gateway Interface (CGI): A standard for external gateway programs to interface with information servers such as HTTP (Hypertext Transfer Protocol) servers used for the World Wide Web.

Classicism: An approach to modeling thinking from the field of cognitive science that employs symbolic processing to model thought processes. See Symbolism.

Cognitive constructivism: A school of thought within constructivism, that postulates that learning occurs as a result of the exploration and discovery by each individual learner. In the view of cognitive constructivists knowledge is a symbolic mental representation in the mind of each individual.

Cognitive psychobiology: Interdisciplinary field of study involving biological neural studies. D. O. Hebb is considered by many to be the father of cognitive psychobiology.

Cognitive science: The interdisciplinary study of mind and intelligence, which attempts to further an understanding of intelligent activities and the nature of thought. The major contributing disciplines to the field include philosophy, psychology, computer science, linguistics, neuroscience, and anthropology.

Cognitivism: Major school of thought that employs an information-processing approach to learning and uses a model based on the input–output information-processing architecture of digital computers. Though cognitivist learning theories are based on active mental processing on the part of learners, such theories still maintain the behaviorist perspective on knowledge, considering knowledge to be both given and absolute.

Computational system: A term used in cognitive science to denote a system that uses discrete mathematics to model cognitive agents and the process of cognition.

Computer assisted (aided) instruction: Usually refers to sequentially ordered "linear programs." CAI generally follows a step-by-step procedural approach to the presentation of subject matter, based on the principles of behaviorist psychology.

Computer-based instruction (CBI): Using computers for training and instruction. However, the term CBI usually refers to instruction that do not use technology from AI. Production rules and expert systems are generally not used for sequencing the elements of information that are presented to the student. This approach generally produces linear sequences of information, and such CBI programs are referred to as "linear programs."

Computer-based learning environments: Systems that use a constructivist approach based on Piaget's theory of active learning, with the objective of providing an environment in which students can develop their own authentic knowledge. Examples of computer-based learning environments are Papert's Mindstorms and Lawler's Microworlds.

Computer-based training (CBT): Developed in the 1950s, CBT bases its training approach on behaviorist psychology theory. CBT "teaches" courses by presenting knowledge to be learned through a step-by-step procedure, leading students from one item to be learned to the next.

Computer-mediated communication: The passing of messages or sharing of information through networking tools, such as email, conferencing, newsgroups, and web sites.

Connectionism: An approach to modeling thinking, developed in the field of cognitive science, that views thought processes as connections between nodes in a distributed network.

Constructionism: A term coined by an MIT researcher to connote the combination of constructivist learning theories with the creation and development of individually designed learning projects.

Constructivism: Major school of thought on the nature of knowledge that views knowledge as a constructed entity developed by each individual. According to constructivist theory, information is transmitted but knowledge cannot be transmitted from teacher to student, parent to child, or any one individual to another; rather, knowledge is (re)constructed by each individual in his/her own mind and is relative, varying through time and space.

Constructivist learning theory: The theory, originally based on the research of Jean Piaget, that holds that learning is the result of an individual's mental construction. The theory posits that individuals learn by actively constructing their own understanding, incorporating new information into the base of knowledge they have already constructed in their own minds.

Content adaptation: Techniques that adapt the content of a page based on the user model; also known as adaptive presentation.

Course management system: A type of online learning system, categorized in terms of its functions of content delivery, assessment, and administration.

Deconstruction: An analytical method to uncover multiple interpretations of text developed by Jacques Derrida, a French philosopher, in the 1960s.

Differential equations: A branch of mathematics used in dynamic systems theory to describe a multidimensional space of potential thoughts and behaviors, traversed by a path of thinking followed by an agent under certain environmental and internal pressures.

Direct guidance: An adaptive navigation technique providing a link to the page that the system determines to be the most suitable next stop along the path to the user's information goal. Usually provided via the "next" button, direct guidance offers a guided tour based on user needs.

Domain model: The component of an adaptive hypermedia application that describes the structure of the information content of the application. The domain model specifies the relationship between the concepts handled by the application and the connection between the concepts and the information fragments and pages.

Dynamic (dynamical) systems theory: The theoretical approach that uses differential equations to describe a multidimensional space of potential thoughts and behaviors, traversed by a path of thinking followed by an agent under certain environmental and internal pressures. Some cognitive scientists view dynamic systems theory as a promising approach to modeling human thinking.

Educational adaptive hypermedia: One of the six major application domains within existing adaptive hypermedia systems. Educational hypermedia constitutes one of the earliest application areas and is still the most widely encountered application domain for adaptive hypermedia systems. Most educational hypermedia systems limit the size of the hyperspace by focusing on a specific course or topic for learning. User modeling-based adaptive hypermedia techniques are useful in educational hypermedia systems since knowledge level varies widely among users, the knowledge of an individual user can expand very quickly, and novice users need navigational assistance even in a limited hyperspace.

Educational hypermedia: One of the six major application domains within existing adaptive hypermedia systems. Educational hypermedia constitutes one of the earliest application areas and is still the most widely encountered application domain for adaptive hypermedia systems. Most educational hypermedia systems limit the size of the hyperspace by focusing on a specific course or topic for learning. User modeling-based adaptive hypermedia techniques are useful in educational hypermedia systems since knowledge level varies widely among users, the knowledge of an individual user can expand very quickly, and novice users need navigational assistance even in a limited hyperspace.

Entry point framework: An educational methodology that accommodates individual differences by providing multiple ways to introduce a topic. While certain entry points activate particular intelligences, a one-to-one correspondence does not exist between entry points and intelligences.

Epistemology: The branch of philosophy that studies knowledge and attempts to answer basic questions about knowledge, such as what distinguishes true or adequate knowledge from false or inadequate knowledge.

Existential/foundational entry point: A way to introduce a topic that allows individuals to approach a topic through addressing fundamental questions, such as the meaning of life. Philosophical issues invite certain learners to engage on a deep level, which piques and holds their interest in studying a particular topic.

Expert model: An intelligent tutoring system component that provides a representation of the knowledge in a way that a person who is skilled in the subject matter represents such as knowledge. In recent intelligent tutoring systems, the expert model is a runnable program with the facility to solve problems in the subject matter domain. The expert model is used to compare the learner's solution to the expert's solution; in this way, the intelligent tutor identifies specific points that the learner does not yet understand or topics the learner has not yet mastered.

Explanation variants: Content adaptation method that involves storing variations of sections of information and presenting each individual with the particular variation that best fits the individual's user model.

Formative evaluation: The evaluation of a working prototype or, in some cases, a rough draft of a system.

g factor: The theory that there exists a single, monolithic, and measurable, general mental ability in humans referred to as *g*.

Generative topics: Topics that are central to one or more disciplines or subjects, accessible and interesting to students, as well as connected to teachers' passions.

Global guidance: A method for adaptive navigation support that helps the user follow the shortest and most direct path to reach the information goal by telling the user which link to follow next or sorting links from a given node according to their relevance to the overall goal.

Global orientation: A method for adaptive navigation support, offering annotation landmarks and hiding non-relevant information so that users understand the structure and position in hyperspace.

Hands-on entry point: A way to introduce a topic that engages learners in constructing experiments with physical materials or through computer simulations. Other hands-on approaches invite learners to learn by building or manipulating a physical manifestation of some aspect of the topic they are studying.

Hypermedia: Technology that focuses on information nodes and the connections between the nodes.

Instrumentalism: Naturalistic understanding and philosophy that was developed by John Dewey based on the underlying belief that thought is the product of the interaction between an organism and the environment and knowledge, guiding and controlling the interaction between the organism and the environment.

Intelligences: Biopsychological potentials for processing information, solving problems, and developing products valued by the culture in which the person resides.

Intelligent educational systems (IES): Systems that advise learners and treat them as collaborators rather than directing them in an authoritarian manner. IES provide learner models that can be inspected and modified by the learners themselves.

Intelligent Computer Aided Instruction (ICAI): Sleeman and Brown consider ICAI to be the same as intelligent tutoring systems.

Intelligent tutoring systems (ITS): An advanced form of ICAI and CBI that attempts to individualize instruction by creating a computer-based learning environment. The environment performs in a manner similar to a human teacher, working with students to indicate when they make errors, offering suggestions on how best to proceed, recommending new topics to study, and collaborating with students on the curriculum. Such systems should be able to analyze student responses and keep track of the preferences and skills of each individual learner, customizing materials to fit the needs of individual students.

Interpersonal entry point: A way to introduce a topic that engages learners with each other so that they can interact, cooperate, work together, or alternately debate and argue with each other. Students learn from each other through group projects, in which each student contributes to the overall effort.

Interpersonal intelligence: A biopsychological potential which involves a person's ability to understand the intentions, motivations, and desires of other people and, therefore, to relate effectively with other people.

Intrapersonal intelligence: A biopsychological potential to understand oneself and to construct an effective working model of personal capabilities and difficulties as well as to employ such knowledge for managing one's life.

Knowledge-based tutoring systems (KBTS): Systems that incorporate knowledge about the subject matter, principles of teaching, characteristics of individual learners, and human–computer interaction.

Learning management system: Online learning system categorized by function, similar to course management systems, which contain content delivery, assessment, and administration functions with an integrated view of all active courses, with assessment and goal tracking facilities.

Learning objects: Components, lessons, modules, courses, or programs that are individually-structured digital or non-digital entities, for use or reference in online learning systems.

Legacy systems: Existing applications or systems within an organization that are not web-based or are not integrated with the web.

Linguistic intelligence: A biopsychological potential which involves the ability to learn and use spoken and written language to process information and achieve specific goals.

Link adaptation: Adaptive hypermedia techniques that modify the links accessible to a user at a particular time; adaptive navigation.

Local guidance: A method for adaptive navigation support that offers suggestions for the most relevant link to follow for the next step, based on the user's preferences, knowledge, and background.

Local orientation: A method for adaptive navigation support that helps users understand their location in hyperspace and nearby information, offering information about nodes available from the current location or limiting navigation possibilities, focusing on the most relevant links.

Logical entry point: A way to introduce a topic that allows learners to deduce the cause and effect of certain occurrences and apply deductive reasoning to understand the relationships among various factors involved in the study of a particular topic.

Logical-mathematical intelligence: A biopsychological potential which involves the ability to conduct logical analysis of problems as well as scientific investigations and to carry out mathematical operations.

Logical positivism: School of thought in philosophy that was widely accepted in the early 1950s, that questioned the value of systematic inquiry into the operation of the mind.

Marxism: The philosophy developed by Karl Marx (1818–1883) that truth can be discerned by analyzing economic structures.

Modernity: A period during the Enlightenment when the worldview was based on using rational, empirical, and objective approaches to discern the truth.

Multimedia technologies: A number of different media-based technologies provide delivery services for online learning. These technologies include: live, streaming video, audio and slides; on-demand pre-recorded video and/ or audio with accompanying graphics; browser-based Web conferencing combined with audio conferencing; interactive graphics, slide shows, audio and video clips, and web pages.

Multiple representations: An educational methodology that is used to convey the definitive aspects of an idea or topic, by modeling them through abstract or natural representation systems. The form of the representation may be closely tied to the physical subject, such as a photographic record, map, or chart, or may provide a formal model. Contrary to established approaches, Gardner argues for a family of representations rather than a single representation that is considered to be the best. Multiple representations allow students to choose elements from known reference areas to represent and model the new topic. The use of multiple representations allows students to understand on a deeper level through developing models of the new subject matter.

Musical intelligence: A biopsychological potential which involves the ability to perform, compose, and appreciate musical patterns.

Narrative entry point: A way to introduce a topic that engages students in learning through relating stories. Linguistic, intrapersonal, and interpersonal intelligences are activated through verbal storytelling, with additional intelligences activated through symbolic narrative forms, including movies and mime.

Naturalist intelligence: A biopsychological potential which involves the ability to recognize and classify many species that constitute the flora and fauna of a person's environment.

Neopragmatist: A philosophical approach adopted by Richard Rorty, similar to the pragmatist view, based on the belief that as humans, we create ourselves and our worlds and that human understanding is based on our interpretation of the world through a variety of paradigms rather than on an objective structure of the mind.

Numerical entry point: A way to introduce a topic that offers students who like to deal with numbers and numerical relations the opportunity to learn through measurement, counting, listing, and determining statistical attributes of the topic being studied.

Ongoing assessment: Asks the question: how will you and your students know what they understand? Students reflect on their own learning experiences throughout the process, and there are multiple ways for students to demonstrate to the teacher and to themselves what they understand.

Online learning: Educational technology using computer-mediated communication facilities that generally arise from the use of Internet and web technology.

Overlay model: The standard type of student model in which a student's knowledge is considered to be a subset of that of a subject matter expert. A technique for student modeling which involves measuring the student's performance against the standard of an expert's model.

Page variants: Content adaptation technique of fragment variants in which a fragment is an entire page. Multiple versions of particular pages exist and are selected based on variables in the user model. Users receive structurally different explanations of concepts based on user model attributes. Easy to implement, this technique offers a variant for each user stereotype.

Papert's principle: Papert's belief that major steps in mental growth are based on acquiring new ways to organize and use what a person already knows, not just on learning new skills.

Perceptron: A system invented by Frank Rosenblatt in 1957 through research in connectionism with which Rosenblatt demonstrated learning by a machine when the Mark I Perceptron "learned" to recognize and identify optical patterns.

Performances of understanding: Asks the question: what will students do to build and demonstrate their understanding? Students can build and demonstrate their understanding through presentations, portfolios, and other approaches to demonstrate to the teacher and to themselves what they have learned.

Pragmatism: A school of thought developed by William James (1842-1910) and adopted by John Dewey. Dewey then developed a theory of knowledge based on pragmatism that encompassed a view of the world as one in which active manipulation of the environment is involved throughout the process of learning.

Primacy effect: A psychological effect that means that students are particularly apt at remembering the starting point in a learning experience.

Postmodernism: A philosophy based on a belief in the plurality of meaning, perspectives, methods, and values, and an appreciation of alternative interpretations. Postmodernists distrust theories that purport to explain why things are the way they are, believing in the existence of multiple truths based on various perspectives and ways of knowing.

Psychoanalytic movement: School of psychology begun by Sigmund Freud (1856–1939), understanding an individual's psyche through an examination of the unconscious.

Self-directed learning: Self-paced, asynchronous online learning with the learner proceeding at his/her own pace through course materials.

Situated learning: Instruction that places an emphasis on the context in which learning occurs and provides students with opportunities to construct new knowledge and understanding in real-life situations, thereby seeking to avoid the decontextualized nature of typical classroom learning.

Social constructivism: A school of thought that stresses the collaborative efforts of groups of learners as sources of learning and considers the mind to be a distributed entity extending beyond the bounds of the human body into the social environment.

Spatial intelligence: The bio psychological capacity to recognize and manipulate patterns in both wide spaces and confined areas.

Stereotype user model: A model used to represent the user's knowledge offering a quick assessment of the user's background knowledge. Stereotype user models can be used to classify a new user and initialize the state.

Structural linguistics: A model of language developed by Ferdinand de Saussure (1857–1913), based on the belief that meaning comes not from analyzing individual words but from considering the structure of a whole language.

Structuralism: A term credited to anthropologist Claude Levi-Strauss (1908-), who applied models of linguistic structure to the study of the customs and myths of society as a whole. Believing that individuals do not control the linguistic, sociological, and psychological structures that shape them and that can be uncovered through systematic investigation, structuralists moved away from the existentialist view that individuals are what they make themselves.

Symbolicism: A school of thought in cognitive science that employs what is now referred to as classicism, using symbolic processing to model thought processes.

Synchronous learning environments: Online learning systems that use audio or video conferencing (or a combination thereof) as their primary delivery modality to support live simultaneous interaction, similar to an in-person instructor-led classroom situation.

Teaching for understanding (TfU) framework: Educational methodology designed to assist teachers in course development. The starting point in teaching for understanding is to develop generative topics, topics that are central to a discipline, and understanding goals to provide focus to the instruction.

Theory of multiple intelligences: The cognitive theory, developed by Howard Gardner, that each individual possesses multiple intelligences rather than one single intelligence. Based on evidence from psychology, biology, and anthropology, Gardner delineates criteria used to define eight specific human intelligences: Linguistic, Logical-Mathematical, Bodily-Kinesthetic, Interpersonal, Intrapersonal, Musical, Spatial, and Naturalist. According to Gardner, these intelligences are both biological and learned or developed. Though everyone possesses these intelligences, individuals differ in which intelligences are more developed than others.

Thinking style: A preferred way of using a person's abilities according to how the individual likes to do something rather than how well he/she can actually carry out a task.

Throughlines: Ideas that are developed across the curriculum.

Understanding goals: What the teacher wants the students to learn; explicit and public goals that are focused on key concepts, methods, purposes, and forms of expression, as well as linked to assessment criteria.

User-adaptive system: An interactive computer system that adapts itself to current users, employing a user model for adaptation purposes.

User model: A component of an adaptive hypermedia application that represents such individual characteristics as the user's preferences, knowledge, goals, and navigation history and may include observations of the user's behavior while using the system.

Web-based online learning: Educational technology using computer-mediated communication facilities based on the World Wide Web.

Source: Extracted from MERIT publications and the Cognitive Early Warning Predictive System and courtesy of http://www.brainjolt.com/multi-intelligent-e-learning/glossary/

Bibliography

http://www.9-11commission.gov/report/
http://www.predictiveanalyticstoday.com/top-15-predictive-analytics-software/
http://www.gartner.com/it-glossary/predictive-analytics
http://spectrum.ieee.org/tech-talk/computing/software/predictive-analytics-and-deciding-who-should-receive-organ-transplants
https://www.cs.cmu.edu/~dmarg/Papers/PhD-Thesis-Margaritis.pdf
https://www.smartgrid.gov/the_smart_grid
http://bayes.cs.ucla.edu/BOOK-99/book-toc.html
http://ftp.cs.ucla.edu/pub/stat_ser/r350.pdf
http://stanford.edu/~ngoodman/papers/LTBC_psychreview_final.pdf
http://www.cs.ubc.ca/~murphyk/Bayes/bnintro.html
AI and human intelligence: https://techcrunch.com/2016/10/12/the-combination-of-human-and-artificial-intelligence-will-define-humanitys-future/
AI in engineering: https://globaljournals.org/GJRE_Volume12/6-Nanotechnology-and-Its-Impact-on-Modern-Computer.pdf
AI in cyber security: http://www.cyberisk.biz/application-artificial-intelligence-in-cyber-security/
NT and national security: http://www.heritage.org/defense/report/nanotechnology-and-national-security-small-changes-big-impact
Smartest cities http://freshome.com/2013/02/07/10-most-impressive-smart-cities-on-earth.
Advantages of nano grid: https://www.greenbiz.com/blog/2014/07/16/greenbiz-101-nothing-small-about-nanogrid-potentials

Chapter 10

Unique Features in Digital Immunity Infrastructure

Introduction

This chapter is a continuation of the previous chapter, but we're going to elaborate on the digital immunity (DI) infrastructure of the future. We call it DI infrastructure because it will be the most viable component to keep the Smart City safe and secure. Antivirus technologies (AVT) have not been able to overcome the flood of cybercrime attacks. In Chapter 4, we covered the problematic, even enigmatic, predicament of AVT. Cybercriminals have come up with ingenious attack strategies to humiliate cybersecurity guards. In today's cybersecurity landscape, it is not possible to prevent all attacks or breaches; today's attackers have significant funding, are patient and sophisticated, and target vulnerabilities in people and processes, as well as technology. Threat actors are constantly inventing new tools and techniques to enable them to get to the information they want and are getting better at identifying gaps and unknown vulnerabilities in an organization's security. The rule of thumb is *antivirus software can be ahead of all the virus writers, so other protection mechanisms should be acquired.*

Let's not forget a couple of things: first, any direct connection to the Internet can mean a direct link to attackers. Second, in the business world, companies are stuck with their preferred AVT vendor. Replacing AVT security software from one vendor to another is a monumental task with significant costs and labor time. Plus, cybercriminals will take advantage of the swap idle time to fire a couple of DDoS missiles. Experience tells us, all AVT vendors claim they are the best, but in fact, they all are selling the same molasses in a different jar.

On Thursday July 17, 2014, Mariette DiChristina, editor in chief and senior vice president of *Scientific American*, served as a witness at the US Senate Committee on Commerce, Science, and Transportation hearing stating "Science is the engine of human prosperity..." So, what is science?

Symbiotic Relation between Science and Technology

Science and technology are two interesting terms that have given us health, education, comfort living, and the misery of crime. Simply speaking, science is knowing, technology is doing. If we didn't have science, we wouldn't have technology. They are closely related by a mathematical relation, as shown below. Technology is the *derivative* of science with respect to time. The goal of *science* is the pursuit of knowledge for its own sake, while the goal of *technology* is to create products that solve problems and improve human life.

$$\text{Technology} = \frac{d(\text{Science})}{dt}$$

Building Blocks of Digital Immunity Infrastructure

Ray Kurzweil eloquently described the artificial intelligence (AI) component in DI as equivalent to the human nervous system: Nanobots are robots that will be the size of human blood cells (seven to eight microns) or even smaller. In his book Are We Spiritual Machines? (Chapter 1: the Evolution of Mind in the Twenty-First Century, 2001), Kurzweil asserted that 44 billion of them could travel through every brain capillary, scanning each relevant neural feature from up close. Using high-speed wireless communication, the nanobots would communicate wirelessly with one another and with computers compiling the brain-scan database. (In other words, the nanobots and computers will all be on a wireless local area network.) Nanobots will be able to travel through the bloodstream, then go in and around our cells and perform various services, such as removing toxins, sweeping out debris, correcting DNA errors, repairing and restoring cell membranes, reversing atherosclerosis, modifying the levels of hormones, neurotransmitters, and other metabolic chemicals, and a myriad of other tasks. For each aging process, we can describe a means for nanobots to reverse the process, down to the level of individual cells, cell components, and molecules.

In the next decade, the building blocks of DI will be made of nanotechnology components: cyborg nanobots, Smart Vaccine ™ nanobots (SVN), nano software, scaled to the molecular level; while Strong AI will offer highly dynamic and autonomous AI agents which will be comparable to the white cells fighters (B-cells, T-cells, memory cells, killer cells, eating cells), which are part of the human immune system. Within a decade, DI infrastructure will be real for Smart Cities.

DI will be a superintelligent machine that will surpass all the malicious cyber-crime activities in intelligence, speed, and efficacy, and will offer Smart Cities the most innovative nanobot-mediated cyber defense. The Smart Vaccine nanorobot army will be programmed to respond wirelessly to attack signals from cloud and grid nanobots, and activate the proper attack strategy. This may sound like science fiction, but given the intelligent exponential acceleration of cybercrime and cyber terrorism, technology will be compelled, under pressure, to respond and deliver DI to Smart Cities. The new superintelligent DI will transcend the limitations of human intelligence by one hundred billion fold.

It should be noted that the new paradigm shift of superintelligent machines will obey Kurzweil's law of accelerating returns, and let's not forget the famous word of caution from I. J. Good: "Let an ultraintelligent machine be defined as a machine that can far surpass all the intellectual activities of any man however clever. Since the design of machines is one of these intellectual activities, an ultraintelligent machine could design even better machines; there would then unquestionably be an 'intelligence explosion,' and the intelligence of man would be left far behind. Thus, the first ultraintelligent machine is the last invention that man need ever make."

If we look at the Internet today, we see a similar paradigm shift of accelerating returns that no one could control; we can only be concerned about its intelligence explosion. The Internet has become a massive inexorable juggernaut crushing anything in its path, or that refuses to disobey its rules.

The architecture of DI infrastructure is monolithic and much more than the sum of its parts. All its enabling technologies will be pathologically connected and will be dedicated to serve a specific function (Figure 10.1).

Today, DI does not exist because Computer Science engineers, CSOs, CIOs and four star CEOs couldn't see the similarities between the Human immune system and DI. Another reason that kept DI in the sarcophagus is that corporate and technology leaders do not know anything about our immune system. But, in the next decade, it will be the *de facto* intelligent defense or nanowall for Smart Cities. It will take a decade before we will be able to fuse Human Intelligence (HI) with machine intelligence at the molecular level. Presently, we do not have the luxury of having SVN that could travel through the nanogrid and enter the operating system (application and memory) and remove hacking locks, ransomware binary executable, rename foreign code, take a copy of the virus code, and block adversary cyborg nanobots from advancing or replicating themselves. In the future, all of this will happen without affecting the performance of the server. Only the system administrator would know about the progress of the fight and would relay the status to the other commanders.

In today's cybersecurity landscape, it is not possible to prevent *all* attacks or breaches. Today's cyberattackers are good software engineers, good planners, and

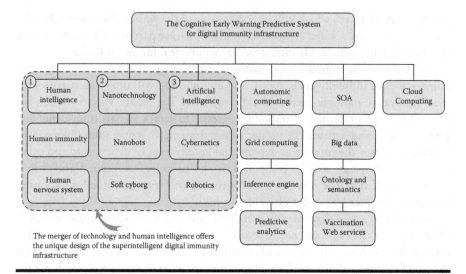

The merger of technology and human intelligence offers the unique design of the superintelligent digital immunity infrastructure

Figure 10.1 DI infrastructure is more than the sum of its parts. These technologies have all been fused into one homogenous infrastructure to create an ultra-intelligent defense system for the Smart City. 1- HI is the primary ingredient which offers the basic security knowledge mixed with AI and used to program SVN armies of the SVG. 2- Nanotechnology is a vital ingredient which is used in the miniaturization and creation the nanobots at the molecular level. 3- AI is responsible for creating the intelligent agents (nanobots) to build the DI infrastructure for the Smart City.

have significant funding. They target vulnerabilities in people as well as technology. The technology today is hysterically hell on wheels, running fast, and any organization that doesn't keep up with it will be left behind.

Advanced technologies offer new capabilities and benefits, but they also introduce new risks, and different technologies are being introduced every day, often outpacing the ability to properly assess risk. Whether the people who conduct these attacks are inside the organization or external to it, they use the technologies in place to their advantage.

DI is the Holy Grail of the Smart City's new generation of intelligent defense. It imposes a big burden of cybercrime lords who will end up with outdated weaponry. But, organized cybercrime will spend millions of dollars to hire money-thirsty software specialists to develop the latest and most advanced attacks. Cybercrime is the hybrid of cutting-edge technology and a Machiavellian mindset. *The Atlantic* magazine, in June 1, 2017, said

> U.S. intelligence agencies say Russian hackers interfered in the U.S. presidential election on behalf of Donald Trump, though they add there's no evidence to suggest those efforts succeeded. Separately,

congressional panels and the FBI are investigating figures close to President Trump for their links to Russia. Meanwhile European intelligence agencies have said Russia is using the same tactics in elections in France, the Netherlands, and Germany in favor of the populist candidates in those countries. Establishment-supported candidates won elections in France and the Netherlands. Germany's elections are in the fall, and Chancellor Angela Merkel is widely expected to win re-election.

Technology 1: Human Intelligence (The Thinking Machine)

In *Time* magazine, Kurzweil says that even though most of the people in the field think we're still several decades away from creating a human-level intelligence, he puts the date at 2029—less than 15 years away.

Kurzweil argues "we are already a human–machine civilization, we already use lower-level AI technology to diagnose disease, provide education, and develop new technologies. A kid in Africa with a smartphone has more intelligent access to knowledge than the President of the United States had 20 years ago."

We cannot put our brain on the shelf and embark on a wild AI goose chase. Time is the element that won't let us do everything at once. DI will be the masterpiece of our biological brain. New generations of the system will still need human navigation. There are two schools of thoughts: one that believes in 30 years, our brain will play second fiddle, and the other school of thought believes that there will be harmony between the biological brain and the AI brain.

Technology 2: Nanotechnology: SVN

Dr. Omid Farokhzad from Harvard Medical School said, "Nanotechnology allows us to do things we are unable to do otherwise. Nanotechnology gives us a 'set of tools.'" Indeed, we will harness nanotechnology to create a new cybersecurity paradigm. In the next two decades, nanotechnology will offer a new era of *nanocomputing*. For example, programmable nanochips could be a formidable defense barricade for corporate servers. These nanochips will have wire connected to surface acoustic wave nanosensors, or guided-mode resonance sensors, to catch anything that would penetrate the data center wirelessly or electronically.

Sequence of Battle between Soft Cyborgs and SVN

Here is the sequence of events of the battle between DDoS soft cyborgs (attackers) and between the SVN army shown in Figure 10.2:

1. DDoS soft cyborgs zombies are approaching the City Smart Grid (CSG) for a massive attack to paralyze the machine-to-machine (M2M) network on the CSG.
2. An alert is issued by the CSG coordination center to the DI Central Coordination Center.
3. The DI coordination center mobilizes an army of SVN to the CSG.
4. SVN get ready to join their partners who are in the CSG patrolling and vaccinating all the systems against a variety of payload.
5. Multiple SVN battalions are heading toward the city, through encrypted wireless and satellite channels.
6. The Smart City coordination center has taken the proper actions to protect the M2M devices on the CSG.
7. The SVN armies confront the soft cyborgs and captures most of them. They will be quarantined, and a sample will be sent to the forensics lab for reverse engineering. The attacks never reached the M2M devices. The SVN learned how the attack payload was developed and learned the strategy of the attack. The SVN adds the strategy of attack to their nanochip library, and at the same time the Virus Knowledge Base (ViKB) acquired more detail about the attack.
8. Autonomically, M2M devices go back to normal and all sensors go back to collecting data.
9. Lesson learned, but the Smart City grid will keep getting massive attacks. Citizens will be educated how to protect the critical devices.

Internet of Nano Things

The Internet of Things (IoT) is a galaxy of interconnected clouds connecting everything to everything else in Smart Cities. It did not fall from the sky, but we created it and now we need to seriously think about. IoT is the most viable technology for Smart Cities, and will certainly benefit from nanochip technology. In the next two decades, IoT devices will be much more sophisticated, molecular, more ergonomic, and come with advanced smart defense circuitry. The interconnection of nanosensors and nanodevices with Internet has led to development of next generation standards based on IoT called "Internet of Nano Things" (IoNT). The integration of nanoscale devices with exiting traditional communication networks with high-speed Internet has led to a new evolution which is termed as IoNT; this will comprise of miniature sensors connected to each other via nano networks to obtain data from objects. So, in turn IoNT will open new doors of research in the area of nanosensors, nano communication, and nanodevices.

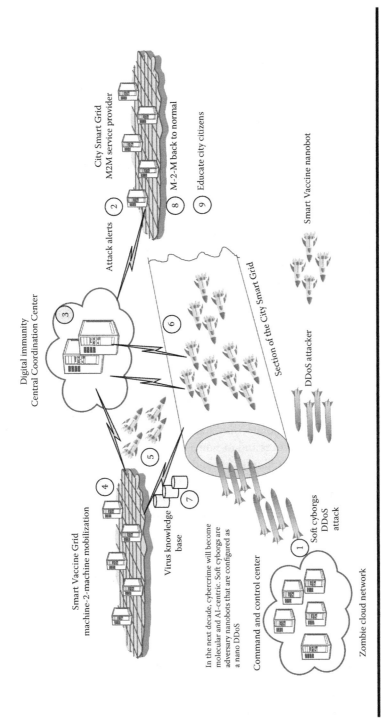

Figure 10.2 **The City Smart Nano Grid is a layered grid with lots of intelligence to manage all the Smart City resources. The figure shows a cross-section of the City Smart Nano Grid (300nm) and a snapshot of the SVN, launched to intercept the attacking soft-cyborgs. We can say that the SVN are the B-cells of DI. (© Copyright 2015, Dr. Rocky Termanini. All rights reserved.)**

The trend and evolution of IoT amazingly coincides with Ray Kurzweil's of evolution theory in his famous book *The Singularity Is Near*. "If you cannot visualize how IoT looks, think of a massive snowball rolling downhill and growing at geometric pace. Or, just look at the sky on a clear night and imagine all these stars are connected together." Now you have the picture of IoT. It comes in three categories:

Category 1: The Home Area Nano Network (HANN)

This is a new emerging technology that connects everything at home as one network with IoT service providers. This is an awesome technology with several tangible benefits. In the next two decades, HANN will be using nanotechnology-nano communication applications plus avail of the merger of Human technology with HI. Homes will be operating automatically and responsively with smart devices. Call it the house of the future.

This is the first incentive to adopt IoT, where all the electric, electronic, solar, and hydro are connected into a home network with systematic sensors to collect operation data and transmit it to the utility providers in Smart Cities. There's a new technology around the corner called "IoNT" which is the next generation of IoT. The main incentives are economic and using standards. Figure 10.3 shows the basic diagram of the HANN with explanatory annotation:

1. The first effort is to connect all the in-home digital devices, such as PCs, mobile phones, entertainment technology, thermostats, home security systems, and smart appliances, into a common network. In the context of energy utilities, HANN is a means for utility companies to extend their reach beyond the meter, and to incorporate the "smart thermostat," direct load control appliances, smart appliances and in-home energy display into utility systems, as well as to enable demand response and energy-efficiency programs.

2. HANN will be connected to a bus of wireless sensors made of nanotechnology circuitry. Each connected device will have its own input. Sensors will transmit data that the receiving end meter will understand.

3. A home monitoring system is a necessary item, to make sure all sensors and devices are working. Checking the system before leaving the house puts the residents ahead of the danger curve.

4. A typical residential gateway. A single Internet connection is shared by multiple HANN devices connected through a modem or WAN to the City's Smart Cloud. The gateway is connected to the Smart Vaccine grid (SVG) and is secured 100%.

5. The SV Nano Grid (SVNG) is an integral part of the Smart City. SVN are guarding the grid and roaming around for hidden nano cyborg trojans.

6. Raw sensor data will be sent wirelessly be sent to Supervisory Control and Data Acquisition (SCADA), for distillation and normalization. While the SV system (CEWPS) is monitoring the transfer of data.

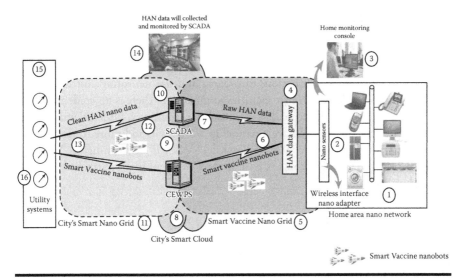

Figure 10.3 Category 1 HANN: Homes will have smart devices and appliances connected to a Home Area Network. The convenience, availability, and reliability of externally-managed cloud computing resources continues to become an appealing choice for many home-dwellers without interest or experience in IT. (© 2014 MERIT CyberSecurity Group. All rights reserved.)

7. SCADA is a control system that uses Programmable Logic Controllers (PLC) which they connect to the gateway and the sensor bus. SCADA collects the HANN data for editing and reformatting, and sends it encrypted to the Smart City utility system where meters will calculate the consumption of energy and the utilization of home devices

8. The city has also a private cloud where HANN data can be stored as an alternative to the city grid.

9. CEWPS system is monitoring the city grid, and collecting information on the activities of the SVN.

10. The city nanogrid and the SV Nano Grid are interlaced and pathologically connected.

11. A squadron of SVN roam around the city grid, looking for soft cyborg trojans.

12. The encrypted data from SCADA and CEWPS ends up in the city utility meter system.

13. Cloud SCADA tightly connect both grids for additional operation management.

14. The meters of IoNT keep track of all the data generated from the HANNs.

15. The Smart City utility meter system generate reports to the central communication center (CCC) of the city.

Category 2: HealthCare Wearable Nanodevice Network (H2M)

Citizens will be wearing devices with molecular nanochip implants that will monitor, analyze, and regulate functions of organs, and use neurotransmitters to send patient data to central health care facilities to make sure there is no epidemic in the city. Figure 10.4 shows the criticality of a blackout in the city. DI SVN will quickly respond. All the devices will have a nanochip which will add more functionalities and security shown in Figure 10.5. Meanwhile, SVN will be roaming the Wearable Device Network (WDN), which is part of the CSG, looking for attackers and collecting battle data.

Category 3: Machine-to-Machine (M2M)

This is going to be the most influential paradigm shift in the history of Smart Cities. The new generation of IoT was developed with nanotechnology, which is a thousand time more efficient than the older generation of IoT. M2M will benefit from the new IoNT which will offer better data collection, data security, and telecom connectivity.

The interconnection of M2M nanodevices will securely be welded into the CSG and connected to the SVG for the most intelligent nano defense and prompt adaptive immunization. Here's a partial list:

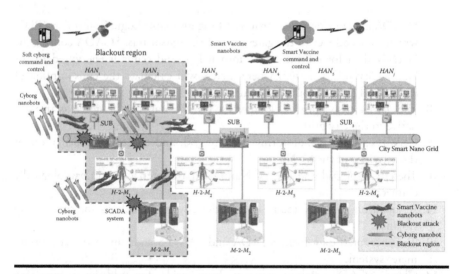

Figure 10.4 The SVN are the B-cells of DI. We represent them as black jets for illustration purpose. They respond to an alert from Command and Control. The Satellite has intercepted a message from the adversary satellite. The attack intended to black out the whole city, but SVN were able to neutralize the adversary cyborg nanobots. (© 2014 MERIT CyberSecurity Group. All rights reserved.)

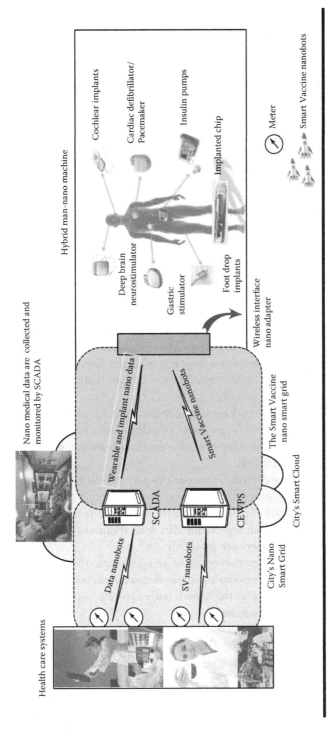

Figure 10.5 Category 2 Man–Nano Machine: Smart wearable and implant medical devices will be securely collected and monitored by SCADA with the gracious support of CEWPS/SV. The integrity and security of the medical data will be one of the biggest advantages of IoT; DI will be the Holy Grail. HIPAA will eventually recommend DI even it will a mandatory requirement for the health care industry. Don't be surprised!

- Business machines
- Office computer equipment
- Telecom connectivity to Internet and the cloud
- Medical equipment (life threatening)
- Driverless cars, metros, drones, airplanes, and control towers
- Interface sensors: These are the components of 'things' that gather and/or disseminate data — be it on location, altitude, velocity, temperature, illumination, motion, power, humidity, blood sugar, air quality, soil moisture … you name it.
- Central servers
- Local scanning devices
- Knowledge engines and storage databases
- Power substations

M2M will rely on an IoNT interconnection tool. Nanobots are communicating with the machines, collecting data, while the SVN are roaming the CSG looking for adversary nanobots, routine vaccinations, and wirelessly reporting progress to the DI CCC. Here are some of the new components of IoNT:

1. Nano-nodes: Nano-nodes are regarded as the smallest and simplest nano-machines which perform various tasks like computation and transmission if the data over short distances and have less memory. Considering body sensor networks, biological sensors fitted in the human body are considered as nano-nodes.
2. Nano-routers: Nano-routers have large computational power as compared to nano-nodes and they act as aggregators of information coming from nano-nodes. Nano-routers also play crucial role in controlling nano-nodes by exchange control commands.
3. Nano-Micro interface devices: These devices perform the task of aggregation of information coming from nano-routers and transmit it to the microscale and vice versa. They act as hybrid devices to communicate in nanoscale using nano communication techniques and also with traditional communication networks with classical network protocols.
4. Gateway: It enables the remote control of an entire nano things network over the Internet. Example: Consider a body sensor network, with the use of gateway. All the sensor data from the human body can be accessed anywhere and everywhere via doctors over the Internet.

All Smart City machines will also be equipped with a nanochip to facilitate secure communication with one another, and report any problems to the city coordination center. M2M will rely on nanotechnology as much as the Internet and the cloud.

Figure 10.6 is a true representation of a nano battle scenario on the cloud. We have the soft cyborg (DDoS) and the SVN, defending three Smart City virtual

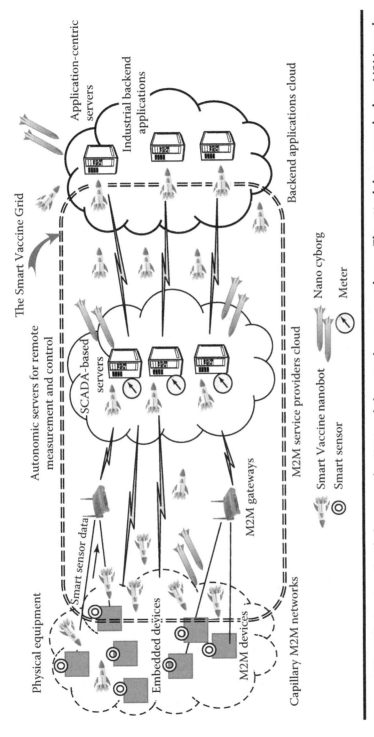

Figure 10.6 **This is a true battle between the SVN and the attackers nano cyborgs. The attack is occurred when M2M service providers are collecting sensor data from the Smart City machines. The SVN were launched from the SVG and intercepted the attackers. It is like the B-Cells defeating attacking pathogens.**

clouds. The first one is the M2M network with sensors, the second one SCADA data collectors cloud which collect data from the M2M net. The third cloud is the backend applications that process the refined data. The following sequence explanation offers more detail on the battle.

1. The M2M embedded devices work peacefully and each device sensor will transmit data to the data collectors in the second cloud.
2. The M2M devices get vaccinated routinely by the SVN, and roam around the cloud for preempted attack
3. M2M sensor data is sent either wirelessly or through modems (using the Internet) to the collecting systems.
4. Sensor data will be metered and normalized for each device.
5. Any attack from the DDoS soft cyborgs will be detected and a squadron of Smart Vaccine (SV) fighters will show up on the battle field.
6. Sensor data will transfer to the SCADA systems which runs autonomically. Data will be transferred back to the appropriate backend application, future demand will be predicted. Summary reports will go to the city coordination center.
7. Attach statistics and the outcome will be analyzed and sent to the DI central coordination for further attack learning and preparation.
8. DDoS attack with nano soft cyborgs will try to raid the SCADA systems. A battle will rage between the SVN and the nano cyborgs. The SVG will protect the Smart City and all nano cyborgs will be taken hostage and cannibalized.
9. Encrypted metered data from SCADA will be sent to the backend applications, under the protection of a squadron of SVN.
10. The SVN roam around the backend application cloud for routine vaccination and make sure that no adversary cyborgs are around for hidden attacks. Although the backend application cloud will be attacked, all battles will be documented and recursive training will give the SVN augmented battle experience and knowledge.
11. The SVG (in dashed line) covers all the three clouds of the Smart City.

Technology 3: Artificial Intelligence, the Ultra-Intelligent Machine

On YouTube, there's an interesting video clip of a cheetah traying to chase a gazelle, where the cat's speed is 75 mph, and the gazelle's top speed is 60 mph. The cheetah closes in on the gazelle, and when the distance between them becomes just a couple of yards, a man running at a speed exceeding 80 mph, grabs the scared gazelle and runs away with it, outpacing the tired cat who stopped, out of breath. We believe there will be a time where man will be able to run 100 yards in 4 seconds!

In 2045, with the help of AI and nanotechnology, the human brain will be augmented. The result will be an exponential speed in processing and storing information one million fold, thus, superintelligence will be formed. The brain will be able to receive sensory neural signals and respond by sending motor neural signals one billionth of a second to the sprinting muscles: quadriceps, hamstrings, glutes, hip flexors, and calves. Intermuscular coordination will also be enhanced one billion-fold. All the problems associated with geometrical and anatomical constraints associated with the transformation of joint rotations, would be resolved including upper leg extension and plantar flexion. The muscle coordination pattern is characterized by a proximo to distal sequence in timing of the monoarticular muscles. Athletes in the next two decades, will redefine the events in the Olympic Games, and new more befitting events will replace the legacy ones.

AI is developing at a staggering pace, and will have the potential to exceed human intelligence within the next 45 years.

Building the Digital Immunity (DI) Infrastructure

"We are now in a position to speed up the learning process by a factor of thousands or millions once again by migrating from biological to nonbiological intelligence. Once a digital neocortex learns a skill, it can transfer that know-how in minutes or even seconds. Ultimately, we will create an artificial neocortex that has the full range and flexibility of its human counterpart."

Ray Kurzweil

"Some people worry that artificial intelligence will make us feel inferior, but then, anybody in his right mind should have an inferiority complex every time he looks at a flower."

Alan Kay

One of the biggest achievements of man, aside from landing on the moon, is to create a digital replica of his brain, and discover what biological intelligence is, and ultimately reaching non-biological superintelligence. We're not there yet. The three words: Brain, intelligence, and mind will be reverse engineered with two decades. The arduous conquest is to build the super intelligent man. Thus, the first ultra-intelligent machine is the last invention that man need ever make.

Anatomy of Digital Immunity (DI)'s Main Components

DI comes with an arsenal of offensive and defensive systems. It is designed specifically to defend, by offense, Smart Cities and large metropolitan areas. The system is in fact an incredible "brain" that controls a multitude of autonomic subsystems that reside on a nanogrid. We often describe this with different configurations, depending on the subject and the content. Figure 10.7 shows how the nine intelligent subsystems headed by the Central Coordination Center (CCC), which acts as the nervous center and control hub.

If we could reverse-engineer the brain and create a superintelligent one, why can't we replicate the Human immune system to create Digital Immune System (DIS) counterpart, for the digital world? DIS is not only an intelligent system, it is a complete infrastructure. The superintelligent DI will replicate the complexity of the Human immune system and recursively will enhance itself with a better DIS.

If we look today at the state-of-the-health of the digital world, we find that the 32% of computers around the world are infected with viruses and malware (malicious software), according to Panda Security. The concept of malware took root in the technology industry, and examples of viruses and worms began to appear on Apple and IBM personal computers in the early 1980s before becoming popularized following the introduction of the World Wide Web and the commercial Internet in the 1990s. Now we have a juggernaut roaming the skies of the Internet slamming right and left everything in its way.

In the next two decades, the number of infected computers will follow an exponential curve, with much more advanced attacks using AI and nanotechnologies. Attacks will also be superintelligent, robotic and cybernetic, while the AVT is moving linearly way behind. A DI machine, will be the Holy Grail to conquer malware. We all know the famous quote "Those who do not learn history are doomed to repeat it"(Figure 10.8).

Speaking of history that we must all remember: During the plague of Athens in 430 BC. The historian Thucydides noted, that people who had recovered from a previous bout of the disease could nurse the sick without contracting the illness a second time. It took 23 centuries of human misery until Edward Jenner discovered the Smallpox vaccine in 1796 AD. Figure 10.9 shows the timeline of the adaptive human immunity pioneers.

The Amazing Reality of the Nanobot

With DI, we're introducing not just a concept, but a complete architecture that will adopted in the near future. No, DI is not science fiction. When Wi-Fi (which is short for Wireless Fidelity) was invented in 1991, it was like magic. Wi-Fi offered wireless networking capability that allows computers, mobile

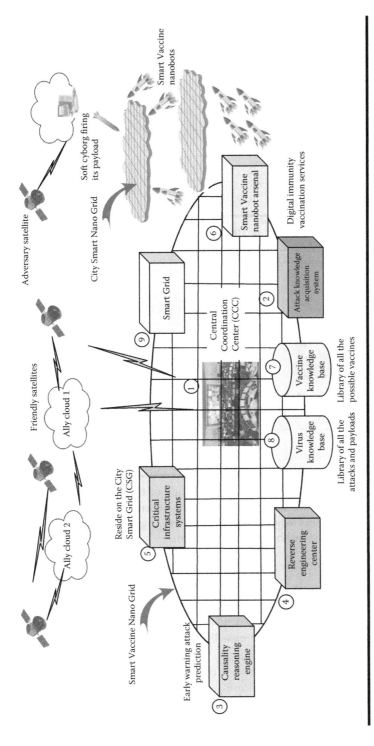

Figure 10.7 The DI infrastructure with all its vital components that operate together to protect the Smart City nanogrid. The pathological integration of 9 unique operating components are equally critical. They receive commands from the central coordination center. During an attack, all the nano armies of SVs (B-Cells) are mobilized and fight together. Their main focus is to protect the critical systems from the attack by vaccination and, at the same time, capture the virus and determine its identity and save it for the next attack. (© 2014 MERIT CyberSecurity Group. All rights reserved.)

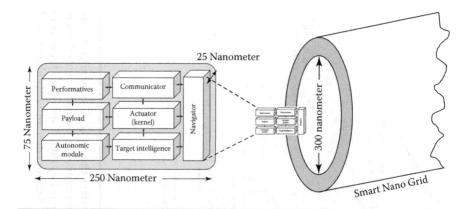

Figure 10.8 The smart nanogrid is 1000 times wider than the nanochip of a cyborg or SV. The nanobots can roam inside the blood and nerve vessels. (© 2014 MERIT CyberSecurity Group. All rights reserved.)

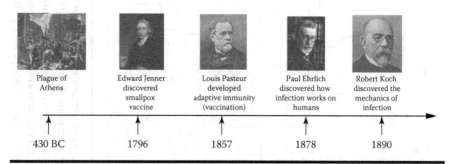

Figure 10.9 A timeline of the pioneers of the study of the human immune system. Not only were they life savers, but humanity savers. No reward could be enough for these crusaders who defied the reaper. Digital immunity will also bring prosperity and peace to the rest of the world.

phones, iPads, game consoles, and other devices to communicate over a "wireless" signal. It was indispensable magic that we cannot live without. Bluetooth is another "disruptive" technology that unites electronic devices, PCs, and cellular industries with a short-range wireless link. Let's not talk about the Internet because it is the mother of all paradigms. Even the prophets 2000 years ago talked about it, but no one understood it then. We all know that "necessity is the mother of invention and stagnation is the father." Actually, social necessity is the driving force behind scientific problem solving. In the case of cybercrime, the remarkable advances in cybercrime and terrorism is the driving force behind the invention of DI.

We consider nanotechnology and AI as two Rosetta stones (not just one) to step into the future and start a new revolution for nano defense technology. Now we are a decade ahead of the AVT. The Holy Grail now is the nanobot.

So, just what is so great about having a robot that measures only six atoms across? We're using nanotechnology to develop the SVN. These magical software objects will keep all the systems in Smart City safe and fully operative. The secret here is that Smart City will be equipped with a nanogrid instead of a conventional grid. Nanogrid is actually the new generation of intelligent grids. No DDoS or any other viral attack will be able to sneak into the nanogrid. The SVN will be the B-cell of the grid and will trap any adversary nano cyborgs. In the next decade, DI with its SVN army will revolutionize cyber defense. All the AVT vendors will hop on the DI bandwagon.

The virus is the most important and diabolical invention of the 21st century. It is the mastery of a new breed of creative "nerds of the third kind," who can hatch an ingenious piece of code to create a technological holocaust for millions of people. He can do it for money, for political or religious reasons.

The first PC virus, *Brain*, appeared in 1986. It was a boot-sector virus which works by modifying the first sector on floppy disks. The infected floppy executes and loads its code into memory, as soon as it is loaded. It doesn't have to be a system disk: any disk will do. The software called BIOS detects the disk in drive A and automatically loads whatever infected code is in the boot sector. The user realizes they've tried to boot from the floppy disk by mistake when they see the message "Non-system disk or disk error, replace and press any key when read." They then remove the disk and continue working, suspecting nothing about what has just happened. The malicious code is already in RAM waiting for the kill.

In today's world of big data, where 2.5 quintillion bytes of data is produced every day, knowing how AI systems capture data, synthesize it, and use it to drive reasoning is most important. The application of these systems to issues of *big data* is what allows us to transform the world of numbers that the machines control into a world of knowledge and insight that we can use.

There's an arduous conquest today to use AI and nanotechnology in the replication of HI to create the digital counterpart. It will take the synergism of hundreds of experts to move from this model to a better version. From Windows 1 (November 20, 1985) to Windows 10 it took 29 years of evolution. Apple Macintosh was born in 1989 and evolved to become the magic iPad Pro in 2017. This a crude analogy but we get the idea. There are lots of hurdles and booby traps along the way. The cockpit dashboard will get perfected and become more AI and nanotechnology centric. Figure 10.10 displays the futuristic trajectory of DIS.

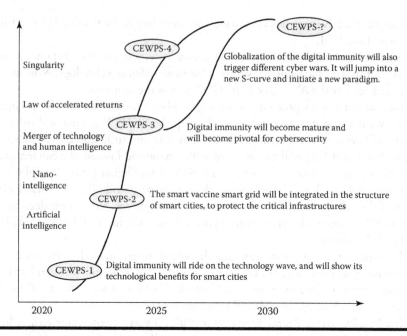

Figure 10.10 No product has ever reached its perfection status after its final assembly and rollout. It is going to take 10 years of maturity before DI reaches perfection. DI for Smart Cities will go through labor pains before an ongoing exponential sequence of cascaded S-curves. (© 2014 MERIT CyberSecurity Group. All rights reserved.)

Glossary

3D printing: A process for making a physical object from a three-dimensional digital model, typically by laying down many successive thin layers of a material.

4th industrial revolution: Or Industry 4.0, is a collective term embracing a number of contemporary automation, data exchange and manufacturing technologies.

Abolitionism: An ethical ideology based upon a perceived obligation to use technology to eliminate involuntary suffering in all sentient life.

Accelerating change: A perceived increase in the rate of technological (and sometimes social and cultural) progress throughout history, which may suggest faster and more profound change in the future.

Anthropocene: Relating to or denoting the current geological age, viewed as the period during which human activity has been the dominant influence on climate and the environment.

Arcology: A portmanteau of "architecture" and "ecology," is a field of creating architectural design principles for very densely populated, ecologically low-impact human habitats.

Artificial general intelligence (AGI): The intelligence of a (hypothetical) machine that could successfully perform any intellectual task that a human being can. It is a primary goal of AI research and an important topic for science fiction writers and futurists.

Artificial intelligence (AI): The theory and development of computer systems able to perform tasks that normally require HI, such as visual perception, speech recognition, decision making, and translation between languages.

Artificial life: The production or action of computer programs or computerized systems that simulate the behavior, population dynamics, or other characteristics of living organisms.

Algorithm: A process or set of rules to be followed in calculations, or other problem-solving operations, especially by a computer.

Android: A robot with a human appearance.

Astronomy: The branch of science that deals with celestial objects, space, and the physical universe as a whole.

Astrophysics: The branch of astronomy concerned with the physical nature of stars and other celestial bodies, and the application of the laws and theories of physics to the interpretation of astronomical observations.

Augmented reality: A live direct or indirect view of a physical, real-world environment whose elements are *augmented* (or supplemented) by computer-generated sensory input such as sound, video, graphics, or GPS data.

Automation: The technique, method, or system of operating or controlling a process by highly automatic means, as by electronic devices, reducing human intervention to a minimum..

Autonomous vehicle: A motor vehicle that uses AI, sensors, and GPS coordinates to drive itself without the active intervention of a human operator.

Basic Income/UBI: A proposed system of social security in which all citizens or residents of a country regularly receive an unconditional sum of money, either from a government or some other public institution, in addition to any income received from elsewhere.

Behavioral science: The scientific study of human and animal behavior.

Big data: A blanket term for any collection of data sets so large and complex that it becomes difficult to process using on-hand database management tools or traditional data processing applications.

Biohacking: The activity of exploiting genetic material experimentally without regard to accepted ethical standards, or for criminal purposes.

Bioinformatics: The science of collecting and analyzing complex biochemical and biological data using mathematics and computer science, as in the study of genomes.

Bioprinting: The 3D printing of biological tissue and organs through the layering of living cells.

Biotechnology: The exploitation of biological processes for industrial and other purposes, especially the genetic manipulation of microorganisms for the production of antibiotics, hormones, and so on.

Blockchain: A decentralized, free-to-access, distributed public database that maintains a continuously growing list of data records that are unchangeable even by operators of the data store's nodes.

Brain–computer interface (BCI): Also known as mind–machine interface (MMI), direct neural interface (DNI), or brain–machine interface (BMI), is a system that allows signals from the brain to direct some external computer or other electronic device.

Carbon nanotube: Large molecules of pure carbon that are long and thin and shaped like tubes, about 1–3 nanometers (1 nm = 1 billionth of a meter) in diameter, and hundreds to thousands of nanometers long.

Chatbot: A computer program designed to simulate conversation with human users, especially over the Internet.

Claytronics: An abstract concept that combines nanoscale robotics and computer science to create individual nanometer-scale computers called claytronic atoms, or catoms, which can interact with each other to form tangible 3D objects that a user can interact with.

Cloud computing: The practice of using a network of remote servers hosted on the Internet to store, manage, and process data, rather than a local server or a personal computer.

Cognitive computing: The simulation of human thought processes in a computerized model. Cognitive computing involves self-learning systems that use data mining, pattern recognition, and natural language processing to mimic the way the human brain works.

Cognitive liberty: Or the "right to mental self-determination" is the freedom of an individual to control his or her own mental processes, cognition, and consciousness.

Cognitive science: The study of thought, learning, and mental organization, which draws on aspects of psychology, linguistics, philosophy, and computer modeling.

Computational biology: The development and application of data-analytical and theoretical methods, mathematical modeling, and computational simulation techniques to the study of biological, behavioral, and social systems.

Computer vision: A field that includes methods for acquiring, processing, analyzing, and understanding images and, in general, high-dimensional data from the real world in order to produce numerical or symbolic information.

Connectome: A comprehensive map of neural connections in the brain, and may be thought of as its "wiring diagram". More broadly, a connectome would include the mapping of all neural connections within an organism's nervous system.

Cosmology: The science of the origin and development of the universe. Modern astronomy is dominated by the Big Bang theory, which brings together observational astronomy and particle physics.

CRISPR: An RNA-guided gene-editing platform that makes use of a bacterially derived protein (Cas9) and a synthetic guide RNA to introduce a double strand break at a specific location within the genome.

Crowdsourcing: The process of obtaining needed services, ideas, or content by soliciting contributions from a large group of people, and especially from an online community, rather than from traditional employees or suppliers.

Cryonics: The low-temperature preservation of humans who cannot be sustained by contemporary medicine, with the hope that healing and resuscitation may be possible in the future.

Cryptocurrency: A digital currency in which encryption techniques are used to regulate the generation of units of currency and verify the transfer of funds, operating independently of a central bank.

Cybernetics: The science of communication and control theory that is concerned especially with the comparative study of automatic control systems (as the nervous system and brain and mechanical-electrical communication systems).

Cyborg: Short for cybernetic organism, it is a piece of software at the molecule scale with the intelligence of a fighter. It is used a zombie in DDoS attacks.

Data science: The extraction of knowledge from large volumes of data that are structured or unstructured, which is a continuation of the field data mining and predictive analytics, also known as knowledge discovery and data mining.

Deep learning: A set of algorithms in machine learning that attempt to model high-level abstractions in data by using architectures composed of multiple non-linear transformations.

Digital currency: An Internet-based form of currency or medium of exchange (i.e., distinct from physical, such as banknotes and coins) that exhibits properties similar to physical currencies, however, allows for instantaneous transactions and borderless transfer-of-ownership.

Digital health: The use of digital technologies such as wireless sensors, smartphones, social networks, and so on. combined with personal health and genetic information to improve the efficiency of health-care, and make medicine more personalized and precise.

Digital immortality: Or "virtual immortality," or "immortality in silico" is storing a person's personality in a more durable media, that is., a computer, and allowing it to communicate with people in the future.

Digital native: A person born or brought up during the age of digital technology and therefore familiar with computers and the Internet from an early age.

Disruptive technology: Any enhanced or completely new technology that helps create a new market and value network that eventually disrupts the traditional business methods and practices, rendering it obsolete.

Dyson sphere: A hypothetical megastructure that completely encompasses a star and captures most or all of its power output.

Emerging technologies: Technologies that are perceived as capable of changing the status quo. These include a variety of technologies such as educational technology, information technology, nanotechnology, biotechnology, cognitive science, robotics, and AI.

Electronic sports (esports): Organized multiplayer video game competitions. The most common video game genres associated with electronic sports are real-time strategy, fighting, first-person shooter, and multiplayer online battle arena.

Existential risk: A hypothetical future event with the potential to inflict serious damage to human well-being on a global scale.

Exoplanet: A planet that orbits a star outside the solar system.

Exponential growth: Growth whose rate becomes ever more rapid in proportion to the growing total number or size.

Extropianism: An evolving framework of values and standards for continuously improving the human condition. Extropians believe that advances in science and technology will someday let people live indefinitely.

Fermi(s) paradox: The apparent contradiction between high estimates of the probability of the existence of extraterrestrial civilization and humanity's lack of contact with, or evidence for, such civilizations.

Friendly artificial intelligence (friendly AI): A hypothetical artificial general intelligence (AGI) that would have a positive rather than negative effect on humanity.

Fusion: Also called nuclear fusion, a thermonuclear reaction in which atomic nuclei of low atomic number fuse to form a heavier nucleus with the release of energy.

Future shock: Physical and psychological distress or disorientation caused by a person's inability to cope with very rapid social and technological change.

Futurology: The study of postulating possible, probable, and preferable future(s), especially from present trends or developments in science, technology, political or social structures, and so on.

Gene therapy: The transplantation of usually genetically altered genes into cells, especially to replace defective genes in the treatment of genetic disorders or to provide a specialized disease-fighting function.

Genetic engineering: The manipulation of DNA to produce new types of organisms, usually by inserting or deleting genes.

Genetically modified organism (GMO): Any organism whose genetic material has been altered using genetic engineering techniques. GMOs are the source of genetically modified foods and are also widely used in scientific research and to produce goods other than food.

Genomics: The branch of molecular biology concerned with the structure, function, evolution, and mapping of genomes.

Genome: The complete set of genes or genetic material present in a cell or organism.

Genome Sequencing: A laboratory process that determines the complete DNA sequence of an organism's genome at a single time.

Geoengineering: The deliberate large-scale manipulation of an environmental process that affects the Earth's climate, in an attempt to counteract the effects of global warming.

Gerontology: The study of the social, psychological, and biological aspects of aging.

Gig economy: An environment in which temporary positions are common and organizations contract with independent workers for short-term engagements.

Global brain: A conceptualization of the worldwide network formed by all the people on this planet together with the information and communication technologies that connect them into an intelligent, self-organizing system.

Graphene: An allotrope of carbon in the form of a two-dimensional, atomic-scale, hexagonal lattice in which one atom forms each vertex.

Grey goo: A hypothetical end-of-the-world scenario involving molecular nanotechnology in which out-of-control self-replicating robots consume all matter on Earth while building more of themselves, a scenario that has been called ecophagy (eating the environment).

Heat death: Of the universe, a state of uniform distribution of energy within a physical system toward a state of maximum entropy, especially viewed as a possible fate of the universe. It is a corollary of the second law of thermodynamics.

Human augmentation: The application of technology to overcome physical or mental limitations of the body, resulting in the temporary or permanent augmentation of a person's abilities and features.

Hyperconnected: The increasing digital interconnection of people (and things) characterized by the widespread or habitual use of devices that have Internet connectivity.

Information Age: Also known as the Computer Age, Digital Age, or New Media Age, a period in human history characterized by the shift from traditional industry that the industrial revolution brought through industrialization, to an economy based on information computerization.

Information technology (IT): The application of computers and telecommunications equipment to store, retrieve, transmit, and manipulate data.

Intelligence amplification (IA): Also referred to as cognitive augmentation and machine augmented intelligence refers to the effective use of information technology in augmenting human intelligence.

Internet of Things (IoT): A proposed development of the Internet in which everyday objects have network connectivity, allowing them to send and receive data.

In vitro: Of a process, performed or taking place in a test tube, culture dish, or elsewhere outside a living organism.

Kardashev scale: A method of measuring a civilization's level of technological advancement, based on the amount of energy a civilization is able to utilize. The scale has three designated categories: Type I, II, and III.

Law of Accelerating Returns: The "returns" of an evolutionary process (such as the speed, cost-effectiveness, or overall "power" of a process) that increase exponentially over time—both for biology and technology.

Life extension science: The study of slowing down or reversing the processes of aging to extend both the maximum and average lifespan.

Li-Fi: A bidirectional, high-speed and fully networked wireless communication technology that uses light-emitting diodes (LEDs) for data transmission.

Machine learning: A subfield of computer science which focuses on the development of algorithms that can learn from and make predictions on data without being explicitly programmed.

Massive open online course (MOOC): A free Web-based distance learning program that is designed for the participation of large numbers of geographically dispersed students.

Materials science: An interdisciplinary field which deals with the study of matter and their properties; as well as the discovery and design of new materials.

Memristor: A type of resistor in which the flow of electrical current in an electronic circuit is determined by the amount of charge that has previously flowed through it.

Metamaterial: A synthetic composite material with a structure such that it exhibits properties not usually found in natural materials, especially a negative refractive index.

Metaverse: A collective virtual shared space, created by the convergence of virtually enhanced physical reality and physically persistent virtual space, including the sum of all virtual worlds, augmented reality, and the Internet.

Mixed reality: The merging of real world and virtual worlds to produce a new environment where physical and digital objects can coexist and interact.

Molecular biology: The branch of biology that deals with the molecular basis of biological activity. It chiefly concerns itself with understanding the interactions between the various systems of a cell, including the interactions between the different types of DNA, RNA, and protein biosynthesis as well as learning how these interactions are regulated.

Molecular manufacturing: A branch of nanotechnology that involves the use of nanoscale (extremely small) tools and non-biological processes to build structures, devices, and systems at the molecular level.

Moore's law: The observation that, over the history of computing hardware, the number of transistors on integrated circuits doubles approximately every two years. This has also been used to suggest exponential increases in "total computing power," "calculations per second," or "calculations per watt of power."

Morphological freedom: A proposed civil right of a person to either maintain or modify their own body, on their own terms, through informed, consensual recourse to, or refusal of, available therapeutic or enabling medical technology.

Nanofactory: A proposed compact molecular manufacturing system, possibly small enough to sit on a desktop, that could build a diverse selection of large-scale atomically precise diamondoid products.

Nanotechnology: The manipulation of matter on an atomic, molecular, and supramolecular scale.

Neural lace: An electronic mesh sensor that integrates with cerebral matter and enables the interaction of neurons with computers.

Neural network: A computer system modeled on the human brain and nervous system.

Neural prosthesis: Any electronic and/or mechanical device that connects with the nervous system and supplements or replaces functions lost by disease or injury.

Neuroscience: Any or all of the sciences, such as neurochemistry and experimental psychology, which deal with the structure or function of the nervous system and brain.

Noosphere: A postulated sphere or stage of evolutionary development dominated by consciousness, the mind, and interpersonal relationships.

Nootropics: Also referred to as *smart drugs, memory enhancers, neuroenhancers, cognitive enhancers*, and *intelligence enhancers*, they are drugs, supplements, nutraceuticals, and functional foods that purportedly improve mental functions such as cognition, memory, intelligence, motivation, attention, and concentration.

Open data: Data that can be freely used, re-used and redistributed by anyone without restrictions from copyright, patents, or other mechanisms of control.

Open source: Denoting software for which the original source code is made freely available and may be redistributed and modified.

Optical computer: A device that uses the photons in visible light or infrared beams, rather than electric current, to perform digital computations.

Optogenetics: The combination of genetics and optics to control well-defined events within specific cells of living tissue.

Particle physics: The branch of physics that studies the nature of the particles that constitute matter (particles with mass) and radiation (massless particles).

Personalized medicine: A medical model that proposes the customization of health care using molecular analysis, with medical decisions, practices, and/or products being tailored to the individual patient.

Post-human: A concept originating in the fields of science fiction, futurology, contemporary art, and philosophy that literally means a person or entity that exists in a state beyond being human.

Post-scarcity: An alternative form of economics or social engineering in which goods, services, and information are universally accessible.

Powered exoskeleton: Also known as powered armor, exoframe, or exosuit, is a mobile machine consisting primarily of an outer framework worn by a person, and powered by a system of motors or hydraulics that delivers at least part of the energy for limb movement.

Programmable matter: Matter which has the ability to change its physical properties (shape, density, moduli, conductivity, optical properties, etc.) in a programmable fashion, based upon user input or autonomous sensing.

Quantified Self: A movement to incorporate technology into data acquisition on aspects of a person's daily life in terms of inputs (e.g., food consumed, quality of surrounding air), states (e.g., mood, arousal, blood oxygen levels), and performance (mental and physical).

Quantum computer: A type of computer that exploits the quantum mechanical properties of subatomic particles to allow a single operation to perform many different computations simultaneously on a large amount of data.

Quantum mechanics: The branch of mechanics that deals with the mathematical description of the motion and interaction of subatomic particles, incorporating the concepts of quantization of energy, wave-particle duality, the uncertainty principle, and the correspondence principle.

Regenerative medicine: Deals with the "process of replacing, engineering or regenerating human cells, tissues, or organs to restore or establish normal function."

Robotics: The branch of technology that deals with the design, construction, operation, and application of robots, as well as computer systems for their control, sensory feedback, and information processing.

Roko's basilisk: A proposition that says an all-powerful AI from the future may retroactively punish those who did not assist in bringing about its existence.

Seasteading: The concept of creating permanent dwellings at sea, called seasteads, outside the territory claimed by the government of any standing nation..

Semantic Web: An extension of the existing World Wide Web. It provides a standardized way of expressing the relationships between web pages, to allow machines to understand the meaning of hyperlinked information.

Senescence: Or biological aging, the process or condition of deterioration with age.

Sharing economy: Also known as collaborative consumption, is an economic model in which individuals are able to borrow or rent assets owned by someone else.

Simulated reality: The hypothesis that reality could be simulated—for example by computer simulation—to a degree indistinguishable from "true" reality. It could contain conscious minds which may or may not be fully aware that they are living inside a simulation.

Singularitarianism: A social movement defined by the belief that a technological singularity—the creation of superintelligence—will likely happen in the medium future, and that deliberate action ought to be taken to ensure that the Singularity benefits humans.

Singularity: Also known as technological singularity, is a hypothetical moment in time when artificial intelligence will have progressed to the point of a greater-than-human intelligence, radically changing civilization, and perhaps human nature.

Smart dust: A collection of microelectromechanical systems forming a simple computer in a container light enough to remain suspended in air, used mainly for information gathering in environments that are hostile to life.

Sousveillance: The recording of an activity by a participant in the activity, typically by way of small wearable or portable personal technologies.

Space elevator: A proposed type of space transportation system conceived as a cable fixed to the equator and reaching into space. A counterweight at the upper end keeps the center of mass well above geostationary orbit level.

Stem cell: An undifferentiated cell of a multicellular organism that is capable of giving rise to indefinitely more cells of the same type, and from which certain other kinds of cell arise by differentiation.

String theory: A theoretical framework in which the point-like particles of particle physics are replaced by one-dimensional objects called strings.

Supercomputer: A particularly powerful data processing (mainframe) computer.

Swarm intelligence (SI): The collective behavior of decentralized, self-organized systems, natural or artificial.

Synthetic biology: The design and construction of biological devices and systems for useful purposes. It is an area of biological research and technology that combines biology and engineering, thus often overlapping with bioengineering and biomedical engineering. It encompasses a variety of different approaches, methodologies, and disciplines with a focus on engineering biology and biotechnology.

Technocracy: A term used to describe an organizational structure or system of governance where decision makers are selected on the basis of technological knowledge.

Technogaianism: A portmanteau word combining "techno-" for technology and "gaian" for Gaia philosophy, is an environmentalist stance of active support for the research, development and use of emerging and future technologies to help restore Earth's environment.

Technological unemployment: Unemployment primarily caused by technological change. Given that technological change generally increases productivity, it is a tenet held in economics since the 19th century that technological change, although it disrupts the careers of individuals and the health of particular firms, produces opportunities for the creation of new, unrelated jobs.

Telemedicine: The remote diagnosis and treatment of patients by means of tele-communications technology.

Telepresence: The use of virtual reality technology, especially for remote control of machinery or for apparent participation in distant event

Telomere: A compound structure at the end of a chromosome composed of a usu-ally repetitive DNA sequence specialized in the replication and stability of DNA molecules. Thus, the processes of cell aging and cell death are regulated in part by telomeres.

Terraforming: Especially in science fiction, to transform (a planet) so as to resem-ble the Earth, so that it can support human life.

Three Laws of Robotics: 1. A robot may not injure a human being or, through inaction, allow a human being to come to harm 2. A robot must obey the orders given by human beings except where such orders would conflict with the First Law 3. A robot must protect its own existence as long as such protection does not conflict with the First or Second Laws.

Transhumanism: Abbreviated as H+ or h+, is an international cultural and intel-lectual movement with an eventual goal of fundamentally transforming the human condition by developing and making widely available tech-nologies to greatly enhance human intellectual, physical, and psychologi-cal capacities.

Turing test: A test for intelligence in a computer, requiring that a human being should be unable to distinguish the machine from another human being by using the replies to questions put to both.

Uncanny valley: Used in reference to the phenomenon whereby a computer-gen-erated figure or humanoid robot bearing a near-identical resemblance to a human being arouses a sense of unease or revulsion in the person viewing it.

Vertical farming: Cultivating plant or animal life within a skyscraper greenhouse or on vertically inclined surfaces. The modern idea of vertical farming uses techniques similar to glass houses, where natural sunlight can be aug-mented with artificial lighting.

Virtual reality (VR): Sometimes referred to as *immersive multimedia*, is a com-puter-simulated environment that can simulate physical presence in places in the real world or imagined worlds. Virtual reality could recreate sensory experiences, including virtual taste, sight, smell, sound, touch, and so on.

Wearable technology: A category of technology devices that can be worn by a consumer and often include tracking information related to health and fitness.

Wetware: Human brain cells or thought processes regarded as analogous to, or in contrast with, computer systems.

Whole Brain Emulation: The hypothetical process of copying mental content (including long-term memory and "self") from a particular brain substrate and copying it to another computational device, such as a digital, analog, quantum-based, or software-based artificial neural network.

Source: Selected terms related to this chapter from www.if4it.com/it-glossary and from MERIT CyberSecurity publications.

Bibliography

Cyber threat: http://www.ey.com/Publication/vwLUAssets/EY-cyber-threat-intelligence-how-to-get-ahead-of-cybercrime/$FILE/EY-cyber-threat-intelligence-how-to-get-ahead-of-cybercrime.pdf

Cheetah chasing a gazelle: https://www.youtube.com/watch?v=M0sSoZHaW-E

Nanobots: http://nanogloss.com/nanobots/what-are-the-capabilities-of-nanobots/#axzz4pWQ6mqDx

Chapter 11

The Ingenious Engineering of the Smart Grid

Introduction

Just to let you know—the urban grid is not an American invention.

A Brief History of the Grid

Hippodamus of Miletus (498–408 BC) was an ancient Greek architect, urban planner, physician, mathematician, meteorologist, and philosopher and is considered the "father of European urban planning" and the namesake of the "Hippodamian plan," or grid plan, of city layout.

According to Aristotle, he was the first urban planner to focus attention on the proper arrangements of cities. He laid out the Piraeus (the port of Athens, for Pericles), with wide streets radiating from the central Agora, which was generally called the Hippodameia in his honor (Figure 11.1). His principles were later adopted in many important cities, such as Alexandria and Antioch. The grid plans attributed to him consisted of series of broad, straight streets, cutting one another at right angles.

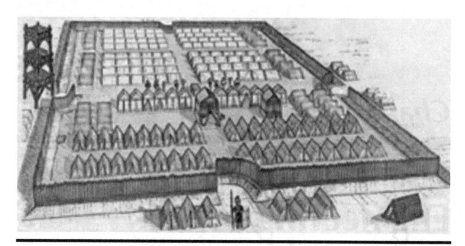

Figure 11.1 Hippodamus of Miletus could have built the best Smart City today. He thought about the grid design before we were born.

It All Started with the Power Grid

A power grid is a network of powerlines, substations, transformers, and associated equipment employed in distributing electricity over a geographical area.

An electrical grid is an interconnected network for delivering electricity from producers to consumers. It consists of generating stations that produce electrical power, high-voltage transmission lines that carry power from distant sources to demand centers, and distribution lines that connect individual customers. Power stations may be located near a fuel source or at a dam site, or take advantage of renewable energy sources, and are often located away from heavily populated areas. They are usually quite large to take advantage of the economies of scale. The electric power that is generated is stepped up to a higher voltage at which it connects to the electric power transmission network. The bulk power transmission network will move the power long distances, sometimes across international boundaries, until it reaches its wholesale customer (usually the company that owns the local electric power distribution network). On arrival at a substation, the power will be stepped down from a transmission level voltage to a distribution level voltage. As it exits the substation, it enters the distribution wiring. Finally, upon arrival at the service location, the power is stepped down again from the distribution voltage to the required service voltage(s). Electrical grids vary in size from covering a single building through national grids that cover whole countries, to transnational grids that can cross continents.

The nervous system, essentially the body's electrical wiring, is a complex collection of nerves and specialized cells known as neurons that transmit signals between different parts of the body.

Anatomy of the Human Grid

The human body is the sum of 13 autonomic cognitive grids that function reliably, but not independently. Each grid gets its directives from the central command—the brain—without any insubordination. Figure 11.2 shows how they work together like the cylinders of a Bugatti.

If you have ever driven a $3 million Bugatti (Chiron), you will appreciate the "one of a kind" engineering of the machine that runs your life.

1. Skeletal system = The slick frame
2. Muscular system = 1600 HP
3. Integumentary system = Outside paint and bumper
4. Digestive system = 16 cylinders, engine cylinders
5. Cardiovascular system = 4 turbochargers
6. Lymphatic system = Body wiring
7. Respiratory system = Radiator
8. Nervous system = Engine wiring
9. Endocrine = (Regulatory) system
10. Reproductive system = Backup tire
11. Immune system = Air filter and air Conditioning
12. Excretory system = Four mufflers and exhaust pipe
13. Urinary system = Fuel pump oil tank

Smart Design Characteristics of the Human Grids

These intelligent heterogeneous grids operate independently but under the supreme command of the brain. They all share superior characteristics and functionalities while serving the body with timely resources:

- They are connected bidirectionally.
- They help each other during distress or a viral battle.
- They transmit production data from sensors in the form of electrical signals to peripheral hubs and to the brain (central command).
- They receive directives and intelligent signals without delay or queues.

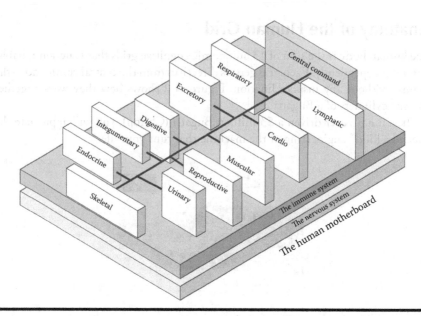

Figure 11.2 **We have stayed away from anatomy—only engineers will understand this unique isometric drawing of the 13 sub-systems in the human body. No, there's no domino effect in the human body—the sub-systems work together with the utmost synergy, but no system can substitute another system. Each of the 13 autonomic systems behaves like an intelligent grid, serving the body with the correct resources at the right time. Only the nervous and the immune systems, which are the brain's deputies, have direct access to all the subordinate systems.** (© 2014 Copyright MERIT CyberSecurity Group. All rights reserved.)

- They protect themselves and fight to the death, and will be mended very quickly.
- They are equipped with a sophisticated alarm system in case of danger or abrupt malfunction.

The skin serves many important functions, including

- Protecting the body against trauma
- Regulating body temperature
- Maintaining water and electrolyte balance
- Sensing painful and pleasant stimuli
- Participating in vitamin D synthesis

To sum it up, the human body is the smartest, most intelligent, and most adaptable in existence.

The most incomprehensible paradox about the human body is its smart constellation of 37 trillion tightly connected cells. National Geographic describes "the great pyramid of Khufu was built with 2.3 million stone blocks." This is a very miniscule number compared to the number of our human cells. It is beyond our imagination that these living nano-organisms are so tightly connected to one another and are simultaneously nourished every microsecond! The immune system alone is the mother of all miracles, for defending the body from massive invaders. The immune system is an incredible learning machine. It learns autonomously to enhance its own performance.

No Smart City today could have an Internet of Things (IoT) with 37 trillion—not even a billion—devices connected to one grid. Rapidly increasing urbanization requires a new paradigm in cyberdefense. This is why digital immunity (DI) systems will be creating a new cyber security paradigm to protect the urban infrastructure as well as the overall quality of life. Such dual objectives are difficult to meet unless future Smart Cities are developed with a dominant contribution from innovative technologies. Using nanoscience and nanotechnology is a natural choice to attain these objectives. Figure 11.3 shows what will happen. The S-curve follows a sigmoid function. I think Ray Kurzweil would concur with our assessment.

Our New Smart Nanogrids

Most definitions of the term "grid" are lopsided, fuzzy, or dislocated. In the traditional sense, a grid is a federation of heterogamous computers loosely coupled through a "wire." The grid is governed by two rules:

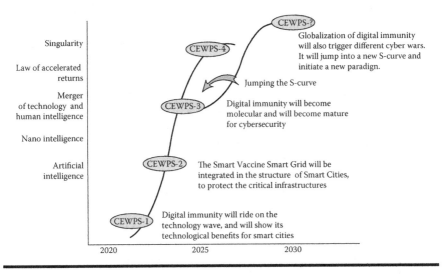

Figure 11.3 The technology S-curve (a sigmoid function) is a powerful tool that can be used to explain how technologies evolve and displace each other. This chart shows the future timeline of digital immunity and how it will evolve before it becomes the de facto of cybersecurity. (© 2014 Copyright MERIT CyberSecurity Group. All rights reserved.)

Rule 1: Each computer on the grid occupies one network "node" only.

Rule 2: All computers on the grid have to collaborate and communicate through a common protocol in order to achieve augmented performance.

The human body also has several nanogrids that work together without conflict. The human brain has 100 billion neurons that operate together, constituting a nervous grid. Actually, this miraculous grid has 100 billion nano computers tied together, processing the electrical signals before sending them to the next neuron. Thus, we can call the nervous grid a smart nanogrid, because it operates at molecular level.

In the 1970s and 1980s, the term *grid* referred only to the power grid. Smart Cities extended the term into a new landscape called the *Internet of Things (IoT)*. As a canonical rule, no Smart City can be built without a reliable and secure power grid. The city power grid is supplied by an external generating plant; the city will have substations with transformers, circuit breakers, supervisory control and data acquisition (SCADA) systems, distribution lines, and (feeder) lines from the power generating plant. The Smart City will have its own grid that connects all electronic and electrical devices in the city with sensors and meters.

The City's main Smart Nano Grid (CSG) is much more than a meshed pipeline connected together. It is totally autonomic, self-healing, and self-managing, offers concrete durability, and has its own AI-centric operating system. The grid has multiple services—not just power. The Smart City Nano Grid (CSG) has many advanced features that make it suitable for Smart City cybersecurity. Here are some of the fascinating properties of carbon nanotubes—the main structure of the nanogrid: They're very strong. Tensile strength is a measure of the amount of force an object can withstand without tearing. The tensile strength of carbon nanotubes is approximately 100 times greater than that of steel of the same diameter. Nanotubes are not only strong but are also elastic. Carbon nanotubes conduct electricity better than metals. When electrons travel through metal, there is some resistance to their movement. This resistance happens when electrons bump into metal atoms. When an electron travels through a carbon nanotube, it's traveling under the rules of quantum mechanics, and so it behaves like a wave traveling down a smooth channel with no atoms to bump into. This quantum movement of an electron within nanotubes is called *ballistic transport*, which is going to be used by Smart Vaccine™ Nanobots (SVNanobots) in fighting adversary Soft Cyborg Nanobots. The Smart Vaccine Nano Grid will have a similar structure to the city nanogrid.

Digital immunity (DI) is the most ingenious technological invention that will make the Smart City immune against most cyberattacks. Without adaptive vaccination to augment our immunity, we would have become extinct a long time ago. Now DI will offer similar protection to the digital world. Let's not forget how vaccination works: the body is injected with a "diluted" virus to teach the natural immune system how to fight and acquire knowledge to fight the real virus.

The City Smart Nano Grid is a complex network of arteries, similar to the human body, which facilitates the connectivity of computing devices, mechanical and digital machines, objects, animals, and people. The grid is designed with nano connections scaled down to the molecular level. All objects are equipped with a nano chip that carries a unique identifier for each object, with its geographic location, type of operation, and type of data, collected without a human-to-human or human-to-computer interface. City's Smart Nano Grid (CSG) will be the first intelligent application of nanotechnology in the domain of cybersecurity.

The Smart City's pioneering intelligent nano defense system, known as the Smart Vaccine Nano Grid (SVG), will be the intelligent nano application to launch digital immunity for the first time. The SVG sits right over the City's Smart Nano Grid (CSG).

The battles between the attackers and the Smart Vaccine army will take place at the molecular level. Distributed denial-of-service (DDoS) attacks will be conducted at the nano level inside the city grid. The battles will be similar to those in the human immune system, where B-cells and T-cells overpower the intruding pathogens and eradicate them. Figure 11.4 is a cross-section of the nanogrid crowded with wide nanotubes to facilitate the movement of the Smart Vaccine Nanobots and to deliver timely vaccination to IoNT devices.

The Grid Magnified Million Times

One day in the near future, you're going to eat your surgeon, because surgery will be performed by an extremely talented and experienced nanobot. Figure 11.5 gives an idea of what the grid will look like in the future. Nanobots will roam freely, looking for the cyborgs (the zombies).

Modern Nano Warfare in a Smart City

Modern nano warfare will be like a conventional air dogfight, but on a molecular scale. B-cells have the same diameter as red cells (7 µm), and they conduct a battle against invading pathogens and annihilate them after knowing their anatomy. In the next two decades, digital immunity will become molecular and even smaller, but it will catch up with malware and defeat it. Figure 11.6 shows how digital immunity engages in a fight like B-cells when an intruder penetrates the body through the skin or the mouth. All the devices (HAN and M-2-M) on the City Smart Grid are registered on both the City Smart Grid and the Smart Vaccine grid. Again, in the next two decades, malware will also use nanotechnology (NT) and artificial intelligence (AI). As a matter of fact, satellite terrorism will be the next (as will be discussed in Chapter 13), and

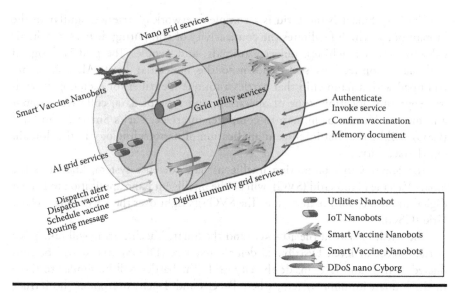

Figure 11.4 A 3D representation of the anatomy of the nanogrid. The City and Smart Vaccine grids are AI-centric nano-operating environments, not just wires and cables. The City Smart Grid is a four-lane highway down-scaled to the molecular level. The attacking cyborgs are encountered by a Smart Vaccine army. The image represents a scenario of a dogfight. We used fighter jets for simplicity and to give readers a live presentation. (© 2014 Copyright MERIT CyberSecurity Group. All rights reserved.)

conventional antivirus technologies (AVT) will be totally ineffective and powerless. In case of a massive nano attack, both grids are prepared and on alert. There's a type of Smart Vaccine that roams around the city grid patrolling the devices and checking if they are vaccinated. All this information is relayed to both control centers. The early warning clouds, which are part of the DI

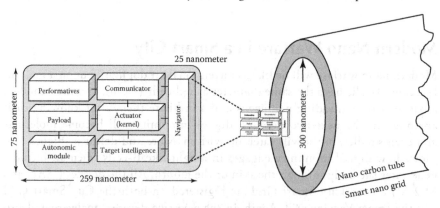

Figure 11.5 The Smart Vaccine Nanobot can easily roam inside blood vessels and nerves. (© 2014 Copyright MERIT CyberSecurity Group. All rights reserved.)

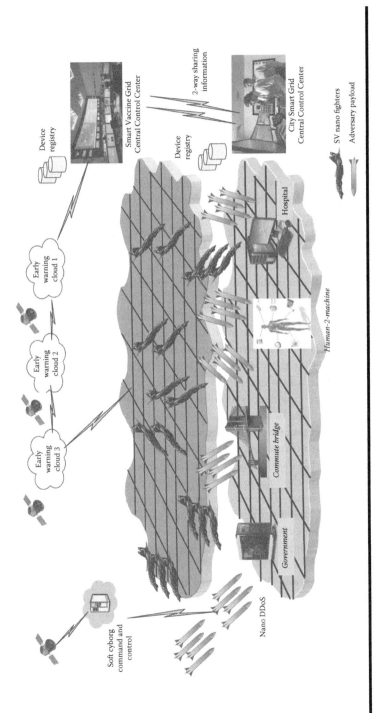

Figure 11.6 Scenario 1: This is a symbolic representation of how digital immunity protects the critical systems in a Smart City. It is all happening at the molecular level. The Smart Vaccine Nano Grid (upper grid) Control Center keeps track of every IoT device connected in the City Smart Nano Grid. Both centers communicate and share battle progress updates and attack warnings. The Smart Vaccine Nano Fighters are the B-cells and T-cells. They take off from their nano grid and penetrate the City Smart Nano Grid. It is good fighting evil. (© 2014 Copyright MERIT CyberSecurity Group. All rights reserved.)

infrastructure, will send encrypted data from previous attacks and forecasts of attacks—quantum key distribution (QKD) technology—to the Central Control Center of both grids.

We're going to describe two scenarios of an attack on a Smart City and demonstrate how the Smart Vaccine Nano Army will handle both types of attacks.

Scenario 1: Attackers Penetrate the City Grid, but Cannot Reach the Targets

Due to the nature of the attack, it looks massive and strategic. The targets are two important government servers. The first one is *The Automated Fingerprint Identification System (AFIS)*, a biometric identification (ID) methodology that uses digital imaging technology to obtain, store, and analyze fingerprint data. The second one is the Pentagon's *Space-Based Infrared System, or SBIRS ("Sibbers")*. SBIRS is a constellation of four satellites parked in orbit above the equator, plus two additional spy satellites that fly over the North Pole. The satellites continue to search for signs of infrared radiation indicating major heat sources—such as missile launches.

Assumptions: The Smart Vaccine Nano Grid Central Control Center (CCC) has collected detailed information on previous nano attacks—most likely from the same assailant who launched similar attacks on banks and hospitals. Predictive analyses have indicated that the organization is state affiliated with a political motif. State-sponsored attacks are a highly rewarding and relatively low-cost/low-risk way to carry out espionage and military operations. The likelihood of being able to attribute attacks back to a particular country with sufficient rigor is extremely low and the success rate of any concerted effort is high. The goal of these attacks is often to obtain information about their targets or access their targets through trusted relationships with a *third-party* company. State-sponsored actors will use standard attack methodologies that are used by other typical cybercrime actors, to camouflage their act. They do this because their work is incredibly professional and is so generic that it cannot be attributed to any particular group. But in this attack scenario, the cybercrime actors have secretly used nanotechnology and artificial intelligence, knowing that an asymmetrical approach will give them the upper hand.

The adversary organization also has access to a geostationary satellite network for information transfer. They use nano DDoS, with a large number of Soft Cyborgs, which have all the instructions for the targets and carry nano payloads. The attack has two fronts: one for the Pentagon SBIRS and one for the FBI's AFIS. The attacking cyborgs know the coordinates of the two targets and are able to penetrate the city grid, but cannot reach the targets because they are intercepted by the Smart Vaccine Nanobots. The DDoS attack fizzles out and the payload is analyzed and reverse engineered for future attacks.

Scenario 2: Attackers Penetrate the City Grid and Are Ready to Compromise the Targets

This attack, shown in Figure 11.7, is pretty serious, because two major systems have been compromised. The first critical system is the FBI's AFIS, which is one of the most critical systems in the United States. First, the AFIS is a repository of criminal history information, fingerprints, and criminal subject photographs, as well as information regarding military and civilian federal employees and other individuals authorized by Congress. The AFIS database had over 74 million records in 2013. Second, it provides positive identification of individuals based on fingerprint submissions (through both ten-print fingerprints and latent fingerprints). Third, it provides tentative identification of individuals based on descriptive information such as name, date of birth, distinctive body markings, and identification numbers. The second target is the critical system of the Pentagon's Small Business Innovation Research (SBIRS). The system is the Air Force's primary missile-warning system, designed to detect launches as well as track missile flight paths and predict impact points. In 2025, SBIRS will have seven missile-warning satellites.

In two decades, satellite terrorism will be as popular as In-N-Out Burger. Adversary terrorism organizations will offer satellite-oriented crime-as-a-service (CaaS). Satellite connection to the Internet will become very fast and will be bundled with robust encryption security. Satellites will also have secure connections to the cloud, as it offers a platform and software as a service. Cybercriminals have much expertise in satellite–cloud–Internet computing and hire NT and AI professionals. In two decades, cybercrime will be a frightening threat to quality of life (QOL) in Smart Cities.

In the next two decades, DI systems will become the Holy Grail of defense for Smart Cities. There are eight types of Intelligent SVNanobots that have specific functions that contribute to the effectiveness of digital immunity. The Smart Vaccine armies (spies, vaccinators, communicators, and paramedics) will use the most advanced nano weaponry and will be able to multiply as the battle requires (like the B-cells). Millions of intelligent nanobots will roam around the city, guarding the grid. They are assigned to specific duties.

A major vulnerability of the Smart City is its connectivity of everything to everything. Cyber terrorists know how the Smart City is connected and know the technology of each critical system and infrastructure. Attacking the power grid and knocking down the substations with the heaviest load will create havoc, cause loss of data, disable street lights and traffic lights, and create huge traffic delays and hysteria among citizens. Armageddon is the best way to describe it.

The best way to knock out the power grid is to create a cascaded blackout, which will bring the whole city into complete darkness. Figures 11.7 and 11.8 illustrate how the terrorists plan to launch the attack.

Here is the sequence of the battle activities (Scenario 2), as shown in Figure 11.7:

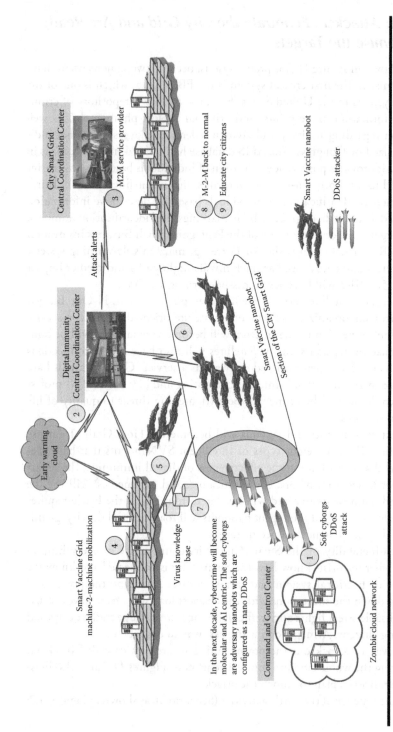

Figure 11.7 Scenario 2: The classic scenario of the nano dogfight. Digital immunity response is triggered by the Smart Vaccine Intelligence Nanobot while they roam around the grid devices, sending information to the SV NanoGrid Central Coordination Center (CCC). Early warning signals come from the satellite through the cloud. An army of Smart Vaccine Nanobots are mobilized and engage with the adversary cyborgs. Casualties will occur, but the SV nanobots are more experienced and have a large variety of fighters. (© 2014 Copyright MERIT CyberSecurity Group. All rights reserved.)

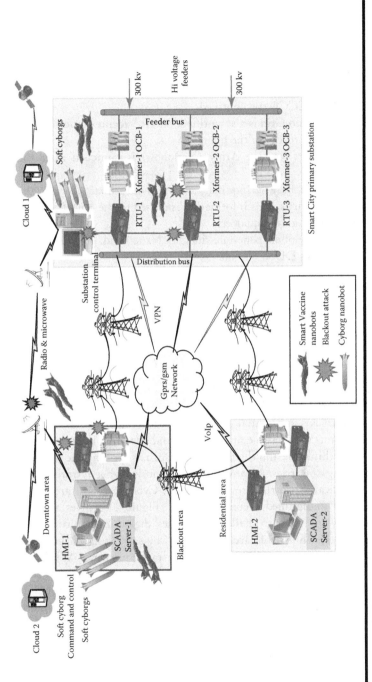

Figure 11.8   Scenario 3: This is how the Smart City gets its electric power from a regional grid. It is almost like a closed system. One of the two 300 KV feeders is a backup, in case of an intentional or unintentional drop in voltage in the regional electrical power supply. All three substations are monitored by a Siemens SCADA system. The adversary geosynchronous satellite—leased from a foreign country—gives the terrorist cloud strategic reconnaissance data on the demography of the city. The massive attack is aimed at the primary and residential substations. Nano cyborgs (soft cyborgs) are launched for both clouds. (© 2014 Copyright MERIT CyberSecurity Group. All rights reserved.)

1. The adversary Command and Control initiates a nano attack using Soft Cyborgs. In the next decade, cybercrime will become molecular and AI-centric. Soft Cyborgs are adversary nanobots that are configured as a nano DDoS.
2. The digital immunity's Early Warning Cloud knows about the incoming attack and notifies the digital immunity CCC.
3. The City Smart Grid CCC is also notified.
4. The Smart Vaccine Nano Grid is also notified. Smart Vaccine Nano Fighters (Nanobots) are getting ready for the fight.
5. A well prepared Smart Vaccine Army (Nanobots) is launched after the attackers.
6. The Virus Knowledge Base is inquired to obtain information about the identity of the attack virus. This information is passed to the Smart Vaccine squadrons before leaving their quarters.
7. The Smart Vaccine Nanobots penetrate the City Nano Grid, going after the attackers (Soft Cyborgs DDoS Nanobots).
8. The City is shielded from the attack, and all machine-to-machine (M2M) device owners are notified.
9. The City issues training pamphlets to all citizens, educating them on how to respond to surprise attacks.

Scenario 3: Attackers Are Going After the City's Power Grid

Technology offers cyber terrorists the same advantages as the cybersecurity administrator. Thus, they learn from each other, but cyber terrorists control the timing of the attack, which is a substantial competitive advantage. In the next two decades, cybercrime actors will become more mature and selective. Their creativity will extend into the unthinkable and the imaginable, such as spoiling the national elections of challenging countries. Meanwhile, their cousin cyber terrorists will concentrate on the critical infrastructures of *IoT cities*. Cyber terrorists are proud of their ingenuity and undignified accomplishments. Figure 11.8 gives a visual description of how they are trying to challenge the cities' digital immunity.

Attackers will use the "house of cards" approach, by secretly modifying the control of the remote terminal unit (RTU) of the central transformer. While the master control screen of the substation shows normal operation, the terrorists increase the load of the central transformer (Cformer-2) through its RTU-2. Nano cyborgs are programmed to do this. Now, the city has only two primary transformers (Xformer-1 and Xformer-3) that cannot accommodate the 300 KV feeders. The oil circuit breakers (OCB-1 and OCB-3) are tripped and the transfer in the downtown areas cannot handle the load; a blackout is triggered. Cloud 2 launches an army of nano cyborgs that are programmed to go after the M2M network. SCADA systems show normal operations until they show the blackout on the screen.

In the next two decades, there will be some interesting blackouts triggered by nano cyborgs unleashed from remote, secret launch pads. The digital immunity system (DIS) will enter its third generation with a new bag of tricks.

Satellites communicate using radio waves to send signals to the antennas on the Earth. The antennas then capture those signals and process the information coming from those signals. Nanochips are becoming the cogs and wheels of all information and communication technology (ICT). Programmable nanochips (PN) have penetrated medicine with bio-nanochips that are effectively used in diagnosis. In the next two decades, we will be able to replace a motherboard on a molecular chip and install a complete AI-centric autonomic operating system on the chip. Wireless communication systems are adopting nanotechnology for cost-effectiveness and speed.

Satellite technology is being used for wireless communication in addition to nanotechnology and artificial intelligence. Satellite communication is self-contained wireless communication technology, spread widely over the world to allow users to stay connected almost anywhere on the Earth. When the signal (a beam of modulated microwave) is sent near the satellite, the satellite amplifies the signal and sends it back to the antenna receiver located on the surface of the Earth. Satellite communication contains two main components: the space segment and the ground segment. The ground segment consists of fixed or mobile transmission, and reception and ancillary equipment; the space segment is mainly the satellite itself.

Internet of NanoThings (IoNT) Connectivity

During the design of a DIS, we looked at the issue of risk and how it can be best managed; we realized that the only way it can be mitigated—not completely eliminated—is to incorporate a Smart Grid, like the human nervous system. There are several unique advantages to a Smart Grid. First, it is an incredible piece of *middleware* to transfer services, data, and alerts. More importantly, a Smart Grid (SG) is the fastest medium to detect attacks, alert other systems on the grid, and provide failover mechanism during abnormal termination.

In the next two decades, all electrical and electronic devices in the city will be connected to smart networks, which will be tied to the master city grid. No device will remain in isolation. All homes, businesses, and academia will be remotely metered for a greener environment, cost reduction, and energy consumption optimization. IoT devices will be sending live data to a central collection system to run predictive analytics models to have better assessment of the overall utility workload in the city of the future. Like the old saying, "if you cannot measure it, you cannot control it." Therefore, the *first* success criteria for Smart Cities is grid connectivity. The *second* success criterion is cognitive cyber defense. Smart Cities need to rely on another grid, which will offer complete protection against Smart Crime. By design, in order to protect a grid, you need another grid. Digital immunity is the best techno solution to conceal the city from persistent attacks and Virus Rain™. Digital immunity will be deployed with the SVG, which will be tightly coupled with the City Smart Grid (CSG). Cognitive and predictive defense will guarantee uninterrupted quality of life in the city. In the next two decades, every Smart City will install digital immunity as the best shield. Smart cities are healthy cities. Many cities that will be tightly welded with the SVG as the cognitive and holistic defense against truly avant-garde crime actors. One of the great contribution to humanity was the discovery of the vaccine. Without adaptive immunity, one-quarter of the human race would be terminally ill. History will repeat itself in the digital world.

Scenario 4: Attackers Are Going After the City's Partial Power Grid

In another scenario (Figure 11.9), the attack is aimed at a residential section of the Smart City. Attackers always try to take the least resistant path to commit their crime.

The IoT Autonomic Adapter

The autonomic adapter (AA) is a marvel of engineering. It is a computing engine, designed with NT components, that reasons, makes its own decisions, and regulates itself in case of internal faults. The AA is an intelligent coupler that ties the device to the Smart Grid. Whenever there's an attack on the grid, the AA will collaborate with the Smart Vaccine Nanobots in fighting the virus nano cyborgs. The AA will play a pivotal role in the inoculation process of all the devices of the IoT. Figure 11.10 describes the futuristic IoT connectivity to the City Smart Grid.

It alerts the IoT device that an attack is taking place on the city grid. The Smart Vaccine Nanobots (army) has already circled the enemy nano cyborgs that were trying to hack the IoT devices and blackout the city. The IoT devices are operating in normal mode and the meters are working properly and sending data to the Grid Coordinating Center.

The AA is the intelligent middleware between the device and the City Smart Grid. It includes seven functional components, as shown in Figure 11.10.

1. *The Sensor*: The interactive component with three functions. First, it sends operational data for collection and analysis to the main server in the city. Second, it alerts the IoT device about attacks and sends help requests through the City Smart Grid to the CCC for immediate response. Third, it collects information about attacks, the nature of the attacking virus, and the damage.

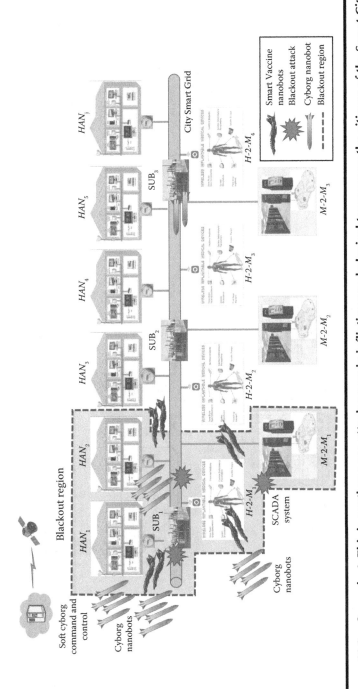

Figure 11.9 Scenario 4: This is another nano attack scenario inflicting psychological terror upon the citizens of the Smart City. Electric power is the life line of the city. Early warning prediction is a survival means to catch the attackers before they reach the city. Sometimes, payloads will reach the edge of the city, but the attack is limited. Once bitten, twice shy. Attack data and strategy will always help for the next time. Digital immunity knowledge bases will translate the attack data into defense by offense.

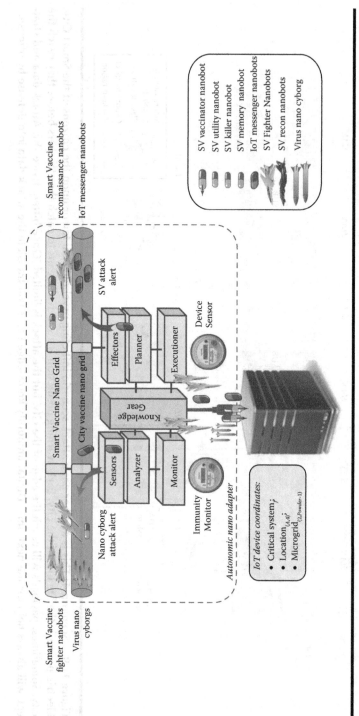

Figure 11.10 Each IoT device is connected to the CSG like an appliance, as well as the SVG, which is the nervous system of CEWPS. Connection is made through the AA, which has all the expert components to carry vaccination services and attack outcomes to the Smart Vaccine Commander. (© 2014 Copyright MERIT CyberSecurity Group. All rights reserved.)

At the same time, the collected information is sent to the knowledge gear to be converted to knowledge.

2. *The Effector*: As the name indicates, it has a list of the vaccination services to be executed due to an attack. Effectors work very closely with the Smart Vaccine Commander during vaccination missions.
3. *The Analyzer*: Provides the mechanism to evaluate the severity of the attack
4. (normal versus attack) based on performance and security metrics and rules.
5. *The Monitor*: Monitors sensor data from IoT devices according to the rules of the analyzer.
6. *The Planner*: Packages a list of vaccination services for the attack and passes them to the commander.
7. *The Executioner*: Collaborates with the SV vaccinators during the inoculation services.
8. *The Knowledge Gear*: Gathers the data activity from the sensor and the effector of the four functional components of the AA and converts it into knowledge that can be discussed between the four components and the Smart Vaccine Commander.

According to Newton's Third Law of Motion, whenever objects A and B interact with each other, they exert forces upon each other. In other words, the law states, "For every action, there is an equal and opposite reaction." Mathematically, this is expressed as

$$F_{AB} = -F_{BA}$$

This is exactly what will be happening in the next two decades, when cybercrime will become more sophisticated using the same technologies as cybersecurity. Malware will be intensely more sophisticated and lethal. Attacks will be more bewildering, enigmatic, and deadly. Nano digital immunity will be the new paradigm and will establish a new science for cyber defense.

Organizational Chart of the Smart Vaccine Nano Army

The Romans had a great army, and the Germans had a phenomenal army, but the United States has the best army. The human immune system has a great army that keeps us healthy. Now digital immunity also has a great army that will keep Smart Cities safe and great places to live.

Figure 11.11 shows the organizational chart of the Smart Vaccine Nano Army. Like the Army, some give orders and some take orders. Each group is responsible for a set of unique services during a confrontation with attacking cyborgs. We all know that our immune system is constantly fighting intruders and exterminating infectious agents.

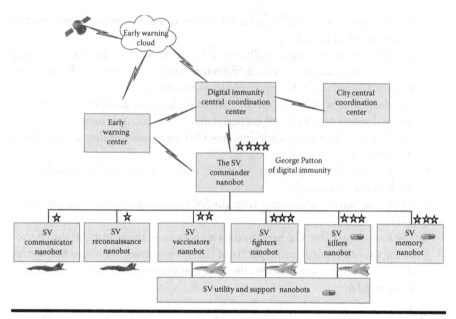

Figure 11.11 Organizational chart of the Smart Vaccine Nano Army. The nanobots that go the battlefield and do all the fighting and risk their lives get three stars. (© 2014 Copyright MERIT CyberSecurity Group. All rights reserved.)

The SV Nano Army has two crucial responsibilities: first, to protect the borders and entries of the Smart City, and second, to inoculate the IoT devices to augment their immunity against future attacks.

The Smart Vaccine Nano Army is a colossal group of autonomic nanobots that could expand to 10 million well-trained in *deep learning* techniques, to recognize types of cyborgs, their formation, their targets, and type of payload. All the fighting will be at a molecular scale.

The SV Reconnaissance Nanobots roam around the CSG during their routine patrol, looking for foreign agents (pathogens) or other microorganisms that could set up Trojans, or ransomware. Nano cyborgs penetrate the city grid to collect strategic intelligence data (about the critical infrastructures) before the attack. The SV Reconnaissance Nanobots call on the SV Memory Nanobots to inform the SV Nano Commander to mobilize the nano army for the upcoming battle. A highly trained army of SV nanobots made up of fighters, vaccinators, killers, and support units leave the SVG heading for the CSG. All the SV Fighter Nanobots can mutate to a stronger army of SV nanobots, if the adversary Nano Cyborgs have the upper hand. These tough SV Fighter Nanobots will be able overcome the Nano Cyborgs, dismantle their programs, reverse engineer their payload into its native code, and pass it to the SV Memory Nanobots, to build the proper vaccine code, and to remember the payload—a vaccine for future attacks. The SV Memory Nanobot will be able to mount a better defense the second time.

The role of the SV Vaccinator Nanobots is just as crucial as fighting the cyborgs. There will be thousands of Vaccinator Nanobots that will go around the city and inoculate all the IoT devices. The nano vaccine, built after reverse engineering the cyborg payload, is a nano program stored on the chip of the SV Vaccinator Nanobot. It moves inside the CSG looking for the autonomic adapter (AA) of IoT devices. After an authenticated handshake, it enters the device, connects permanently to the security module, and downloads the nano vaccine code. The SV Vaccinator Nanobot will trigger a full intelligent scan to make sure that the device has not been infected. The SV Vaccinator Nanobot will establish contact with the digital immunity headquarters to be prepared for future attacks. Every time the device receives data from the grid, the SV Vaccinator Nanobot will run a heuristic check and make sure the arriving data does not carry hidden nano cyborgs.

At the beginning of the battle, in addition to the SV Fighter Nanobot, there are two types of SV nanobots that contribute to the eradication of the attack. The first group is the SV Support Nanobots, which are responsible for the cleanup after the battle; and the second group is the SV Killer Nanobots, which are responsible for collecting all the hostile code of the nano cyborgs and sending it to the SV Memory Nanobots for storage in the knowledge base. This will help in the recognition of future attacks.

Nanotechnology has added a new dimension to cybersecurity. We're harnessing nature's superpower. Nanochips made of millions of nanotubes will be the building blocks of the digital immunity Cognitive Early Warning Predictive system (CEWPS). We will be able to build 32 nanometer chips with nanolithography that can hold 995 million transistors. Nano programming will also be the mainstream in the world of software engineering. We will be able to cram 10 million instructions of code on one nanochip.

A Real-Time Screen of the CEWPS during an Attack

Smart Cities are the most tempting places for organized cybercriminals. Our body is constantly bombarded with vicious viral attacks, but we don't feel the attacks because we have a great defense system. The immune system continually learns about pathogens and diseases and keeps the B-cells trained. The digital immune system augments the intelligence of the Smart Vaccine Nanobots so they are ready for the next encounter.

We have all noticed that the modern cars of today (including driverless) are garnished with an incredible dashboard that can do anything for you. An array of dynamic digital windows of information keep the driver safe.

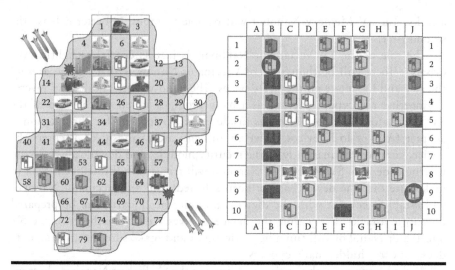

Figure 11.12 **This real-time screen shows at the main dashboard of the system administrator. This screen is one of the remarkable real-time screens that should be in the war room, showing where the IOT devices and the critical infrastructure systems are. The screen shows the location and time of the cyborg attack on the Smart City. The screen on the right highlights the moments before the attack will take place. The response of the SV Fighter Nanobots is lightning fast and will intercept and neutralize the attackers.**

In the next two decades, digital immunity will become so intelligent that it will be able to run for itself as "normal utility."

Figure 11.12 is a real-time view of what is going on in the city. The two attacks couldn't reach the city because they were eradicated by the Smart Vaccine Nanobots and their payloads were sent for forensics. The Central Coordination Center was informed about the status of the battle.

Glossary

Arc method: One of the synthesis methods for carbon nanotubes (CNTs). This method creates CNTs through arc vaporization of two carbon rods placed end to end, separated by approximately 1 mm, in an enclosure that is usually filled with inert gas (helium, argon) at low pressure (between 50 and 700 mbar). Recent investigations have shown that it is also possible to create CNTs with the arc method in liquid nitrogen. A direct current of 50–100 A, driven by a potential difference of approximately 20 V, creates a high temperature discharge between the two electrodes. The discharge vaporizes the surface of one of the carbon electrodes and forms a small rod-shaped deposit on the other electrode. Producing CNTs in high yield depends on the uniformity of the plasma arc, and the temperature of the deposit forming on the carbon electrode (Wilson et al., 2002). CNTs have many unique and interesting properties.

Assembler: A molecular manufacturing device capable of positioning molecules through chemical reactions.

Atom: The smallest unit of a chemical element, about a third of a nanometer in diameter. Atoms are the basis for molecules and solid objects.

Atomic force microscope: An imaging instrument used to "magnify" at the molecular level through mechanical tracing of surface contours.

Automated engineering: Engineering done by computer systems without the input of humans.

Automated manufacturing: Manufacturing at the nano-level by assemblers and replicators by themselves.

Bulk technology: Manipulation and fabrication of large groups of molecules.

Carbon nanotubes (CNTs): Single-walled (SWNTs), double-walled (DWNTs), and multiwalled (MWNTs) varieties. CNTs can best be described as a graphene sheet rolled into a one-dimensional structure with axial symmetry. CNTs are one of the primary building blocks that will be critical to the Nanotechnology Revolution. CNTs have many unique and interesting properties.

Cell pharmacology: The administration of drugs to precise locations in the patient by means of a nanomachine.

Cell surgery: Precise surgery done by the modification of cell structures by a nanomachine.

Cell: A small structural unit, surrounded by a membrane, making up living things.

Chemical vapor deposition (CVD): One of the synthesis methods for carbon nanotubes. Large numbers of CNTs can be formed by catalytic CVD of acetylene over Co and Fe catalysts supported on silica or zeolite. The carbon deposition activity seems to relate to the cobalt content of the catalyst, whereas the CNTs' selectivity seems to be a function of the pH in catalyst preparation. Fullerenes and bundles of SWNTs were also found among the MWNTs produced on the carbon/zeolite catalyst (Wilson et al., 2002). CNTs have many unique and interesting properties.

Derivatization of nanotubes: See Functionalization of nanotubes.

Dispersion of nanotubes: A term to describe getting the carbon nanotubes into a well dispersed, liquid state, sometimes referred to as getting the nanotubes into suspension or getting the nanotubes into solution.

DNA: DNA molecules carry the genetic information necessary for the organization and functioning of most living cells and control the inheritance of characteristics.

DWNTs: An abbreviation for double-walled carbon nanotubes.

Enabling science and technologies: Areas of research relevant to a particular goal, such as nanotechnology.

Enzymes: Naturally occurring chemical substances in the human body that help a chemical reaction take place.

Exploratory engineering: Looking into designs and analysis of systems that will be possible in the future as our tools and processes are refined.

Fullerenes: A spherical carbon molecule in which the carbon atoms are arranged in a soccer ball shape. C_{60} was the first fullerene of the now thirty or more fullerene families. In a C_{60} structure, there are 60 carbon atoms and a number of five-membered rings isolated by six-membered rings.

Functionalization of nanotubes: Also known as Derivatization of nanotubes. MWNTs or SWNTs that have received post-production processing to add chemical functional groups to the ends and sidewalls of the nanotubes.

Immune machines: Nanomachines applied for medical uses by aiding a patient's immune system, changing or destroying viruses and bacteria.

Industrial-grade nanotubes: Large quantities, up to metric tons (1,000,000 g) of MWNTs in either >85 wt% or >95 wt% purity.

Laser method: One of the synthesis methods for carbon nanotubes. "In 1996, a dual-pulsed laser vaporization technique was developed, which produced SWNTs in gram quantities and yields of >70 wt% purity. Samples were prepared by laser vaporization of graphite rods with a 50:50 catalyst mixture of Co and Ni (particle size ~1 μm) at 1200°C in flowing argon, followed by heat treatment in a vacuum at 1000°C to remove the C_{60} and other fullerenes. The initial laser vaporization pulse was followed by a second pulse, to vaporize the target more uniformly. The use of two successive laser pulses minimizes the amount of carbon deposited as soot. The second laser pulse breaks up the larger particles ablated by the first one, and feeds them into the growing nanotube structure." (Wilson et al., 2002).

Microtechnology: Working with structures, proteins, and molecular groups in the micrometer range.

Molecular electronics: An electronic system that is able to operate using single electrons for power. Further refined by the use of multiple parts at the nanoscale as opposed to current technology of etching "parts" from a single substance.

Molecular machine: A machine that is atomically precise and of nanometer size, can also be used to describe naturally produced devices.

Molecular manipulator: A device combining a proximal probe mechanism for atomically precise positioning with a molecule binding site on the tip; can serve as the basis for building complex structures by positional synthesis.

Molecular manufacturing: Manufacturing using molecular machinery, giving molecule-by-molecule control of products and by-products via positional chemical synthesis.

Molecular medicine: A variety of pharmaceutical techniques and therapies in use today.

Molecular nanotechnology: Thorough, inexpensive control of the structure of matter based on molecule-by-molecule control of products and by-products; the products and processes of molecular manufacturing, including molecular machinery.

Molecular recognition: A chemical term referring to processes in which molecules adhere in a highly specific way, forming a larger structure; an enabling technology for nanotechnology.

Molecular surgery or molecular repair: Analysis and physical correction of molecular structures in the body using medical nano machines.

Molecular systems engineering: Design, analysis, and construction of systems of molecular parts working together to carry out a useful purpose.

Molecule: Group of atoms held together by chemical bonds; the typical unit manipulated by nanotechnology.

Molecular nanotechnology: Term to describe the manipulation and fabrication of single or small groups of atoms and molecules.

MWNTs: An abbreviation for multiwalled carbon nanotubes, which come in different diameters.

Nano: A prefix meaning one billionth (1/1,000,000,000).

Nano computer: A computer with parts built on a molecular scale.

Nanoelectronics: Electronics on a nanometer scale, whether made by current techniques or nanotechnology; includes both molecular electronics and nanoscale devices resembling today's semiconductor devices.

Nanomachine: An artificial molecular machine created through molecular manufacturing.

Nanomanufacturing: See molecular manufacturing.

Nanometer: One billionth of a meter or 1/1000 of a micrometer.

Nanosurgery: A generic term including molecular repair and cell surgery.

Nanotechnology: Originally used to define any work done on the molecular scale, or one billionth of a meter. This term is now used broadly (and loosely) for anything that is really small (usually smaller than a micrometer).

Positional synthesis: Control of chemical reactions by precisely positioning the reactive molecules; the basic principle of assemblers.

Protein design, protein engineering: The design and construction of new proteins; an enabling technology for nanotechnology.

Proximal probes: A family of devices capable of fine positional control and sensing, including scanning tunneling and atomic force microscopes; an enabling technology for nanotechnology.

Scanning tunneling microscope: An instrument able to image conducting surfaces to atomic accuracy; has been used to pin molecules to a surface.

Self-assembly: It is predicted that we may soon develop "smart molecules" that will be able to self-assemble to form different materials. Current research has been focusing on the use of chemical bonds that are well known and widely understood.

Short nanotubes: Short nanotubes are 0.5–2.0 μm long, instead of the regular length of nanotubes, which are ~50 μm.

Smart materials and products: Here, materials and products capable of relatively complex behavior due to the incorporation of nanocomputers and nano-machines. Also used for products having some ability to respond to the environment.

SWNTs: Abbreviation for single-walled carbon nanotubes.

Virtual reality system: A combination of computer and interface devices (goggles, gloves, etc.) that present a user with the illusion of being in a three-dimensional world of computer-generated objects.

Virus: A parasite that invades cells and takes over their molecular machinery in order to copy itself. Also, a program that may act maliciously on its own or through execution.

Reference

Wilson, M., Kannangara, K., Smith, G., Simmons, M., Raguse, B. (2002). *Nanotechnology: Basic Science and Emerging Technologies*, London: Chapman and Hall.

Chapter 12

Defense Strategies of Smart Cities: Smart Defense by Smart Offense

History of Defense

From the dawn of history, walls and moats were the best fortifications usually used to protect a city, town, or other settlement from potential aggressors. From very early history to modern times, walls have been a near necessity for every city. Exceptions were few, but neither ancient Sparta nor ancient Rome had walls for a long time, choosing to rely on their militaries for defense instead.

With the development of firearms came the necessity to expand the existing installation, which occurred in multiples stages. Firstly, additional, half-circular towers were added in the interstices between the walls and pre-walls in which a handful of cannons could be placed. Soon after, bastions were added in strategically relevant positions, such as at the gates or corners. Therefore, new, star forts with numerous cannons and thick earth walls reinforced by stone were built. These could resist cannon fire for prolonged periods of time. However, these massive fortifications severely limited the growth of the cities, as it was much more difficult to move them compared to the simple walls previously employed. To make matters worse, it was forbidden to build outside the city gates for strategic reasons, and the cities became more and more densely populated as a result.

Department of Homeland Risk Lexicon

In 2010, the Department of Homeland Security published an interesting document on terms and definitions called the DHS Risk Lexicon (2010 edition). This is the second edition of the DHS Risk Lexicon and represents an update of the version published in September 2008. More than 70 terms and definitions were included in the first edition; the 2010 edition includes 50 new terms and definitions in addition to the revised definitions of the 23 original terms.

It was produced by the DHS Risk Steering Committee (RSC). The RSC, chaired by the Undersecretary for the National Protection and Programs Directorate and administered by the Office of Risk Management and Analysis (RMA), has produced a DHS Risk Lexicon with definitions for terms that are fundamental to the practice of homeland security risk management and analysis. The RSC created the Risk Lexicon Working Group (RLWG) to represent the DHS risk community of the Chemicals of Interest (COI) in the development of this professional risk lexicon.

The RSC is the risk governance structure for the DHS, with membership from across the department. All terms in the DHS Risk Lexicon were completed using this process and represent the collective work of the DHS risk COI. The DHS Risk Lexicon terms and definitions will be included as part of the DHS Lexicon, and future additions and revisions will be coordinated by the RSC and RLWG in collaboration with the DHS Lexicon Program.

The Lexicon is a 69-page document containing in detail all the security and vulnerability terms with examples (https://www.dhs.gov/xlibrary/assets/dhs-risk-lex-icon-2010.pdf). We reviewed it and extracted some of its content that applies to this book.

- *Defense*: According to Sigmund Freud, "a defense mechanism is an unconscious psychological mechanism that reduces anxiety arising from unacceptable or potentially harmful stimuli." He was one of the first proponents of this construct.
- *Security*: Defined as "reducing the risk to critical infrastructure by physical means or defensive cyber measures to intrusions, attacks, or the effects of natural or man-made disasters."
- *Fear*: A strong emotion caused by great worry about something dangerous, painful, or unknown that is happening or might happen.
- *Resilience*: Defined as "the ability to prepare for and adapt to changing conditions and withstand and recover rapidly from disruptions, it includes the ability to withstand and recover from deliberate attacks, accidents, or naturally occurring threats or incidents."
- *Risk*: Defined as "the potential for an unwanted outcome resulting from an incident, event, or occurrence, as determined by its likelihood (a function of threats and vulnerabilities) and the associated consequences."

■ *Risk management*: Defined as "the process of identifying, analyzing, and communicating risk and accepting, avoiding, transferring, or controlling it to an acceptable level at an acceptable cost."

The Need for Numerical Metrics

This book includes information on operational research of analytical methods to help make better decisions. The world is built with math and probabilities that we cannot evade or eliminate. These problem-solving techniques are universal and apply to any project and design. The Oxford Dictionary defines the term "defect" as a "Frailty or shortcoming that prevents an item from being complete."

We start with the term "vulnerability," which is often is used as a qualitative metric such as when used in a critical infrastructure homeland security context. It is difficult to define because (1) various homeland security decision makers define and use metrics for vulnerability in different ways to support their decisions, and (2) cascading consequences, interdependencies, and systems issues can lead to computational complexities that make the idea and valuation of isolated vulnerabilities of little or no use to decision makers:

$$\text{Risk} = \frac{\text{Threat} \times \text{Vulnerability}}{\text{Countermeasures}} \times \text{Impact}$$

The risk equation that we use is quite simple: risk equals impact multiplied by probability weighed against the cost (risk = impact × probability/cost). Impact is the effect on the organization should a risk event occur. Probability is the likelihood (threat) the event could occur within a given time frame. Cost (countermeasures) is the amount it takes to mitigate or reduce the risk to an acceptable level.

Simplistically, we can say: risk is the probability that a threat will exploit a vulnerability to cause harm to an asset. This is represented by

$$R = f(T, V, A)$$

where:
T = threat
V = vulnerability
A = asset

Vulnerability can also be defined as the conditional probability of success given an attack for a given scenario:

$$\text{Probability} \left(\text{Success}|\text{Attack}\right) = P(S|A)$$

Risk Computation

Commonly defined, risk is the potential for an unwanted outcome resulting from an incident, event, or occurrence, as determined by its likelihood and the associated consequences. Quantitatively, risk is estimated as the expected value of loss from one or more scenarios multiplied by the likelihood or frequency of those scenarios. A scenario describes an incident (attack, accident, or natural disaster) and what specifically is being attacked or affected. The probability or frequency of a scenario and the associated consequences are calculated with respect to a domain, which defines the extent of the effects of calculations. The domain is defined either geographically, or functionally (e.g., cascading, interdependent effects), or both. The domain also includes the time horizon (e.g., immediate, 1 week, and 5 years).

As an example, consider a set of attack scenarios comprising cyber terrorists, using a Stuxnet-like worm, to attack a grid of power plants that supplies energy to 5 million people in the metropolitan city, and the estimated consequence that include astronomical loss of the business, major logistic chaos, and a severe economic impact until conditions are normalized. Another example could be a set of scenarios involving hurricanes that strike the East Coast from June through November of a given year, and the domain could be the national electrical grid and the costs and economic consequences due to the associated large-scale power outages.

To compute a probabilistic risk assessment, a set of attack scenarios is specified. For each attack scenario, a probability of occurrence is determined and the expected value of the consequences (EVC) given the attack occurrence is calculated. The following relationship is a mathematical formula for a probabilistic risk assessment:

$$\text{Risk}(\text{Scenario } S, \text{ Domain } D) = \sum_{\text{Scenarios } S} P(\text{Scenarios } S, \text{ Domain } D)$$

$$\times EVC(\text{Scenarios } S, \text{ Domain } D)$$

In case a quantitative risk metric is given to restrict the condition of the attack, then the risk of the attack becomes conditional. This is called the conditional risk associated with that attack. The conditional risk, defined as the expected value of loss given that the scenario occurs, is calculated as follows:

Conditional Risk = Probability that an attack is successful given that it occurs

$$\times \text{Consequences of the attack given that it is successful}$$

or symbolically

$$\text{Risk} = P(\text{successful attack}) \times \text{Impact of successful attack}$$

When dealing with layered defenses, for example, in the power grid, the probability of an attack successfully penetrating the outer layer of defense is not a condition of successfully penetrating any previous layer. For all layers of defense contained within this outer layer, the probabilities are a condition of the sequence of previously penetrated layers.

For example, in a two-layer defense—*F1 (firewall 1)* and *F2 (firewall 2)*—the joint probability of successfully penetrating both *F1* and *F2* is $P(F1) \times P(F2|F1)$. That is, the unconditional probability of successfully penetrating *F1* is multiplied by the probability of successfully penetrating *F2*, given that *F1* has been successfully penetrated. This general formula can be extended to accommodate multiple layers.

The Rise of the Nano Machine: AI, the Future of Cybersecurity

The need for a new cybersecurity direction is necessary since IT professionals know signature matching is no longer an effective means to identifying current attacks. Artificial intelligence (AI) has impacted our day-to-day lives for years, whether that's automated voice calls or virtual personal assistants—like Siri—or even self-driving cars.

Eliminating human error is a key driver behind bringing artificial intelligence to security through intelligent video analytics. Humans can easily get distracted, generally have short attention spans, and often find it difficult to focus on multiple things at once—a bank of security screens.

The next step is to implement AI and nanotechnology into cybersecurity ecosystems. The need for a cybersecurity overhaul is necessary as cyber terrorists can easily conceal their attacks from these signature matching security systems. Anti-virus technologies (AVT) have done an excellent job defending an older generation of software applications, but AVT became ineffective in tackling sophisticated and elaborate cyber invasions on business and government servers. Upgrading the current AVT software will only provide short-term relief. Primers to reduce wrinkles and acne and face powder to conceal small flaws or blemishes aren't going to work.

A radical approach is mandatory to secure the skies of Smart Cities. The book *The Cognitive Early Warning Predictive System (CEWPS)* (published by CRC Press, 2015) introduces a new cybersecurity paradigm called digital immunity (DI), which introduces a new infrastructure designed with AI and nanotechnology (NT). Digital immunity infrastructure (DII) replicates the human immune system and is considered the Holy Grail of cybersecurity for Smart Cities. DI is not only disruptive technology, but it is a technological revolution that will bring constructive change to our business world and societal fabric. Once the benefits prevail, it will become the de facto of cyber defense.

Kurzweil's Singularity as Transcendence

There's a bizarre myth going around creating a wave of jitters around the globe, that so-called AI is going to create computers that are smarter than people. The whole idea was created by the genius Ray Kurzweil and his mind-boggling prediction that by adding computer intelligence to our intelligence, with the help of nanobots, our brains will make us "Godlike." Once we're cyborgs, he says, we'll be funnier, sexier, and more loving. All this accelerated evolution is going to happen in the 2030s! Ray Kurzweil published his bestselling book *The Singularity Is Near*, in which stunningly and systematically Kurzweil predicts when humans will transcend biology. His book is an exquisite version of the Iliad discussing the molecular merger of technology and human intelligence.

Right now, we are in the midst of a machine intelligence renaissance. Engineering has given us computers that perform tasks that, until recently, could be done only by people. The software revolution has given us "expert" code that identifies faces at border crossings and matches them against passports or that labels people and objects in photographs posted to social media. Algorithms can teach themselves to play animated video games. A camera and chip embedded in top-of-the-line sedans let the vehicles drive autonomously on the open road. IBM's Deep Blue beat the world's reigning chess champion in 1997, while IBM's Watson accomplished the same for the quiz show *Jeopardy* in 2011. They were taught by trial and error.

Our defense strategy for Smart Cities is to develop a superintelligent DII. The Smart City is a central model for stepwise refinement, to test all engineering projects and computer science systems. DI is one of the projects that will demonstrate its success. We refer to DI as an infrastructure because it is a collection of intelligent components—like a surgical team—that work together pathologically and synchronically. The superintelligent DI is designed to surpass the intelligence of 50 cybercrime Einsteins who will try to sabotage the glamour of the Smart City. The uniqueness of DI is in its molecular structure using nanobots (nano robots) wired with AI programs to perform a specific defense service. As described earlier, nanobots are microscopic robots that will be the size of human blood cells (7–8 μm) or even smaller. Forty-four billion of them could travel through every brain capillary.

There are kinds of nanobots that coexist with DII. The first kind is the *Smart Vaccine Nanobot (SVNanobot)*, and the second kind is the *adversary nanobot (also known as the nano cyborgs or cyborg nanobots)*. On both sides of the battle, Nanobots will be using high-speed wireless to communicate with one another and their higher command. Satellites will also be part of communication. In the next two decades, DI will go down to a nanoscale with its new nanobot armies. Information warfare will become totally nanotechnology centric. Figure 12.1 shows a Smart Vaccine Nanobot and its counterpart cyborg nanobot. the two nanobots look similar, but they belong to two different camps. The exponential acceleration in information technologies created two diametrically opposed technological vectors. One vector builds a digital immunity system with a new design immersed with strong AI

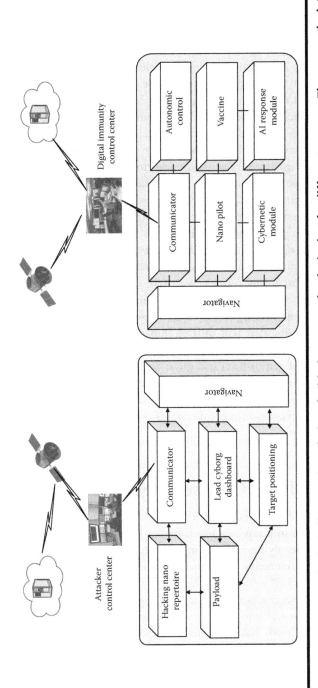

Figure 12.1 Two amazingly similar nanobots designed with the same technologies but for different purpose. The one on the left is the Soft Cyborg Nanobot (we use it to represent the attacker), and the one on the right is the Smart Vaccine Nanobot, which is the city defender. (© 2014 Copyright MERIT CyberSecurity Group. All rights reserved.)

and NT. The second vector is the accelerated proliferation and modernization of malware, also toward strong AI and NT. In two decades, the cyber terror organizers will buy or secretly syphon most of the technologies used in digital immunity.

The DII is a vivid example of strong AI technology. Strong AI is a term used to describe a specific approach in artificial intelligence development. Strong AI's goal is to develop artificial intelligence where the machine's intellectual capability is functionally equal to a human's. We learned how the human immune system operates and how it acquires more experience from historical defense episodes, and replicated how the B-cells and C-cells build scalable armies to defend the body from infection and invading viruses, bacteria, and other microbes that crawl into the body. DI will learn from its mistakes and through stepwise refinement, new algorithms, and expert reasoning rules, DI will become the most resilient layer of defense for Smart Cities. Combined with nanotechnology nanobot services, DI will develop multiple ways of approaching each attack, just as humans do.

Initially, the first prototype will be built in a real testbed environment, by computer science engineers, and then this superintelligent DI infrastructure will reconfigure itself recursively into a better infrastructure! Thus, the first superintelligent DI is the last invention that man will ever need to make, but DI will remain docile and obedient enough to tell its master engineers how to keep it under control. It is an amazing phenomenon, how human intelligence creates an ultra-intelligent machine that will shift us into a new paradigm. Again, to completely mitigate cyber threats and cyberattacks, our DII will be smarter than a whole stadium full of genius-level bad guys. So, in two decades, DI will surpass human intelligence in defeating malware and put an end to the human misery. Within three decades, SV nanobots will have the power and intelligence to convert adversary nano cyborgs into good cyborgs. This is the ultimate quality of life for citizens of the world.

AVT, the Achilles of Cybersecurity

Given current cyber defense technologies vis-à-vis escalating cybercrime, cybersecurity machines have to jump to a much higher level. We will therefore examine the implications of deploying artificial intelligence nanobots for the best cognitive cyber defense and guaranteeing the promise of a better quality of life for the citizens of Smart Cities.

Thus, our sole objective is to build a stunning cybernetic engineering defense that will be ahead of its time for several decades. Information, communication technologies (ICT) already has the hi-tech components needed to build an expert autonomic *geodefense* environment that will put an end to all global moaning and groaning, caused by the inability of antivirus technologies (AVT) to offer cybercrime and its cousin cyber terrorism a one-way ticket to Gehenna. We believe there are several crucial reasons for this enigmatic dilemma:

- AVT has been focusing on winning the first place in a distracting race. Each vendor claims he is the best of the pack.
- AVT products are designed specifically for individual accounts-copying IBM. The Smart City needs a blanket account to cover all its IoT devices.
- AVT products are still reactive by design with limited heuristics and a touch of neural technology. They haven't yet reached the AI or NT domains.
- AVT products are not holistically designed from the top down. Over time, most vendors have kept adding heterogeneous modules from different technologies. Customers were not enthusiastic about half-cooked upgrades. Everyone remembers Microsoft's zero-day nightmare. For example, Symantec oversold Endpoint Protection 14, which was not capable of stopping all smart DDoS cyberattacks.
- Every year, there are over 300 seminars, summits, conferences, and symposia on cybersecurity that resemble farmers' markets. Most of them are organized by salesmen. These conferences generate substantial revenues for hotels and resorts.
- CIOs and CSOs attend these social meetings to exchange ideas, but there is little value-added synergism or collaboration.
- Consulting and data analysis companies endorse the AVT vendor of their choice. It is a marketing contract more than a presentation of new technology products.
- Even the government doesn't have a universal reference architecture to protect Smart Cities. The NIST 800 Series, for example, is a set of 200 voluminous documents that describe US federal government computer security policies, procedures, and guidelines. The publications can be useful as guidelines for enforcement of security rules and as legal references in case of litigation involving security issues.
- The National Institute of Standards and Technology (NIST) are faced with two technical barriers. First, many current Smart City ICT deployments are based on custom systems that are not interoperable or portable across cities. Second, the architectural design efforts of ISO/IEC JTC1, IEC, IEEE, ITU, and consortia have no common denominator or convergence. The NIST are solving this with a consensus *framework* to produce a standardized solution for Smart Cities. The contention between AVT vendors and NIST continues.
- IoT connectivity in the Smart City is a critical success factor that will only be achieved through an intelligent grid which is real-time responsive, cognitive, recursively learning from its past episodes, self-governing, self-repairing, fully scalable, and progressively augments its intelligence over time.
- All the energy and expense spent on research in medicine, health care, and epidemiology have unfortunately not inspired anyone to look at their own *healthy* body and to wonder how immunity has protected the marvelous anatomical infrastructure! No one has done this.

Postulates of Digital Immunity Infrastructure (DI)

Everyone takes it for granted that the human body would not function or even survive if all its components operated independently in isolation without intelligent control messages from the brain telling them what to do. The nervous and immune systems jointly act as the intelligent transport grids to accomplish their orderly assignments to all the components to work together! If either grid went out of balance, we would be sick and deranged.

Here's a revelation that's worth mentioning: During the plague of Athens in 430 BC, the historian Thucydides noted that people who had recovered from a previous bout of the disease could nurse the sick without contracting the illness a second time. In 1857, Louis Pasteur developed acquired immunity through vaccination. It was not until 1891 that Robert Koch proved this, for which he was awarded a Nobel Prize in 1905. His contribution to humanity is much more significant than that of Einstein or Newton. Without adaptive immunity through vaccination, humans would have drastically fallen in jeopardy. What is the moral of the story? We need to build DI to save the digital world.

Based on the concerns that we have listed above, we would like to draft the following postulates:

Postulate 1: Smart Cities need smart grids to manage IoT and control cybercrime.

Postulate 2: IoT devices need a smart grid to manage energy consumption and establish *data collection* metering criteria for quality of living.

Postulate 3: Smart Cities would not be safe with an intelligent security grid. In fact, Smart Cities' security will deteriorate without an intelligent security grid.

Postulate 4: Replication of the cognitive human immune system would be the best solutions to defend Smart Cities.

Postulate 5: DII will be AI-NT-hybrid enabled. These two disruptive technologies will build DI with a unique futuristic security ecosystem with much advanced defense weaponry, which Smart Cities deserve for their citizens.

The Rationale of Defense by Offense

The Department of Defense has published an interesting document titled "Department of Defense Cyber strategy, April 2015." The purpose of this cyber strategy is to guide the development of DOD's cyber forces and strengthen our cyber defense and cyber deterrence posture. It focuses on building cyber capabilities and organizations for DOD's three missions: to defend DOD networks, critical systems, and information; defend the homeland and US national interests against cyberattacks if there are significant consequences; and support operational and contingency plans.

Although the document's title is "Cyber Strategy," it was purely academic, focusing on cross-organizational principles and protocols. The document was like the rest of the government's highly structured documents, with no technical depth or reference to any of the disruptive technologies such as nanoscience and artificial intelligence applications; not even a word on how to defend Smart Cities.

It's great to know that all branches of the US military are currently conducting nanotechnology research, including the Defense Advanced Research Projects Agency (DARPA), Office of Naval Research (ONR), Army Research Office (ARO), and Air Force Office of Scientific Research (AFOSR). The Air Force is heavily involved in the research of composite materials. Among other projects, the Navy Research Laboratory's Institute for Nanoscience has studied quantum dots for application in nanophononics and identifying biological materials. In May 2003, the Army and the Massachusetts Institute of Technology opened the Institute for Soldier Nanotechnologies, a joint research collaboration to develop technologies to better protect soldiers.

With all these disparate nanotechnology research activities in every industry, DII will eventually emerge as a universal reality. Other security projects have not met the expectations of the business world. In the next two decades, all Smart Cities will use DI infrastructure and cybersecurity will take a different orbital direction away from AVT.

So, defense by offense is that proactivity (a strong offensive action) instead of a passive attitude will preoccupy the opposition and ultimately hinder its ability to mount an opposing counterattack, leading to a strategic advantage. If a pathogen (attacking virus) can evade immunologic surveillance and invade a cell successfully, the cell releases a "stress" signal that attracts natural killer (NK) cells to the vicinity. Those NK cells release mediators that induce cell death in the infected cell, which also results in the death of the pathogen. The early "preemptive" attack triggered by the stress signal is the best form of defense.

Digital immunity utilizes its own "defense by offense" strategy. First, all the devices and critical infrastructure systems are connected—with backup routes—to the City Smart Nano Grid. At the same time, the Smart Vaccine Smart Nano Grid is active and the SV Reconnaissance Nanobots are roaming around and monitoring the City Smart Nano Grid. The early warning system is constantly studying the previous attacks and learning from their payloads. When an alert signal is issued, the Smart Vaccine Fighter Nanobots will go into "preemptive" mode as the attacking cyborg nanobots get closer to the Smart City's grid or any of the IoT devices.

Figure 12.2a and 12.2b show how the human immune system can be a reference model to design a digital immune system.

Let's summarize the events (Figure 12.2a):

1. The bee stings the finger and injects its poison.
2. The sensory electrical signal travels to the brain.

3. The brain issues a command to send medical nanobots to the site of the accident.
4. The brain notifies the lymphatics network and the immune system.
5. The B-cells are mobilized as well as the medical nanobots.
6. They create the antibody since they know the chemistry of the poison.
7. The vaccine is carried to the site (victim's finger).
8. The killer cells are also mobilized and ready to go to war.
9. The poison is located and captured.
10. The killer cells have been notified.
11. The poison is quarantined.
12. The waste of the attacker is eaten by the killer cells.

Figure 12.2b is another awesome scenario of a fight to the death between Smart Vaccine Nanobots and their adversaries, who are fighting with the same technology. Sooner or later, smart cybercrime organizers will pay millions of dollars to hire NT and AI hands-on specialists to build the most creative and lethal nanobots. Today,

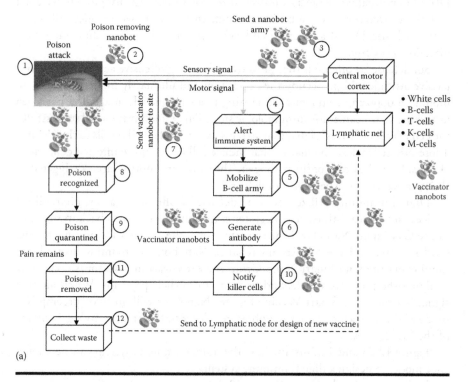

(a)

Figure 12.2 (a) The human immune system is a great reference model to design its counterpart for the digital immune infrastructure of a Smart City. Nanotechnology's magic agents (nanobots) are doing wonders for us; they are going to heal us from all diseases and enhance our longevity by 100 years.

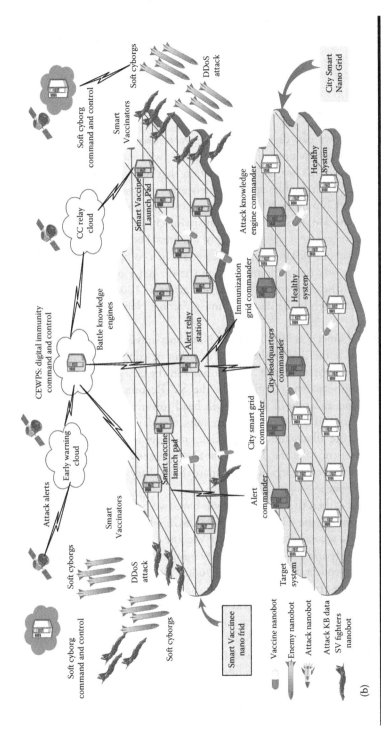

Figure 12.2 (b) What happens in our body when we're hit with a viral attack. The attack starts after penetration of the pathogen, which begins to multiply, mutate, and expand. The wound starts to swell, early warning cells will issue the alert, and the B-cells will be mobilized and head toward the battle field. The payload (antigen) will be matched and the vaccine is created, which will kill the attacking virus. This image describes a raging battle. The approach is the same: the early warning cloud issues the warning, the vaccine nanobots respond, and payloads never reach their targets. (© 2014 Copyright MERIT CyberSecurity Group. All rights reserved.)

we are witnessing unsolvable cybercrimes and this trend will continue. Fortunately, DI system will be the only right mechanism for blocking the attacks and learning from their payloads.

Structure of the Smart Nanogrid

With nanotechnology we can design a single atom transistor of an infinitesimal size of 300 nm. This puts Moore's law in the grave, with no more than simple 18-month doubling. Moore's law is the observation that the number of transistors in a dense integrated circuit doubles approximately every two years. By comparison, IBM's 5 Nano Meter Chip holds 30 billion transistors (https://latesthackingnews. com/2017/06/05/ibms-5-nano-meter-chip-consisting-30-billion-transistors-just-size-sim-card/). A nanometer is one billionth of a meter (1×10^{-9} m). In comparison, a human hair is about 100,000 nm in diameter. On a comparative scale, if the diameter of a marble was one nanometer, then the diameter of the Earth would be about one meter. The diameter of the largest artery is 100,000 mm, and the smallest one is 0.1 mm, while the size of a Smart Vaccine Nanobot varies from 75 to 400 nm.

The smart grid diameter is 300,000 mm. Nanobots and SV Fighter Nanobots will roam freely inside the grid without any queuing or congestion. Figure 12.3 shows a size comparison between the SV nanobot and the city grid.

SV Fighter Nanobots, when notified by the SV Reconnaissance Nanobots, will be mobilized and an army of fighters will head toward the battle sight. The nanogrids (Smart City and Smart Vaccine) are huge compared to the size of nanobots. The grid structure allows the nano particles to move around because all the nanogrid tubes are open. Like the T-cells, the SV Fighter Nanobots are eager to surround the enemy's nano cyborgs and terminate them. They have been trained to defend the city by offence.

As was described earlier, the Smart City will have two Smart tightly connected nanogrids. The first one is the City Smart Grid (CSG), which connects all the city (IoT) devices; and the second one is the Smart Vaccine Grid (SVG), where the SV Fighter Nanobots reside and get organized. They monitor the city grid while roaming around the city to collect data and respond to IoT attacks inside the City Smart Grid with an invincible army of fighting nanobots.

We refer to the digital immunity grid as *infrastructure* because it is a crucial structure for the safety of the city, which cannot survive if it is constantly vulnerable to invasion from hostile nano cyborgs. The nanogrid is in fact a collection of many micro grids connected together, which offer reliability and scalability.

The DII is a unique type of nano architecture, way ahead of its time, designed with special molecular material called *carbon nanotubes*. Figure 12.4 shows a cross-section of the smart nanogrid. The City Smart Grid (CSG) is also a nano

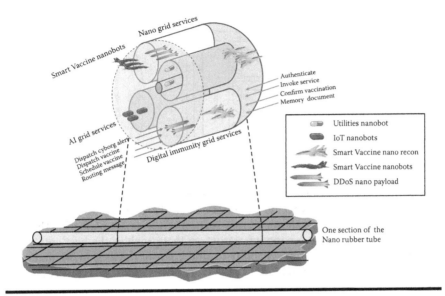

Figure 12.3 **The City Smart Nano Grid is made of nano rubber tube, not copper wire, containing a nebula of communication lines to carry messages, alerts, and battles between the Smart Vaccine Nanobots and the adversary cyborgs. The city grid is tightly coupled to the Digital Immunity Grid (not shown here). The battle takes place in the city's nanogrid. (© 2014 Copyright MERIT CyberSecurity Group. All rights reserved.)**

infrastructure that provides the best cost-effective energy saving and better reliability to all the sensor devices, M2M, and critical systems.

Carbon nanotubes have electrical properties similar to metals. In fact, they are better conductors than the copper normally used in electrical wire, or any other metal. Nanobots move freely, performing their assignments and communicating with other nanobots.

Deployment Strategy of Smart City Nano Defense

It is much easier to build a Smart City than to build a smart grid. With the lack of intelligent defense, the city will be an easy target for continual attacks and disruption of quality of life. Put simply, a Smart City is only as good as its smart grid. Thus, we define the City Smart NanoGrid (CSG) as the integration of

$$\text{Nano Technologies (NT)} + \text{Artificial Intelligence (AI)} + \text{Digital Immunity}$$

$$+ \text{Human Knowledge} + \text{City Science}$$

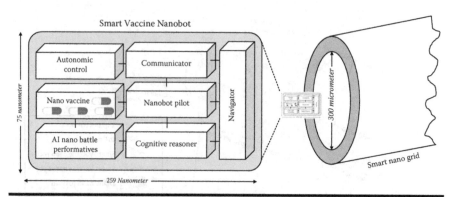

Figure 12.4 The Smart Vaccine Nanobot can easily roam inside the blood and nerve vessels. This image shows a cross-section of the smart nanogrid. The City Smart Grid (CSG) is also a nano infrastructure that provides the best cost-effective energy saving and better reliability to all the sensor devices, M2M, and critical systems. (© 2014 Copyright MERIT CyberSecurity Group. All rights reserved.)

The result of this cohesive integration is an ultra-sophisticated defense of unique structure, beyond the present capabilities. In the science fiction world of Star Trek, replicators can produce practically any physical object, from weapons to a steaming cup of Earl Grey tea (hot!). Long considered to be exclusively the product of science fiction, today some people believe replicators are on the real-time horizon via the technologies of nanotechnology and *3D printing*. When this molecular manufacturing reaches its potential, the technology will drastically change the world.

Nano cyber defense (NCD) ushers nanotechnologies into cybersecurity. It is a revolutionary concept to replace antivirus technologies (AVT) with new weaponry. Computing will go down to the atomic level. We're taking the grid down to the nanoscale level with dimensions of 100 nm (1×10^{-9}). Nanorobotics will allow us to design and build nano robots. Figure 12.4 shows the immense size differential between the grid and nanobots.

The battlefield (Figure 12.5) will be inside the nanogrid. Smart grids will become nano rubber tubes with multiple intercity and bidirectional highways. Smart Vaccine Nano Reconnaissance Nanobots will alarm the control centers to mobilize the defense stage. Like T-cells and B-cells, a trained army of SV Fighter Nanobots will head toward the aggressors. The SV fighters already have knowledge of the attackers and their payloads. This is the secret of nano digital immunity.

Nothing will be visible to the naked eye, but the contribution of immunization will be appreciable and attacks will be neutralized. Let us not underestimate the adroitness of cyber assailants. It will not be a surprise if they fabricate another horizontal strategy to penetrate the Smart City. During a massive attack, the adversary nano cyborgs will mutate to another form and multiply. Part of the Smart City may be damaged from the attack, but the nanogrid will reconfigure itself autonomically and remain operative. The citizens will know about the attack, but their devices

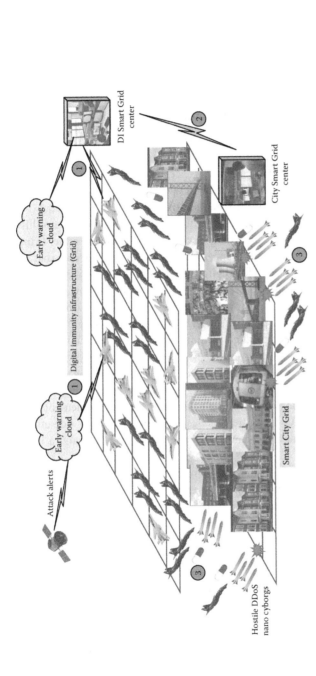

Figure 12.5 In the next two decades, by around 2040, modern cyber warfare will be fought at molecular (B-cell) level, spreading payloads of nanogerms and toxins with nano cyborgs! Digital immunity nanobots (aka Smart Vaccine Nanobots, SV nanobots) will fight with adversary nanobots (aka soft cyborgs), capture them, reverse engineer their payloads, and learn how to prevent similar future attacks. (© 2014 Copyright MERIT CyberSecurity Group. All rights reserved.)

1. Reconnaissance nanobot informs DI Smart grid center about the DDoS attacks
2. DI Smart grid informs the city grid about the attack and SV fighters are mobilized
3. The SV Fighter Nanobots engage with the attackers and defense by office in initiated

will remain connected and the meters will continue to collect data. Human immunity works in the same way. Efficacious vaccines not only protect the immunized, but can also reduce disease among unimmunized individuals in the community through "indirect effects" or "herd protection."

How to Build the Nano Smart Grid

Times have changed and computing is accelerating fast, bringing us new things to improve our life. The gravitational force of the Internet is inescapable. But now, nanotechnology combined with artificial intelligence are an overwhelming double-barrel force sweeping aside the old and replacing it with more captivating, although disruptive, quality of life, comfort, health, and security.

In the next two decades, nano computing will become the new paradigm shift. Computer processors and memory are going down to the molecular scale, bringing speed, reliability, and higher performance/cost. It seems inconceivable that the floppy disk was once the flag-bearer for digital storage devices. A 3.5-inch floppy disk could store a measly 1.44 megabytes of data—not even enough to fit a single mp3 music file. Today, a small one-gigabyte (1000 megabytes) USB flash drive can store about 200 songs. Inside that drive, electrical charges that encode the data are applied to areas across a silicon chip called memory cells, each of which is made up of transistors.

DII is the stunning invention of the 21st century that takes the defense of Smart Cities to the highest level. We're designing the whole defense system at the molecular scale. Nanotechnology is a wonder of our era. We can implement wonders using nanotechnology. We can cure diseases like cancer without side effects, develop invisible cloaks and develop bulletproof suits that can withstand a bullet from a machine gun.

In the next two decades, nanotechnology will give a new meaning to computing. The production of a working *quantum computer* has become a real possibility thanks to recent developments in the field nanotechnology. It may be a little difficult to comprehend that the bit cell size of the nano chip measures 2 × 3 nm, carrying a terabyte-per-chip. In 1995, Richard Feynman eloquently defined nanoelectronics: "There is plenty of room to make [computers] smaller ... nothing that I can see in the physical laws ... says the computer elements cannot be made enormously smaller than they are now. In fact, there may be certain advantages."

Blueprint of the Design of Digital Immunity Infrastructure

The blueprint of the DII design, as shown in Figure 12.6 has six consecutive groups of vertical activities that replicate the human immune/nervous systems. Before setting up a DII, a Smart City must be selected, and the project must be approved by

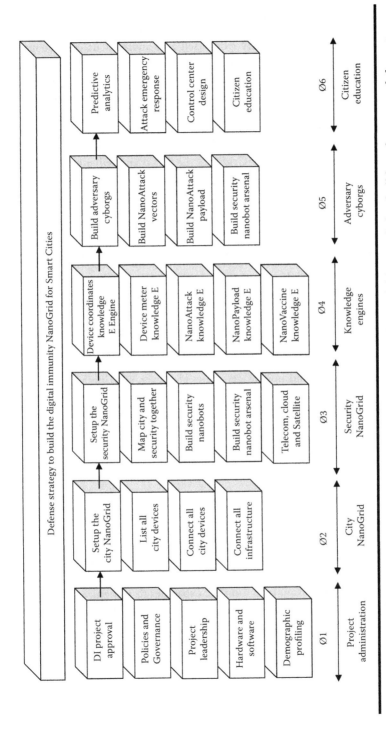

Figure 12.6 The systematic and holistic representation of all the design activities needed to build a robust nano defense to protect a Smart City.

the city managers. DI is a complex endeavor with many technological challenges. Nanotechnology and artificial intelligence can set up an intelligent security infrastructure that will learn recursively from itself and augment its competence and experience. Scaling down to the molecular level, this will open the door for cybercrime to become nanocentric and launch a new era of attacks. The most brilliant feature of DI is the arsenal of the Smart Vaccine Nanobots, which are the wonder of technology and imagination. They work in a military formation, on assigned tasks, during the war against the adversary cyborgs. Nano battles will not be science fiction anymore. The DI NanoGrid (aka the Smart Vaccine Grid (SVG)) is tightly coupled with the City Smart NanoGrid (aka the CSG) and will also have an intelligent NanoGrid to anchor all the IoT devices and to have all the critical systems of the city's infrastructure under its tight security.

Why Do We Need a Blueprint for Defense Strategy?

Mikhail Tal, the famous chess master once said, "You must take your opponent into a deep dark forest where 2 + 2 = 5, and the path leading out is only wide enough for one."

Here's another interesting quote from the father of modern management, Peter Drucker, "The best way to predict your future is to create it."

The moral of these quotes is very simple: you need a very powerful flashlight to know your destination and how to get there. However, crafting a robust strategy to shield Smart Cities for cyberattacks is quite different. In 1974, Evel Knievel, the famous performer and international icon, he failed an attempted canyon jump across Snake River Canyon in the Skycycle X-2, a steam-powered rocket. In the same year, the Frenchman Philippe Petit completed an unbelievable tightrope walk between the Twin Towers. Success or failure depends on the strategy of execution.

$$\text{Strategy} = \text{Human Intelligence} + \text{Visioning} + \text{Goals} + \text{Technology} + \text{Experience} + \text{Risk}$$

Human Intelligence: This is the most crucial component of the polynomial. It is the multifaceted cognitive abilities to learn from concepts, understand, apply logic, and reason, including the capacities to recognize patterns, comprehend ideas, plan, problem solve, make decisions, retain information, and use language to communicate. Intelligence enables humans to experience and think.

Visioning: This is the multidimensional process of seeing a picture mentally. It is an interactive team-oriented activity, to draw a composite picture that majority agrees upon. Visioning is generated from the ability of the analyst to describe an object assembled in his mind.

Goals: These are milestones established in the future that need to be reached. Time, level of effort, and risk are the three attributes used to rank the goal.

Technology: This is the mixture of knowledge, engineering, and science combined to introduce a new generation of products, often disruptive, into the business world and at home. Technology moves forward, improving with time. New products have better quality and performance. The computing industry is leading the way with exponential enhancements. The world is accepting new technologies and dumping old ones. New technology companies have emerged, promoting change, while established business companies are resisting change.

Experience: As time moves forward 24 hours per day, any event that took place prior to that will be registered as a historical experience. Experience is additive and accumulative. It will help during the planning of a new strategy. Experience is an invaluable component.

Risk: The engineering definition of risk is the product of the probability of an undesirable event occurring during the deployment of the strategy, and assessment of the expected harm from the event occurring. Put in a different way, risk is the probability that a threat will generate some vulnerability that will slow down a project. Numerically, risk can be represented as:

$$\text{Risk} = \frac{\text{Threat} \times \text{Vulnerability}}{\text{Countermeasures}} \times \text{Impact}$$

In the final analysis, a successful defense strategy is one that has all the factors that contribute to success and examines all the possible vulnerabilities, assesses the damage incurred, and minimizes their impact during the progress of the project.

Building a Robust Nano Defense for a Smart City

Even the old Egyptians had to draw a systematic and holistic plan before erecting the famous pyramids. To build a Digital Immunity NanoGrid for a Smart City, six major, sequentially and vertically built phases must be completed successfully (Figure 12.6).

Phase 1: Project administration, policies and regulations
Phase 2: Building the City Smart NanoGrid
Phase 3: Building the DII or the Smart Vaccine Grid
Phase 4: Building the knowledge engines that will be used for metering data collection, attack data
Phase 5: Building a Nano Attack Scenario (cyborgs against Smart Vaccine Warriors)
Phase 6: Predictive analytics, citizen education, and attack response

Glossary

Adenosine triphosphate (ATP): Organic molecule that stores energy in a biological cell.

Amines: Organic compounds used as attachment points for molecular structures.

Amphiphile: A molecule that has two distinct parts; a hydrophilic (water-loving) head and a hydrophobic (water-fearing) tail.

Atom: Smallest particle of an element, composed of three types of charged particles: protons (positive), neutrons (neutral), and electrons (negative).

Atomic force microscope (AFM): A scanning probe instrument that measures the atomic force acting on its tip as it moves along the surface of a sample.

Band gap: The energy difference between the top of the valence band and the bottom of the conduction band in semiconductors and insulators. In insulators, the band gap is large—it requires a lot of energy to move valence electrons to the conduction band. In semiconductors, the band gap is not as large; it doesn't require as much energy to move electrons from the valence band to the conduction band. Adding impurities to the semiconductor (called doping) can change the band gap and the amount of energy needed to move electrons. In conductors (metals), the valence band and conduction band overlap, resulting in no band gap.

Benzene: A ring of six carbon atoms, each with one hydrogen atom.

Bioactive materials: Materials capable of interacting with living tissue.

Bioavailability: The extent to which a drug successfully targets specific cells. Used in measuring the effectiveness of drug delivery.

Biometrics: Identification based on personal features such as face recognition or fingerprint.

Biomimetic: Applying systems found in nature to the design of engineering systems and modern technology. Velcro is an example of a biomimetic: the plastic hooks and loops resemble plant burrs (hooks) that cling to animal fur and clothing (loops).

Biosensor: A sensor that detects biological molecules such as proteins.

Bottom-up fabrication: A construction process that works with the smallest units of a material first (in this context, atoms) and builds them up into the form of the final product. Compare top-down fabrication.

Bucky ball: Short for buckminsterfullerene; a molecule containing 60 carbon atoms in a soccer-ball orientation. Also known as fullerene or C60.

Bucky paper: A randomly oriented network of carbon nanotubes formed into a flat sheet.

Cantilever: A solid beam allowed to oscillate at one end. Used in atomic force microscopes (AFMs).

Carbon nanotube: A graphite sheet rolled up into a tube.

Catalyst: A substance that reduces the amount of energy required during a chemical reaction. Its presence increases the rate of reaction without the consuming the catalyst.

Chirality: In the context of this book, chirality is the "twist" of a carbon nanotube. Twisting carbon nanotubes down the length of the tube gives them unique properties that depend upon the degree of the twist. (For example, specific twists make a nanotube either metallic or semiconducting.)

Colloidal self-assembly: A process by which colloids assemble themselves into useful alignments; used in developing photonic crystals.

Colloids: Very small particles (within the 1 nm to 1000 nm range) that remain dispersed in a liquid for a long time. Their small size prevents them from being filtered easily or settled rapidly.

Colorimetric sensors: Sensors that provide an indicator for quick macroscopic analysis by changing color.

Composite: An engineered material composed of two or more components.

Conduction band: The energy at which electrons can move freely through the material.

Covalent bond: Atoms that bond sharing two electrons.

Curing: Process of hardening. In this context, heat is added to a liquid polymer to harden it.

Cyborg: A nano cybernetic robot (nanobot); usually represents the horrific attackers who perform devious attacks. The Smart Vaccine is a good robot who defends the city.

Data mining: Sifting through large amounts of data, trying to find relationships and patterns within the information.

Decoherence: The breakdown of quantum properties (super position and entanglement) changing the behavior of the system from quantum mechanical to classical physics. This is usually the result when a quantum mechanical system interacts with its environment.

Dendrimer: An artificial, polymer-based molecule that resembles a foam ball with tree sprigs shooting out of it in every direction. Contains a great number of voids between the sprigs, which allows it to carry drug molecules.

Deoxyribonucleic acid (DNA): The nucleic acid that carries the genetic blueprint for all forms of cellular life.

Diffraction: The spreading or bending of light as it passes by an object. An example of diffraction is using a prism to spread sunlight into a spectrum of color.

Digital immunity (DI): The general term for vaccinating Smart City devices in the grid.

Doping: Adding specific impurities ("dopants") to give a material desired properties—as in the process that creates either n-type or p-type silicon.

Electrochromatics: Materials that change color when energized by an electrical current.

Electroluminescence: Converting electrical energy into light.

Electron-beam lithography (EBL): Fabrication method that uses a tight beam of electrons to form nanoscale features on a substrate.

Electro-osmosis: A method that uses an electric field to move liquids through a nano channel. The sides of the nano channel's wall are charged, allowing the liquid to slip through at a constant rate.

Electrophoresis: A method of using an electric field to move particles through a nano channel and separate them by size. The particles move at a rate inverse to their mass: the larger ones are slower than the smaller ones.

Endocytosis: A process whereby cells absorb particles by enveloping them with the help of vesicles formed from the cell wall.

Enigma: A mystery wrapped in a riddle. "Atomic interactions at the nano-scale are an enigma that is yet to be fully understood." According to Dr. Richard Feynman, pioneer of quantum computing, nanotechnology and women are both enigmas.

Entanglement: Relationship in which the quantum states of two or more objects are always described with reference to each other, even if they're physically separate.

Exocytosis: The removal of particles by enveloping them in a vesicle and releasing them outside the cell wall.

Extreme ultraviolet (EUV): Light whose wavelengths are in the range of 10–200 nm, outside the higher end of the visible spectrum.

Fabrication: Creating something physical. In the context of this book, the actual manufacture of computer processors.

Fiber optics: Technology that uses light pulses through thin glass fibers at high speeds.

Field-effect transistor: The most common type of transistor used in computer processors. It has a gate that controls whether it's a 1 or a 0.

Fluorescence: A property of some molecules to absorb one wavelength of light and then emit light at a higher wavelength.

Fullerene: A molecule containing 60 carbon atoms in a soccer-ball orientation. Also known as buckminsterfullerene, Bucky ball, or C60.

Functionalization: Attaching groups of molecules to a surface to serve a specific purpose.

Graphite: A flat sheet of benzene rings attached together.

Gray goo: Nanotech disaster scenario in which myriads of self-replicating nano assemblers make uncountable copies of themselves and consume the earth: "gray" because they're machines; "goo" because their small size makes them look like a thick liquid when taken together.

Hemoglobin: Oxygen-carrying protein in blood cells.

Holographic data-storage system (HDSS): High-capacity data storage, using pages of data rather than lines of data. This type of memory has both high capacity and high transfer rates.

Hybridization: The process of joining two complementary strands of DNA together to form a double-stranded molecule.

Hydrodynamic focusing: "Water-loving" materials that are soluble in water. In a molecule, the part of the molecule that is attracted to water molecules.

Hydrophilic: "Water-loving" materials that are soluble in water. In a molecule, the part of the molecule that is attracted to water molecules.

Hydrophobic: "Water-fearing" materials that do not dissolve in water. In a molecule, the part of the molecule that is repulsed by water molecules.

Hysteresis: A property of magnetism: the magnetic effect doesn't disappear when an applied magnetic field is withdrawn.

Impedance: The degree to which a wire resists the flow of electricity.

In vitro: Biological or medical experiments done outside the body, usually in a Petri dish.

In vivo: Biological or medical experiments done within a living subject.

Lab-on-a-chip: Product that results from miniaturizing the processes of a lab (such as fluid analysis) into the space of a microchip.

Laminar flow: Smooth and regular fluid flow. Opposite of turbulence.

Laser: Acronym for "light amplification through stimulated emission of radiation." An intense, powerful beam of light produced by this process is made up of nearly parallel waves.

Liposome: A spherical vesicle composed of a phospholipid bilayer, used to deliver drugs or genetic material into a cell.

Magnetic random-access memory (MRAM): Random-access memory that's based on magnets instead of capacitors. This type of memory is fast and nonvolatile (i.e., it doesn't disappear when you turn off the power), and uses less energy.

Magnetic tunnel junction (MTJ): A type of magnetic random-access memory (MRAM).

Metallofullerene: A metal atom caged in a fullerene.

Metrology: The study of measurements.

Micelles: Spherical micro-structures consisting of amphiphiles.

Microelectromechanical system (MEMS): A mechanical system or machine that exists at the micro-level.

Microfluidics: The study of the behavior of fluids at volumes thousands of times smaller than in a common droplet. Fluid at this level is very viscous; water moves like honey.

Molecular electronics: Using organic molecules instead of silicon to make much smaller, faster, energy-stingier computer processors and memory components.

Molecule: Two or more atoms chemically bonded together.

Multiwalled carbon nanotubes (MWNT): Multiple carbon nanotubes within each other.

Nano: Greek for "dwarf," meaning one billionth.

Nanometer (nm): One billionth of a meter.

Nano shells: Gold-coated silica spheres which, when injected into the bloodstream, attach themselves to cancer cells. The nano shells are then illuminated with a laser, giving off heat and killing the tumor cells.

Nanotechnology: Technology development at the atomic and molecular range (1 nm to 100 nm) to create and use structures, devices, and systems that have novel properties because of their small size.

Nanowire: Very small wires composed of either metals or semiconductors.

Optical tweezers: A strongly focused laser beam used to grasp and move micro- and nano-size translucent particles.

Organic molecules: Carbon-based molecules that make up the solid portions of living things, as well as certain materials such as plastics and oil.

Organic surfaces: Surfaces that are nonmetallic, such as skin, wood, or fabric.

Oxidation: Chemically combining oxygen with another substance; fire and rust are two examples.

Parallel processing: Simultaneous execution of the same task on multiple processors. Fast, nanoscale processors could make this technique possible on an unprecedented scale, as in the quantum computer.

Pharmacogenetics: The study of how a patient's genetic make-up will affect his or her response to medicines.

Phospholipids: Naturally occurring amphiphiles that make up human cell walls.

Photolithography: A computer-processor fabrication technique that uses light to expose a photosensitive film, resulting in the needed pattern of circuits at a much smaller scale.

Photon: A particle that is a packet of light.

Photonic band gap: A band gap that corresponds to a specific wavelength of light used in photonic crystals. Photons that have this particular wavelength have to travel within this photonic band gap, restricted from the surrounding material. Useful for diverting light at the molecular level.

Photonic crystal: A "light insulator"—materials that control how much (or what kind of) light is allowed to pass through the nanocrystal.

Photonics: The science of manipulating photons.

Photoresist: A substance that becomes soluble when exposed to light. Used in photolithography.

Piezoelectric transducer (PZT): A material that expands and contracts according to the amount of electric current that travels through it.

Plasma: A gas made of charged particles. An example of naturally occurring plasma is lightning. You may have seen plasma lamps—glass globes with sparks shooting around inside.

Polymers: Plastic—large molecules made from many smaller molecules usually composed of carbon atoms bonded in long chains.

Quantum computer: A computer that exploits the quantum mechanical nature of particles, such as electrons or atomic nuclei, to manipulate information as quantum sized bits (q-ubit). This quantum computer will be able to perform quick operations in parallel solving problems that can't be solved with today's computer (e.g., factoring large numbers).

Quantum cryptography: Cryptography scheme that relies on quantum mechanics to ensure accurate key exchange and prevent eavesdropping.

Quantum dot: A semiconductor nanocrystal that exhibits quantum behavior in optical or electrical processes.

Quantum mechanics: In physics, a theory that describes physical interactions between atoms more accurately than classical physics, often with results that seem strange from an everyday frame of reference.

Quantum tunneling: A quantum-mechanical effect of transitioning through a state that classical physics would forbid. An analogy is throwing a ball at a wall and having it appear on the other side.

Quantum: In atomic physics, a discrete and basic unit, similar to the way an individual electron is the basic unit of electricity. Plural form is quanta.

q-ubit: Quantum bit—the smallest unit in quantum computing.

Random-access memory (RAM): Memory storage that accesses data anywhere on the storage medium.

Repeaters: In-line amplifiers that take fading light or electrical signals and resend them with more power.

Respirocytes: Tiny mechanical spheres used to store and release oxygen directly within the bloodstream.

Scanning electron microscope (SEM): Electron microscope that creates images of nanoscale features by bombarding the surface of a sample with a stream of electrons, scanning back and forth, and reading the reflected electrons as they bounce off the surface.

Scanning probe microscope: An instrument that studies the properties of surfaces at the atomic level by scanning an atomically sharp probe over the sample. This produces an image of the sample's topography with atomic resolution.

Scanning tunneling microscope (STM): The first scanning probe instrument—measures electrons tunneling between a scanning tip and a conducting surface.

Schottky barrier: Area of resistance to electrical conduction, occurring at the junction between the metal wires and the semiconductor in a computer processor.

Self-assembled monolayers (SAMs): A single layer of atoms or molecules that has assembled itself under controlled conditions. This makes it possible to design surfaces at the molecular scale.

Self-assembly: Process that creates the specific conditions under which atoms and molecules spontaneously arrange themselves into a final product. An example of self-assembly is the automatic arrangement of phospholipids into a cell wall.

Semiconductor: Material that has more electrical conductivity than an insulator (which has no conductivity) but less than a conductor; it can be made to insulate or conduct electricity in patterns, as in a computer processor.

Shape-memory alloy (SMA): A metal alloy that remembers its geometry. After it is deformed, it is heater to a specific temperature and regains its original geometry by itself.

Single-electron transistor (SET): A transistor that switches between on and off (in computer terms, 1 and 0) by using a single electron—much smaller than a traditional transistor, which uses many electrons to switch.

Single-walled carbon nanotube (SWNT): A carbon nanotube with one wall. Compare multiwalled carbon nanotube.

Smart Vaccine: A nano object used in digital immunity as the agent that performs vaccination on IoT attached to the Smart City. Is called the Holy Grail of cybersecurity.

Soft lithography: A process that uses polymers for molding and printing micro- and nanostructures. Pioneered by George Whitesides and used for microfluidics and its descendant, nanofluidics.

Spectrometers: Tools that reveal the composition of things by measuring the light absorbed or emitted by atoms or molecules.

Spintronics: "Spin-based electronics" that exploits not only an electron's charge but also its spin.

Sputter deposition: A method of creating a thin film of metal by sputtering fine particles onto a surface.

Stent: An expandable wire mesh used to keep a blood vessel open.

Strained silicon: New method of improving processor speed by stretching individual silicon atoms apart so electrons flow through a transistor faster with little resistance. Compare superconductor.

Substrate: The supporting surface that serves as a base.

Superconductor: A material through which electricity flows with zero resistance.

Superlattice: A crystal formed of thin layers. A natural example is graphite.

Superposition: When an object simultaneously possesses two or more values of a specified quantity. Useful in the development of quantum computers.

Surface tension: The pull of a liquid into its most compact form to minimize the amount of energy used, keeping the surface area to a minimum.

Surfactants: "Surface-active" molecules that reduce the surface tension between two liquids. Surfactants are used in many detergents as a dispersant between oil and water.

Tetra pods: Pyramid-shaped nanocrystals that resemble children's jacks.

Top-down fabrication: A construction process in which we first work at the large scale and then cut away until we have a smaller product. This is similar to a sculptor cutting away at a block of marble producing the final product, a statue. Compare bottom-up fabrication.

Transistor: A switch that determines whether a bit is a 1 or a 0.

Uncertainty principle: In quantum mechanics, a principle made famous by Werner Heisenberg: Measuring one property in a quantum state will perturb another property. You can, for example, measure the position or momentum of an electron—but not both at once.

Valence electrons: The electrons in the outermost shell of an atom. These electrons largely dictate the chemical reactions of the atom.

van der Waals: Weak electrostatic forces between atoms.

Vesicles: Micelles with two layers: a reverse micelle surrounded by a regular micelle. Resembles the walls of biological cells.

Viscosity: The measure of resistance of a fluid—its "thickness."

Water window: A range of frequencies in the electromagnetic spectrum that are most easily transmitted through water, making them suitable for optical imaging (800–1300 nm).

Wavelength: In physics, the distance between one wave peak and the next in a transmitted wave of radiant energy. Typically measured in nanometers.

Source: Selected terms related to this chapter from www.if4it.com/it-glossary and from publications and educational seminars of MERIT CyberSecurity.

Bibliography

http://www.fieldservicematters.com/adventures-in-artificial-intelligence-machine-learning/

Nanotechnology and defense: http://www.heritage.org/defense/report/nanotechnology-and-national-security-small-changes-big-impact

http://www.information-age.com/rise-machine-ai-future-security-123461783/

Kurzweil: http://www.huffingtonpost.com/entry/ray-kurzweil-nanobots-brain-godlike_us_560555a0e4b0af3706dbe1e2

Conceptual model of smart grid: http://electrical-engineering-portal.com/conceptual-model-of-smart-grid-framework-by-iec

Nano thermology: http://www.heritage.org/defense/report/nanotechnology-and-national-security-small-changes-big-impact

https://scholar.lib.vt.edu/ejournals/JOTS/v41/v41n1/pdf/tate.pdf

http://www.information-age.com/role-ai-cyber-security-123465795/

Conceptual model of nano defense: http://electrical-engineering-portal.com/conceptual-model-of-smart-grid-framework-by-iec

Working with nano: https://www.nano.gov/nanotech-101/what/working-nanoscale

Amazing nanotechnology: http://www.33rdsquare.com/2013/04/the-amazing-potential-of-nanotechnology.html

Chapter 13

Cyber Terrorism Launched against Smart Cities

We all remember General George Patton's famous quote: "May God have mercy upon my enemies, because I won't..."

Introduction

In August 2000, Dorothy Denning, from Georgetown University, at a testimony before the Special Oversight Panel on Terrorism Committee on Armed Services at the US House of Representatives, eloquently defined the term cyber terrorism:

> Cyber terrorism is the convergence of cyberspace and terrorism. It refers to unlawful attacks and threats of attack against computers, networks, and the information stored therein when done to intimidate or coerce a government or its people in furtherance of political or social objectives. Further, to qualify as cyberterrorism, an attack should result in violence against persons or property, or at least cause enough harm to generate fear. Attacks that lead to death or bodily injury, explosions, or severe economic loss would be examples. Serious attacks against critical infrastructures could be acts of cyberterrorism, depending on their impact. Attacks that disrupt nonessential services or that are mainly a costly nuisance would not be defined as cyber terrorism.

As the Internet and associated digital technologies continue their expansion throughout social life, the "cyber" prefix has been applied to a growing list of diverse activities and phenomena. Among these we find the notorious term "cyber terrorism."

It's been over a quarter of century of agonizing uphill battle against cyber terrorism, and we need to think out of the box. Our thinking should shift from vertical to lateral. We need to detach our affinity from cybersecurity and cyber terrorism and move to *nanosecurity* and *nano terrorism*—written this way as aphoristic labels.

The United States is the undisputed king of nanotechnology (NT), and is just another example of why the country is regarded as the only real-world superpower. It is definitely the best country in nanotechnology. The time is ripe to extend the realm of NT into cyber terrorism and have control over this seven-headed dragon.

Perspectives of Nano Technology

In order to provide the necessary perspective, the following working definitions of nanotechnology, and its distinction from nanoscience, are listed below.

Nanotechnology: When you go down to the molecular scale, you have better control over the matter. Nanotechnology is considered to be, more so than ever, a technology that will have great impact on all aspects of culture and society. Nanotechnology is the application of nanoscience—plain and simple. You will see many different forms of the above definitions in the media and scientific literature, but essentially all the definitions, after distillation and purification, crystallize into a few key forms—in particular that nanotechnology consists of materials with small dimensions, remarkable properties, and great potential.

Nanotechnology: Based on the manipulation, control, and integration of atoms and molecules to form materials, structures, components, devices, and systems at the nanoscale, is the application of nanoscience, especially to industrial and commercial objectives.

Nanotechnology: Is a horizontal enabling convergent technology that will impact the development of enhanced materials and devices.

Nanotechnology: Will require that a new genre of partnerships be formed among and between business, academe, and government. It will focus study and effort on potential societal implications of a new and certainly disruptive technology. Nanotechnology is predicted to significantly impact the wealth and security of nations. Nanotechnology is the next industrial revolution.

Nanoscale: The nanoscale, based on the nanometer (nm) or one-billionth of a meter, exists specifically between 1 and 100 nm. In the general sense, materials with at least one dimension below one micron but greater than one nanometer can be considered as nanoscale materials.

Nanoscience: Exists specifically between 1 and 100 nm. In the general sense, materials with at least one dimension below one micron but greater than one nanometer can be considered as nanoscale materials.

Nanoscience: Nanoscience is the study of nanoscale materials—materials that exhibit remarkable properties, functionality, and phenomena due to the influence of small dimensions. Nanoscience is similar to materials science in that it is an integrated convergence of academic disciplines. There are a couple of major distinctions between the two: size and biology. We understand size by now but we also understand that materials science traditionally does not include biological topics.

The United States is the leader in artificial intelligence (AI) and nanotechnology (NT), but we haven't seen substantial advancement in the domain of cybersecurity. Although the United States is second to none in the whole spectrum of military as well, massive cyberattacks could inflict more damage and fear than a squadron of F-35s. The Chinese military stole US plans to the technically sophisticated F-35 Joint Strike Fighter, allowing Beijing to create the copycat J-31. Hackers with connections to the Iranian government were charged earlier this year for attacks on US banks and a dam in New York. North Korean operatives released a trove of damaging emails from Sony as the entertainment company planned to release a comedy with an unflattering portrayal of the country's leader. Russia, with its massive cyber army, is widely suspected in a hack of the Democratic National Committee that undermined the integrity of the US election.

The United States, as of right now, is not fully prepared to match incidents like these. The United States has to focus on AI and NT to leapfrog forward and demonstrate its might in protecting its inventions and heritage. Furthermore, it would be the biggest contributor to global peace. Albert Einstein once said, "We cannot solve our problems with the same thinking we used when we created them. No problem can be solved from the same level of consciousness that created it. If I had an hour to solve a problem, I'd spend 55 minutes thinking about the problem and 5 minutes thinking about solutions." We need to get out of the antivirus technology (AVT) bubble and head toward a brighter security future with the help of AI and NT.

Adding Insult to Injury

We recognize with lament two facts related to US cybersecurity. First, the reason we still have cyber terrorism is because we're not capable of defeating it, or even to control it. The second reason is that the United States is the inventor of the Internet and we gave it to the world on a silver platter. Now the United States is playing third fiddle and is not able to regain the leadership it deserves.

Take for example the arrogant countries of Russia, China, Iran, and North Korea which are routinely launching cyberattacks on peaceful cities, robbing technology data from private companies or spying on military sites by using online tools to spread twisted propaganda, and hiring unethical computer technicians (mercenaries) to do the dirty work. There are over 1500 training centers and academies to teach radicals how to become cyber fighters and militants. It is like training dogs to be killer machines; students are mind-programmed to use the most lethal tools of the Devil.

The techno-espionage is not going to slow down. The Silicon Valley located in the San Francisco Bay area has been suffering from a shortage of computer specialists. Every month, 51 new tech companies are launched and looking for top-notch computer specialists. There are over 16,000 technical positions open according to a *Silicon Valley Business Journal* report in August 2015. These hi-tech companies lure specialists from competitors, outsource projects, or hire from abroad. This opens the front gate to major potential espionage and intellectual property theft. It is a horrific technical bleeding that has no effective solution.

As time goes by, US cybersecurity will become more fragmented and out of synch with the pace of technology. Adversaries will disguise their Internet and mask their identities and serial information wars will occur. Smart Cities will innocently be easy targets of serial cyber assaults with new breeds of cyber terrorism. Thus, the United States should finally wake up and shift the focus toward using nanotechnology and build a new cybersecurity architecture for the nation's critical infrastructures and Smart Cities. Let's remember, nanotechnology is expected to change the way we live. In that sense, it can be considered to be revolutionary. Nanotechnology is also the product of the natural evolutionary process of miniaturization. The immersion of nanotechnology into cybersecurity will be a great wild invention that will save the face of America. More importantly, nano cybersecurity will transform the most parlous cyberattacks into domesticated cyborgs serving the Smart City of the future. We will expand on this subject later in this chapter.

Anatomy of Cyber Terrorism

Nearly 75% of the world's population practices one of the five most influential religions of the world: Buddhism, Christianity, Hinduism, Islam, and Judaism. The Internet is the keystone and the sole causality of cyber terrorism.

Here's the causality relationship of cyber terrorism, which precedes its effect, and includes the factors that were involved in the intervention:

$$\text{Hostility} = \text{Religion Fanaticism} + \text{Political Conflict}$$

$$+ \text{Social Revenge} + \text{Territorial Gain}$$

$$+ \text{Radical Activists} + \text{Intimidation} + \text{Technological Rivalry}$$

These are some of the major exogenous reasons that will lead to cyber terrorism. Obviously, cyber terrorists who belong to radical organizations will not be intimidated to reveal their terror act. Often, government-sponsored cyber terrorism acts will be denied or politely kept silent. It has been said that tomorrow's terrorist may be able to do more damage with a keyboard than with a bomb.

Cyber Terrorism Attraction to Smart Cities

How Do Cyber Terrorists Plan an Attack?

Not all Smart Cities will be attacked by hacking professionals. Only selected Smart Cities will be carefully studied before the attack launch. Vulnerability varies with the size of the city and all its components such as the number of citizens, traffic intensity, law enforcement, traffic lights, banks, government buildings, energy data collection, the level of connectivity, the number of critical infrastructures, and the sophistication of the power grid.

To plan an attack on a Smart City, attackers use a well-known graphical method called the directed acyclic graph (DAG, a graph without a cycle). It is made of nodes, which are represented as circles or ovals. Edges are the connections between the nodes. An edge connects two nodes. They are usually represented by lines, or lines with arrows. A directed acyclic graph has a topological ordering which means that the nodes are ordered in sequence—the starting node has a lower value than the ending node. The DAG is a probabilistic causality graph that shows how events are happening according to their respective probabilities of occurrence. Figures 13.1a,b show how cyber terrorists have used causality methods to acquire higher visibility and confidence on the incoming attack.

How Can We Quantitatively Measure the Success of a Cyberattack?

The success of a cyberattack is measured by the risk and vulnerability of a critical system.

Risk R is defined as a set of triplets:

$$R = \{(s_i, p_i, x_i)\}, \quad i = 1, 2, \ldots, N$$

where:

s_i is the scenario identification or description
p_i is the probability of that scenario
x_i is the consequence or evaluation measure of that scenario, i.e., the measure of damage

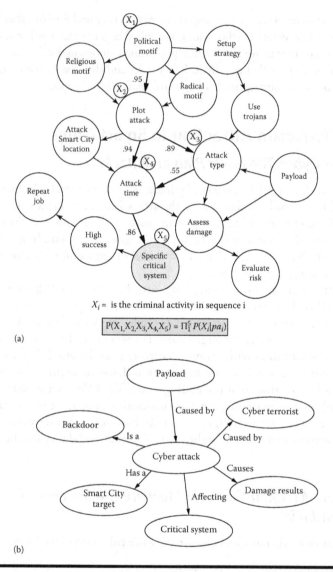

(a)

$X_i =$ is the criminal activity in sequence i

$$P(X_1, X_2, X_3, X_4, X_5) = \Pi_1^5 \, P(X_i | pa_i)$$

(b)

Figure 13.1 **(a) This directed acyclic graph represents a knowledge model of a cyberattack. It is also called the Bayesian network model. All cyberattacks can be transformed into this model. Ontology is the technique that is used to convert a cyberattack into a knowledge model. Web Ontology Language (OWL) does the conversion. The Semantic Resource Description Framework (RDF) stores it in the Attack Knowledge Base. The vertices (circles) represent the variables (criminal activity), and the arcs (arrows) represent the causal relationship between the activities. (b) Usually cyberattacks have six attributes that are semantically related to one another. We can use the ontology technique to group similar cyberattacks and convert them into a "knowledge model," as was explained in Chapter 9.**

Commonly defined, risk is the potential for an unwanted outcome resulting from an incident, event, or occurrence, as determined by its likelihood and the associated consequences. Quantitatively, risk is estimated as the expected value of loss from one or more scenarios multiplied by the likelihood or frequency of those scenarios. A scenario describes an incident (attack, accident, or natural disaster) and what specifically is being attacked or affected. The probability or frequency of a scenario and the associated consequences are calculated with respect to a domain, which defines the extent of the effects of calculations. The domain is defined either geographically, or functionally (e.g., cascading, interdependent effects), or both. The domain also includes the time horizon (for example, immediate, 1 week, or 5 years).

To compute a probabilistic risk assessment, a set of attack scenarios is specified. For each attack scenario, a probability of occurrence is determined and the Expected Value of the Consequences (EVC) given the attack occurrence is calculated. The following relationship is a mathematical formula for a probabilistic risk assessment:

$$\text{Risk (Scenario } S, \text{ Domain } D) = \sum_{\text{Scenario } S} P(\text{Scenario } S, \text{ Domain } D)$$
$$\times EVC(\text{Scenario } S, \text{ Domain } D)$$

In case a quantitative risk metric is given to restrict the condition of the attack, then the risk of the attack becomes conditional. This is called the conditional risk associated with that attack. The conditional risk, defined as the expected value of loss given that the scenario occurs, is calculated as follows:

Conditional Risk = Probability that an attack is successful given that it occurs

$$\times \text{Consequences of the attack given that it is successful}$$

Or symbolically:

$$\text{Risk} = P(\text{successful attack}) \times \text{Impact of successful attack}$$

Vulnerability can also be defined as the conditional probability of success given an attack for a given scenario:

$$\text{Probability (Success|Attack)} = P(S|A)$$

What Is the Planning Cycle for a Cyberattack?

The cyber terror strategists will draft the plan and evaluate every risk and outcome associated with the attack. Figure 13.2 shows the systematic six phases of the

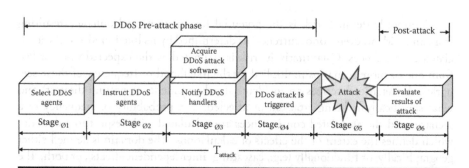

Figure 13.2 The systematic six phases of the DDoS cyberattack. The attack is as good as its plan. One successful attack will breed more wicked terror with more experience and higher technology. Most attacks follow the same pattern. The DDoS attacker has to have a large reservoir of knowledge, a bulletproof plan, and wide-angle vision. Skipping one stage makes the attack less successful. (© 2014 Copyright MERIT CyberSecurity Group. All rights reserved.)

cyberattack. There are six consecutive stages to a cyberattack. The attack is just as good as its plan. One successful attack will breed more wicked terror with more experience and higher technology. Most attacks follow the same pattern.

The Futuristic Architecture of Nano Digital Immunity

The future is here, and we're going through an unprecedented global technological acceleration and intelligence explosion. There is no "cast in concrete" charted course for technology; only innovation drives it forward. Albert Einstein was right when he said, "Technological progress is like an axe in the hands of a pathological psychopath."

The most fascinating revelation about the Internet is its immersion in the atomic world of nanotechnology. The evolution of computer technology is truly amazing. As the old saying goes, "necessity is the mother of invention." It started out with punch card computing with chain printing, then it moved into dial-up computing with laser printing, then cyber computing with 3D printing, and finally into a bright day with nano computing and artificial intelligence. Malware kept abreast of the best technologies and it built a space of its own to promote organized crime, with a new breed of cyber terrorism, and satellite and botnet terrorism. The world has been plagued with intrusive software engines that package hostile vectors loaded with a timed payload of Trojans, rootkits, worms, backdoors, and distributed denial-of-service attacks. The new revelation of *Crime-as-a-Service (CaaS)* created a new portfolio of disruptive and disturbing "booby traps" that rob our banks, swipe our medical records, blackmail our citizens, narcotize our youth, and robotize our minds. Not only that, but cybercrime has drilled deep holes into the business world and tarnished the credibility of many major companies with "zero-day" bugs.

Cyber terrorists leave nothing to the imagination. To these rogue actors, Smart Cities are a live coliseum where they can demonstrate their superior cyber terror skills to the rest of the world. Since Smart Cities' communication arteries connect the Internet to everything, the malware hell-raisers are happy to see that in Smart Cities *the eggs are all in one basket.* The cyber terrorists will use the city grid to lead them to the selected target. They don't want to use their hands to commit any crimes; they let Internet do the nasty stuff.

When the cyber terrorists zoom in on a city, their strategy of attack is to paralyze the city and spread fear. They look for the most indispensable systems:

- Smart energy: More efficient energy production, grid-centric distribution, smart devices, and metering—at the city, building, and home levels
- Critical infrastructure systems
- Internet of Things devices
- Smart parking: Monitoring of parking space availability in the city
- Smart lighting: Intelligent and weather adaptive street lights
- Smart City traffic: Monitoring of vehicle traffic and congestion and pedestrian levels to optimize driving and walking routes
- Smartphone detection: Detect smart phones and in general any device that works with Wi-Fi or Bluetooth interfaces
- Smart roads: Intelligent highways with warning messages and diversions according to climate conditions and unexpected events like accidents or traffic jams

Cyber terrorists are aware of the latest advances in nano technology and artificial intelligence, and they have shown time and time again their eagerness and technical skills to leverage these two emerging technologies to their advantage, as a golden opportunity too good to pass up. They have embarked on an aggressive mission to jump on the nano technology bandwagon and bring their evil acts to the molecular level. They form intelligence teams to collect any material on the topic of NT and AI as related to cybersecurity. They also form research teams to discuss nano security with academia and software companies. They have visited half a dozen Smart Cities around the world, to examine how critical infrastructure is protected. They have also hired a team of specialists in AI and NT to develop the nano software that is called *Nano Soft Cyborg* or *Cyborg Nanobot.*

The mischievous attackers are not resting on their laurels; they are in the war room brainstorming and blueprinting the next attack. Figure 13.3 shows how cybercrime and terrorism have evolved and become more lethal and sophisticated. 3G nano applications will be assembled symmetrically by the attackers and deployed in Smart Cities.

Cyber terrorism is well funded by adversary nations to lead asymmetric warfare against the United States and its allies. Cyber terrorists are

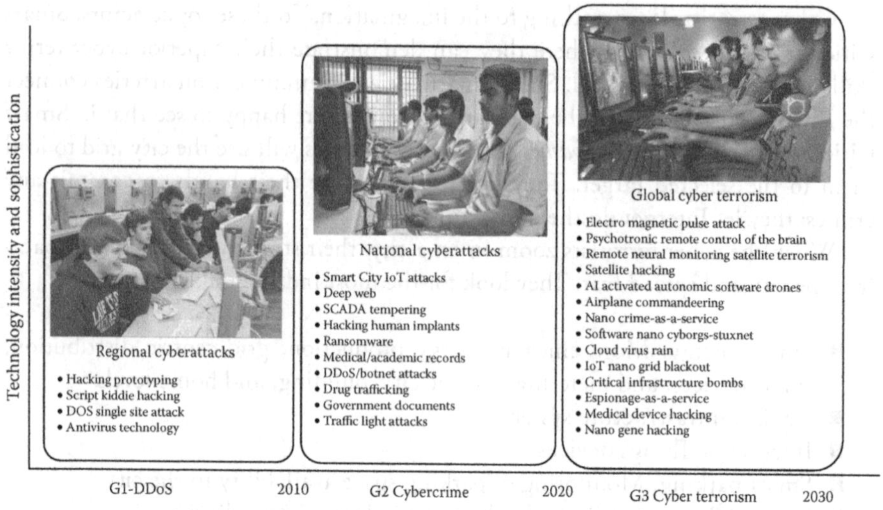

Figure 13.3 The technological progress from the first generation all the way to the third one. 3G cyber terrorism is the most challenging because of two formidable technologies (AI and NT) that have brought cybercrime to the molecular level, where matter can be controlled better. In 2030, cyber terrorism will be totally immersed in these two technologies. Both sides will be using it. (© 2014 Copyright MERIT CyberSecurity Group. All rights reserved.)

cross-pollinated professionals who are Western-educated and have a solid engineering and computer science background. The Russian cyberpower invaded the United States in a humiliating way when it meddled in the presidential elections. It left the United States in turmoil and increased people's distrust in the government.

Attack Scenario of the Virus Nano Rain™

We're introducing a new terror term: Virus Nano Rain (VNR). It is a monsoon of heavy viral rains hitting a region in successive waves and carrying a big load of any kind of nano malware, starting with a variety of nanobots carrying Trojans, backdoors, viruses, worms, ransomware, credit card finders, password readers, backup erasers, dormant Trojans, and customized stealth nano software. It is a million times more damaging than DDoS because it is remotely monitored and has an intricate molecular structure. In the next decade, VNR will be used during conflicts between nations. This attack scenario describes how cyberspace warfare can cripple most activities in metropolitan areas and Smart Cities, with nano terrorism weaponry. Out of necessity of survival, Smart Cities of the future will also be equipped with nano digital immunity.

On July 4, 2025, the city of San Francisco, California—the second largest city in the state—is hit by an unusual type of massive cyberattack (no one knows it is a nano attack) assembled at molecular scale.

The nano attack hits the heart of city, shown in Figure 13.3— and the financial district and shuts down the traffic systems of Oakland—the San Francisco Bridge, the Golden Gate bridge, and the Bay Area Rapid Transit (BART). 107 city blocks lose their traffic lights and a large portion of city becomes horribly gridlocked. It is like the four horsemen of the apocalypse or the final battle of Armageddon.

The nano attack has been packaged by top-notch professionals (researchers, professors, and software engineers) who know NT and AI and were once residents of the city. They know the city and its critical infrastructures and the level of its vulnerability (Figure 13.4). San Francisco is a special city, known for its natural beauty; it is positioned on the western side of the bay, with rolling hills, and blessed with a magnificent view of the Pacific Ocean on its west. The city is very proud of its famous bridges and its BART Metro system. They are considered the main traffic arteries and most critical infrastructure. Pacific Gas & Electric (PG&E) gets its power for the city from the Hetch Hetchy reservoir in Yosemite National Park, which also supplies water to the city. Here are some of the statistics forecast for 2025 that were provided by the SF Public Utility Commission, prior to the attack:

Population	1,200,000
Homes	600,000
Registered vehicles	600,000
Hospitals	23
Energy types	Geothermal, hydraulic, wind, solar, bio-waste
Energy consumption	8968 million kwh
Distribution substations	11 tied to geothermal main power plant
Internet of Things	2,800,000 sensor devices
Systems on the grid	3000 servers
SCADA systems	35

After thorough examination and planning, and at zero hour, the nano attack starts from Satellite 1 and Satellite 2. They connect with cloud 1 and cloud 2 and 200,000 malicious software nano cyborgs, from the arsenals 1 and 2, are mobilized and ready to be launched in 10 waves at different locations of

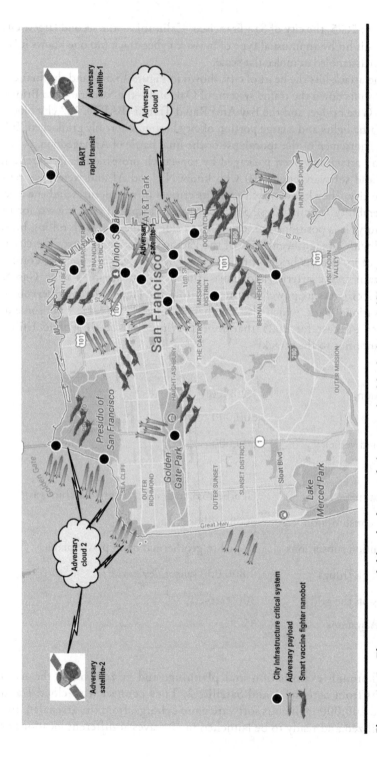

Figure 13.4 The nano attack hits the heart of city. 107 city blocks lose traffic lights and a large portion of the city becomes horribly gridlocked. It is like the four horsemen of the apocalypse, or the final battle of Armageddon. (© 2014 Copyright MERIT CyberSecurity Group. All rights reserved.)

the city. The destination is the city grid. All the enemy cyborgs are designed at nanoscale (75 nm), which make them easy to move about the city grid (800 mm).

Strategy of Attack

The main objective of the attack is to achieve rapid dominance with "shock and awe" and spread fear, commotion and anger at the city municipality for neglecting to protect the city from massive attacks. The execution of the attack has to be prompted with no mistakes. The nano attack is guided by nano commanders as follows:

Squad 1: Crack the Bay bridge central toll system, causing a delay of 4 hours.

Squad 2: Crack the Golden Gate Central toll system, causing a delay of 8 hours.

Squad 3: Deactivate the remote terminal units (RTUs) and programmable logic controllers (PLCs) at the main substation at the financial center. Load the dummy "Normal Operation" screens. One of the Transformers will overheat and stop.

Squad 4: Crack the control terminal at the Mission District substation. One of the transformers will overheat and the main circuit breaker will trip and the overload will create a black out.

Squad 5: Hijack 3000 machines and turn them into slave zombies to launch a DDoS at the Embarcadero Center.

Squad 6: Monitor the cascaded black out at the Presidio substation that provides power to IoT devices.

Squad 7: Crack the sensor data collection metering system for all the sensors at the Sunset District.

Squad 8: Crack the sensor data collection metering system for all the sensors at the Fisherman's Wharf district.

Squad 9: Hack the communications of Sutro Tower, which serves the city and most telecom companies in the area. Hack Internet communication with clouds and satellites.

Squad 10: Disruption of emergency central servers, police stations and firemen.

The nano attack catches the city by surprise and the city administrators contact the Central Coordination Center (CCC) of the Smart vaccine nano grid for help. The Computer Emergency Response Team (CERT) estimates over 200,000 different types of deadly viruses have been unleashed from the cyborg nanobots to paralyze the city. Later, Stanford University Medical Center do some nano forensics and conclude that the attack on the city is of a nano nature and refer to it as VNR.

VNR is a new high-tech hybrid phenomenon fabricated with cutting-edge components of NT and AI. It contains a large collection of autonomic software agents to guide the rain to hit their targets with great precision and paralyze every movement in the city, in addition to crippling the most congested critical infrastructures in the city, like the Golden Gate Bridge and the BART Metro system.

In March 2012, the Russian defense minister Anatoli Serdjukov said, "The development of weaponry based on new physics principles: direct-energy weapons, geophysical weapons, wave-energy weapons, genetic weapons, psychotronic weapons, etc., is part of the state arms procurement program for 2011–2020" (Voice of Russia).

We showed (in Chapter 12) how NT is going to play a pivotal role in the fabrication of the cybersecurity of the future.

Cyber Terrorism Shifting to High Gear

The cyber terrorists will have a massive arsenal of the most creative nano weapons for any conceivable nano war. Here is a synopsis of the most prominent applications carried out by adversary nano cyborgs:

Internet of Things (IoT) Grid Blackout: Cyber terrorists will go after the Smart City grid. It connects all the IoT devices through sensors. If the grid is attacked by an army of nano cyborgs, then once the grid is impacted or partially blacked out, then most of the IoT devices will be out of order.

Electromagnetic Pulse (EMP) Attack: This is an intense burst of electromagnetic energy caused by an abrupt and rapid acceleration of charged particles. It can knock down the power in a city, fry servers, and delete storage data.

Satellite Hacking: New hackers could pull off a cyberattack by taking remote control of a satellite or by spoofing or jamming its signals. Another tricky threat is to have an adversary satellite fire a stream of hostile software at the city satellites and jam the communication with the ground station.

Remote Neural Monitoring Satellite Terrorism: This a very efficient method of controlling the human brain. Remote neural monitoring (RNM) is expected to revolutionize cybercrime and cyber terrorism. Research has shown that the human intellect thinks at a speed of about 5 kilobits per second and, therefore, does not have the capability to compete with supercomputers acting via satellites, implants, and biotelemetry. The human brain has a characteristic set of bioelectric resonance structures. By using supercomputers, the RNM system can home link to it and send hostile messages through an embedded individual's nervous system in order to affect their behavior in a specific way. This could be applied to doctors performing critical surgeries, commercial pilots, politicians, and drivers.

Corrupt government and corporate elements will use RNM satellite technology, also known as satellite terrorism, to harass, torture, and terrorize individuals. In some instances, these criminals are utilizing a bogus, illegal so-called "investigation" in an attempt to cover up the crime. Once the RNM satellite technology is locked on the individual, this false, bogus "investigation" is nothing more than repetitive harassment, torture, and terrorism, which can last for years, with the goals of causing induced insanity or hoping that the victim commits suicide.

Medical Device Nano Hacking: Medical systems hacks are scary, but medical device hacks could be even worse. Researchers in Belgium and the UK have demonstrated that in the next decade (not two decades), it will be possible to transmit a squad of life-threatening nano soft cyborgs to implant medical devices such as pacemakers, defibrillators, and insulin pumps and make them secretly defective. Nano soft cyborgs will be smuggled into the hospital network (antivirus defense will be useless), reach the bioengineering lab, and implant a timed payload to distort the reading of critical devices such as X-rays, blood gas analyzers, and communications devices.

DNA Nano Hacking: DNA is nature's own nano engineered computer, and its ability to store information and conduct logical manipulations at the molecular level has already been exploited in specialized "DNA computers." A DNA computer is essentially a test tube filled with water containing trillions of DNA molecules, with each molecule acting as a computer. A team of biologists could be well paid to successfully infect a nanobot with malware coded into a strand of DNA. In the next decade, DNA-based nano code injection attacks will be reality. Adversaries will be able to compromise computational biology programs.

Nano Gene Hacking: New gene-editing technologies are revolutionizing biology by giving scientists the tools to dramatically alter organisms' DNA and resulting physical traits. What will we do with this new power? DNA is the compiler of life itself. Everything that has life was created by that compiler. So, nanobiologists can modify the compiler itself and change what it was compiling, regardless of the instructions within the program. In the next two decades, this type of terrorism will be like the assassination of selected leaders. The hacking will be done through satellites.

Nano Crime-as-a-Service: The classic crime-as-a-service will become ineffective in the next two decades. The nano version will be à la mode. Cyber terrorists will be so versed in nanotechnology that they will upgrade their skills and sell their services to other countries or adversaries.

Nano Software Cyborgs: In the next two decades, most effective attacks are going to using AI and NT. Nano software cyborgs are autonomic software agents that can be smuggled into a critical system or infrastructure and deactivate an important module. The Smart Vaccine™ is also from the family of cyborgs, but it is the dynamic agent that is responsible for the immunization of the critical systems.

Commercial Airplane Commandeering: Hackers could commandeer new planes through passenger Wi-Fi. Terrorists with extensive experience in avionics or airplane manufacturing could alter the configuration of the firewall that separates the passenger Wi-Fi network from the cockpit avionics system. The Wi-Fi systems in these planes connect to the world outside the plane, opening the door for malicious actors to also remotely harm the plane's system. Just imagine, a nano virus or malware planted in websites visited by passengers could provide an opportunity for a malicious attacker to access the IP-connected onboard information system through their infected machines. Satellites are another hell-raising means to send hostile messages to one of the terrorist passengers. Modern transportation systems, including planes, trains, and automobiles, are becoming increasingly computerized and therefore susceptible to some of the same vulnerabilities and attacks that have long plagued desktop and laptop systems.

Psychotronic Remote Control of the Brain: In wars in the next decade, adversaries will be using psychotronic weapons programs. The development of psychotropic weapons—wave devices that control human thoughts, feelings, and behavior—has started and these will be used by malicious actors.

How Long Will It Take a City to Become a Smart City?

The instantaneous magic has not arrived yet. It will take at least 10–15 years for a normal city to be labeled "Smart." Figure 13.5 shows the trend in technology harnessing. The most retarding factor in the equation is people. Urbanization may be difficult for some people who were lured to move in. Too much organization will be hard to adjust to and will be hard to absorb. The biggest challenge is fighting new crimes. Smart Cities will create new cybercrimes beyond imagination from the Internet. The younger generation will have broader access to the cyber world and this will lead to new crimes.

Take, for example, the impact of AI and NT on young digital natives. These young cybernauts will be living on chat farms and become regular invisible netizens, and will have access to everything there: cash, ID theft, ransomware, pornography and sex, online dating, and bullying. Now, stepping into the nano world will give them more flexibility to commit crime. The time of nano cybercrime will come soon and these webheads will invent more intelligent nanobots that can be used to assail academic, medical, government, and financial records. These mouse potatoes will be addicted to power games, which in fact are the fastest way to learn problem solving and patience.

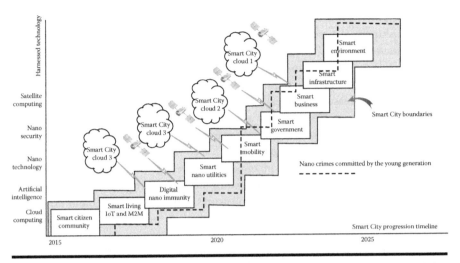

Figure 13.5 Smart Cities will not be fully realized reality overnight. Implementation of a complete blueprint will take some years. The city starts with the easy steps and keeps adding more complex applications as time goes by. New technologies are deployed to enhance the quality of life of the citizens, and at the same time, to increase the security of the city. There will be two enabling technologies (satellite and cloud) that provide robust and intelligent nano shields to the city. The dashed line represents the new nano crimes committed by young digital natives. (© 2014 Copyright MERIT CyberSecurity Group. All rights reserved.)

Glossary

Acheson–Lilienthal Proposal: See Baruch Plan.

Air-launched cruise missile (ALCM): A missile designed to be launched from an aircraft and jet-engine powered throughout its flight. As with all cruise missiles, its range is a function of payload, propulsion, and fuel volume, and can thus vary greatly. Under the START I Treaty, the term "long-range ALCM" means an air-launched cruise missile with a range in excess of 600 km.

Alpha particle: A positively charged particle ejected spontaneously from the nuclei of some radioactive isotopes. It is a helium nucleus that has a mass number of 4 and an electrostatic charge of +2e. It has low penetrating power and a short range (a few centimeters in air). The most energetic alpha particle will generally fail to penetrate the dead layers of cells covering the skin and can be easily stopped by a sheet of paper. Alpha particles are hazardous when an alpha-emitting isotope is inside the body.

Anti-Ballistic Missile (ABM) Treaty: Signed by the United States and the Soviet Union on May 26, 1972, entered into force on October 3, 1972. It constrained strategic missile defenses to a total of 200 launchers and interceptors per country, which were divided between two widely separated deployment areas. These restrictions were intended to prevent the establishment of a nationwide defense, and the creation of a base for deploying such a defense. The treaty was modified in 1974, reducing the permitted deployment areas to one per country. The United States withdrew from the ABM Treaty in 2002.

Arms control: Measures, typically bilateral or multilateral, taken to control or reduce weapon systems or armed forces. Such limitations or reductions are typically taken to increase stability between countries, reducing the likelihood or intensity of an arms race. They might affect the size, type, configuration, production, or performance characteristics of a weapon system, or the size, organization, equipment, deployment, or employment of armed forces. Arms control measures typically include monitoring and verification provisions, and may also include provisions to increase transparency between the parties.

Asymmetric response or asymmetric warfare: Tactics employed by a country or organization to attack an opponent with greater military power. Asymmetric response or warfare will typically involve the use of unconventional weapons or strategy. An example would be the use of suicide bombers against the US military in Iraq.

Atom: The smallest unit of an element, which cannot be divided or broken up by chemical means, and has all the chemical properties of that element. It consists of a central core of protons and neutrons, called the nucleus. In atomic models, electrons revolve in orbits around the nucleus. Atoms are the fundamental building blocks of elements.

Atomic: Pertaining to an atom, which is the basic unit of matter, consisting of a dense nucleus of protons and neutrons and a cloud of electrons surrounding it.

Atomic bomb: See Nuclear weapon.

Atomic energy: See Nuclear energy.

Atoms for Peace: A US program announced by President Dwight D. Eisenhower at the United Nations on December 8, 1953, to share nuclear materials and technology for peaceful purposes with other countries. This program required countries receiving nuclear materials to agree to inspections of the transferred technology to ensure it was not used for military purposes. The program was formally established in 1954, following the passage of the Atomic Energy Act, and ended abruptly in 1974 following India's first nuclear test.

Aum Shinrikyo: A Japanese religious cult that attempted six failed biological attacks (five using incorrectly produced botulinum toxin, and one using incorrectly produced anthrax) and 12 chemical attacks (five using sarin, five using VX, one using phosgene, and one using hydrogen cyanide) from 1990 to 1995. The deadliest of these attacks was the sarin attack on the Tokyo subway system, which killed 12 people and injured 1039 people on March 20, 1995. Under cult leader Shoko Asahara, Aum Shinrikyo's membership numbered in the tens of thousands, and the cult held assets in the range of $300 million to $1 billion.

Ballistic missile: A delivery vehicle powered by a liquid- or solid-fueled rocket that primarily travels in a ballistic (free-fall) trajectory. The flight of a ballistic missile includes three phases: (1) boost phase, where the rocket generates thrust to launch the missile into flight; (2) midcourse phase, where the missile coasts in an arc under the influence of gravity; and (3) terminal phase, in which the missile descends toward its target. Ballistic missiles can be characterized by three key parameters: range, payload, and circular error probable (CEP), or targeting precision. Ballistic missiles are primarily intended for use against ground targets.

Ballistic missile defense (BMD): All active and passive measures designed to detect, identify, track, and defeat incoming ballistic missiles, in both strategic and theater tactical roles, during any portion of their flight trajectory (boost, post-boost, mid-course, or terminal phase) or to nullify or reduce their effectiveness in destroying their targets.

Baruch Plan: Initially known as the Acheson–Lilienthal proposal, this was a US initiative to outlaw nuclear weapons and to internationalize global stocks of fissile material for use in peaceful nuclear programs. After Bernard Baruch proposed the plan in 1946 at the United Nations, the United States and the Soviet Union held negotiations on the program but never reached agreement.

Beta particle: A charged particle emitted from a nucleus during certain types of radioactive decay, with a mass much smaller than that of a proton or a neutron. A negatively charged beta particle is identical to an electron. A positively charged beta particle is called a positron. Large amounts of beta radiation may cause skin burns, and beta emitters are harmful if they enter the body. Beta particles may be stopped by thin sheets of metal or plastic.

Boomer: See Nuclear-powered ballistic missile submarines.

Boosted fission nuclear weapon: A type of nuclear weapon with a higher explosive yield than a regular fission weapon. A small amount of fusion fuel in the weapon increases the neutron flux, leading to a larger amount of the fissionable material undergoing fission, typically resulting in a higher yielding weapon.

Boost phase: The part of a ballistic missile's flight path that begins at launch, and may last from 5 minutes to 80 seconds, depending on the sophistication of the missile. During the boost phase, the booster and sustainer engines operate, and the warheads have not yet been deployed.

Breakout: This is the time required to produce enough weapons-grade uranium (WGU) for one nuclear weapon; it has most recently been applied to the Iran Nuclear agreement. See Joint Comprehensive Plan of Action.

Bunker Busters: See Robust Nuclear Earth Penetrator (RNEP).

Centrifuge: A machine used to enrich uranium by rapidly spinning a cylinder (known as a rotor and containing uranium hexafluoride gas) inside another cylinder (called the casing).

Chain reaction (fission): A process in which neutrons are absorbed by fissionable material and the neutrons released as a result of fission go on to cause more fissions. A self-sustaining chain reaction is one where the number of neutrons released from fission in one period of time (or generation) is enough to cause the same number of fissions in the following generation, taking into account that some neutrons will be absorbed by non-fissionable material or escape the region of fissionable material. Nuclear reactors, as well as nuclear weapons, utilize chain reactions.

Circular error probable (CEP): An indicator of a weapon system's accuracy, measured as the radius of the circle in which half of all warheads fired at a target will fall.

Cold Start Doctrine: A military strategy devised by India, intended to allow India's conventional forces to perform holding attacks in order to prevent a nuclear retaliation from Pakistan in case of a conflict. It involved, among other changes, basing sufficient conventional forces close to the India–Pakistan border to allow for rapid mobilization in case of an attack.

Comprehensive Nuclear Test Ban Treaty (CTBT): Opened for signature in 1996 at the UN General Assembly, the CTBT prohibits all nuclear testing if it enters into force. The treaty establishes the Comprehensive Test Ban Treaty Organization (CTBTO) to ensure the implementation of its provisions and verify compliance through a global monitoring system upon entry into force. Pending the treaty's entry into force, the Preparatory Commission of the CTBTO is charged with establishing the International Monitoring System (IMS) and promoting treaty ratifications. CTBT entry into force is contingent on ratification by 44 Annex II states.

Conventional warfare: War conducted with conventional weapons only.

Conventional weapons: Weapons and military equipment, including small arms and light weapons, tanks, artillery rockets, aircraft, torpedoes, mines, and cluster munitions that do not use biological agents, chemical agents, nuclear explosives, or kinetic energy weapons to damage targets.

Cooperative Threat Reduction (Nunn–Lugar) Program: A US Department of Defense (DOD) program established in 1992 by the US Congress, through legislation sponsored primarily by Senators Sam Nunn and Richard Lugar. It is the largest and most diverse US program addressing former Soviet Union weapons of mass destruction threats. The program has focused primarily on (1) destroying vehicles for delivering nuclear weapons (e.g., missiles and aircraft), their launchers (such as silos and submarines), and their related facilities; (2) securing former Soviet nuclear weapons and their components; and (3) destroying Russian chemical weapons. The term is often used generically to refer to all US nonproliferation programs in the former Soviet Union—and sometimes beyond— including those implemented by the US Departments of Energy, Commerce, and State. The program's scope has expanded to include threat reduction efforts in geographical areas outside the former Soviet Union.

Counterforce targeting: War planning that envisions strikes on an enemy's military and industrial targets.

Counter value targeting: War planning that envisions strikes on an enemy's civilian population centers.

Credibility trap: Derived from game theory, credibility trap describes a situation where a leader has made a threat to another country. Once the threat has been made, the leader may feel compelled to follow through despite changing circumstances, in order to maintain the believe in the credibility of future threats.

Critical: A state where the number of neutrons in each period of time, or generation, remains constant. When a nuclear reactor is "steady-state," or operating at normal power levels for extended periods of time, it is in this state.

Critical mass: The minimum amount of concentrated fissionable material required to sustain a chain reaction. See Chain reaction.

Cruise missile: An unmanned self-propelled guided vehicle that sustains flight through aerodynamic lift for most of its flight path. There are subsonic and supersonic cruise missiles currently deployed in conventional and nuclear arsenals, while conventional hypersonic cruise missiles are currently in development. These can be launched from the air, submarines, or the ground. Although they carry smaller payloads, travel at slower speeds, and cover lesser ranges than ballistic missiles, cruise missiles can be programmed to travel along customized flight paths and to evade missile defense systems.

Cruise missile submarines (SSGN): SSGN is the US Navy hull classification symbol for a nuclear-powered cruise missile submarine. The SS denotes a submarine, the G denotes a "guided missile," and the N denotes nuclear power. The Soviet Navy had several submarines that were also called SSGNs by Western observers.

Deterrence: The actions of a state or group of states to dissuade a potential adversary from initiating an attack or conflict through the credible threat of retaliation. To be effective, a deterrence strategy should demonstrate to an adversary that the costs of an attack would outweigh any potential gains. See Extended deterrence and Nuclear deterrence.

Dirty bomb: See Radiological dispersal device (RDD).

Disarmament: Though there is no agreed-upon legal definition of what disarmament entails within the context of international agreements, a general definition is the process of reducing the quantity and/or capabilities of military weapons and/or military forces.

Diversion: The clandestine removal or appropriation of materials or technologies for use in projects or weapons programs that violate either a state's treaty obligations or an end use agreement reached between the state and the country from which the material or technology originated.

Dual-use technology: Technology that has both civilian and military applications. For example, many of the precursor chemicals used in the manufacture of chemical weapons have legitimate civilian industrial uses, such as the production of pesticides or ink for ballpoint pens.

Electromagnetic pulse (EMP): A sharp pulse of radio-frequency (long wavelength) radiation produced when an explosion occurs in an asymmetrical environment, especially at or near the earth's surface or at high altitudes. The intense electric and magnetic fields can damage unprotected electrical and electronic equipment over a large area.

Electron: An elementary particle with a negative charge and a mass of 0.00055 amu (atomic mass units). Electrons surround the positively charged nucleus and determine the chemical properties of the atom.

Enriched uranium: Uranium with an increased concentration of the isotope U-235, relative to natural uranium. Natural uranium contains 0.7% U-235, whereas nuclear weapons typically require uranium enriched to very high levels (see Highly enriched uranium and Weapons-grade). Nuclear power plant fuel typically uses uranium enriched to 3%–5% U-235, material that is not sufficiently enriched to be used for nuclear weapons.

Extended deterrence: A country protected from potential adversaries by the nuclear weapons-backed security guarantee of an ally is said to be under an (extended deterrence) nuclear umbrella. See Deterrence.

Fallout: The process of the descent to the earth's surface of particles contaminated with radioactive material from a radioactive cloud. The term is also applied in a collective sense to the contaminated particulate matter itself. The early (or local) fallout is defined, somewhat arbitrarily, as those particles which reach the earth within 24 hours after a nuclear explosion. The delayed (or worldwide) fallout consists of the smaller particles which ascend into the upper troposphere and stratosphere, to be carried by winds to all parts of the earth. The delayed fallout is brought to earth, mainly by rain and snow, over extended periods ranging from months to years, and can contaminate the animal food-chain.

First strike: The launch of a surprise attack intended to considerably weaken or destroy an adversary's military infrastructure or nuclear forces, and thus severely reduce the adversary's ability to attack or retaliate.

First-strike capability: The ability of a country to launch a first strike against an adversary.

First-use: The introduction of nuclear weapons, or other weapons of mass destruction, into a conflict. In agreeing to a "no-first-use" policy, a country states that it will not use nuclear weapons first, but only under retaliatory circumstances. See No-first-use.

Fissile material: A type of fissionable material capable of sustaining a chain reaction by undergoing fission upon the absorption of low-energy (or thermal) neutrons. Uranium-235, plutonium-239, and uranium-233 are the most prominently discussed fissile materials for peaceful and nuclear weapons purposes.

Fission: The splitting of the nucleus of a heavy atom into two lighter nuclei (called fission fragments). It is accompanied by the release of neutrons, gamma rays, and fission fragments with large amounts of kinetic energy. It is usually triggered by absorption of a neutron, but in some cases may be induced by protons, gamma rays or other particles.

Fission bomb: A nuclear bomb based on the concept of releasing energy through the fission (splitting) of heavy isotopes, such as uranium-235 or plutonium-239.

Fleet ballistic missile submarine (SSBN): A nuclear-powered submarine designed to deliver ballistic missile attacks against assigned targets from either a submerged or surfaced condition.

Fuel cycle: A term for the full spectrum of processes associated with utilizing nuclear fission reactions for peaceful or military purposes. The "front-end" of the uranium-plutonium nuclear fuel cycle includes uranium mining and milling, conversion, enrichment, and fuel fabrication. The fuel is used in a nuclear reactor to produce neutrons that can, for example, produce thermal reactions to generate electricity or propulsion, or produce fissile materials for weapons. The "back end" of the nuclear fuel cycle refers to spent fuel being stored in spent fuel pools, possible reprocessing of the spent fuel, and ultimately long-term storage in a geological or other repository.

Fusion: Nuclear fusion is a type of nuclear reaction in which two atomic nuclei combine to form a heavier nucleus, releasing energy. For a fusion reaction to take place, the nuclei, which are positively charged, must have enough kinetic energy to overcome their electrostatic force of repulsion (also called the Coulomb barrier). Thermonuclear fusion of deuterium and tritium will produce a helium nucleus and an energetic neutron. This is one basis of the hydrogen bomb, which employs a brief, uncontrolled thermonuclear fusion reaction. A great effort is now underway to harness thermonuclear fusion as a source of power.

Gamma radiation: High-energy, short wavelength, electromagnetic radiation emitted from the nucleus. Gamma radiation frequently accompanies alpha and beta emissions and always accompanies fission. Gamma rays are very penetrating and are best stopped or shielded by dense materials, such as lead or depleted uranium. Gamma rays are similar to X-rays but have higher energies.

Gun-type (nuclear) weapon: A device in which two or more pieces of fissionable material, each smaller than a critical mass, are brought together very rapidly to form a supercritical mass which can explode as the result of a rapidly expanding fission chain reaction.

Half-life: The time in which one-half of the atoms of a particular radioactive substance decay. Measured half-lives vary from millionths of a second to billions of years, depending on the isotope.

High alert: A state of readiness of nuclear forces sufficient to launch an immediate attack.

Highly enriched uranium (HEU): Refers to uranium with a concentration of more than 20% of the isotope U-235. Achieved via the process of enrichment. See Enriched uranium.

Hydrogen bomb: See Nuclear weapon and Thermonuclear weapon.

Improvised nuclear device (IND): A device that uses a simple, untested design to attempt to create a nuclear explosion.

Intercontinental ballistic missile (ICBM): A ballistic missile with a range greater than 5500 km. See Ballistic missile.

Intermediate-Range Nuclear Forces (INF) Treaty: A treaty between the United States and the former Soviet Union, signed on December 8, 1987, which entered into force on June 1, 1988. It aimed to eliminate and ban all ground-launched ballistic and cruise missiles with a range of 300–3400 miles (500–5500 km). The treaty required the United States and the Soviet Union to conduct inspections at each other's sites during the elimination of treaty-limited items (TLI). By May 1991, all intermediate-range and shorter-range missiles, launchers, related support equipment, and support structures were eliminated.

International Atomic Energy Agency (IAEA): Founded in 1957 and based in Vienna, Austria, the IAEA is an autonomous international organization in the United Nations system. The Agency's mandate is the promotion of peaceful uses of nuclear energy, technical assistance in this area, and verification that nuclear materials and technology stay in peaceful use. Article III of the Nuclear Non-Proliferation Treaty (NPT) requires non-nuclear weapon states party to the NPT to accept safeguards administered by the IAEA. The IAEA consists of three principal organs: the General Conference (of member states), the Board of Governors, and the Secretariat.

Isotope: Any two or more forms of an element having identical or very closely related chemical properties and the same atomic number (the same number of protons in their nuclei), but different atomic weights or mass numbers (a different number of neutrons in their nuclei). Uranium-238 and uranium-235 are isotopes of uranium.

Just War Doctrine: This doctrine considers a war morally justifiable if it meets a series of criteria. *Jus ad bellum* refers to "the right to go to war" and *jus in bello* is the set of criteria relating to the "right conduct in war."

Kiloton (kT): A term used to quantify the energy of a nuclear explosion that is equivalent to the explosion of 1000 tons of trinitrotoluene (TNT) conventional explosive.

Limited Test Ban Treaty: Also known as the Partial Test Ban Treaty, the Treaty Banning Nuclear Weapons Tests in the Atmosphere, in Outer Space and Under Water prohibits nuclear weapons tests "or any other nuclear explosion" in the atmosphere, in outer space, and under water. While the treaty does not ban tests underground, it does prohibit nuclear explosions in this environment if they cause "radioactive debris to be present outside the territorial limits of the State under whose jurisdiction or control" the explosions were conducted. The treaty is of unlimited duration.

Low enriched uranium (LEU): Refers to uranium with a concentration of the isotope U-235 that is higher than that found in natural uranium but lower than 20% LEU (usually 3%–5%). LEU is used as fuel for many nuclear reactor designs.

Low-Yield Nuclear Earth Penetrator: See Robust Nuclear Earth Penetrator.

Megaton (MT): The energy equivalent released by 1000 kilotons (1,000,000 tons) of trinitrotoluene (TNT) explosive. Typically used as the unit of measurement to express the amount of energy released by a nuclear bomb.

Mid phase (or midcourse phase): The second phase in the flight path of a ballistic missile, following the boost and preceding the terminal phase. The midcourse phase is the longest phase in the flight path of a ballistic missile. For an ICBM, it lasts about 20 minutes. Its relatively long duration has rendered the midcourse phase the preferred point for interception by ballistic missile defense systems.

Multiple independently targetable reentry vehicle (MIRV): An offensive ballistic missile system with multiple warheads, each of which can strike a separate target and can be launched by a single booster rocket.

Mutual deterrence: A condition of deterrence that exists between two adversaries. See Deterrence.

Mutually assured destruction (MAD): A term originating in the Cold War, which described the deterrence relationship between the United States and the Soviet Union beginning in the 1950s. MAD assumed that both sides possessed an assured second-strike capability such that a nuclear first strike by either side would provide no strategic advantage—because both states would suffer unacceptably high damage in the ensuing nuclear war.

National technical means (NTM): Satellites, aircraft, electronic, and seismic monitoring devices used to monitor the activities of other states, including treaty compliance and movement of troops and equipment. Some agreements include measures that explicitly prohibit tampering with other parties' NTM.

Neutron: An uncharged particle with a mass slightly greater than that of the proton, and found in the nucleus of every atom heavier than hydrogen-1.

New START: A treaty between the United States and Russia on further limitations and reductions of strategic offensive weapons, signed on April 8, 2010, which entered into force on February 5, 2011. Under the New START provisions, the two sides have to reduce the number of deployed strategic warheads and the number of deployed strategic delivery vehicles within seven years of the treaty's entry into force. The treaty's verification measures are based on the earlier verification system created under START I. New START supersedes the Moscow Treaty, and its duration is 10 years, with an option of extension for up to 5 years. See Strategic Arms Reduction Treaty.

No-First-Use: A pledge on the part of a nuclear weapon state not to be the first party to use nuclear weapons in a conflict or crisis. No-first-use guarantees may be made in unilateral statements, bilateral, or multilateral agreements, or as part of a treaty creating a nuclear-weapon-free zone.

Nonproliferation: Measures to prevent the spread of biological, chemical, and/or nuclear weapons and their delivery systems. See Proliferation.

Nonproliferation Treaty (NPT): Signed in 1968, the Treaty on the Non-Proliferation of Nuclear Weapons (NPT) is the most widely adhered to international security agreement. The "three pillars" of the NPT are nuclear disarmament, nonproliferation, and peaceful uses of nuclear energy. Article VI of the NPT commits states possessing nuclear weapons to negotiate in good faith toward halting the arms race and the complete elimination of nuclear weapons. The Treaty stipulates that non-nuclear-weapon states will not seek to acquire nuclear weapons, and will accept International Atomic Energy Agency safeguards on their nuclear activities, while nuclear weapon states commit not to transfer nuclear weapons to other states. All states have a right to the peaceful use of nuclear energy, and should assist one another in its development. The NPT provides for conferences of member states to review treaty implementation at 5-year intervals. Initially of a 25-year duration, the NPT was extended indefinitely in 1995.

Non-strategic nuclear weapons: See Tactical nuclear weapons.

North American Aerospace (formerly Air) Defense Command (NORAD): Established in 1957, a bi-national air defense organization between the United States and Canada. Originally aimed at deterring threats from Soviet bombers and ICBMs, NORAD has expanded following the end of the Cold War and the attacks of 9/11, and now provides for aerospace warnings from aircraft, missiles, and space vehicles as well as risks emanating from the interior of North America. NORAD, headquartered at Peterson Air Force Base near Colorado Springs, Colorado, is broken down into three regional commands: the Alaskan NORAD Region (ANR), the Canadian NORAD Region (CANR), and the Continental US NORAD Region (CONR).

North Atlantic Treaty Organization (NATO): The North Atlantic Treaty Organization is a military alliance that was formed in 1949 to help deter the Soviet Union from attacking Europe. The Alliance is based on the North Atlantic Treaty, which was signed in Washington on April 4, 1949. The treaty originally created an alliance of 10 European and two North American independent states, but today NATO has 28 members who have committed to maintaining and developing their defense capabilities, to consulting on issues of mutual security concern, and to the principle of collective self-defense. NATO is also engaged in out-of-area security operations, most notably in Afghanistan, where Alliance forces operate alongside other non-NATO countries as part of the International Security Assistance Force (ISAF).

NSC-68: National Security Council document 68 was a top-secret policy paper presented to President Truman in 1950. It outlined a broad strategic approach to counter the Soviet Union and global Communist expansion. In contrast to the famous X article from George Kennan, it de-emphasized containment and promoted military strength as the primary means. However, it firmly rejected calls for a preventive war against the Soviet Union.

Nuclear deterrence: Deterrence that relies on nuclear weapons to inhibit an adversary from attacking with their nuclear weapons. See Mutually assured destruction.

Nuclear Posture Review: Under a mandate from the US Congress, the Department of Defense regularly conducts a comprehensive Nuclear Posture Review to set forth the direction of US nuclear weapons policies. To date, the United States has completed three Nuclear Posture Reviews (in 1994, 2002, and 2010).

Nuclear-powered ballistic missile submarines (SSBN): A nuclear-powered submarine designed to deliver ballistic missile attacks against assigned targets from either a submerged or surfaced condition (informally called "boomers").

Nuclear Security Summits: A series of international summits that emerged out of US President Barack Obama's call in April 2009 to "secure all vulnerable nuclear material around the world within four years." The summit process focuses on strengthening international cooperation to prevent nuclear terrorism, thwarting nuclear materials trafficking, and enhancing nuclear materials security.

Nuclear Suppliers Group (NSG): The NSG was established in 1975, and its members commit themselves to exporting sensitive nuclear technologies only to countries that adhere to strict nonproliferation standards.

Nuclear umbrella: See Extended deterrence.

Nuclear weapon: A device that releases nuclear energy in an explosive manner as the result of nuclear chain reactions involving fission, or fission and fusion, of atomic nuclei. Such weapons are also sometimes referred to as atomic bombs (a fission-based weapon), or boosted fission weapons (a fission-based weapon deriving a slightly higher yield from a small fusion reaction), or hydrogen bombs/thermonuclear weapons (a weapon deriving a significant portion of its energy from fusion reactions).

Nucleus: The central, positively charged region of an atom. Except for the nucleus of ordinary hydrogen (or hydrogen-1), which has only a proton, all atomic nuclei contain both protons and neutrons. The number of protons determines the total positive charge or atomic number. This number is the same for all the atomic nuclei of a given chemical element. The total number of neutrons and protons is called the mass number or atomic mass number.

Nunn–Lugar Program: See Cooperative Threat Reduction Program.

Partial Test Ban Treaty (PTBT): See Limited Test Ban Treaty (LTBT).

Peaceful nuclear explosion (PNE): PNEs are nuclear explosions carried out for non-military purposes, such as the construction of harbors or canals. PNEs are technically indistinguishable from nuclear explosions of a military nature. Although Article V of the Treaty on the Non-Proliferation of Nuclear Weapons (NPT) allows for PNEs, no significant peaceful benefits of these explosions (that outweigh the drawbacks) have been discovered. In the Final Document of the 2000 NPT Review Conference, the state parties agreed that Article V of the NPT is to be interpreted in light of the Comprehensive Nuclear Test Ban Treaty, which will ban all nuclear explosions, including PNEs, once it enters into force.

Plutonium (Pu): A transuranic element with atomic number 94, produced when uranium is irradiated in a reactor. It is used primarily in nuclear weapons and, along with uranium, in mixed-oxide (MOX) fuel. Plutonium-239, a fissile isotope, is the most suitable isotope for use in nuclear weapons.

Prague Speech: Refers to the speech given by US President Barack Obama in April 2009 at Hradčany Square, Prague, the Czech Republic. In the speech, Obama stated "America's commitment to seek the peace and security of a world without nuclear weapons." He noted that "the United States will take concrete steps towards a world without nuclear weapons." The Prague speech served as the framework for the 2010 Nuclear Posture Review and subsequent US arms control efforts.

Preemptive military action: An attack launched to preempt expected aggression by an enemy. In the context of nuclear weapons, this would involve striking nuclear arsenals or facilities to eliminate them before broader hostilities ensue.

Preventive war: Preventive wars or attacks are launched in response to less immediate threats than faced in preemptive military action. A preventive attack is not motivated by the desire to strike first rather than second but rather the desire to fight sooner rather than later.

Proliferation (of weapons of mass destruction): The spread of biological, chemical, and/or nuclear weapons, and their delivery systems. Horizontal proliferation refers to the spread of WMD to states that have not previously possessed them. Vertical proliferation refers to an increase in the quantity or capabilities of existing WMD arsenals within a state.

Proton: A particle with a positive electric charge located in the nucleus of an atom.

Radiation (ionizing): Radiation that has sufficient energy to remove electrons from substances that it passes through, forming ions. May include alpha particles, beta particles, gamma rays, X-rays, neutrons, high-speed electrons, high-speed protons, and other particles capable of producing ions.

Radiation syndrome (also called radiation sickness): The complex of symptoms resulting from excessive exposure of the human body to acute ionizing radiation. The earliest symptoms may include nausea, fatigue, vomiting, and diarrhea, which may be followed by loss of hair, hemorrhage, inflammation of the mouth and throat, and a general loss of energy. In severe cases, where the radiation has been approximately 1000 rad (acute dose) or more, death may occur within two to four weeks. Those who survive six weeks after the receipt of a single large dose of radiation to the whole body may generally be expected to recover. Over the long-term, there are also stochastic health effects from radiation exposure (in contrast to acute effects), meaning an increased probability of cancers and other negative effects on a person's health.

Radioactive decay: The spontaneous emission of energy and/or particles from the nucleus of a radioactive atom. This is most often in the form of either alpha or beta particles, gamma radiation, or spontaneous fission where the nucleus undergoes fission without the bombardment of a particle or photon. Each radioactive isotope has an associated half-life, and the amount of radioactive material decreases over time as the material decays.

Radioactivity: The spontaneous emission of radiation, generally alpha or beta particles, often accompanied by gamma rays, from the nucleus of an unstable isotope.

Radioisotope: An unstable isotope of an element that decays or disintegrates spontaneously, emitting energy (radiation). Approximately 5000 natural and artificial radioisotopes have been identified. Some radioisotopes, such as Molybdenum-99, are used for medical applications, such as diagnostics. These isotopes are created by the irradiation of targets in research reactors.

Radiological dispersal device (RDD): Any device, other than a nuclear explosive device, designed to spread radioactive material (sometimes called a dirty bomb).

Radiological terrorism: Terrorist acts intended to release harmful radiation, through sabotage of a nuclear facility or the detonation of a radiological dispersal device (RDD). See Radiological dispersal device.

Reentry phase: The portion of the trajectory of a ballistic missile or space vehicle when the vehicle reenters the earth's atmosphere.

Reentry vehicle (RV): A nuclear warhead on a ballistic missile specially designed to reenter the earth's atmosphere in the terminal portion of the missile's trajectory.

Reprocessing: The chemical treatment of spent nuclear fuel to separate the remaining usable plutonium and uranium for re-fabrication into fuel, or alternatively, to extract the plutonium for use in nuclear weapons.

Robust Nuclear Earth Penetrator (RNEP): A US program during the George W. Bush administration that envisioned the development of a "bunker buster" nuclear weapon that would penetrate deep into the earth prior to detonation in order to destroy deeply buried and hardened targets. The RNEP was never built.

Sea-launched cruise missile (SLCM): Refers to cruise missiles with conventional or nuclear payloads that are launched from submarines.

Second-strike capability: The ability of a country's nuclear forces to survive a first strike and be available to retaliate. A robust second-strike capability is believed to deter against a first strike.

Silo: Hardened underground facility for housing and launching a ballistic missile.

Single Integrated Operational Plan (SIOP): The nuclear war plan for an integrated response to a nuclear attack on the United States. In 1960, the US Joint Strategic Target Planning Staff completed the SIOP-62. Since then, a version of the SIOP war plan has dictated how US nuclear forces would be used in a conflict. With guidance from the President, the Secretary of Defense, and the Joint Chiefs of Staff, the Staff of the U.S. Strategic Command (STRATCOM) works out the details of the SIOP. STRATCOM designs and maintains the list of targets for nuclear attacks. The Pentagon formally changed the name of the SIOP in 2003, to OPLAN 8044 Revision (FY).

SLBM: Submarine-launched ballistic missile.

SSBN: ship, submersible, ballistic, nuclear: A hull classification for a submarine capable of launching a ballistic missile. The N, or nuclear, refers to the ship's propulsion system. SSBNs are generally reserved for strategic vessels, as most submarine-launched ballistic missiles carry nuclear payloads. A non-strategic vessel carries the designation SSN, or attack submarine.

SSGN: ship, submersible, guided, nuclear: A hull classification for a submarine that carries guided cruise missiles. The N, or nuclear, refers to the ship's propulsion system. Also known as attack submarines, SSGNs serve a conventional military support role and are often used for special forces transportation.

Stockpile Life Extension Program (LEP): The LEP is a National Nuclear Security Administration (NNSA) program aimed at extending the lifetime and guaranteeing the reliability of the US nuclear stockpile.

Stockpile Stewardship Program: NNSA programs associated with research, design, development, and testing of US nuclear weapons, and the assessment and certification of their safety and reliability. These activities include the Stockpile Life Extension Program (LEP).

Strategic Arms Limitations Talks (SALT I & II): A series of discussions between the Soviet Union and the United States aimed at limiting missile systems and other strategic armaments. The first round of talks (SALT I) was held from 1969 to 1972, and concluded with the May 20, 1971 signing of the Anti-Ballistic Missile (ABM) Treaty and the Interim Agreement limiting strategic offensive arms. SALT II was held from 1972 to 1979. The SALT II Treaty was signed on June 18, 1979, but was not ratified by either country, although both committed to abiding by its limits.

Strategic Arms Reduction Treaty (START I, II, & III): Refers to negotiations between the United States and the Soviet Union/Russian Federation, held between 1982 and 1993 to limit and reduce the numbers of strategic offensive nuclear weapons in each country's nuclear arsenal. The talks culminated in the 1991 START I Treaty, which entered into force in December 1994, and the 1993 START II Treaty. Although START II was ratified by the two countries, it never entered into force. In 1997, U.S. President Bill Clinton and Russian President Boris Yeltsin discussed the possibility of a START III treaty to make further weapons reductions, but negotiations resulted in a stalemate. Following the U.S. withdrawal from the Anti-Ballistic Missile Treaty (ABM) in 2002, Russia declared START II void. START I expired on 5 December 2009, and was followed by the New START treaty. See New START and the Trilateral Statement.

Strategic bomber: A long-range aircraft designed to drop large amounts of explosive power—either conventional or nuclear—on enemy territory.

Strategic Defense Initiative (SDI): Launched by US President Ronald Reagan in March 1983, the SDI was aimed at studying the feasibility of research and development of defensive measures against ballistic missiles, with the ultimate goal of establishing a national missile defense system that would protect the United States from ballistic missile attacks. Colloquially called "Star Wars." See Anti-Ballistic Missile Treaty, Ballistic missile.

Strategic nuclear warhead: A high-yield nuclear warhead placed on a long-range delivery system, such as a land-based intercontinental ballistic missile (ICBMs), a submarine-launched ballistic missile (SLBMs), or a strategic bomber.

Strategic nuclear weapons: Nuclear weapons that can be employed to directly strike an opponent's country, and in particular their nuclear weapons. Strategic nuclear weapons are the basis of *nuclear deterrence* (sometimes called mutually assured destruction). The theory of nuclear deterrence holds that if a country possesses a nuclear arsenal that can survive a *first strike*, and thus could be used to retaliate, this will effectively inhibit the enemy from attempting such a strike. Thus, the mission of strategic nuclear weapons is to prevent the use of nuclear weapons and therefore a nuclear war. The key feature of strategic nuclear weapons is not their design or the size of the warhead, but their targets, their delivery systems (strategic bombers, ICBMS, SLBMs), and how they are based.

Sub-critical mass: A mass of fissionable material that is smaller than that required for a self-sustaining chain reaction.

Submarine-launched ballistic missile (SLBM): A ballistic missile that is carried on and launched from a submarine.

Supercritical mass: A mass of fissionable material that is larger than the amount needed to sustain a fission chain reaction. The detonation mechanism of a nuclear weapon relies on the creation of a supercritical mass of fissile material.

Surgical attack or surgical strike: An attack designed to have limited impact beyond the immediate military target, minimizing collateral damage.

Tactical nuclear weapons: Short-range nuclear weapons, such as artillery shells, bombs, and short-range missiles, deployed for use in battlefield operations (as opposed to strategic nuclear weapons).

Terminal phase: The third and final phase of the flight path of a ballistic missile. Refers to the trajectory of the warhead, now decoupled from the missile, as it re-enters the earth's atmosphere and proceeds to its target.

Theater ballistic missile: Short- or medium-range ballistic missiles with a range between 300 and 3500 km.

Thermonuclear weapon: A nuclear weapon in which the fusion of light nuclei, such as deuterium and tritium, leads to a significantly higher explosive yield than in a regular fission weapon. Thermonuclear weapons are sometimes referred to as staged weapons, because the initial fission reaction (the first stage) creates the condition under which the thermonuclear reaction can occur (the second stage). Also archaically referred to as a hydrogen bomb.

Throw-weight: Throw-weight refers to the weight of the payload that a missile is capable of delivering, and it is a measure of the destructive potential of a ballistic missile.

Treaty between the United States of America and the Russian Federation on Strategic Offensive Reductions (SORT): Also known as the Treaty of Moscow, SORT was an operationally deployed offensive strategic arms reduction treaty between the United States of America and the Russian Federation. The Treaty was in force from June 2004 until February 2011, when it was superseded by the New START treaty. The Treaty stipulated that the United States and Russia both had to reduce their strategic arsenals to between 1700 and 2200 warheads each, but did not stipulate the destruction of delivery vehicles or the warheads.

Triad: The concept of the triad integrates three forms of nuclear weapons deployment: intercontinental ballistic missiles (ICBMs), sea-launched ballistic missiles (SLBMs), and strategic bombers. The 2002 US Nuclear Posture Review announced the development of a New Triad, which included the following "legs": the first leg included non-nuclear and nuclear strike capabilities; the second leg included active and passive defense mechanisms, including ballistic missile defenses; and the third leg included responsive defense infrastructure, as part of an effort to better meet more amorphous and untraditional threats.

Trilateral Statement: Signed by US President Bill Clinton, Russian President Boris Yeltsin, and Ukrainian President Leonid Kravchuk in January 1994, the Trilateral Statement on the Non-Proliferation of Weapons of Mass Destruction and the Means of Their Delivery committed Ukraine to rid itself of nuclear weapons and to transfer 200 SS-19 and SS-24 warheads to Russia over a ten-month period. The Trilateral Statement also specified that Ukraine was to deactivate its SS-24s within the same ten-month period. The United States and Russia agreed to guarantee Ukraine's borders and grant Ukraine security guarantees provided that Ukraine joined the NPT as a non-nuclear weapon state. Ukraine finished transferring its nuclear weapons to Russia in 1996 and acceded to the NPT as a non-nuclear weapon state in 1994. Also see Strategic Arms Reductions Talks.

Unauthorized launch: The launch of a (nuclear) missile absent the authorization of the leadership legally endowed with such decision-making power. The term generally refers to an accidental or unintended launch that occurs because of faulty intelligence, systematic or mechanical failures, or the mistaken actions of military personnel.

Unmanned aerial vehicle (UAV): Remotely piloted or self-piloted aircraft that can take on various intelligence or combat roles such as reconnaissance or targeted missiles strikes (sometimes called "drones"). The rapid proliferation of UAVs has raised concerns that they might serve as a delivery vehicle for a terrorist strike involving WMD.

Uranium: Uranium is a metal with the atomic number 92. See Enriched uranium, Low enriched uranium, and Highly enriched uranium.

Warsaw Pact: Created in 1955 by the Soviet Union and its six Central European satellites, this military and political security alliance was the counterpart of NATO. It was formally dissolved on April 1, 1991.

Weapons-grade material: Refers to the nuclear materials that are most suitable for the manufacture of nuclear weapons, e.g., uranium (U) enriched to 90% U-235 or plutonium (Pu) that is primarily composed of Pu-239 and contains less than 7% Pu-240. Crude nuclear weapons (i.e., improvised nuclear devices) could be fabricated from lower-grade materials.

WMD (weapons of mass destruction): Typically refers to nuclear, biological, or chemical weapons, though there is some debate as to whether chemical weapons qualify as weapons of "mass destruction."

X Article: A paper published anonymously in *Foreign Affairs* in 1947. Written by a US diplomat, George Kennan, it outlined a long-term strategy for dealing with the Soviet Union that emphasized containment. It argued that the Soviet system was fundamentally opposed to capitalism and democracy and that economic and military strength would be required to counteract Soviet expansionism.

Yield: The total amount of energy released by a nuclear explosion, generally measured in equivalent tons of trinitrotoluene (TNT). A kiloton is equivalent to 1000 tons of TNT; a megaton is equivalent to one million tons of TNT.

We thank the James Martin Center for Nonproliferation Studies at the Middlebury Institute of International Studies at Monterey for the use of its glossary, developed independently for the Nuclear Threat Initiative.

Source: Collection of terms from www.if4it.com/it-glossary and from Knowledge Base of presentations from MERIT CyberSecurity Consulting.

Bibliography

The psychotropics war: http://www.organised-crime-of-covert-electronic-assault-nz.com/uploads/8/4/5/0/8450814/elinspectadorarticle_-_putin_.pdf

America losing the cyber war: https://www.scientificamerican.com/article/anonymous-s-cyber-war-with-isis-could-compromise-terrorism-intelligence/

Define terrorism: https://ctc.usma.edu/posts/defining-cyberterrorism-capturing-a-broad-range-of-activities-in-cyberspace

Stuxnet: http://www.csoonline.com/article/2134162/malware-cybercrime/stuxnet-creators-defined-21st-century-warfare.html

Review of the definition of risk: http://www.iiakm.org/ojakm/articles/2015/volume3_3/OJAKM_Volume3_3pp17-26.pdf

Types of terrorism: https://www.thoughtco.com/types-of-terrorism-3209376

http://www.globalresearch.ca/psychotronic-and-electromagnetic-weapons-remote-control-of-the-human-nervous-system/5319111

https://www.fda.gov/MedicalDevices/ucm106367.htm

Chapter 14

Epilogue: Where Are We Headed with the Cyber Nightmare?

Cyber Nightmare is a relative term that depends on which technology we're talking about. We're still in the second generation of malware misery. The worst is yet to come.

Which Is the Most Powerful Army in the World?

What a silly question. An all-out fight may be the only real way to compare military strength, but fortunately, the world hasn't had many opportunities lately. In fact, there are many influencing variables to determine the mightiest army at a global level. In the most unsurprising countdown to date, the United States of America is number one when it comes to military power. The Unites States has a perfect combination of military personnel numbers and military tool numbers.

However, we turned to the *Global Firepower Index*, a ranking of 106 nations based on more than 50 factors—including each country's military budget, manpower, and the amount of equipment each country has in its respective arsenal, and its natural resources. The complete Global Firepower list for 2017 puts the military powers of the world into full perspective.

The finalized Global Firepower ranking relies on over 50 factors to determine a given nation's Power Index *PwrIndx* score. Our formula allows smaller, though more technologically advanced, nations to compete with larger, lesser-developed ones. Modifiers (in the form of bonuses and penalties) are added to further refine the list.

The Best Army's Criteria

Some items to observe in regard to the finalized ranking:

- Ranking *does not simply rely on the total number of weapons* available to any one country but rather focuses on *weapon diversity* within the number totals to provide a better balance of firepower available (i.e., fielding 100 minesweepers does not equal the strategic and tactical value of fielding 10 aircraft carriers).
- *Nuclear stockpiles* are NOT taken into account but recognized/suspected nuclear powers receive a bonus.
- *Geographical factors, logistical flexibility, natural resources* and local industry influence the final ranking.
- *Available manpower* is a key consideration; nations with large populations tend to rank higher.
- Land-locked nations are NOT penalized for *lack of a navy*; naval powers ARE penalized for lack of diversity in available assets.
- *NATO allies* receive a slight bonus due to the theoretical sharing of resources.
- *Current political/military leadership* is NOT taken into account.

Collectively applying the factors cited above, we selected the first 10 nations with the most effective cyber armies:

1. United States
2. Russia
3. China
4. India
5. Israel
6. United Kingdom
7. North Korea
8. Germany
9. Turkey
10. Egypt

As a canonical rule: *The best army is the one that wins every battle, anytime anywhere.* There's a strong correlation between the US diagonal foreign policy and the logarithmic escalation of cyber terrorism.

The Institute of Terrorism and Research—a consortium between the USA and Israel in Fort Washington, Pennsylvania—reports that there are 3500 jihadi organizations and schools to produce cross-pollinated terrorists, and most likely they have 3500 missile launch websites. Of course, not all of them are invisible. The thing is, it is easy to hide or spoof the originating website. The Deep Web has hundreds of cyber armies anonymously planning to highjack the whole world.

Another canonical rule: *It is possible for a conventional army to win every battle, anytime anywhere, but in the cyber world, victory rules have drastically different criteria.* The USA is still suffering from the fear of massive cyber terrorism, as James Clapper, director of national intelligence thinks that cyber terrorism is the leading worldwide threat to US security. The US Cyber Command will be given more autonomy and visibility as a separate entity, after splitting off from the intelligence-focused National Security Agency. Hopefully, this will intensify America's ability to wage cyberwar against cyber terrorism armies in the world. The new US Cyber Command move reflects the escalating threat of cyberattacks and intrusions from other nation states, terrorist groups, and hackers, and comes as the USA faces ever-widening fears about Russian hacking following Moscow's efforts to meddle in the 2016 American election.

The USA has long operated "slow tempo" in cyberspace, using it to collect information, disrupt enemy networks, and aid conventional military missions. But as other nations and foes expand their use of cyber spying and attacks, the USA is determined to improve its ability to incorporate cyber operations into its everyday warfighting. Unfortunately, the USA is ranked 10th in the world in cybersecurity technology, behind Russia, China, Iran, North Korea, Syria, and other countries. It is embarrassing to mention.

The Cyber Terrorism Armies, Enlisted in the Hall of Infamy

Here is a list of the six deadliest terrorist groups that are operating today, and no doubt feature prominently on Washington's radar:

1 The Islamic State of Iraq and Syria (ISIS)

They are the most hated by the West. It takes a special kind of terrorist organization to force the world's most powerful and professional military into action halfway around the globe. The Islamic State of Iraq and the Levant (ISIL, ISIS, or simply the Islamic State) is exactly this type of organization: strong enough to rout several divisions of a national army, and rich enough to sustain their operations at an impressive pace. ISIS knows enough about Islam to be dangerous. The problem with ISIS is that they are masked and in combat fatigue. ISIS doesn't have diplomats and political representatives. This Islamic State jihadism is not a holy war but an unholy mess. You'll often hear the term *Cyber Caliphate* used when there's a mention of ISIS and cyber. It is also referred to as the Islamic State Hacking

Division or The United Cyber Caliphate. All these nicknames represent a loose group of anarchists that acts as the cyber army for ISIS.

The Cyber Caliphate was started by Junaid Hussain, a British national, who was later killed in a US airstrike in Raqqa, Iraq. The 'pioneer' of the Cyber Jihad was Anwar al-Awlaki, the so-called "bin Laden of the internet." Anwar al-Awlaki is credited with coining the term *creative terrorism*. He was deactivated in September 2011 in Yemen.

On September 12, 2014, CNN reported that the Central Intelligence Agency (CIA) estimated ISIS to have 31,000 fighters. ISIS has single-handedly swept across an area of the Middle East roughly the size of Belgium. The swift and easy capture of Iraq's second-largest city, Mosul, which used to be Saddam Hussein's hometown, by several thousand ISIL fighters in June 2014 had the effect of not only embarrassing the Iraqi government in the eyes of its people, but also revealing how poorly led and pathetic the Iraqi security forces had become. On September 12, 2014, President Barack Obama authorized targeted airstrikes against ISIL positions. President Obama's action created the collapse of several divisions of the Iraqi army, which resulted in the creation of ISIL. This action made ISIL more jihadistic and pervasive (Figures 14.1 and 14.2).

A major difference between ISIL and the litany of other Islamist terrorist organizations competing for fundraising and recruits is that the former is succeeding in well-timed and deliberate suicidal missions, that not even Al-Qaeda could accomplish; they are capturing territory, holding that territory, and declaring an Islamic caliphate in the very heart of the Arab world. And ISIL is doing it in the most brutal way imaginable: rounding up and executing anyone who shows the slightest bit of resistance to its domination. At least four cases of mass killings by ISIL terrorists

Figure 14.1 A website of an ISIS member of the Dark Web. ISIS has over 250 websites around the world in every language. They deal with Bitcoin and Altcoin. They have 3000 operatives in the United States, with 100 US bank accounts. In the ISIS organization, there are the militants who appear on the websites and TV, and there are the leaders and the thinkers who plan the attacks.

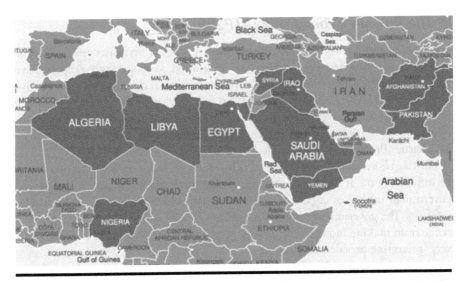

Figure 14.2 The world is suffering not only from biological diseases, but also the fundamentalist terror organization called ISIS—a major threat. Technology has enriched their viciousness. Jihadi warriors are fighting to reoccupy the Middle East to establish their caliphate. Many of these warriors are emigrating to provoke the West with jihad in order to bring about the countdown to the apocalypse.

have been documented, including the execution of 250 Syrian troops in August after the group captured the al-Tabqa air base. On August 12, 2014, over 200 Iraqi tribesmen were massacred west of Ramadi in what can only be described as an attempt by ISIL to extinguish any competitor, however passive, who dares to rise up and challenge its authority. What's clear is that ISIS and its monstrosities won't be defeated by the same powers that brought it to Iraq and Syria in the first place, or whose open and covert war-making has fostered it in the years since. Endless Western military interventions in the Middle East have brought only destruction and division.

Combined with a Treasury Department study that assesses ISIL's crude oil revenue at a value of US$1 million per day, it's safe to say that the United States and the coalition it has assembled has a lot of work ahead of them. ISIS, as an organization, obviously needs money. Cybercrime pays and, in fact, can be considered to be a more reliable source of revenue for the terrorist organization as opposed to, for example, oil sales—which are now declining. ISIS's income has fallen by about a third (mid-2016) compared to the same time last year. Revenue for the militant group fell to US$56 million a month in March from around US$80 million a month in the middle of 2015; hence their need to embark on greater cybercrime.

Speaking of historic heritage, ISIS says it is destroying museums because, according to their ideology, they have to destroy every statue that is a symbol of worship; but the real reason behind the destruction is they don't have much money right now.

2 The Russian Cyber Army (ATP28)

Since Democratic National Committee (DNC) officials first discovered, on June 16, 2016, their data networks had been compromised, a group of cyber experts have collected evidence that the Russian government was responsible. Representative Jamie Raskin, D-MD., declared last month at a hearing of the House Committee on Oversight and Government Reform that "Russian President Vladimir Putin figured that he was no military match for the United States, but he could launch a Manhattan Project for cyber-attacks."

In the United States, the FBI and other agencies focus on how criminals may be infiltrating or, at the very least, influencing government offices. In Russia, the government infiltrates organized crime and establishes a reciprocal business relationship. The government provides protection in exchange for favors. Favors may range from making money to using a gang to implement state interests. 2016 was a very interesting presidential election year.

At the beginning, in May 2016, DNC officials noticed unusual activity in their network. CrowdStrike cybersecurity was hired to investigate, and quickly it found that a group of hackers had, in late April, gained access to the systems of the committee's opposition-research team, from which the group had stolen two files containing information on Donald J. Trump, who became the Republican nominee for president. The investigators determined that the hackers were part of APT 28, a group well known among cybersecurity experts. The name is short for *Advanced Persistent Threat*, which usually refers to government hackers. Officials in the United States, UK, Israel, and Germany have all told the *Financial Times* that they believe APT 28 is run by Russia's sprawling military intelligence arm, the GRU. Moscow has consistently denied any connection to APT 28.

David Satter is a recognized authority on Russian organized crime. He documented, in his book *Darkness at Dawn* (Yale University Press), the *Russian Business Network* (RBN) as a cybercrime provider. Satter recently wrote an article on the suspected ties between Russian organized crime and the Russian police as seen in the rising unsolved murder rate of journalists in the Russian Federation; their work had become too problematic for the authorities to manage ("Who Murdered These Russian Journalists?," Forbes.com, December 26, 2008). Satter used the case of the murdered journalist Anna Politkovskaya to illustrate his point (Figure 14.3).

3 The Syrian Electronic Army

Syria, one of the highly visible Arab countries in the Middle East, has been the target of constant cyber espionage and crime by the Western world. The Syrian government decided to build a data center to retaliate and respond to these cyber-attacks, consisting of a group of talented hackers from within and outside Syria (Figure 14.4a and 14.4b). Initial training and support came from Iran and Russia.

Figure 14.3 This is the friendly web, one of 20 Russian websites. This is not the one where they do the secret trade for opium and drugs. Russians use the Dark Web, the Deep Web, Bitcoin, and the mighty dollar.

The group of hackers named themselves the Syrian Electronic Army (SEA) to support the government of Syrian President Bashar al-Assad. Technical investigation shows that the Army's official website is hosted by SCS-NET, the Internet service provider of the Syrian Computer Society (SCS).

The SEA surfaced in 2011 and it grabbed the world's attention by hacking the Associated Press's Twitter account and briefly wiping $136 billion from stock exchanges. The SEA rose to notoriety throughout 2013 after hacking a number of high-profile Twitter accounts and websites, including those of *The New York Times*, *The Washington Post*, and *The Guardian*. On April 23, 2013, SEA hackers broke into the Associated Press Twitter account and posted a bogus story about an explosion at the White House. That created a hectic denial of service (DoS) when millions of Twitter users logged in to find out what happened.

The White House says that the SEA is not that sophisticated, but the SEA has a bigger plan to become truly cyber terrorism savvy. The SEA is trained and financially supported by Iran and Russia, who consider themselves well positioned in the world of cyber terror. Russia has a huge global network made of 120,000 cells around the world.

After successfully hacking radio stations NPR and CBS, and the Associated Press, people want to know more about the Syrian Electronic Army. Are they real? How can anyone cause the Dow to drop 150 points with a single tweet? How could the White House claim the SEA is not sophisticated?

Recently, the SEA has been touted in underground circles as one of the top 10 most skilled hacking teams in the world. Tactics commonly used by the group include phishing, website hacking, and compromising Facebook and Twitter accounts. Harvard University, a victim of the SEA, stated on September 27, 2011, that a "sophisticated individual or group" is behind the attacks of the SEA.

(a)

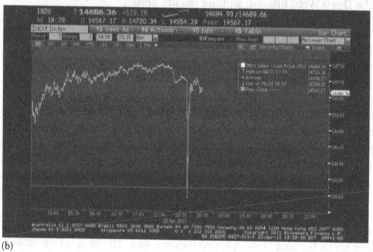

(b)

Figure 14.4 **(a) This is one of the visible websites representing the Syrian government, active in defacing other sites, spamming, and ransomware, based in Tartous and Lattakieh. The electronic army has 4000 active members. (b) A chart showing the Dow Jones plunge in the moments after the bogus AP tweet was sent from the agency's hacked account.**

The SEA has a significant web presence. The group uses their website to coordinate group membership and report on operations that have been carried out. The SEA runs two leak sites where they dump information from various hacks. One is included on their primary website and the second separate site discloses leaks related to Qatar. The primary leak site was launched on January 23, 2013.

The SEA completed targeted attacks during summer 2012 that used Skype to distribute Dark Comet RAT malware to the Syrian opposition. The malware masqueraded as a Skype encryption application. This tool was used to track the IP, location, and personal information of dissidents. The information collected on the dissident was then sent to an IP address located in Damascus, Syria, owned by the Syrian Telecommunications Establishment (216.6.0.28). A website hosted at the same IP address also served a tool called AntiHacker, which was purported to be a tool to defend against hackers for the opposition, but was in fact DarkComet. The Electronic Frontier Foundation (EFF) reported that during the Syrian Internet shutdown in November 2012, this IP address was one of the few still reachable in the Syrian IP address space. This IP address no longer appears to be hosting this malware. PDF files that appear to be lists of opposition members have also been distributed, but they too actually installed the malware in the background. Once the creator of DarkComet learned of the use by the Syrian government, development and the distribution sites were shut down.

BlackShades Remote Controller, a commercial tool, has also been used by the SEA. Similar to the fake social media sites, these tools are used to collect information on the individual by accessing the user's local PC.

It is believed the SEA uses Havij, an automated SQL Injection exploit tool, to compromise websites. SQL Injection is the leading attack vector for compromising websites. The SEA, with its website http://sea.sy/index/en, also has its own Black Hat Group. It uses the very latest technologies including SEANux, which is an Ubuntu-based Linux with a modified Gnome Shell interface, icons, and GTK theme. Basically, defacing a website simply means that you replace the *index.html* file of the target site with your file. Then all the users who open it will see the defaced pages. It is charged up with penetration testing and privacy tools and other potent missiles. The SEA is made up of a group of top-notch computer geeks to support the government of Syria's President Bashar al-Assad, in collaboration with the Iranians, Chinese, and North Koreans. It uses spamming, website defacement, malware, phishing, and DoS attacks.

The SEA claimed responsibility for recently hacking into the critical infrastructure of the Israeli city Haifa. The group also runs a WikiLeaks-type site and has released documents that some activists and researchers say led to the persecution of revolutionary leaders. Syrian President Bashar al-Assad has publicly endorsed the SEA as a "virtual army" to complement the real army. The HP researchers also found evidence that the government is providing support to the SEA, something both parties deny. In one case, a young man who was targeted for recruitment was told that he could avoid serving in the regular army if he entered the SEA.

So far, the SEA has not penetrated the nanotechnology domain. The Russians and the North Koreans have been providing the Syrian hackers with third-generation tools (3G cyber nano terrorism) to get into the nano world of crime.

4 The Chinese Cyber Army

China is known as the slickest country in cyber spying! The Chinese government has been spotted with its hand in the cookie jar, being involved in a number of high-profile cases of espionage, primarily through the use of a "global virtual network" of students, business people, scientists, diplomats, and engineers from within the Chinese diaspora (outside the mainland). A defector in Belgium, purportedly an agent, claimed that there were hundreds of spies in industries throughout Europe and the United States, and on his defection to Australia, Chinese diplomat Chen Yonglin said there were over 1000 such spies in that country. And as usual, after every attack, China continues to deny this, playing the victim card. China has immensely expanded its cyber capabilities and is in the process of integrating it with its military to ensure increased education of its soldiers in cyber warfare.

The Chinese have been masters of espionage and spying. Every member of the Chinese Cyber Army is an employee with a specific assignment to steal intellectual property, advanced technologies, trade secrets, military secrets (compromises have included the theft of secrets regarding the F-35 and F-22 jets, the B-2 bomber, and space-based laser systems), information on critical infrastructure, and engineering design blueprints. The Chinese espionage network is made of 540,000 agents capturing information on everything strategic, technological, or military (Figure 14.5).

Figure 14.5 The Chinese website as a static screen, but in fact it has a secret key for entry. The Chinese are considered very experienced in cybercrime. The Chinese hackers have a permanent account with the Chinese government. They teach other electronic armies all the tricks of malware.

5 North Korean Cyber Army

Since early 2014, North Korea has been hacking computers of South Korean firms and government agencies quite frequently. Some experts say they are planting malicious code under a long-term plan laying groundwork for a massive cyberattack against its rival. *Bureau 121* is the North Korean cyber warfare agency; it is staffed by some of North Korea's most talented computer experts and is run by the Korean military. A defector indicated that the agency has about 1800 specialists. Many of the bureau's hackers are hand-picked graduates of the University of Automation, Pyongyang. While these specialists are scattered around the world, their families benefit from special privileges at home. Most of the collected military data has to do with satellite technology and ballistic military engineering. The North Korean Cyber Army operates in complete secrecy and has a direct connection with Kim Jong-un.

6 The Iran Cyber Army

Iran now has the world's fourth biggest cyber army, as claimed by an official of the Islamic Revolutionary Guard Corps (IRGC), stressing that the IRGC's cyber power is seen as a major counterbalance to that of the United States and Israel in the region. The Israel-based Institute for National Security Studies (INSS) said that, "IRGC clearly makes the country one of the best and most advanced nations when it comes to cyberwar. In a case of escalation between Iran and the West, Iran will likely aim to launch a cyber-attack against critical infrastructures in the United States and its allies, including energy infrastructures, financial institutions, transportation systems, and others."

Iran's cyber army has launched a cyberattack against critical infrastructures in the United States and its allies, including energy infrastructures, financial institutions, transportation systems, and others. In order to realize the goals of its strategy, Iran has allocated about $1 billion to develop and acquire technology and recruit and train experts. The country has an extensive network of educational and academic research institutions dealing with information technology, computer engineering, electronic engineering, and math.

It is worth mentioning that Iran's cyber army was able to acquire, from a third party, a copy of the source code of the famous worm Stuxnet. (The Russian Sergey Ulasen collaborated with the Iranians to explain the internal details of Stuxnet.)

In addition, the government operates its own institute—the Iran Telecommunications Research Center—the research and professional branch of the *Information and Communications Ministry*. The institute trains and operates advanced research teams in various fields, including information security. Another government body is the *Technology Cooperation Officer*, which belongs to the President's bureau, and initiates information technology research projects. This body has been identified by the European Union and others in the West as involved in the Iranian nuclear program. The Iranian cyberspace system comprises a large number of cyber organizations, formally related to various establishment institutions and involved in numerous fields.

One central organization with a primarily defensive orientation is the Cyber Defense Command, operating under Iran's Passive Defensive Organization, affiliated with the General Staff of the Armed Forces. Alongside military personnel, this cyberspace organization includes representatives of government ministries, such as the ministries of communications, defense, intelligence, and industry, and its main goal is to develop a defensive doctrine against cyberspace threats.

Another cyberspace body of a defensive nature is the MAHER Information Security Center, operating under the aegis of the communications and information technology ministry. The center is in charge of operating rapid response teams in case of emergencies and cyberattacks. Iran also has a Committee for Identifying Unauthorized Sites and FETA, the police cyberspace unit, which in addition to dealing with Internet crime also monitors and controls Iranian Internet usage, with emphasis on Internet cafés throughout the country that allow relatively anonymous web surfing.

The picture is less clear regarding Iran's offensive cyberspace capabilities. Clearly the capabilities of the Revolutionary Guard make Iran one of the most advanced nations in the field of cyberspace warfare, with capabilities, inter alia, to install malicious code in counterfeit computer software, to block computer communications networks, to develop viruses and tools for penetrating computers to gather intelligence, and to develop tools with delayed action mechanisms or mechanisms connected to control servers. There is also evidence of links between the Revolutionary Guard and hacker groups in Iran and abroad that operate against the enemies of the regime at home and around the world. The use of outsourcing allows the Revolutionary Guard and Iran to maintain distance and deniability about Iran's involvement in cyberspace warfare.

Iran's cyber army has transitioned to retaliatory action. Secretary Panetta's recent statement on the need to close accounts with those responsible for this attack demonstrates this, but what ultimately counts is the test of action and not of words. The focus of Iran's cyberspace activity directed against Israel and other countries in the West requires appropriate defensive arrangements, beginning with an up-to-date doctrine of cyberspace defense. The attackers' sophistication requires intelligence-based defenses as well as the generic ones.

In light of developments in Iran, the State of Israel must place the issue of Iranian cyberspace activity among its highest intelligence priorities, in order to identify advance preparations and foil attacks before they are underway. Similar to the Iranian nuclear program, the challenge is not Israel's alone, but rather that of many other states in the West as well as the Gulf states. It is therefore necessary to initiate broad interstate cooperation to gather intelligence and foil Iranian cyber activity (Figure 14.6).

Figure 14.6 The Iran Cyber Army is one of the most active collaborators with the Chinese and Russians.

What Drives a Country to Develop a Cyber Army?

Just imagine, one F-22 can annihilate the strongest Roman army of 200,000 foot soldiers in 5 minutes. Obviously, modern armies would make quick work of any ancient military, but we should judge an army based on how well they dominated in their time. In the old days, an empire built an army for three reasons: (1) to defend itself, (2) to invade other empires, and (3) to defend itself and defeat weak empires.

If we were to ask Vint Cerf or Leonard Kleinrock what they think about the Internet of today, they would say that "The internet wasn't designed to do the things we're asking of it now…". No prophet could have predicted the nebulosity of this man-made beast. The hyper exponential evolution of the Internet has led us to a truly unimaginable époque, as eloquently envisioned by Ray Kurzweil: "The universe will wake up and patterns of matter and energy in the universe will become saturated with intelligence processes and knowledge…Technology will expand and master all our biology methods, including Human Intelligence. Nanotechnology has given us the tools…we will be able to adjust our anatomy and adjust our biological systems to remain healthy forever. Not only will we live to be healthier and longer, but more importantly, more intelligent."

Historically, the purpose of the military has been to defend the nation's borders against invasion and external attack. And yet if you look at the most recent US military encounters in Afghanistan, Iraq, and Libya, it is clear that the military was not used for this purpose. None of those countries were about to invade our nation's borders.

The factors that influence the might of the conventional army are listed in the following relationship:

$$\text{Military Might} = \text{Number of Troops} + \text{Size of Arsenal}$$
$$+ \text{Advanced Arms Technology} + \text{Leadership}$$
$$+ \text{Military Strategy}$$

This relationship doesn't apply to cyber military might, which has different influencing factors:

$$\text{Electronic Army Might} = \text{Hacking Knowlege} + \text{Spying \& Reconnaissance}$$
$$+ \text{Digital Immunity} + \text{Internet Knowledge} + \text{Cryptography}$$
$$+ \text{Artificial Intelligence} + \text{Nanotechnology}$$
$$+ \text{Big Data} + \text{Telecom Knowledge} + \text{Cyberattack History}$$

The Dream Cyberattacks for the Cyber Armies of the World

The definition of cyber terrorism has become "rigid" like a rubber band. It is stretched in every direction and domain, with an increasingly fuzzy meaning and lots of smoke and mirrors. It incorporates premeditated, politically motivated attacks by subnational groups, clandestine agents, or individuals against information and computer systems, computer programs, and data that result in violence against non-combatant targets.

Religious terrorists are motivated by the belief that they will go straight to paradise if they're killed in the name of jihad. We witnessed this in the chilling poem carried by one of the 9/11 hijackers:

> Oh God, open all Paradise doors for me. Oh God who answers prayers and answers those who ask you, I am asking you for your help. I am asking you for forgiveness. I am asking you to lighten my way. I am asking you to lift the burden I feel. Oh God, you who open all doors, please open all doors to me, open all venues for me, open all avenues for me. God, I trust in you. God, I lay myself in your hands.

Thus, cyber terrorism is an act of hellish audacity and fearlessness, where the mischievous actor will deliberately shut down all his vital systems before he commits the destined act, ignoring all the human dignities.

The world today as shown in Figure 14.7 has 35 active electronic army centers (EAC) that belong to 55 countries run by dictatorship regimes. However, we believe that each of the 191 countries of the world has a cybersecurity group that runs clandestine projects for its government.

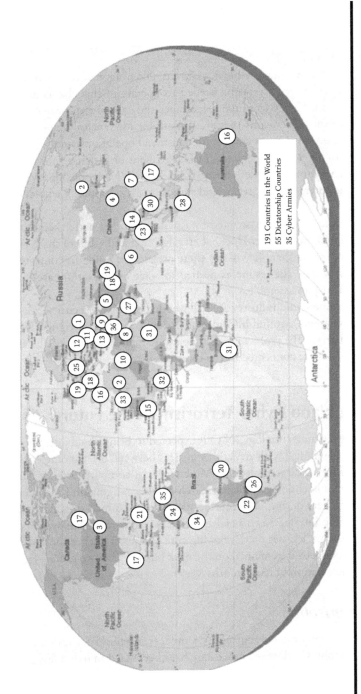

Figure 14.7 The world's façade is stained with 35 cyber armies that are drilling terror holes into our societal fabric. They're bitting the hand of Vint Cerf and Leonard Kleinrock. (From: www.quora.com/What-countries-are-currently-ruled-by-dictatorships.)

As of late 2016, more than 30 nations have developed offensive cyberattack capabilities. The proliferation of cyber capabilities coupled with new warfighting technologies will increase the incidence of standoff and remote operations, especially in the initial phases of conflict.

The National Security Agency, in particular, has taken aggressive measures to hire and retain the cybersecurity talent needed to operate in this challenging environment. In addition, Cyber Command leverages the capacity and capabilities of 133 Cyber Mission Force teams that are responsible for synchronizing and executing cyber operations to support combatant command operations, and for the defense and security of service component and Department of Defense information networks. Cyber Command has established close working relationships with both international and interagency partners and stands ready to support a whole of nation response.

Cyberattacks like those being perpetrated by Russia and other nations cannot be fought in conventional ways. Roger Hockenberry, founder and CEO of the consulting firm Cognitio, insists that, "I will say these attacks are going to continue and they will grow in scale." The resources needed to wage cyber warfare are "so commoditized they're easy to assemble."

Much of the government and industry are still wedded to "legacy security" that aims to build walls or "moats" around information systems, as if they are guarding a castle, says Hockenberry. "The problem is that moats are ineffective," especially as more systems and devices are connected to the Internet.

Crystal-Balling Nano Cyber Terrorism in the Future

In the coming decades, nanotechnology (NT) is expected to bring about a technological revolution. NT will deal with structures of sizes between 0.1 nanometer (a single atom) and 100 nm (a large molecule). More recently, computer science has become involved in nanotechnology. Such research is wide ranging and includes software engineering, networking, Internet security, image processing, virtual reality, human–machine interfaces, artificial intelligence, and intelligent systems. Although most of the work focuses on developing core computer science tools and applications, nano cybersecurity remained on the back burner. The two crucial factors that energized the creation of nanosecurity were:

Factor 1: Miniaturization

Miniaturization of microprocessors is currently in process at nanometer scales. For example, computer graphics and image processing have been used in nanomanipulators that provide researchers an interactive system interface to scanning probe microscopes. Conventional methods to miniaturize the size of transistors in silicon microprocessor chips will soon reach its limit, and the modification of today's top-down technology to produce (from large to small size) nanoscale structures is difficult and expensive. Feynman and Drexler proposed a new style of technology, which assembles individual atoms or molecules into a refined product. Drexler coined the term *molecular technology* or bottom-up technology (from small to large). This bottom-up technology will be the answer for the computer industry and, in particular, for cybersecurity.

Factor 2: Malware

Antivirus technology is ready to retire and become a legacy sculpture on the shelf. No antivirus software can keep ahead of all the virus writers, so other protection mechanisms are needed. Spyware is often not detected and some spyware such as key logging and rootkit software is very dangerous. A free one might be better than a commercial one. One reputable antivirus software, used by tens of thousands of businesses and millions of home users, shut down an untold number of computers around the world after it mistakenly identified core parts of Microsoft Windows as threats. The company confirmed that the software is suffering from senility. On May 28, 2012, computer security labs in Iran, Russia, and Hungary announced the discovery of Flame, "the most complex malware ever found," according to Hungary's CrySyS Lab. Duqu and Stuxnet raised the stakes in the cyber battles being fought in the Middle East—but now what might be the most sophisticated cyber weapon yet has been unleashed. The Flame cyber espionage worm came to the attention of Kaspersky Lab while they were tracking another malware, which was deleting sensitive information across the Middle East. While searching for that code—nicknamed Wiper—Kaspersky discovered the new malware codenamed Worm.Win32.Flame.

Flame shares many characteristics with notorious cyber weapons Duqu and Stuxnet. While its features are different, the geography and careful targeting of attacks coupled with the usage of specific software vulnerabilities seem to put it alongside those familiar "super-weapons" currently deployed in the Middle East by unknown perpetrators. Flame can easily be described as one of the most complex threats ever discovered. It's big and incredibly sophisticated. It pretty much redefines the notion of cyberwar and cyber espionage.

In May 2012, Kaspersky found out that Flame had initially infected approximately 1000 machines, with victims including governmental organizations, educational institutions, and private individuals. At that time, 65% of the infections happened in Iran, Israel, the Palestinian Territories, Sudan, Syria, Lebanon, Saudi Arabia, and Egypt, with a "huge majority of targets" within Iran. Flame has also been reported in Europe and North America. Flame supports a "kill" command that wipes all traces of the malware from the computer. The initial infections of Flame stopped operating after its public exposure, and the "kill" command was sent. The creators of the Flame malware have sent a "suicide" command that removes it from some infected computers.

The New Dawn for Cybersecurity

Nanotechnology has indeed promised a great future for humanity. We can recognize Dr. Richard Feynman as the father of nanotechnology with his famous speech "There's Plenty of Room at the Bottom," from a lecture at an American Physical Society meeting at Caltech on December 29, 1959, along with Dr. Eric Drexler, who was strongly influenced by ideas on limits to growth. He introduced the terms "nanotechnology" and "molecular engineering" in his book *Engines of Creation*. According to Feynman, building products with atomic precision by bottom-up technology could offer a dramatic increase in potential and a decrease in environmental impact, which would improve our way of life. A simple example of the potential benefits of nanotechnology is that information on paper can be packed into much smaller spaces so that less pollution from discarding that paper will be produced. The aspect that would be directly beneficial to humankind is nanomedicine, which involves medical research at the nanoscale. For example, a group of programmable nano robots (nanobots) could flow along our bloodstreams without harming our bodies, being injected to treat our bodies from within.

Then came the big shock: "The Next Big Thing Is Really Small." Nanotechnology and artificial intelligence will be the best pillars to promote and support cybersecurity. We're already having intelligent conversations with our cell phones, and in the months and years to come, artificial intelligence (AI) will allow us to communicate with our biological cells and calibrate our DNA, and even augment our intelligence. The United States has the biggest technology think tank in the world and in the next decade nanotechnology and AI will be the prime components of digital immunity, which will be molecular and immersed in all our computing devices. On a more grandiose scale, NT and AI will make great contributions to Smart Cities. Remember, AI is the computer science that specializes in making computers behave like humans. Thus, AI will replicate the human immune system and create digital immunity (DI) for the digital world. DI will have the intelligence of the machine and the intelligence of an immunologist fused together. Smart Cities will be the prime beneficiaries of DI.

The Smart City will be armed with a magical shield that will trap and immobilize smuggling attackers like a bear trap.

Molecular Warfare to Defend Smart Cities

Molecular war is invisible, as it is in the human body. When we get sick, we know a big war is raging in our body between the assailants and the city grid defenders. These are the first symptoms of sickness: higher temperature and sluggish mobility.

A hypothetical cyber nano attack on the city of San Francisco will demonstrate how professional cyber terrorists will perform their evil act. It is a coalition of cyber terrorists who have been studying the selection of the proper city. San Francisco is on a peninsula that sits on seven hills between the Pacific Ocean and the East Bay. San Francisco has two iconic bridges and a first-class rapid transit metro (Bay Area Rapid Transit, BART) system. These are the only three main "direct" arteries that connect the city to Marin County and the city of Oakland. San Francisco is a vulnerable city, as described by Jack London ("Not in history has a modern imperial city been so completely destroyed. San Francisco is gone.") after the 1906 earthquake and fire, caused by the notorious San Andreas Fault. The bridges leading to the city suffer from nerve-wrecking commute gridlock starting at 4:30 AM every day of the week. According to the California Department of Transportation (Cal Tran), every day 425,000 cars cross the Golden Gate and Bay Bridges, and the number is increasing 15% each year. If anything happens to the structure of these two bridges, the city will have a catastrophe of biblical proportions.

The BART, which opened in 1972, should also be added to the list of the critical infrastructures of the Bay Area. It has a total of 112 miles of tracks. System wide, there are approximately 32 miles of aerial track, 52 miles of track at grade, and about 28 miles of subway track, with a third rail propulsion power of 1000 volt DC electricity. BART runs 70 trains concurrently and is monitored directly from the Operations Control Center located in Oakland across the bay. BART trains run on hydroelectric and solar energy. Daily commute ridership across the bay to San Francisco is 215,000 on weekdays.

San Francisco International Airport is also considered as major infrastructure. It is the largest airport in Northern California and is located 14 miles from downtown San Francisco. It handles 700 flights per day.

Plan of Attack

The famous scientist Charles Darwin said, regarding survival, "It is not the strongest of the species that survives, nor the most intelligent that survives. It is the one that is most adaptable to change."

We can add another dimension to his famous quote by saying, "Since cyber terror is always going after newly born smart cities, cybersecurity will make cities most adaptable to change!"

Cyberattacks are like germs in the air or in the water; they have been in existence since the creation of the universe. A good *defense by offense* is the most effective approach to win the battle and the war. In other words, learning from previous attacks will augment knowledge about future attacks. This is how the human body acquires knowledge about invading pathogens, through adaptive vaccination.

San Francisco is one of the most attractive cities in the world, despite its geological fragility due to earthquake faults. It was decided to hire a unique think-tank experts from Stanford University and University of California, Berkeley, to install a duplex of nano grid over the city. The first one is the City Nano Grid (CNG) for infrastructure and the IoT of most of the city, as shown in Figure 14.8a. The second one is the Digital Immunity Nano Grid (DIG). The two grids are pathologically

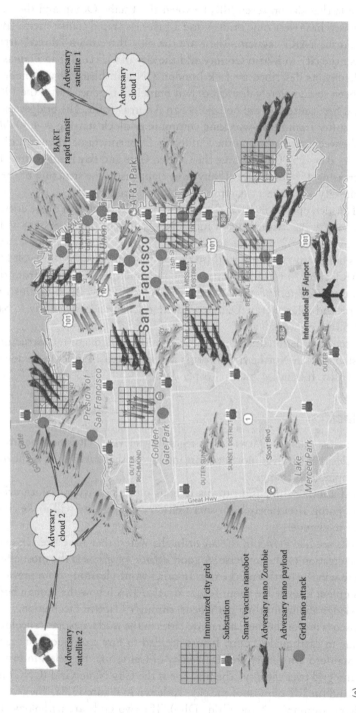

Figure 14.8 (a) A typical cyberwar inside the city nanogrid of San Francisco. All the fighting between the Smart Vaccine Immunity Nanobots and the Adversary Zombies takes place on the city smart grid at the molecular scale.

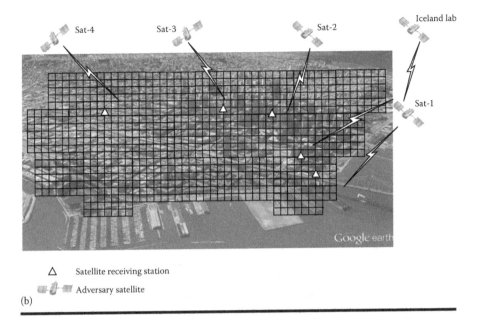

connected, similarly to the nervous system and the immune system. The nano grid is made of cross-carbon nanotubes, as shown in Figure 14.8b, which are known for their extraordinary thermal conductivity and mechanical and electrical properties.

Quantum computers are exponentially faster than modern computers. A super-computer trying to find one phone number in a database of all the world's phone books would take a month, while a quantum computer could do it in 27 minutes (Figure 14.9).

Nano-RAM is a proprietary computer memory technology from the company Nantero. On January 2, 2018, the *Daily Mail* Australia reported the IBM chip contains 5.4 billion transistors and uses just 70 milliwatts.

The transistors will be 100 times smaller than the thickness of a human hair. It is a type of nonvolatile random-access memory based on the position of carbon nanotubes deposited on a chip-like substrate. In theory, the small size of the nano-tubes allows for very high-density memories. Nantero also refers to it as NRAM.

The silicon transistors in computers may be replaced in ten years by transistors based on carbon nanotubes. By replacing silicon transistors with transistors base on nanotubes, we will get faster, smaller and more energy-efficient computers.

HewlettPackard is developing a memory device that uses nanowires coated with titanium dioxide. One group of these nanowires is deposited parallel to another group. When a perpendicular nanowire is laid over a group of parallel wires, at each intersection a device called a memristor is formed. A memristor can be used as a

Single carbon nanotube

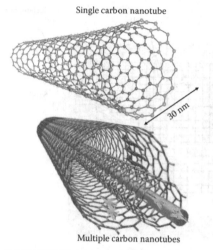

30 nm

Multiple carbon nanotubes

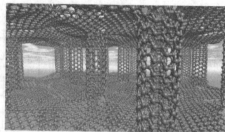

Cross carbon nanotubes grid model

Figure 14.9 **The nanogrid is made of carbon nanotubes tied together. It is similar to a subway tunnel with a multitude of other nanotubes. It is a fascinating world that has become visible in the world of digital immunity.**

single-component memory cell in an integrated circuit. By reducing the diameter of the nanowires, researchers believe memristor memory chips can achieve higher memory density than flash memory chips. Magnetic nanowires made of an alloy of iron and nickel are being used to create dense memory devices.

In the next decade, molecular and quantum cybersecurity will be the de facto approach in Smart Cities to neutralize nano cyber terrorism, which will be characterized by its highly sophisticated symmetry and stunning technological advances.

In our hypothetical attack, a group of professional hackers from an adversary East European nation—given the name Maglev, from the name of Shanghai Maglev, the fastest electric train in the world—have noticed that San Francisco is becoming a Smart City of the West and have decided to deploy their multiple distributed nano attacks in the afternoon (3:30 PM) of a busy weekday: July 7.

The Maglev team comprises seven top-notch officers of the adversary nation's Electronic Army, two PhD graduates in computer science, an AI guru from a reputable Silicon Valley company, a nanotechnologist who went back to his native country after 5 years of classified research in military nanotechnology for the Department of Defense, three scientists who worked on loan for three years before going to back to their country in the Middle East, at one of the best labs in genetics and cybernetics, four scientists from Eastern Europe who worked on research in artificial intelligence and robotics, two satellite telecommunication gurus who worked on contract to the military, a motherboard electronic engineer who has invented cyber bombs and prototypes in electromagnetic pulse devices (EMP), and finally, two software engineers who specialize in encryption and autonomic grid computing. Although

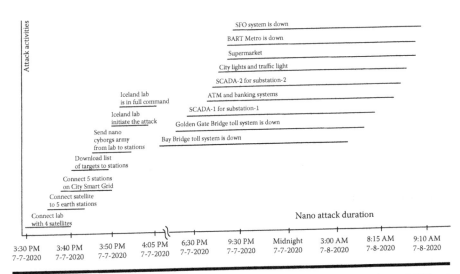

Figure 14.10 **The nano attack on San Francisco, California on July 7, 2020, at 3:30 PM. The timeline is split into the setup section, first, and the attack itself, the second section.**

the team members are not cyber terrorists by all means, they have been approached by a business "front" in Sofia, Bulgaria, and have agreed to work to upgrade the Electronic Army with new technologies ahead of the rest of the world, and to experiment on three Smart Cities in the United States. A modern lab is set up in Iceland for the project. The length of the engagement is one year. The price is 40 million dollars! It is pretty much like the TV series of *Mission Impossible*, but three technology generations ahead.

Here's the sequence of events for the cyberattack on San Francisco. Figure 14.10 gives a visual representation of the nano attack.

1. Establish five spy stations (called Base-1) in the city to study how the city lives and where the critical spots are, and when.
2. Establish encrypted communication between the lab in Iceland and the four satellites.
3. Establish encrypted communication between the four satellites and Base-1.
4. Download the list of the targets from Iceland through the satellites to Base-1. The list contains the toll systems for the two bridges, and BART, and three SCADA systems connected to three distribution substations in the city.
5. Download the adversary software nanobots (nano cyborgs) from the satellites and store them temporarily on a holding server connected to the city grid. These nano cyborgs were developed by the team in the Iceland lab. These cyborgs are the type that will replicate themselves and mutate into a new type of cyborg.
6. The team in Iceland is in full control and ready to start the attack.

Glossary

Aerogel: A silicon-based foam composed mostly of air. Often called "frozen smoke" or "blue smoke," aerogels have extremely low thermal conductivity, which gives them extraordinary insulating properties. They are the lowest-density solids known on earth.

Aerosol: A suspension of fine particles (0.01–10 μm) of a solid or liquid in a gas.

Aggregation: A collection of individual units or particles gathered together into a mass or body.

Alkali metals: A group of soft, very reactive elements that includes lithium, sodium, and potassium.

Alumina: A ceramic material made of aluminum oxide. Alumina is often used as a substrate, or underlying layer, for experiments. Alumina can be mixed with various amounts of titania (titanium dioxide) to change its properties as a substrate.

Aluminum: A silvery-white, metallic element with good conductive and thermal properties.

Atomic force microscope (AFM): A scanning probe microscopy instrument capable of revealing the structure of samples. The AFM uses a sharp metal tip positioned over a conducting or non-conducting substrate, and the surface topography is mapped out by measuring the mechanical force exerted on the tip. See Scanning probe microscopy.

Biomimetics: The study of the structure and function of biological substances to develop man-made systems that mimic natural ones; imitating, copying, or learning from biological systems to create new materials and technologies.

Biopolymer: A polymer found in nature. DNA and RNA are examples of naturally occurring biopolymers. See also Polymer.

Biosensor: A sensor used to detect a biological substance (e.g., bacteria, blood gases, or hormones). Biosensors often make use of sensors that are themselves made of biological materials or of materials that are derived from or mimic biological materials.

Biosynthesis: The process by which living organisms produce chemical compounds.

Block copolymers: Self-assembled material composed of long sequences of "blocks" of the same monomer unit, covalently bound to sequences of unlike type.

Buckyball: See fullerene.

Carbon: A nonmetallic element found in all living things. Carbon is part of all organic compounds and, in combined form, of many inorganic substances. Diamonds, graphite, and fullerenes are pure forms of carbon.

Carbon nanotubes: Long, thin cylinders of carbon, discovered in 1991 by S. Iijima. These large macromolecules are unique for their size, shape, and remarkable physical properties. They can be thought of as a sheet of graphite (a hexagonal lattice of carbon) rolled into a cylinder. The physical properties are still being discovered. Nanotubes have a very broad range of electronic, thermal, and structural properties that change depending on the different kinds of nanotube (defined by its diameter, length, and chirality, or twist). To make things more interesting, besides having a single cylindrical wall (single-walled nanotubes or SWNTs), nanotubes can have multiple walls (MWNTs)—cylinders inside the other cylinders. Sometimes referred to simply as nano tubes.

Cell: A small, usually microscopic, membrane-bound structure that is the fundamental unit of all living things. Organisms can be made up of one cell (unicellular; bacteria, for example) or many cells (multicellular; human beings, for example, which are made up of an estimated 100,000 billion cells).

Cell adhesion: The bonding of cells to surfaces or to other cells. Protein molecules at the surface of cells are generally the glue involved in cell adhesion.

Cell recognition: The process by which a cell in a multicellular organism interprets its surroundings.

Characterization: Analysis of critical features of an object or concept.

Chemical vapor deposition (CVD): A technique used to deposit thin layers of coatings on a substrate. In CVD, chemicals are vaporized and then applied to the substrate using an inert gas such as nitrogen as a carrier. CVD is used in the production of microchips, integrated circuits, sensors, and protective coatings.

Chemical vapor transport: A technique similar to CVD used to grow crystal structures.

Chemisorption: The process by which a liquid or gas is chemically bonded to the surface of a solid.

Colloids: Very fine solid particles that will not settle out of a solution or medium. Smoke is an example of a colloid, being solid particles suspended in a gas. Colloids are the intermediate stage between a truly dissolved particle and a suspended solid, which will settle out of solution.

Composite: A material made from two or more components that has properties different from the constituent materials. Composite materials have two phases: matrix (continuous) phase and dispersed phase (particulates, fibers). For example, steel-reinforced cement is a composite material. The concrete is the matrix phase and the steel rods are the dispersed phase. The composite material is much stronger than either of the phases separately.

Computational chemistry: A branch of theoretical chemistry with the goal of creating computer programs to calculate the properties of molecules (such as total energy, dipole moment, and vibrational frequencies) and to apply these programs to concrete chemical objects.

Copolymerization: The process of using more than one type of monomer in the production of a polymer, resulting in a product with properties different from either monomer. See Monomer and Polymer.

Crystallography: The process of growing crystals.

Dendrimer: A polymer with multiple branches. Dendrimers are synthetic 3-D macromolecular structures that interact with cells, enabling scientists to probe, diagnose, treat, or manipulate cells on the nanoscale. From the Greek word dendra, meaning tree.

Dip-pen nanolithography (DPN): A method for nanoscale patterning of surfaces by the transfer of a material from the tip of an atomic force microscope onto the surface. Developed by Professor Chad A. Mirkin, the DPN allows researchers to precisely lay down or "write" chemicals, metals, biological macromolecules, and other molecular "inks" with nanometer dimensions and precision on a surface.

DNA (deoxyribonucleic acid): The molecule that encodes genetic information, found in the cell's nucleus.

DNA cleavage: The cutting or breaking of a DNA strand.

DNA recognition: The ability of one DNA molecule to "recognize" and attach to another molecule that has a complementary shape.

DNA replication: The process of making copies of DNA strands prior to cell division using existing DNA as a template for the newly created strands.

DNA structures: DNA frameworks occurring in nature, i.e., double helix, cruciform, left-handed DNA, multistranded structures. Also, microarrays of small dots of DNA on surfaces.

Doping: In electronics, the addition of impurities to a semiconductor to achieve a desired characteristic, often altering its conductivity dramatically. Also known as semiconductor doping.

drug delivery: The use of physical, chemical, and biological components to deliver controlled amounts of a therapeutic agent.

Electrochemical methods: Experimental methods used to study the physical and chemical phenomena associated with electron transfer at the interface of an electrode and a solution. Electrochemical methods are used to obtain analytical or fundamental information regarding electroactive species in solution. Four main types of electrochemical methods are potentiometry, voltammetry, coulometry, and conductimetry.

Electrochemical properties: The characteristics of materials that occur when (1) an electric current is passed through a material and produces chemical changes and (2) a chemical reaction is used to produce an electric current, as in a battery.

Electroluminescence (EL): The light produced by some materials—mainly semiconductors—when exposed to an electric field. In this process, the electric field excites electrons in the material, which then emit the excess energy in the form of photons. Light-emitting diodes (LEDs) are the most well-known example of EL.

Electron diffraction: A surface science technique used to examine solids by firing a beam of electrons at a sample and observing the electron deflection from the sample's atomic nuclei.

Electron microscopy: The visual examination of very small structures with a device that forms greatly magnified images of objects by using electrons rather than light to create an image. An electron microscope focuses a beam of electrons at an object and detects the actions of electrons as they scatter off the surface to form an image.

Electron transfer: The passage of an electron from one constituent of a system to another, as from one molecule or ion to another. Applications include photography, xerography, and dye-sensitized injection solar cells.

Electron transport: The manipulation of individual electrons. Nanolithography techniques allow single electrons to be transported at very low temperatures in specially designed circuits.

Electron tunneling: The passage of electrons through a barrier that, according to the principles of classical mechanics, cannot be breached. An example of electron tunneling is the passage of an electron through a thin insulating barrier between two superconductors. Electron tunneling is a pure quantum-mechanical effect that cannot be explained by a classical theory.

Electro-optics: The study of the influence of an electric field on the optical properties of matter—especially in crystalline form—such as transmission, emission, and absorption of light. Also known as optoelectronics.

Electrophoresis: A method of separating large molecules, such as DNA fragments or proteins, from a mixture of similar molecules by passing an electric current through a medium containing the molecules. Depending on its electrical charge and size, each kind of molecule travels through the medium at a different rate, allowing separation.

Encapsulation: The condition of being enclosed or the process of enclosing.

Epitaxy: The growth of a crystal layer of one mineral on the crystal base of another mineral in such a manner that the crystalline orientation of the layer mimics that of the substrate.

Excited states: In quantum mechanics, all levels of energy above the lowest or ground state (also known as equilibrium). Excited states are ranked in order of increasing energy; that is, the second excited state has higher energy than the first.

Ferroelectrics: Crystalline substances that have a permanent spontaneous electric polarization (electric dipole moment per cubic centimeter) that can be reversed by an electric field.

Ferro fluid: A fluid in which fine particles of iron, magnetite or cobalt are suspended, typically in an oil. A ferrofluid is superparamagnetic and can create liquid seals held in position by magnetic fields. One application of ferrofluids is to keep dust off the drive shafts of magnetic disk drives. Ferrofluids were invented by NASA as a way to control the flow of liquid fuels in space.

Ferromagnetic materials: Substances, including a number of crystalline materials, that are characterized by a possible permanent magnetization.

Ferromagnetism: A phenomenon by which a material can exhibit spontaneous magnetization. One of the strongest forms of magnetism, ferromagnetism is responsible for most of the magnetic behavior encountered in everyday life and is the basis for all permanent magnets.

Field effect: The local change from the normal value produced by an electric field in the charge-carrier concentration of a semiconductor.

Field emission: The emission of electrons from the surface of a metallic conductor into a vacuum (or into an insulator) under the influence of a strong electric field. In field emission, electrons penetrate through the potential surface barrier by virtue of the quantum-mechanical tunnel effect. Also known as cold emission. See also Electron tunneling.

Fluorescence: The process in which molecules or matter absorb high-energy photons and then emit lower-energy photons. The difference in energy causes molecular vibrations.

Fluorescence spectroscopy: A technique to measure the interaction of radiant energy with matter by passing emitted fluorescent light through a monochromator to record the fluorescence emission spectrum.

Fluorescent probe: A stain used for tagging and labeling biological cells to detect structures, molecules, or proteins within the cell. Also, single-stranded pieces of DNA, with enzymatically incorporated fluorescent tags, affixed in a microscopic array (DNA microarray).

Fuel cell: An electrical cell that converts the intrinsic chemical free energy of a fuel into direct-current electrical energy in a continuous catalytic process. Fuel cells extract the chemical energy bound in fuel and, in combination with air as an oxidant, transform it into electricity. Researchers are hoping to develop fuel cells that could take the place of combustion engines, thereby reducing the world dependence on fossil fuels.

Fullerene: A molecular form of pure carbon that takes the form of a hollow cage-like structure with pentagonal and hexagonal faces. The most abundant form of fullerenes is carbon-60 (C60), a naturally occurring form of carbon with 60 carbon atoms arranged in a spherical structure that allows each of the molecule's 60 atomic corners to bond with other molecules. Larger fullerenes may contain from 70 to 500 carbon atoms. Named for R. Buckminster Fuller for his writing on geodesic domes; also referred to as "buckyballs."

Gas-phase reactions: A class of chemical reactions that occur in a single gaseous phase based on the physical state of the substances present. Examples include the combination of common household gas and oxygen to produce a flame.

Gene expression: The transcription, translation, and phenotypic manifestation of a gene.

Gene sequencing: Technology used to interpret the sequence of the nucleotides (adenine, cytosine, guanine, and thymine) in a DNA sample from bands on an X-ray film image. Scientists use a combination of lasers, high-precision optics, and computer software to determine the sequence of fluorescently tagged DNA molecules.

Gene technology: Techniques that allow experimenters to manipulate specific genes within an organism and determine the effect this has on the functioning of the organism.

Genomics: The study of the genetic content of organisms.

Green chemistry: The use of chemical products and processes that reduce or eliminate substances hazardous to human health or the environment, creating no waste or generating only benign waste.

Heterogeneous catalysis: A chemical process in which the catalyst and the reactant are present in separate phases. Usually the catalyst is a solid, the reactants and products are in gaseous or liquid phases, and the catalytic reaction occurs on the surface of the solid.

High-throughput screening (HTS): An assortment of technologies used to identify small molecules. HTS is often used in drug development to screen potential sources for novel molecules. It is capable of processing a wide variety of input samples and track data for each.

Homogeneous catalysis: A process in which a catalyst is in the same phase—usually a gas or liquid—as the reactant. Catalysis of the transformation of organic molecules by acids or bases is one of the most widespread types of homogeneous catalysis.

Hydrogen bonding: The interaction of a hydrogen atom with another atom, influencing the physical properties and three-dimensional structure of a chemical substance. Hydrogen bonding generally occurs between atoms of hydrogen and nitrogen, oxygen, or fluorine. An important example of a hydrogen bonding is the formation of the DNA double helix.

Hydrophilic effect: Having an affinity for, attracting, adsorbing, or absorbing water. Hydrophilic effect occurs when a liquid comes into contact with another phase—typically a solid substrate, if it attracts the liquid molecules—causing the liquid to attain a relatively large contact area with the substrate.

Hydrophobic effect: Lacking an affinity for, repelling, or failing to adsorb or absorb water. Hydrophobic effect occurs when a liquid comes into contact with another phase—typically a solid substrate, if it exerts a repulsive force onto the liquid—causing the liquid to retract from the surface, with relatively little contact area between liquid and substrate.

Infrared (IR) spectroscopy: A technique in which infrared light is passed through matter and some of the light is absorbed by inciting molecular vibration. The difference between the incident and the emitted radiation reveals structural and functional data about the molecule.

Ion channel: A protein-coated pore in a cell membrane that selectively regulates the diffusion of ions into and out of the cell, allowing only certain ion species to pass through the membrane.

Ion conductors: The discharge of charged particles in a fluid electrolyte to conduct an electrical current.

Junctions: In electronics, the interface between two different types of materials within diodes, transistors, and other semiconductor devices.

Lab-on-a-chip devices: Miniaturized analytical systems that integrate a chemical laboratory on a chip. Lab-on-a-chip technology enables portable devices for point-of-care (or on-site) medical diagnostics and environmental monitoring.

Langmuir–Blodgett (LB) films: Ultrathin films (monolayers and isolated molecular layers) created by nanofabrication. An LB film can consist of a single layer or many, up to a depth of several visible-light wavelengths. The term Langmuir–Blodgett comes from the names of a research scientist and his assistant, Irving Langmuir and Katherine Blodgett, who discovered unique properties of thin films in the early 1900s. Such films exhibit various electrochemical and photochemical properties. This has led some researchers to pursue LB films as a possible structure for integrated circuits (ICs). Ultimately, it might be possible to construct an LB-film memory chip in which each data bit is represented by a single molecule. Complex switching networks might be fabricated onto multilayer LB-film chips.

Lattice: In crystallography, a regular periodic arrangement of atoms in three-dimensional space.

LED (light-emitting diode): A semiconductor device that converts electrical energy into electromagnetic radiation. The LED emits light of a particular frequency (hence a particular color) depending on the physical characteristics of the semiconductor used. See Electroluminescence.

Liposome: A type of nanoparticle made from fat molecules surrounding a core of water. Liposomes were the first nanoparticles used to create unique therapeutic agents.

Liquid phase separation: A method of extracting one liquid from another, generally through the use of solvents.

Lithography: The process of imprinting patterns on materials. Derived from Greek, the term lithography means literally "writing on stone." Nanolithography refers to etching, writing, or printing at the microscopic level, where the dimensions of characters are on the order of nanometers (units of 10^{-9} meter, or millionths of a millimeter).

Luminescence: Cool light emitted by sources as a result of the movement of electrons from more energetic states to less energetic states. There are many types of luminescence. Chemiluminescence is produced by certain chemical reactions. Electroluminescence is produced by electric discharges, which may appear when silk or fur is stroked or when adhesive surfaces are separated. Triboluminescence is produced by rubbing or crushing crystals.

Macromolecule: A very large molecule composed of hundreds or thousands of atoms.

Magnetism: The force of attraction or repulsion between various substances, especially those made of iron and certain other metals. Magnetism is the result of the motion of electrons in the atoms.

Mass spectrometer: A device used to identify the kinds of molecules present in a given substance: the molecules are ionized and passed through an electromagnetic field. The way in which they are deflected is indicative of their mass and identity.

Microcontact printing: A technique that uses a silicone stamp to deposit molecules on surfaces in patterns with microscale features.

Microfluidic device: A device that has one or more channels with at least one dimension less than 1 mm. Common fluids used in microfluidic devices include whole blood samples, bacterial cell suspensions, protein or antibody solutions, and various buffers. The small amounts of samples needed and relative inexpensiveness of microfluidic devices make them attractive for biomedical research and creating clinically useful technologies. One of the long-term goals in the field of microfluidics is to create integrated, portable clinical diagnostic devices for home and bedside use, thereby eliminating time-consuming laboratory analysis procedures.

Microfluidics: A multidisciplinary field that studies the behavior of fluids at volumes thousands of times smaller than a drop. Microfluidic components form the basis of "lab-on-a-chip" devices capable of performing several different functions. Microfluidics is critical in the development of gene chip and protein chip technology.

Micromachining: The use of standard semiconductor technologies along with special processes to fabricate miniature mechanical devices and components on silicon and other materials. See Micromolding.

Micromolding: A method of fabricating microsystems using tiny molds to cast materials. Micromolding serves as an alternative to micromachining. See Micromachining.

MOCVD (metal-organic chemical vapor deposition): A technique for growing thin layers of compound semiconductors in which metal-organic compounds are decomposed near the surface of a heated substrate wafer.

Molecular beam epitaxy: Method used to grow layers of materials of atomic-scale thickness on surfaces.

Molecular imprinting: A process by which functional monomers are allowed to self-assemble around a template molecule and locked into place. The template molecule is then removed, leaving behind a cavity that is complementary in shape and functionality as the template molecule, which will bind molecules identical to the template.

Monomer: A small molecule that may become chemically bonded to other monomers to form a polymer; from Greek mono "one" and meros "part."

Nano characterization: The understanding of the chemical and physical properties of atomic and nanoscale materials.

Nanocomposites: Materials that result from the intimate mixture of two or more nanophase materials. See Composite.

Nanocrystal line materials: Solids with small domains of crystallinity within the amorphous phase. Applications include optical electronics and solar cells.

Nanoelectromechanical systems (NEMS): A generic term to describe nanoscale electrical/mechanical devices.

Nanofiber: A polymer membrane formed by electrospinning, with filament diameters of 150–200 nm. Also called nanomesh, it is used in air and liquid filtration applications.

Nanofluidics: The control of nanoscale amounts of fluids.

Nanolithography: Writing nanoscale patterns. See Lithography.

Nanomanipulation: The process of manipulating items at an atomic or molecular scale in order to produce precise structures.

Nanomaterials: Nanoscale particles, films, and composites designed and assembled in controlled ways.

Nanometer: A unit of measurement equal to one-billionth of one meter. The head of a pin is about 1 million nanometers across. A human hair is about 60,000 nm in diameter, and a DNA molecule is between 2 and 12 nm wide.

Nanoparticles: Particles ranging from 1 to 100 nm in diameter. Semiconductor nanoparticles up to 20 nm in diameter are often called quantum dots, nanocrystals, or Q-particles.

Nanoporous materials: Engineered materials with nanoscale holes, used in filters, sensors, and diffraction gratings. In DNA sequencing, nonporous materials have tiny holes that allow DNA to pass through one strand at a time. In biology, complex protein assemblies that span cell membranes allow ionic transport across the otherwise impermeable lipid bilayer.

Nano shell: A nanoparticle that has a metallic shell surrounding a semiconductor. Nano shells are being investigated for use in treating cancer.

Nanostructures: Structures made from nanomaterials.

Nanotubes: Long, thin cylinders of carbon, discovered in 1991 by S. Iijima. These large macromolecules are unique for their size, shape, and remarkable physical properties. They can be thought of as a sheet of graphite (a hexagonal lattice of carbon) rolled into a cylinder. The physical properties are still being discovered. Nanotubes have a very broad range of electronic, thermal, and structural properties that change depending on the different kinds of nanotube (defined by its diameter, length, and chirality, or twist). To make things more interesting, besides having a single cylindrical wall (single-walled nanotubes or SWNTs), nanotubes can have multiple walls (MWNTs)—cylinders inside the other cylinders. Usually referred to as carbon nanotubes, also known as nanorods. Applications for carbon nanotubes include high-density data storage, nanoscale electronics, and flexible solar cells.

NMR (nuclear magnetic resonance) spectroscopy: Analytical technique used to determine the structure of molecules. In NMR, the molecule is placed within a strong magnetic field to align the atomic nuclei. An oscillating electromagnetic field is applied, and the radiation absorbed or emitted by the molecule is measured. Not all atoms can be detected using NMR because the nuclei must have non-zero magnetic moments.

Noncovalent interactions: first recognized by J. D. van der Waals in the nineteenth century. In contrast to the covalent interactions, noncovalent interactions are weak interactions that bind together different kinds of building blocks into supramolecular entities. Also referred to as van der Waals interactions.

Oxidation: Process in which a molecule loses one or more electrons to another component of the reaction.

Phase: A part of a sample of matter that is in contact with other parts but is separate from them. Properties within a phase are homogeneous (uniform). For example, oil and vinegar salad dressing contains two phases: an oil-rich liquid and a vinegar-rich liquid. Shaking the bottle breaks the phases up into tiny droplets, but there are still two distinct phases.

Phase diagram: A map that shows which phases of a sample are most stable for a given set of conditions. Phases are depicted as regions on the map; the borderlines between regions correspond to conditions where the phases can coexist in equilibrium.

Phase transport: The movement of heat, mass, and momentum in a medium.

Photoluminescence: Light excited in a body by some form of electromagnetic radiation in the ultraviolet, visible, or infrared regions of the electromagnetic spectrum. See Electroluminescence, LED, and Luminescence.

Piezoelectric: Dielectric crystal that produces a voltage when subjected to mechanical stress or can change shape when subjected to a voltage.

Polymer: A macromolecule formed from a long chain of molecules called monomers; a high-molecular-weight material composed of repeating sub-units. Polymers may be organic, inorganic, or organometallic, and synthetic or natural in origin. See Biopolymer.

Polymerase chain reaction: A technique for copying and amplifying the complementary strands of a target DNA molecule.

Polymorphism: The property of a chemical substance crystallizing into two or more forms having different structures, such as diamond, graphite, and fullerenes from carbon. Also known as pleomorphic.

Protein: Large organic molecules involved in all aspects of cell structure and function.

Proteomics: The separation, identification, and characterization of the complete set of proteins present in the various cells of an organism; the design and construction of new proteins.

Quantum confinement effect: Atoms caged inside nanocrystals.

Quantum dot: A nanoscale crystalline structure made from cadmium selenide that absorbs white light and then re-emits it a couple of nanoseconds later in a specific color. The quantum dot was originally investigated for possible computer applications. Recently, researchers have been investigating the use of quantum dots for medical applications, using the molecule-sized crystals as probes to track antibodies, viruses, proteins, or DNA within the human body.

Raman spectroscopy: Analysis of the intensity of Raman scattering, in which light is scattered as it passes through a material medium and suffers a change in frequency and a random alteration in phase. The resulting information is useful for determining molecular structure.

Reduction: In analytical chemistry, the preparation of one or more subsamples from a sample of material that is to be analyzed chemically. In chemistry, reduction refers to the reaction of hydrogen with another substance or the chemical reaction in which an element gains an electron.

Resists: Elements used in performing photolithography experiments. Resists are polymer materials spun onto a substrate. When exposed to UV light, the polymer in the resist cross-links. When treated with a solvent, the cross-linked portion of the resist dissolves, leaving the desired pattern.

RNA (ribonucleic acid): A long linear polymer of nucleotides found mainly in the cytoplasm of a cell that transmits genetic information from DNA to the cytoplasm and controls certain chemical processes in the cell.

RNA structures: Molecules that act as scaffolds upon which proteins are assembled to form functional ribosomes. RNA structures include a variety of single-stranded and double-stranded structures that result in complex three-dimensional structures.

Scaffold: Three-dimensional biodegradable polymers engineered for cell growth.

Scanning probe microscopy (SPM): Experimental techniques used to image both organic and inorganic surfaces with (near) atomic resolution. Includes atomic force microscopes and scanning tunneling microscopes.

Scanning tunneling microscope (STM): A scanning probe microscopy instrument capable of revealing the structure of samples. The STM uses a sharp metal tip positioned over a conducting substrate with a small potential difference applied between them. The gap between the tip and substrate surface is small enough so that electrons can tunnel between the tip and the surface. The tip is then scanned across the surface and adjusted to keep a contact current flowing. By recording the tip height at each location, a "map" of the sample surface is obtained.

Second-harmonic generation (SHG): The light that results when a beam of monochromatic light hits an asymmetrical surface. The second-harmonic light is at a frequency twice that of the incident light and allows the study of surface phenomena such as molecular adsorption, aggregation, and orientation as well as of buried interfaces.

Self-assembled monolayers (SAMs): Monomolecular films that form or self-assemble after immersing a substrate into a solution of an active surfactant.

Self-assembly: At the molecular level, the spontaneous gathering of molecules into well-defined, stable, structures that are held together by intermolecular forces. In chemical solutions, self-assembly (also called Brownian assembly) results from the random motion of molecules and the affinity of their binding sites for one another. Self-assembly also refers to the joining of complementary surfaces in nanomolecular interaction. Developing simple, efficient methods to organize molecules and molecular clusters into precise, predetermined structures is an important area of nanotechnology exploration.

Simulation: A broad collection of methods used to study and analyze the behavior and performance of actual or theoretical systems. Simulation provides a mechanism for predicting computationally useful functional properties of systems, including thermodynamic, thermochemical, spectroscopic, mechanical, and transport properties.

Single-molecule studies: The analysis of individual molecular properties in contrast with the study of bulk properties.

Single-source precursors: In materials science, the starting materials for semiconductor devices; powdered materials with uniform chemical composition throughout the mixture.

Sol-gel materials: Gels, glasses, and ceramic powders synthesized through the sol-gel process; organic–inorganic composite materials.

Sol-gel process: A chemical synthesis technique for preparing gels, glasses, and ceramic powders generally involving the use of metal alkoxides.

Solid-state reactions: Transformations that occur in and between solids and between solids and other phases to produce solids.

Substrate: A wafer that is the basis for subsequent processing operations in the fabrication of semiconductor devices.

Superconductor: An object or substance that conducts electricity with zero resistance.

Super hydrophobicity: Extreme water repellence. See Hydrophobic effect.

Synthesis: Any process or reaction for building up a complex compound by the union of simpler compounds or elements.

Synthetic methods: Techniques for the design and creation of new materials in the laboratory.

Template: In cell and molecular biology, the macromolecular model for the synthesis of another macromolecule.

Template synthesis: The engineered design and creation of materials of controlled size, shape, and surface chemistry.

Thin film: A film one molecule thick; often referred to as a monolayer.

Transmission electron microscopy (TEM): The use of electron high-energy beams to achieve magnification close to atomic observation. See Electron microscopy.

UV/VIS (ultraviolet-visible) spectroscopy/spectrophotometry: Method to determine concentrations of an absorbing species in solution. This technique uses light in the visible and adjacent near ultraviolet (UV) and near infrared (NIR) ranges to achieve this quantitative analysis.

Vesicles: In cell biology, a relatively small and enclosed compartment, separated from the cytosol by at least one lipid bilayer. Vesicles store, transport, or digest cellular products and wastes.

Wetting: In electronics, coating a contact surface with an adherent film of mercury. In metallurgy, wetting refers to spreading liquid filler metal or flux on a solid base metal. Wetting occurs if a liquid is in contact with another phase, typically a solid substrate, with the substrate exerting an attractive force on the liquid molecules.

X-ray analysis: The use of X-ray radiation to detect heavy elements in the presence of lighter ones, to give critical-edge absorption to identify elemental composition, and to identify crystal structures by diffraction patterns.

X-ray diffraction: The scattering of X-rays from a crystal, resulting in an interference pattern used to determine the structure of the crystal.

Source: Selected terms related to this chapter from www.if4it.com/it-glossary and from publications and educational seminars of MERIT CyberSecurity.

Bibliography

http://www.globalfirepower.com/

http://www.military.com/daily-news/2017/07/16/military-cyber-operations-headed-revamp-long-delay.html

http://resources.infosecinstitute.com/isis-cyber-capabilities/#gref

http://www.bbc.com/news/world-middle-east-22287326

https://en.wikipedia.org/wiki/Syrian_Electronic_Army

http://www.telegraph.co.uk/news/worldnews/middleeast/syria/10014982/Who-is-the-Syrian-Electronic-Army.html

https://www.slideshare.net/HackRead/irans-cyber-war-skills

What makes a country decide on a cyber army?: https://www.wsj.com/articles/cataloging-the-worlds-cyberforces-1444610710

http://citeseerx.ist.psu.edu/viewdoc/download?doi=10.1.1.95.4960&rep=rep1&type=pdf

Strongest armies: https://historylist.wordpress.com/2008/03/11/what-is-the-best-military-in-world-history/

US military and hacking: http://www.businessinsider.com/us-military-cyberwar-2016-5

US cyber army: http://idstch.com/home5/international-defence-security-and-technology/cyber/many-countries-investing-in-cyber-warfare-programs-and-developing-military-cyber-commands/

Benefits of nanotechnology: http://ice.chem.wisc.edu/Small%20Science/From_Small_
Science_Comes_Big_Decisions/Choices_files/Military.pdf

Computer science in NT: http://citeseerx.ist.psu.edu/viewdoc/download?doi=10.1.1.95.496
0&rep=rep1&type=pdf

Genetically engineered bioweapon: http://dujs.dartmouth.edu/2013/03/genetically-engi-
neered-bioweapons-a-new-breed-of-weapons-for-modern-warfare/#.WXt4yITys08

Being cynical about the word "smart": https://mathbabe.org/2016/06/20/adding-another-
layer-of-cynicism-to-the-smart-city-revolution/

Artificial neural network: https://www.techopedia.com/definition/5967/artificial-neural-
network-ann

Electronic warfare in operations: http://usacac.army.mil/cac2/Repository/FM336/FM336.pdf

Nano computers: https://www.google.com/search?q=nanocomputers&oq=nanocomputer
&aqs=chrome.0.0j69i57j0l4.5085j0j7&sourceid=chrome&ie=UTF-8

Epilogue: http://blogs.discovermagazine.com/80beats/2011/02/09/harvard-engineers-build-
tiny-processors-out-of-nanowires/#.WX2sN4TytEY

http://www.heritage.org/defense/report/nanotechnology-and-national-security-small-
changes-big-impact

Trump–Russia connection: https://www.vox.com/mischiefs-of-faction/2017/3/6/14820506/
trump-russia-network-mapped

Appendix

The Human Immune System: The Master Blueprint

The human body is one symbiotic unit, it all works together. Nothing is separate from another—what a brilliant house to live in! When fully contemplating the magic of our body systems, we are often filled with awe and wonder. One of the fascinating features of adaptive immunity (through vaccination) is the autonomic faculty of storing historical attack episodes as a deep learning process to recognize future attacks. This *immunologic memory* allows your immune system to respond much more effectively when you meet a particular pathogen again. The T-cells, also called *CD4 cells*, coordinate your entire adaptive immune response. Helper T-cells receive signals from the white blood cells of your innate defenses, such as the dendritic cells and phagocytes, and relay those signals to the fighters of your adaptive defenses: the B-cells and cytotoxic T-cells. The B-cells are activated when they detect a foreign pathogen with their B-cell receptors and when they receive signals from helper T-cells. They're activated to form two types of cells: plasma cells and memory cells. The plasma cells produce antibodies, which are defensive proteins that bind specifically to antigens. Antibody proteins have a forked structure, like the letter Y, with a binding site for an antigen at each tip of the Y. Your immune system releases the antibodies that plasma cells produce into the blood, where they can circulate around the body. Anything in the body that's tagged with antibodies—such as invading pathogens—is marked for destruction by the immune system. The cytotoxic T-cells, also called *CD8 cells* or *cytotoxic T lymphocytes* (CTLs), come into play if microbes try to hide inside your cells so that the antibodies can't find them. Cytotoxic T-cells can detect foreign antigens on the surface of an infected host cell. When these cells discover an infected cell, they send signals that tell the infected cell to commit suicide—a necessary sacrifice in order to destroy the hidden microbes. CD8 T-cells also tell abnormal cells within your body to die, thus preventing them from becoming cancerous.

Of all these types of white blood cells, your helper T-cells are probably the most important. *Antigen-presenting cells* like dendritic cells and macrophages from your innate immunity activate helper T-cells by showing them bits of molecules from pathogens. After they're activated, your helper T-cells multiply and release communicating molecules called *cytokines* that stimulate both cytotoxic T-cells and B-cells. Thus, without the action of helper T-cells, your entire immune system would fail.

The HIV virus infects helper T-cells, slowly reducing their numbers until a person who's infected with the virus doesn't have enough helper T-cells to activate his or her adaptive immunity. At this point, the person develops *acquired immunodeficiency syndrome*, better known as AIDS. After AIDS has developed, the person is very susceptible to infection and certain cancers, which ultimately causes death.

The activation of helper T-cells and the other cells that make up your immune system involves several steps:

1. Antigen-presenting cells attach pieces of a foreign antigen to proteins called MHC2 proteins that they display on their surface.
2. Antigen-presenting cells also produce molecules like cytokines, signaling that they've detected a foreign antigen.
3. Helper T-cells bind to the displayed antigen using a receptor called a T-cell receptor.
4. After helper T-cells recognize an antigen and receive the signals from antigen-presenting cells, they activate and multiply and then activate cytotoxic T-cells and B-cells. Helper T-cells also send signals to phagocytes that cause them to become more efficient killers.

Index